W9-BWS-890

Case Studies in Contemporary Criticism

EDITH WHARTON

The House of Mirth

Case Studies in Contemporary Criticism

SERIES EDITOR: *Ross C Murfin*

Charlotte Brontë, *Jane Eyre*
EDITED BY Beth Newman, Southern Methodist University

Emily Brontë, *Wuthering Heights*
EDITED BY Linda H. Peterson, Yale University

Geoffrey Chaucer, *The Wife of Bath*
EDITED BY Peter G. Beidler, Lehigh University

Kate Chopin, *The Awakening*
EDITED BY Nancy A. Walker, Vanderbilt University

Joseph Conrad, *Heart of Darkness,* Second Edition
EDITED BY Ross C Murfin, Southern Methodist University

Joseph Conrad, *The Secret Sharer*
EDITED BY Daniel R Schwarz, Cornell University

Charles Dickens, *Great Expectations*
EDITED BY Janice Carlisle, Tulane University

E. M. Forster, *Howards End*
EDITED BY Alistair M. Duckworth, University of Florida

Thomas Hardy, *Tess of the d'Urbervilles*
EDITED BY John Paul Riquelme, Boston University

Nathaniel Hawthorne, *The Scarlet Letter*
EDITED BY Ross C Murfin, Southern Methodist University

Henry James, *The Turn of the Screw*
EDITED BY Peter G. Beidler, Lehigh University

James Joyce, *The Dead*
EDITED BY Daniel R. Schwarz, Cornell University

James Joyce, *A Portrait of the Artist as a Young Man*
EDITED BY R. B. Kershner, University of Florida

A Companion to James Joyce's Ulysses
EDITED BY Margot Norris, University of California, Irvine

Thomas Mann, *Death in Venice*
EDITED BY Naomi Ritter, University of Missouri

William Shakespeare, *Hamlet*
EDITED BY Susanne L. Wofford, University of Wisconsin–Madison

Mary Shelley, *Frankenstein*
EDITED BY Johanna M. Smith, University of Texas at Arlington

Jonathan Swift, *Gulliver's Travels*
EDITED BY Christopher Fox, University of Notre Dame

Edith Wharton, *The House of Mirth*
EDITED BY Shari Benstock, University of Miami

Case Studies in Contemporary Criticism

SERIES EDITOR: Ross C Murfin, *Southern Methodist University*

EDITH WHARTON
The House of Mirth

**Complete, Authoritative Text with
Biographical and Historical Contexts,
Critical History, and Essays from
Five Contemporary Critical Perspectives**

EDITED BY

Shari Benstock
University of Miami

Bedford/St. Martin's
BOSTON ◆ NEW YORK

For Bedford/St. Martin's

Publisher: Charles H. Christensen
Associate Publisher/General Manager: Joan E. Feinberg
Managing Editor: Elizabeth M. Schaaf
Developmental Editor: Stephen A. Scipione
Production Editor: Andrea Goldman
Copyeditor: Kate Layzer
Text Design: Sandra Rigney, The Book Department
Cover Design: Richard Emery Design, Inc.

Library of Congress Catalog Card Number: 92–75895

Manufactured in the United States of America.

4 3 2 1
j i h g

For information, write: Bedford/St. Martin's, 75 Arlington Street, Boston, MA 02116 (617–426–7440)

ISBN: 0–312–06234–6 (paperback)
ISBN: 0–312–10633–5 (hardcover)

Published and distributed outside North America by:

MACMILLAN PRESS LTD.
Houndmills, Basingstoke, Hampshire RG21 2XS and London
Companies and representatives throughout the world.

ISBN: 0–333–60891–7

Acknowledgments

Dimock, Wai-chee. "Debasing Exchange: Edith Wharton's *The House of Mirth*." In *Modern Critical Views: Edith Wharton,* Ed. Harold Bloom. New York: Chelsea House, 1986, 123–37.

Restuccia, Frances L. "The Name of the Lily: Edith Wharton's Feminism(s)." *Contemporary Literature* 28, no. 2 (1987): 222–38.

Page 440 photo. *Mrs. Lloyd* by Sir Joshua Reynolds, 1775. Lord Rothschild's Private Collection.

About the Series

Case Studies in Contemporary Criticism provide college students with an entrée into the current critical and theoretical ferment in literary studies. Each volume reprints the complete text of a classic literary work and presents critical essays that approach the work from different theoretical perspectives, together with the editors' introductions to both the literary work and the critics' theoretical perspectives.

The volume editor of each *Case Study* has selected and prepared an authoritative text of the classic work, written an introduction to the work's biographical and historical contexts, and surveyed the critical responses to the work since its initial publication. Thus situated biographically, historically, and critically, the work is examined in five critical essays, each representing a theoretical perspective of importance to contemporary literary studies. These essays, prepared especially for undergraduates by exemplary critics, show theory in praxis; whether written by established scholars or exceptional young critics, they demonstrate how current theoretical approaches can generate compelling readings of great literature.

As series editor, I have prepared introductions, with bibliographies, to the theoretical perspectives represented in the five critical essays. Each introduction presents the principal concepts of a particular theory in their historical context and discusses the major figures and key works that have influenced their formulation. It is my hope that these introductions will reveal to students that good criticism is informed by a set of coherent assumptions, and will encourage them to recognize and examine their own assumptions about literature. Finally, I have compiled a glossary of key terms that recur in these volumes and in the discourse of contemporary theory and criticism. We hope that the *Case Studies in Contemporary Criticism* series will reaffirm the richness of its literary works, even as it introduces invigorating new ways to mine their apparently inexhaustible wealth.

Ross C Murfin
Series Editor
Southern Methodist University

About This Volume

The text of *The House of Mirth* is reprinted from the original 1905 Charles Scribner's Sons edition, corrected by Edith Wharton from the serialized version in *Scribner's Magazine* that ran from January to November 1905. Joshua Reynolds's Portrait of Mrs. Lloyd (1775) did not appear in the original edition of the novel, which was illustrated by A. B. Wenzell. Edith Wharton disliked the practice of illustrating novels and was often critical of the visual images of her heroes and heroines. Illustration, however, was a trademark of magazine publication, and since all but one of her novels was serialized, she had to fall in with this convention. In fact, despite her belief that illustrations cheapened the level of good literature, she was served by some of the best artists in the trade; however, I have acquiesced to her desires and reprinted the text without illustrations.

Part Two of this volume includes five critical articles, each of which represents a contemporary mode of reading *The House of Mirth*. Two of the essays have been published previously. Wai-chee Dimock's "Debasing Exchange," which here represents Marxist critique, first appeared in *PMLA* in 1985. Frances Restuccia's "The Name of the Lily," which appears here under the flag of feminist criticism (under which all five essays might also fly) first appeared in *Contemporary Literature* in 1987. The remaining three essays were written especially for this volume. Margot Norris's "Death by Speculation" illustrates deconstructive reading practices, and is to my knowledge the first deconstructive analysis of *The House of Mirth* to appear in print. Ellie Ragland Sullivan's "The Daughter's Dilemma" examines Lily Bart's crisis of gender from the perspective of Jacques Lacan's theories of psychosexuality, and in so doing breaks new ground on theories of hysteria and the meaning of sublimation. Freud and Lacan often used literature to explain or exemplify problems in psychic structures or to find their way to new stages of thinking; for example, Lacan theorized the "symptom," the fourth term of the psychoanalytic field, by means of James Joyce's *Finnegans Wake*. Edith Wharton might be surprised that her novel has served as an entrance into the psychoanalytic field; she herself was curious about Freud's discoveries, especially as they touched on the difficult issues of gender and sexuality. Lillian Robinson's "The Traffic in Women" provides a cultural critique of *The House of Mirth* within the terms of Wharton's own cultural history. One might say that cultural criticism was the first mode of reading her novel, a perspective brought to it perforce by readers who lived within its historical frame. Ninety years later, on the eve of a new century and in the wake of enormous social and cultural change and new theories of reading and writing, cultural criticism remains a powerful a way of reading Lily Bart both in and out of her time. Collectively these essays demonstrate the rich complexity of *The House of Mirth* and also the complex richness of contemporary ways of reading and writing.

Acknowledgments

I first want to thank the contributors to this volume for their enthusiasm and cooperation at all stages of the work. This group includes some friends of many years whose writing on the literature of women's lives has guided my own work; to them I owe more, intellectually and personally, than I can ever adequately repay. My next debt is to the editorial group at Bedford Books, who cheerfully and patiently helped me through every stage of the publication process. Virtually all my work on the book was done while on sabbatical and away from the University of Miami, and I am grateful to Belinda Ghitis and Suzanne Ferris for their assistance in providing bibliographies and difficult-to-find texts. Finally, I thank my dean and friend, Ross Murfin, for asking me to contribute to *The Scarlet Letter* volume he so ably edited and then requesting that I edit *The House of Mirth*. A cheerier, more dedicated editor and critic would be hard to find. I appreciate Ellie Ragland Sullivan's help on glossary definitions of Lacanian terms. My thanks also to Edvige

Giunta for photographic assistance reproducing the Joshua Reynolds portrait of Mrs. Lloyd. Finally, Nancy Walker's edition of Kate Chopin's *The Awakening* in this series provided insights into contextualizing American women writers at the turn of the century.

Preparation of this volume has coincided with research and writing of my forthcoming biography of Edith Wharton, a work of more than five years' research that makes extensive use of unpublished materials and new information about her health and finances, her development as a writer, her husband's mental breakdown and his inherited estate, her parentage and relations with her parents and brothers, and the circumstances of her love affair with William Morton Fullerton. This material changes significantly some of the dominant assumptions about Edith Wharton's life and work, changes hinted at in my two essays in this volume. I am grateful to the Beinecke Library, Yale University, the Lilly Library, Indiana University, Princeton University libraries, and to the Edith Wharton Estate for permission to quote from their sources. Information on Dr. S. Weir Mitchell comes from the Archives of the College of Physicians of Philadelphia. Information on Dr. George McClellan can be found in the archives of Jefferson Medical College, Philadelphia.

Shari Benstock
University of Miami

Contents

About the Series   v

About This Volume   vii

PART ONE

The House of Mirth:
The Complete Text

Introduction: Biographical and Historical Contexts   3

The Complete Text   25

PART TWO

The House of Mirth:
A Case Study in Contemporary Criticism

A Critical History of *The House of Mirth*   309

Cultural Criticism and *The House of Mirth*   326

What Is Cultural Criticism?   326
Cultural Criticism: A Selected Bibliography   337

A Cultural Perspective:
   LILLIAN S. ROBINSON, The Traffic in Women: A Cultural Critique
   of *The House of Mirth* 340

Marxist Criticism and *The House of Mirth* 359

What Is Marxist Criticism? 359
Marxist Criticism: A Selected Bibliography 372
A Marxist Perspective:
   WAI-CHEE DIMOCK, Debasing Exchange: Edith Wharton's
   The House of Mirth 375

Feminist Criticism and *The House of Mirth* 391

What Is Feminist Criticism? 391
Feminist Criticism: A Selected Bibliography 398
A Feminist Perspective:
   FRANCES L. RESTUCCIA, The Name of the Lily: Edith Wharton's
   Feminism(s) 404

Deconstruction and *The House of Mirth* 419

What Is Deconstruction? 419
Deconstruction: A Selected Bibliography 429
A Deconstructionist Perspective:
   MARGOT NORRIS, Death by Speculation: Deconstructing
   The House of Mirth 431

Psychoanalytic Criticism and *The House of Mirth* 447

What Is Psychoanalytic Criticism? 447
Psychoanalytic Criticism: A Selected Bibliography 459
A Psychoanalytic Perspective:
   ELLIE RAGLAND SULLIVAN, The Daughter's Dilemma:
   Psychoanalytic Interpretation and Edith Wharton's *The House of
   Mirth* 464

Glossary of Critical and Theoretical Terms 483

About the Contributors 497

Case Studies in Contemporary Criticism

EDITH WHARTON

The House of Mirth

PART ONE

The House of Mirth:
The Complete Text

Introduction:
Biographical and
Historical Contexts

Edith Wharton was born on January 24, 1862, in New York City, the third child and only daughter of George Frederic Jones and Lucretia Stevens Rhinelander. Christened Edith Newbold Jones, she was descended from wealthy Anglo-Dutch merchant families who had established New York society, and her family lived on the income from George Jones's Manhattan real-estate investments. At her daughter's birth, Lucretia Jones was nearly thirty-seven years old, a prominent society matron married for seventeen years and the mother of two sons, aged sixteen and twelve. The pregnancy was unexpected and perhaps unwanted. Her daughter's birth allowed Mrs. Jones, a handsome but indolent woman, to withdraw briefly from the winter season of dinners and theater parties, but by spring she had returned to her busy social schedule. From her earliest years Edith was cared for by an Irish nurse ("Doyley"); her later education was guided by a German governess, Anna Bahlmann, who eventually became her secretary.

Raised virtually as an only child, Edith was by her own account indulged and overprotected by her wealthy, frivolous parents. While she loved games and outdoor activities, she also lived actively within her own mind and imagination, and often felt lonely and different from those around her. "All the people I have known who have cared for 'les choses de l'esprit' [things of the mind] have found some degree of sympathy & companionship either in their families or among their youthful friends. But I never exchanged a word with a really intelligent human being until I was over twenty," she wrote in "Life and I," an early draft version of her memoir, *A Backward Glance*. She described her childhood and youth as "an intellectual desert" ("Life" 1082–83, 1089).

Edith's creativity and intelligence were far in advance of her age. She discovered in childhood her talent as an observer of the domestic and social scenes around her, and entertained herself by inventing stories in which her parents and their associates were the main characters. She called this "making up," a display of narrative and imaginative powers that at first amused her parents, then worried them, because the urgent necessity to "make up" seemed to overpower the young child. Years later, her husband, Edward R. Wharton, was also disconcerted by the spell that storytelling held for his wife: he feared it, seeing it as a form of "witchcraft," Edith Wharton remarked to a friend (Tyler 33). By adolescence she had learned to hide her writing activities, and even in adulthood she divided her day between writing, a strictly private activity that occupied her mornings, and social activities that filled her afternoons and evenings.

As a little girl, Edith loved words long before she could understand their meanings. George Jones taught her to read when she was six and later gave her access to his private six-hundred-volume library of books on history, art, archeology, and poetry, including translations of the classics. Except for the works of Sir Walter Scott and Benjamin Disraeli, two nineteenth-century British writers, there were no novels on the library shelves. Lucretia Jones, who read only novels and works on horticulture, censored her daughter's reading. She did not want Edith exposed to the domestic and erotic subject matter of fiction and required that she obtain her approval before reading any novel. Wanting to please her mother and afraid of Lucretia's anger, which showed itself in icy disapproval and heightened criticism, Edith obeyed. She never read a novel without first asking permission until she was married ("Life" 1083).

The early interest Edith displayed in narrative fiction was not likely to have met with Lucretia Jones's encouragement. In 1873, at age eleven, she had begun to write a story of social observation, the mode that would later become her special provenance as a novelist. It opened with a dialogue between two society women:

"Oh, how do you do, Mrs. Brown?" said Mrs. Tomkins. "If only I had known you were going to call I should have tidied up the drawing-room."

Young Edith showed the opening sentences of the story to her mother, who remarked coldly, "Drawing rooms are always tidy" (*Glance* 73). The domestic subject matter and conversational dialogue of this vignette mimed stories that Edith may have read in local newspapers such as *The Mercury* of Newport, Rhode Island, where the Joneses had a summer house.

Lucretia Jones trained her daughter in all the reigning modes of decorum, custom, and propriety. Taking note of Edith's early writings, which ranged from stories to sentimental poetry, blank-verse tragedies, even sermons ("Life" 1090), Mrs. Jones adhered to conventional beliefs of the day regarding proper conduct for young ladies with literary talents: they might write occasional poetry without compromising their place in society. She and George Frederic therefore rewarded their daughter's poetic gifts. In 1878, when Edith was sixteen years old, Mr. Jones arranged to have privately printed a selection of his daughter's poems entitled *Verses*. We can imagine that Edith was pleased, and perhaps a little embarrassed, by this attention. She wanted real publication, and in 1879, the year of her debut into New York-Newport society, several of her poems were accepted for publication. One appeared in the New York *World* newspaper under the pseudonym "Eadgyth"; a seventy-two line poem based on a story she had read in the press, "Only a Child" recounted the suicide of a twelve-year-old boy who had been locked into solitary confinement in a Philadelphia orphanage. Four others were accepted for publication by William Dean Howells, editor of the prestigious literary magazine, *The Atlantic Monthly*. Of the four other poems, only one appeared over Edith's signature, perhaps because her parents, her editors, or she herself preferred that her name not appear. The reasons for masking her identity are not known.

Endowed with a keen eye for social circumstances and a talent for storytelling, Edith could not turn away for long from narrative fiction. Two years before she became a published poet, she had secretly composed a thirty-thousand-word novella, *Fast and Loose*. A tale of love's trials, it was exactly the kind of story her mother would not have wanted her to read, much less to write. An irony of Edith's early literary development is that she *wrote* a novella before she had ever *read* one. Signed with the pseudonym "David Olivieri," it was written as an entertainment for her friend Emelyn Washburn, daughter of the rector of Calvary Church in Manhattan, where George Frederic Jones and Edith often attended afternoon services. Several years older than Edith, Emelyn saw that her young friend was "starving for mental nourishment"; she introduced her to Dante's *Divine Comedy*, and together they read Nordic and Anglo-Saxon poetry ("Life" 1085).

Fast and Loose is a comic send-up of eighteenth-century romances, its plot contrived and its narrative mode stylized and stiff. In a gesture of self-mockery, Edith appended to the text a series of invented reviews that parodied the hypercritical attitudes of literary journals but also incorporated her mother's deriding voice as an instrument of satire. A fabricated review from "The Nation" that perfectly mimicked the authoritative, judgmental tone adopted by critics enumerated Edith's own failures as a fiction writer: "Every character is a failure, the plot a vacuum, the style spiritless, the dialogue vague, the sentiment weak, and the whole thing a fiasco."

Tersely judicious, this comic mode became the signature of Edith Wharton's social criticism. She was famous in her own time for searing retorts to bores and hangers-on, and her social satires combined wit with stinging reproof. The very voice that amused her friends and struck fear in her enemies, however, had once been turned on Edith. Lucretia Jones tried to mold her daughter to society's measurements by derisive laughter countered with unexpected flashes of approval. This treatment confused Edith and crippled her emotional development, even as it served as the crucible of her art. As a child she was acutely aware of the differences between herself and others. Prone to illness, she thought she was defective; red-haired and small, she did not resemble other members of her family and therefore considered herself less good-looking than they, even less "bright"! Teased and taunted by her older brothers, she was also subjected to a "perpetual cross-fire of criticism" from her mother. All this had the effect of making her "a painfully shy self-conscious" and conscientious child ("Life" 1089–90).

Reacting to these "outward miseries," she turned inward and tried to nourish herself intellectually ("Life" 1090). If her mother was less than encouraging about her literary interests, George Frederic Jones steadfastly encouraged them, and in gratitude she retained fond memories of him. After his death in 1882, Lucretia Jones retreated from society and clung close to her children, especially Edith, who lived with her mother until her marriage in 1885 and then resided in a house on her mother's Newport estate until 1893 — by which time Edith Wharton was thirty-one years old. Three years later, Edith's elder brother Frederic was divorced in a scandalous lawsuit that threatened the family's place in New York-Newport society. The divorce divided family allegiances, and Lucretia followed Frederic to Paris, where she died in 1901 after a three-year illness, during which her daughter visited her several times. Lucretia died never knowing how disaffected her daughter was, how she resented her mother's lifelong effort to mold her into her own image — a woman of society and fashion.

It took enormous courage and persistence for Wharton to overcome Old New York society's attitudes about women's social place and the proper forms of creative expression. She did not publish her first story until she was twenty-nine, and she was thirty-seven when her first book-length literary work, a short story collection entitled *The Greater Inclination*, appeared from Scribner's. It was this book that gave her a sense of herself and "broke the chains which had held [her] so long in a kind of torpor" (*Glance* 122). During the years of her long literary apprenticeship, she often doubted her abilities and was confused about the directions of her life. Still she continued writing, even as society gossips ridiculed her literary pretensions or claimed that it was Edith's secretary, Anna Bahlmann, who wrote the books to which Edith Wharton signed her name (Tyler 6).

I

In many ways Edith Newbold Jones was a child of her times, shaped by the cultural and moral doctrines of the day in America, especially the prevailing attitudes toward women. But European culture suited far better her tastes and disposition, a discovery she made during the six childhood years (1866–1872) that she traveled abroad with her family. This was the formative period of Edith's tastes and personality, and years later, when she returned to live in Europe as an adult, she was in some deeply satisfying way returning "home."

The post-Civil War depression in the real-estate market, during which time the Jones family rented out their homes in New York and Newport, occasioned this long European tour. They spent the first year in Rome (1867), then traveled in Spain and settled for two years in Paris in 1868 (the year Edith's brother Henry entered Trinity Hall College, Cambridge). In 1871, the family settled in Florence for a year before returning to New York. During this time, Edith learned Italian, French, and German, and at age eight she was reading the New Testament in German.

At Wildbad in 1870, where Lucretia Jones took a spa cure popular among society ladies, Edith fell ill with typhoid fever and lay for weeks at the point of death. She described this illness as "the dividing line between my little-childhood, & the next stage" ("Life" 1079). During

the long months of her convalescence, she occupied her time with
books, one of which profoundly disturbed her. Although she disliked
children's literature (and Lucretia Jones agreed that these stories were
sometimes injurious because they used "bad English"), two of her
friends gave her a "robber story" as a get-well token. To please them,
she read it, and the effects on her feverish imagination were disastrous.
So badly was she frightened that she fell into a serious relapse and was
again at the point of death. When she finally emerged from the second
fever, it was to a world "haunted by formless horrors," a "dark undefinable menace, forever dogging my steps, lurking & threatening" ("Life"
1079). This event changed Edith from a fearless child to one who for some
years lived in a chronic state of anxiety, even terror. Grateful to her parents
for not trying to "harden" her and for not scolding or ridiculing her for
her fears, she nonetheless believed that her fears and self-doubts — her
seeming lack of courage — marked her as someone different and diminished ("Life" 1080). Ashamed of her weakness, she connected her fear
and lack of courage with the powers of certain stories.

The woman who became a renowned writer of ghost stories could
not, until she was twenty-seven years old, sleep in a room that contained
a ghost story. She admitted that she "frequently had to burn books of
this kind, because it frightened me to know that they were downstairs in
the library!" ("Life" 1080). The symptoms of the deadly typhoid —
nausea, fatigue, weight loss, and lassitude — reappeared later and were
particularly severe in the 1890s.

R. W. B. Lewis, in his influential biography, writes that Edith Wharton suffered a series of psychological breakdowns in her thirties that
culminated in her decision in autumn 1898 to undergo the rest cure
developed by Dr. S. Weir Mitchell, a prominent Philadelphia neurolo-
gist who specialized in diseases of the nerves. His therapy included mas-
sage and electric treatments, a high-fat diet, and enforced rest during
which patients were forbidden to do creative work of any kind. His cli-
ents (mostly women) were removed from their domestic and social en-
vironments and placed in hospitals or rest homes where they were not
allowed visitors (Lewis 82–84). Alice James and Charlotte Perkins Gilman took the cure (Gilman drew on her experiences in "The Yellow
Wallpaper"); while undergoing a similar treatment in England, Virginia
Woolf tried to commit suicide.

After a period of ill health in Newport during the summer of 1898,
Wharton suddenly announced to her editors at Scribner's that she was
departing for Philadelphia to take a long rest cure. Because she knew
Dr. Mitchell slightly from Newport, where he summered, and because

he was a fiction writer who had begun to follow her emergence onto the literary scene, it seemed a safe guess that she was under his care in Philadelphia, although no medical records or correspondence exist to confirm this assumption. The claim quickly became a "fact" of Wharton biographical studies, underwritten by the popular belief that artists are unstable and prone to depression and that women artists are particularly vulnerable to psychic collapse because they face enormous social pressure to conform to the domestic expectations of marriage and motherhood. As a young matron, Edith Wharton tried to fashion her life to society's expectations and also to fulfill her desire to write. She divided her life into two parts, making a conspicuous show of her social and charitable activities while keeping her writing an absolutely private act. When she became a successful author in the early 1900s, she passed lightly over her literary accomplishments, giving people the impression that writing was a hobby rather that the most important commitment of her life.

Her divided life might have led to the kind of psychological stress that the Weir Mitchell cure hoped to ease. But when she stepped off the train in Philadelphia that October afternoon in 1898, she believed that she had suffered a heart attack caused by repeated bouts of flu and colds. She took rooms for herself and her husband at the Stenton Hotel, and there, for the next three months, she was visited by Dr. George McClellan, a well-known professor of anatomy and surgery at the Jefferson Medical College of Philadelphia, who tried to discover the causes of her ill health. Freed from social and domestic obligations, she spent her days reading, resting, and writing short stories. Her heart was fine, Dr. McClellan declared. Her nausea and weight loss were caused by drainage from infected tonsils, and she later took medical treatments and steam inhalations for this condition. Instead of returning to New York, where the winter season was in full swing, she and her husband, Teddy, spent the spring in Washington D.C., where they bicycled and took long walks. Her throat and respiratory ailments recurred often, both in times of stress and during periods of tranquility, and these illnesses eventually did irreparable damage to her heart.

Although Edith Wharton faced difficult challenges in her development as a woman and as a writer, there is no evidence that she experienced psychological breakdowns. She used writing as a means of working through and mastering the complex social situation in which she lived. She continued to write, despite lack of encouragement, jealousy, and the dissapproval of Old New York matrons.

The small, inbred society into which Edith Newbold Jones was

born, no less than the Gilded Age society that replaced it, fed on gossip
and whispered stories of social improprieties and moral failures. Lucretia
Jones had a lifelong horror of gossip; even so, several rumors about her
and her daughter wound their way sinuously, and ominously, through
New York society. One story was true: Edith Wharton's marriage to
Teddy Wharton existed in name only — the couple did not maintain
sexual relations.[1] Other stories concerned Lucretia's private life, and
although their truth has yet to be proven, one of them made a deep
impression on Wharton. Long after her parents were dead, she learned
what certain of her friends had whispered about for many years — that
she was probably not her father's daughter. It was said that she was the
child of an Englishman, her older brothers' tutor, a man she described
as "extremely cultivated" (*Glance* 49). Among her close friends, two
women she had known since childhood knew of the story as did a New
York cousin whom Wharton saw frequently during her European years
(Tyler passim; Lewis 535–39).

On the surface the story seems unlikely, given Lucretia Jones's con-
ventionality. Yet Wharton took it seriously, even making efforts to find
the man in his native English village, only to discover that he was dead.
In its general outline (and its mystery), the rumor resembles stories that
she wrote, tales of illicit love affairs within the proper world of Old New
York society ("That Good May Come"), liaisons that produced children who later discovered the secret of their birth or in other ways were
affected by their "irregular parentage" ("The Old Maid" and "His
Father's Son"). If Edith Wharton were the child of an adulterous union
between a society matron in her mid-thirties and a young Englishman,
then the truth of her mother's double sexual standards, the reality of the
Jones's marriage, the conditions of Wharton's upbringing, and her
parents' attitudes and feelings toward her would have further contributed to her intense sense of otherness. Her strange parentage might also
explain intellectual gifts and literary talents heretofore unknown in either the Schermerhorn-Jones or the Rhinelander-Stevens families. Iron-

[1]Ogden Codman Jr. to Sarah Codman, 19 March 1901. Codman, the Boston architect and designer who helped create interiors for two of Edith's homes (Land's End in
Newport and The Mount in Lenox, Massachusetts) and with whom she wrote *The Decoration of Houses* (Scribner's, 1897), enjoyed collecting stories about her. Indebted to her
because she had helped establish his reputation by recommending his work to her rich
friends, he was also possessive, jealous, and pathologically avaricious. His letters to his
mother, Sarah Fletcher Bradlee Codman, gleefully recount demeaning personal attacks
on Edith and her writing made by people in her social circle. See the Codman Family
Papers, Society for the Preservation of New England Antiquities, Boston, Massachusetts
(SPNEA).

ically, Wharton's only literary "relation" was her husband's distant cousin, the Philadelphia writer Anna Wharton.

If the story were true, then Lucretia Jones's concern for discretion and accepted proprieties was not merely conventional. In these circumstances, she would not have wanted her daughter writing stories that might "tell tales" on the family. As an adult, Wharton did not hesitate to tell tales on those around her, to recast family members in her fictions and draw recognizable portraits of her contemporaries. For example, Mrs. William Sloane — Emily Vanderbilt Sloane, granddaughter of Commodore Cornelius Vanderbilt, scion of the rich and famous Gilded Age family — was not pleased by Wharton's short story "The Line of Least Resistance," published in autumn 1900 in *Lippincott's Magazine*. Set in Newport, it gave a thinly veiled account of Emily Sloane's sister-in-law Jessie, who had left her husband Henry (William Sloane's brother) and two daughters in order to marry Perry Belmont, descendent of a wealthy family reputed to have Jewish origins. Society closed its doors against Jessie Belmont, and her affair and its aftermath were a cautionary tale in society; shortly after Wharton's story appeared, her friend Walter Berry wrote to ask whether anyone had yet "fitted the key" to it (Berry to EW).

A founder of Lenox, Massachusetts, summer society, Mrs. Sloane used her considerable social powers to turn the town against Edith Wharton at the very moment the Whartons were in the process of building a home on an estate at the edge of Lenox. Snubbed by the community, Wharton was forced to write Emily Sloane a letter of apology. She did not allow "The Line of Least Resistance" to be reprinted in her lifetime (Ogden Codman to Sarah Codman, 25 February 1901).

II

Edith Wharton was both a historian and a social critic of the world in which she lived, and her stories are not only (or even) records of personal invective. They pull away the mask of pietistic convention of the old families (like her own) and expose the greed of status-seeking new-breed industrialists and business tycoons who succeeded in buying social prominence by intermarrying with the "Knickerbockers." Her fiction casts a cool, clearsighted glance at the false values of the modern world with a special focus on the limited possibilities for women's lives and the loss of selfhood that success in society meant both for women and men. This is one theme of *The House of Mirth*. In her own life, then,

Wharton turned her back on her mother's platitudes (and hypocrisies) and followed instead her own desire to expand her intellectual and cultural horizons, to achieve independence of spirit, emotional equilibrium, and artistic maturity.

In upbringing and education, Wharton followed the patterns common for women of her social class — but with two important variations. She had a longer experience of Europe earlier than did most young women, who sometimes did not travel abroad until making the Grand Tour just prior to their debut in society, and she read well beyond the fixed limits for women training to become society matrons. Rather than limiting herself to the predictable accomplishments in music, painting, and needlepoint, mastering the delicacies of bread-and-butter notes and the graces of *salon* French and Italian, she charted another course for herself — the one reserved in her time for young men. With the exception of the required languages for a gentleman's education, Latin and Greek (a loss she always regretted), Wharton had followed the curriculum of university studies that her brother Henry undertook at Cambridge University and that her husband, Teddy Wharton, followed at Harvard: philology, philosophy and logic, religion, science, history and art history, archeology, ancient and modern poetry, and drama. She particularly loved the German and Anglo-Saxon poetic sagas, and she learned Middle High German and Anglo-Saxon in order to read them.

The difference between her experiences and those of her brothers and husband was that she did all this at a far earlier age than they did and without the aid of a tutor who guided her reading and discussed it with her. By fifteen, she had read virtually everything by the German writer Johann Wolfgang von Goethe; his work in natural science spurred her lifelong interest in the history of evolution and the origin of plants. She went on to become a landscape designer of merit, creating three acclaimed gardens. She also encouraged her niece, Beatrix Jones Farrand, who became one of the first American woman to practice landscape architecture as a profession.

Wharton's interest in domestic architecture, interior decoration, and garden design was a direct response to the aesthetic charm of Europe and a reaction against the bleak brick and iron of American cities. It was not contemporary Europe that most satisfied her, but rather the neoclassical formality of the eighteenth century, which as a child she had observed in architecture, garden design, painting, and sculpture in the cities she visited. Her stories and novels provide visual records of architectural details and interior furnishings. *The House of Mirth*, for example, is a devastating commentary on (and also an accurate record of)

New York taste at the beginning of this century. When she returned with her parents from Europe in 1872, she experienced "bitter disappointment" at her impressions of America: "'*How ugly it is!*' I have never since thought otherwise, or felt otherwise than as an exile in America" ("Life" 1080–81).

Because of continuing financial problems, which had begun during the Civil War, the Jones family did not travel in Europe during the next eight years. They instead divided their time between New York City and a home they had built in Newport just before the war. By the time Mr. Jones's failing health took them to the south of France in November 1880, Edith had already been "out" in society for nearly two years. Lucretia had advanced the debut (Edith came out in January 1879, when she had just turned seventeen) because she feared that the family's financial difficulties would force them to give up their New York home. She wanted Edith to establish her place in New York-Newport society before these problems became known. But Edith did not have a successful launch into the marriage market. In her extreme shyness she turned away potential suitors (most of them her brother Henry's friends) with a frozen glare or a curt nod of rejection when they asked her to dance.

By early 1880, however, things had changed. Helped by her sister-in-law, Mary Cadwalader Jones, she had joined a group of lively young people that included the popular Henry Leyden Stevens, twenty-one-year-old son of Mrs. Paran Stevens. Although Mrs. Stevens did not come from the leisured classes (her father was a successful grocer in Lowell, Massachusetts), at age nineteen she had married a wealthy Boston widower, a hotel owner in his late forties who did not share his wife's passion for society. Mrs. Stevens, who was to play an injurious role in Edith Jones's young life, could have stepped straight from the pages of *The House of Mirth*. (She did appear in *The Age of Innocence* and *New Year's Day* as Mrs. Lemuel Struthers, widow of a man who made his fortune selling shoe polish.) Lily Bart's mother, recalled briefly in the novel, is a paler version of this indefatigable social climber. By 1880, Mrs. Stevens, who had been a widow for several years, made a successful match for her beautiful daughter, Mary Fisk Stevens, with a titled Englishman. What she felt about her son's initial interest in "Pussy" Jones we do not know, but by the time the Jones family left New York for Cannes in November, gossips conjectured that Edith and young Harry Stevens were engaged.

They were not, and Edith did not see him again for almost a year, when they met in Venice and renewed their friendship. He then followed the Jones family back to Cannes, where he stayed throughout

George Frederic's final illness and death in March 1882. When Edith and her mother returned to Newport, the courtship was taken up again. Henry Stevens was very much in love (Edith was less enamored), and in August Mrs. Stevens announced the engagement of her son. Then suddenly in October, the month they were to be married, *Town Topics*, a gossipy magazine of high society, reported that the marriage had been postponed indefinitely. Rumors flew between New York and Newport as to the causes for this sudden change of plans. The reported reason for the broken engagement was an "alleged preponderance of intellectuality on the part of the intended bride." Edith was described as "an ambitious authoress"; Mr. Stevens, according to the report, found "ambition a grievous fault" (Lewis 45).

Biographers and critics have speculated that Mrs. Stevens broke up the romance because she wanted to maintain complete control of her son's inheritance of more than a million dollars. Whatever the private reasons for the annulled engagement, Edith was publicly made to bear responsibility for it, and Mrs. Stevens, who believed that she had been snubbed by the Joneses and their friends, no doubt enjoyed holding Edith up to ridicule. Her message, delivered by *Town Topics*, was unambiguous: young women wishing to marry well must hide any intellectual or literary desires and ambitions they might have. In the wake of the broken engagement and the gossip that followed, Lucretia Jones quickly removed Edith to Paris.

When they returned to New York in January 1883, Edith — thin and pinched looking — feared re-entry into New York society and another season on the ballroom circuit. This was her fourth season "out"; after two seasons' absence from New York, January 1883 constituted a second debut, and she met the cold stares of the matrons who believed that she had broken off her engagement to an eminently eligible young man because of her literary ambitions. In truth, Edith was deeply discouraged about her literary prospects. She continued to read, but her "dream of a literary career . . . [had] faded into unreality" (*Glance* 76).

When summer came, Lucretia avoided Newport, with its painful memories of the previous year, and instead visited the Frederic Joneses in Bar Harbor. It was here that Edith met two men who would play important roles in her life. One of them she would marry; the other, Walter Van Rensselaer Berry, she called "the love of all my life" (Wharton "Diary"). Handsome and tall (six foot three to Edith's five foot four), intelligent, with a dry wit and observing blue eyes, he would become her closest male friend and among the first to encourage her literary work and intellectual pursuits. He was himself an ambitious young man preparing to study law at Columbia University. Although there was romance in the air in summer 1883, she responded to a love letter he wrote her by setting terms of friendship rather than courtship (Tyler 20).

Another man with his eye on Edith that summer was Edward Robbins Wharton, a Boston gentleman of leisure who for more than a decade had been a summer visitor in the Jones house in Newport as a guest of Henry Jones. A man much like Edith's brother, he was easygoing and friendly, loved the outdoors, and had a fondness for animals, as did Edith, who felt comfortable with him. His playful sense of humor and gaiety made him seem far younger than his thirty-three years. Lucretia was particularly fond of him and encouraged his interest in her daughter. After a two-year courtship, they were married in April 1885. Less than three months after the Wharton marriage, Henry Leyden Stevens died from complications of tuberculosis, and his mother gained complete control of the family fortune that would have been his. Gossips had it that he died of a broken heart.

The newlywed Whartons moved into Pencraig Cottage, a small house on Lucretia Jones's estate at Newport, where they lived for the next eight years. Lucretia, sometimes visited by her son Henry, resided at Pencraig, the big house a few hundred yards away. In Newport, Edith Wharton fashioned herself as a society matron, giving dinner parties, working for charitable causes, attending tennis matches (her favorite spectator sport), riding her horse or bicycling on the winding paths along the sea cliffs. Except that she did not have children, she took the role to which women of her class were destined, the role her mother desired for her.

Wharton was now a married woman, but she had not yet left home or broken away from the mother-daughter tie that had bound her for so many years. This proximity to her mother was determined not only by unresolved emotional issues but also by economic factors. Wharton had married a man who had not yet come into his legacy (he would not do so until he was fifty-nine years old), and her own inheritance was in trust. Only when she fell heir to a surprise bequest from a distant Jones cousin in 1888 were she and Teddy able to rent a small house in New York for visits to the city, and later buy their own home — Land's End — in Newport. Each spring they traveled for four months in Europe, primarily in Italy, where Wharton pursued her interests in eighteenth-century architecture and garden design.

Photographs of a gaunt, hollow-eyed Edith Wharton provide graphic evidence that her Newport years were difficult ones. Writing eased her lack of power to control her life, but it was also a source of insecurity. She wrote poems and composed short stories as exercises in narrative method; working alone and without guidance and encouragement, however, she often lost heart.

Gradually, however, she gained self-assurance, helped by encouraging editors and friends. Her commitment to the rigors of the writing life during her mid-thirties as well as her literary success can be seen in the publications that preceded *The House of Mirth*. These included *The Decoration of Houses* (1897), *The Greater Inclination* (1899, a short story collection), *The Touchstone* (1900, a novella), *Crucial Instances* (1901, a short story collection), *The Valley of Decision* (1902, a two-volume novel set in eighteenth-century Italy), *Sanctuary* (1903, a novella), *The Descent of Man* (1904, a short story collection), *Italian Villas and Their Gardens* (1904) and *Italian Backgrounds* (1905), two studies of Italian achitecture and culture.

During these years, Wharton's most important literary mentors were her editors at Scribner's, Edward L. Burlingame and William Crary Brownell, and Walter Berry, by this time a successful lawyer in Washington, D.C. Charles Eliot Norton, retired professor of fine arts at Harvard, an expert on the Italian renaissance and medieval art and literature, was an enthusiastic reader of her work as was his daughter Sara, who had become one of Wharton's closest friends. Sara saved Wharton's letters over their long friendship, letters that reveal Wharton's literary and artistic interests and track her life events. In 1893 Wharton met the French novelist Paul Bourget, who introduced her to a French reading audience by helping her find a translator and Paris publisher for *The House of Mirth*, which appeared as *Les Heureux du monde* in 1907. By the early years of this century she had also become a friend of Henry James, a man twenty years her senior, to whose writing hers is still most often compared.

In 1902, although they did not yet know each other well, Wharton sent James a copy of *The Valley of Decision*. He responded appreciatively, adding that he longed to talk with her about the novel. He then proceeded to "admonish" her toward "the *American Subject*": "Don't pass it by — the immediate, the real, the ours, the yours, the novelist's that it waits for" (17 Aug. 1902, Powers 34). He had urged her toward the study of American life in 1900, when she sent him a copy of "The Line of Least Resistance," which she thought the best thing she had yet written (26 Oct. 1900, Powers 32–33).

Even in 1900 James's advice was too late. She had already mapped out a novel entitled "Disintegration," set in modern day New York and Long Island. She put it aside to write *The Valley of Decision* but returned to it in autumn 1902, writing seventy pages of the story before abandoning it — despite Edward L. Burlingame's enthusiasm for her subject and her methods. After another delay brought about by work on The Mount, the house she was building in Lenox, she began to write *The House of Mirth* and worked steadily from September to December 1903. ("Disintegration" was eventually revised and incorporated twenty years later into *The Mother's Recompense.*)

Progress on *The House of Mirth* stalled when Teddy Wharton fell ill with symptoms very much like the ones Wharton had suffered for so many years — nausea, weakness, and headaches. Biographers have been misled into thinking that Teddy and Edith both suffered from neurosis, or neurasthenia, as it was then called. Twice in one year he experienced fatigue and nervousness brought on by management and financial worries associated with building The Mount. These breakdowns were the first signs of the bipolar disease (manic-depression) that eventually incapacitated him, a disease he inherited from his father, who spent the last eight years of his life in McLean's Asylum outside Boston, where he died in 1891 of melancholia. Whereas Edith Wharton's anxieties were associated primarily with her efforts to become a professional writer and her unhappiness with the trivialities of society life (in today's medical terminology her stress was "situational"), Teddy's disease had biogenetic roots and eventually destroyed his sanity.

During this same period, Wharton was angered by reviews of her recent work in which her writing was compared to that of Henry James. Discouraged, she wrote to William Crary Brownell on 25 June 1904: "the continued cry that I am an echo of Mr. James (whose books of the last ten years I can't read, much as I delight in the man), & the assumption that the people I write about are not 'real' because they are not navvies & char-women, makes me feel rather hopeless. I write what I see, what I happen to be nearest to, which is surely better than doing cowboys de chic" (Lewis, *Letters* 91). In late summer 1904, Wharton summoned her courage and began again on her novel. On October 7, she reported to Edward Burlingame that she was "fatuously pleased with 'The House of Mirth'" (unpublished letter from Wharton). In a rare moment of pride, she predicted large sales for the book — a prediction that came true. Reader reaction to *The House of Mirth* confirmed that she had been correct in staying close to her New York subject: the best-selling novel was most admired for its verisimilitude.

For its early readers, the strength of *The House of Mirth*, which in her "*donnée* book" she had called "A Moment's Ornament" and then "The Year of the Rose" (suggesting the transitory nature of woman's beauty and feminine appeal) and later thought of calling "Costs," lay in its detailed portrait of society life. Readers saw the novel's characters as living people whose activities might have been chronicled daily in new.s- paper society columns. These were the fortunate few who congregated in damask-lined drawing-rooms of Fifth Avenue and gathered for long weekends in palatial country houses along the Hudson River, entertaining each other playing *tableaux vivants* (a kind of charade that takes scenes from paintings as its subject matter), gambling at auction bridge, dancing after dinner, and — when the oil lamps had been turned down for the evening — slipping down corridors for secret assignations.

Although Edith Wharton's personal values were those of an earlier, less affluent, less worldly community (a world only briefly glimpsed in the novel), she understood the double standard of "modern" society's mores — the tensions between private desires and public codes of behavior. Like Lily Bart, she could not live or write within these contradictions, and she decided to leave America. After 1912, she returned only twice to the United States — once to attend her niece Beatrix's wedding (1913) and again in 1923 to accept an honorary doctorate of letters from Yale University, the first woman to be so honored.

III

Unlike Lily Bart, who is effectively disinherited by her aunt, Edith Wharton was heir to three separate fortunes from her family. Only one of these, however, was at her direct disposal. Teddy Wharton and Henry Jones, the trustees of the estate she inherited from her parents, controlled its expenditures until her divorce in 1913, when Walter Berry and a New York cousin became co-trustees. In 1909, Teddy secretly took fifty thousand dollars from his wife's trust to buy a house in Boston, in which he established (according to the confession he later made to Edith) a mistress and several actresses. Although he later repaid the money, this strange event (a sign of his mental disease), his violent mood swings, and his verbal abuse of Edith led her to divorce him. They had been married almost twenty-eight years, and she admitted to friends that this decision was the most difficult of her life. She felt a "spiritual responsibility" for Teddy (Tyler 28), and thus divorce, which went against her moral and religious beliefs, was particularly difficult to accept. Her friends and legal advisors warned her, however, that Teddy's mental illness could lead him to further fiscal and personal irresponsibility.

If Wharton's trust monies were never fully at her disposal, she had always had a free hand with the substantial earnings generated from her writing. Beginning with *The House of Mirth*, literary royalties alone provided an average yearly income of one hundred fifty thousand dollars at today's rates. She used the royalties on *The House of Mirth* to buy her way out of America and establish a new life among the intellectual elite of Europe. Economic freedom provided by monies she had *earned* gave her independence and self-determination unavailable to the women characters of her fiction and to most women of her time. One wonders what the future might have held for Lily Bart if she had been able to earn economic independence. Would she have built a life of cultured elegance and shared her wealth with those less fortunate, as did Edith, or would she have continued her pursuit of society's pleasures and vanities?

Whatever Edith Wharton and Lily Bart shared by their common social, cultural, and historical contexts, the author and her heroine were distinctly unlike each other in personality and in personal goals. In contrast to Lily, Edith Wharton was intellectually and emotionally independent, a woman who reasoned her emotions and had a clearsighted view of the moral and ethical choices of life. Rather than allowing herself to drift in the moral shallows of high society, she charted a path toward artistry and authorship. Still, the society that was complicit in shaping Lily Bart also played a role in Edith Wharton's slow and painful emergence as writer and social critic.

Wharton struggled over the ending of *The House of Mirth*, and she finally decided on a closing to the novel that does not figure either-or choices either for Lily or the society she inhabits. Yet the meaning of her fate flickers within the terms the novel sets for her life and lifestyle. Lily cannot be extricated from her social, and therefore moral, contexts. The novel poses the question of human subjectivity in terms of social morality, and we should not underestimate the courage required for Wharton to hold the mirror of art up to her own social set, the society in which she lived and moved. Although her values were those of an earlier, less affluent, and less worldly community, she understood the double standard of "modern" society's mores, the tensions between personal desires and public codes of behavior that trap Lily.

Wharton rewrote the dénouement of the novel of manners to reflect these tensions. The classic ending of comedy (in which marriage renews society and extends its power) and tragedy (where death is a cleansing and renewing social force) draw together in a single closing image in *The House of Mirth* that combines both meanings. There is no place for

Lily Bart outside of marriage or the conventions that lead to marriage, no exit from "the house of mirth," as most reviewers noted when the novel was published. Wharton firmly believed the family to be the core unit of civilized society, and the effect of shifting social mores on familial relations was always a major theme of her fiction. Although she realized that marriage fostered women's economic and emotional dependence on men, and that parents often behaved irresponsibly with regard to their children, she could envision no other form of social organization so well suited to nurturing and preserving civilization.

In the thirty years of active publishing that followed *The House of Mirth*, Edith Wharton risked addressing other subjects considered unfeminine, immoral, or outside her range of experience — mercy killings, child abuse, incest, illegitimacy, and divorce. But on only one other occasion did she sacrifice a woman to the cause of social criticism. In *The Fruit of the Tree* (the novel that followed *The House of Mirth*), a work of social conscience, Wharton examined the abuses of power and profit motives of New England mills. Her heroine, Justine Brent, a surgical nurse with strong ethical convictions and a version of the Edith Wharton who walked surgical wards and established hospices for the tuberculous during World War I, commits a mercy killing. She takes the life of her childhood friend Bessy Westmore, a woman, like Lily Bart, made to society's measure, whose injury in a riding accident has induced paraplegia. The story was taken from a real-life incident involving a friend in Lenox, and to set the economic background of the story, Wharton interviewed workers at a textile mill in North Adams, Massachusetts. This novel asks similar questions to those posed by *The House of Mirth*: Is Justine a hero or a murderer? (Is Lily's final gesture intentional or accidental?) To what degree was Bessy/Lily a victim of society's false, self-serving morality, and in what degree did these women contribute to their own fates?

Rather than disposing of her future heroines, Wharton imagined a more tragic, less merciful future for them: they suffered through the dry seasons of unhappy marriages. This kind of suffering, a slow spiritual death, mirrored the pain she experienced in her own marriage, especially in its last years. Marriage became an instrument of torture in Wharton's later fictions, and even modern, quick-fix divorces did little to alter the psychological pain in which her heroines faced their destinies. There are several reasons for the shift in her perspective on the marriage question. Her love affair with William Morton Fullerton between 1907 and 1911 opened her to a heretofore unknown world of women's experiences that included the pleasures (and power) of sexual desire.

She saw the danger of confusing sex with love or love with marriage; her own divorce made her realize that marital ties can never successfully be untied; she came to believe that suffering deepened and broadened the spiritual and creative life.

As the years went on, Wharton insisted ever more outspokenly in her writings on the ethical referentiality of art. Yet in her personal life she was slowly caught up in the very money-seeking conventions that her art decried — caught in these conventions *by* her art. During the first World War she used all the social and economic privileges at her disposal and expended all her energy on helping homeless refugees. Ill and exhausted after the war (she suffered a major heart attack in 1918, following a severe case of pneumonia), she moved to the country in order to devote herself full-time to writing — the career that in her own life-narrative had replaced the marriage plot that was so often the subject of her fictions. In order to support her new life, she began publishing in the "pictorials," popular magazines that paid large sums for serialized novels. She was delighted to rediscover her earning power, but she also found herself working harder, faster, and under greater pressures than ever to support herself and those who depended on her — her household staff, war dependents, and relations, primarily Minnie Jones and Beatrix. It is not an exaggeration to say that Edith's financial dependence on the American publishing market (which collapsed with the 1929 stock market crash) and the effort to meet its demanding publishing schedules created a vicious cycle of overwork and illness that eventually killed her.

Nineteen twenty-nine marked the reverse of her fortunes, as it did for many Americans in Europe. In the spring she suffered a stroke (the first of several); six months later, the Wall Street panic reduced the value of the dollar and the French franc, and the New York real-estate market that provided her investment income began to crumble. By 1934 her literary income was cut by seventy-five percent, she owed income and property taxes both in France and the United States, and her health was in serious decline. She struggled valiantly to keep ahead of her debts by continuing to write — and often writing well, as her memoir *A Backward Glance* and the posthumously published *The Buccaneers* attest. The huge success of *The House of Mirth* some thirty years earlier had forged a link in her mind between the creative powers of authorship and the social and economic power writing gave her. To lose the financial power of the pen, a fear that had long haunted her, was to lose the chance of fulfilling the desires that fed her creativity (travel, gardens, beautiful homes) and of sharing her bounty with friends.

Like Lily Bart, Wharton's last desire was to settle her affairs and be freed from all responsibility. She turned over tax, finance, and literary estate burdens to longtime friends, arranged her funeral service, said goodbye to loved ones, and died peacefully in the late afternoon of August 11, 1937. Her life and death contrasted markedly with the plights of all her heroines. She acknowledged the costs (and rewards) of taking responsibility for all the dimensions of her life, from worldly desires to artistic creativity, from moral imperatives to the dictates of social conscience. She had lived a thoughtful, self-conscious life, and her death at age seventy-five was not, as Lily Bart's might have been, either a tragedy of lost opportunities or merely the last in a series of "careless compromises" (DuPlessis 17). Obituaries and memoirs heaped praise on her work, acclaiming her as the most prominent of American women writers and the only one to have attained a truly international stature. A Chevalier of the French Legion of Honor and decorated by the Belgian government for her war work, she was also a hero for her public service and ambassadorial activities. She died as she lived — a woman of courage, strong morals, high ideals, and fixed beliefs.

WORKS CITED

Berry, Walter. Unpublished letter to Edith Wharton, Friday eve, 1900. Part of Edith Wharton Collection, Bieneke Library, Yale University.

Codman, Ogden, Jr. Codman Family Papers, Society for the Preservation of New England Antiquities, Boston, Massachusetts (SPNEA).

DuPlessis, Rachel Blau. *Writing Beyond the Ending: Narrative Strategies of Twentieth-Century Women Writers.* Bloomington: Indiana UP, 1985.

Lewis, R. W. B. *Edith Wharton: A Biography.* New York: Harper, 1975.

Lewis, R. W. B., and Nancy Lewis, eds. *The Letters of Edith Wharton.* New York: Scribner's, 1988.

Powers, Lyall H., ed. *Henry James and Edith Wharton, Letters: 1900–1915.* New York: Scribner's, 1990.

Tyler, Elisina. Untitled report of Edith Wharton's last days. Edith Wharton Collection, Lilly Library, Indiana University.

Wharton, Edith. *A Backward Glance.* New York: Scribner's, 1934.

————. "Diary," Edith Wharton Collection, Lilly Library, Indiana University.

————. *Fast and Loose: A Novelette by David Olivieri*. Ed. Viola Hopkins Winner. Charlottesville: UP of Virginia, 1977.

————. "Life and I." *Edith Wharton: Novellas and Other Writings*. Ed. Cynthia Griffin Wolff. New York: Library of America, 1990.

————. Unpublished letter from Edith Wharton to Edward L. Burlington, Scribner's Archive, Princeton Universities Libraries.

The House of Mirth

BOOK I

I

Selden paused in surprise. In the afternoon rush of the Grand Central Station his eyes had been refreshed by the sight of Miss Lily Bart.

It was a Monday in early September, and he was returning to his work from a hurried dip into the country; but what was Miss Bart doing in town at that season? If she had appeared to be catching a train, he might have inferred that he had come on her in the act of transition between one and another of the country-houses which disputed her presence after the close of the Newport season; but her desultory air perplexed him. She stood apart from the crowd, letting it drift by her to the platform or the street, and wearing an air of irresolution which might, as he surmised, be the mask of a very definite purpose. It struck him at once that she was waiting for some one, but he hardly knew why the idea arrested him. There was nothing new about Lily Bart, yet he could never see her without a faint movement of interest: it was characteristic of her that she always roused speculation, that her simplest acts seemed the result of far-reaching intentions.

An impulse of curiosity made him turn out of his direct line to the door, and stroll past her. He knew that if she did not wish to be seen she would contrive to elude him; and it amused him to think of putting her skill to the test.

"Mr. Selden—what good luck!"

She came forward smiling, eager almost, in her resolve to intercept him. One or two persons, in brushing past them, lingered to look; for Miss Bart was a figure to arrest even the suburban traveller rushing to his last train.

Selden had never seen her more radiant. Her vivid head, relieved against the dull tints of the crowd, made her more conspicuous than in a ball-room, and under her dark hat and veil she regained the girlish smoothness, the purity of tint, that she was beginning to lose after eleven years of late hours and indefatigable dancing. Was it really eleven years, Selden found himself wondering, and had she indeed reached the nine-and-twentieth birthday with which her rivals credited her?

"What luck!" she repeated. "How nice of you to come to my rescue!"

He responded joyfully that to do so was his mission in life, and asked what form the rescue was to take.

"Oh, almost any—even to sitting on a bench and talking to me. One sits out a cotillion—why not sit out a train? It is n't a bit hotter here than in Mrs. Van Osburgh's conservatory—and some of the women are not a bit uglier."

She broke off, laughing, to explain that she had come up to town from Tuxedo, on her way to the Gus Trenors' at Bellomont, and had missed the three-fifteen train to Rhinebeck.

"And there is n't another till half-past five." She consulted the little jewelled watch among her laces. "Just two hours to wait. And I don't know what to do with myself. My maid came up this morning to do some shopping for me, and was to go on to Bellomont at one o'clock, and my aunt's house is closed, and I don't know a soul in town." She glanced plaintively about the station. "It *is* hotter than Mrs. Van Osburgh's, after all. If you can spare the time, do take me somewhere for a breath of air."

He declared himself entirely at her disposal: the adventure struck him as diverting. As a spectator, he had always enjoyed Lily Bart; and his course lay so far out of her orbit that it amused him to be drawn for a moment into the sudden intimacy which her proposal implied.

"Shall we go over to Sherry's for a cup of tea?"

She smiled assentingly, and then made a slight grimace.

"So many people come up to town on a Monday—one is sure to meet a lot of bores. I 'm as old as the hills, of course, and it ought not to make any difference; but if *I 'm* old enough, you 're not," she objected gaily. "I 'm dying for tea—but is n't there a quieter place?"

He answered her smile, which rested on him vividly. Her discretions interested him almost as much as her imprudences: he was so sure that both were part of the same carefully-elaborated plan. In judging Miss Bart, he had always made use of the "argument from design."

"The resources of New York are rather meagre," he said; "but I 'll find a hansom first, and then we 'll invent something."

He led her through the throng of returning holiday-makers, past sallow-faced girls in preposterous hats, and flat-chested women struggling with paper bundles and palm-leaf fans. Was it possible that she belonged to the same race? The dinginess, the crudity of this average section of womanhood made him feel how highly specialized she was.

A rapid shower had cooled the air, and clouds still hung refreshingly over the moist street.

"How delicious! Let us walk a little," she said as they emerged from the station.

They turned into Madison Avenue and began to stroll northward. As she moved beside him, with her long light step, Selden was conscious of taking a luxurious pleasure in her nearness: in the modelling of her little ear, the crisp upward wave of her hair—was it ever so slightly brightened by art?—and the thick planting of her straight black lashes. Everything about her was at once vigorous and exquisite, at once strong and fine. He had a confused sense that she must have cost a great deal to make, that a great many dull and ugly people must, in some mysterious way, have been sacrificed to produce her. He was aware that the qualities distinguishing her from the herd of her sex were chiefly external: as though a fine glaze of beauty and fastidiousness had been applied to vulgar clay. Yet the analogy left him unsatisfied, for a coarse texture will not take a high finish; and was it not possible that the material was fine, but that circumstance had fashioned it into a futile shape?

As he reached this point in his speculations the sun came out, and her lifted parasol cut off his enjoyment. A moment or two later she paused with a sigh.

"Oh, dear, I 'm so hot and thirsty—and what a hideous place New York is!" She looked despairingly up and down the dreary thoroughfare. "Other cities put on their best clothes in summer, but New York

seems to sit in its shirt-sleeves." Her eyes wandered down one of the
side-streets. "Some one has had the humanity to plant a few trees over
there. Let us go into the shade."

"I am glad my street meets with your approval," said Selden as they
turned the corner.

"Your street? Do you live here?"

She glanced with interest along the new brick and limestone house-
fronts, fantastically varied in obedience to the American craving for novelty, but fresh and inviting with their awnings and flower-boxes.

"Ah, yes—to be sure: *The Benedick*. What a nice-looking building!
I don't think I 've ever seen it before." She looked across at the flat-
house with its marble porch and pseudo-Georgian façade. "Which are
your windows? Those with the awnings down?"

"On the top floor—yes."

"And that nice little balcony is yours? How cool it looks up there!"

He paused a moment. "Come up and see," he suggested. "I can
give you a cup of tea in no time—and you won't meet any bores."

Her colour deepened—she still had the art of blushing at the right
time—but she took the suggestion as lightly as it was made.

"Why not? It 's too tempting—I 'll take the risk," she declared.

"Oh, I 'm not dangerous," he said in the same key. In truth, he had
never liked her as well as as that moment. He knew she had accepted
without afterthought: he could never be a factor in her calculations, and
there was a surprise, a refreshment almost, in the spontaneity of her
consent.

On the threshold he paused a moment, feeling for his latch-key.

"There 's no one here; but I have a servant who is supposed to come
in the mornings, and it 's just possible he may have put out the tea-
things and provided some cake."

He ushered her into a slip of a hall hung with old prints. She noticed
the letters and notes heaped on the table among his gloves and sticks;
then she found herself in a small library, dark but cheerful, with its walls
of books, a pleasantly faded Turkey rug, a littered desk, and, as he had
foretold, a tea-tray on a low table near the window. A breeze had
sprung up, swaying inward the muslin curtains, and bringing a fresh
scent of mignonette and petunias from the flower-box on the balcony.

Lily sank with a sigh into one of the shabby leather chairs.

"How delicious to have a place like this all to one's self! What a
miserable thing it is to be a woman." She leaned back in a luxury of
discontent.

Selden was rummaging in a cupboard for the cake.

"Even women," he said, "have been known to enjoy the privileges of a flat."

"Oh, governesses—or widows. But not girls—not poor, miserable, marriageable girls!"

"I even know a girl who lives in a flat."

She sat up in surprise. "You do?"

"I do," he assured her, emerging from the cupboard with the sought-for cake.

"Oh, I know—you mean Gerty Farish." She smiled a little unkindly. "But I said *marriageable*—and besides, she has a horrid little place, and no maid, and such queer things to eat. Her cook does the washing and the food tastes of soap. I should hate that, you know."

"You should n't dine with her on wash-days." said Selden, cutting the cake.

They both laughed, and he knelt by the table to light the lamp under the kettle, which she measured out the tea into a little tea-pot of green glaze. As he watched her hand, polished as a bit of old ivory, with its slender pink nails, and the sapphire bracelet slipping over her wrist, he was struck with the irony of suggesting to her such a life as his cousin Gertrude Farish had chosen. She was so evidently the victim of the civilization which had produced her, that the links of her bracelet seemed like manacles chaining her to her fate.

She seemed to read his thought. "It was horrid of me to say that of Gerty," she said with charming compunction. "I forgot she was your cousin. But we 're so different, you know: she likes being good, and I like being happy. And besides, she is free and I am not. If I were, I daresay I could manage to be happy even in her flat. It must be pure bliss to arrange the furniture just as one likes, and give all the horrors to the ash-man. If I could only do over my aunt's drawing-room I know I should be a better woman."

"Is it so very bad?" he asked sympathetically.

She smiled at him across the tea-pot which she was holding up to be filled.

"That shows how seldom you come there. Why don't you come oftener?"

"When I do come, it 's not to look at Mrs. Peniston's furniture."

"Nonsense," she said, "You don't come at all—and yet we get on so well when we meet."

"Perhaps that 's the reason," he answered promptly. "I 'm afraid I have n't any cream, you know—shall you mind a slice of lemon instead?"

"I shall like it better." She waited while he cut the lemon and dropped a thin disk into her cup. "But that is not the reason," she insisted.

"The reason for what?"

"For your never coming." She leaned forward with a shade of perplexity in her charming eyes. "I wish I knew—I wish I could make you out. Of course I know there are men who don't like me—one can tell that at a glance. And there are others who are afraid of me: they think I want to marry them." She smiled up at him frankly. "But I don't think you dislike me—and you can't possibly think I want to marry you."

"No—I absolve you of that," he agreed.

"Well, then——?"

He had carried his cup to the fireplace, and stood leaning against the chimney-piece and looking down on her with an air of indolent amusement. The provocation in her eyes increased his amusement—he had not supposed she would waste her powder on such small game; but perhaps she was only keeping her hand in; or perhaps a girl of her type had no conversation but of the personal kind. At any rate, she was amazingly pretty, and he had asked her to tea and must live up to his obligations.

"Well, then," he said with a plunge," perhaps *that 's* the reason."

"What?"

"The fact that you don't want to marry me. Perhaps I don't regard it as such a strong inducement to go and see you." He felt a slight shiver down his spine as he ventured this, but her laugh reassured him.

"Dear Mr. Selden, that was n't worthy of you. It 's stupid of you to make love to me, and it is n't like you to be stupid." She leaned back, sipping her tea with an air so enchantingly judicial that, if they h.d been in her aunt's drawing-room, he might almost have tried to disprove her deduction.

"Don't you see," she continued, "that there are men enough to say pleasant things to me, and that what I want is a friend who won't be afraid to say disagreeable ones when I need them? Sometimes I have fancied you might be that friend—I don't know why, except that you are neither a prig nor a bounder, and that I should n't have to pretend with you or be on my guard against you." Her voice had dropped to a note of seriousness, and she sat gazing up at him with the troubled gravity of a child.

"You don't know how much I need such a friend," she said. "My aunt is full of copy-book axioms, but they were all meant to apply to conduct in the early fifties. I always feel that to live up to them would include wearing book-muslin with gigot sleeves. And the other women—my best friends—well, they use me or abuse me; but they don't care a straw what happens to me. I 've been about too long—people are getting tired of me; they are beginning to say I ought to marry."

There was a moment's pause, during which Selden meditated one or two replies calculated to add a momentary zest to the situation; but he rejected them in favour of the simple question: "Well, why don't you?"

She coloured and laughed. "Ah, I see you *are* a friend after all, and that is one of the disagreeable things I was asking for."

"It was n't meant to be disagreeable," he returned amicably. "Is n't marriage your vocation? Is n't it what you 're all brought up for?"

She sighed. "I suppose so. What else is there?"

"Exactly. And so why not take the plunge and have it over?"

She shrugged her shoulders. "You speak as if I ought to marry the first man who came along."

"I did n't mean to imply that you are as hard put to it as that. But there must be some one with the requisite qualifications."

She shook her head wearily. "I threw away one or two good chances when I first came out—I suppose every girl does; and you know I am horribly poor—and very expensive. I must have a great deal of money."

Selden had turned to reach for a cigarette-box on the mantelpiece.

"What 's become of Dillworth?" he asked.

"Oh, his mother was frightened—she was afraid I should have all the family jewels reset. And she wanted me to promise that I would n't do over the drawing-room."

"The very thing you are marrying for!"

"Exactly. So she packed him off to India."

"Hard luck—but you can do better than Dillworth."

He offered the box, and she took out three or four cigarettes, putting one between her lips and slipping the others into a little gold case attached to her long pearl chain.

"Have I time? Just a whiff, then." She leaned forward, holding the tip of her cigarette to his. As she did so, he noted, with a purely impersonal enjoyment, how evenly the black lashes were set in her smooth white lids, and how the purplish shade beneath them melted into the pure pallour of the cheek.

She began to saunter about the room, examining the bookshelves between the puffs of her cigarette-smoke. Some of the volumes had the ripe tints of good tooling and old morocco, and her eyes lingered on them caressingly, not with the appreciation of the expert, but with the pleasure in agreeable tones and textures that was one of her inmost susceptibilities. Suddenly her expression changed from desultory enjoyment to active conjecture, and she turned to Selden with a question.

"You collect, don't you—you know about first editions and things?"

"As much as a man may who has no money to spend. Now and then I pick up something in the rubbish heap; and I go and look on at the big sales."

She had again addressed herself to the shelves, but her eyes now swept them inattentively, and he saw that she was preoccupied with a new idea.

"And Americana—do you collect Americana?"

Selden stared and laughed.

"No, that 's rather out of my line. I 'm not really a collector, you see; I simply like to have good editions of the books I am fond of."

She made a slight grimace. "And Americana are horribly dull, I suppose?"

"I should fancy so—except to the historian. But your real collector values a thing for its rarity. I don't suppose the buyers of Americana sit up reading them all night—old Jefferson Gryce certainly did n't."

She was listening with keen attention. "And yet they fetch fabulous prices, don't they? It seems so odd to want to pay a lot for an ugly badly-printed book that one is never going to read! And I suppose most of the owners of Americana are not historians either?"

"No; very few of the historians can afford to buy them. They have to use those in the public libraries or in private collections. It seems to be the mere rarity that attracts the average collector."

He had seated himself on an arm of the chair near which she was standing, and she continued to question him, asking which were the rarest volumes, whether the Jefferson Gryce collection was really considered the finest in the world, and what was the largest price ever fetched by a single volume.

It was so pleasant to sit there looking up at her, as she lifted now one book and then another from the shelves, fluttering the pages between her fingers, while her drooping profile was outlined against the warm background of old bindings, that he talked on without pausing to wonder at her sudden interest in so unsuggestive a subject. But he could never be long with her without trying to find a reason for what she was doing, and as she replaced his first edition of La Bruyère and turned away from the bookcases, he began to ask himself what she had been driving at. Her next question was not of a nature to enlighten him. She

paused before him with a smile which seemed at once designed to admit
him to her familiarity, and to remind him of the restrictions it imposed.

"Don't you ever mind," she asked suddenly, "not being rich
enough to buy all the books you want?"

He followed her glance about the room, with its worn furniture and
shabby walls.

"Don't I just? Do you take me for a saint on a pillar?"

"And having to work—do you mind that?"

"Oh, the work itself is not so bad—I'm rather fond of the law."

"No; but the being tied down: the routine—don't you ever want to
get away, to see new places and people?"

"Horribly—especially when I see all my friends rushing to the
steamer."

She drew a sympathetic breath. "But do you mind enough—to
marry to get out of it?"

Selden broke into a laugh. "God forbid!" he declared.

She rose with a sigh, tossing her cigarette into the grate.

"Ah, there's the difference—a girl must, a man may if he chooses."
She surveyed him critically. "Your coat's a little shabby—but who
cares? It doesn't keep people from asking you to dine. If I were shabby
no one would have me: a woman is asked out as much for her clothes as
for herself. The clothes are the background, the frame, if you like: they
don't make success, but they are a part of it. Who wants a dingy woman?
We are expected to be pretty and well-dressed till we drop—and if we
can't keep it up alone, we have to go into partnership."

Selden glanced at her with amusement: it was impossible, even with
her lovely eyes imploring him, to take a sentimental view of her case.

"Ah, well, there must be plenty of capital on the look-out for such
an investment. Perhaps you'll meet your fate tonight at the Trenors'."

She returned his look interrogatively.

"I thought you might be going there—oh, not in that capacity! But
there are to be a lot of your set—Gwen Van Osburgh, the Wetheralls,
Lady Cressida Raith—and the George Dorsets."

She paused a moment before the last name, and shot a query
through her lashes; but he remained imperturbable.

"Mrs. Trenor asked me; but I can't get away till the end of the week;
and those big parties bore me."

"Ah, so they do me," she exclaimed.

"Then why go?"

"It's part of the business—you forget! And besides, if I did n't, I
should be playir bézique with my aunt at Richfield Springs."

"That 's almost as bad as marrying Dillworth," he agreed, and they both laughed for pure pleasure in their sudden intimacy.

She glanced at the clock.

"Dear me! I must be off. It 's after five."

She paused before the mantelpiece, studying herself in the mirror while she adjusted her veil. The attitude revealed the long slope of her slender sides, which gave a kind of wild-wood grace to her outline — as though she were a captured dryad subdued to the conventions of the drawing-room; and Selden reflected that it was the same streak of sylvan freedom in her nature that lent such savour to her artificiality.

He followed her across the room to the entrance-hall; but on the threshold she held out her hand with a gesture of leave-taking.

"It 's been delightful; and now you will have to return my visit."

"But don't you want me to see you to the station?"

"No; good bye here, please."

She let her hand lie in his a moment, smiling up at him adorably.

"Good bye, then — and good luck at Bellomont!" he said, opening the door for her.

On the landing she paused to look about her. There were a thousand chances to one against her meeting anybody, but one could never tell, and she always paid for her rare indiscretions by a violent reaction of prudence. There was no one in sight, however, but a char-woman who was scrubbing the stairs. Her own stout person and its surrounding implements took up so much room that Lily, to pass her, had to gather up her skirts and brush against the wall. As she did so, the woman paused in her work and looked up curiously, resting her clenched red fists on the wet cloth she had just drawn from her pail. She had a broad sallow face, slightly pitted with small-pox, and thin straw-coloured hair through which her scalp shone unpleasantly.

"I beg your pardon," said Lily, intending by her politeness to convey a criticism of the other's manner.

The woman, without answering, pushed her pail aside, and continued to stare as Miss Bart swept by with a murmur of silken linings. Lily felt herself flushing under the look. What did the creature suppose? Could one never do the simplest, the most harmless thing, without subjecting one's self to some odious conjecture? Half way down the next flight, she smiled to think that a char-woman's stare should so perturb her. The poor thing was probably dazzled by such as unwonted apparition. But *were* such apparitions unwonted on Selden's stairs? Miss Bart was not familiar with the moral code of bachelors' flat-houses, and her colour rose again as it occurred to her that the woman's persistent gaze implied a groping among past associations. But she put aside the thought with a smile at her own fears, and hastened downward, wondering if she should find a cab short of Fifth Avenue.

Under the Georgian porch she paused again, scanning the street for a hansom. None was in sight, but as she reached the sidewalk she ran against a small glossy-looking man with a gardenia in his coat, who raised his hat with a surprised exclamation.

"Miss Bart? Well—of all people! This *is* luck," he declared; and she caught a twinkle of amused curiosity between his screwed-up lids.

"Oh, Mr. Rosedale—how are you?" she said, perceiving that the irrepressible annoyance on her face was reflected in the sudden intimacy of his smile.

Mr. Rosedale stood scanning her with interest and approval. He was a plump rosy man of the blond Jewish type, with smart London clothes fitting him like upholstery, and small sidelong eyes which gave him the air of appraising people as if they were bric-a-brac. He glanced up interrogatively at the porch of the Benedick.

"Been up to town for a little shopping, I suppose?" he said, in a tone which had the familiarity of a touch.

Miss Bart shrank from it slightly, and then flung herself into precipitate explanations.

"Yes—I came up to see my dress-maker. I am just on my way to catch the train to the Trenors'."

"Ah—your dress-maker; just so," he said blandly. "I did n't know there were any dress-makers in the Benedick."

"The Benedick?" She looked gently puzzled. "Is that the name of this building?"

"Yes, that 's the name: I believe it 's an old word for bachelor, is n't it? I happen to own the building—that 's the way I know." His smile deepened as he added with increasing assurance: "But you must let me take you to the station. The Trenors are at Bellomont, of course? You 've barely time to catch the five-forty. The dress-maker kept you waiting, I suppose."

Lily stiffened under the pleasantry.

"Oh, thanks," she stammered; and at that moment her eye caught a hansom drifting down Madison Avenue, and she hailed it with a desperate gesture.

"You 're very kind; but I could n't think of troubling you," she said, extending her hand to Mr. Rosedale; and heedless of his protestations, she sprang into the rescuing vehicle, and called out a breathless order to the driver.

II

In the hansom she leaned back with a sigh.

Why must a girl pay so dearly for her least escape from routine? Why could one never do a natural thing without having to screen it behind a structure of artifice? She had yielded to a passing impulse in going to Lawrence Selden's rooms, and it was so seldom that she could allow herself the luxury of an impulse! This one, at any rate, was going to cost her rather more than she could afford. She was vexed to see that, in spite of so many years of vigilance, she had blundered twice within five minutes. That stupid story about her dress-maker was bad enough—it would have been so simple to tell Rosedale that she had been taking tea with Selden! The mere statement of the fact would have rendered it innocuous. But, after having let herself be surprised in a falsehood, it was doubly stupid to snub the witness of her discomfiture. If she had had the presence of mind to let Rosedale drive her to the station, the concession might have purchased his silence. He had his race's accuracy in the appraisal of values, and to be seen walking down the platform at the crowded afternoon hour in the company of Miss Lily Bart would have been money in his pocket, as he might himself have phrased it. He knew, of course, that there would be a large house-party at Bellomont, and the possibility of being taken for one of Mrs. Trenor's guests was doubtless included in his calculations. Mr. Rosedale was still at a stage in his social ascent when it was of importance to produce such impressions.

The provoking part was that Lily knew all this—knew how easy it would have been to silence him on the spot, and how difficult it might be to do so afterward. Mr. Simon Rosedale was a man who made it his business to know everything about every one, whose idea of showing himself to be at home in society was to display an inconvenient familiarity with the habits of those with whom he wished to be thought intimate. Lily was sure that within twenty-four hours the story of her visiting her dress-maker at the Benedick would be in active circulation among Mr. Rosedale's acquaintants. The worst of it was that she had always snubbed and ignored him. On his first appearance—when her improvident cousin, Jack Stepney, had obtained for him (in return for favours too easily guessed) a card to one of the vast impersonal Van Osburgh "crushes"—Rosedale, with that mixture of artistic sensibility and business astuteness which characterizes his race, had instantly gravitated toward Miss Bart. She understood his motives, for her own course was guided by as nice calculations. Training and experience had taught her to be hospitable to newcomers, since the most unpromising might be useful later on, and there were plenty of available *oubliettes* to swallow them if they were not. But some intuitive repugnance, getting the better of years of social discipline, had made her push Mr. Rosedale into his *oubliette* without a trial. He had left behind only the ripple of amusement which his speedy despatch had caused among her friends; and though later (to shift the metaphor) he reappeared lower down the stream, it was only in fleeting glimpses, with long submergences between.

Hitherto Lily had been undisturbed by scruples. In her little set Mr. Rosedale had been pronounced "impossible," and Jack Stepney roundly snubbed for his attempt to pay his debts in dinner invitations. Even Mrs. Trenor, whose taste for variety had led her into some hazardous experiments, resisted Jack's attempts to disguise Mr. Rosedale as a novelty, and declared that he was the same little Jew who had been served up and rejected at the social board a dozen times within her memory; and while Judy Trenor was obdurate there was small chance of Mr. Rosedale's penetrating beyond the outer limbo of the Van Osburgh crushes. Jack gave up the contest with a laughing "You 'll see," and, sticking manfully to his guns, showed himself with Rosedale at the fashionable restaurants, in company with the personally vivid if socially obscure ladies who are available for such purposes. But the attempt had hitherto been vain, and as Rosedale undoubtedly paid for the dinners, the laugh remained with his debtor.

Mr. Rosedale, it will be seen, was thus far not a factor to be feared—unless one put one's self in his power. And this was precisely what Miss Bart had done. Her clumsy fib had let him see that she had something to conceal; and she was sure he had a score to settle with her. Something in his smile told her he had not forgotten. She turned from the thought with a little shiver, but it hung on her all the way to the station, and dogged her down the platform with the persistency of Mr. Rosedale himself.

She had just time to take her seat before the train started; but having arranged herself in her corner with the instinctive feeling for effect which never forsook her, she glanced about in the hope of seeing some other member of the Trenors' party. She wanted to get away from herself, and conversation was the only means of escape that she knew.

Her search was rewarded by the discovery of a very blond young man with a soft reddish beard, who, at the other end of the carriage, appeared to be dissembling himself behind an unfolded newspaper. Lily's eye brightened, and a faint smile relaxed the drawn lines of her mouth. She had known that Mr. Percy Gryce was to be at Bellomont, but she had not counted on the luck of having him to herself in the train; and the fact banished all perturbing thoughts of Mr. Rosedale. Perhaps, after all, the day was to end more favourably than it had begun.

She began to cut the pages of a novel, tranquilly studying her prey through downcast lashes while she organized a method of attack. Something in his attitude of conscious absorption told her that he was aware of her presence: no one had ever been quite so engrossed in an evening paper! She guessed that he was too shy to come up to her, and that she would have to devise some means of approach which should not appear to be an advance on her part. It amused her to think that any one as rich as Mr. Percy Gryce should be shy; but she was gifted with treasures of indulgence for such idiosyncrasies, and besides, his timidity might serve her purpose better than too much assurance. She had the art of giving self-confidence to the embarrassed, but she was not equally sure of being able to embarrass the self-confident.

She waited till the train had emerged from the tunnel and was racing between the ragged edges of the northern suburbs. Then, as it lowered its speed near Yonkers, she rose from her seat and drifted slowly down the carriage. As she passed Mr. Gryce, the train gave a lurch, and he was aware of a slender hand gripping the back of his chair. He rose with a start, his ingenuous face looking as though it had been dipped in crimson: even the reddish tint in his beard seemed to deepen.

The train swayed again, almost flinging Miss Bart into his arms. She steadied herself with a laugh and drew back; but he was enveloped in the scent of her dress, and his shoulder had felt her fugitive touch.

"Oh, Mr. Gryce, is it you? I'm so sorry—I was trying to find the porter and get some tea."

She held out her hand as the train resumed its level rush, and they stood exchanging a few words in the aisle. Yes—he was going to Bellomont. He had heard she was to be of the party—he blushed again as he admitted it. And was he to be there for a whole week? How delightful!

But at this point one or two belated passengers from the last station forced their way into the carriage, and Lily had to retreat to her seat.

"The chair next to mine is empty—do take it," she said over her shoulder; and Mr. Gryce, with considerable embarrassment, succeeded in effecting an exchange which enabled him to transport himself and his bags to her side.

"Ah—and here is the porter, and perhaps we can have some tea."

She signalled to that official, and in a moment, with the ease that seemed to attend the fulfilment of all her wishes, a little table had been set up between the seats, and she had helped Mr. Gryce to bestow his encumbering properties beneath it.

When the tea came he watched her in silent fascination while her hands flitted above the tray, looking miraculously fine and slender in contrast to the coarse china and lumpy bread. It seemed wonderful to him that any one should perform with such careless ease the difficult task of making tea in public in a lurching train. He would never have dared to order it for himself, lest he should attract the notice of his fellow-passengers; but, secure in the shelter of her conspicuousness, he sipped the inky draught with a delicious sense of exhilaration.

Lily, with the flavour of Selden's caravan tea on her lips, had no great fancy to drown it in the railway brew which seemed such nectar to her companion; but, rightly judging that one of the charms of tea is the fact of drinking it together, she proceeded to give the last touch to Mr. Gryce's enjoyment by smiling at him across her lifted cup.

"Is it quite right—I have n't made it too strong?" she asked solicitously; and he replied with conviction that he had never tasted better tea.

"I daresay it is true," she reflected; and her imagination was fired by the thought that Mr. Gryce, who might have sounded the depths of the most complex self-indulgence, was perhaps actually taking his first journey alone with a pretty woman.

It struck her as providential that she should be the instrument of his initiation. Some girls would not have known how to manage him. They would have over-emphasized the novelty of the adventure, trying to make him feel in it the zest of an escapade. But Lily's methods were more delicate. She remembered that her cousin Jack Stepney had once defined Mr. Gryce as the young man who had promised his mother never to go out in the rain without his overshoes; and acting on this hint, she resolved to impart a gently domestic air to the scene, in the hope that her companion, instead of feeling that he was doing something reckless or unusual, would merely be led to dwell on the advantage of always having a companion to make one's tea in the train.

But in spite of her efforts, conversation flagged after the tray had been removed, and she was driven to take a fresh measurement of Mr. Gryce's limitations. It was not, after all, opportunity but imagination that he lacked: he had a mental palate which would never learn to distinguish between railway tea and nectar. There was, however, one topic she could rely on: one spring that she had only to touch to set his simple machinery in motion. She had refrained from touching it because it was a last resource, and she had relied on other arts to stimulate other sensations; but as a settled look of dulness began to creep over his candid features, she saw that extreme measures were necessary.

"And how," she said, leaning forward, "are you getting on with your Americana?"

His eye became a degree less opaque: it was as though an incipient film had been removed from it, and she felt the pride of a skilful operator.

"I 've got a few new things," he said, suffused with pleasure, but lowering his voice as though he feared his fellow-passengers might be in league to despoil him.

She returned a sympathetic enquiry, and gradually he was drawn on to talk of his latest purchases. It was the one subject which enabled him to forget himself, or allowed him, rather, to remember himself without constraint, because he was at home in it, and could assert a superiority that there were few to dispute. Hardly any of his acquaintances cared for Americana, or knew anything about them; and the consciousness of this ignorance threw Mr. Gryce's knowledge into agreeable relief. The only difficulty was to introduce the topic and to keep it to the front; most people showed no desire to have their ignorance dispelled, and Mr. Gryce was like a merchant whose warehouses are crammed with an unmarketable commodity.

But Miss Bart, it appeared, really did want to know about Americana; and moreover, she was already sufficiently informed to make the task of farther instruction as easy as it was agreeable. She questioned him intelligently, she heard him submissively; and, prepared for the look of lassitude which usually crept over his listeners' faces, he grew eloquent under her receptive gaze. The "points" she had had the presence of mind to glean from Selden, in anticipation of this very contingency, were serving her to such good purpose that she began to think her visit to him had been the luckiest incident of the day. She had once more shown her talent for profiting by the unexpected, and dangerous theories as to the advisability of yielding to impulse were germinating under the surface of smiling attention which she continued to present to her companion.

Mr. Gryce's sensations, if less definite, were equally agreeable. He felt the confused titillation with which the lower organisms welcome the gratification of their needs, and all his senses floundered in a vague well-being, through which Miss Bart's personality was dimly but pleasantly perceptible.

Mr. Gryce's interest in Americana had not originated with himself: it was impossible to think of him as evolving any taste of his own. An uncle had left him a collection already noted among bibliophiles; the existence of the collection was the only fact that had ever shed glory on the name of Gryce, and the nephew took as much pride in his inheritance as though it had been his own work. Indeed, he gradually came to regard it as such, and to feel a sense of personal complacency when he chanced on any reference to the Gryce Americana. Anxious as he was to avoid personal notice, he took, in the printed mention of his name, a pleasure so exquisite and excessive that it seemed a compensation for his shrinking from publicity.

To enjoy the sensation as often as possible, he subscribed to all the reviews dealing with book-collecting in general, and American history in particular, and as allusions to his library abounded in the pages of these journals, which formed his only reading, he came to regard himself as figuring prominently in the public eye, and to enjoy the thought of the interest which would be excited if the persons he met in the street, or sat among in travelling, were suddenly to be told that he was the possessor of the Gryce Americana.

Most timidities have such secret compensations, and Miss Bart was discerning enough to know that the inner vanity is generally in proportion to the outer self-depreciation. With a more confident person she would not have dared to dwell so long on one topic, or to show such exaggerated interest in it; but she had rightly guessed that Mr. Gryce's egoism was a thirsty soil, requiring constant nurture from without. Miss Bart had the gift of following an undercurrent of thought while she appeared to be sailing on the surface of conversation; and in this case her mental excursion took the form of a rapid survey of Mr. Percy Gryce's future as combined with her own. The Gryces were from Albany, and but lately introduced to the metropolis, where the mother and son had come, after old Jefferson Gryce's death, to take possession of his house in Madison Avenue — an appalling house, all brown stone without and black walnut within, with the Gryce library in a fire-proof annex that looked like a mausoleum. Lily, however, knew all about them: young Mr. Gryce's arrival had fluttered the maternal breasts of New York, and when a girl has no mother to palpitate for her she must needs be on the alert for herself. Lily, therefore, had not only contrived to put herself in the young man's way, but had made the acquaintance of Mrs. Gryce, a monumental woman with the voice of a pulpit orator and a mind preoccupied with the iniquities of her servants, who came sometimes to sit with Mrs. Peniston and learn from that lady how she managed to prevent the kitchenmaid's smuggling groceries out of the house. Mrs. Gryce had a kind of impersonal benevolence: cases of individual need she regarded with suspicion, but she subscribed to Institutions when their annual reports showed an impressive surplus. Her domestic duties were manifold, for they extended from furtive inspections of the servants' bedrooms to unannounced descents to the cellar; but she had never allowed herself many pleasures. Once, however, she had had a special edition of the Sarum Rule printed in rubric and presented to every clergyman in the diocese; and the gilt album in which their letters of thanks were pasted formed the chief ornament of her drawing-room table.

Percy had been brought up in the principles which so excellent a woman was sure to inculcate. Every form of prudence and suspicion had been grafted on a nature originally reluctant and cautious, with the result that it would have seemed hardly needful for Mrs. Gryce to extract his promise about the overshoes, so little likely was he to hazard himself abroad in the rain. After attaining his majority, and coming into the fortune which the late Mr. Gryce had made out of a patent device for excluding fresh air from hotels, the young man continued to live with his mother in Albany; but on Jefferson Gryce's death, when another large property passed into her son's hands, Mrs. Gryce thought that what she called his "interests" demanded his presence in New York. She accordingly installed herself in the Madison Avenue house, and Percy, whose sense of duty was not inferior to his mother's, spent all his week days in the handsome Broad Street office where a batch of pale men on small salaries had grown grey in the management of the Gryce estate, and where he was initiated with becoming reverence into every detail of the art of accumulation.

As far as Lily could learn, this had hitherto been Mr. Gryce's only occupation, and she might have been pardoned for thinking it not too hard a task to interest a young man who had been kept on such low diet. At any rate, she felt herself so completely in command of the situation that she yielded to a sense of security in which all fear of Mr. Rosedale, and of the difficulties on which that fear was contingent, vanished beyond the edge of thought.

The stopping of the train at Garrisons would not have distracted her from these thoughts, had she not caught a sudden look of distress in her companion's eye. His seat faced toward the door, and she guessed that he had been perturbed by the approach of an acquaintance; a fact confirmed by the turning of heads and general sense of commotion which her own entrance into a railway-carriage was apt to produce.

She knew the symptoms at once, and was not surprised to be hailed by the high notes of a pretty woman, who entered the train accompanied by a maid, a bull-terrier, and a footman staggering under a load of bags and dressing-cases.

"Oh, Lily—are you going to Bellomont? Then you can't let me have your seat, I suppose? But I *must* have a seat in this carriage—porter, you must find me a place at once. Can't some one be put somewhere else? I want to be with my friends. Oh, how do you do, Mr. Gryce? Do please make him understand that I must have a seat next to you and Lily."

Mrs. George Dorset, regardless of the mild efforts of a traveller with a carpet-bag, who was doing his best to make room for her by getting out of the train, stood in the middle of the aisle, diffusing about her that general sense of exasperation which a pretty woman on her travels not infrequently creates.

She was smaller and thinner than Lily Bart, with a restless pliability of pose, as if she could have been crumpled up and run through a ring, like the sinuous draperies she affected. Her small pale face seemed the mere setting of a pair of dark exaggerated eyes, of which the visionary gaze contrasted curiously with her self-assertive tone and gestures; so that, as one of her friends observed, she was like a disembodied spirit who took up a great deal of room.

Having finally discovered that the seat adjoining Miss Bart's was at her disposal, she possessed herself of it with a farther displacement of her surroundings, explaining meanwhile that she had come across from Mount Kisco in her motor-car that morning, and had been kicking her heels for an hour at Garrisons, without even the alleviation of a cigarette, her brute of a husband having neglected to replenish her case before they parted that morning.

"And at this hour of the day I don't suppose you 've a single one left, have you, Lily?" she plaintively concluded.

Miss Bart caught the startled glance of Mr. Percy Gryce, whose own lips were never defiled by tobacco.

"What an absurd question, Bertha!" she exclaimed, blushing at the thought of the store she had laid in at Lawrence Selden's.

"Why, don't you smoke? Since when have you given it up? What— you never———And you don't either, Mr. Gryce? Ah, of course— how stupid of me—I understand."

And Mrs. Dorset leaned back against her travelling cushions with a smile which made Lily wish there had been no vacant seat beside her own.

III

Bridge at Bellomont usually lasted till the small hours; and when Lily went to bed that night she had played too long for her own good.

Feeling no desire for the self-communion which awaited her in her room, she lingered on the broad stairway, looking down into the hall below, where the last card-players were grouped about the tray of tall glasses and silver-collared decanters which the butler had just placed on a low table near the fire.

The hall was arcaded, with a gallery supported on columns of pale yellow marble. Tall clumps of flowering plants were grouped against a background of dark foliage in the angles of the walls. On the crimson carpet a deer-hound and two or three spaniels dozed luxuriously before the fire, and the light from the great central lantern overhead shed a brightness on the women's hair and struck sparks from their jewels as they moved.

There were moments when such scenes delighted Lily, when they gratified her sense of beauty and her craving for the external finish of life; there were others when they gave a sharper edge to the meagreness of her own opportunities. This was one of the moments when the sense of contrast was uppermost, and she turned away impatiently as Mrs. George Dorset, glittering in serpentine spangles, drew Percy Gryce in her wake to a confidential nook beneath the gallery.

It was not that Miss Bart was afraid of losing her newly-acquired hold over Mr. Gryce. Mrs. Dorset might startle or dazzle him, but she had neither the skill nor the patience to effect his capture. She was too self-engrossed to penetrate the recesses of his shyness, and besides, why should she care to give herself the trouble? At most it might amuse her to make sport of his simplicity for an evening—after that he would be merely a burden to her, and knowing this, she was far too experienced to encourage him. But the mere thought of that other woman, who could take a man up and toss him aside as she willed, without having to regard him as a possible factor in her plans, filled Lily Bart with envy. She had been bored all the afternoon by Percy Gryce—the mere thought seemed to waken an echo of his droning voice—but she could not ignore him on the morrow, she must follow up her success, must submit to more boredom, must be ready with fresh compliances and adaptabilities, and all on the bare chance that he might ultimately decide to do her the honour of boring her for life.

It was a hateful fate—but how escape from it? What choice had she? To be herself, or a Gerty Farish. As she entered her bedroom, with its softly-shaded lights, her lace dressing-gown lying across the silken bed-spread, her little embroidered slippers before the fire, a vase of carnations filling the air with perfume, and the last novels and magazines lying uncut on a table beside the reading-lamp, she had a vision of Miss Farish's cramped flat, with its cheap conveniences and hideous wall-papers. No; she was not made for mean and shabby surroundings, for the squalid compromises of poverty. Her whole being dilated in an atmosphere of luxury; it was the background she required, the only climate she could breathe in. But the luxury of others was not what she wanted. A few years ago it had sufficed her: she had taken her daily meed of pleasure without caring who provided it. Now she was beginning to chafe at the obligations it imposed, to feel herself a mere pensioner on the splendour which had once seemed to belong to her. There were even moments when she was conscious of having to pay her way.

For a long time she had refused to play bridge. She knew she could not afford it, and she was afraid of acquiring so expensive a taste. She had seen the danger exemplified in more than one of her associates — in young Ned Silverton, for instance, the charming fair boy now seated in abject rapture at the elbow of Mrs. Fisher, a striking divorcée with eyes and gowns as emphatic as the head-lines of her "case." Lily could remember when young Silverton had stumbled into their circle, with the air of a strayed Arcadian who has published charming sonnets in his college journal. Since then he had developed a taste for Mrs. Fisher and bridge, and the latter at least had involved him in expenses from which he had been more than once rescued by harassed maiden sisters, who treasured the sonnets, and went without sugar in their tea to keep their darling afloat. Ned's case was familiar to Lily: she had seen his charming eyes — which had a good deal more poetry in them than the sonnets — change from surprise to amusement, and from amusement to anxiety, as he passed under the spell of the terrible god of chance; and she was afraid of discovering the same symptoms in her own case.

For in the last year she had found that her hostesses expected her to take a place at the card-table. It was one of the taxes she had to pay for their prolonged hospitality, and for the dresses and trinkets which occasionally replenished her insufficient wardrobe. And since she had played regularly the passion had grown on her. Once or twice of late she had won a large sum, and instead of keeping it against future losses, had spent it in dress or jewelry; and the desire to atone for this imprudence, combined with the increasing exhilaration of the game, drove her to risk higher stakes at each fresh venture. She tried to excuse herself on the plea that, in the Trenor set, if one played at all one must either play high or be set down as priggish or stingy; but she knew that the gambling passion was upon her, and that in her present surroundings there was small hope of resisting it.

Tonight the luck had been persistently bad, and the little gold purse which hung among her trinkets was almost empty when she returned to her room. She unlocked the wardrobe, and taking out her jewel-case, looked under the tray for the roll of bills from which she had replenished the purse before going down to dinner. Only twenty dollars were left: the discovery was so startling that for a moment she fancied she must have been robbed. Then she took paper and pencil, and seating herself at the writing-table, tried to reckon up what she had spent during the day. Her head was throbbing with fatigue, and she had to go over the figures again and again; but at last it became clear to her that she had lost three hundred dollars at cards. She took out her chequebook to see if her balance was larger than she remembered, but found she had erred in the other direction. Then she returned to her calculations; but figure as she would, she could not conjure back the vanished three hundred dollars. It was the sum she had set aside to pacify her dress-maker — unless she should decide to use it as a sop to the jeweller. At any rate, she had so many uses for it that its very insufficiency had caused her to play high in the hope of doubling it. But of course she had lost — she who needed every penny, while Bertha Dorset, whose husband showered money on her, must have pocketed at least five hundred, and Judy Trenor, who could have afforded to lose a thousand a night, had left the table clutching such a heap of bills that she had been unable to shake hands with her guests when they bade her good night.

A world in which such things could be seemed a miserable place to Lily Bart; but then she had never been able to understand the laws of a universe which was so ready to leave her out of its calculations.

She began to undress without ringing for her maid, whom she had sent to bed. She had been long enough in bondage to other people's pleasure to be considerate of those who depended on hers, and in her bitter moods it sometimes struck her that she and her maid were in the same position, except that the latter received her wages more regularly.

As she sat before the mirror brushing her hair, her face looked hollow and pale, and she was frightened by two little lines near her mouth, faint flaws in the smooth curve of the cheek.

"Oh, I must stop worrying!" she exclaimed. "Unless it's the electric light——" she reflected, springing up from her seat and lighting the candles on the dressing-table.

She turned out the wall-lights, and peered at herself between the candle-flames. The white oval of her face swam out waveringly from a background of shadows, the uncertain light blurring it like a haze; but the two lines about the mouth remained.

Lily rose and undressed in haste.

"It is only because I am tired and have such odious things to think about," she kept repeating; and it seemed an added injustice that petty cares should leave a trace on the beauty which was her only defence against them.

But the odious things were there, and remained with her. She returned wearily to the thought of Percy Gryce, as a wayfarer picks up a heavy load and toils on after a brief rest. She was almost sure she had "landed" him: a few days' work and she would win her reward. But the reward itself seemed unpalatable just then: she could get no zest from the thought of victory. It would be a rest from worry, no more — and how little that would have seemed to her a few years earlier! Her ambitions had shrunk gradually in the desiccating air of failure. But why had she failed? Was it her own fault or that of destiny?

She remembered how her mother, after they had lost their money, used to say to her with a kind of fierce vindictiveness: "But you 'll get it all back — you 'll get it all back, with your face." . . . The remembrance roused a whole train of association, and she lay in the darkness reconstructing the past out of which her present had grown.

A house in which no one ever dined at home unless there was "company"; a door-bell perpetually ringing; a hall-table showered with square envelopes which were opened in haste, and oblong envelopes which were allowed to gather dust in the depths of a bronze jar; a series of French and English maids giving warning amid a chaos of hurriedly-ransacked wardrobes and dress-closets; an equally changing dynasty of nurses and footmen; quarrels in the pantry, the kitchen and the drawing-room; precipitate trips to Europe, and returns with gorged trunks and days of interminable unpacking; semi-annual discussions as to where the summer should be spent, grey interludes of economy and brilliant reactions of expense — such was the setting of Lily Bart's first memories.

Ruling the turbulent element called home was the vigorous and determined figure of a mother still young enough to dance her ball-dresses to rags, while the hazy outline of a neutral-tinted father filled an intermediate space between the butler and the man who came to wind the clocks. Even to the eyes of infancy, Mrs. Hudson Bart had appeared young; but Lily could not recall the time when her father had not been bald and slightly stooping, with streaks of grey in his hair, and a tired walk. It was a shock to her to learn afterward that he was but two years older than her mother.

Lily seldom saw her father by daylight. All day he was "down town"; and in winter it was long after nightfall when she heard his fagged step on the stairs and his hand on the school-room door. He would kiss her in silence, and ask one or two questions of the nurse or the governess; then Mrs. Bart's maid would come to remind him that he was dining out, and he would hurry away with a nod to Lily. In summer, when he joined them for a Sunday at Newport or Southampton, he was even more effaced and silent than in winter. It seemed to tire him to rest, and he would sit for hours staring at the sea-line from a quiet corner of the verandah, while the clatter of his wife's existence went on unheeded a few feet off. Generally, however, Mrs. Bart and Lily went to Europe for the summer, and before the steamer was half way over Mr. Bart had dipped below the horizon. Sometimes his daughter heard him denounced for having neglected to forward Mrs. Bart's remittances; but for the most part he was never mentioned or thought of till his patient stooping figure presented itself on the New York dock as a buffer between the magnitude of his wife's luggage and the restrictions of the American custom-house.

In this desultory yet agitated fashion life went on through Lily's teens: a zig-zag broken course down which the family craft glided on a rapid current of amusement, tugged at by the underflow of a perpetual need—the need of more money. Lily could not recall the time when there had been money enough, and in some vague way her father seemed always to blame for the deficiency. It could certainly not be the fault of Mrs. Bart, who was spoken of by her friends as a "wonderful manager." Mrs. Bart was famous for the unlimited effect she produced on limited means; and to the lady and her acquaintances there was something heroic in living as though one were much richer than one's bank-book denoted.

Lily was naturally proud of her mother's aptitude in this line: she had been brought up in the faith that, whatever it cost, one must have a good cook, and be what Mrs. Bart called "decently dressed." Mrs. Bart's worst reproach to her husband was to ask him if he expected her to "live like a pig"; and his replying in the negative was always regarded as a justification for cabling to Paris for an extra dress or two, and telephoning to the jeweller that he might, after all, send home the turquoise bracelet which Mrs. Bart had looked at that morning.

Lily knew people who "lived like pigs," and their appearance and surroundings justified her mother's repugnance to that form of existence. They were mostly cousins, who inhabited dingy houses with engravings from Cole's Voyage of Life on the drawing-room walls, and slatternly parlour-maids who said "I 'll go and see" to visitors calling at an hour when all right-minded persons are conventionally if not actually out. The disgusting part of it was that many of these cousins were rich, so that Lily imbibed the idea that if people lived like pigs it was from choice, and through the lack of any proper standard of conduct. This gave her a sense of reflected superiority, and she did not need Mrs. Bart's comments on the family frumps and misers to foster her naturally lively taste for splendour.

Lily was nineteen when circumstances caused her to revise her view of the universe.

The previous year she had made a dazzling début fringed by a heavy thunder-cloud of bills. The light of the début still lingered on the horizon, but the cloud had thickened; and suddenly it broke. The suddenness added to the horror; and there were still times when Lily relived with painful vividness every detail of the day on which the blow fell. She and her mother had been seated at the luncheon-table, over the *chaufroix* and cold salmon of the previous night's dinner: it was one of Mrs. Bart's few economies to consume in private the expensive remnants of her hospitality. Lily was feeling the pleasant languor which is youth's penalty for dancing till dawn; but her mother, in spite of a few lines about the mouth, and under the yellow waves on her temples, was as alert, determined and high in colour as if she had risen from an untroubled sleep.

In the centre of the table, between the melting *marrons glacés* and candied cherries, a pyramid of American Beauties lifted their vigorous stems; they held their heads as high as Mrs. Bart, but their rose-colour had turned to a dissipated purple, and Lily's sense of fitness was disturbed by their reappearance on the luncheon-table.

"I really think, mother," she said reproachfully, "we might afford a few fresh flowers for luncheon. Just some jonquils or lilies-of-the-valley———"

Mrs. Bart stared. Her own fastidiousness had its eye fixed on the world, and she did not care how the luncheon-table looked when there was no one present at it but the family. But she smiled at her daughter's innocence.

"Lilies-of-the-valley," she said calmly, "cost two dollars a dozen at this season."

Lily was not impressed. She knew very little of the value of money.

"It would not take more than six dozen to fill that bowl," she argued.

"Six dozen what?" asked her father's voice in the doorway.

The two women looked up in surprise; though it was a Saturday, the sight of Mr. Bart at luncheon was an unwonted one. But neither his wife nor his daughter was sufficiently interested to ask an explanation.

Mr. Bart dropped into a chair, and sat gazing absently at the fragment of jellied salmon which the butler had placed before him.

"I was only saying," Lily began, "that I hate to see faded flowers at luncheon; and mother says a bunch of lilies-of-the-valley would not cost more than twelve dollars. May n't I tell the florist to send a few every day?"

She leaned confidently toward her father: he seldom refused her anything, and Mrs. Bart had taught her to plead with him when her own entreaties failed.

Mr. Bart sat motionless, his gaze still fixed on the salmon, and his lower jaw dropped; he looked even paler than usual, and his thin hair lay in untidy streaks on his forehead. Suddenly he looked at his daughter and laughed. The laugh was so strange that Lily coloured under it: she disliked being ridiculed, and her father seemed to see something ridiculous in the request. Perhaps he thought it foolish that she should trouble him about such a trifle.

"Twelve dollars—twelve dollars a day for flowers? Oh, certainly, my dear—give him an order for twelve hundred." He continued to laugh.

Mrs. Bart gave him a quick glance.

"You need n't wait, Poleworth—I will ring for you," she said to the butler.

The butler withdrew with an air of silent disapproval, leaving the remains of the *chaufroix* on the sideboard.

"What is the matter, Hudson? Are you ill?" said Mrs. Bart severely.

She had no tolerance for scenes which were not of her own making, and it was odious to her that her husband should make a show of himself before the servants.

"Are you ill?" she repeated.

"Ill?—— No, I 'm ruined," he said.

Lily made a frightened sound, and Mrs. Bart rose to her feet.

"Ruined——?" she cried; but controlling herself instantly, she turned a calm face to Lily.

"Shut the pantry door," she said.

Lily obeyed, and when she turned back into the room her father was sitting with both elbows on the table, the plate of salmon between them, and his head bowed on his hands.

Mrs. Bart stood over him with a white face which made her hair unnaturally yellow. She looked at Lily as the latter approached: her look was terrible, but her voice was modulated to a ghastly cheerfulness.

"Your father is not well—he does n't know what he is saying. It is nothing—but you had better go upstairs; and don't talk to the servants," she added.

Lily obeyed; she always obeyed when her mother spoke in that voice. She had not been deceived by Mrs. Bart's words: she knew at once that they were ruined. In the dark hours which followed, that awful fact overshadowed even her father's slow and difficult dying. To his wife he no longer counted: he had become extinct when he ceased to fulfil his purpose, and she sat at his side with the provisional air of a traveller who waits for a belated train to start. Lily's feelings were softer: she pitied him in a frightened ineffectual way. But the fact that he was for the most part unconscious, and that his attention, when she stole into the room, drifted away from her after a moment, made him even more of a stranger than in the nursery days when he had never come home till after dark. She seemed always to have seen him through a blur—first of sleepiness, then of distance and indifference—and now the fog had thickened till he was almost indistinguishable. If she could have performed any little services for him, or have exchanged with him a few of those affecting words which an extensive perusal of fiction had led her to connect with such occasions, the filial instinct might have stirred in her; but her pity, finding no active expression, remained in a state of spectatorship, overshadowed by her mother's grim unflagging resentment. Every look and act of Mrs. Bart's seemed to say: "You are sorry for him now—but you will feel differently when you see what he has done to us."

It was a relief to Lily when her father died.

Then a long winter set in. There was a little money left, but to Mrs. Bart it seemed worse than nothing—the mere mockery of what she was entitled to. What was the use of living if one had to live like a pig? She sank into a kind of furious apathy, a state of inert anger against fate. Her faculty for "managing" deserted her, or she no longer took sufficient pride in it to exert it. It was well enough to "manage" when by so doing one could keep one's own carriage; but when one's best contrivance did not conceal the fact that one had to go on foot, the effort was no longer worth making.

Lily and her mother wandered from place to place, now paying long visits to relations whose house-keeping Mrs. Bart criticized, and who deplored the fact that she let Lily breakfast in bed when the girl had no prospects before her, and now vegetating in cheap continental refuges, where Mrs. Bart held herself fiercely aloof from the frugal tea-tables of her companions in misfortune. She was especially careful to avoid her old friends and the scenes of her former successes. To be poor seemed to her such a confession of failure that it amounted to disgrace; and she detected a note of condescension in the friendliest advances.

Only one thought consoled her, and that was the contemplation of Lily's beauty. She studied it with a kind of passion, as though it were some weapon she had slowly fashioned for her vengeance. It was the last asset in their fortunes, the nucleus around which their life was to be rebuilt. She watched it jealously, as though it were her own property and Lily its mere custodian; and she tried to instil into the latter a sense of the responsibility that such a charge involved. She followed in imagination the career of other beauties, pointing out to her daughter what might be achieved through such a gift, and dwelling on the awful warning of those who, in spite of it, had failed to get what they wanted: to Mrs. Bart, only stupidity could explain the lamentable dénouement of some of her examples. She was not above the inconsistency of charging fate, rather than herself, with her own misfortunes; but she inveighed so acrimoniously against love-matches that Lily would have fancied her own marriage had been of that nature, had not Mrs. Bart frequently assured her that she had been "talked into it" — by whom, she never made clear.

Lily was duly impressed by the magnitude of her opportunities. The dinginess of her present life threw into enchanting relief the existence to which she felt herself entitled. To a less illuminated intelligence Mrs. Bart's counsels might have been dangerous; but Lily understood that beauty is only the raw material of conquest, and that to convert it into success other arts are required. She knew that to betray any sense of superiority was a subtler form of the stupidity her mother denounced, and it did not take her long to learn that a beauty needs more tact than the possessor of an average set of features.

Her ambitions were not as crude as Mrs. Bart's. It had been among that lady's grievances that her husband—in the early days, before he was too tired—had wasted his evenings in what she vaguely described as "reading poetry"; and among the effects packed off to auction after his death were a score or two of dingy volumes which had struggled for existence among the boots and medicine bottles of his dressing-room shelves. There was in Lily a vein of sentiment, perhaps transmitted from this source, which gave an idealizing touch to her most prosaic purposes. She liked to think of her beauty as a power for good, as giving her the opportunity to attain a position where she should make her influence felt in the vague diffusion of refinement and good taste. She was fond of pictures and flowers, and of sentimental fiction, and she could not help thinking that the possession of such tastes ennobled her desire for worldly advantages. She would not indeed have cared to marry a man who was merely rich: she was secretly ashamed of her mother's crude passion for money. Lily's preference would have been for an English nobleman with political ambitions and vast estates; or, for second choice, an Italian prince with a castle in the Apennines and an hereditary office in the Vatican. Lost causes had a romantic charm for her, and she liked to picture herself as standing aloof from the vulgar press of the Quirinal, and sacrificing her pleasure to the claims of an immemorial tradition. . . .

How long ago and how far off it all seemed! Those ambitions were hardly more futile and childish than the earlier ones which had centred about the possession of a French jointed doll with real hair. Was it only ten years since she had wavered in imagination between the English earl and the Italian prince? Relentlessly her mind travelled on over the dreary interval. . . .

After two years of hungry roaming Mrs. Bart had died—died of a deep disgust. She had hated dinginess, and it was her fate to be dingy. Her visions of a brilliant marriage for Lily had faded after the first year.

"People can't marry you if they don't see you—and how can they see you in these holes where we 're stuck?" That was the burden of her lament; and her last adjuration to her daughter was to escape from dinginess if she could.

"Don't let it creep up on you and drag you down. Fight your way out of it somehow—you 're young and can do it," she insisted.

She had died during one of their brief visits to New York, and there Lily at once became the centre of a family council composed of the wealthy relatives whom she had been taught to despise for living like pigs. It may be that they had an inkling of the sentiments in which she had been brought up, for none of them manifested a very lively desire for her company; indeed, the question threatened to remain unsolved till Mrs. Peniston with a sigh announced: "I 'll try her for a year."

Every one was surprised, but one and all concealed their surprise, lest Mrs. Peniston should be alarmed by it into reconsidering her decision.

Mrs. Peniston was Mr. Bart's widowed sister, and if she was by no means the richest of the family group, its other members nevertheless abounded in reasons why she was clearly destined by Providence to assume the charge of Lily. In the first place she was alone, and it would be charming for her to have a young companion. Then she sometimes travelled, and Lily's familiarity with foreign customs — deplored as a misfortune by her more conservative relatives — would at least enable her to act as a kind of courier. But as a matter of fact Mrs. Peniston had not been affected by these considerations. She had taken the girl simply because no one else would have her, and because she had the kind of moral *mauvaise honte* which makes the public display of selfishness difficult, though it does not interfere with its private indulgence. It would have been impossible for Mrs. Peniston to be heroic on a desert island, but with the eyes of her little world upon her she took a certain pleasure in her act.

She reaped the reward to which disinterestedness is entitled, and found an agreeable companion in her niece. She had expected to find Lily headstrong, critical and "foreign" — for even Mrs. Peniston, though she occasionally went abroad, had the family dread of foreignness — but the girl showed a pliancy, which, to a more penetrating mind than her aunt's, might have been less reassuring than the open selfishness of youth. Misfortune had made Lily supple instead of hardening her, and a pliable substance is less easy to break than a stiff one.

Mrs. Peniston, however, did not suffer from her niece's adaptability. Lily had no intention of taking advantage of her aunt's good nature. She was in truth grateful for the refuge offered her: Mrs. Peniston's opulent interior was at least not externally dingy. But dinginess is a quality which assumes all manner of disguises; and Lily soon found that it was as latent in the expensive routine of her aunt's life as in the makeshift existence of a continental pension.

Mrs. Peniston was one of the episodical persons who form the padding of life. It was impossible to believe that she had herself ever been a focus of activities. The most vivid thing about her was the fact that her grandmother had been a Van Alstyne. This connection with the well-fed and industrious stock of early New York revealed itself in the glacial neatness of Mrs. Peniston's drawing-room and in the excellence of her cuisine. She belonged to the class of old New Yorkers who have always lived well, dressed expensively, and done little else; and to these inherited obligations Mrs. Peniston faithfully conformed. She had always been a looker-on at life, and her mind resembled one of those little mirrors which her Dutch ancestors were accustomed to affix to their upper windows, so that from the depths of an impenetrable domesticity they might see what was happening in the street.

Mrs. Peniston was the owner of a country-place in New Jersey, but she had never lived there since her husband's death—a remote event, which appeared to dwell in her memory chiefly as a dividing point in the personal reminiscences that formed the staple of her conversation. She was a woman who remembered dates with intensity, and could tell at a moment's notice whether the drawing-room curtains had been renewed before or after Mr. Peniston's last illness.

Mrs. Peniston thought the country lonely and trees damp, and cherished a vague fear of meeting a bull. To guard against such contingencies she frequented the more populous watering-places, where she installed herself impersonally in a hired house and looked on at life through the matting screen of her verandah. In the care of such a guardian, it soon became clear to Lily that she was to enjoy only the material advantages of good food and expensive clothing; and, though far from underrating these, she would gladly have exchanged them for what Mrs. Bart had taught her to regard as opportunities. She sighed to think what her mother's fierce energies would have accomplished, had they been coupled with Mrs. Peniston's resources. Lily had abundant energy of her own, but it was restricted by the necessity of adapting herself to her aunt's habits. She saw that at all costs she must keep Mrs. Peniston's favour till, as Mrs. Bart would have phrased it, she could stand on her own legs. Lily had to mind for the vagabond life of the poor relation, and to adapt herself to Mrs. Peniston she had, to some degree, to assume that lady's passive attitude. She had fancied at first that it would be easy to draw her aunt into the whirl of her own activities, but there was a static force in Mrs. Peniston against which her niece's efforts spent themselves in vain. To attempt to bring her into active relation with life was like tugging at a piece of furniture which has been screwed to the floor. She did not, indeed, expect Lily to remain equally immovable: she had all the American guardian's indulgence for the volatility of youth. She had indulgence also for certain other habits of her niece's. It seemed to her natural that Lily should spend all her money on dress, and she supplemented the girl's scanty income by occasional "handsome presents" meant to be applied to the same purpose. Lily, who was intensely practical, would have preferred a fixed allowance; but Mrs. Peniston liked the periodical recurrence of gratitude evoked by unexpected cheques, and was perhaps shrewd enough to perceive that such a method of giving kept alive in her niece of salutary sense of dependence.

Beyond this, Mrs. Peniston had not felt called upon to do anything for her charge: she had simply stood aside and let her take the field. Lily had taken it, at first with the confidence of assured possessorship, then with gradually narrowing demands, till now she found herself actually struggling for a foothold on the broad space which had once seemed her own for the asking. How it happened she did not yet know. Sometimes she thought it was because Mrs. Peniston had been too passive, and again she feared it was because she herself had not been passive enough. Had she shown an undue eagerness for victory? Had she lacked patience, pliancy and dissimulation? Whether she charged herself with these faults or absolved herself from them, made no difference in the sum-total of her failure. Younger and plainer girls had been married off by dozens, and she was nine-and-twenty, and still Miss Bart.

She was beginning to have fits of angry rebellion against fate, when she longed to drop out of the race and make an independent life for herself. But what manner of life would it be? She had barely enough money to pay her dress-makers' bills and her gambling debts; and none of the desultory interests which she dignified with the name of tastes was pronounced enough to enable her to live contentedly in obscurity. Ah, no—she was too intelligent not to be honest with herself. She knew that she hated dinginess as much as her mother had hated it, and to her last breath she meant to fight against it, dragging herself up again and again above its flood till she gained the bright pinnacles of success which presented such a slippery surface to her clutch.

IV

The next morning, on her breakfast tray, Miss Bart found a note from her hostess.

"Dearest Lily," it ran, "if it is not too much of a bore to be down by ten, will you come to my sitting-room to help me with some tiresome things?"

Lily tossed aside the note and subsided on her pillows with a sigh. It *was* a bore to be down by ten—an hour regarded at Bellomont as vaguely synchronous with sunrise—and she knew too well the nature of the tiresome things in question. Miss Pragg, the secretary, had been called away, and there would be notes and dinner-cards to write, lost addresses to hunt up, and other social drudgery to perform. It was understood that Miss Bart should fill the gap in such emergencies, and she usually recognized the obligation without a murmur.

Today, however, it renewed the sense of servitude which the previous night's review of her cheque-book had produced. Everything in her surroundings ministered to feelings of ease and amenity. The windows stood open to the sparkling freshness of the September morning, and between the yellow boughs she caught a perspective of hedges and parterres leading by degrees of lessening formality to the free undulations of the park. Her maid had kindled a little fire on the hearth, and it contended cheerfully with the sunlight which slanted across the moss-green carpet and caressed the curved sides of an old marquetry desk. Near the bed stood a table holding her breakfast tray, with its harmonious porcelain and silver, a handful of violets in a slender glass, and the morning paper folded beneath her letters. There was nothing new to Lily in these tokens of a studied luxury; but, though they formed a part of her atmosphere, she never lost her sensitiveness to their charm. Mere display left her with a sense of superior distinction; but she felt an affinity to all the subtler manifestations of wealth.

Mrs. Trenor's summons, however, suddenly recalled her state of dependence, and she rose and dressed in a mood of irritability that she was usually too prudent to indulge. She knew that such emotions leave lines on the face as well as in the character, and she had meant to take warning by the little creases which her midnight survey had revealed.

The matter-of-course tone of Mrs. Trenor's greeting deepened her irritation. If one did drag one's self out of bed at such an hour, and come down fresh and radiant to the monotony of note-writing, some special recognition of the sacrifice seemed fitting. But Mrs. Trenor's tone showed no consciousness of the fact.

"Oh, Lily, that 's nice of you," she merely sighed across the chaos of letters, bills and other domestic documents which gave an incongruously commercial touch to the slender elegance of her writing-table.

"There are such lots of horrors this morning," she added, clearing a space in the centre of the confusion and rising to yield her seat to Miss Bart.

Mrs. Trenor was a tall fair woman, whose height just saved her from redundancy. Her rosy blondness had survived some forty years of futile activity without showing much trace of ill-usage except in a diminished play of feature. It was difficult to define her beyond saying that she seemed to exist only as a hostess, not so much from any exaggerated instinct of hospitality as because she could not sustain life except in a crowd. The collective nature of her interests exempted her from the ordinary rivalries of her sex, and she knew no more personal emotion than that of hatred for the woman who presumed to give bigger dinners or have more amusing house-parties than herself. As her social talents, backed by Mr. Trenor's bank-account, almost always assured her ulti-mate triumph in such competitions, success had developed in her an unscrupulous good nature toward the rest of her sex, and in Miss Bart's utilitarian classification of her friends, Mrs. Trenor ranked as the woman who was least likely to "go back" on her.

"It was simply inhuman of Pragg to go off now," Mrs. Trenor de-clared, as her friend seated herself at the desk. "She says her sister is going to have a baby—as if that were anything to having a house-party! I 'm sure I shall get most horribly mixed up and there will be some awful rows. When I was down at Tuxedo I asked a lot of people for next week, and I 've mislaid the list and can't remember who is coming. And this week is going to be a horrid failure too—and Gwen Van Osburgh will go back and tell her mother how bored people were. I did n't mean to ask the Wetheralls—that was a blunder of Gus's. They disapprove of Carry Fisher, you know. As if one could help having Carry Fisher! It *was* foolish of her to get that second divorce—Carry always overdoes things—but she said the only way to get a penny out of Fisher was to divorce him and make him pay alimony. And poor Carry has to consider every dollar. It 's really absurd of Alice Wetherall to make such a fuss about meeting her, when one thinks of what society is coming to. Some one said the other day that there was a divorce and a case of appendicitis in every family one knows. Besides, Carry is the only person who can keep Gus in a good humour when we have bores in the house. Have you noticed that *all* the husbands like her? All, I mean, except her own. It 's rather clever of her to have made a specialty of devoting herself to dull people—the field is such a large one, and she has it practically to herself. She finds compensations, no doubt—I know she borrows money of Gus—but then I 'd *pay* her to keep him in a good humour, so I can't complain, after all."

Mrs. Trenor paused to enjoy the spectacle of Miss Bart's efforts to unravel her tangled correspondence.

"But it is n't only the Wetheralls and Carry," she resumed, with a fresh note of lament. "The truth is, I 'm awfully disappointed in Lady Cressida Raith."

"Disappointed? Had n't you known her before?"

"Mercy, no—never saw her till yesterday. Lady Skiddaw sent her over with letters to the Van Osburghs, and I heard that Maria Van Os-burgh was asking a big party to meet her this week, so I thought it would be fun to get her away, and Jack Stepney, who knew her in India, managed it for me. Maria was furious, and actually had the impudence to make Gwen invite herself here, so that they should n't be *quite* out of it—if I 'd known what Lady Cressida was like, they could have had her and welcome! But I thought any friend of the Skiddaws' was sure to be amusing. You remember what fun Lady Skiddaw was? There were times when I simply had to send the girls out of the room. Besides, Lady Cressida is the Duchess of Beltshire's sister, and I naturally supposed she was the same sort; but you never can tell in those English families. They are so big that there 's room for all kinds, and it turns out that Lady Cressida is the moral one—married a clergyman and does missionary work in the East End. Think of my taking such a lot of trouble about a clergyman's wife, who wears Indian jewelry and botanizes! She made Gus take her all through the glass-houses yesterday, and bothered him to death by asking him the names of the plants. Fancy treating Gus as if he were the gardener!"

Mrs. Trenor brought this out in a *crescendo* of indignation.

"Oh, well, perhaps Lady Cressida will reconcile the Wetheralls to meeting Carry Fisher," said Miss Bart pacifically.

"I 'm sure I hope so! But she is boring all the men horribly, and if she takes to distributing tracts, as I hear she does, it will be too depressing. The worst of it is that she would have been so useful at the right time. You know we have to have the Bishop once a year, and she would have given just the right tone to things. I always have horrid luck about the Bishop's visits," added Mrs. Trenor, whose present misery was being fed by a rapidly rising tide of reminiscence; "last year, when he came, Gus forgot all about his being here, and brought home the Ned Wintons and the Farleys—five divorces and six sets of children between them!"

"When is Lady Cressida going?" Lily enquired.

Mrs. Trenor cast up her eyes in despair. "My dear, if one only knew! I was in such a hurry to get her away from Maria that I actually forgot to name a date, and Gus says she told some one she meant to stop here all winter."

"To stop here? In this house?"

"Don't be silly—in America. But if no one else asks her—you know they *never* go to hotels."

"Perhaps Gus only said it to frighten you."

"No—I heard her tell Bertha Dorset that she had six months to put in while her husband was taking the cure in the Engadine. You should have seen Bertha look vacant! But it 's no joke, you know—if she stays here all the autumn she 'll spoil everything, and Maria Van Osburgh will simply exult."

At this affecting vision Mrs. Trenor's voice trembled with self-pity.

"Oh, Judy—as if any one were ever bored at Bellomont!" Miss Bart tactfully protested. "You know perfectly well that, if Mrs. Van Osburgh were to get all the right people and leave you with all the wrong ones, you 'd manage to make things go off, and she would n't."

Such an assurance would usually have restored Mrs. Trenor's complacency; but on this occasion it did not chase the cloud from her brow.

"It is n't only Lady Cressida," she lamented. "Everything has gone wrong this week. I can see that Bertha Dorset is furious with me."

"Furious with you? Why?"

"Because I told her that Lawrence Selden was coming; but he would n't, after all, and she's quite unreasonable enough to think it 's my fault."

Miss Bart put down her pen and sat absently gazing at the note she had begun.

"I thought that was all over," she said.

"So it is, on his side. And of course Bertha has n't been idle since. But I fancy she 's out of a job just at present—and some one gave me a hint that I had better ask Lawrence. Well, I *did* ask him—but I could n't make him come; and now I suppose she 'll take it out of me by being perfectly nasty to every one else."

"Oh, she may take it out of *him* by being perfectly charming—to some one else."

Mrs. Trenor shook her head dolefully. "She knows he would n't mind. And who else is there? Alice Wetherall won't let Lucius out of her sight. Ned Silverton can't take his eyes off Carry Fisher—poor boy! Gus is bored by Bertha, Jack Stepney knows her too well—and—well, to be sure, there 's Percy Gryce!"

She sat up smiling at the thought.

Miss Bart's countenance did not reflect the smile.

"Oh, she and Mr. Gryce would not be likely to hit it off."

"You mean that she 'd shock him and he 'd bore her? Well, that 's not such a bad beginning, you know. But I hope she won't take it into her head to be nice to him, for I asked him here on purpose for you."

Lily laughed. "*Merci du compliment!* I should certainly have no show against Bertha."

"Do you think I am uncomplimentary? I 'm not really, you know. Every one knows you 're a thousand times handsomer and cleverer than Bertha; but then you 're not nasty. And for always getting what she wants in the long run, commend me to a nasty woman."

Miss Bart stared in affected reproval. "I thought you were so fond of Bertha."

"Oh, I am—it 's much safer to be fond of dangerous people. But she *is* dangerous—and if I ever saw her up to mischief it 's now. I can tell by poor George's manner. That man is a perfect barometer—he always knows when Bertha is going to——"

"To fall?" Miss Bart suggested.

"Don't be shocking! You know he believes in her still. And of course I don't say there 's any real harm in Bertha. Only she delights in making people miserable, and especially poor George."

"Well, he seems cut out for the part—I don't wonder she likes more cheerful companionship."

"Oh, George is not as dismal as you think. If Bertha did n't worry him he would be quite different. Or if she 'd leave him alone, and let him arrange his life as he pleases. But she does n't dare lose her hold of him on account of the money, and so when *he* is n't jealous she pretends to be."

Miss Bart went on writing in silence, and her hostess sat following her train of thought with frowning intensity.

"Do you know," she exclaimed after a long pause, "I believe I 'll call up Lawrence on the telephone and tell him he simply *must* come?"

"Oh, don't," said Lily, with a quick suffusion of colour. The blush surprised her almost as much as it did her hostess, who, though not commonly observant of facial changes, sat staring at her with puzzled eyes.

"Good gracious, Lily, how handsome you are!——Why? Do you dislike him so much?"

"Not at all; I like him. But if you are actuated by the benevolent intention of protecting me from Bertha—I don't think I need your protection."

Mrs. Trenor sat up with an exclamation. "Lily!—— *Percy*? Do you mean to say you 've actually done it?"

Miss Bart smiled, "I only mean to say that Mr. Gryce and I are getting to be very good friends."

"H'm—I see." Mrs. Trenor fixed a rapt eye upon her. "You know they say he has eight hundred thousand a year—and spends nothing, except on some rubbishy old books. And his mother has heart-disease and will leave him a lot more. *Oh, Lily, do go slowly,*" her friend adjured her.

Miss Bart continued to smile without annoyance. "I should n't, for instance," she remarked, "be in any haste to tell him that he had a lot of rubbishy old books."

"No, of course not; I know you 're wonderful about getting up people's subjects. But he 's horribly shy, and easily shocked, and—and——"

"Why don't you say it, Judy? I have the reputation of being on the hunt for a rich husband?"

"Oh, I don't mean that; he would n't believe it of you—at first," said Mrs. Trenor, with candid shrewdness. "But you know things are rather lively here at times—I must give Jack and Gus a hint—and if he thought you were what his mother would call fast—oh, well, you know what I mean. Don't wear your scarlet *crêpe-de-chine* for dinner, and don't smoke if you can help it, Lily dear!"

Lily pushed aside her finished work with a dry smile. "You 're very kind, Judy: I 'll lock up my cigarettes and wear that last year's dress you sent me this morning. And if you are really interested in my career, perhaps you 'll be kind enough not to ask me to play bridge again this evening."

"Bridge? Does he mind bridge, too? Oh, Lily, what an awful life you 'll lead! But of course I won't—why did n't you give me a hint last night? There 's nothing I would n't do, you poor duck, to see you happy!"

And Mrs. Trenor, glowing with her sex's eagerness to smooth the course of true love, enveloped Lily in a long embrace.

"You 're quite sure," she added solicitously, as the latter extricated herself, "that you would n't like me to telephone for Lawrence Selden?"

"Quite sure," said Lily.

The next three days demonstrated to her own complete satisfaction Miss Bart's ability to manage her affairs without extraneous aid.

As she sat, on the Saturday afternoon, on the terrace at Bellomont, she smiled at Mrs. Trenor's fear that she might go too fast. If such a warning had ever been needful, the years had taught her a salutary lesson, and she flattered herself that she now knew how to adapt her pace to the object of pursuit. In the case of Mr. Gryce she had found it well to flutter ahead, losing herself elusively and luring him on from depth to depth of unconscious intimacy. The surrounding atmosphere was propitious to this scheme of courtship. Mrs. Trenor, true to her word, had shown no signs of expecting Lily at the bridge-table, and had even hinted to the other card-players that they were to betray no surprise at her unwonted defection. In consequence of this hint, Lily found herself the centre of that feminine solicitude which envelops a young woman in the mating season. A solitude was tacitly created for her in the crowded existence of Bellomont, and her friends could not have shown a greater readiness for self-effacement had her wooing been adorned with all the attributes of romance. In Lily's set this conduct implied a sympathetic comprehension of her motives, and Mr. Gryce rose in her esteem as she saw the consideration he inspired.

The terrace at Bellomont on a September afternoon was a spot propitious to sentimental musings, and as Miss Bart stood leaning against the balustrade above the sunken garden, at a little distance from the animated group about the tea-table, she might have been lost in the mazes of an inarticulate happiness. In reality, her thoughts were finding definite utterance in the tranquil recapitulation of the blessings in store for her. From where she stood she could see them embodied in the form of Mr. Gryce, who, in a light overcoat and muffler, sat somewhat nervously on the edge of his chair, while Carry Fisher, with all the energy of eye and gesture with which nature and art had combined to endow her, pressed on him the duty of taking part in the task of municipal reform.

Mrs. Fisher's latest hobby was municipal reform. It had been preceded by an equal zeal for socialism, which had in turn replaced an energetic advocacy of Christian Science. Mrs. Fisher was small, fiery and dramatic; and her hands and eyes were admirable instruments in the service of whatever cause she happened to espouse. She had, however, the fault common to enthusiasts of ignoring any slackness of response on the part of her hearers, and Lily was amused by her unconsciousness of the resistance displayed in every angle of Mr. Gryce's attitude. Lily herself knew that his mind was divided between the dread of catching cold if he remained out of doors too long at that hour, and the fear that, if he retreated to the house, Mrs. Fisher might follow him up with a paper to be signed. Mr. Gryce had a constitutional dislike to what he called "committing himself," and tenderly as he cherished his health, he evidently concluded that it was safer to stay out of reach of pen and ink till chance released him from Mrs. Fisher's toils. Meanwhile he cast agonized glances in the direction of Miss Bart, whose only response was to sink into an attitude of more graceful abstraction. She had learned the value of contrast in throwing her charms into relief, and was fully aware of the extent to which Mrs. Fisher's volubility was enhancing her own repose.

She was roused from her musings by the approach of her cousin Jack Stepney who, at Gwen Van Osburgh's side, was returning across the garden from the tennis court.

The couple in question were engaged in the same kind of romance in which Lily figured, and the latter felt a certain annoyance in contemplating what seemed to her a caricature of her own situation. Miss Van Osburgh was a large girl with flat surfaces and no high lights: Jack Stepney had once said of her that she was as reliable as roast mutton. His own taste was in the line of less solid and more highly-seasoned diet; but hunger makes any fare palatable, and there had been times when Mr. Stepney had been reduced to a crust.

Lily considered with interest the expression of their faces: the girl's turned toward her companion's like an empty plate held up to be filled, while the man lounging at her side already betrayed the encroaching boredom which would presently crack the thin veneer of his smile.

"How impatient men are!" Lily reflected. "All Jack has to do to get everything he wants is to keep quiet and let that girl marry him; whereas I have to calculate and contrive, and retreat and advance, as if I were going through an intricate dance, where one misstep would throw me hopelessly out of time."

As they drew nearer she was whimsically struck by a kind of family likeness between Miss Van Osburgh and Percy Gryce. There was no resemblance of feature. Gryce was handsome in a didactic way—he looked like a clever pupil's drawing from a plaster-cast—while Gwen's countenance had no more modelling than a face painted on a toy balloon. But the deeper affinity was unmistakable: the two had the same prejudices and ideals, and the same quality of making other standards non-existent by ignoring them. This attribute was common to most of Lily's set: they had a force of negation which eliminated everything beyond their own range of perception. Gryce and Miss Van Osburgh were, in short, made for each other by every law of moral and physical correspondence——"Yet they would n't look at each other," Lily mused, "they never do. Each of them wants a creature of a different race, of Jack's race and mine, with all sorts of intuitions, sensations, and perceptions that they don't even guess the existence of. And they always get what they want."

She stood talking with her cousin and Miss Van Osburgh, till a slight cloud on the latter's brow advised her that even cousinly amenities were subject to suspicion, and Miss Bart, mindful of the necessity of not exciting enmities at this crucial point of her career, dropped aside while the happy couple proceeded toward the tea-table.

Seating herself on the upper step of the terrace, Lily leaned her head against the honeysuckles wreathing the balustrade. The fragrance of the late blossoms seemed an emanation of the tranquil scene, a landscape tutored to the last degree of rural elegance. In the foreground glowed the warm tints of the gardens. Beyond the lawn, with its pyramidal pale-gold maples and velvety firs, sloped pastures dotted with cattle; and through a long glade the river widened like a lake under the silver light of September. Lily did not want to join the circle about the tea-table. They represented the future she had chosen, and she was content with it, but in no haste to anticipate its joys. The certainty that she could marry Percy Gryce when she pleased had lifted a heavy load from her mind, and her money troubles were too recent for their removal not to leave a sense of relief which a less discerning intelligence might have taken for happiness. Her vulgar cares were at an end. She would be able to arrange her life as she pleased, to soar into that empyrean of security where creditors cannot penetrate. She would have smarter gowns than Judy Trenor, and far, far more jewels than Bertha Dorset. She would be free forever from the shifts, the expedients, the humiliations of the relatively poor. Instead of having to flatter, she would be flattered; instead of being grateful, she would receive thanks. There were old scores she could pay off as well as old benefits she could return. And she had no doubts as to the extent of her power. She knew that Mr. Gryce was of the small chary type most inaccessible to impulses and emotions. He had the kind of character in which prudence is a vice, and good advice the most dangerous nourishment. But Lily had known the species before: she was aware that such a guarded nature must find one huge outlet of egoism, and she determined to be to him what his Americana had hitherto been: the one possession in which he took sufficient pride to spend money on it. She knew that this generosity to self is one of the forms of meanness, and she resolved so to identify herself with her husband's vanity that to gratify her wishes would be to him the most exquisite form of self-indulgence. The system might at first necessitate a resort to some of the very shifts and expedients from which she intended it should free her; but she felt sure that in a short time she would be able to play the game in her own way. How should she have distrusted her powers? Her beauty itself was not the mere ephemeral possession it might have been in the hands of inexperience: her skill in enhancing it, the care she took of it, the use she made of it, seemed to give it a kind of permanence. She felt she could trust it to carry her through to the end.

And the end, on the whole, was worth while. Life was not the mockery she had thought it three days ago. There was room for her, after all, in this crowded selfish world of pleasure whence, so short a time since, her poverty had seemed to exclude her. These people whom she had ridiculed and yet envied were glad to make a place for her in the charmed circle about which all her desires revolved. They were not as brutal and self-engrossed as she had fancied—or rather, since it would no longer be necessary to flatter and humour them, that side of their nature became less conspicuous. Society is a revolving body which is apt to be judged according to its place in each man's heaven; and at present it was turning its illuminated face to Lily.

In the rosy glow it diffused her companions seemed full of amiable qualities. She liked their elegance, their lightness, their lack of emphasis: even the self-assurance which at times was so like obtuseness now seemed the natural sign of social ascendency. They were lords of the only world she cared for, and they were ready to admit her to their ranks and let her lord it with them. Already she felt within her a stealing allegiance to their standards, an acceptance of their limitations, a disbelief in the things they did not believe in, a contemptuous pity for the people who were not able to live as they lived.

The early sunset was slanting across the park. Through the boughs of the long avenue beyond the gardens she caught the flash of wheels, and divined that more visitors were approaching. There was a movement behind her, a scattering of steps and voices: it was evident that the party about the tea-table was breaking up. Presently she heard a tread behind her on the terrace. She supposed that Mr. Gryce had at last found means to escape from his predicament, and she smiled at the significance of his coming to join her instead of beating an instant retreat to the fire-side.

She turned to give him the welcome which such gallantry deserved; but her greeting wavered into a blush of wonder, for the man who had approached her was Lawrence Selden.

"You see I came after all," he said; but before she had time to answer, Mrs. Dorset, breaking away from a lifeless colloquy with her host, had stepped between them with a little gesture of appropriation.

V

The observance of Sunday at Bellomont was chiefly marked by the punctual appearance of the smart omnibus destined to convey the household to the little church at the gates. Whether any one got into the omnibus or not was a matter of secondary importance, since by standing there it not only bore witness to the orthodox intentions of the family, but made Mrs. Trenor feel, when she finally heard it drive away, that she had somehow vicariously made use of it.

It was Mrs. Trenor's theory that her daughters actually did go to church every Sunday; but their French governess's convictions calling her to the rival fane, and the fatigues of the week keeping their mother in her room till luncheon, there was seldom any one present to verify the fact. Now and then, in a spasmodic burst of virtue—when the house had been too uproarious over night—Gus Trenor forced his genial bulk into a tight frock-coat and routed his daughters from their slumbers; but habitually, as Lily explained to Mr. Gryce, this parental duty was forgotten till the church bells were ringing across the park, and the omnibus had driven away empty.

Lily had hinted to Mr. Gryce that this neglect of religious observances was repugnant to her early traditions, and that during her visits to Bellomont she regularly accompanied Muriel and Hilda to church. This tallied with the assurance, also confidentially imparted, that, never having played bridge before, she had been "dragged into it" on the night of her arrival, and had lost an appalling amount of money in consequence of her ignorance of the game and of the rules of betting. Mr. Gryce was undoubtedly enjoying Bellomont. He liked the ease and glitter of the life, and the lustre conferred on him by being a member of this group of rich and conspicuous people. But he thought it a very materialistic society; there were times when he was frightened by the talk of the men and the looks of the ladies, and he was glad to find that Miss Bart, for all her ease and self-possession, was not at home in so ambiguous an atmosphere. For this reason he had been especially pleased to learn that she would, as usual, attend the young Trenors to church on Sunday morning; and as he paced the gravel sweep before the door, his light overcoat on his arm and his prayer-book in one carefully-gloved hand, he reflected agreeably on the strength of character which kept her true to her early training in surroundings so subversive to religious principles.

For a long time Mr. Gryce and the omnibus had the gravel sweep to themselves; but, far from regretting this deplorable indifference on the part of the other guests, he found himself nourishing the hope that Miss Bart might be unaccompanied. The precious minutes were flying, however; the big chestnuts pawed the ground and flecked their impatient sides with foam; the coachman seemed to be slowly petrifying on the box, and the groom on the doorstep; and still the lady did not come. Suddenly, however, there was a sound of voices and a rustle of skirts in the doorway, and Mr. Gryce, restoring his watch to his pocket, turned with a nervous start; but it was only to find himself handing Mrs. Wetherall into the carriage.

The Wetheralls always went to church. They belonged to the vast group of human automata who go through life without neglecting to perform a single one of the gestures executed by the surrounding puppets. It is true that the Bellomont puppets did not go to church; but others equally important did—and Mr. and Mrs. Wetherall's circle was so large that God was included in their visiting-list. They appeared, therefore, punctual and resigned, with the air of people bound for a dull "At Home," and after them Hilda and Muriel straggled, yawning and pinning each other's veils and ribbons as they came. They had promised Lily to go to church with her, they declared, and Lily was such a dear old duck that they did n't mind doing it to please her, though they could n't fancy what had put the idea in her head, and though for their own part they would much rather have played lawn tennis with Jack and Gwen, if she had n't told them she was coming. The Misses Trenor were followed by Lady Cressida Raith, a weather-beaten person in Liberty silk and ethnological trinkets, who, on seeing the omnibus, expressed her surprise that they were not to walk across the park; but at Mrs. Wetherall's horrified protest that the church was a mile away, her ladyship, after a glance at the height of the other's heels, acquiesced in the necessity of driving, and poor Mr. Gryce found himself rolling off between four ladies for whose spiritual welfare he felt not the least concern.

It might have afforded him some consolation could he have known that Miss Bart had really meant to go to church. She had even risen earlier than usual in the execution of her purpose. She had an idea that the sight of her in a grey gown of devotional cut, with her famous lashes drooped above a prayer-book, would put the finishing touch to Mr. Gryce's subjugation, and render inevitable a certain incident which she had resolved should form a part of the walk they were to take together after luncheon. Her intentions in short had never been more definite; but poor Lily, for all the hard glaze of her exterior, was inwardly as malleable as wax. Her faculty for adapting herself, for entering into other people's feelings, if it served her now and then in small contingencies, hampered her in the decisive moments of life. She was like a water-plant in the flux of the tides, and today the whole current of her mood was carrying her toward Lawrence Selden. Why had he come? Was it to see herself or Bertha Dorset? It was the last question which, at that moment, should have engaged her. She might better have contented herself with thinking that he had simply responded to the despairing summons of his hostess, anxious to interpose him between herself and the ill-humour of Mrs. Dorset. But Lily had not rested till she learned from Mrs. Trenor that Selden had come of his own accord.

"He did n't even wire me—he just happened to find the trap at the

station. Perhaps it 's not over with Bertha after all," Mrs. Trenor musingly concluded; and went away to arrange her dinner-cards accordingly.

Perhaps it was not, Lily reflected; but it should be soon, unless she
had lost her cunning. If Selden had come at Mrs. Dorset's call, it was at
her own that he would stay. So much the previous evening had told her.
Mrs. Trenor, true to her simple principle of making her married friends
happy, had placed Selden and Mrs. Dorset next to each other at dinner;
but, in obedience to the time-honoured traditions of the match-maker,
she had separated Lily and Mr. Gryce, sending in the former with
George Dorset, while Mr. Gryce was coupled with Gwen Van Osburgh.

George Dorset's talk did not interfere with the range of his
neighbour's thoughts. He was a mournful dyspeptic, intent on finding
out the deleterious ingredients of every dish and diverted from this care
only by the sound of his wife's voice. On this occasion, however, Mrs.
Dorset took no part in the general conversation. She sat talking in low
murmurs with Selden, and turning a contemptuous and denuded shoulder toward her host, who, far from resenting his exclusion, plunged into
the excesses of the *menu* with the joyous irresponsibility of a free man.
To Mr. Dorset, however, his wife's attitude was a subject of such evident concern that, when he was not scraping the sauce from his fish, or
scooping the moist bread-crumbs from the interior of his roll, he sat
straining his thin neck for a glimpse of her between the lights.

Mrs. Trenor, as it chanced, had placed the husband and wife on
opposite sides of the table, and Lily was therefore able to observe Mrs.
Dorset also, and by carrying her glance a few feet farther, to set up a
rapid comparison between Lawrence Selden and Mr. Gryce. It was that
comparison which was her undoing. Why else had she suddenly grown
interested in Selden? She had known him for eight years or more: ever
since her return to America he had formed a part of her background.
She had always been glad to sit next to him at dinner, had found him
more agreeable than most men, and had vaguely wished that he possessed the other qualities needful to fix her attention; but till now she
had been too busy with her own affairs to regard him as more than one
of the pleasant accessories of life. Miss Bart was a keen reader of her own
heart, and she saw that her sudden preoccupation with Selden was due
to the fact that his presence shed a new light on her surroundings. Not
that he was notably brilliant or exceptional; in his own profession he was
surpassed by more than one man who had bored Lily through many a
weary dinner. It was rather that he had preserved a certain social detachment, a happy air of viewing the show objectively, of having points of

contact outside the great gilt cage in which they were all huddled for the mob to gape at. How alluring the world outside the cage appeared to Lily, as she heard its door clan on her! In reality, as she knew, the door never clanged: it stood always open; but most of the captives were like flies in a bottle, and having once flown in, could never regain their freedom. It was Selden's distinction that he had never forgotten the way out.

That was the secret of his way of readjusting her vision. Lily, turning her eyes from him, found herself scanning her little world through his retina: it was a though the pink lamps had been shut off and the dusty daylight let in. She looked down the long table, studying its occupants one by one, from Gus Trenor, with his heavy carnivorous head sunk between his shoulders, as he preyed on a jellied plover, to his wife, at the opposite end of the long bank of orchids, suggestive, with her glaring good-looks, of a jeweller's window lit by electricity. And between the two, what a long stretch of vacuity! How dreary and trivial these people were! Lily reviewed them with a scornful impatience: Carry Fisher, with her shoulders, her eyes, her divorces, her general air of embodying a "spicy paragraph"; young Silverton, who had meant to live on proofreading and write an epic, and who now lived on his friends and had become critical of truffles; Alice Wetherall, an animated visiting-list, whose most fervid convictions turned on the wording of invitations and the engraving of dinner-cards; Wetherall, with his perpetual nervous nod of acquiescence, his air of agreeing with people before he knew what they were saying; Jack Stepney, with his confident smile and anxious eyes, half way between the sheriff and an heiress; Gwen Van Osburgh, with all the guileless confidence of a young girl who has always been told that there is no one richer than her father.

Lily smiled at her classification of her friends. How different they had seemed to her a few hours ago! Then they had symbolized what she was gaining, now they stood for what she was giving up. That very afternoon they had seemed full of brilliant qualities; now she saw that they were merely dull in a loud way. Under the glitter of their opportunities she saw the poverty of their achievement. It was not that she wanted them to be more disinterested; but she would have liked them to be more picturesque. And she had a shamed recollection of the way in which, a few hours since, she had felt the centripetal force of their standards. She closed her eyes an instant, and the vacuous routine of the life she had chosen stretched before her like a long white road without dip or turning: it was true she was to roll over it in a carriage instead of trudging it on foot, but sometimes the pedestrian enjoys the diversion of a short cut which is denied to those on wheels.

She was roused by a chuckle which Mr. Dorset seemed to eject from the depths of his lean throat.

"I say, do look at her," he exclaimed, turning to Miss Bart with lugubrious merriment—"I beg your pardon, but do just look at my wife making a fool of that poor devil over there! One would really suppose she was gone on him—and it 's all the other way round, I assure you."

Thus adjured, Lily turned her eyes on the spectacle which was affording Mr. Dorset such legitimate mirth. It certainly appeared, as he said, that Mrs. Dorset was the more active participant in the scene: her neighbour seemed to receive her advances with a temperate zest which did not distract him from his dinner. The sight restored Lily's good humour, and knowing the peculiar disguise which Mr. Dorset's marital fears assumed, she asked gaily: "Are n't you horribly jealous of her?"

Dorset greeted the sally with delight. "Oh, abominably—you 've just hit it—keeps me awake at night. The doctors tell me that 's what has knocked my digestion out—being so infernally jealous of her.—I can't eat a mouthful of this stuff, you know," he added suddenly, pushing back his plate with a clouded countenance; and Lily, unfailingly adaptable, accorded her radiant attention to his prolonged denunciation of other people's cooks, with a supplementary tirade on the toxic qualities of melted butter.

It was not often that he found so ready an ear; and, being a man as well as a dyspeptic, it may be that as he poured his grievances into it he was not insensible to its rosy symmetry. At any rate he engaged Lily so long that the sweets were being handed when she caught a phrase on her other side, where Miss Corby, the comic woman of the company, was bantering Jack Stepney on his approaching engagement. Miss Corby's rôle was jocularity: she always entered the conversation with a handspring.

"And of course you 'll have Sim Rosedale as best man!" Lily heard her fling out as the climax of her prognostications; and Stepney responded, as if struck: "Jove, that 's an idea. What a thumping present I 'd get out of him!"

Sim Rosedale! The name, made more odious by its diminutive, obtruded itself on Lily's thoughts like a leer. It stood for one of the many hated possibilities hovering on the edge of life. If she did not marry Percy Gryce, the day might come when she would have to be civil to

such men as Rosedale. *If she did not marry him?* But she meant to marry
him — she was sure of him and sure of herself. She drew back with a
shiver from the pleasant paths in which her thoughts had been straying,
and set her feet once more in the middle of the long white road. . . .
When she went upstairs that night she found that the late post had
brought her a fresh batch of bills. Mrs. Peniston, who was a conscientious woman, had forwarded them all to Bellomont.

Miss Bart, accordingly, rose the next morning with the most earnest
conviction that it was her duty to go to church. She tore herself betimes
from the lingering enjoyment of her breakfast-tray, rang to have her
grey gown laid out, and despatched her maid to borrow a prayer-book
from Mrs. Trenor.

But her course was too purely reasonable not to contain the germs
of rebellion. No sooner were her preparations made than they roused a
smothered sense of resistance. A small spark was enough to kindle Lily's
imagination, and the sight of the grey dress and the borrowed prayer-
book flashed a long light down the years. She would have to go to
church with Percy Gryce every Sunday. They would have a front pew in
the most expensive church in New York, and his name would figure
handsomely in the list of parish charities. In a few years, when he grew
stouter, he would be made a warden. Once in the winter the rector
would come to dine, and her husband would beg her to go over the list
and see that no *divorcées* were included, except those who had showed
signs of penitence by being re-married to the very wealthy. There was
nothing especially arduous in this round of religious obligations; but it
stood for a fraction of that great bulk of boredom which loomed across
her path. And who could consent to be bored on such a morning? Lily
had slept well, and her bath had filled her with a pleasant glow, which
was becomingly reflected in the clear curve of her cheek. No lines were
visible this morning, or else the glass was at a happier angle.

And the day was the accomplice of her mood: it was a day for impulse and truancy. The light air seemed full of powdered gold; below
the dewy bloom of the lawns the woodlands blushed and smouldered,
and the hills across the river swam in molten blue. Every drop of blood
in Lily's veins invited her to happiness.

The sound of wheels roused her from these musings, and leaning
behind her shutters she saw the omnibus take up its freight. She was too
late, then — but the fact did not alarm her. A glimpse of Mr. Gryce's
crestfallen face even suggested that she had done wisely in absenting
herself, since the disappointment he so candidly betrayed would surely

whet his appetite for the afternoon walk. That walk she did not mean to miss; one glance at the bills on her writing-table was enough to recall its necessity. But meanwhile she had the morning to herself, and could muse pleasantly on the disposal of its hours. She was familiar enough with the habits of Bellomont to know that she was likely to have a free field till luncheon. She had seen the Wetheralls, the Trenor girls and Lady Cressida packed safely into the omnibus; Judy Trenor was sure to be having her hair shampooed; Carry Fisher had doubtless carried off her host for a drive; Ned Silverton was probably smoking the cigarette of young despair in his bedroom; and Kate Corby was certain to be playing tennis with Jack Stepney and Miss Van Osburgh. Of the ladies, this left only Mrs. Dorset unaccounted for, and Mrs. Dorset never came down till luncheon: her doctors, she averred, had forbidden her to expose herself to the crude air of the morning.

To the remaining members of the party Lily gave no special thought; wherever they were, they were not likely to interfere with her plans. These, for the moment, took the shape of assuming a dress somewhat more rustic and summerlike in style than the garment she had first selected, and rustling downstairs, sunshade in hand, with the disengaged air of a lady in quest of exercise. The great hall was empty but for the knot of dogs by the fire, who, taking in at a glance the outdoor aspect of Miss Bart, were upon her at once with lavish offers of companionship. She put aside the ramping paws which conveyed these offers, and assuring the joyous volunteers that she might presently have a use for their company, sauntered on through the empty drawing-room to the library at the end of the house. The library was almost the only surviving portion of the old manor-house of Bellomont: a long spacious room, revealing the traditions of the mother-country in its classically-cased doors, the Dutch tiles of the chimney, and the elaborate hob-grate with its shining brass urns. A few family portraits of lantern-jawed gentlemen in tie-wigs, and ladies with large head-dresses and small bodies, hung between the shelves lined with pleasantly-shabby books: books mostly contemporaneous with the ancestors in question, and to which the subsequent Trenors had made no perceptible additions. The library at Bellomont was in fact never used for reading, though it had a certain popularity as a smoking-room or a quiet retreat for flirtation. It had occurred to Lily, however, that it might on this occasion have been resorted to by the only member of the party in the least likely to put it to its original use. She advanced noiselessly over the dense old rug scattered with easy-chairs, and before she reached the middle of the room she saw that she had not been mistaken. Lawrence Selden was in fact seated at its farther end; but though a book lay on his knee, his attention was not engaged with it, but directed to a lady whose lace-clad figure, as she leaned back in an adjoining chair, detached itself with exaggerated slimness against the dusky leather of the upholstery.

Lily paused as she caught sight of the group; for a moment she seemed about to withdraw, but thinking better of this, she announced her approach by a slight shake of her skirts which made the couple raise their heads, Mrs. Dorset with a look of frank displeasure, and Selden with his usual quiet smile. The sight of his composure had a disturbing effect on Lily; but to be disturbed was in her case to make a more brilliant effort at self-possession.

"Dear me, am I late?" she asked, putting a hand in his as he advanced to greet her.

"Late for what?" enquired Mrs. Dorset tartly. "Not for luncheon, certainly—but perhaps you had an earlier engagement?"

"Yes, I had," said Lily confidingly.

"Really? Perhaps I am in the way, then? But Mr. Selden is entirely at your disposal." Mrs. Dorset was pale with temper, and her antagonist felt a certain pleasure in prolonging her distress.

"Oh, dear, no—do stay," she said good-humouredly. "I don't in the least want to drive you away."

"You 're awfully good, dear, but I never interfere with Mr. Selden's engagements."

The remark was uttered with a little air of proprietorship not lost on its object, who concealed a faint blush of annoyance by stooping to pick up the book he had dropped at Lily's approach. The latter's eyes widened charmingly and she broke into a light laugh.

"But I have no engagement with Mr. Selden! My engagement was to go to church; and I 'm afraid the omnibus has started without me. *Has* it started, do you know?"

She turned to Selden, who replied that he had heard it drive away some time since.

"Ah, then I shall have to walk; I promised Hilda and Muriel to go to church with them. It 's too late to walk there, you say? Well, I shall have the credit of trying, at any rate—and the advantage of escaping part of the service. I 'm not so sorry for myself, after all!"

And with a bright nod to the couple on whom she had intruded, Miss Bart strolled through the glass doors and carried her rustling grace down the long perspective of the garden walk.

She was taking her way churchward, but at no very quick pace; a fact not lost on one of her observers, who stood in the doorway looking after her with an air of puzzled amusement. The truth is that she was conscious of a somewhat keen shock of disappointment. All her plans for the day had been built on the assumption that it was to see her that Selden had come to Bellomont. She had expected, when she came downstairs, to find him on the watch for her; and she had found him, instead, in a situation which might well denote that he had been on the watch for another lady. Was it possible, after all, that he had come for Bertha Dorset? The latter had acted on the assumption to the extent of appearing at an hour when she never showed herself to ordinary mortals, and Lily, for the moment, saw no way of putting her in the wrong. It did not occur to her that Selden might have been actuated merely by the desire to spend a Sunday out of town: women never learn to dispense with the sentimental motive in their judgments of men. But Lily was not easily disconcerted; competition put her on her mettle, and she reflected that Selden's coming, if it did not declare him to be still in Mrs. Dorset's toils, showed him to be so completely free from them that he was not afraid of her proximity.

These thoughts so engaged her that she fell into a gait hardly likely to carry her to church before the sermon, and at length, having passed from the gardens to the wood-path beyond, so far forgot her intention as to sink into a rustic seat at a bend of the walk. The spot was charming, and Lily was not insensible to the charm, or to the fact that her presence enhanced it; but she was not accustomed to taste the joys of solitude except in company, and the combination of a handsome girl and a romantic scene struck her as too good to be wasted. No one, however, appeared to profit by the opportunity; and after a half hour of fruitless waiting she rose and wandered on. She felt a stealing sense of fatigue as she walked; the sparkle had died out of her, and the taste of life was stale on her lips. She hardly knew what she had been seeking, or why the failure to find it had so blotted the light from her sky: she was only aware of a vague sense of failure, of an inner isolation deeper than the loneliness about her.

Her footsteps flagged, and she stood gazing listlessly ahead, digging the ferny edge of the path with the tip of her sunshade. As she did so a step sounded behind her, and she saw Selden at her side.

"How fast you walk!" he remarked. "I thought I should never catch up with you."

She answered gaily: "You must be quite breathless! I 've been sitting under that tree for an hour."

"Waiting for me, I hope?" he rejoined; and she said with a vague laugh:

"Well—waiting to see if you would come."

"I seize the distinction, but I don't mind it, since doing the one involved doing the other. But were n't you sure that I should come?"

"If I waited long enough—but you see I had only a limited time to give to the experiment."

"Why limited? Limited by luncheon?"

"No; by my other engagement."

"Your engagement to go to church with Muriel and Hilda?"

"No; but to come home from church with another person."

"Ah, I see; I might have known you were fully provided with alternatives. And is the other person coming home this way?"

Lily laughed again. "That 's just what I don't know; and to find out, it is my business to get to church before the service is over."

"Exactly; and it is my business to prevent your doing so; in which case the other person, piqued by your absence, will form the desperate resolve of driving back in the omnibus."

Lily received this with fresh appreciation; his nonsense was like the bubbling of her inner mood. "Is that what you would do in such an emergency?" she enquired.

Selden looked at her with solemnity. "I am here to prove to you," he cried, "what I am capable of doing in an emergency!"

"Walking a mile in an hour—you must own that the omnibus would be quicker!"

"Ah—but will he find you in the end? That 's the only test of success."

They looked at each other with the same luxury of enjoyment that they had felt in exchanging absurdities over his tea-table; but suddenly Lily's face changed, and she said: "Well, if it is, he has succeeded."

Selden, following her glance, perceived a party of people advancing toward them from the farther bend of the path. Lady Cressida had evidently insisted on walking home, and the rest of the church-goers had thought it their duty to accompany her. Lily's companion looked rapidly from one to the other of the two men of the party; Wetherall walking respectfully at Lady Cressida's side with his little sidelong look of nervous attention, and Percy Gryce bringing up the rear with Mrs. Wetherall and the Trenors.

"Ah—now I see why you were getting up your Americana!" Selden exclaimed with a note of the freest admiration; but the blush with which the sally was received checked whatever amplifications he had meant to give it.

That Lily Bart should object to being bantered about her suitors, or even about her means of attracting them, was so new to Selden that he had a momentary flash of surprise, which lit up a number of possibilities; but she rose gallantly to the defence of her confusion, by saying, as its object approached: "That was why I was waiting for you — to thank you for having given me so many points!"

"Ah, you can hardly do justice to the subject in such a short time," said Selden, as the Trenor girls caught sight of Miss Bart; and while she signalled a response to their boisterous greeting, he added quickly: "Won't you devote your afternoon to it? You know I must be off to-morrow morning. We 'll take a walk, and you can thank me at your leisure."

VI

The afternoon was perfect. A deeper stillness possessed the air, and the glitter of the American autumn was tempered by a haze which diffused the brightness without dulling it.

In the woody hollows of the park there was already a faint chill; but as the ground rose the air grew lighter, and ascending the long slopes beyond the high-road, Lily and her companion reached a zone of lingering summer. The path wound across a meadow with scattered trees; then it dipped into a lane plumed with asters and purpling sprays of bramble, whence, through the light quiver of ash-leaves, the country unrolled itself in pastoral distances.

Higher up, the lane showed thickening tufts of fern and of the creeping glossy verdure of shaded slopes; trees began to overhang it, and the shade deepened to the checkered dusk of a beech-grove. The boles of the trees stood well apart, with only a light feathering of undergrowth; the path wound along the edge of the wood, now and then looking out on a sunlit pasture or on an orchard spangled with fruit.

Lily had no real intimacy with nature, but she had a passion for the appropriate and could be keenly sensitive to a scene which was the fitting background of her own sensations. The landscape outspread below her seemed an enlargement of her present mood, and she found something of herself in its calmness, its breadth, its long free reaches. On the nearer slopes the sugar-maples wavered like pyres of light; lower down was a massing of grey orchards, and here and there the lingering green of an oak-grove. Two or three red farm-houses dozed under the apple-trees, and the white wooden spire of a village church showed beyond the shoulder of the hill; while far below, in a haze of dust, the high-road ran between the fields.

"Let us sit here," Selden suggested, as they reached an open ledge of rock above which the beeches rose steeply between mossy boulders.

Lily dropped down on the rock, glowing with her long climb. She sat quiet, her lips parted by the stress of the ascent, her eyes wandering peacefully over the broken ranges of the landscape. Selden stretched himself on the grass at her feet, tilting his hat against the level sun-rays, and clasping his hands behind his head, which rested against the side of the rock. He had no wish to make her talk; her quick-breathing silence seemed a part of the general hush and harmony of things. In his own mind there was only a lazy sense of pleasure, veiling the sharp edges of sensation as the September haze veiled the scene at their feet. But Lily, though her attitude was as calm as his, was throbbing inwardly with a rush of thoughts. There were in her at the moment two beings, one drawing deep breaths of freedom and exhilaration, the other gasping for air in a little black prison-house of fears. But gradually the captive's gasps grew fainter, or the other paid less heed to them: the horizon expanded, the air grew stronger, and the free spirit quivered for flight.

She could not herself have explained the sense of buoyancy which seemed to lift and swing her above the sun-suffused world at her feet. Was it love, she wondered, or a mere fortuitous combination of happy thoughts and sensations? How much of it was owing to the spell of the perfect afternoon, the scent of the fading woods, the thought of the dulness she had fled from? Lily had no definite experience by which to test the quality of her feelings. She had several times been in love with fortunes or careers, but only once with a man. That was years ago, when she first came out, and had been smitten with a romantic passion for a young gentleman named Herbert Melson, who had blue eyes and a little wave in his hair. Mr. Melson, who was possessed of no other negotiable securities, had hastened to employ these in capturing the eldest Miss Van Osburgh: since then he had grown stout and wheezy, and was given to telling anecdotes about his children. If Lily recalled this early emotion it was not to compare it with that which now possessed her; the only point of comparison was the sense of lightness, of emancipation, which she remembered feeling, in the whirl of a waltz or the seclusion of a conservatory, during the brief course of her youthful romance. She had not known again till today that lightness, that glow of freedom; but now it was something more than a blind groping of the blood. The peculiar charm of her feeling for Selden was that she understood it; she could put her finger on every link of the chain that was drawing them together. Though his popularity was of the quiet kind, felt rather than actively expressed among his friends, she had never mistaken his incon-

spicuousness for obscurity. His reputed cultivation was generally regarded as a slight obstacle to easy intercourse, but Lily, who prided herself on her broad-minded recognition of literature, and always carried
an Omar Khayam in her travelling-bag, was attracted by this attribute,
which she felt would have had its distinction in an older society. It was,
moreover, one of his gifts to look his part; to have a height which lifted
his head above the crowd, and the keenly-modelled dark features which,
in a land of amorphous types, gave him the air of belonging to a more
specialized race, of carrying the impress of a concentrated past. Expansive persons found him a little dry, and very young girls thought him
sarcastic; but this air of friendly aloofness, as far removed as possible
from any assertion of personal advantage, was the quality which piqued
Lily's interest. Everything about him accorded with the fastidious element in her taste, even to the light irony with which he surveyed what
seemed to her most sacred. She admired him most of all, perhaps, for
being able to convey as distinct a sense of superiority as the richest man
she had ever met.

It was the unconscious prolongation of this thought which led her
to say presently, with a laugh: "I have broken two engagements for you
today. How many have you broken for me?"

"None," said Selden calmly. "My only engagement at Bellomont
was with you."

She glanced down at him, faintly smiling.

"Did you really come to Bellomont to see me?"

"Of course I did."

Her look deepened meditatively. "Why?" she murmured, with an
accent which took all tinge of coquetry from the question.

"Because you 're such a wonderful spectacle: I always like to see
what you are doing."

"How do you know what I should be doing if you were not here?"

Selden smiled. "I don't flatter myself that my coming has deflected
your course of action by a hair's breadth."

"That 's absurd—since, if you were not here, I could obviously not
be taking a walk with you."

"No; but your taking a walk with me is only another way of making
use of your material. You are an artist and I happen to be the bit of
colour you are using today. It 's a part of your cleverness to be able to
produce premeditated effects extemporaneously."

Lily smiled also: his words were too acute not to strike her sense of
humour. It was true that she meant to use the accident of his presence
as part of a very definite effect; or that, at least, was the secret pretext she

had found for breaking her promise to walk with Mr. Gryce. She had sometimes been accused of being too eager—even Judy Trenor had warned her to go slowly. Well, she would not be too eager in this case; she would give her suitor a longer taste of suspense. Where duty and inclination jumped together, it was not in Lily's nature to hold them asunder. She had excused herself from the walk on the plea of a headache: the horrid headache which, in the morning, had prevented her venturing to church. Her appearance at luncheon justified the excuse. She looked languid, full of a suffering sweetness; she carried a scent-bottle in her hand. Mr. Gryce was new to such manifestations; he wondered rather nervously if she were delicate, having far-reaching fears about the future of his progeny. But sympathy won the day, and he besought her not to expose herself: he always connected the outer air with ideas of exposure.

Lily had received his sympathy with languid gratitude, urging him, since she should be such poor company, to join the rest of the party who, after luncheon, were starting in automobiles on a visit to the Van Osburghs at Peekskill. Mr. Gryce was touched by her disinterestedness, and, to escape from the threatened vacuity of the afternoon, had taken her advice and departed mournfully, in a dust-hood and goggles: as the motor-car plunged down the avenue she smiled at his resemblance to a baffled beetle.

Selden had watched her manœuvres with lazy amusement. She had made no reply to his suggestion that they should spend the afternoon together, but as her plan unfolded itself he felt fairly confident of being included in it. The house was empty when at length he heard her step on the stair and strolled out of the billiard-room to join her. She had on a hat and walking-dress, and the dogs were bounding at her feet.

"I thought, after all, the air might do me good," she explained; and he agreed that so simple a remedy was worth trying.

The excursionists would be gone at least four hours; Lily and Selden had the whole afternoon before them, and the sense of leisure and safety gave the last touch of lightness to her spirit. With so much time to talk, and no definite object to be led up to, she could taste the rare joys of mental vagrancy.

She felt so free from ulterior motives that she took up his charge with a touch of resentment.

"I don't know," she said, "why you are always accusing me of premeditation."

"I thought you confessed to it: you told me the other day that you had to follow a certain line—and if one does a thing at all it is a merit to do it thoroughly."

"If you mean that a girl who has no one to think for her is obliged to think for herself, I am quite willing to accept the imputation. But you must find me a dismal kind of person if you suppose that I never yield to an impulse."

"Ah, but I don't suppose that: have n't I told you that your genius lies in converting impulses into intentions?"

"My genius?" she echoed with a sudden note of weariness. "Is there any final test of genius but success? And I certainly have n't succeeded."

Selden pushed his hat back and took a side-glance at her. "Success—what is success? I shall be interested to have your definition."

"Success?" She hesitated. "Why, to get as much as one can out of life, I suppose. It 's a relative quality, after all. Is n't that your idea of it?"

"My idea of it? God forbid!" He sat up with sudden energy, resting his elbows on his knees and staring out upon the mellow fields. "My idea of success," he said, "is personal freedom."

"Freedom? Freedom from worries?"

"From everything—from money, from poverty, from ease and anxiety, from all the material accidents. To keep a kind of republic of the spirit—that 's what I call success."

She leaned forward with a responsive flash. "I know—I know—it 's strange; but that 's just what I 've been feeling today."

He met her eyes with the latent sweetness of his. "Is the feeling so rare with you?" she said.

She blushed a little under his gaze. "You think me horribly sordid, don't you? But perhaps it 's rather that I never had any choice. There was no one, I mean, to tell me about the republic of the spirit."

"There never is—it 's a country one has to find the way to one's self."

"But I should never have found my way there if you had n't told me."

"Ah, there are sign-posts—but one has to know how to read them."

"Well, I have known, I have known!" she cried with a glow of eagerness. "Whenever I see you, I find myself spelling out a letter of the sign—and yesterday—last evening at dinner—I suddenly saw a little way into your republic."

Selden was still looking at her, but with a changed eye. Hitherto he had found, in her presence and her talk, the æsthetic amusement which a reflective man is apt to seek in desultory intercourse with pretty women. His attitude had been one of admiring spectatorship, and he would have been almost sorry to detect in her any emotional weakness which should interfere with the fulfilment of her aims. But now the hint of this weakness had become the most interesting thing about her. He had come on her that morning in a moment of disarray; her face had been pale and altered, and the diminution of her beauty had lent her a poignant charm. *That is how she looks when she is alone!* had been his first thought; and the second was to note in her the change which his coming produced. It was the danger-point of their intercourse that he could not doubt the spontaneity of her liking. From whatever angle he viewed their dawning intimacy, he could not see it as part of her scheme of life; and to be the unforeseen element in a career so accurately planned was stimulating even to a man who had renounced sentimental experiments.

"Well," he said, "did it make you want to see more? Are you going to become one of us?"

He had drawn out his cigarettes as he spoke, and she reached her hand toward the case.

"Oh, do give me one—I have n't smoked for days!"

"Why such unnatural abstinence? Everybody smokes at Bellomont."

"Yes—but it is not considered becoming in a *jeune fille à marier;* and at the present moment I am a *jeune fille à marier.*"

"Ah, then I 'm afraid we can't let you into the republic."

"Why not? Is it a celibate order?"

"Not in the least, though I 'm bound to say there are not many married people in it. But you will marry some one very rich, and it 's as hard for rich people to get into as the kingdom of heaven."

"That 's unjust, I think, because, as I understand it, one of the conditions of citizenship is not think too much about money, and the only way not to think about money is to have a great deal of it."

"You might as well say that the only way not to think about air is to have enough to breathe. That is true enough in a sense; but your lungs are thinking about the air, if you are not. And so it is with your rich people—they may not be thinking of money, but they 're breathing it all the while; take them into another element and see how they squirm and gasp!"

Lily sat gazing absently through the blue rings of her cigarette-smoke.

"It seems to me," she said at length, "that you spend a good deal of your time in the element you disapprove of."

Selden received this thrust without discomposure. "Yes; but I have tried to remain amphibious: it's all right as long as one's lungs can work in another air. The real alchemy consists in being able to turn gold back again into something else; and that's the secret that most of your friends have lost."

Lily mused. "Don't you think," she rejoined after a moment, "that the people who find fault with society are too apt to regard it as an end and not a means, just as the people who despise money speak as if its only use were to be kept in bags and gloated over? Is n't it fairer to look at them both as opportunities, which may be used either stupidly or intelligently, according to the capacity of the user?"

"That is certainly the sane view; but the queer thing about society is that the people who regard it as an end are those who are in it, and not the critics on the fence. It's just the other way with most shows—the audience may be under the illusion, but the actors know that real life is on the other side of the footlights. The people who take society as an escape from work are putting it to its proper use; but when it becomes the thing worked for it distorts all the relations of life." Selden raised himself on his elbow. "Good heavens!" he went on, "I don't underrate the decorative side of life. It seems to me the sense of splendour has justified itself by what it has produced. The worst of it is that so much human nature is used up in the process. If we 're all the raw stuff of the cosmic effects, one would rather be the fire that tempers a sword than the fish that dyes a purple cloak. And a society like ours wastes such good material in producing its little patch of purple! Look at a boy like Ned Silverton—he's really too good to be used to refurbish anybody's social shabbiness. There's a lad just setting out to discover the universe: is n't it a pity he should end by finding it in Mrs. Fisher's drawing-room?"

"Ned is a dear boy, and I hope he will keep his illusions long enough to write some nice poetry about them; but do you think it is only in society that he is likely to lose them?"

Selden answered her with a shrug. "Why do we call all our generous ideas illusions, and the mean ones truths? Is n't it a sufficient condemnation of society to find one's self accepting such phraseology? I very nearly acquired the jargon at Silverton's age, and I know how names can alter the colour of beliefs."

She had never heard him speak with such energy of affirmation. His habitual touch was that of the eclectic, who lightly turns over and compares; and she was moved by this sudden glimpse into the laboratory where his faiths were formed.

"Ah, you are as bad as the other sectarians," she exclaimed; "why do you call your republic a republic? It is a close corporation, and you create arbitrary objections in order to keep people out."

"It is not *my* republic; if it were, I should have a *coup d'état* and seat you on the throne."

"Whereas, in reality, you think I can never even get my foot across the threshold? Oh, I understand what you mean. You despise my ambitions—you think them unworthy of me!"

Selden smiled, but not ironically. "Well, is n't that a tribute? I think them quite worthy of most of the people who live by them."

She had turned to gaze on him gravely. "But is n't it possible that, if I had the opportunities of these people, I might make a better use of them? Money stands for all kinds of things—its purchasing quality is n't limited to diamonds and motor-cars."

"Not in the least: you might expiate your enjoyment of them by founding a hospital."

"But if you think they are what I should really enjoy, you must think my ambitions are good enough for me."

Selden met this appeal with a laugh. "Ah, my dear Miss Bart, I am not divine Providence, to guarantee your enjoying the things you are trying to get!"

"Then the best you can say for me is, that after struggling to get them I probably shan't like them?" She drew a deep breath. "What a miserable future you foresee for me!"

"Well—have you never foreseen it for yourself?"

The slow colour rose to her cheek, not a blush of excitement but drawn from the deep wells of feeling; it was as if the effort of her spirit had produced it.

"Often and often," she said. "But it looks so much darker when you show it to me!"

He made no answer to this exclamation, and for a while they sat silent, while something throbbed between them in the wide quiet of the air. But suddenly she turned on him with a kind of vehemence.

"Why do you do this to me?" she cried. "Why do you make the things I have chosen seem hateful to me, if you have nothing to give me instead?"

The words roused Selden from the musing fit into which he had fallen. He himself did not know why he had led their talk along such lines; it was the last use he would have imagined himself making of an afternoon's solitude with Miss Bart. But it was one of those moments when neither seemed to speak deliberately, when an indwelling voice in each called to the other across unsounded depths of feeling.

"No, I have nothing to give you instead," he said, sitting up and turning so that he faced her. "If I had, it should be yours, you know."

She received this abrupt declaration in a way even stranger than the manner of its making: she dropped her face on her hands and he saw that for a moment she wept.

It was for a moment only, however; for when he leaned nearer and drew down her hands with a gesture less passionate than grave, she turned on him a face softened but not disfigured by emotion, and he said to himself, somewhat cruelly, that even her weeping was an art.

The reflection steadied his voice as he asked, between pity and irony: "Isn't it natural that I should try to belittle all the things I can't offer you?"

Her face brightened at this, but she drew her hand away, not with a gesture of coquetry, but as though renouncing something to which she had no claim.

"But you belittle *me,* don't you," she returned gently, "in being so sure they are the only things I care for?"

Selden felt an inner start; but it was only the last quiver of his egoism. Almost at once he answered quite simply: "But you do care for them, don't you? And no wishing of mine can alter that."

He had so completely ceased to consider how far this might carry him, that he had a distinct sense of disappointment when she turned on him a face sparkling with derision.

"Ah," she cried, "for all your fine phrases you're really as great a coward as I am, for you wouldn't have made one of them if you hadn't been so sure of my answer."

The shock of this retort had the effect of crystallizing Selden's wavering intentions.

"I am not so sure of your answer," he said quietly. "And I do you the justice to believe that you are not either."

It was her turn to look at him with surprise; and after a moment — "Do you want to marry me?" she asked.

He broke into a laugh. "No, I don't want to — but perhaps I should if you did!"

"That's what I told you — you're so sure of me that you can amuse yourself with experiments." She drew back the hand he had regained, and sat looking down on him sadly.

"I am not making experiments," he returned. "Or if I am, it is not on you but on myself. I don't know what effect they are going to have on me — but if marrying you is one of them, I will take the risk."

She smiled faintly. "It would be a great risk, certainly — I have never concealed from you how great."

"Ah, it 's you who are the coward!" he exclaimed.

She had risen, and he stood facing her with his eyes on hers. The soft isolation of the falling day enveloped them: they seemed lifted into a finer air. All the exquisite influences of the hour trembled in their veins, and drew them to each other as the loosened leaves were drawn to the earth.

"It 's you who are the coward," he repeated, catching her hands in his.

She leaned on him for a moment, as if with a drop of tired wings: he felt as though her heart were beating rather with the stress of a long flight than the thrill of new distances. Then, drawing back with a little smile of warning — "I shall look hideous in dowdy clothes; but I can trim my own hats," she declared.

They stood silent for a while after this, smiling at each other like adventurous children who have climbed to a forbidden height from which they discover a new world. The actual world at their feet was veiling itself in dimness, and across the valley a clear moon rose in the denser blue.

Suddenly they heard a remote sound, like the hum of a giant insect, and following the high-road, which wound whiter through the surrounding twilight, a black object rushed across their vision.

Lily started from her attitude of absorption; her smile faded and she began to move toward the lane.

"I had no idea it was so late! We shall not be back till after dark," she said, almost impatiently.

Selden was looking at her with surprise: it took him a moment to regain his usual view of her; then he said, with an uncontrollable note of dryness: "That was not one of our party; the motor was going the other way."

"I know — I know ——" She paused, and he saw her redden through the twilight. "But I told them I was not well — that I should not go out. Let us go down!" she murmured.

Selden continued to look at her; then he drew his cigarette-case from his pocket and slowly lit a cigarette. It seemed to him necessary, at that moment, to proclaim, by some habitual gesture of this sort, his recovered hold on the actual: he had an almost puerile wish to let his companion see that, their flight over, he had landed on his feet.

She waited while the spark flickered under his curved palm; then he held out the cigarettes to her.

She took one with an unsteady hand, and putting it to her lips, leaned forward to draw her light from his. In the indistinctness the little red gleam lit up the lower part of her face, and he saw her mouth tremble into a smile.

"Were you serious?" she asked, with an old thrill of gaiety which she might have caught up, in haste, from a heap of stock inflections, without having time to select the just note.

Selden's voice was under better control. "Why not?" he returned. "You see I took no risks in being so." And as she continued to stand before him, a little pale under the retort, he added quickly: "Let us go down."

VII

It spoke much for the depth of Mrs. Trenor's friendship that her voice, in admonishing Miss Bart, took the same note of personal despair as if she had been lamenting the collapse of a house-party.

"All I can say is, Lily, that I can't make you out!" She leaned back, sighing, in the morning abandon of lace and muslin, turning an indifferent shoulder to the heaped-up importunities of her desk, while she considered, with the eye of a physician who has given up the case, the erect exterior of the patient confronting her.

"If you had n't told me you were going in for him seriously—but I 'm sure you made that plain enough from the beginning! Why else did you ask me to let you off bridge, and to keep away Carry and Kate Corby? I don't suppose you did it because he amused you; we could none of us imagine your putting up with him for a moment unless you meant to marry him. And I 'm sure everybody played fair! They all wanted to help it along. Even Bertha kept her hands off—I will say that—till Lawrence came down and you dragged him away from her. After that she had a right to retaliate—why on earth did you interfere with her? You 've known Lawrence Selden for years—why did you behave as if you had just discovered him? If you had a grudge against Bertha it was a stupid time to show it—you could have paid her back just as well after you were married! I told you Bertha was dangerous. She was in an odious mood when she came here, but Lawrence's turning up put her in a good humour, and if you'd only let her think he came for *her* it would have never occurred to her to play you this trick. Oh, Lily, you 'll never do anything if you 're not serious!"

Miss Bart accepted this exhortation in a spirit of the purest impartiality. Why should she have been angry? It was the voice of her own conscience which spoke to her through Mrs. Trenor's reproachful accents. But even to her own conscience she must trump up a semblance of defence.

"I only took a day off—I thought he meant to stay on all this week, and I knew Mr. Selden was leaving this morning."

Mrs. Trenor brushed aside the plea with a gesture which laid bare its weakness.

"He did mean to stay—that 's the worse of it. It shows that he 's run away from you; that Bertha 's done her work and poisoned him thoroughly."

Lily gave a slight laugh. "Oh, if he 's running I 'll overtake him!"

Her friend threw out an arresting hand. "Whatever you do, Lily, do nothing!"

Miss Bart received the warning with a smile. "I don't mean, literally, to take the next train. There are ways——" But she did not go on to specify them.

Mrs. Trenor sharply corrected the tense. "There *were* ways—plenty of them! I did n't suppose you needed to have them pointed out. But don't deceive yourself—he 's thoroughly frightened. He has run straight home to his mother, and she 'll protect him!"

"Oh, to the death," Lily agreed, dimpling at the vision.

"How you can *laugh*——" her friend rebuked her; and she dropped back to a soberer perception of things with the question: "What was it Bertha really told him?"

"Don't ask me—horrors! She seemed to have raked up everything. Oh, you know what I mean—of course there is n't anything, *really;* but I suppose she brought in Prince Varigliano—and Lord Hubert—and there was some story of your having borrowed money of old Ned Van Alstyne: did you ever?"

"He is my father's cousin," Miss Bart interposed.

"Well, of course she left *that* out. It seems Ned told Carry Fisher; and she told Bertha, naturally. They 're all alike, you know: they hold their tongues for years, and you think you 're safe, but when their opportunity comes they remember everything."

Lily had grown pale: her voice had a harsh note in it. "It was some money I lost at bridge at the Van Osburghs'. I repaid it, of course."

"Ah, well, they would n't remember that; besides, it was the idea of the gambling debt that frightened Percy. Oh, Bertha knew her man—she knew just what to tell him!"

In this strain Mrs. Trenor continued for nearly an hour to admonish her friend. Miss Bart listened with admirable equanimity. Her naturally good temper had been disciplined by years of enforced compliance, since she had almost always had to attain her ends by the circuitous path of other people's; and, being naturally inclined to face unpleasant facts as soon as they presented themselves, she was not sorry to hear an impartial statement of what her folly was likely to cost, the more so as her own thoughts were still insisting on the other side of the case. Presented in the light of Mrs. Trenor's vigorous comments, the reckoning was certainly a formidable one, and Lily, as she listened, found herself gradually reverting to her friend's view of the situation. Mrs. Trenor's words were moreover emphasized for her hearer by anxieties which she herself could scarcely guess. Affluence, unless stimulated by a keen imagination, forms but the vaguest notion of the practical strain of poverty. Judy knew it must be "horrid" for poor Lily to have to stop to consider whether she could afford real lace on her petticoats, and not to have a motor-car and a steam-yacht at her orders; but the daily friction of unpaid bills, the daily nibble of small temptations to expenditure, were trials as far out of her experience as the domestic problems of the charwoman. Mrs. Trenor's unconsciousness of the real stress of the situation had the effect of making it more galling to Lily. While her friend reproached her for missing the opportunity to eclipse her rivals, she was once more battling in imagination with the mounting tide of indebtedness from which she had so nearly escaped. What wind of folly had driven her out again on those dark seas?

If anything was needed to put the last touch to her self-abasement it was the sense of the way her old life was opening its ruts again to receive her. Yesterday her fancy had fluttered free pinions above a choice of occupations; now she had to drop to the level of the familiar routine, in which moments of seeming brilliancy and freedom alternated with long hours of subjection.

She laid a deprecating hand on her friend's. "Dear Judy! I 'm sorry to have been such a bore, and you are very good to me. But you must have some letters for me to answer—let me at least be useful."

She settled herself at the desk, and Mrs. Trenor accepted her resumption of the morning's task with a sigh which implied that, after all, she had proved herself unfit for higher uses.

The luncheon table showed a depleted circle. All the men but Jack Stepney and Dorset had returned to town (it seemed to Lily a last touch of irony that Selden and Percy Gryce should have gone in the same train), and Lady Cressida and the attendant Wetheralls had been despatched by motor to lunch at a distant country-house. At such moments of diminished interest it was usual for Mrs. Dorset to keep her room till the afternoon; but on this occasion she drifted in when luncheon was half over, hollowed-eyed and drooping, but with an edge of malice under her indifference.

She raised her eyebrows as she looked about the table. "How few of us are left! I do so enjoy the quiet—don't you, Lily? I wish the men would always stop away—it 's really much nicer without them. Oh, you don't count, George: one does n't have to talk to one's husband. But I thought Mr. Gryce was to stay for the rest of the week?" she added enquiringly. "Did n't he intend to, Judy? He's such a nice boy—I wonder what drove him away? He is rather shy, and I 'm afraid we may have shocked him: he has been brought up in such an old-fashioned way. Do you know, Lily, he told me had never seen a girl play cards for money till he saw you doing it the other night? And he lives on the interest of his income, and always has a lot left over to invest!"

Mrs. Fisher leaned forward eagerly. "I do believe it is some one's duty to educate that young man. It is shocking that he has never been made to realize his duties as a citizen. Every wealthy man should be compelled to study the laws of his country."

Mrs. Dorset glanced at her quietly. "I think he *has* studied the divorce laws. He told me he had promised the Bishop to sign some kind of a petition against divorce."

Mrs. Fisher reddened under her powder, and Stepney said with a laughing glance at Miss Bart: "I suppose he is thinking of marriage, and wants to tinker up the old ship before he goes aboard."

His betrothed looked shocked at the metaphor, and George Dorset exclaimed with a sardonic growl: "Poor devil! It is n't the ship that will do for him, it 's the crew."

"Or the stowaways," said Miss Corby brightly. "If I contemplated a voyage with him I should try to start with a friend in the hold."

Miss Van Osburgh's vague feeling of pique was struggling for appropriate expression. "I 'm sure I don't see why you laugh at him; I think he 's very nice," she exclaimed; "and, at any rate, a girl who married him would always have enough to be comfortable."

She looked puzzled at the redoubled laughter which hailed her words, but it might have consoled her to know how deeply they had sunk into the breast of one of her hearers.

Comfortable! At that moment the word was more eloquent to Lily Bart than any other in the language. She could not even pause to smile over the heiress's view of a colossal fortune as a mere shelter against want: her mind was filled with the vision of what that shelter might have been to her. Mrs. Dorset's pin-pricks did not smart, for her own irony cut deeper: no one could hurt her as much as she was hurting herself, for no one else—not even Judy Trenor—knew the full magnitude of her folly.

She was roused from these unprofitable considerations by a whispered request from her hostess, who drew her apart as they left the luncheon-table.

"Lily, dear, if you 've nothing special to do, may I tell Carry Fisher that you intend to drive to the station and fetch Gus? He will be back at four, and I know she has it in her mind to meet him. Of course, I 'm very glad to have him amused, but I happen to know that she had bled him rather severely since she 's been here, and she is so keen about going to fetch him that I fancy she must have got a lot more bills this morning. It seems to me," Mrs. Trenor feelingly concluded, "that most of her alimony is paid by other women's husbands!"

Miss Bart, on her way to the station, had leisure to muse over her friend's words, and their peculiar application to herself. Why should she have to suffer for having once, for a few hours, borrowed money of an elderly cousin, when a woman like Carry Fisher could make a living unrebuked from the good-nature of her men friends and the tolerance of their wives? It all turned on the tiresome distinction between what a married woman might, and a girl might not, do. Of course it was shocking for a married woman to borrow money—and Lily was expertly aware of the implication involved—but still, it was the mere *malum prohibitum* which the world decries but condones, and which, though it may be punished by private vengeance, does not provoke the collective disapprobation of society. To Miss Bart, in short, no such opportunities were possible. She could of course borrow from her women friends—a hundred here or there, at the utmost—but they were more ready to give a gown or a trinket, and looked a little askance when she hinted her preference for a cheque. Women are not generous lenders, and those among whom her lot was cast were either in the same case as herself, or else too far removed from it to understand its necessities. The result of her meditations was the decision to join her aunt at Richfield. She could not remain at Bellomont without playing bridge, and being involved in other expenses; and to continue her usual series of autumn visits would merely prolong the same difficulties. She had reached a point where abrupt retrenchment was necessary, and the only cheap life was a dull life. She would start the next morning for Richfield.

At the station she thought Gus Trenor seemed surprised, and not wholly unrelieved, to see her. She yielded up the reins of the light run-about in which she had driven over, and as he climbed heavily to her side, crushing her into a scant third of the seat, he said: "Halloo! It is n't often you honour me. You must have been uncommonly hard up for something to do."

The afternoon was warm, and propinquity made her more than usu-ally conscious that he was red and massive, and that beads of moisture had caused the dust of the train to adhere unpleasantly to the broad expanse of cheek and neck which he turned to her; but she was aware also, from the look in his small dull eyes, that the contact with her fresh-ness and slenderness was as agreeable to him as the sight of a cooling beverage.

The perception of this fact helped her to answer gaily: "It 's not often I have the chance. There are too many ladies to dispute the privi-lege with me."

"The privilege of driving me home? Well, I 'm glad you won the race, anyhow. But I know what really happened—my wife sent you. Now did n't she?"

He had the dull man's unexpected flashes of astuteness, and Lily could not help joining in the laugh with which he had pounced on the truth.

"You see, Judy thinks I 'm the safest person for you to be with; and she 's quite right," she rejoined.

"Oh, is she, though? If she is, it 's because you would n't waste your time on an old hulk like me. We married men have to put up with what we can get: all the prizes are for the clever chaps who 've kept a free foot. Let me light a cigar, will you? I 've had a beastly day of it."

He drew up in the shade of the village street, and passed the reins to her while he held a match to his cigar. The little flame under his hand cast a deeper crimson on his puffing face, and Lily averted her eyes with a momentary feeling of repugnance. And yet some women thought him handsome!

As she handed back the reins, she said sympathetically: "Did you have such a lot of tiresome things to do?"

"I should say so—rather!" Trenor, who was seldom listened to, ei-ther by his wife or her friends, settled down into the rare enjoyment of a confidential talk. "You don't know how a fellow has to hustle to keep this kind of thing going." He waved his whip in the direction of the Bellomont acres, which lay outspread before them in opulent undula-tions. "Judy has no idea of what she spends—not that there is n't plenty to keep the thing going," he interrupted himself, "but a man has got to keep his eyes open and pick up all the tips he can. My father and mother used to live like fighting-cocks on their income, and put by a good bit of it too—luckily for me—but at the pace we go now, I don't know where I should be if it were n't for taking a flyer now and then. The women all think—I mean Judy thinks—I 've nothing to do but to go down town once a month and cut off coupons, but the truth is it takes a devilish lot of hard work to keep the machinery running. Not that I ought to complain to-day, though," he went on after a moment, "for I did a very neat stroke of business, thanks to Stepney's friend Rosedale: by the way, Miss Lily, I wish you 'd try to persuade Judy to be decently civil to that chap. He 's going to be rich enough to buy us all out one of these days, and if she 'd only ask him to dine now and then I could get almost anything out of him. The man is mad to know the people who don't want to know him, and when a fellow 's in that state there is nothing he won't do for the first woman who takes him up."

Lily hesitated a moment. The first part of her companion's discourse had started an interesting train of thought, which was rudely interrupted by the mention of Mr. Rosedale's name. She uttered a faint protest.

"But you know Jack did try to take him about, and he was impossible."

"Oh, hang it—because he 's fat and shiny, and has a shoppy manner! Well, all I can say is that the people who are clever enough to be civil to him now will make a mighty good thing of it. A few years from now he 'll be in it whether we want him or not, and then he won't be giving away a half-a-million tip for a dinner."

Lily's mind had reverted from the intrusive personality of Mr. Rosedale to the train of thought set in motion by Trenor's first words. This vast mysterious Wall Street world of "tips" and "deals"—might she not find in it the means of escape from her dreary predicament? She had often heard of women making money in this way through their friends: she had no more notion than most of her sex of the exact nature of the transaction, and its vagueness seemed to diminish its indelicacy. She could not, indeed, imagine herself, in any extremity, stooping to extract a "tip" from Mr. Rosedale; but at her side was a man in possession of that precious commodity, and who, as the husband of her dearest friend, stood to her in a relation of almost fraternal intimacy.

In her inmost heart Lily knew it was not by appealing to the fraternal instinct that she was likely to move Gus Trenor; but this way of explaining the situation helped to drape its crudity, and she was always scrupulous about keeping up appearances to herself. Her personal fastidiousness had a moral equivalent, and when she made a tour of inspection in her own mind there were certain closed doors she did not open.

As they reached the gates of Bellomont she turned to Trenor with a smile.

"The afternoon is so perfect—don't you want to drive me a little farther? I 've been rather out of spirits all day, and it 's so restful to be away from people, with some one who won't mind if I 'm a little dull."

She looked so plaintively lovely as she proferred the request, so trustfully sure of his sympathy and understanding, that Trenor felt himself wishing that his wife could see how other women treated him—not battered wire-pullers like Mrs. Fisher, but a girl that most men would have given their boots to get such a look from.

"Out of spirits? Why on earth should you ever be out of spirits? Is your last box of Doucet dresses a failure, or did Judy rook you out of everything at bridge last night?"

Lily shook her head with a sigh. "I have had to give up Doucet; and bridge too—I can't afford it. In fact I can't afford any of the things my friends do, and I am afraid Judy often thinks me a bore because I don't play cards any longer, and because I am not as smartly dressed as the other women. But you will think me a bore too if I talk to you about my worries, and I only mention them because I want you to do me a favour—the very greatest of favours."

Her eyes sought his once more, and she smiled inwardly at the tinge of apprehension that she read in them.

"Why, of course—if it 's anything I can manage——" He broke off, and she guessed that his enjoyment was disturbed by the remembrance of Mrs. Fisher's methods.

"The greatest of favours," she rejoined gently. "The fact is, Judy is angry with me, and I want you to make my peace."

"Angry with you? Oh, come, nonsense——" his relief broke through in a laugh. "Why, you know she 's devoted to you."

"She is the best friend I have, and that is why I mind having to vex her. But I daresay you know what she has wanted me to do. She has set her heart—poor dear—on my marrying—marrying a great deal of money."

She paused with a slight falter of embarrassment, and Trenor, turning abruptly, fixed on her a look of growing intelligence.

"A great deal of money? Oh, by Jove—you don't mean Gryce? What—you do? Oh, no, of course I won't mention it—you can trust me to keep my mouth shut—but Gryce—good Lord, *Gryce!* Did Judy really think you could bring yourself to marry that portentous little ass? But you could n't, eh? And so you gave him the sack, and that 's the reason why he lit out by the first train this morning?" He leaned back, spreading himself farther across the seat, as if dilated by the joyful sense of his own discernment. "How on earth could Judy think you would do such a thing? *I* could have told her you 'd never put up with such a little milksop!"

Lily sighed more deeply. "I sometimes think," she murmured, "that men understand a woman's motives better than other women do."

"Some men—I 'm certain of it! I could have *told* Judy," he repeated, exulting in the implied superiority over his wife.

"I thought you would understand; that 's why I wanted to speak to you," Miss Bart rejoined. "I *can't* make that kind of marriage; it 's impossible. But neither can I go on living as all the women in my set do. I am almost entirely dependent on my aunt, and though she is very kind to me she makes me no regular allowance, and lately I 've lost money at cards, and I don't dare tell her about it. I have paid my card debts, of course, but there is hardly anything left for my other expenses, and if I go on with my present life I shall be in horrible difficulties. I have a tiny income of my own, but I 'm afraid it 's badly invested, for it seems to bring in less every year, and I am so ignorant of money matters that I don't know if my aunt's agent, who looks after it, is a good adviser." She paused a moment, and added in a lighter tone: "I did n't mean to bore you with all this, but I want your help in making Judy understand that I can't, at present, go on living as one must live among you all. I am going away tomorrow to join my aunt at Richfield, and I shall stay there for the rest of the autumn, and dismiss my maid and learn how to mend my own clothes."

At this picture of loveliness in distress, the pathos of which was heightened by the light touch with which it was drawn, a murmur of indignant sympathy broke from Trenor. Twenty-four hours earlier, if his wife had consulted him on the subject of Miss Bart's future, he would have said that a girl with extravagant tastes and no money had better marry the first rich man she could get; but with the subject of discussion at his side, turning to him for sympathy, making him feel that he understood her better than her dearest friends, and confirming the assurance by the appeal of her exquisite nearness, he was ready to swear that such a marriage was a desecration, and that, as a man of honour, he was bound to do all he could to protect her from the results of her disinterestedness. This impulse was reinforced by the reflection that if she had married Gryce she would have been surrounded by flattery and approval, whereas, having refused to sacrifice herself to expediency, she was left to bear the whole cost of her resistance. Hang it, if he could find a way out of such difficulties for a professional sponge like Carry Fisher, who was simply a mental habit corresponding to the physical titillations of the cigarette or the cock-tail, he could surely do as much for a girl who appealed to his highest sympathies, and who brought her troubles to him with the trustfulness of a child.

Trenor and Miss Bart prolonged their drive till long after sunset; and before it was over he had tried, with some show of success, to prove to her that, if she would only trust him, he could make a handsome sum of money for her without endangering the small amount she possessed. She was too genuinely ignorant of the manipulations of the stock-market to understand his technical explanations, or even perhaps to perceive that certain points in them were slurred; the haziness enveloping the transaction served as a veil for her embarrassment, and through the general blur her hopes dilated like lamps in a fog. She understood only that her modest investments were to be mysteriously multiplied without risk to herself; and the assurance that this miracle would take place within a short time, that there would be no tedious interval for suspense and reaction, relieved her of her lingering scruples.

Again she felt the lightening of her load, and with it the release of repressed activities. Her immediate worries conjured, it was easy to resolve that she would never again find herself in such straits, and as the need of economy and self-denial receded from her foreground she felt herself ready to meet any other demand which life might make. Even the immediate one of letting Trenor, as they drove homeward, lean a little nearer and rest his hand reassuringly on hers, cost her only a momentary shiver of reluctance. It was part of the game to make him feel that her appeal had been an uncalculated impulse, provoked by the liking he inspired; and the renewed sense of power in handling men, while it consoled her wounded vanity, helped also to obscure the thought of the claim at which his manner hinted. He was a coarse dull man who, under all his show of authority, was a mere supernumerary in the costly show for which his money paid: surely, to a clever girl, it would be easy to hold him by his vanity, and so keep the obligation on his side.

VIII

The first thousand dollar cheque which Lily received with a blotted scrawl from Gus Trenor strengthened her self-confidence in the exact degree to which it effaced her debts.

The transaction had justified itself by its results: she saw now how absurd it would have been to let any primitive scruple deprive her of this easy means of appeasing her creditors. Lily felt really virtuous as she dispensed the sum in sops to her tradesmen, and the fact that a fresh order accompanied each payment did not lessen her sense of disinterestedness. How many women, in her place, would have given the orders without making the payment!

She had found it reassuringly easy to keep Trenor in a good humour. To listen to his stories, to receive his confidences and laugh at his jokes, seemed for the moment all that was required of her, and the complacency with which her hostess regarded these attentions freed them of the least hint of ambiguity. Mrs. Trenor evidently assumed that Lily's growing intimacy with her husband was simply an indirect way of returning her own kindness.

"I 'm so glad you and Gus have become such good friends," she said approvingly. "It 's too delightful of you to be so nice to him, and put up with all his tiresome stories. I know what they are, because I had to listen to them when we were engaged—I 'm sure he is telling the same ones still. And now I shan't always have to be asking Carry Fisher here to keep him in a good-humour. She 's a perfect vulture, you know, and she has n't the least moral sense. She is always getting Gus to speculate for her, and I 'm sure she never pays when she loses."

Miss Bart could shudder at this state of things without the embarrassment of a personal application. Her own position was surely quite different. There could be no question of her not paying when she lost, since Trenor had assured her that she was certain not to lose. In sending her the cheque he had explained that he had made five thousand for her out of Rosedale's "tip," and had put four thousand back in the same venture, as there was the promise of another "big rise"; she understood therefore that he was now speculating with her own money, and that she consequently owed him no more than the gratitude which such a trifling service demanded. She vaguely supposed that, to raise the first sum, he had borrowed on her securities; but this was a point over which her curiosity did not linger. It was concentrated, for the moment, on the probable date of the next "big rise."

The news of this event was received by her some weeks later, on the occasion of Jack Stepney's marriage to Miss Van Osburgh. As a cousin of the bridegroom, Miss Bart had been asked to act as bridesmaid; but she had declined on the plea that, since she was much taller than the other attendant virgins, her presence might mar the symmetry of the group. The truth was, she had attended too many brides to the altar:

when next seen there she meant to be the chief figure in the ceremony. She knew the pleasantries made at the expense of young girls who have been too long before the public, and she was resolved to avoid such assumptions of youthfulness as might lead people to think her older than she really was.

The Van Osburgh marriage was celebrated in the village church near the paternal estate on the Hudson. It was the "simple country wedding" to which guests are convoyed in special trains, and from which the hordes of the uninvited have to be fended off by the intervention of the police. While these sylvan rites were taking place, in a church packed with fashion and festooned with orchids, the representatives of the press were threading their way, note-book in hand, through the labyrinth of wedding presents, and the agent of a cinematograph syndicate was setting up his apparatus at the church door. It was the kind of scene in which Lily had often pictured herself as taking the principal part, and on this occasion the fact that she was once more merely a casual spectator, instead of the mystically veiled figure occupying the centre of attention, strengthened her resolve to assume the latter part before the year was over. The fact that her immediate anxieties were relieved did not blind her to a possibility of their recurrence; it merely gave her enough buoyancy to rise once more above her doubts and feel a renewed faith in her beauty, her power, and her general fitness to attract a brilliant destiny. It could not be that one conscious of such aptitudes for mastery and enjoyment was doomed to a perpetuity of failure; and her mistakes looked easily reparable in the light of her restored self-confidence.

A special appositeness was given to these reflections by the discovery, in a neighbouring pew, of the serious profile and neatly-trimmed beard of Mr. Percy Gryce. There was something almost bridal in his own aspect: his large white gardenia had a symbolic air that struck Lily as a good omen. After all, seen in an assemblage of his kind he was not ridiculous-looking: a friendly critic might have called his heaviness weighty, and he was at his best in the attitude of vacant passivity which brings out the oddities of the restless. She fancied he was the kind of man whose sentimental associations would be stirred by the conventional imagery of a wedding, and she pictured herself, in the seclusion of the Van Osburgh conservatories, playing skilfully upon sensibilities thus prepared for her touch. In fact, when she looked at the other women about her, and recalled the image she had brought away from her own glass, it did not seem as though any special skill would be needed to repair her blunder and bring him once more to her feet.

The sight of Selden's dark head, in a pew almost facing her, disturbed for a moment the balance of her complacency. The rise of her blood as their eyes met was succeeded by a contrary motion, a wave of resistance and withdrawal. She did not wish to see him again, not because she feared his influence, but because his presence always had the effect of cheapening her aspirations, of throwing her whole world out of focus. Besides, he was a living reminder of the worst mistake in her career, and the fact that he had been its cause did not soften her feelings toward him. She could still imagine an ideal state of existence in which, all else being superadded, intercourse with Selden might be the last touch of luxury; but in the world as it was, such a privilege was likely to cost more than it was worth.

"Lily, dear, I never saw you look so lovely! You look as if something delightful had just happened to you!"

The young lady who thus formulated her admiration of her brilliant friend did not, in her own person, suggest such happy possibilities. Miss Gertrude Farish, in fact, typified the mediocre and the ineffectual. If there were compensating qualities in her wide frank glance and the freshness of her smile, these were qualities which only the sympathetic observer would perceive before noticing that her eyes were of a workaday grey and her lips without haunting curves. Lily's own view of her wavered between pity for her limitations and impatience at her cheerful acceptance of them. To Miss Bart, as to her mother, acquiescence in dinginess was evidence of stupidity; and there were moments when, in the consciousness of her own power to look and to be so exactly what the occasion required, she almost felt that other girls were plain and inferior from choice. Certainly no one need have confessed such acquiescence in her lot as was revealed in the "useful" colour of Gerty Farish's gown and the subdued lines of her hat: it is almost as stupid to let your clothes betray that you know you are ugly as to have them proclaim that you think you are beautiful.

Of course, being fatally poor and dingy, it was wise of Gerty to have taken up philanthropy and symphony concerts; but there was something irritating in her assumption that existence yielded no higher pleasures, and that one might get as much interest and excitement out of life in a cramped flat as in the splendours of the Van Osburgh establishment. Today, however, her chirping enthusiasms did not irritate Lily. They seemed only to throw her own exceptionalness into becoming relief, and give a soaring vastness to her scheme of life.

"Do let us go and take a peep at the presents before everyone else leaves the dining-room!" suggested Miss Farish, linking her arm in her friend's. It was characteristic of her to take a sentimental and unenvious interest in all the details of a wedding: she was the kind of person who always kept her handkerchief out during the service, and departed clutching a box of wedding-cake.

"Is n't everything beautifully done?" she pursued, as they entered the distant drawing-room assigned to the display of Miss Van Osburgh's bridal spoils. "I always say no one does things better than cousin Grace! Did you ever taste anything more delicious than that *mousse* of lobster with champagne sauce? I made up my mind weeks ago that I would n't miss this wedding, and just fancy how delightfully it all came about. When Lawrence Selden heard I was coming, he insisted on fetching me himself and driving me to the station, and when we go back this evening I am to dine with him at Sherry's. I really feel as excited as if I were getting married myself!"

Lily smiled: she knew that Selden had always been kind to his dull cousin, and she had sometimes wondered why he wasted so much time in such an unremunerative manner; but now the thought gave her a vague pleasure.

"Do you see him often?" she asked.

"Yes; he is very good about dropping in on Sundays. And now and then we do a play together; but lately I have n't seen much of him. He does n't look well, and he seems nervous and unsettled. The dear fellow! I do wish he would marry some nice girl. I told him so today, but he said he did n't care for the really nice ones, and the other kind did n't care for him—but that was just his joke, of course. He could never marry a girl who *was n't* nice. Oh, my dear, did you ever see such pearls?"

They had paused before the table on which the bride's jewels were displayed, and Lily's heart gave an envious throb as she caught the refraction of light from their surfaces—the milky gleam of perfectly matched pearls, the flash of rubies relieved against contrasting velvet, the intense blue rays of sapphires kindled into light by surrounding diamonds: all these precious tints enhanced and deepened by the varied art of their setting. The glow of the stones warmed Lily's veins like wine. More completely than any other expression of wealth they symbolized the life she longed to lead, the life of fastidious aloofness and refinement in which every detail should have the finish of a jewel, and the whole form a harmonious setting to her own jewel-like rareness.

"Oh, Lily, do look at this diamond pendant—it 's as big as a dinner-plate! Who can have given it?" Miss Farish bent short-sightedly over the accompanying card. "*Mr. Simon Rosedale.* What, that horrid man? Oh, yes—I remember he 's a friend of Jack's, and I suppose cousin

Grace had to ask him here today; but she must rather hate having to let Gwen accept such a present from him."

Lily smiled. She doubted Mrs. Van Osburgh's reluctance, but was aware of Miss Farish's habit of ascribing her own delicacies of feeling to the persons least likely to be encumbered by them.

"Well, if Gwen does n't care to be seen wearing it she can always exchange it for something else," she remarked.

"Ah, here is something so much prettier," Miss Farish continued. "Do look at this exquisite white sapphire. I 'm sure the person who chose it must have taken particular pains. What is the name? Percy Gryce? Ah, then I 'm not surprised!" She smiled significantly as she replaced the card. "Of course you 've heard that he 's perfectly devoted to Evie Van Osburgh? Cousin Grace is so pleased about it — it 's quite a romance! He met her first at the George Dorsets', only about six weeks ago, and it 's just the nicest possible marriage for dear Evie. Oh, I don't mean the money — of course she has plenty of her own — but she 's such a quiet stay-at-home kind of girl, and it seems he has just the same tastes; so they are exactly suited to each other."

Lily stood staring vacantly at the white sapphire on its velvet bed. Evie Van Osburgh and Percy Gryce? The names rang derisively through her brain. *Evie Van Osburgh?* The youngest, dumpiest, dullest of the four dull and dumpy daughters whom Mrs. Van Osburgh, with unsurpassed astuteness, had "placed" one by one in enviable niches of existence! Ah, lucky girls who grow up in the shelter of a mother's love — a mother who knows how to contrive opportunities without conceding favours, how to take advantage of propinquity without allowing appetite to be dulled by habit! The cleverest girl may miscalculate where her own interests are concerned, may yield too much at one moment and withdraw too far at the next: it takes a mother's unerring vigilance and foresight to land her daughters safely in the arms of wealth and suitability.

Lily's passing light-heartedness sank beneath a renewed sense of failure. Life was too stupid, too blundering! Why should Percy Gryce's millions be joined to another great fortune, why should this clumsy girl be put in possession of powers she would never know how to use?

She was roused from these speculations by a familiar touch on her arm, and turning saw Gus Trenor beside here. She felt a thrill of vexation: what right had he to touch her? Luckily Gerty Farish had wandered off to the next table, and they were alone.

Trenor, looking stouter than ever in his tight frock-coat, and unbecomingly flushed by the bridal libations, gazed at her with undisguised approval.

"By Jove, Lily, you do look a stunner!" He had slipped insensibly into the use of her Christian name, and she had never found the right moment to correct him. Besides, in her set all the men and women called each other by their Christian names; it was only on Trenor's lips that the familiar address had an unpleasant significance.

"Well," he continued, still jovially impervious to her annoyance, "have you made up your mind which of these little trinkets you mean to duplicate at Tiffany's tomorrow? I 've got a cheque for you in my pocket that will go a long way in that line!"

Lily gave him a startled look: his voice was louder than usual, and the room was beginning to fill with people. But as her glance assured her that they were still beyond ear-shot a sense of pleasure replaced her apprehension.

"Another dividend?" she asked, smiling and drawing near him in the desire not to be overhead.

"Well, not exactly: I sold out on the rise and I 've pulled off four thou' for you. Not so bad for a beginner, eh? I suppose you 'll begin to think you 're a pretty knowing speculator. And perhaps you won't think poor old Gus such an awful ass as some people do."

"I think you the kindest of friends; but I can't thank you properly now."

She let her eyes shine into his with a look that made up for the hand-clasp he would have claimed if they had been alone—and how glad she was that they were not! The news filled her with the glow produced by a sudden cessation of physical pain. The world was not so stupid and blundering after all: now and then a stroke of luck came to the unluckiest. At the thought her spirits began to rise: it was characteristic of her that one trifling piece of good fortune should give wings to all her hopes. Instantly came the reflection that Percy Gryce was not irretrievably lost; and she smiled to think of the excitement of recapturing him from Evie Van Osburgh. What chance could such a simpleton have against her if she chose to exert herself? She glanced about, hoping to catch a glimpse of Gryce; but her eyes lit instead on the glossy countenance of Mr. Rosedale, who was slipping through the crowd with an air half obsequious, half obtrusive, as though, the moment his presence was recognized, it would swell to the dimensions of the room.

Not wishing to be the means of effecting this enlargement, Lily quickly transferred her glance to Trenor, to whom the expression of her gratitude seemed not to have brought the complete gratification she had meant it to give.

"Hang thanking me — I don't want to be thanked, but I *should* like the chance to say two words to you now and then," he grumbled. "I thought you were going to spend the whole autumn with us, and I 've hardly laid eyes on you for the last month. Why can't you come back to Bellomont this evening? We 're all alone, and Judy is as cross as two sticks. Do come and cheer a fellow up. If you say yes I 'll run you over in the motor and you can telephone your maid to bring your traps from town by the next train."

Lily shook her head with a charming semblance of regret. "I wish I could — but it 's quite impossible. My aunt has come back to town, and I must be with her for the next few days."

"Well, I 've seen a good deal less of you since we 've got to be such pals than I used to when you were Judy's friend," he continued with unconscious penetration.

"When I was Judy's friend?" Am I not her friend still? Really, you say the most absurd things! If I were always at Bellomont you would tire of me much sooner than Judy — but come and see me at my aunt's the next afternoon you are in town; then we can have a nice quiet talk, and you can tell me how I had better invest my fortune."

It was true that, during the last three or four weeks, she had absented herself from Bellomont on the pretext of having other visits to pay; but she now began to feel that the reckoning she had thus contrived to evade had rolled up interest in the interval.

The prospect of the nice quiet talk did not appear as all-sufficing to Trenor as she had hoped, and his brows continued to lower as he said: "Oh, I don't know that I can promise you a fresh tip every day. But there 's one thing you might do for me; and that is, just to be a little civil to Rosedale. Judy has promised to ask him to dine when we get to town, but I can't induce her to have him at Bellomont, and if you would let me bring him up now it would make a lot of difference. I don't believe two women have spoken to him this afternoon, and I can tell you he 's a chap it pays to be decent to."

Miss Bart made an impatient movement, but suppressed the words which seemed about to accompany it. After all, this was an unexpectedly easy way of acquitting her debt; and had she not reasons of her own for wishing to be civil to Mr. Rosedale?

"Oh, bring him by all means," she said smiling; "perhaps I can get a tip out of him on my own account."

Trenor paused abruptly, and his eyes fixed themselves on hers with a look which made her change colour.

"I say, you know—you 'll please remember he 's a blooming bounder," he said; and with a slight laugh she turned toward the open window near which they had been standing.

The throng in the room had increased, and she felt a desire for space and fresh air. Both of these she found on the terrace, where only a few men were lingering over cigarettes and liqueur, while scattered couples strolled across the lawn to the autumn-tinted borders of the flower-garden.

As she emerged, a man moved toward her from the knot of smokers, and she found herself face to face with Selden. The stir of the pulses which his nearness always caused was increased by a slight sense of constraint. They had not met since their Sunday afternoon walk at Bellomont, and that episode was still so vivid to her that she could hardly believe him to be less conscious of it. But his greeting expressed no more than the satisfaction which every pretty woman expects to see reflected in masculine eyes; and the discovery, if distasteful to her vanity, was reassuring to her nerves. Between the relief of her escape from Trenor, and the vague apprehension of her meeting with Rosedale, it was pleasant to rest a moment on the sense of complete understanding which Lawrence Selden's manner always conveyed.

"This is luck" he said smiling. "I was wondering if I should be able to have a word with you before the special snatches us away. I came with Gerty Farish, and promised not to let her miss the train, but I am sure she is still extracting sentimental solace from the wedding presents. She appears to regard their number and value as evidence of the disinterested affection of the contracting parties."

There was not the least trace of embarrassment in his voice, and as he spoke, leaning slightly against the jamb of the window, and letting his eyes rest on her in the frank enjoyment of her grace, she felt with a faint chill of regret that he had gone back without an effort to the footing on which they had stood before their last talk together. Her vanity was stung by the sight of his unscathed smile. She longed to be to him something more than a piece of sentient prettiness, a passing diversion to his eye and brain; and the longing betrayed itself in her reply.

"Ah," she said, "I envy Gerty that power she has of dressing up with romance all our ugly and prosaic arrangements! I have never recovered my self-respect since you showed me how poor and unimportant my ambitions were."

The words were hardly spoken when she realized their infelicity. It seemed to be her fate to appear at her worst to Selden.

"I thought, on the contrary," he returned lightly, "that I had been the means of proving they were more important to you than anything else."

It was as if the eager current of her being had been checked by a sudden obstacle which drove it back upon itself. She looked at him helplessly, like a hurt or frightened child: this real self of hers, which he had the faculty of drawing out of the depths, was so little accustomed to go alone!

The appeal of her helplessness touched in him, as it always did, a latent chord of inclination. It would have meant nothing to him to discover that his nearness made her more brilliant, but this glimpse of a twilight mood to which he alone had the clue seemed once more to set him in a world apart with her.

"At least you can't think worse things of me than you say!" she exclaimed with a trembling laugh; but before he could answer, the flow of comprehension between them was abruptly stayed by the reappearance of Gus Trenor, who advanced with Mr. Rosedale in his wake.

"Hang it, Lily, I thought you 'd given me the slip: Rosedale and I have been hunting all over for you!"

His voice had a note of conjugal familiarity: Miss Bart fancied she detected in Rosedale's eye a twinkling perception of the fact, and the idea turned her dislike of him to repugnance.

She returned his profound bow with a slight nod, made more disdainful by the sense of Selden's surprise that she should number Rosedale among her acquaintances. Trenor had turned away, and his companion continued to stand before Miss Bart, alert and expectant, his lips parted in a smile at whatever she might be about to say, and his very back conscious of the privilege of being seen with her.

It was the moment for tact; for the quick bridging over of gaps; but Selden still leaned against the window, a detached observer of the scene, and under the spell of his observation Lily felt herself powerless to exert her usual arts. The dread of Selden's suspecting that there was any need for her to propitiate such a man as Rosedale checked the trivial phrases of politeness. Rosedale still stood before her in an expectant attitude, and she continued to face him in silence, her glance just level with his polished baldness. The look put the finishing touch to what her silence implied.

He reddened slowly, shifting from one foot to the other, fingered the plump black pearl in his tie, and gave a nervous twist to his moustache; then, running his eye over her, he drew back, and said, with a side-glance at Selden: "Upon my soul, I never saw a more ripping get-up. Is that the last creation of the dress-maker you go to see at the Benedick? If so, I wonder all the other women don't go to her too!"

The words were projected sharply against Lily's silence, and she saw in a flash that her own act had given them their emphasis. In ordinary talk they might have passed unheeded; but following on her prolonged pause they acquired a special meaning. She felt, without looking, that Selden had immediately seized it, and would inevitably connect the allusion with her visit to himself. The consciousness increased her irritation against Rosedale, but also her feeling that now, if ever, was the moment to propitiate him, hateful as it was to do so in Selden's presence.

"How do you know the other women don't go to my dress-maker?" she returned. "You see I 'm not afraid to give her address to my friends!"

Her glance and accent so plainly included Rosedale in this privileged circle that his small eyes puckered with gratification, and a knowing smile drew up his moustache.

"By Jove, you need n't be!" he declared. "You could give 'em the whole outfit and win at a canter!"

"Ah, that 's nice of you; and it would be nicer still if you would carry me off to a quiet corner, and get me a glass of lemonade or some innocent drink before we all have to rush for the train."

She turned away as she spoke, letting him strut at her side through the gathering groups on the terrace, while every nerve in her throbbed with the consciousness of what Selden must have thought of the scene.

But under her angry sense of the perverseness of things, and the light surface of her talk with Rosedale, a third idea persisted: she did not mean to leave without an attempt to discover the truth about Percy Gryce. Chance, or perhaps his own resolve, had kept them apart since his hasty withdrawal from Bellomont; but Miss Bart was an expert in making the most of the unexpected, and the distasteful incidents of the last few minutes — the revelation to Selden of precisely that part of her life which she most wished him to ignore — increased her longing for shelter, for escape from such humiliating contingencies. Any definite situation would be more tolerable than this buffeting of chances, which kept her in an attitude of uneasy alertness toward every possibility of life.

Indoors there was a general sense of dispersal in the air, as of an audience gathering itself up for departure after the principal actors had left the stage; but among the remaining groups, Lily could discover neither Gryce nor the youngest Miss Van Osburgh. That both should be missing struck her with foreboding; and she charmed Mr. Rosedale by proposing that they should make their way to the conservatories at the farther end of the house. There were just enough people left in the long suite of rooms to make their progress conspicuous, and Lily was aware of being followed by looks of amusement and interrogation, which glanced off as harmlessly from her indifference as from her companion's self-satisfaction. She cared very little at that moment about being seen with Rosedale: all her thoughts were centered on the object of her search. The latter, however, was not discoverable in the conservatories, and Lily, oppressed by a sudden conviction of failure, was casting about for a way to rid herself of her now superfluous companion, when they came upon Mrs. Van Osburgh, flushed and exhausted, but beaming with the consciousness of duty performed.

She glanced at them a moment with the benign but vacant eye of the tired hostess, to whom her guests have become mere whirling spots in a kaleidoscope of fatigue; then her attention became suddenly fixed, and she seized on Miss Bart with a confidential gesture.

"My dear Lily, I have n't had time for a word with you, and now I suppose you are just off. Have you seen Evie? She 's been looking everywhere for you: she wanted to tell you her little secret; but I daresay you have guessed it already. The engagement is not to be announced till next week—but you are such a friend of Mr. Gryce's that they both wished you to be the first to know of their happiness."

IX

In Mrs. Peniston's youth, fashion had returned to town in October; therefore on the tenth day of the month the blinds of her Fifth Avenue residence were drawn up, and the eyes of the Dying Gladiator in bronze who occupied the drawing-room window resumed their survey of that deserted thoroughfare.

The first two weeks after her return represented to Mrs. Peniston the domestic equivalent of a religious retreat. She "went through" the linen and blankets in the precise spirit of the penitent exploring the inner folds of conscience; she sought for moths as the stricken soul seeks for lurking infirmities. The topmost shelf of every closet was made to yield up its secret, cellar and coal-bin were probed to their darkest depths and, as a final stage in the lustral rites, the entire house was swathed in penitential white and deluged with expiatory soapsuds.

It was on this phase of the proceedings that Miss Bart entered on the afternoon of her return from the Van Osburgh wedding. The journey back to town had not been calculated to soothe her nerves. Though Evie Van Osburgh's engagement was still officially a secret, it was one of which the innumerable intimate friends of the family were already possessed; and the trainful of returning guests buzzed with allusions and anticipations. Lily was acutely aware of her own part in this drama of innuendo: she knew the exact quality of the amusement the situation evoked. The crude forms in which her friends took their pleasure included a loud enjoyment of such complications: the zest of surprising destiny in the act of playing a practical joke. Lily knew well enough how to bear herself in difficult situations. She had, to a shade, the exact manner between victory and defeat: every insinuation was shed without an effort by the bright indifference of her manner. But she was beginning to feel the strain of the attitude; the reaction was more rapid, and she lapsed to a deeper self-disgust.

As was always the case with her, this moral repulsion found a physical outlet in a quickened distaste for her surroundings. She revolted from the complacent ugliness of Mrs. Peniston's black walnut, from the slippery gloss of the vestibule tiles, and the mingled odour of sapolio and furniture-polish that met her at the door.

The stairs were still carpetless, and on the way up to her room she was arrested on the landing by an encroaching tide of soapsuds. Gathering up her skirts, she drew aside with an impatient gesture; and as she did so she had the odd sensation of having already found herself in the same situation but in different surroundings. It seemed to her that she was again descending the staircase from Selden's rooms; and looking down to remonstrate with the dispenser of the soapy flood, she found herself met by a lifted stare which had once before confronted her under similar circumstances. It was the char-woman of the Benedick who, resting on crimson elbows, examined her with the same unflinching curiosity, the same apparent reluctance to let her pass. On this occasion, however, Miss Bart was on her own ground.

"Don't you see that I wish to go by? Please move your pail," she said sharply.

The woman at first seemed not to hear; then, without a word of excuse, she pushed back her pail and dragged a wet floor-cloth across the landing, keeping her eyes fixed on Lily while the latter swept by. It was insufferable that Mrs. Peniston should have such creatures about the house; and Lily entered her room resolved that the woman should be dismissed that evening.

Mrs. Peniston, however, was at the moment inaccessible to remonstrance: since early morning she had been shut up with her maid, going over her furs, a process which formed the culminating episode in the drama of household renovation. In the evening also Lily found herself alone, for her aunt, who rarely dined out, had responded to the summons of a Van Alstyne cousin who was passing through town. The house, in its state of unnatural immaculateness and order, was as dreary as a tomb, and as Lily, turning from her brief repast between shrouded sideboards, wandered into the newly-uncovered glare of the drawing-room she felt as though she were buried alive in the stifling limits of Mrs. Peniston's existence.

She usually contrived to avoid being at home during the season of domestic renewal. On the present occasion, however, a variety of reasons had combined to bring her to town; and foremost among them was the fact that she had fewer invitations than usual for the autumn. She had so long been accustomed to pass from one country-house to another, till the close of the holidays brought her friends to town, that the unfilled gaps of time confronting her produced a sharp sense of waning popularity. It was as she had said to Selden—people were tired of her. They would welcome her in a new character, but as Miss Bart they knew her by heart. She knew herself by heart too, and was sick of the old story. There were moments when she longed blindly for anything different, anything strange, remote and untried; but the utmost reach of her imagination did not go beyond picturing her usual life in a new setting. She could not figure herself as anywhere but in a drawing-room, diffusing elegance as a flower sheds perfume.

Meanwhile, as October advanced she had to face the alternative of returning to the Trenors or joining her aunt in town. Even the desolating dulness of New York in October, and the soapy discomforts of Mrs. Peniston's interior, seemed preferable to what might await her at Bellomont; and with an air of heroic devotion she announced her intention of remaining with her aunt till the holidays.

Sacrifices of this nature are sometimes received with feelings as mixed as those which actuate them; and Mrs. Peniston remarked to her confidential maid that, if any of the family were to be with her at such a crisis (though for forty years she had been thought competent to see to the hanging of her own curtains), she would certainly have preferred Miss Grace to Miss Lily. Grace Stepney was an obscure cousin, of adaptable manners and vicarious interests, who "ran in" to sit with Mrs. Peniston when Lily dined out too continuously; who played bézique, picked up dropped stitches, read out the deaths from the Times, and sincerely admired the purple satin drawing-room curtains, the Dying Gladiator in the window, and the seven-by-five painting of Niagara which represented the one artistic excess of Mr. Peniston's temperate career.

Mrs. Peniston, under ordinary circumstances, was as much bored by her excellent cousin as the recipient of such services usually is by the person who performs them. She greatly preferred the brilliant and unreliable Lily, who did not know one end of a crochet-needle from the other, and had frequently wounded her susceptibilities by suggesting that the drawing-room should be "done over." But when it came to hunting for missing napkins, or helping to decide whether the back-stairs needed re-carpeting, Grace's judgment was certainly sounder than Lily's: not to mention the fact that the latter resented the smell of beeswax and brown soap, and behaved as though she thought a house ought to keep clean of itself, without extraneous assistance.

Seated under the cheerless blaze of the drawing-room chandelier — Mrs. Peniston never lit the lamps unless there was "company" — Lily seemed to watch her own figure retreating down vistas of neutral-tinted dulness to a middle age like Grace Stepney's. When she ceased to amuse Judy Trenor and her friends she would have to fall back on amusing Mrs. Peniston; whichever way she looked she saw only a future of servitude to the whims of others, never the possibility of asserting her own eager individuality.

A ring at the door-bell, sounding emphatically through the empty house, roused her suddenly to the extent of her boredom. It was as though all the weariness of the past months had culminated in the vacuity of that interminable evening. If only the ring meant a summons from the outer world — a token that she was still remembered and wanted!

After some delay a parlour-maid presented herself with the announcement that there was a person outside who was asking to see Miss Bart; and on Lily's pressing for a more specific description, she added: It 's Mrs. Haffen, Miss; she won't say what she wants."

Lily, to whom the name conveyed nothing, opened the door upon a woman in a battered bonnet, who stood firmly planted under the hall-light. The glare of the unshaded gas shone familiarly on her pock-marked face and the reddish baldness visible through thin strands of straw-coloured hair. Lily looked at the char-woman in surprise.

"Do you wish to see me?" she asked.

"I should like to say a word to you, Miss." The tone was neither aggressive nor conciliatory: it revealed nothing of the speaker's errand. Nevertheless, some precautionary instinct warned Lily to withdraw beyond ear-shot of the hovering parlour-maid.

She signed to Mrs. Haffen to follow her into the drawing-room, and closed the door when they had entered.

"What is it that you wish?" she enquired.

The char-woman, after the manner of her kind, stood with her arms folded in her shawl. Unwinding the latter, she produced a small parcel wrapped in dirty newspaper.

"I have something here that you might like to see, Miss Bart." She spoke the name with an unpleasant emphasis, as though her knowing it made a part of her reason for being there. To Lily the intonation sounded like a threat.

"You have found something belonging to me?" she asked, extending her hand.

Mrs. Haffen drew back. "Well, if it comes to that, I guess it's mine as much as anybody's," she returned.

Lily looked at her perplexedly. She was sure, now, that her visitor's manner conveyed a threat; but, expert as she was in certain directions, there was nothing in her experience to prepare her for the exact significance of the present scene. She felt, however, that it must be ended as promptly as possible.

"I don't understand; if this parcel is not mine, why have you asked for me?"

The woman was unabashed by the question. She was evidently prepared to answer it, but like all her class she had to go a long way back to make a beginning, and it was only after a pause that she replied: "My husband was janitor to the Benedick till the first of the month; since then he can't get nothing to do."

Lily remained silent and she continued: "It wasn't no fault of our own, neither: the agent had another man he wanted the place for, and we was put out, bag and baggage, just to suit his fancy. I had a long sickness last winter, and an operation that ate up all we'd put by; and it's hard for me and the children, Haffen being so long out of a job."

After all, then, she had come only to ask Miss Bart to find a place for her husband; or, more probably, to seek the young lady's intervention with Mrs. Peniston. Lily had such an air of always getting what she wanted that she was used to being appealed to as an intermediary, and, relieved of her vague apprehension, she took refuge in the conventional formula.

"I am sorry you have been in trouble," she said.

"Oh, that we have, Miss, and it's on'y just beginning. If on'y we'd 'a got another situation—but the agent he's dead against us. It ain't no fault of ours, neither, but——"

At this point Lily's impatience overcame her. "If you have anything
to say to me——" she interposed.

The woman's resentment of the rebuff seemed to spur her lagging
ideas.

"Yes, Miss; I 'm coming to that," she said. She paused again, with
her eyes on Lily, and then continued, in a tone of diffuse narrative:
"When we was at the Benedick I had charge of some of the gentlemen's
rooms; leastways, I swep' 'em out on Saturdays. Some of the gentlemen
got the greatest sight of letters: I never saw the like of it. Their waste-
paper baskets 'd be fairly brimming, and papers falling over on the floor.
Maybe havin' so many is how they get so careless. Some of 'em is worse
than others. Mr. Selden, Mr. Lawrence Selden, he was always one of the
carefullest: burnt his letters in winter, and tore 'em in little bits in summer. But sometimes he 'd have so many he 'd just bunch 'em together,
the way the others did, and tear the lot through once—like this."

While she spoke she had loosened the string from the parcel in her
hand, and now she drew forth a letter which she laid on the table between Miss Bart and herself. As she had said, the letter was torn in two;
but with a rapid gesture she laid the torn edges together and smoothed
out the page.

A wave of indignation swept over Lily. She felt herself in the presence of something vile, as yet but dimly conjectured—the kind of vile-
ness of which people whispered, but which she had never thought of as
touching her own life. She drew back with a motion of disgust, but her
withdrawal was checked by a sudden discovery: under the glare of Mrs.
Peniston's chandelier she had recognized the hand-writing of the letter.
It was a large disjointed hand, with a flourish of masculinity which but
slightly disguised its rambling weakness, and the words, scrawled in
heavy ink on pale-tinted note-paper, smote on Lily's ear as though she
had heard them spoken.

At first she did not grasp the full import of the situation. She understood only that before her lay a letter written by Bertha Dorset, and
addressed, presumably, to Lawrence Selden. There was no date, but the
blackness of the ink proved the writing to be comparatively recent. The
packet in Mrs. Haffen's hand doubtless contained more letters of the
same kind—a dozen, Lily conjectured from its thickness. The letter before her was short, but its few words, which had leapt into her brain
before she was conscious of reading them, told a long history—a history over which, for the last four years, the friends of the writer had
smiled and shrugged, viewing it merely as one among the countless

"good situations" of the mundane comedy. Now the other side presented itself to Lily, the volcanic nether side of the surface over which conjecture and innuendo glide so lightly till the first fissure turns their whisper to a shriek. Lily knew that there is nothing society resents so much as having given its protection to those who have not known how to profit by it: it is for having betrayed its connivance that the body social punishes the offender who is found out. And in this case there was no doubt of the issue. The code of Lily's world decreed that a woman's husband should be the only judge of her conduct: she was technically above suspicion while she had the shelter of his approval, or even of his indifference. But with a man of George Dorset's temper there could be no thought of condonation—the possessor of his wife's letters could overthrow with a touch the whole structure of her existence. And into what hands Bertha Dorset's secret had been delivered! For a moment the irony of the coincidence tinged Lily's disgust with a confused sense of triumph. But the disgust prevailed—all her instinctive resistances, of taste, of training, of blind inherited scruples, rose against the other feeling. Her strongest sense was one of personal contamination.

She moved away, as though to put as much distance as possible between herself and her visitor. "I know nothing of these letters," she said; "I have no idea why you have brought them here."

Mrs. Haffen faced her steadily. "I 'll tell you why, Miss. I brought 'em to you to sell, because I ain't got no other way of raising money, and if we don't pay our rent by tomorrow night we 'll be put out. I never done anythin' of the kind before, and if you 'd speak to Mr. Selden or to Mr. Rosedale about getting Haffen taken on again at the Benedick—I seen you talking to Mr. Rosedale on the steps that day you come out of Mr. Selden's rooms——"

The blood rushed to Lily's forehead. She understood now—Mrs. Haffen supposed her to be the writer of the letters. In the first leap of her anger she was about to ring and order the woman out; but an obscure impulse restrained her. The mention of Selden's name had started a new train of thought. Bertha Dorset's letters were nothing to her—they might go where the current of chance carried them! But Selden was inextricably involved in their fate. Men do not, at worst, suffer much from such exposure; and in this instance the flash of divination which had carried the meaning of the letters to Lily's brain had revealed also that they were appeals—repeated and therefore probably unanswered—for the renewal of a tie which time had evidently relaxed. Nevertheless, the fact that the correspondence had been allowed to fall into strange hands would convict Selden of negligence in a matter where the world holds it least pardonable; and there were graver risks to consider where a man of Dorset's ticklish balance was concerned.

If she weighed all these things it was unconsciously: she was aware only of feeling that Selden would wish the letters rescued, and that therefore she must obtain possession of them. Beyond that her mind did not travel. She had, indeed, a quick vision of returning the packet to Bertha Dorset, and of the opportunities the restitution offered; but this thought lit up abysses from which she shrank back ashamed.

Meanwhile Mrs. Haffen, prompt to perceive her hesitation, had already opened the packet and ranged its contents on the table. All the letters had been pieced together with strips of thin paper. Some were in small fragments, the others merely torn in half. Though there were not many, thus spread out they nearly covered the table. Lily's glance fell on a word here and there — then she said in a low voice: "What do you wish me to pay you?"

Mrs. Haffen's face reddened with satisfaction. It was clear that the young lady was badly frightened, and Mrs. Haffen was the woman to make the most of such fears. Anticipating an easier victory than she had foreseen, she named an exorbitant sum.

But Miss Bart showed herself a less ready prey than might have been expected from her imprudent opening. She refused to pay the price named, and after a moment's hesitation, met it by a counter-offer of half the amount.

Mrs. Haffen immediately stiffened. Her hand travelled toward the outspread letters, and folding them slowly, she made as though to restore them to their wrapping.

"I guess they 're worth more to you than to me, Miss, but the poor has got to live as well as the rich," she observed sententiously.

Lily was throbbing with fear, but the insinuation fortified her resistance.

"You are mistaken," she said indifferently. "I have offered all I am willing to give for the letters; but there may be other ways of getting them."

Mrs. Haffen raised a suspicious glance: she was too experienced not to know that the traffic she was engaged in had perils as great as its rewards, and she had a vision of the elaborate machinery of revenge which a word of this commanding young lady's might set in motion.

She applied the corner of her shawl to her eyes, and murmured through it that no good came of bearing too hard on the poor, but that for her part she had never been mixed up in such a business before, and that on her honour as a Christian all she and Haffen had thought of was that the letters must n't go any farther.

Lily stood motionless, keeping between herself and the char-woman the greatest distance compatible with the need of speaking in low tones. The idea of bargaining for the letters was intolerable to her, but she knew that, if she appeared to weaken, Mrs. Haffen would at once increase her original demand.

She could never afterward recall how long the duel lasted, or what was the decisive stroke which finally, after a lapse of time recorded in minutes by the clock, in hours by the precipitate beat of her pulses, put her in possession of the letters; she knew only that the door had finally closed, and that she stood alone with the packet in her hand.

She had no idea of reading the letters; even to unfold Mrs. Haffen's dirty newspaper would have seemed degrading. But what did she intend to do with its contents? The recipient of the letters had meant to destroy them, and it was her duty to carry out his intention. She had no right to keep them — to do so was to lessen whatever merit lay in having secured their possession. But how destroy them so effectually that there should be no second risk of their falling in such hands? Mrs. Peniston's icy drawing-room grate shone with a forbidding lustre: the fire, like the lamps, was never lit except when there was company.

Miss Bart was turning to carry the letters upstairs when she heard the opening of the outer door, and her aunt entered the drawing-room. Mrs. Peniston was a small plump woman, with a colourless skin lined with trivial wrinkles. Her grey hair was arranged with precision, and her clothes looked excessively new and yet slightly old-fashioned. They were always black and tightly fitting, with an expensive glitter: she was the kind of woman who wore jet at breakfast. Lily had never seen her when she was not cuirassed in shining black, with small tight boots, and an air of being packed and ready to start; yet she never started.

She looked about the drawing-room with an expression of minute scrutiny. "I saw a streak of light under one of the blinds as I drove up: it 's extraordinary that I can never teach that woman to draw them down evenly."

Having corrected the irregularity, she seated herself on one of the glossy purple arm-chairs; Mrs. Peniston always sat on a chair, never in it. Then she turned her glance to Miss Bart.

"My dear, you look tired; I suppose it 's the excitement of the wedding. Cornelia Van Alstyne was full of it: Molly was there, and Gerty Farish ran in for a minute to tell us about it. I think it was odd, their serving melons before the *consommé:* a wedding breakfast should always begin with *consommé*. Molly did n't care for the bridesmaids' dresses. She had it straight from Julia Melson that they cost three hundred dollars apiece at Céleste's, but she says they did n't look it. I 'm glad you decided not to be a bridesmaid; that shade of salmon-pink would n't have suited you."

Mrs. Peniston delighted in discussing the minutest details of festivities in which she had not taken part. Nothing would have induced her to undergo the exertion and fatigue of attending the Van Osburgh wedding, but so great was her interest in the event that, having heard two versions of it, she now prepared to extract a third from her niece. Lily, however, had been deplorably careless in noting the particulars of the entertainment. She had failed to observe the colour of Mrs. Van Osburgh's gown, and could not even say whether the old Van Osburgh's Sèvres had been used at the bride's table: Mrs. Peniston, in short, found that she was of more service as a listener than as a narrator.

"Really, Lily, I don't see why you took the trouble to go to the wedding, if you don't remember what happened or whom you saw there. When I was a girl I used to keep the *menu* of every dinner I went to, and write the names of the people on the back; and I never threw away my cotillion favours till after your uncle's death, when it seemed unsuitable to have so many coloured things about the house. I had a whole closet-full, I remember; and I can tell to this day what balls I got them at. Molly Van Alstyne reminds me of what I was at that age; it 's wonderful how she notices. She was able to tell her mother exactly how the wedding-dress was cut, and we knew at once, from the fold in the back, that it must have come from Paquin."

Mrs. Peniston rose abruptly, and, advancing to the ormolu clock surmounted by a helmeted Minerva, which throned on the chimney-piece between two malachite vases, passed her lace handkerchief between the helmet and its visor.

"I knew it—the parlour-maid never dusts there!" she exclaimed, triumphantly displaying a minute spot on the handkerchief; then, re-seating herself, she went on: "Molly thought Mrs. Dorset the best-dressed woman at the wedding. I 've no doubt her dress *did* cost more than any one else's, but I can't quite like the idea—a combination of sable and *point de Milan*. It seems she goes to a new man in Paris, who won't take an order till his client has spent a day with him at his villa at Neuilly. He says he must study his subject's home life—a most peculiar arrangement, I should say! But Mrs. Dorset told Molly about it herself: she said the villa was full of the most exquisite things and she was really sorry to leave. Molly said she never saw her looking better; she was in tremendous spirits, and said she had made a match between Evie Van Osburgh and Percy Gryce. She really seems to have a very good influence on young men. I hear she is interesting herself now in that silly Silverton boy, who has had his head turned by Carry Fisher, and has been gambling so dreadfully. Well, as I was saying, Evie is really engaged: Mrs. Dorset had her to stay with Percy Gryce, and managed it all, and Grace Van Osburgh is in the seventh heaven—she had almost despaired of marrying Evie."

Mrs. Peniston again paused, but this time her scrutiny addressed itself, not to the furniture, but to her niece.

"Cornelia Van Alstyne was so surprised: she had heard that you were to marry young Gryce. She saw the Wetheralls just after they had stopped with you at Bellomont, and Alice Wetherall was quite sure there was an engagement. She said that when Mr. Gryce left unexpectedly one morning, they all thought he had rushed to town for the ring."

Lily rose and moved toward the door.

"I believe I *am* tired: I think I will go to bed," she said; and Mrs. Peniston, suddenly distracted by the discovery that the easel sustaining the late Mr. Peniston's crayon-portrait was not exactly in line with the sofa in front of it, presented an absent-minded brow to her kiss.

In her own room Lily turned up the gas-jet and glanced toward the grate. It was as brilliantly polished as the one below, but here at least she could burn a few papers with less risk of incurring her aunt's disapproval. She made no immediate motion to do so, however, but dropping into a chair looked wearily about her. Her room was large and comfortably-furnished—it was the envy and admiration of poor Grace Stepney, who boarded; but, contrasted with the light tints and luxurious appointments of the guest-rooms where so many weeks of Lily's existence were spent, it seemed as dreary as a prison. The monumental wardrobe and bedstead of black walnut had migrated from Mr. Peniston's bedroom, and the magenta "flock" wall-paper, of a pattern dear to the early 'sixties, was hung with large steel engravings of an anecdotic character. Lily had tried to mitigate this charmless background by a few frivolous touches, in the shape of a lace-decked toilet table and a little painted desk surmounted by photographs; but the futility of the attempt struck her as she looked about the room. What a contrast to the subtle elegance of the setting she had pictured for herself—an apartment which should surpass the complicated luxury of her friends' surroundings by the whole extent of that artistic sensibility which made her feel herself their superior; in which every tint and line should combine to enhance her beauty and give distinction to her leisure! Once more the haunting sense of physical ugliness was intensified by her mental depression, so that each piece of the offending furniture seemed to thrust forth its most aggressive angle.

Her aunt's words had told her nothing new; but they had revived the vision of Bertha Dorset, smiling, flattered, victorious, holding her up to ridicule by insinuations intelligible to every member of their little group. The thought of the ridicule struck deeper than any other sensation: Lily knew every turn of the allusive jargon which could flay its victims without the shedding of blood. Her cheek burned at the recollection, and she rose and caught up the letters. She no longer meant to destroy them: that intention had been effaced by the quick corrosion of Mrs. Peniston's words.

Instead, she approached her desk, and lighting a taper, tied and sealed the packet; then she opened the wardrobe, drew out a despatch-box, and deposited the letters within it. As she did so, it struck her with a flash of irony that she was indebted to Gus Trenor for the means of buying them.

X

The autumn dragged on monotonously. Miss Bart had received one or two notes from Judy Trenor, reproaching her for not returning to Bellomont; but she replied evasively, alleging the obligation to remain with her aunt. In truth, however, she was fast wearying of her solitary existence with Mrs. Peniston, and only the excitement of spending her newly-acquired money lightened the dulness of the days.

All her life Lily had seen money go out as quickly as it came in, and whatever theories she cultivated as to the prudence of setting aside a part of her gains, she had unhappily no saving vision of the risks of the opposite course. It was a keen satisfaction to feel that, for a few months at least, she would be independent of her friends' bounty, that she could show herself abroad without wondering whether some penetrating eye would detect in her dress the traces of Judy Trenor's refurbished splendour. The fact that the money freed her temporarily from all minor obligations obscured her sense of the greater one it represented, and having never before known what it was to command so large a sum, she lingered delectably over the amusement of spending it.

It was on one of these occasions that, leaving a shop where she had spent an hour of deliberation over a dressing-case of the most complicated elegance, she ran across Miss Farish, who had entered the same establishment with the modest object of having her watch repaired. Lily

was feeling unusually virtuous. She had decided to defer the purchase of
the dressing-case till she should receive the bill for her new opera-cloak,
and the resolve made her feel much richer than when she had entered
the shop. In this mood of self-approval she had a sympathetic eye for
others, and she was struck by her friend's air of dejection.

Miss Farish, it appeared, had just left the committee-meeting of a
struggling charity in which she was interested. The object of the association was to provide comfortable lodgings, with a reading-room and
other modest distractions, where young women of the class employed
in down town offices might find a home when out of work, or in need
of rest, and the first year's financial report showed so deplorably small a
balance that Miss Farish, who was convinced of the urgency of the
work, felt proportionately discouraged by the small amount of interest
it aroused. The other-regarding sentiments had not been cultivated in
Lily, and she was often bored by the relation of her friend's philanthropic efforts, but today her quick dramatizing fancy seized on the
contrast between her own situation and that represented by some of
Gerty's "cases." These were young girls, like herself; some perhaps
pretty, some not without a trace of her finer sensibilities. She pictured
herself leading such a life as theirs — a life in which achievement seemed
as squalid as failure — and the vision made her shudder sympathetically.
The price of the dressing-case was still in her pocket; and drawing out
her little gold purse she slipped a liberal fraction of the amount into
Miss Farish's hand.

The satisfaction derived from this act was all that the most ardent
moralist could have desired. Lily felt a new interest in herself as a person
of charitable instincts: she had never before thought of doing good with
the wealth she had so often dreamed of possessing, but now her horizon
was enlarged by the vision of a prodigal philanthropy. Moreover, by
some obscure process of logic, she felt that her momentary burst of generosity had justified all previous extravagances, and excused any in
which she might subsequently indulge. Miss Farish's surprise and gratitude confirmed this feeling, and Lily parted from her with a sense of
self-esteem which she naturally mistook for the fruits of altruism.

About this time she was farther cheered by an invitation to spend
the Thanksgiving week at a camp in the Adirondacks. The invitation was
one which, a year earlier, would have provoked a less ready response, for
the party, though organized by Mrs. Fisher, was ostensibly given by a
lady of obscure origin and indomitable social ambitions, whose acquaintance Lily had hitherto avoided. Now, however, she was disposed
to coincide with Mrs. Fisher's view, that it did n't matter who gave the

party, as long as things were well done; and doing things well (under competent direction) was Mrs. Wellington Bry's strong point. The lady (whose consort was known as "Welly" Bry on the Stock Exchange and in sporting circles) had already sacrificed one husband, and sundry minor considerations, to her determination to get on; and, having obtained a hold on Carry Fisher, she was astute enough to perceive the wisdom of committing herself entirely to that lady's guidance. Everything, accordingly, was well done, for there was no limit to Mrs. Fisher's prodigality when she was not spending her own money, and as she remarked to her pupil, a good cook was the best introduction to society. If the company was not as select as the *cuisine,* the Welly Brys at least had the satisfaction of figuring for the first time in the society columns in company with one or two noticeable names; and foremost among these was of course Miss Bart's. The young lady was treated by her hosts with corresponding deference; and she was in the mood when such attentions are acceptable, whatever their source. Mrs. Bry's admiration was a mirror in which Lily's self-complacency recovered its lost outline. No insect hangs its nest on threads as frail as those which will sustain the weight of human vanity; and the sense of being of importance among the insignificant was enough to restore to Miss Bart the gratifying consciousness of power. If these people paid court to her it proved that she was still conspicuous in the world to which they aspired; and she was not above a certain enjoyment in dazzling them by her fineness, in developing their puzzled perception of her superiorities.

Perhaps, however, her enjoyment proceeded more than she was aware from the physical stimulus of the excursion, the challenge of crisp cold and hard exercise, the responsive thrill of her body to the influences of the winter woods. She returned to town in a glow of rejuvenation, conscious of a clearer colour in her cheeks, a fresh elasticity in her muscles. The future seemed full of a vague promise, and all her apprehensions were swept out of sight on the buoyant current of her mood.

A few days after her return to town she had the unpleasant surprise of a visit from Mr. Rosedale. He came late, at the confidential hour when the tea-table still lingers by the fire in friendly expectancy; and his manner showed a readiness to adapt itself to the intimacy of the occasion.

Lily, who had a vague sense of his being somehow connected with her lucky speculations, tried to give him the welcome he expected; but there was something in the quality of his geniality which chilled her own, and she was conscious of marking each step in their acquaintance by a fresh blunder.

Mr. Rosedale—making himself promptly at home in an adjoining easy-chair, and sipping his tea critically, with the comment: "You ought to go to my man for something really good"—appeared totally unconscious of the repugnance which kept her in frozen erectness behind the urn. It was perhaps her very manner of holding herself aloof that appealed to his collector's passion for the rare and unattainable. He gave, at any rate, no sign of resenting it and seemed prepared to supply in his own manner all the ease that was lacking in hers.

His object in calling was to ask her to go to the opera in his box on the opening night, and seeing her hesitate he said persuasively: "Mrs. Fisher is coming, and I 've secured a tremendous admirer of yours, who 'll never forgive me if you don't accept."

As Lily's silence left him with this allusion on his hands, he added with a confidential smile: "Gus Trenor has promised to come to town on purpose. I fancy he 'd go a good deal farther for the pleasure of seeing you."

Miss Bart felt an inward motion of annoyance: it was distasteful enough to hear her name coupled with Trenor's, and on Rosedale's lips the allusion was peculiarly unpleasant.

"The Trenors are my best friends—I think we should all go a long way to see each other," she said, absorbing herself in the preparation of fresh tea.

Her visitor's smile grew increasingly intimate. "Well, I was n't thinking of Mrs. Trenor at the moment—they say Gus does n't always, you know." Then, dimly conscious that he had not struck the right note, he added, with a well-meant effort at diversion: "How 's your luck been going in Wall Street, by the way? I hear Gus pulled off a nice little pile for you last month."

Lily put down the tea-caddy with an abrupt gesture. She felt that her hands were trembling, and clasped them on her knee to steady them; but her lip trembled too, and for a moment she was afraid the tremor might communicate itself to her voice. When she spoke, however, it was in a tone of perfect lightness.

"Ah, yes—I had a little bit of money to invest, and Mr. Trenor, who helps me about such matters, advised my putting it in stocks instead of a mortgage, as my aunt's agent wanted me to do; and as it happened, I made a lucky 'turn'—is that what you call it? For you make a great many yourself. I believe."

She was smiling back at him now, relaxing the tension of her attitude, and admitting him, by imperceptible gradations of glance and manner, a step farther toward intimacy. The protective instinct always nerved her to successful dissimulation, and it was not the first time she had used her beauty to divert attention from an inconvenient topic.

When Mr. Rosedale took leave, he carried with him, not only her acceptance of his invitation, but a general sense of having comported himself in a way calculated to advance his cause. He had always believed he had a light touch and a knowing way with women, and the prompt manner in which Miss Bart (as he would have phrased it) had "come into line," confirmed his confidence in his powers of handling the skittish sex. Her way of glossing over the transaction with Trenor he regarded at once as a tribute to his own acuteness, and a confirmation of his suspicions. The girl was evidently nervous, and Mr. Rosedale, if he saw no other means of advancing his acquaintance with her, was not above taking advantage of her nervousness.

He left Lily to a passion of disgust and fear. It seemed incredible that Gus Trenor should have spoken of her to Rosedale. With all his faults, Trenor had the safeguard of his traditions, and was the less likely to overstep them because they were so purely instinctive. But Lily recalled with a pang that there were convivial moments when, as Judy had confided to her, Gus "talked foolishly": in one of these, no doubt, the fatal word had slipped from him. As for Rosedale, she did not, after the first shock, greatly care what conclusions he had drawn. Though usually adroit enough where her own interests were concerned, she made the mistake, not uncommon to persons in whom the social habits are instinctive, of supposing that the inability to acquire them quickly implies a general dulness. Because a blue-bottle bangs irrationally against a window-pane, the drawing-room naturalist may forget that under less artificial conditions it is capable of measuring distances and drawing conclusions with all the accuracy needful to its welfare; and the fact that Mr. Rosedale's drawing-room manner lacked perspective made Lily class him with Trenor and the other dull men she knew, and assume that a little flattery, and the occasional acceptance of his hospitality, would suffice to render him innocuous. However, there could be no doubt of the expediency of showing herself in his box on the opening night of the opera; and after all, since Judy Trenor had promised to take him up that winter, it was as well to reap the advantage of being first in the field.

For a day or two after Rosedale's visit, Lily's thoughts were dogged by the consciousness of Trenor's shadowy claim, and she wished she had a clearer notion of the exact nature of the transaction which seemed to have put her in his power; but her mind shrank from any unusual application, and she was always helplessly puzzled by figures. Moreover she had not seen Trenor since the day of the Van Osburgh wedding, and in his continued absence the trace of Rosedale's words was soon effaced by other impressions.

When the opening night of the opera came, her apprehensions had so completely vanished that the sight of Trenor's ruddy countenance in the back of Mr. Rosedale's box filled her with a sense of pleasant reassurance. Lily had not quite reconciled herself to the necessity of appearing as Rosedale's guest on so conspicuous an occasion, and it was a relief to find herself supported by any one of her own set—for Mrs. Fisher's social habits were too promiscuous for her presence to justify Miss Bart's.

To Lily, always inspirited by the prospect of showing her beauty in public, and conscious tonight of all the added enhancements of dress, the insistency of Trenor's gaze merged itself in the general stream of admiring looks of which she felt herself the centre. Ah, it was good to be young, to be radiant, to glow with the sense of slenderness, strength and elasticity, of well-poised lines and happy tints, to feel one's self lifted to a height apart by that incommunicable grace which is the bodily counterpart of genius!

All means seemed justifiable to attain such an end, or rather, by a happy shifting of lights with which practice had familiarized Miss Bart, the cause shrank to a pin-point in the general brightness of the effect. But brilliant young ladies, a little blinded by their own effulgence, are apt to forget that the modest satellite drowned in their light is still performing its own revolutions and generating heat at its own rate. If Lily's poetic enjoyment of the moment was undisturbed by the base thought that her gown and opera cloak had been indirectly paid for by Gus Trenor, the latter had not sufficient poetry in his composition to lose sight of these prosaic facts. He knew only that he had never seen Lily look smarter in her life, that there was n't a woman in the house who showed off good clothes as she did, and that hitherto he, to whom she owed the opportunity of making this display, had reaped no return beyond that of gazing at her in company with several hundred other pairs of eyes.

It came to Lily therefore as a disagreeable surprise when, in the back of the box, where they found themselves alone between two acts, Trenor said, without preamble, and in a tone of sulky authority: "Look here, Lily, how is a fellow ever to see anything of you? I 'm in town three or four days in the week, and you know a line to the club will always find me, bJt you don't seem to remember my existence nowadays unless you want to get a tip out of me."

The fact that the remark was in distinctly bad taste did not make it any easier to answer, for Lily was vividly aware that it was not the moment for that drawing up of her slim figure and surprised lifting of the brows by which she usually quelled incipient signs of familiarity.

"I 'm very much flattered by your wanting to see me," she returned, essaying lightness instead, "but, unless you have mislaid my address, it would have been easy to find me any afternoon at my aunt's—in fact, I rather expected you to look me up there."

If she hoped to mollify him by this last concession the attempt was a failure, for he only replied, with the familiar lowering of the brows that made him look his dullest when he was angry: "Hang going to your aunt's, and wasting the afternoon listening to a lot of other chaps talking to you! You know I 'm not the kind to sit in a crowd and jaw—I 'd always rather clear out when that sort of circus is going on. But why can't we go off somewhere on a little lark together—a nice quiet little expedition like that drive at Bellomont, the day you met me at the station?"

He leaned unpleasantly close in order to convey this suggestion, and she fancied she caught a significant aroma which explained the dark flush on his face and the glistening dampness of his forehead.

The idea that any rash answer might provoke an unpleasant outburst tempered her disgust with caution, and she answered with a laugh: "I don't see how one can very well take country drives in town, but I am not always surrounded by an admiring throng, and if you will let me know what afternoon you are coming I will arrange things so that we can have a nice quiet talk."

"Hang talking! That's what you always say," returned Trenor, whose expletives lacked variety. "You put me off with that at the Van Osburgh wedding—but the plain English of it is that, now you 've got what you wanted out of me, you 'd rather have any other fellow about."

His voice had risen sharply with the last words, and Lily flushed with annoyance, but she kept command of the situation and laid a persuasive hand on his arm.

"Don't be foolish, Gus; I can't let you talk to me in that ridiculous way. If you really want to see me, why should n't we take a walk in the Park some afternoon? I agree with you that it 's amusing to be rustic in town, and if you like I 'll meet you there, and we 'll go and feed the squirrels, and you shall take me out on the lake in the steam-gondola."

She smiled as she spoke, letting her eyes rest on his in a way that took the edge from her banter and made him suddenly malleable to her will.

"All right, then: that 's a go. Will you come tomorrow? Tomorrow at three o'clock, at the end of the Mall? I 'll be there sharp, remember; you won't go back on me, Lily?"

But to Miss Bart's relief the repetition of her promise was cut short by the opening of the box door to admit George Dorset.

Trenor sulkily yielded his place, and Lily turned a brilliant smile on the newcomer. She had not talked with Dorset since their visit at Bellomont, but something in his look and manner told her that he recalled the friendly footing on which they had last met. He was not a man to whom the expression of admiration came easily: his long sallow face and distrustful eyes seemed always barricaded against the expansive emotions. But, where her own influence was concerned, Lily's intuitions sent out thread-like feelers, and as she made room for him on the narrow sofa she was sure he found a dumb pleasure in being near her. Few women took the trouble to make themselves agreeable to Dorset, and Lily had been kind to him at Bellomont, and was now smiling on him with a divine renewal of kindness.

"Well, here we are, in for another six months of caterwauling," he began complainingly. "Not a shade of difference between this year and last, except that the women have got new clothes and the singers have n't got new voices. My wife 's musical, you know—puts me through a course of this every winter. It is n't so bad on Italian nights—then she comes late, and there 's time to digest. But when they give Wagner we have to rush dinner, and I pay up for it. And the draughts are damnable—asphyxia in front and pleurisy in the back. There 's Trenor leaving the box without drawing the curtain! With a hide like that draughts don't make any difference. Did you ever watch Trenor eat? If you did, you 'd wonder why he 's alive; I suppose he 's leather inside too.—But I came to say that my wife wants you to come down to our place next Sunday. Do for heaven's sake say yes. She 's got a lot of bores coming—intellectual ones, I mean; that 's her new line, you know, and I 'm not sure it ain't worse than the music. Some of 'em have long hair, and they start an argument with the soup, and don't notice when things are handed to them. The consequence is the dinner gets cold, and I have dyspepsia. That silly ass Silverton brings them to the house—he writes poetry, you know, and Bertha and he are getting tremendously thick. She could write better than any of 'em if she chose, and I don't blame her for wanting clever fellows about; all I say is: 'Don't let me see 'em eat!'"

The gist of this strange communication gave Lily a distinct thrill of

pleasure. Under ordinary circumstances, there would have been nothing surprising in an invitation from Bertha Dorset; but since the
Bellomont episode an unavowed hostility had kept the two women
apart. Now, with a start of inner wonder, Lily felt that her thirst for
retaliation had died out. *If you would forgive your enemy,* says the Malay
proverb, *first inflict a hurt on him;* and Lily was experiencing the truth
of the apothegm. If she had destroyed Mrs. Dorset's letters, she might
have continued to hate her; but the fact that they remained in her possession had fed her resentment to satiety.

She uttered a smiling acceptance, hailing in the renewal of the tie an
escape from Trenor's importunities.

XI

Meanwhile the holidays had gone by and the season was beginning.
Fifth Avenue had become a nightly torrent of carriages surging upward
to the fashionable quarters about the Park, where illuminated windows
and outspread awnings betokened the usual routine of hospitality.
Other tributary currents crossed the main stream, bearing their freight
to the theatres, restaurants, or opera; and Mrs. Peniston, from the se-
cluded watch-tower of her upper window, could tell to a nicety just
when the chronic volume of sound was increased by the sudden influx
setting toward a Van Osburgh ball, or when the multiplication of
wheels meant merely that the opera was over, or that there was a big
supper at Sherry's.

Mrs. Peniston followed the rise and culmination of the season as
keenly as the most active sharer in its gaieties; and, as a looker-on, she
enjoyed opportunities of comparison and generalization such as those
who take part must proverbially forego. No one could have kept a more
accurate record of social fluctuations, or have put a more unerring finger on the distinguishing features of each season: its dulness, its extravagance, its lack of balls or excess of divorces. She had a special memory
for the vicissitudes of the "new people" who rose to the surface with
each recurring tide, and were either submerged beneath its rush or
landed triumphantly beyond the reach of envious breakers; and she was
apt to display a remarkable retrospective insight into their ultimate fate,
so that, when they had fulfilled their destiny, she was almost always able
to say to Grace Stepney — the recipient of her prophecies — that she had
known exactly what would happen.

This particular season Mrs. Peniston would have characterized as
that in which everybody "felt poor" except the Welly Brys and Mr.

Simon Rosedale. It had been a bad autumn in Wall Street, where prices fell in accordance with that peculiar law which proves railway stocks and bales of cotton to be more sensitive to the allotment of executive power than many estimable citizens trained to all the advantages of self-government. Even fortunes supposed to be independent of the market either betrayed a secret dependence on it, or suffered from a sympathetic affection: fashion sulked in its countryhouses, or came to town incognito, general entertainments were discountenanced, and informality and short dinners became the fashion.

But society, amused for a while at playing Cinderella, soon wearied of the hearthside rôle, and welcomed the Fairy Godmother in the shape of any magician powerful enough to turn the shrunken pumpkin back again into the golden coach. The mere fact of growing richer at a time when most people's investments are shrinking, is calculated to attract envious attention; and according to Wall Street rumours, Welly Bry and Rosedale had found the secret of performing this miracle.

Rosedale, in particular, was said to have doubled his fortune, and there was talk of his buying the newly-finished house of one of the victims of the crash, who, in the space of twelve short months, had made the same number of millions, built a house in Fifth Avenue, filled a picture-gallery with old masters, entertained all New York in it, and been smuggled out of the country between a trained nurse and a doctor, while his creditors mounted guard over the old masters, and his guests explained to each other that they had dined with him only because they wanted to see the pictures. Mr. Rosedale meant to have a less meteoric career. He knew he should have to go slowly, and the instincts of his race fitted him to suffer rebuffs and put up with delays. But he was prompt to perceive that the general dulness of the season afforded him an unusual opportunity to shine, and he set about with patient industry to form a background for his growing glory. Mrs. Fisher was of immense service to him at this period. She had set off so many newcomers on the social stage that she was like one of those pieces of stock scenery which tell the experienced spectator exactly what is going to take place. But Mr. Rosedale wanted, in the long run, a more individual environment. He was sensitive to shades of difference which Miss Bart would never have credited him with perceiving, because he had no corresponding variations of manner; and it was becoming more and more clear to him that Miss Bart herself possessed precisely the complementary qualities needed to round off his social personality.

Such details did not fall within the range of Mrs. Peniston's vision. Like many minds of panoramic sweep, hers was apt to overlook the *minutiæ* of the foreground, and she was much more likely to know where Carry Fisher had found the Welly Brys' *chef* for them, than what was happening to her own niece. She was not, however, without purveyors of information ready to supplement her deficiencies. Grace Stepney's mind was like a kind of moral fly-paper, to which the buzzing items of gossip were drawn by a fatal attraction, and where they hung fast in the toils of an inexorable memory. Lily would have been surprised to know how many trivial facts concerning herself were lodged in Miss Stepney's head. She was quite aware that she was of interest to dingy people, but she assumed that there is only one form of dinginess, and that admiration for brilliancy is the natural expression of its inferior state. She knew that Gerty Farish admired her blindly, and therefore supposed that she inspired the same sentiments in Grace Stepney, whom she classified as a Gerty Farish without the saving traits of youth and enthusiasm.

In reality, the two differed from each other as much as they differed from the object of their mutual contemplation. Miss Farish's heart was a fountain of tender illusions, Miss Stepney's a precise register of facts as manifested in their relation to herself. She had sensibilities which, to Lily, would have seemed comic in a person with a freckled nose and red eyelids, who lived in a boarding-house and admired Mrs. Peniston's drawing-room; but poor Grace's limitations gave them a more concentrated inner life, as poor soil starves certain plants into intenser efflorescence. She had in truth no abstract propensity to malice: she did not dislike Lily because the latter was brilliant and predominant, but because she thought that Lily disliked her. It is less mortifying to believe one's self unpopular than insignificant, and vanity prefers to assume that indifference is a latent form of unfriendliness. Even such scant civilities as Lily accorded to Mr. Rosedale would have made Miss Stepney her friend for life; but how could she foresee that such a friend was worth cultivating? How, moreover, can a young woman who has never been ignored measure the pang which this injury inflicts? And, lastly, how could Lily, accustomed to choose between a pressure of engagements, guess that she had mortally offended Miss Stepney by causing her to be excluded from one of Mrs. Peniston's infrequent dinner-parties?

Mrs. Peniston disliked giving dinners, but she had a high sense of family obligation, and on the Jack Stepneys' return from their honeymoon she felt it incumbent upon her to light the drawing-room lamps and extract her best silver from the Safe Deposit vaults. Mrs. Peniston's rare entertainments were preceded by days of heart-rending vacillation as to every detail of the feast, from the seating of the guests to the pattern of the table-cloth, and in the course of one of these preliminary discussions she had imprudently suggested to her cousin Grace that, as the dinner was a family affair, she might be included in it. For a week the prospect had lighted up Miss Stepney's colourless existence; then she had been given to understand that it would be more convenient to have her another day. Miss Stepney knew exactly what had happened. Lily, to whom family reunions were occasions of unalloyed dulness, had persuaded her aunt that a dinner of "smart" people would be much more to the taste of the young couple, and Mrs. Peniston, who leaned helplessly on her niece in social matters, had been prevailed upon to pronounce Grace's exile. After all, Grace could come any other day; why should she mind being put off?

It was precisely because Miss Stepney could come any other day— and because she knew her relations were in the secret of her unoccupied evenings—that this incident loomed gigantically on her horizon. She was aware that she had Lily to thank for it; and dull resentment was turned to active animosity.

Mrs. Peniston, on whom she had looked in a day or two after the dinner, laid down her crochet-work and turned abruptly from her oblique survey of Fifth Avenue.

"Gus Trenor?—Lily and Gus Trenor?" she said, growing so suddenly pale that her visitor was almost alarmed.

"Oh, cousin Julia . . . of course I don't mean . . . "

"I don't know what you *do* mean," said Mrs. Peniston, with a frightened quiver in her small fretful voice. "Such things were never heard of in my day. And my own niece! I 'm not sure I understand you. Do people say he 's in love with her?"

Mrs. Peniston's horror was genuine. Though she boasted an unequalled familiarity with the secret chronicles of society, she had the innocence of the school-girl who regards wickedness as a part of "history," and to whom it never occurs that the scandals she reads of in lesson-hours may be repeating themselves in the next street. Mrs. Peniston had kept her imagination shrouded, like the drawing-room furniture. She knew, of course, that society was "very much changed," and that many women her mother would have thought "peculiar" were now in a position to be critical about their visiting-lists; she had discussed the perils of divorce with her rector, and had felt thankful at times that Lily was still unmarried; but the idea that any scandal could attach to a young girl's name, above all that it could be lightly coupled with that of a married man, was so new to her that she was as much aghast as if she had been accused of leaving her carpets down all summer, or of violating any of the other cardinal laws of housekeeping.

Miss Stepney, when her first fright had subsided, began to feel the superiority that greater breadth of mind confers. It was really pitiable to be as ignorant of the world as Mrs. Peniston!

She smiled at the latter's question. "People always say unpleasant things—and certainly they 're a great deal together. A friend of mine met them the other afternoon in the Park—quite late, after the lamps were lit. It 's a pity Lily makes herself so conspicuous."

"*Conspicuous!*" gasped Mrs. Peniston. She bent forward, lowering her voice to mitigate the horror. "What sort of things do they say? That he means to get a divorce and marry her?"

Grace Stepney laughed outright. "Dear me, no! He would hardly do that. It—it 's a flirtation—nothing more."

"A flirtation? Between my niece and a married man? Do you mean to tell me that, with Lily's looks and advantages, she could find no better use for her time than to waste it on a fat stupid man almost old enough to be her father?" This argument had such a convincing ring that it gave Mrs. Peniston sufficient reassurance to pick up her work, while she waited for Grace Stepney to rally her scattered forces.

But Miss Stepney was on the spot in an instant. "That 's the worst of it—people say she is n't wasting her time! Every one knows, as you say, that Lily is too handsome and—and charming—to devote herself to a man like Gus Trenor unless——"

"Unless?" echoed Mrs. Peniston.

Her visitor drew breath nervously. It was agreeable to shock Mrs. Peniston, but not to shock her to the verge of anger. Miss Stepney was not sufficiently familiar with the classic drama to have recalled in advance how bearers of bad tidings are proverbially received, but she now had a rapid vision of forfeited dinners and a reduced wardrobe as the possible consequence of her disinterestedness. To the honour of her sex, however, hatred of Lily prevailed over more personal considerations. Mrs. Peniston had chosen the wrong moment to boast of her niece's charms.

"Unless," said Grace, leaning forward to speak with low-toned emphasis, "unless there are material advantages to be gained by making herself agreeable to him."

She felt that the moment was tremendous, and remembered suddenly that Mrs. Peniston's black brocade, with the cut jet fringe, would have been hers at the end of the season.

Mrs. Peniston put down her work again. Another aspect of the same idea had presented itself to her, and she felt that it was beneath her dignity to have her nerves racked by a dependent relative who wore her old clothes.

"If you take pleasure in annoying me by mysterious insinuations," she said coldly, "you might at least have chosen a more suitable time than just as I am recovering from the strain of giving a large dinner."

The mention of the dinner dispelled Miss Stepney's last scruples. "I don't know why I should be accused of taking pleasure in telling you about Lily. I was sure I should n't get any thanks for it," she returned with a flare of temper. "But I have some family feeling left, and as you are the only person who has any authority over Lily, I thought you ought to know what is being said of her."

"Well," said Mrs. Peniston, "what I complain of is that you have n't told me yet what *is* being said."

"I did n't suppose I should have to put it so plainly. People say that Gus Trenor pays her bills."

"Pays her bills—her bills?" Mrs. Peniston broke into a laugh. "I can't imagine where you can have picked up such rubbish. Lily has her own income—and I provide for her very handsomely——"

"Oh, we all know that," interposed Miss Stepney drily. "But Lily wears a great many smart gowns——"

"I like her to be well-dressed—it 's only suitable!"

"Certainly; but then there are her gambling debts besides."

Miss Stepney, in the beginning, had not meant to bring up this point; but Mrs. Peniston had only her own incredulity to blame. She was like the stiff-necked unbelievers of Scripture, who must be annihilated to be convinced.

"Gambling debts? Lily?" Mrs. Peniston's voice shook with anger and bewilderment. She wondered whether Grace Stepney had gone out of her mind. "What do you mean by her gambling debts?"

"Simply that if one plays bridge for money in Lily's set one is liable to lose a great deal—and I don't suppose Lily always wins."

"Who told you that my niece played cards for money?"

"Mercy, cousin Julia, don't look at me as if I were trying to turn you against Lily! Everybody knows she is crazy about bridge. Mrs. Gryce told me herself that it was her gambling that frightened Percy Gryce—it seems he was really taken with her at first. But, of course, among Lily's friends it 's quite the custom for girls to play for money. In fact, people are inclined to excuse her on that account——"

"To excuse her for what?"

"For being hard up—and accepting attentions from men like Gus Trenor—and George Dorset——"

Mrs. Peniston gave another cry. "George Dorset? Is there any one else? I should like to know the worst, if you please."

"Don't put it in that way, cousin Julia. Lately Lily has been a good deal with the Dorsets, and he seems to admire her—but of course that 's only natural. And I 'm sure there is no truth in the horrid things people say; but she *has* been spending a great deal of money this winter. Evie Van Osburgh was at Céleste's ordering her trousseau the other day— yes, the marriage takes place next month—and she told me that Céleste showed her the most exquisite things she was just sending home to Lily. And people say that Judy Trenor has quarrelled with her on account of Gus; but I 'm sure I 'm sorry I spoke, though I only meant it as a kindness."

Mrs. Peniston's genuine incredulity enabled her to dismiss Miss Stepney with a disdain which boded ill for that lady's prospect of succeeding to the black brocade; but minds impenetrable to reason have generally some crack through which suspicion filters, and her visitor's insinuations did not glide off as easily as she had expected. Mrs. Peniston disliked scenes, and her determination to avoid them had always led her to hold herself aloof from the details of Lily's life. In her youth, girls had not been supposed to require close supervision. They were generally assumed to be taken up with the legitimate business of courtship and marriage, and interference in such affairs on the part of their natural guardians was considered as unwarrantable as a spectator's suddenly joining in a game. There had of course been "fast" girls even in Mrs. Peniston's early experience; but their fastness, at worst, was understood to be a mere excess of animal spirits, against which there could be no graver charge than that of being "unladylike." The modern fastness appeared synonymous with immorality, and the mere idea of immorality was as offensive to Mrs. Peniston as a smell of cooking in the drawing-room: it was one of the conceptions her mind refused to admit.

She had no immediate intention of repeating to Lily what she had heard, or even of trying to ascertain its truth by means of discreet interrogation. To do so might be to provoke a scene; and a scene, in the shaken state of Mrs. Peniston's nerves, with the effects of her dinner not worn off, and her mind still tremulous with new impressions, was a risk she deemed it her duty to avoid. But there remained in her thoughts a settled deposit of resentment against her niece, all the denser because it was not to be cleared by explanation or discussion. It was horrible of a young girl to let herself be talked about; however unfounded the charges against her, she must be to blame for their having been made. Mrs. Peniston felt as if there had been a contagious illness in the house, and she was doomed to sit shivering among her contaminated furniture.

XII

Miss Bart had in fact been treading a devious way, and none of her critics could have been more alive to the fact than herself; but she had a fatalistic sense of being drawn from one wrong turning to another, without ever perceiving the right road till it was too late to take it.

Lily, who considered herself above narrow prejudices, had not imagined that the fact of letting Gus Trenor make a little money for her would ever disturb her self-complacency. And the fact in itself still seemed harmless enough; only it was a fertile source of harmful complications. As she exhausted the amusement of spending the money these complications became more pressing, and Lily, whose mind could be severely logical in tracing the causes of her ill-luck to others, justified herself by the thought that she owed all her troubles to the enmity of Bertha Dorset. This enmity, however, had apparently expired in a renewal of friendliness between the two women. Lily's visit to the Dorsets had resulted, for both, in the discovery that they could be of use to each other; and the civilized instinct finds a subtler pleasure in making use of its antagonist than in confounding him. Mrs. Dorset was, in fact, engaged in a new sentimental experiment, of which Mrs. Fisher's late property, Ned Silverton, was the rosy victim; and at such moments, as Judy Trenor had once remarked, she felt a peculiar need of distracting her husband's attention. Dorset was as difficult to amuse as a savage; but even his self-engrossment was not proof against Lily's arts, or rather these were especially adapted to soothe an uneasy egoism. Her experience with Percy Gryce stood her in good stead in ministering to Dorset's humours, and if the incentive to please was less urgent, the difficulties of her situation were teaching her to make much of minor opportunities.

Intimacy with the Dorsets was not likely to lessen such difficulties on the material side. Mrs. Dorset had none of Judy Trenor's lavish impulses, and Dorset's admiration was not likely to express itself in financial "tips," even had Lily cared to renew her experiences in that line. What she required, for the moment, of the Dorsets' friendship, was simply its social sanction. She knew that people were beginning to talk of her; but this fact did not alarm her as it had alarmed Mrs. Peniston. In her set such gossip was not unusual, and a handsome girl who flirted with a married man was merely assumed to be pressing to the limit of her opportunities. It was Trenor himself who frightened her. Their walk in the Park had not been a success. Trenor had married young, and since his marriage his intercourse with women had not taken the form of the sentimental small-talk which doubles upon itself like the paths in a maze. He was first puzzled and then irritated to find himself always led back to the same starting-point, and Lily felt that she was gradually losing control of the situation. Trenor was in truth in an unmanageable mood. In spite of his understanding with Rosedale he had been somewhat heavily "touched" by the fall in stocks; his household expenses weighed on him, and he seemed to be meeting, on all sides, a sullen opposition to his wishes, instead of the easy good luck he had hitherto encountered.

Mrs. Trenor was still at Bellomont, keeping the town-house open, and descending on it now and then for a taste of the world, but preferring the recurrent excitement of week-end parties to the restrictions of a dull season. Since the holidays she had not urged Lily to return to Bellomont, and the first time they met in town Lily fancied there was a shade of coldness in her manner. Was it merely the expression of her displeasure at Miss Bart's neglect, or had disquieting rumours reached her? The latter contingency seemed improbable, yet Lily was not without a sense of uneasiness. If her roaming sympathies had struck root anywhere, it was in her friendship with Judy Trenor. She believed in the sincerity of her friend's affection, though it sometimes showed itself in self-interested ways, and she shrank with peculiar reluctance from any risk of estranging it. But, aside from this, she was keenly conscious of the way in which such an estrangement would react on herself. The fact that Gus Trenor was Judy's husband was at times Lily's strongest reason for disliking him, and for resenting the obligation under which he had placed her.

To set her doubts at rest, Miss Bart, soon after the New Year, "proposed" herself for a week-end at Bellomont. She had learned in advance that the presence of a large party would protect her from too great assiduity on Trenor's part, and his wife's telegraphic "come by all means" seemed to assure her of her usual welcome.

Judy received her amicably. The cares of a large party always prevailed over personal feelings, and Lily saw no change in her hostess's manner. Nevertheless, she was soon aware that the experiment of coming to Bellomont was destined not to be successful. The party was made up of what Mrs. Trenor called "poky people"—her generic name for persons who did not play bridge—and, it being her habit to group all such obstructionists in one class, she usually invited them together, regardless of their other characteristics. The result was apt to be an irreducible combination of persons having no other quality in common than their abstinence from bridge, and the antagonisms developed in a group lacking the one taste which might have amalgamated them, were in this case aggravated by bad weather, and by the ill-concealed boredom of their host and hostess. In such emergencies, Judy would usually have turned to Lily to fuse the discordant elements; and Miss Bart, assuming that such a service was expected of her, threw herself into it with her accustomed zeal. But at the outset she perceived a subtle resistance to her efforts. If Mrs. Trenor's manner toward her was unchanged, there was certainly a faint coldness in that of the other ladies. An occasional caustic allusion to "your friends the Wellington Brys," or to "the little Jew who has bought the Greiner house—some one told us you knew him, Miss Bart,"—showed Lily that she was in disfavour with that portion of society which, while contributing least to its amusement, has assumed the right to decide what forms that amusement shall take. The indication was a slight one, and a year ago Lily would have smiled at it, trusting to the charm of her personality to dispel any prejudice against her. But now she had grown sensitive to criticism and less confident in her power of disarming it. She knew, moreover, that if the ladies at Bellomont permitted themselves to criticize her friends openly, it was a proof that they were not afraid of subjecting her to the same treatment behind her back. The nervous dread lest anything in Trenor's manner should seem to justify their disapproval made her seek every pretext for avoiding him, and she left Bellomont conscious of having failed in every purpose which had taken her there.

In town she returned to preoccupations which, for the moment, had the happy effect of banishing troublesome thoughts. The Welly Brys, after much debate, and anxious counsel with their newly acquired friends, had decided on the bold move of giving a general entertainment. To attack society collectively, when one's means of approach are limited to a few acquaintances, is like advancing into a strange country with an insufficient number of scouts; but such rash tactics have sometimes led to brilliant victories, and the Brys had determined to put their fate to the touch. Mrs. Fisher, to whom they had entrusted the conduct of the affair, had decided that *tableaux vivants* and expensive music were the two baits most likely to attract the desired prey, and after prolonged negotiations, and the kind of wire-pulling in which she was known to excel, she had induced a dozen fashionable women to exhibit themselves in a series of pictures which, by a farther miracle of persuasion, the distinguished portrait painter, Paul Morpeth, had been prevailed upon to organize.

Lily was in her element on such occasions. Under Morpeth's guidance her vivid plastic sense, hitherto nurtured on no higher food than dress-making and upholstery, found eager expression in the disposal of draperies, the study of attitudes, the shifting of lights and shadows. Her dramatic instinct was roused by the choice of subjects, and the gorgeous reproductions of historic dress stirred an imagination which only visual impressions could reach. But keenest of all was the exhilaration of displaying her own beauty under a new aspect: of showing that her loveliness was no mere fixed quality, but an element shaping all emotions to fresh forms of grace.

Mrs. Fisher's measures had been well-taken, and society, surprised in a dull moment, succumbed to the temptation of Mrs. Bry's hospitality. The protesting minority were forgotten in the throng which abjured and came; and the audience was almost as brilliant as the show.

Lawrence Selden was among those who had yielded to the proffered inducements. If he did not often act on the accepted social axiom that a man may go where he pleases, it was because he had long since learned that his pleasures were mainly to be found in a small group of the like-minded. But he enjoyed spectacular effects, and was not insensible to the part money plays in their production: all he asked was that the very rich should live up to their calling as stage-managers, and not spend their money in a dull way. This the Brys could certainly not be charged with doing. Their recently built house, whatever it might lack as a frame for domesticity, was almost as well-designed for the display of a festal assemblage as one of those airy pleasure-halls which the Italian architects improvised to set off the hospitality of princes. The air of improvisation was in fact strikingly present: so recent, so rapidly-evoked was the whole *mise-en-scène* that one had to touch the marble columns to learn they were not of cardboard, to seat one's self in one of the damask-and-gold arm-chairs to be sure it was not painted against the wall.

Selden, who had put one of these seats to the test, found himself, from an angle of the ball-room, surveying the scene with frank enjoyment. The company, in obedience to the decorative instinct which calls for fine clothes in fine surroundings, had dressed rather with an eye to Mrs. Bry's background than to herself. The seated throng, filling the immense room without undue crowding, presented a surface of rich tissues and jewelled shoulders in harmony with the festooned and gilded walls, and the flushed splendours of the Venetian ceiling. At the

farther end of the room a stage had been constructed behind a prosce-
nium arch curtained with folds of old damask; but in the pause before
the parting of the folds there was little thought of what they might reveal, for every woman who had accepted Mrs. Bry's invitation was engaged in trying to find out how many of her friends had done the same.

Gerty Farish, seated next to Selden, was lost in that indiscriminate
and uncritical enjoyment so irritating to Miss Bart's finer perceptions. It
may be that Selden's nearness had something to do with the quality of
his cousin's pleasure; but Miss Farish was so little accustomed to refer
her enjoyment of such scenes to her own share in them, that she was
merely conscious of a deeper sense of contentment.

"Was n't it dear of Lily to get me an invitation? Of course it would
never have occurred to Carry Fisher to put me on the list, and I should
have been so sorry to miss seeing it all—and especially Lily herself.
Some one told me the ceiling was by Veronese—you would know, of
course, Lawrence. I suppose it 's very beautiful, but his women are so
dreadfully fat. Goddesses? Well, I can only say that if they'd been mortals and had to wear corsets, it would have been better for them. I think
our women are much handsomer. And this room is wonderfully becoming—every one looks so well! Did you ever see such jewels? Do look at
Mrs. George Dorset's pearls—I suppose the smallest of them would
pay the rent of our Girls' Club for a year. Not that I ought to complain
about the club; every one has been so wonderfully kind. Did I tell you
that Lily had given us three hundred dollars? Was n't it splendid of her?
And then she collected a lot of money from her friends—Mrs. Bry gave
us five hundred, and Mr. Rosedale a thousand. I wish Lily were not so
nice to Mr. Rosedale, but she says it 's no use being rude to him, because he does n't see the difference. She really can't bear to hurt
people's feelings—it makes me so angry when I hear her called cold and
conceited! The girls at the club don't call her that. Do you know she has
been there with me twice?—yes, Lily! And you should have seen their
eyes! One of them said it was as good as a day in the country just to look
at her. And she sat there, and laughed and talked with them—not a bit
as if she were being *charitable,* you know, but as if she liked it as much
as they did. They 've been asking ever since when she 's coming back;
and she 's promised me——oh!"

Miss Farish's confidences were cut short by the parting of the curtain on the first *tableau*—a group of nymphs dancing across flower-
strewn sward in the rhythmic postures of Botticelli's Spring. *Tableaux
vivants* depend for their effect not only on the happy disposal of lights
and the delusive interposition of layers of gauze, but on a corresponding

adjustment of the mental vision. To unfurnished minds they remain, in spite of every enhancement of art, only a superior kind of wax-works; but to the responsive fancy they may give magic glimpses of the boundary world between fact and imagination. Selden's mind was of this order: he could yield to vision-making influences as completely as a child to the spell of a fairy-tale. Mrs. Bry's *tableaux* wanted none of the qualities which go to the producing of such illusions, and under Morpeth's organizing hand the pictures succeeded each other with the rhythmic march of some splendid frieze, in which the fugitive curves of living flesh and the wandering light of young eyes have been subdued to plastic harmony without losing the charm of life.

The scenes were taken from old pictures, and the participators had been cleverly fitted with characters suited to their types. No one, for instance, could have made a more typical Goya than Carry Fisher, with her short dark-skinned face, the exaggerated glow of her eyes, the provocation of her frankly-painted smile. A brilliant Miss Smedden from Brooklyn showed to perfection the sumptuous curves of Titian's Daughter, lifting her gold salver laden with grapes above the harmonizing gold of rippled hair and rich brocade, and a young Mrs. Van Alstyne, who showed the frailer Dutch type, with high blue-veined forehead and pale eyes and lashes, made a characteristic Vandyck, in black satin, against a curtained archway. Then there were Kauffmann nymphs garlanding the altar of Love; a Veronese supper, all sheeny textures, pearl-woven heads and marble architecture; and a Watteau group of lute-playing comedians, lounging by a fountain in a sunlit glade.

Each evanescent picture touched the vision-building faculty in Selden, leading him so far down the vistas of fancy that even Gerty Farish's running commentary—"Oh, how lovely Lulu Melson looks!" or: "That must be Kate Corby, to the right there, in purple"—did not break the spell of the illusion. Indeed, so skilfully had the personality of the actors been subdued to the scenes they figured in that even the least imaginative of the audience must have felt a thrill of contrast when the curtain suddenly parted on a picture which was simply and undisguisedly the portrait of Miss Bart.

Here there could be no mistaking the predominance of personality— the unanimous "Oh!" of the spectators was a tribute, not to the brushwork of Reynolds's "Mrs. Lloyd" but to the flesh and blood loveliness of Lily Bart. She had shown her artistic intelligence in selecting a type so like her own that she could embody the person represented without ceasing to be herself. It was as though she had stepped, not out of, but into, Reynolds's canvas, banishing the phantom of his dead beauty by the beams of her living grace. The impulse to show herself in a splendid setting—she had thought for a moment of representing Tiepolo's Cleopatra—had yielded to the truer instinct of trusting to her unassisted beauty, and she had purposely chosen a picture without distracting accessories of dress or surroundings. Her pale draperies, and the background of foliage against which she stood, served only to relieve the long dryad-like curves that swept upward from her poised foot to her lifted arm. The noble buoyancy of her attitude, its suggestion of soaring grace, revealed the touch of poetry in her beauty that Selden always felt in her presence, yet lost the sense of when he was not with her. Its expression was now so vivid that for the first time he seemed to see before him the real Lily Bart, divested of the trivialities of her little world, and catching for a moment a note of that eternal harmony of which her beauty was a part.

"Deuced bold thing to show herself in that get-up; but, gad, there is n't a break in the lines anywhere, and I suppose she wanted us to know it!"

These words, uttered by that experienced connoisseur, Mr. Ned Van Alstyne, whose scented white moustache had brushed Selden's shoulder whenever the parting of the curtains presented any exceptional opportunity for the study of the female outline, affected their hearer in an unexpected way. It was not the first time that Selden had heard Lily's beauty lightly remarked on, and hitherto the tone of the comments had imperceptibly coloured his view of her. But now it woke only a motion of indignant contempt. This was the world she lived in, these were the standards by which she was fated to be measured! Does one go to Caliban for a judgment on Miranda?

In the long moment before the curtain fell, he had time to feel the whole tragedy of her life. It was as though her beauty, thus detached from all that cheapened and vulgarized it, had held out suppliant hands to him from the world in which he and she had once met for a moment, and where he felt an overmastering longing to be with her again.

He was roused by the pressure of ecstatic fingers. "Was n't she too beautiful, Lawrence? Don't you like her best in that simple dress? It makes her look like the real Lily—the Lily I know."

He met Gerty Farish's brimming gaze. "The Lily *we* know," he corrected; and his cousin, beaming at the implied understanding, exclaimed joyfully: "I 'll tell her that! She always says you dislike her."

The performance over, Selden's first impulse was to seek Miss Bart. During the interlude of music which succeeded the *tableaux,* the actors had seated themselves here and there in the audience, diversifying its conventional appearance by the varied picturesqueness of their dress. Lily, however, was not among them, and her absence served to protract the effect she had produced on Selden: it would have broken the spell to see her too soon in the surroundings from which accident had so happily detached her. They had not met since the day of the Van Osburgh wedding, and on his side the avoidance had been intentional. Tonight, however, he knew that, sooner or later, he should find himself at her side; and though he let the dispersing crowd drift him whither it would, without making an immediate effort to reach her, his procrastination was not due to any lingering resistance, but to the desire to luxuriate a moment in the sense of complete surrender.

Lily had not an instant's doubt as to the meaning of the murmur greeting her appearance. No other *tableau* had been received with that precise note of approval: it had obviously been called forth by herself, and not by the picture she impersonated. She had feared at the last moment that she was risking too much in dispensing with the advantages of a more sumptuous setting, and the completeness of her triumph gave her an intoxicating sense of recovered power. Not caring to diminish the impression she had produced, she held herself aloof from the audience till the movement of dispersal before supper, and thus had a second opportunity of showing herself to advantage, as the throng poured slowly into the empty drawing-room where she was standing.

She was soon the centre of a group which increased and renewed itself as the circulation became general, and the individual comments on her success were a delightful prolongation of the collective applause. At such moments she lost something of her natural fastidiousness, and cared less for the quality of the admiration received than for its quantity. Differences of personality were merged in a warm atmosphere of praise, in which her beauty expanded like a flower in sunlight; and if Selden had approached a moment or two sooner he would have seen her turning on Ned Van Alstyne and George Dorset the look he had dreamed of capturing for himself.

Fortune willed, however, that the hurried approach of Mrs. Fisher, as whose aide-de-camp Van Alstyne was acting, should break up the group before Selden reached the threshold of the room. One or two of the men wandered off in search of their partners for supper, and the others, noticing Selden's approach, gave way to him in accordance with the tacit free-masonry of the ball-room. Lily was therefore standing alone when he reached her; and finding the expected look in her eye, he had the satisfaction of supposing he had kindled it. The look did indeed deepen as it rested on him, for even in that moment of self-intoxication Lily felt the quicker beat of life that his nearness always produced. She read, too, in his answering gaze the delicious confirmation of her triumph, and for the moment it seemed to her that it was for him only she cared to be beautiful.

Selden had given her his arm without speaking. She took it in silence, and they moved away, not toward the supper-room, but against the tide which was setting thither. The faces about her flowed by like the streaming images of sleep: she hardly noticed where Selden was leading her, till they passed through a glass doorway at the end of the long suite of rooms and stood suddenly in the fragrant hush of a garden. Gravel grated beneath their feet, and about them was the transparent dimness of a midsummer night. Hanging lights made emerald caverns in the depths of foliage, and whitened the spray of a fountain falling among lilies. The magic place was deserted: there was no sound but the plash of the water on the lily-pads, and a distant drift of music that might have been blown across a sleeping lake.

Selden and Lily stood still, accepting the unreality of the scene as a part of their own dream-like sensations. It would not have surprised them to feel a summer breeze on their faces, or to see the lights among the boughs reduplicated in the arch of a starry sky. The strange solitude about them was no stranger than the sweetness of being alone in it together.

At length Lily withdrew her hand, and moved away a step, so that her white-robed slimness was outlined against the dusk of the branches. Selden followed her, and still without speaking they seated themselves on a bench beside the fountain.

Suddenly she raised her eyes with the beseeching earnestness of a child. "You never speak to me—you think hard things of me," she murmured.

"I think of you at any rate, God knows!" he said.

"Then why do we never see each other? Why can't we be friends? You promised once to help me," she continued in the same tone, as though the words were drawn from her unwillingly.

"The only way I can help you is by loving you," Selden said in a low voice.

She made no reply, but her face turned to him with the soft motion of a flower. His own met it slowly, and their lips touched.

She drew back and rose from her seat. Selden rose too, and they stood facing each other. Suddenly she caught his hand and pressed it a moment against her cheek.

"Ah, love me, love me — but don't tell me so!" she sighed with her eyes in his; and before he could speak she had turned and slipped through the arch of boughs, disappearing in the brightness of the room beyond.

Selden stood where she had left him. He knew too well the transiency of exquisite moments to attempt to follow her; but presently he reëntered the house and made his way through the deserted rooms to the door. A few sumptuously-cloaked ladies were already gathered in the marble vestibule, and in the coat-room he found Van Alstyne and Gus Trenor.

The former, at Selden's approach, paused in the careful selection of a cigar from one of the silver boxes invitingly set out near the door.

"Hallo, Selden, going too? You 're an Epicurean like myself, I see: you don't want to see all those goddesses gobbling terrapin. Gad, what a show of good-looking women; but not one of 'em could touch that little cousin of mine. Talk of jewels — what 's a woman want with jewels when she 's got herself to show? The trouble is that all these fal-bals they wear cover up their figures when they 've got 'em. I never knew till tonight what an outline Lily has."

"It 's not her fault if everybody don't know it now," growled Trenor, flushed with the struggle of getting into his fur-lined coat. "Damned bad taste, I call it — no, no cigar for me. You can't tell what you 're smoking in one of these new houses — likely as not the *chef* buys the cigars. Stay for supper? Not if I know it! When people crowd their rooms so that you can't get near any one you want to speak to, I 'd as soon sup in the elevated at the rush hour. My wife was dead right to stay away: she says life 's too short to spend it in breaking in new people."

XIII

Lily woke from happy dreams to find two notes at her bed-side.

One was from Mrs. Trenor, who announced that she was coming to town that afternoon for a flying visit, and hoped Miss Bart would be able to dine with her. The other was from Selden. He wrote briefly that an important case called him to Albany, whence he would be unable to return till the evening, and asked Lily to let him know at what hour on the following day she would see him.

Lily, leaning back among her pillows, gazed musingly at his letter. The scene in the Brys' conservatory had been like a part of her dreams; she had not expected to wake to such evidence of its reality. Her first movement was one of annoyance: this unforeseen act of Selden's added another complication to life. It was so unlike him to yield to such an irrational impulse! Did he really mean to ask her to marry him? She had once shown him the impossibility of such a hope, and his subsequent behaviour seemed to prove that he had accepted the situation with a reasonableness somewhat mortifying to her vanity. It was all the more agreeable to find that this reasonableness was maintained only at the cost of not seeing her; but, though nothing in life was as sweet as the sense of her power over him, she saw the danger of allowing the episode of the previous night to have a sequel. Since she could not marry him, it would be kinder to him, as well as easier for herself, to write a line amicably evading his request to see her: he was not the man to mistake such a hint, and when next they met it would be on their usual friendly footing.

Lily sprang out of bed, and went straight to her desk. She wanted to write at once, while she could trust to the strength of her resolve. She was still languid from her brief sleep and the exhilaration of the evening, and the sight of Selden's writing brought back the culminating moment of her triumph: the moment when she had read in his eyes that no philosophy was proof against her power. It would be pleasant to have that sensation again . . . no one else could give it to her in its fulness; and she could not bear to mar her mood of luxurious retrospection by an act of definite refusal. She took up her pen and wrote hastily: *"Tomorrow at four";* murmuring to herself, as she slipped the sheet into its envelope: "I can easily put him off when tomorrow comes."

Judy Trenor's summons was very welcome to Lily. It was the first time she had received a direct communication from Bellomont since the close of her last visit there, and she was still visited by the dread of having incurred Judy's displeasure. But this characteristic command seemed to reëstablish their former relations; and Lily smiled at the thought that her friend had probably summoned her in order to hear about the Brys' entertainment. Mrs. Trenor had absented herself from the feast, perhaps for the reason so frankly enunciated by her husband, perhaps because, as Mrs. Fisher somewhat differently put it, she "could n't bear new people when she had n't discovered them herself." At any rate, though she remained haughtily at Bellomont, Lily suspected in her a devouring eagerness to hear of what she had missed, and to learn exactly in what measure Mrs. Wellington Bry had surpassed all previous competitors for social recognition. Lily was quite ready to gratify this curiosity, but it happened that she was dining out. She determined, however, to see Mrs. Trenor for a few moments, and ringing for her maid she despatched a telegram to say that she would be with her friend that evening at ten.

She was dining with Mrs. Fisher, who had gathered at an informal feast a few of the performers of the previous evening. There was to be plantation music in the studio after dinner—for Mrs. Fisher, despairing of the republic, had taken up modelling, and annexed to her small crowded house a spacious apartment, which, whatever its uses in her hours of plastic inspiration, served at other times for the exercise of an indefatigable hospitality. Lily was reluctant to leave, for the dinner was amusing, and she would have liked to lounge over a cigarette and hear a few songs; but she could not break her engagement with Judy, and shortly after ten she asked her hostess to ring for a hansom, and drove up Fifth Avenue to the Trenors'.

She waited long enough on the doorstep to wonder that Judy's presence in town was not signalized by a greater promptness in admitting her; and her surprise was increased when, instead of the expected footman, pushing his shoulders into a tardy coat, a shabby care-taking person in calico let her into the shrouded hall. Trenor, however, appeared at once on the threshold of the drawing-room, welcoming her with unusual volubility while he relieved her of her cloak and drew her into the room.

"Come along to the den; it 's the only comfortable place in the house. Does n't this room look as if it was waiting for the body to be brought down? Can't see why Judy keeps the house wrapped up in this awful slippery white stuff—it 's enough to give a fellow pneumonia to walk through these rooms on a cold day. You look a little pinched yourself, by the way: it 's rather a sharp night out. I noticed it walking up from the club. Come along, and I 'll give you a nip of brandy, and you can toast yourself over the fire and try some of my new Egyptians—that little Turkish chap at the Embassy put me on to a brand that I want you to try, and if you like 'em I 'll get out a lot for you: they don't have 'em here yet, but I 'll cable."

He led her through the house to the large room at the back, where Mrs. Trenor usually sat, and where, even in her absence, there was an air of occupancy. Here, as usual, were flowers, newspapers, a littered writing-table, and a general aspect of lamp-lit familiarity, so that it was a surprise not to see Judy's energetic figure start up from the arm-chair near the fire.

It was apparently Trenor himself who had been occupying the seat in question, for it was overhung by a cloud of cigar smoke, and near it stood one of those intricate folding tables which British ingenuity has devised to facilitate the circulation of tobacco and spirits. The sight of such appliances in a drawing-room was not unusual in Lily's set, where smoking and drinking were unrestricted by considerations of time and place, and her first movement was to help herself to one of the cigarettes recommended by Trenor, while she checked his loquacity by asking, with a surprised glance: "Where 's Judy?"

Trenor, a little heated by his unusual flow of words, and perhaps by prolonged propinquity with the decanters, was bending over the latter to decipher their silver labels.

"Here, now, Lily, just a drop of cognac in a little fizzy water—you do look pinched, you know: I swear the end of your nose is red. I 'll take another glass to keep you company—Judy?—Why, you see, Judy 's got a devil of a headache—quite knocked out with it, poor thing—she asked me to explain—make it all right, you know—Do come up to the fire, though; you look dead-beat, really. Now do let me make you comfortable, there 's a good girl."

He had taken her hand, half-banteringly, and was drawing her toward a low seat by the hearth; but she stopped and freed herself quietly.

"Do you mean to say that Judy 's not well enough to see me? Does n't she want me to go upstairs?"

Trenor drained the glass he had filled for himself, and paused to set it down before he answered.

"Why, no—the fact is, she 's not up to seeing anybody. It came on suddenly, you know, and she asked me to tell you how awfully sorry she was—if she 'd known where you were dining she 'd have sent you word."

"She did know where I was dining; I mentioned it in my telegram. But it does n't matter, of course. I suppose if she 's so poorly she won't go back to Bellomont in the morning, and I can come and see her then."

"Yes: exactly—that 's capital. I 'll tell her you 'll pop in tomorrow morning. And now do sit down a minute, there 's a dear, and let 's have a nice quiet jaw together. You won't take a drop, just for sociability? Tell me what you think of that cigarette. Why, don't you like it? What are you chucking it away for?"

"I am chucking it away because I must go, if you 'll have the goodness to call a cab for me," Lily returned with a smile.

She did not like Trenor's unusual excitability, with its too evident explanation, and the thought of being alone with him, with her friend out of reach upstairs, at the other end of the great empty house, did not conduce to a desire to prolong their *tête-à-tête*.

But Trenor, with a promptness which did not escape her, had moved between herself and the door.

"Why must you go, I should like to know? If Judy 'd been here you 'd have sat gossiping till all hours—and you can't even give me five minutes! It 's always the same story. Last night I could n't get near you—I went to that damned vulgar party just to see you, and there was everybody talking about you, and asking me if I 'd ever seen anything so stunning, and when I tried to come up and say a word, you never took any notice, but just went on laughing and joking with a lot of asses who only wanted to be able to swagger about afterward, and look knowing when you were mentioned."

He paused, flushed by his diatribe, and fixing on her a look in which resentment was the ingredient she least disliked. But she had regained her presence of mind, and stood composedly in the middle of the room, while her slight smile seemed to put an ever increasing distance between herself and Trenor.

Across it she said: "Don't be absurd, Gus. It 's past eleven, and I must really ask you to ring for a cab."

He remained immovable, with the lowering forehead she had grown to detest.

"And supposing I won't ring for one—what 'll you do then?"

"I shall go upstairs to Judy if you force me to disturb her."

Trenor drew a step nearer and laid his hand on her arm. "Look here, Lily: won't you give me five minutes of your own accord?"

"Not tonight, Gus: you——"

"Very good, then: I 'll take 'em. And as many more as I want." He had squared himself on the threshold, his hands thrust deep in his pockets. He nodded toward the chair on the hearth.

"Go and sit down there, please: I 've got a word to say to you."

Lily's quick temper was getting the better of her fears. She drew herself up and moved toward the door.

"If you have anything to say to me, you must say it another time. I shall go up to Judy unless you call a cab for me at once."

He burst into a laugh. "Go upstairs and welcome, my dear; but you won't find Judy. She ain't there."

Lily cast a startled look upon him. "Do you mean that Judy is not in the house—not in town?" she exclaimed.

"That 's just what I do mean," returned Trenor, his bluster sinking to sullenness under her look.

"Nonsense—I don't believe you. I am going upstairs," she said impatiently.

He drew unexpectedly aside, letting her reach the threshold unimpeded.

"Go up and welcome; but my wife is at Bellomont."

But Lily had a flash of reassurance. "If she had n't come she would have sent me word——"

"She did; she telephoned me this afternoon to let you know."

"I received no message."

"I did n't send any."

The two measured each other for a moment, but Lily still saw her opponent through a blur of scorn that made all other considerations indistinct.

"I can't imagine your object in playing such a stupid trick on me; but if you have fully gratified your peculiar sense of humour I must again ask you to send for a cab."

It was the wrong note, and she knew it as she spoke. To be stung by irony it is not necessary to understand it, and the angry streaks on Trenor's face might have been raised by an actual lash.

"Look here, Lily, don't take that high and mighty tone with me." He had again moved toward the door, and in her instinctive shrinking from him she let him regain command of the threshold. "I *did* play a trick on you; I own up to it; but if you think I 'm ashamed you 're mistaken. Lord knows I 've been patient enough—I 've hung round and looked like an ass. And all the while you were letting a lot of other fellows make up to you . . . letting 'em make fun of me, I daresay . . . I 'm not sharp, and can't dress my friends up to look funny, as you do . . . but I can tell when it 's being done to me . . . I can tell fast enough when I 'm made a fool of . . . "

"Ah, I should n't have thought that!" flashed from Lily; but her laugh dropped to silence under his look.

"No; you would n't have thought it; but you 'll know better now. That 's what you 're here for tonight. I 've been waiting for a quiet time to talk things over, and now I 've got it I mean to make you hear me out."

His first rush of inarticulate resentment had been followed by a steadiness and concentration of tone more disconcerting to Lily than the excitement preceding it. For a moment her presence of mind forsook her. She had more than once been in situations where a quick sword-play of wit had been needful to cover her retreat; but her frightened heart-throbs told her that here such skill would not avail.

To gain time she repeated: "I don't understand what you want."

Trenor had pushed a chair between herself and the door. He threw himself in it, and leaned back, looking up at her.

"I 'll tell you what I want: I want to know just where you and I stand. Hang it, the man who pays for the dinner is generally allowed to have a seat at table."

She flamed with anger and abasement, and the sickening need of having to conciliate where she longed to humble.

"I don't know what you mean—but you must see, Gus, that I can't stay here talking to you at this hour——"

"Gad, you go to men's houses fast enough in broad daylight—strikes me you 're not always so deuced careful of appearances."

The brutality of the thrust gave her the sense of dizziness that follows on a physical blow. Rosedale had spoken then—this was the way men talked of her—She felt suddenly weak and defenceless: there was a throb of self-pity in her throat. But all the while another self was sharpening her to vigilance, whispering the terrified warning that every word and gesture must be measured.

"If you have brought me here to say insulting things——" she began.

Trenor laughed. "Don't talk stage-rot. I don't want to insult you. But a man 's got his feelings—and you 've played with mine too long. I did n't begin this business—kept out of the way, and left the track clear for the other chaps, till you rummaged me out and set to work to make an ass of me—and an easy job you had of it, too. That 's the trouble—it was too easy for you—you got reckless—thought you could turn me inside out, and chuck me in the gutter like an empty purse. But, by gad, that ain't playing fair: that 's dodging the rules of the game. Of course I know now what you wanted—it was n't my beautiful eyes you were after—but I tell you what, Miss Lily, you 've got to pay up for making me think so——"

He rose, squaring his shoulders aggressively, and stepped toward her with a reddening brow; but she held her footing, though every nerve tore at her to retreat as he advanced.

"Pay up?" she faltered. "Do you mean that I owe you money?"

He laughed again. "Oh, I 'm not asking for payment in kind. But there 's such a thing as fair play—and interest on one's money—and hang me if I 've had as much as a look from you——"

"Your money? What have I to do with your money? You advised me how to invest mine . . . you must have seen I knew nothing of business . . . you told me it was all right——"

"It *was* all right—it is, Lily: you 're welcome to all of it, and ten times more. I 'm only asking for a word of thanks from you." He was closer still, with a hand that grew formidable; and the frightened self in her was dragging the other down.

"I *have* thanked you; I 've shown I was grateful. What more have you done than any friend might do, or any one accept from a friend?"

Trenor caught her up with a sneer. "I don't doubt you 've accepted as much before—and chucked the other chaps as you 'd like to chuck me. I don't care how you settled your score with them—if you fooled 'em I 'm that much to the good. Don't stare at me like that—I know I 'm not talking the way a man is supposed to talk to a girl—but, hang it, if you don't like it you can stop me quick enough—you know I 'm mad about you—damn the money, there 's plenty more of it—if *that* bothers you . . . I was a brute, Lily—Lily!—just look at me——"

Over and over her the sea of humiliation broke—wave crashing on wave so close that the moral shame was one with the physical dread. It seemed to her that self-esteem would have made her invulnerable—that it was her own dishonour which put a fearful solitude about her.

His touch was a shock to her drowning consciousness. She drew back from him with a desperate assumption of scorn.

"I 've told you I don't understand—but if I owe you money you shall be paid—— "

Trenor's face darkened to rage: her recoil of abhorrence had called out the primitive man.

"Ah—you 'll borrow from Selden or Rosedale—and take your chances of fooling them as you 've fooled me! Unless—unless you 've settled your other scores already—and I 'm the only one left out in the cold!"

She stood silent, frozen to her place. The words—the words were worse than the touch! Her heart was beating all over her body—in her throat, her limbs, her helpless useless hands. Her eyes travelled despairingly about the room—they lit on the bell, and she remembered that help was in call. Yes, but scandal with it—a hideous mustering of tongues. No, she must fight her way out alone. It was enough that the servants knew her to be in the house with Trenor—there must be nothing to excite conjecture in her way of leaving it.

She raised her head, and achieved a last clear look at him.

"I am here alone with you," she said." What more have you to say?"

To her surprise, Trenor answered the look with a speechless stare. With his last gust of words the flame had died out, leaving him chill and humbled. It was as though a cold air had dispersed the fumes of his libations, and the situation loomed before him black and naked as the ruins of a fire. Old habits, old restraints, the hand of inherited order, plucked back the bewildered mind which passion had jolted from its ruts. Trenor's eye had the haggard look of the sleep-walker waked on a deathly ledge.

"Go home! Go away from here——" he stammered, and turning his back on her walked toward the hearth.

The sharp release from her fears restored Lily to immediate lucidity. The collapse of Trenor's will left her in control, and she heard herself, in a voice that was her own yet outside herself, bidding him ring for the servant, bidding him give the order for a hansom, directing him to put her in it when it came. Whence the strength came to her she knew not; but an insistent voice warned her that she must leave the house openly, and nerved her, in the hall before the hovering caretaker, to exchange light words with Trenor, and charge him with the usual messages for Judy, while all the while she shook with inward loathing. On the doorstep, with the street before her, she felt a mad throb of liberation, intoxicating as the prisoner's first draught of free air; but the clearness of brain continued, and she noted the mute aspect of Fifth Avenue, guessed at the lateness of the hour, and even observed a man's figure — was there something half-familiar in its outline? — which, as she entered the hansom, turned from the opposite corner and vanished in the obscurity of the side street.

But with the turn of the wheels reaction came, and shuddering darkness closed on her. "I can't think — I can't think," she moaned, and leaned her head against the rattling side of the cab. She seemed a stranger to herself, or rather there were two selves in her, the one she had always known, and a new abhorrent being to which it found itself chained. She had once picked up, in a house where she was staying, a translation of the *Eumenides,* and her imagination had been seized by the high terror of the scene where Orestes, in the cave of the oracle, finds his implacable huntresses asleep, and snatches an hour's repose. Yes, the Furies might sometimes sleep, but they were there, always there in the dark corners, and now they were awake and the iron clang of their wings was in her brain . . . She opened her eyes and saw the streets passing — the familiar alien streets. All she looked on was the same and yet changed. There was a great gulf fixed between today and yesterday. Everything in the past seemed simple, natural, full of daylight — and she was alone in a place of darkness and pollution. — Alone! It was the loneliness that frightened her. Her eyes fell on an illuminated clock at a street corner, and she saw that the hands marked the half hour after eleven. Only half-past eleven—there were hours and hours left of the night! And she must spend them alone, shuddering sleepless on her bed. Her soft nature recoiled from this ordeal, which had none of the stimulus of conflict to goad her through it. Oh, the slow cold drip of the minutes on her head! She had a vision of herself lying on the black walnut bed—and the darkness would frighten her, and if she left the light burning the dreary details of the room would brand themselves forever on her brain. She had always hated her room at Mrs. Peniston's—its ugliness, its impersonality, the fact that nothing in it was really hers. To a torn heart uncomforted by human nearness a room may open almost human arms, and the being to whom no four walls mean more than any others, is, at such hours, expatriate everywhere.

Lily had no heart to lean on. Her relation with her aunt was as superficial as that of chance lodgers who pass on the stairs. But even had the two been in closer contact, it was impossible to think of Mrs. Peniston's mind as offering shelter or comprehension to such misery as Lily's. As the pain that can be told is but half a pain, so the pity that questions has little healing in its touch. What Lily craved was the darkness made by enfolding arms, the silence which is not solitude, but compassion holding its breath.

She started up and looked forth on the passing streets. Gerty!— they were nearing Gerty's corner. If only she could reach there before this labouring anguish burst from her breast to her lips—if only she could feel the hold of Gerty's arms while she shook in the ague-fit of fear that was coming upon her! She pushed up the door in the roof and called the address to the driver. It was not so late—Gerty might still be waking. And even if she were not, the sound of the bell would penetrate every recess of her tiny apartment, and rouse her to answer her friend's call.

XIV

Gerty Farish, the morning after the Wellington Brys' entertainment, woke from dreams as happy as Lily's. If they were less vivid in hue, more subdued to the half-tints of her personality and her experience, they were for that very reason better suited to her mental vision. Such flashes of joy as Lily moved in would have blinded Miss Farish, who was accustomed, in the way of happiness, to such scant light as shone through the cracks of other people's lives.

Now she was the centre of a little illumination of her own: a mild but unmistakable beam, compounded of Lawrence Selden's growing kindness to herself and the discovery that he extended his liking to Lily Bart. If these two factors seem incompatible to the student of feminine psychology, it must be remembered that Gerty had always been a parasite in the moral order, living on the crumbs of other tables, and content to look through the window at the banquet spread for her friends. Now that she was enjoying a little private feast of her own, it would have seemed incredibly selfish not to lay a plate for a friend; and there was no one with whom she would rather have shared her enjoyment than Miss Bart.

As to the nature of Selden's growing kindness, Gerty would no more have dared to define it than she would have tried to learn a butterfly's colours by knocking the dust from its wings. To seize on the wonder would be to brush off its bloom, and perhaps see it fade and stiffen in her hand: better the sense of beauty palpitating out of reach, while she held her breath and watched where it would alight. Yet Selden's manner at the Brys' had brought the flutter of wings so close that they seemed to be beating in her own heart. She had never seen him so alert, so responsive, so attentive to what she had to say. His habitual manner had an absent-minded kindliness which she accepted, and was grateful for, as the liveliest sentiment her presence was likely to inspire; but she was quick to feel in him a change implying that for once she could give pleasure as well as receive it.

And it was so delightful that this higher degree of sympathy should be reached through their interest in Lily Bart! Gerty's affection for her friend—a sentiment that had learned to keep itself alive on the scantiest diet—had grown to active adoration since Lily's restless curiosity had drawn her into the circle of Miss Farish's work. Lily's taste of beneficence had wakened in her a momentary appetite for well-doing. Her visit to the Girls' Club had first brought her in contact with the dramatic contrasts of life. She had always accepted with philosophic calm the fact that such existences as hers were pedestalled on foundations of obscure humanity. The dreary limbo of dinginess lay all around and beneath that little illuminated circle in which life reached its finest efflorescence, as the mud and sleet of a winter night enclose a hot-house filled with tropical flowers. All this was in the natural order of things, and the orchid basking in its artificially created atmosphere could round the delicate curves of its petals undisturbed by the ice on the panes.

But it is one thing to live comfortably with the abstract conception of poverty, another to be brought in contact with its human embodiments. Lily had never conceived of these victims of fate otherwise than in the mass. That the mass was composed of individual lives, innumera-

ble separate centres of sensation, with her own eager reachings for pleasure, her own fierce revulsions from pain — that some of these bundles
of feeling were clothed in shapes not so unlike her own, with eyes meant
to look on gladness, and young lips shaped for love — this discovery
gave Lily one of those sudden shocks of pity that sometimes decentral-
ize a life. Lily's nature was incapable of such renewal: she could feel
other demands only through her own, and no pain was long vivid which
did not press on an answering nerve. But for the moment she was drawn
out of herself by the interest of her direct relation with a world so unlike
her own. She had supplemented her first gift by personal assistance to
one or two of Miss Farish's most appealing subjects, and the admiration
and interest her presence excited among the tired workers at the club
ministered in a new form to her insatiable desire to please.

Gerty Farish was not a close enough reader of character to disen-
tangle the mixed threads of which Lily's philanthropy was woven. She
supposed her beautiful friend to be actuated by the same motive as herself — that sharpening of the moral vision which makes all human suffering so near and insistent that the other aspects of life fade into remote-
ness. Gerty lived by such simple formulas that she did not hesitate to
class her friend's state with the emotional "change of heart" to which
her dealings with the poor had accustomed her; and she rejoiced in the
thought that she had been the humble instrument of this renewal. Now
she had an answer to all criticisms of Lily's conduct: as she had said, she
knew "the real Lily," and the discovery that Selden shared her knowledge raised her placid acceptance of life to a dazzled sense of its possibilities — a sense farther enlarged, in the course of the afternoon, by the
receipt of a telegram from Selden asking if he might dine with her that
evening.

While Gerty was lost in the happy bustle which this announcement
produced in her small household, Selden was at one with her in thinking with intensity of Lily Bart. The case which had called him to Albany
was not complicated enough to absorb all his attention, and he had the
professional faculty of keeping a part of his mind free when its services
were not needed. This part — which at the moment seemed dangerously like the whole — was filled to the brim with the sensations of the
previous evening. Selden understood the symptoms: he recognized the
fact that he was paying up, as there had always been a chance of his
having to pay up, for the voluntary exclusions of his past. He had meant
to keep free from permanent ties, not from any poverty of feeling, but
because, in a different way, he was, as much as Lily, the victim of his
environment. There had been a germ of truth in his declaration to Gerty

Farish that he had never wanted to marry a "nice" girl: the adjective connoting, in his cousin's vocabulary, certain utilitarian qualities which are apt to preclude the luxury of charm. Now it had been Selden's fate to have a charming mother: her graceful portrait, all smiles and Cashmere, still emitted a faded scent of the undefinable quality. His father was the kind of man who delights in a charming woman: who quotes her, stimulates her, and keeps her perennially charming. Neither one of the couple cared for money, but their disdain of it took the form of always spending a little more than was prudent. If their house was shabby, it was exquisitely kept; if there were good books on the shelves there were also good dishes on the table. Selden senior had an eye for a picture, his wife an understanding of old lace; and both were so conscious of restraint and discrimination in buying that they never quite knew how it was that the bills mounted up.

Though many of Selden's friends would have called his parents poor, he had grown up in an atmosphere where restricted means were felt only as a check on aimless profusion: where the few possessions were so good that their rarity gave them a merited relief, and abstinence was combined with elegance in a way exemplified by Mrs. Selden's knack of wearing her old velvet as if it were new. A man has the advantage of being delivered early from the home point of view, and before Selden left college he had learned that there are as many different ways of going without money as of spending it. Unfortunately, he found no way as agreeable as that practised at home; and his views of womankind in especial were tinged by the remembrance of the one woman who had given him his sense of "values." It was from her that he inherited his detachment from the sumptuary side of life: the stoic's carelessness of material things, combined with the Epicurean's pleasure in them. Life shorn of either feeling appeared to him a diminished thing; and nowhere was the blending of the two ingredients so essential as in the character of a pretty woman.

It had always seemed to Selden that experience offered a great deal besides the sentimental adventure, yet he could vividly conceive of a love which should broaden and deepen till it became the central fact of life. What he could not accept, in his own case, was the makeshift alternative of a relation that should be less than this: that should leave some portions of his nature unsatisfied, while it put an undue strain on others. He would not, in other words, yield to the growth of an affection which might appeal to pity yet leave the understanding untouched: sympathy should no more delude him than a trick of the eyes, the grace of helplessness than a curve of the cheek.

But now—that little *but* passed like a sponge over all his vows. His reasoned-out resistances seemed for the moment so much less important than the question as to when Lily would receive his note! He yielded himself to the charm of trivial preoccupations, wondering at what hour her reply would be sent, with what words it would begin. As to its import he had no doubt—he was as sure of her surrender as of his own. And so he had leisure to muse on all its exquisite details, as a hard worker, on a holiday morning, might lie still and watch the beam of light travel gradually across his room. But if the new light dazzled, it did not blind him. He could still discern the outline of facts, though his own relation to them had changed. He was no less conscious than before of what was said of Lily Bart, but he could separate the woman he knew from the vulgar estimate of her. His mind turned to Gerty Farish's words, and the wisdom of the world seemed a groping thing beside the insight of innocence. *Blessed are the pure in heart, for they shall see God*—even the hidden god in their neighbour's breast! Selden was in the state of impassioned self-absorption that the first surrender to love produces. His craving was for the companionship of one whose point of view should justify his own, who should confirm, by deliberate observation, the truth to which his intuitions had leaped. He could not wait for the midday recess, but seized a moment's leisure in court to scribble his telegram to Gerty Farish.

Reaching town, he was driven direct to his club, where he hoped a note from Miss Bart might await him. But his box contained only a line of rapturous assent from Gerty, and he was turning away disappointed when he was hailed by a voice from the smoking room.

"Hallo, Lawrence! Dining here? Take a bit with me—I 've ordered a canvas-back."

He discovered Trenor, in his day clothes, sitting, with a tall glass at his elbow, behind the folds of a sporting journal.

Selden thanked him, but pleaded an engagement.

"Hang it, I believe every man in town has an engagement tonight. I shall have the club to myself. You know how I 'm living this winter, rattling round in that empty house. My wife meant to come to town today, but she 's put it off again, and how is a fellow to dine alone in a room with the looking-glasses covered, and nothing but a bottle of Harvey sauce on the side-board? I say, Lawrence, chuck your engagement and take pity on me—it gives me the blue devils to dine alone, and there 's nobody but that canting ass Wetherall in the club."

"Sorry, Gus—I can't do it."

As Selden turned away, he noticed the dark flush on Trenor's face,

the unpleasant moisture of his intensely white forehead, the way his jewelled rings were wedged in the creases of his fat red fingers. Certainly
the beast was predominating—the beast at the bottom of the glass.
And he had heard this man's name coupled with Lily's! Bah—the
thought sickened him; all the way back to his rooms he was haunted by
the sight of Trenor's fat creased hands———

On his table lay the note: Lily had sent it to his rooms. He knew
what was in it before he broke the seal—a grey seal with *Beyond!* beneath a flying ship. Ah, he would take her beyond—beyond the ugliness, the pettiness, the attrition and corrosion of the soul———

Gerty's little sitting-room sparkled with welcome when Selden entered
it. Its modest "effects," compact of enamel paint and ingenuity, spoke
to him in the language just then sweetest to his ear. It is surprising
how little narrow walls and a low ceiling matter, when the roof of the
soul has suddenly been raised. Gerty sparkled too; or at least shone
with a tempered radiance. He had never before noticed that she had
"points"—really, some good fellow might do worse . . . Over the little
dinner (and here, again, the effects were wonderful) he told her she
ought to marry—he was in a mood to pair off the whole world. She had
made the caramel custard with her own hands? It was sinful to keep such
gifts to herself. He reflected with a throb of pride that Lily could trim
her own hats—she had told him so the day of their walk at Bellomont.

He did not speak of Lily till after dinner. During the little repast he
kept the talk on his hostess, who, fluttered at being the centre of observation, shone as rosy as the candle-shades she had manufactured for the
occasion. Selden evinced an extraordinary interest in her household arrangements: complimented her on the ingenuity with which she had
utilized every inch of her small quarters, asked how her servant managed
about afternoons out, learned that one may improvise delicious dinners
in a chafing-dish, and uttered thoughtful generalizations on the burden
of a large establishment.

When they were in the sitting-room again, where they fitted as
snugly as bits in a puzzle, and she had brewed the coffee, and poured it
into her grandmother's egg-shell cups, his eye, as he leaned back, basking in the warm fragrance, lighted on a recent photograph of Miss Bart,
and the desired transition was effected without an effort. The photograph was well enough—but to catch her as she had looked last night!
Gerty agreed with him—never had she been so radiant. But could photography capture that light? There had been a new look in her face—
something different; yes, Selden agreed there had been something dif-

ferent. The coffee was so exquisite that he asked for a second cup: such a contrast to the watery stuff at the club! Ah, your poor bachelor with his impersonal club fare, alternating with the equally impersonal *cuisine* of the dinner-party! A man who lived in lodgings missed the best part of life — he pictured the flavourless solitude of Trenor's repast, and felt a moment's compassion for the man . . . But to return to Lily — and again and again he returned, questioning, conjecturing, leading Gerty on, draining her inmost thoughts of their stored tenderness for her friend.

At first she poured herself out unstintingly, happy in this perfect communion of their sympathies. His understanding of Lily helped to confirm her own belief in her friend. They dwelt together on the fact that Lily had had no chance. Gerty instanced her generous impulses — her restlessness and discontent. The fact that her life had never satisfied her proved that she was made for better things. She might have married more than once — the conventional rich marriage which she had been taught to consider the sole end of existence — but when the opportunity came she had always shrunk from it. Percy Gryce, for instance, had been in love with her — every one at Bellomont had supposed them to be engaged, and her dismissal of him was thought inexplicable. This view of the Gryce incident chimed too well with Selden's mood not to be instantly adopted by him, with a flash of retrospective contempt for what had once seemed the obvious solution. If rejection there had been — and he wondered now that he had ever doubted it! — then he held the key to the secret, and the hillsides of Bellomont were lit up, not with sunset, but with dawn. It was he who had wavered and disowned the face of opportunity — and the joy now warming his breast might have been a familiar inmate if he had captured it in its first flight.

It was at this point, perhaps, that a joy just trying its wings in Gerty's heart dropped to earth and lay still. She sat facing Selden, repeating mechanically: "No, she has never been understood——" and all the while she herself seemed to be sitting in the centre of a great glare of comprehension. The little confidential room, where a moment ago their thoughts had touched elbows like their chairs, grew to unfriendly vastness, separating her from Selden by all the length of her new vision of the future — and that future stretched out interminably, with her lonely figure toiling down it, a mere speck on the solitude.

"She is herself with a few people only; and you are one of them," she heard Selden saying. And again: "Be good to her, Gerty, won't you?" and: "She has it in her to become whatever she is believed to be — you 'll help her by believing the best of her?"

The words beat on Gerty's brain like the sound of a language which has seemed familiar at a distance, but on approaching is found to be unintelligible. He had come to talk to her of Lily—that was all! There had been a third at the feast she had spread for him, and that third had taken her own place. She tried to follow what he was saying, to cling to her own part in the talk—but it was all as meaningless as the boom of waves in a drowning head, and she felt, as the drowning may feel, that to sink would be nothing beside the pain of struggling to keep up.

Selden rose, and she drew a deep breath, feeling that soon she could yield to the blessed waves.

"Mrs. Fisher's? You say she was dining there? There 's music afterward; I believe I had a card from her." He glanced at the foolish pink-faced clock that was drumming out this hideous hour. "A quarter past ten? I might look in there now; the Fisher evenings are amusing. I have n't kept you up too late, Gerty? You look tired—I 've rambled on and bored you." And in the unwonted overflow of his feelings, he left a cousinly kiss upon her cheek.

At Mrs. Fisher's, through the cigar-smoke of the studio, a dozen voices greeted Selden. A song was pending as he entered, and he dropped into a seat near his hostess, his eyes roaming in search of Miss Bart. But she was not there, and the discovery gave him a pang out of all proportion to its seriousness; since the note in his breast-pocket assured him that at four the next day they would meet. To his impatience it seemed immeasurably long to wait, and half-ashamed of the impulse, he leaned to Mrs. Fisher to ask, as the music ceased, if Miss Bart had not dined with her.

"Lily? She 's just gone. She had to run off, I forget where. Was n't she wonderful last night?"

"Who 's that? Lily?" asked Jack Stepney, from the depths of a neighbouring arm-chair. "Really, you know, I 'm no prude, but when it comes to a girl standing there as if she was up at auction—I thought seriously of speaking to cousin Julia."

"You did n't know Jack had become our social censor?" Mrs. Fisher said to Selden with a laugh; and Stepney spluttered, amid the general derision: "But she 's a cousin, hang it, and when a man 's married—*Town Talk* was full of her this morning."

"Yes: lively reading that was," said Mr. Ned Van Alstyne, stroking his moustache to hide the smile behind it. "Buy the dirty sheet? No, of course not; some fellow showed it to me—but I 'd heard the stories before. When a girl 's as good-looking as that she 'd better marry; then no questions are asked. In our imperfectly organized society there is no provision as yet for the young woman who claims the privileges of marriage without assuming its obligations."

"Well, I understand Lily is about to assume them in the shape of Mr. Rosedale," Mrs. Fisher said with a laugh.

"Rosedale—good heavens!" exclaimed Van Alstyne, dropping his eye-glass. "Stepney, that 's your fault for foisting the brute on us."

"Oh, confound it, you know, we don't *marry* Rosedale in our family," Stepney languidly protested; but his wife, who sat in oppressive bridal finery at the other side of the room, quelled him with the judicial reflection: "In Lily's circumstances it 's a mistake to have too high a standard."

"I hear even Rosedale has been scared by the talk lately," Mrs. Fisher rejoined; "but the sight of her last night sent him off his head. What do you think he said to me after her *tableau*? 'My God, Mrs. Fisher, if I could get Paul Morpeth to paint her like that, the picture 'd appreciate a hundred per cent in ten years."

"By Jove,—but is n't she about somewhere?" exclaimed Van Alstyne, restoring his glass with an uneasy glance.

"No; she ran off while you were all missing the punch down stairs. Where was she going, by the way? What 's on tonight? I had n't heard of anything."

"Oh, not a party, I think," said an inexperienced young Farish who had arrived late. "I put her in her cab as I was coming in, and she gave the driver the Trenors' address."

"The Trenors'?" exclaimed Mrs. Jack Stepney. "Why, the house is closed—Judy telephoned me from Bellomont this evening."

"Did she? That 's queer. I 'm sure I 'm not mistaken. Well, come now, Trenor 's there, anyhow—I—oh, well—the fact is, I 've no head for numbers," he broke off, admonished by the nudge of an adjoining foot, and the smile that circled the room.

In its unpleasant light Selden had risen and was shaking hands with his hostess. The air of the place stifled him, and he wondered why he had stayed in it so long.

On the doorstep he stood still, remembering a phrase of Lily's: "It seems to me you spend a good deal of time in the element you disapprove of."

Well—what had brought him there but the quest of her? It was her element, not his. But he would lift her out of it, take her beyond! That *Beyond!* on her letter was like a cry for rescue. He knew that Perseus's task is not done when he has loosed Andromeda's chains, for her limbs are numb with bondage, and she cannot rise and walk, but clings to him with dragging arms as he beats back to land with his burden. Well, he had strength for both—it was her weakness which had put the strength in him. It was not, alas, a clean rush of waves they had to win through, but a clogging morass of old associations and habits, and for the moment its vapours were in his throat. But he would see clearer, breathe freer in her presence: she was at once the dead weight at his breast and the spar which should float them to safety. He smiled at the whirl of metaphor with which he was trying to build up a defence against the influences of the last hour. It was pitiable that he, who knew the mixed motives on which social judgments depend, should still feel himself so swayed by them. How could he lift Lily to a freer vision of life, if his own view of her was to be coloured by any mind in which he saw her reflected?

The moral oppression had produced a physical craving for air, and he strode on, opening his lungs to the reverberating coldness of the night. At the corner of Fifth Avenue Van Alstyne hailed him with an offer of company.

"Walking? A good thing to blow the smoke out of one's head. Now that women have taken to tobacco we live in a bath of nicotine. It would be a curious thing to study the effect of cigarettes on the relation of the sexes. Smoke is almost as great a solvent as divorce: both tend to obscure the moral issue."

Nothing could have been less consonant with Selden's mood than Van Alstyne's after-dinner aphorisms, but as long as the latter confined himself to generalities his listener's nerves were in control. Happily Van Alstyne prided himself on his summing up of social aspects, and with Selden for audience was eager to show the sureness of his touch. Mrs. Fisher lived in an East side street near the Park, and as the two men walked down Fifth Avenue the new architectural developments of that versatile thoroughfare invited Van Alstyne's comment.

"That Greiner house, now—a typical rung in the social ladder! The man who built it came from a *milieu* where all the dishes are put on the table at once. His façade is a complete architectural meal; if he had omitted a style his friends might have thought the money had given out. Not a bad purchase for Rosedale, though: attracts attention, and awes the Western sight-seer. By and bye he 'll get out of that phase, and want something that the crowd will pass and the few pause before. Especially if he marries my clever cousin——"

Selden dashed in with the query: "And the Wellington Brys'? Rather clever of its kind, don't you think?"

They were just beneath the wide white façade, with its rich restraint of line, which suggested the clever corseting of a redundant figure.

"That 's the next stage: the desire to imply that one has been to Europe, and has a standard. I 'm sure Mrs. Bry thinks her house a copy of the *Trianon;* in America every marble house with gilt furniture is thought to be a copy of the *Trianon.* What a clever chap that architect is, though — how he takes his client's measure! He has put the whole of Mrs. Bry in his use of the composite order. Now for the Trenors, you remember, he chose the Corinthian: exuberant, but based on the best precedent. The Trenor house is one of his best things — does n't look like a banqueting-hall turned inside out. I hear Mrs. Trenor wants to build out a new ball-room, and that divergence from Gus on that point keeps her at Bellomont. The dimensions of the Brys' ball-room must rankle: you may be sure she knows 'em as well as if she 'd been there last night with a yard-measure. Who said she was in town, by the way? That Farish boy? She is n't, I know; Mrs. Stepney was right; the house is dark, you see: I suppose Gus lives in the back."

He had halted opposite the Trenors' corner, and Selden perforce stayed his steps also. The house loomed obscure and uninhabited; only an oblong gleam above the door spoke of provisional occupancy.

"They 've bought the house at the back: it gives them a hundred and fifty feet in the side street. There 's where the ball-room 's to be, with a gallery connecting it: billiard-room and so on above. I suggested changing the entrance, and carrying the drawing-room across the whole Fifth Avenue front; you see the front door corresponds with the windows —— "

The walking-stick which Van Alstyne swung in demonstration dropped to a startled "Hallo!" as the door opened and two figures were seen silhouetted against the hall-light. At the same moment a hansom halted at the curb-stone, and one of the figures floated down to it in a haze of evening draperies; while the other, black and bulky, remained persistently projected against the light.

For an immeasurable second the two spectators of the incident were silent; then the house-door closed, the hansom rolled off, and the whole scene slipped by as if with the turn of a stereopticon.

Van Alstyne dropped his eye-glass with a low whistle.

"A — hem — nothing of this, eh, Selden? As one of the family, I know I may count on you — appearances are deceptive — and Fifth Avenue is so imperfectly lighted —— "

"Goodnight," said Selden, turning sharply down the side street without seeing the other's extended hand.

Alone with her cousin's kiss, Gerty stared upon her thoughts. He had kissed her before—but not with another woman on his lips. If he had spared her that she could have drowned quietly, welcoming the dark flood as it submerged her. But now the flood was shot through with glory, and it was harder to drown at sunrise than in darkness. Gerty hid her face from the light, but it pierced to the crannies of her soul. She had been so contented, life had seemed so simple and sufficient—why had he come to trouble her with new hopes? And Lily—Lily, her best friend! Woman-like, she accused the woman. Perhaps, had it not been for Lily, her fond imagining might have become truth. Selden had always liked her—had understood and sympathized with the modest independence of her life. He, who had the reputation of weighing all things in the nice balance of fastidious perceptions, had been uncritical and simple in his view of her: his cleverness had never overawed her because she had felt at home in his heart. And now she was thrust out, and the door barred against her by Lily's hand! Lily, for whose admission there she herself had pleaded! The situation was lighted up by a dreary flash of irony. She knew Selden—she saw how the force of her faith in Lily must have helped to dispel his hesitations. She remembered, too, how Lily had talked of him—she saw herself bringing the two together, making them known to each other. On Selden's part, no doubt, the wound inflicted was inconscient; he had never guessed her foolish secret; but Lily—Lily must have known! When, in such matters, are a woman's perceptions at fault? And if she knew, then she had deliberately despoiled her friend, and in mere wantonness of power, since, even to Gerty's suddenly flaming jealousy, it seemed incredible that Lily should wish to be Selden's wife. Lily might be incapable of marrying for money, but she was equally incapable of living without it, and Selden's eager investigations into the small economies of house-keeping made him appear to Gerty as tragically duped as herself.

She remained long in her sitting-room, where the embers were crumbling to cold grey, and the lamp paled under its gay shade. Just beneath it stood the photograph of Lily Bart, looking out imperially on the cheap gim-cracks, the cramped furniture of the little room. Could Selden picture her in such an interior? Gerty felt the poverty, the insignificance of her surroundings: she beheld her life as it must appear to Lily. And the cruelty of Lily's judgments smote upon her memory. She saw that she had dressed her idol with attributes of her own making. When had Lily ever really felt, or pitied, or understood? All she wanted was the taste of new experiences: she seemed like some cruel creature experimenting in a laboratory.

The pink-faced clock drummed out another hour, and Gerty rose with a start. She had an appointment early the next morning with a district visitor on the East side. She put out her lamp, covered the fire, and went into her bedroom to undress. In the little glass above her dressing-table she saw her face reflected against the shadows of the room, and tears blotted the reflection. What right had she to dream the dreams of loveliness? A dull face invited a dull fate. She cried quietly as she undressed, laying aside her clothes with her habitual precision, setting everything in order for the next day, when the old life must be taken up as though there had been no break in its routine. Her servant did not come till eight o'clock, and she prepared her own tea-tray and placed it beside the bed. Then she locked the door of the flat, extinguished her light and lay down. But on her bed sleep would not come, and she lay face to face with the fact that she hated Lily Bart. It closed with her in the darkness like some formless evil to be blindly grappled with. Reason, judgment, renunciation, all the sane daylight forces, were beaten back in the sharp struggle for self-preservation. She wanted happiness—wanted it as fiercely and unscrupulously as Lily did, but without Lily's power of obtaining it. And in her conscious impotence she lay shivering, and hated her friend——

A ring at the door-bell caught her to her feet. She struck a light and stood startled, listening. For a moment her heart beat incoherently, then she felt the sobering touch of fact, and remembered that such calls were not unknown in her charitable work. She flung on her dressing-gown to answer the summons, and unlocking her door, confronted the shining vision of Lily Bart.

Gerty's first movement was one of revulsion. She shrank back as though Lily's presence flashed too sudden a light upon her misery. Then she heard her name in a cry, had a glimpse of her friend's face, and felt herself caught and clung to.

"Lily—what is it?" she exclaimed.

Miss Bart released her, and stood breathing brokenly, like one who has gained shelter after a long flight.

"I was so cold—I could n't go home. Have you a fire?"

Gerty's compassionate instincts, responding to the swift call of habit, swept aside all her reluctances. Lily was simply some one who needed help—for what reason, there was no time to pause and conjecture:

disciplined sympathy checked the wonder on Gerty's lips, and made her draw her friend silently into the sitting-room and seat her by the darkened hearth.

"There is kindling wood here: the fire will burn in a minute."

She knelt down, and the flame leapt under her rapid hands. It flashed strangely through the tears which still blurred her eyes, and smote on the white ruin of Lily's face. The girls looked at each other in silence; then Lily repeated: "I could n't go home."

"No—no—you came here, dear! You 're cold and tired—sit quiet, and I 'll make you some tea."

Gerty had unconsciously adopted the soothing note of her trade: all personal feeling was merged in the sense of ministry, and experience had taught her that the bleeding must be stayed before the wound is probed.

Lily sat quiet, leaning to the fire: the clatter of cups behind her soothed her as familiar noises hush a child whom silence has kept wakeful. But when Gerty stood at her side with the tea she pushed it away, and turned an estranged eye on the familiar room.

"I came here because I could n't bear to be alone," she said.

Gerty set down the cup and knelt beside her.

"Lily! Something has happened—can't you tell me?"

"I could n't bear to lie awake in my room till morning. I hate my room at Aunt Julia's—so I came here——"

She stirred suddenly, broke from her apathy, and clung to Gerty in a fresh burst of fear.

"Oh, Gerty, the furies . . . you know the noise of their wings—alone, at night, in the dark? But you don't know—there is nothing to make the dark dreadful to you——"

The words, flashing back on Gerty's last hours, struck from her a faint derisive murmur; but Lily, in the blaze of her own misery, was blinded to everything outside it.

"You 'll let me stay? I shan't mind when daylight comes—Is it late? Is the night nearly over? It must be awful to be sleepless—everything stands by the bed and stares——"

Miss Farish caught her straying hands. "Lily, look at me! Something has happened—an accident? You have been frightened—what has frightened you? Tell me if you can—a word or two—so that I can help you."

Lily shook her head.

"I am not frightened: that 's not the word. Can you imagine looking into your glass some morning and seeing a disfigurement—some hideous change that has come to you while you slept? Well, I seem to myself like that—I can't bear to see myself in my own thoughts—I hate ugliness, you know—I 've always turned from it—but I can't explain to you—you would n't understand."

She lifted her head and her eyes fell on the clock.

"How long the night is! And I know I shan't sleep tomorrow. Some one told me my father used to lie sleepless and think of horrors. And he was not wicked, only unfortunate—and I see now how he must have suffered, lying alone with his thoughts! But I am bad—a bad girl—all my thoughts are bad—I have always had bad people about me. Is that any excuse? I thought I could manage my own life—I was proud—proud! but now I 'm on their level——"

Sobs shook her, and she bowed to them like a tree in a dry storm.

Gerty knelt beside her, waiting, with the patience born of experience, till this gust of misery should loosen fresh speech. She had first imagined some physical shock, some peril of the crowded streets, since Lily was presumably on her way home from Carry Fisher's; but she now saw that other nerve-centres were smitten, and her mind trembled back from conjecture.

Lily's sobs ceased, and she lifted her head.

"There are bad girls in your slums. Tell me—do they ever pick themselves up? Ever forget, and feel as they did before?"

"Lily! you must n't speak so—you 're dreaming."

"Don't they always go from bad to worse? There 's no turning back—your old self rejects you, and shuts you out."

She rose, stretching her arms as if in utter physical weariness. "Go to bed, dear! You work hard and get up early. I 'll watch here by the fire, and you 'll leave the light, and your door open. All I want is to feel that you are near me." She laid both hands on Gerty's shoulders, with a smile that was like sunrise on a sea strewn with wreckage.

"I can't leave you, Lily. Come and lie on my bed. Your hands are frozen—you must undress and be made warm " Gerty paused with sudden compunction. "But Mrs. Peniston—it 's past midnight! What will she think?"

"She goes to bed. I have a latch-key. It does n't matter—I can't go back there."

"There 's no need to: you shall stay here. But you must tell me where you have been. Listen, Lily—it will help you to speak!" She regained Miss Bart's hands, and pressed them against her. "Try to tell me—it will clear your poor head. Listen—you were dining at Carry Fisher's." Gerty paused and added with a flash of heroism: "Lawrence Selden went from here to find you."

At the word, Lily's face melted from locked anguish to the open misery of a child. Her lips trembled and her gaze widened with tears.

"He went to find me? And I missed him! Oh, Gerty, he tried to help me. He told me—he warned me long ago—he foresaw that I should grow hateful to myself!"

The name, as Gerty saw with a clutch at the heart, had loosened the springs of self-pity in her friend's dry breast, and tear by tear Lily poured out the measure of her anguish. She had dropped sideways in Gerty's big arm-chair, her head buried where lately Selden's had leaned, in a beauty of abandonment that drove home to Gerty's aching senses the inevitableness of her own defeat. Ah, it needed no deliberate purpose on Lily's part to rob her of her dream! To look on that prone loveliness was to see in it a natural force, to recognize that love and power belong to such as Lily, as renunciation and service are the lot of those they despoil. But if Selden's infatuation seemed a fatal necessity, the effect that his name produced shook Gerty's steadfastness with a last pang. Men pass through such superhuman loves and outlive them: they are the proba-tion subduing the heart to human joys. How gladly Gerty would have welcomed the ministry of healing: how willingly have soothed the sufferer back to tolerance of life! But Lily's self-betrayal took this last hope from her. The mortal maid on the shore is helpless against the siren who loves her prey: such victims are floated back dead from their adventure.

Lily sprang up and caught her with strong hands. "Gerty, you know him—you understand him—tell me; if I went to him, if I told him everything—if I said: 'I am bad through and through—I want admira-tion, I want excitement, I want money—' yes, *money!* That 's my shame, Gerty—and it 's known, it 's said of me—it 's what men think of me—If I said it all to him—told him the whole story—said plainly: 'I 've sunk lower than the lowest, for I 've taken what they take, and not paid as they pay'—oh, Gerty, you know him, you can speak for him: if I told him everything would he loathe me? Or would he pity me, and understand me, and save me from loathing myself?"

Gerty stood cold and passive. She knew the hour of her probation had come, and her poor heart beat wildly against its destiny. As a dark river sweeps by under a lightning flash, she saw her chance of happiness surge past under a flash of temptation. What prevented her from saying: "He is like other men"? She was not so sure of him, after all! But to do so would have been like blaspheming her love. She could not put him before herself in any light but the noblest: she must trust him to the height of her own passion.

"Yes: I know him; he will help you," she said; and in a moment Lily's passion was weeping itself out against her breast.

There was but one bed in the little flat, and the two girls lay down on it side by side when Gerty had unlaced Lily's dress and persuaded her to put her lips to the warm tea. The light extinguished, they lay still in the darkness, Gerty shrinking to the outer edge of the narrow couch to avoid contact with her bed-fellow. Knowing that Lily disliked to be caressed, she had long ago learned to check her demonstrative impulses toward her friend. But tonight every fibre in her body shrank from Lily's nearness: it was torture to listen to her breathing, and feel the sheet stir with it. As Lily turned, and settled to completer rest, a strand of her hair swept Gerty's cheek with its fragrance. Everything about her was warm and soft and scented: even the strains of her grief became her as rain-drops do the beaten rose. But as Gerty lay with arms drawn down her side, in the motionless narrowness of an effigy, she felt a stir of sobs from the breathing warmth beside her, and Lily flung out her hand, groped for her friend's, and held it fast.

"Hold me, Gerty, hold me, or I shall think of things," she moaned; and Gerty silently slipped an arm under her, pillowing her head in its hollow as a mother makes a nest for a tossing child. In the warm hollow Lily lay still and her breathing grew low and regular. Her hand still clung to Gerty's as if to ward off evil dreams, but the hold of her fingers relaxed, her head sank deeper into its shelter, and Gerty felt that she slept.

XV

When Lily woke she had the bed to herself, and the winter light was in the room.

She sat up, bewildered by the strangeness of her surroundings; then memory returned, and she looked about her with a shiver. In the cold slant of light reflected from the back wall of a neighbouring building, she saw her evening dress and opera cloak lying in a tawdry heap on a chair. Finery laid off is as unappetizing as the remains of a feast, and it occurred to Lily that, at home, her maid's vigilance had always spared her the sight of such incongruities. Her body ached with fatigue, and with the constriction of her attitude in Gerty's bed. All through her troubled sleep she had been conscious of having no space to toss in, and the long effort to remain motionless made her feel as if she had spent her night in a train.

This sense of physical discomfort was the first to assert itself; then she perceived, beneath it, a corresponding mental prostration, a languor of horror more insufferable than the first rush of her disgust. The thought of having to wake every morning with this weight on her breast roused her tired mind to fresh effort. She must find some way out of the slough into which she had stumbled: it was not so much compunction as the dread of her morning thoughts that pressed on her the need of action. But she was unutterably tired; it was weariness to think connectedly. She lay back, looking about the poor slit of a room with a renewal of physical distaste. The outer air, penned between high buildings, brought no freshness through the window; steam-heat was beginning to sing in a coil of dingy pipes, and a smell of cooking penetrated the crack of the door.

The door opened, and Gerty, dressed and hatted, entered with a cup of tea. Her face looked sallow and swollen in the dreary light, and her dull hair shaded imperceptibly into the tones of her skin.

She glanced shyly at Lily, asking in an embarrassed tone how she felt; Lily answered with the same constraint, and raised herself up to drink the tea.

"I must have been over-tired last night; I think I had a nervous attack in the carriage," she said, as the drink brought clearness to her sluggish thoughts.

"You were not well; I am so glad you came here," Gerty returned.

"But how am I to get home? And Aunt Julia——?"

"She knows; I telephoned early, and your maid has brought your things. But won't you eat something? I scrambled the eggs myself."

Lily could not eat; but the tea strengthened her to rise and dress under her maid's searching gaze. It was a relief to her that Gerty was obliged to hasten away: the two kissed silently, but without a trace of the previous night's emotion.

Lily found Mrs. Peniston in a state of agitation. She had sent for Grace Stepney and was taking digitalis. Lily breasted the storm of enquiries as best she could, explaining that she had had an attack of faintness on her way back from Carry Fisher's; that, fearing she would not have strength to reach home, she had gone to Miss Farish's instead; but that a quiet night had restored her, and that she had no need of a doctor.

This was a relief to Mrs. Peniston, who could give herself up to her own symptoms, and Lily was advised to go and lie down, her aunt's panacea for all physical and moral disorders. In the solitude of her own room she was brought back to a sharp contemplation of facts. Her daylight view of them necessarily differed from the cloudy vision of the night. The winged furies were now prowling gossips who dropped in on each other for tea. But her fears seemed the uglier, thus shorn of their vagueness; and besides, she had to act, not rave. For the first time she forced herself to reckon up the exact amount of her debt to Trenor; and the result of this hateful computation was the discovery that she had, in all, received nine thousand dollars from him. The flimsy pretext on which it had been given and received shrivelled up in the blaze of her shame: she knew that not a penny of it was her own, and that to restore her self-respect she must at once repay the whole amount. The inability thus to solace her outraged feelings gave her a paralyzing sense of insignificance. She was realizing for the first time that a woman's dignity may cost more to keep than her carriage; and that the maintenance of a moral attribute should be dependent on dollars and cents, made the world appear a more sordid place than she had conceived it.

After luncheon, when Grace Stepney's prying eyes had been removed, Lily asked for a word with her aunt. The two ladies went upstairs to the sitting-room, where Mrs. Peniston seated herself in her black satin arm-chair tufted with yellow buttons, beside a bead-work table bearing a bronze box with a miniature of Beatrice Cenci in the lid. Lily felt for these objects the same distaste which the prisoner may entertain for the fittings of the court-room. It was here that her aunt received her rare confidences, and the pink-eye smirk of the turbaned Beatrice was associated in her mind with the gradual fading of the smile from Mrs. Peniston's lips. The lady's dread of a scene gave her an inexorableness which the greatest strength of character could not have produced, since it was independent of all considerations of right or wrong; and knowing this, Lily seldom ventured to assail it. She had never felt less like making the attempt than on the present occasion; but she had sought in vain for any other means of escape from an intolerable situation.

Mrs. Peniston examined her critically. "You 're a bad colour, Lily: this incessant rushing about is beginning to tell on you," she said.

Miss Bart saw an opening. "I don't think it 's that, Aunt Julia; I 've had worries," she replied.

"Ah," said Mrs. Peniston, shutting her lips with the snap of a purse closing against a beggar.

"I 'm sorry to bother you with them," Lily continued, "but I really believe my faintness last night was brought on partly by anxious thoughts——"

"I should have said Carry Fisher's cook was enough to account for it. She has a woman who was with Maria Melson in 1891 — the spring of the year we went to Aix — and I remember dining there two days before we sailed, and feeling *sure* the coppers had n't been scoured."

"I don't think I ate much; I can't eat or sleep." Lily paused, and then said abruptly: "The fact is, Aunt Julia, I owe some money."

Mrs. Peniston's face clouded perceptibly, but did not express the astonishment her niece had expected. She was silent and Lily was forced to continue: "I have been foolish —— "

"No doubt you have: extremely foolish," Mrs. Peniston interposed. "I fail to see how any one with your income, and no expenses — not to mention the handsome presents I 've always given you —— "

"Oh, you 've been most generous, Aunt Julia; I shall never forget your kindness. But perhaps you don't quite realize the expense a girl is put to nowadays —— "

"I don't realize that *you* are put to any expense except for your clothes and your railway fares. I expect you to be handsomely dressed; but I paid Céleste's bill for you last October."

Lily hesitated: her aunt's implacable memory had never been more inconvenient. "You were as kind as possible; but I have had to get a few things since —— "

"What kind of things? Clothes? How much have you spent? Let me see the bill — I daresay the woman is swindling you."

"Oh, no, I think not: clothes have grown so frightfully expensive; and one needs so many different kinds, with country visits, and golf and skating, and Aiken and Tuxedo —— "

"Let me see the bill," Mrs. Peniston repeated.

Lily hesitated again. In the first place, Mme. Céleste had not yet sent in her account, and secondly, the amount it represented was only a fraction of the sum that Lily needed.

"She has n't sent in the bill for my winter things, but I *know* it 's large; and there are one or two other things; I 've been careless and imprudent — I 'm frightened to think of what I owe —— "

She raised the troubled loveliness of her face to Mrs. Peniston, vainly hoping that a sight so moving to the other sex might not be without effect upon her own. But the effect produced was that of making Mrs. Peniston shrink back apprehensively.

"Really, Lily, you are old enough to manage your own affairs, and after frightening me to death by your performance of last night you might at least choose a better time to worry me with such matters." Mrs. Peniston glanced at the clock, and swallowed a tablet of digitalis.

"If you owe Céleste another thousand, she may send me her account," she added, as though to end the discussion at any cost.

"I am very sorry, Aunt Julia; I hate to trouble you at such a time; but I have really no choice—I ought to have spoken sooner—I owe a great deal more than a thousand dollars."

"A great deal more? Do you owe two? She must have robbed you!"

"I told you it was not only Céleste. I—there are other bills—more pressing—that must be settled."

"What on earth have you been buying? Jewelry? You must have gone off your head," said Mrs. Peniston with asperity. "But if you have run into debt, you must suffer the consequences, and put aside your monthly income till your bills are paid. If you stay quietly here until next spring, instead of racing about all over the country, you will have no expenses at all, and surely in four or five months you can settle the rest of your bills if I pay the dress-maker now."

Lily was again silent. She knew she could not hope to extract even a thousand dollars from Mrs. Peniston on the mere plea of paying Céleste's bill: Mrs. Peniston would expect to go over the dress-maker's account, and would make out the cheque to her and not to Lily. And yet the money must be obtained before the day was over!

"The debts I speak of are—different—not like tradesmen's bills," she began confusedly; but Mrs. Peniston's look made her almost afraid to continue. Could it be that her aunt suspected anything? The idea precipitated Lily's avowal.

"The fact is, I 've played cards a good deal—bridge; the women all do it; girls too—it 's expected. Sometimes I 've won—won a good deal—but lately I 've been unlucky—and of course such debts can't be paid off gradually——"

She paused: Mrs. Peniston's face seemed to be petrifying as she listened.

"Cards—you 've played cards for money? It 's true, then: when I was told so I would n't believe it. I won't ask if the other horrors I was told were true too; I 've heard enough for the state of my nerves. When I think of the example you 've had in this house! But I suppose it 's your foreign bringing-up—no one knew where your mother picked up her friends. And her Sundays were a scandal—that I know." Mrs. Peniston wheeled round suddenly. "You play cards on Sunday?"

Lily flushed with the recollection of certain rainy Sundays at Bellomont and with the Dorsets.

"You 're hard on me, Aunt Julia: I have never really cared for cards, but a girl hates to be thought priggish and superior, and one drifts into doing what the others do. I 've had a dreadful lesson, and if you 'll help me out this time I promise you——"

Mrs. Peniston raised her hand warningly. "You need n't make any promises: it 's unnecessary. When I offered you a home I did n't undertake to pay your gambling debts."

"Aunt Julia! You don't mean that you won't help me?"

"I shall certainly not do anything to give the impression that I countenance your behaviour. If you really owe your dress-maker, I will settle with her—beyond that I recognize no obligation to assume your debts."

Lily had risen, and stood pale and quivering before her aunt. Pride stormed in her, but humiliation forced the cry from her lips: "Aunt Julia, I shall be disgraced—I——" But she could go no farther. If her aunt turned such a stony ear to the fiction of the gambling debts, in what spirit would she receive the terrible avowal of the truth?

"I consider that you *are* disgraced, Lily: disgraced by your conduct far more than by its results. You say your friends have persuaded you to play cards with them; well, they may as well learn a lesson too. They can probably afford to lose a little money—and at any rate, I am not going to waste any of mine in paying them. And now I must ask you to leave me—this scene has been extremely painful, and I have my own health to consider. Draw down the blinds, please; and tell Jennings I will see no one this afternoon but Grace Stepney."

Lily went up to her own room and bolted the door. She was trembling with fear and anger—the rush of the furies' wings was in her ears. She walked up and down the room with blind irregular steps. The last door of escape was closed—she felt herself shut in with her dishonour——

Suddenly her wild pacing brought her before the clock on the chimney-piece. Its hands stood at half-past three, and she remembered that Selden was to come to her at four. She had meant to put him off with a word—but now her heart leaped at the thought of seeing him. Was there not a promise of rescue in his love? As she had lain at Gerty's side the night before, she had thought of his coming, and of the sweetness of weeping out her pain upon his breast. Of course she had meant to clear herself of its consequences before she met him—she had never really doubted that Mrs. Peniston would come to her aid. And she had felt, even in the full storm of her misery, that Selden's love could not be her ultimate refuge; only it would be so sweet to take a moment's shelter there, while she gathered fresh strength to go on.

But now his love was her only hope, and as she sat alone with her wretchedness the thought of confiding in him became as seductive as the river's flow to the suicide. The first plunge would be terrible — but afterward, what blessedness might come! She remembered Gerty's words: "I know him — he will help you"; and her mind clung to them as a sick person might cling to a healing relic. Oh, if he really understood — if he would help her to gather up her broken life, and put it together in some new semblance in which no trace of the past should remain! He had always made her feel that she was worthy of better things, and she had never been in greater need of such solace. Once and again she shrank at the thought of imperilling his love by her confession: for love was what she needed — it would take the glow of passion to weld together the shattered fragments of her self-esteem. But she recurred to Gerty's words and held fast to them. She was sure that Gerty knew Selden's feeling for her, and it had never dawned upon her blindness that Gerty's own judgment of him was coloured by emotions far more ardent than her own.

Four o'clock found her in the drawing-room: she was sure that Selden would be punctual. but the hour came and passed — it moved on feverishly, measured by her impatient heart-beats. She had time to take a fresh survey of her wretchedness, and to fluctuate anew between the impulse to confide in Selden and the dread of destroying his illusions. But as the minutes passed the need of throwing herself on his comprehension became more urgent: she could not bear the weight of her misery alone. There would be a perilous moment, perhaps: but could she not trust to her beauty to bridge it over, to land her safe in the shelter of his devotion?

But the hour sped on and Selden did not come. Doubtless he had been detained, or had misread her hurriedly scrawled note, taking the four for a five. The ringing of the door-bell a few minutes after five confirmed this supposition, and made Lily hastily resolve to write more legibly in future. The sound of steps in the hall, and of the butler's voice preceding them, poured fresh energy into her veins. She felt herself once more the alert and competent moulder of emergencies, and the remembrance of her power over Selden flushed her with sudden confidence. But when the drawing-room door opened it was Rosedale who came in.

The reaction caused her a sharp pang, but after a passing movement of irritation at the clumsiness of fate, and at her own carelessness in not denying the door to all but Selden, she controlled herself and greeted Rosedale amicably. It was annoying that Selden, when he came, should find that particular visitor in possession, but Lily was mistress of the art

of ridding herself of superfluous company, and to her present mood
Rosedale seemed distinctly negligible.

His own view of the situation forced itself upon her after a few
moments' conversation. She had caught at the Brys' entertainment as
an easy impersonal subject, likely to tide them over the interval till Selden appeared, but Mr. Rosedale, tenaciously planted beside the tea-
table, his hands in his pockets, his legs a little too freely extended, at
once gave the topic a personal turn.

"Pretty well done—well, yes, I suppose it was: Welly Bry's got his
back up and don't mean to let go till he 's got the hang of the thing. Of
course, there were things here and there—things Mrs. Fisher could n't
be expected to see to—the champagne was n't cold, and the coats got
mixed in the coat-room. I would have spent more money on the music.
But that 's my character: if I want a thing I 'm willing to pay: I don't go
up to the counter, and then wonder if the article 's worth the price. I
would n't be satisfied to entertain like the Welly Brys; I 'd want something that would look more easy and natural, more as if I took it in my
stride. And it takes just two things to do that, Miss Bart: money, and the
right woman to spend it."

He paused, and examined her attentively while she affected to re-
arrange the tea-cups.

"I 've got the money," he continued, clearing his throat, "and what
I want is the woman—and I mean to have her too."

He leaned forward a little, resting his hands on the head of his
walking-stick. He had seen men of Ned Van Alstyne's type bring their
hats and sticks into a drawing-room, and he thought it added a touch of
elegant familiarity to their appearance.

Lily was silent, smiling faintly, with the eyes absently resting on his
face. She was in reality reflecting that a declaration would take some
time to make, and that Selden must surely appear before the moment of
refusal had been reached. Her brooding look, as of a mind withdrawn
yet not averted, seemed to Mr. Rosedale full of a subtle encouragement.
He would not have liked any evidence of eagerness.

"I mean to have her too," he repeated, with a laugh intended to
strengthen his self-assurance. "I generally *have* got what I wanted in life,
Miss Bart. I wanted money, and I 've got more than I know how to
invest; and now the money does n't seem to be of any account unless I
can spend it on the right woman. That 's what I want to do with it: I
want my wife to make all the other women feel small. I 'd never grudge
a dollar that was spent on that. But it is n't every woman can do it, no
matter how much you spend on her. There was a girl in some history

book who wanted gold shields, or something, and the fellows threw 'em at her, and she was crushed under 'em: they killed her. Well, that 's true enough: some women looked buried under their jewelry. What I want is a woman who 'll hold her head higher the more diamonds I put on it. And when I looked at you the other night at the Brys', in that plain white dress, looking as if you had a crown on, I said to myself: 'By gad, if she had one she 'd wear it as if it grew on her.'"

Still Lily did not speak, and he continued, warming with his theme: "Tell you what it is, though, that kind of woman costs more than all the rest of 'em put together. If a woman 's going to ignore her pearls, they want to be better than anybody else's—and so it is with everything else. You know what I mean—you know it 's only the showy things that are cheap. Well, I should want my wife to be able to take the earth for granted if she wanted to. I know there 's one thing vulgar about money, and that 's the thinking about it; and my wife would never have to demean herself in that way." He paused, and then added, with an unfortunate lapse to an earlier manner: "I guess you know the lady I 've got in view, Miss Bart."

Lily raised her head, brightening a little under the challenge. Even through the dark tumult of her thoughts, the clink of Mr. Rosedale's millions had a faintly seductive note. Oh, for enough of them to cancel her one miserable debt! But the man behind them grew increasingly repugnant in the light of Selden's expected coming. The contrast was too grotesque: she could scarcely suppress the smile it provoked. She decided that directness would be best.

"If you mean me, Mr. Rosedale, I am very grateful—very much flattered; but I don't know what I have ever done to make you think——"

"Oh, if you mean you 're not dead in love with me, I 've got sense enough left to see that. And I ain't talking to you as if you were—I presume I know the kind of talk that 's expected under those circumstances. I 'm confoundedly gone on you—that 's about the size of it—and I 'm just giving you a plain business statement of the consequences. You 're not very fond of me—yet—but you 're fond of luxury, and style, and amusement, and of not having to worry about cash. You like to have a good time, and not to have to settle for it; and what I propose to do is to provide for the good time and do the settling."

He paused, and she returned with a chilling smile: "You are mistaken in one point, Mr. Rosedale: whatever I enjoy I am prepared to settle for."

She spoke with the intention of making him see that, if his words implied a tentative allusion to her private affairs, she was prepared to meet and repudiate it. But if he recognized her meaning it failed to abash him, and he went on in the same tone: "I did n't mean to give offence; excuse me if I 've spoken too plainly. But why ain't you straight with me—why do you put up that kind of bluff? You know there 've been times when you were bothered—damned bothered—and as a girl gets older, and things keep moving along, why, before she knows it, the things she wants are liable to move past her and not come back. I don't say it 's anywhere near that with you yet; but you 've had a taste of bothers that a girl like yourself ought never to have known about, and what I 'm offering you is the chance to turn your back on them once for all."

The colour burned in Lily's face as he ended; there was no mistaking the point he meant to make, and to permit it to pass unheeded was a fatal confession of weakness, while to resent it too openly was to risk offending him at a perilous moment. Indignation quivered on her lip; but it was quelled by the secret voice which warned her that she must not quarrel with him. He knew too much about her, and even at the moment when it was essential that he should show himself at his best, he did not scruple to let her see how much he knew. How then would he use his power when her expression of contempt had dispelled his one motive for restraint? Her whole future might hinge on her way of answering him: she had to stop and consider that, in the stress of her other anxieties, as a breathless fugitive may have to pause at the cross-roads and try to decide coolly which turn to take.

"You are quite right, Mr. Rosedale. I *have* had bothers; and I am grateful to you for wanting to relieve me of them. It is not always easy to be quite independent and self-respecting when one is poor and lives among rich people; I have been careless about money, and have worried about my bills. But I should be selfish and ungrateful if I made that a reason for accepting all you offer, with no better return to make than the desire to be free from my anxieties. You must give me time—time to think of your kindness—and of what I could give you in return for it——"

She held out her hand with a charming gesture in which dismissal was shorn of its rigour. Its hint of future leniency made Rosedale rise in obedience to it, a little flushed with his unhoped-for success, and disciplined by the tradition of his blood to accept what was conceded, without undue haste to press for more. Something in his prompt acquiescence frightened her; she felt behind it the stored force of a patience that might subdue the strongest will. But at least they had parted amicably, and he was out of the house without meeting Selden—Selden, whose continued absence now smote her with a new alarm. Rosedale had remained over an hour, and she understood that it was now too late to hope for Selden. He would write explaining his absence, of course; there would be a note from him by the late post. But her confession would have to be postponed; and the chill of the delay settled heavily on her fagged spirit.

It lay heavier when the postman's last ring brought no note for her, and she had to go upstairs to a lonely night—a night as grim and sleepless as her tortured fancy had pictured it to Gerty. She had never learned to live with her own thoughts, and to be confronted with them through such hours of lucid misery made the confused wretchedness of her previous vigil seem easily bearable.

Daylight disbanded the phantom crew, and made it clear to her that she would hear from Selden before noon; but the day passed without his writing or coming. Lily remained at home, lunching and dining alone with her aunt, who complained of flutterings of the heart, and talked icily on general topics. Mrs. Peniston went to bed early, and when she had gone Lily sat down and wrote a note to Selden. She was about to ring for a messenger to despatch it when her eye fell on a paragraph in the evening paper which lay at her elbow: "Mr. Lawrence Selden was among the passengers sailing this afternoon for Havana and the West Indies on the Windward Liner Antilles."

She laid down the paper and sat motionless, staring at her note. She understood now that he was never coming—that he had gone away because he was afraid that he might come. She rose, and walking across the floor stood gazing at herself for a long time in the brightly-lit mirror above the mantelpiece. The lines in her face came out terribly—she looked old; and when a girl looks old to herself, how does she look to other people? She moved away, and began to wander aimlessly about the room, fitting her steps with mechanical precision between the monstrous roses of Mrs. Peniston's Axminster. Suddenly she noticed that the pen with which she had written to Selden still rested against the uncovered ink-stand. She seated herself again, and taking out an envelope, addressed it rapidly to Rosedale. Then she laid out a sheet of paper, and sat over it with suspended pen. It had been easy enough to write the date, and "Dear Mr. Rosedale"—but after that her inspiration flagged. She meant to tell him to come to her, but the words refused to shape themselves. At length she began: "I have been thinking——" then she laid the pen down, and sat with her elbows on the table and her face hidden in her hands.

Suddenly she started up at the sound of the door-bell. It was not late—barely ten o'clock—and there might still be a note from Selden, or a message—or he might be there himself, on the other side of the door! The announcement of his sailing might have been a mistake—it might be another Lawrence Selden who had gone to Havana—all these possibilities had time to flash through her mind, and build up the conviction that she was after all to see or hear from him, before the drawing-room door opened to admit a servant carrying a telegram.

Lily tore it open with shaking hands, and read Bertha Dorset's name below the message: "Sailing unexpectedly tomorrow. Will you join us on a cruise in Mediterranean?"

BOOK II

I

It came vividly to Selden on the Casino steps that Monte Carlo had, more than any other place he knew, the gift of accommodating itself to each man's humour.

His own, at the moment, lent it a festive readiness of welcome that might well, in a disenchanted eye, have turned to paint and facility. So frank an appeal for participation—so outspoken a recognition of the holiday vein in human nature—struck refreshingly on a mind jaded by prolonged hard work in surroundings made for the discipline of the senses. As he surveyed the white square set in an exotic coquetry of architecture, the studied tropicality of the gardens, the groups loitering in the foreground against mauve mountains which suggested a sublime stage-setting forgotten in a hurried shifting of scenes—as he took in the whole outspread effect of light and leisure, he felt a movement of revulsion from the last few months of his life.

The New York winter had presented an interminable perspective of snow-burdened days, reaching toward a spring of raw sunshine and furious air, when the ugliness of things rasped the eye as the gritty wind ground into the skin. Selden, immersed in his work, had told himself that external conditions did not matter to a man in his state, and that cold and ugliness were a good tonic for relaxed sensibilities. When an urgent case summoned him abroad to confer with a client in Paris, he broke reluctantly with the routine of the office; and it was only now that, having despatched his business, and slipped away for a week in the south, he began to feel the renewed zest of spectatorship that is the solace of those who take an objective interest in life.

The multiplicity of its appeals—the perpetual surprise of its contrasts and resemblances! All these tricks and turns of the show were upon him with a spring as he descended the Casino steps and paused on the pavement at its doors. He had not been abroad for seven years—and what changes the renewed contact produced! If the central depths were untouched, hardly a pin-point of surface remained the same. And this was the very place to bring out the completeness of the renewal. The sublimities, the perpetuities, might have left him as he was: but this tent pitched for a day's revelry spread a roof of oblivion between himself and his fixed sky.

It was mid-April, and one felt that the revelry had reached its climax and that the desultory groups in the square and gardens would soon dissolve and re-form in other scenes. Meanwhile the last moments of the performance seemed to gain an added brightness from the hovering threat of the curtain. The quality of the air, the exuberance of the flowers, the blue intensity of sea and sky, produced the effect of a closing *tableau*, when all the lights are turned on at once. This impression was presently heightened by the way in which a consciously conspicuous group of people advanced to the middle front, and stood before Selden with the air of the chief performers gathered together by the exigencies of the final effect. Their appearance confirmed the impression that the show had been staged regardless of expense, and emphasized its resemblance to one of those "costume-plays" in which the protagonists walk through the passions without displacing a drapery. The ladies stood in unrelated attitudes calculated to isolate their effects, and the men hung about them as irrelevantly as stage heroes whose tailors are named in the programme. It was Selden himself who unwittingly fused the group by arresting the attention of one of its members.

"Why, Mr. Selden!" Mrs. Fisher exclaimed in surprise; and with a gesture toward Mrs. Jack Stepney and Mrs. Wellington Bry, she added plaintively: "We 're starving to death because we can't decide where to lunch."

Welcomed into their group, and made the confidant of their difficulty, Selden learned with amusement that there were several places where one might miss something by not lunching, or forfeit something by lunching; so that eating actually became a minor consideration on the very spot consecrated to its rites.

"Of course one gets the best things at the *Terrasse*—but that looks as if one had n't any other reason for being there: the Americans who don't know any one always rush for the best food. And the Duchess of Beltshire has taken up Bécassin's lately," Mrs. Bry earnestly summed up.

Mrs. Bry, to Mrs. Fisher's despair, had not progressed beyond the point of weighing her social alternatives in public. She could not acquire the air of doing things because she wanted to, and making her choice the final seal of their fitness.

Mr. Bry, a short pale man, with a business face and leisure clothes, met the dilemma hilariously.

"I guess the Duchess goes where it 's cheapest, unless she can get her meal paid for. If you offered to blow her off at the *Terrasse* she 'd turn up fast enough."

But Mrs. Jack Stepney interposed. "The Grand Dukes go to that little place at the Condamine. Lord Hubert says it 's the only restaurant in Europe where they can cook peas."

Lord Hubert Dacey, a slender shabby-looking man, with a charming worn smile, and the air of having spent his best years in piloting the wealthy to the right restaurant, assented with gentle emphasis: "It 's quite that."

"*Peas?*" said Mr. Bry contemptuously. "Can they cook terrapin? It just shows," he continued, "what these European markets are, when a fellow can make a reputation cooking peas!"

Jack Stepney intervened with authority. "I don't know that I quite agree with Dacey: there 's a little hole in Paris, off the Quai Voltaire — but in any case, I can't advise the Condamine *gargote;* at least not with ladies."

Stepney, since his marriage, had thickened and grown prudish, as the Van Osburgh husbands were apt to do; but his wife, to his surprise and discomfiture, had developed an earth-shaking fastness of gait which left him trailing breathlessly in her wake.

"That 's where we 'll go then!" she declared, with a heavy toss of her plumage. "I 'm so tired of the *Terrasse:* it 's as dull as one of mother's dinners. And Lord Hubert has promised to tell us who all the awful people are at the other place — has n't he, Carry? Now, Jack, don't look so solemn!"

"Well," said Mrs. Bry, "all I want to know is who their dress-makers are."

"No doubt Dacey can tell you that too," remarked Stepney, with an ironic intention which the other received with the light murmur, "I can at least *find out,* my dear fellow"; and Mrs. Bry having declared that she could n't walk another step, the party hailed two or three of the light phaetons which hover attentively on the confines of the gardens, and rattled off in procession toward the Condamine.

Their destination was one of the little restaurants overhanging the boulevard which dips steeply down from Monte Carlo to the low intermediate quarter along the quay. From the window in which they presently found themselves installed, they overlooked the intense blue curve of the harbour, set between the verdure of twin promontories: to the right, the cliff of Monaco, topped by the mediæval silhouette of its church and castle, to the left the terraces and pinnacles of the gambling-house. Between the two, the waters of the bay were furrowed by a light coming and going of pleasure-craft, through which, just at the culminating moment of luncheon, the majestic advance of a great steam-yacht drew the company's attention from the peas.

"By Jove, I believe that 's the Dorsets back!" Stepney exclaimed; and Lord Hubert, dropping his single eye-glass, corroborated: "It 's the Sabrina—yes."

"So soon? They were to spend a month in Sicily," Mrs. Fisher observed.

"I guess they feel as if they had: there 's only one up-to-date hotel in the whole place," said Mr. Bry disparagingly.

"It was Ned Silverton's idea—but poor Dorset and Lily Bart must have been horribly bored." Mrs. Fisher added in an undertone to Selden: "I do hope there has n't been a row."

"It 's most awfully jolly having Miss Bart back," said Lord Hubert, in his mild deliberate voice; and Mrs. Bry added ingenuously: "I daresay the Duchess will dine with us, now that Lily 's here."

"The Duchess admires her immensely: I 'm sure she 'd be charmed to have it arranged," Lord Hubert agreed, with the professional promptness of the man accustomed to draw his profit from facilitating social contacts: Selden was struck by the businesslike change in his manner.

"Lily has been a tremendous success here," Mrs. Fisher continued, still addressing herself confidentially to Selden. "She looks ten years younger—I never saw her so handsome. Lady Skiddaw took her everywhere in Cannes, and the Crown Princess of Macedonia had her to stop for a week at Cimiez. People say that was one reason why Bertha whisked the yacht off to Sicily: the Crown Princess did n't take much notice of her, and she could n't bear to look on at Lily's triumph."

Selden made no reply. He was vaguely aware that Miss Bart was cruising in the Mediterranean with the Dorsets, but it had not occurred to him that there was any chance of running across her on the Riviera, where the season was virtually at an end. As he leaned back, silently contemplating his filigree cup of Turkish coffee, he was trying to put some order in his thoughts, to tell himself how the news of her nearness was really affecting him. He had a personal detachment enabling him, even in moments of emotional high-pressure, to get a fairly clear view of his feelings, and he was sincerely surprised by the disturbance which the sight of the Sabrina had produced in him. He had reason to think that his three months of engrossing professional work, following on the sharp shock of his disillusionment, had cleared his mind of its sentimental vapours. The feeling he had nourished and given prominence to was one of thankfulness for his escape: he was like a traveller so grateful for rescue from a dangerous accident that at first he is hardly conscious of his bruises. Now he suddenly felt the latent ache, and realized that after all he had not come off unhurt.

An hour later, at Mrs. Fisher's side in the Casino gardens, he was trying to find fresh reasons for forgetting the injury received in the contemplation of the peril avoided. The party had dispersed with the loitering indecision characteristic of social movements at Monte Carlo, where the whole place, and the long gilded hours of the day, seem to offer an infinity of ways of being idle. Lord Hubert Dacey had finally gone off in quest of the Duchess of Beltshire, charged by Mrs. Bry with the delicate negotiation of securing the lady's presence at dinner, the Stepneys had left for Nice in their motor-car, and Mr. Bry had departed to take his place in the pigeon-shooting match which was at the moment engaging his highest faculties.

Mrs. Bry, who had a tendency to grow red and stertorous after luncheon, had been judiciously prevailed upon by Carry Fisher to withdraw to her hotel for an hour's repose: and Selden and his companion were thus left to a stroll propitious to confidences. The stroll soon resolved itself into a tranquil session on a bench overhung with laurel and Banksian roses, from which they caught a dazzle of blue sea between marble balusters, and the fiery shafts of cactus-blossoms shooting meteor-like from the rock. The soft shade of their niche, and the adjacent glitter of the air, were conducive to an easy lounging mood, and to the smoking of many cigarettes; and Selden, yielding to these influences, suffered Mrs. Fisher to unfold to him the history of her recent experiences. She had come abroad with the Welly Brys at the moment when fashion flees the inclemency of the New York spring. The Brys, intoxicated by their first success, already thirsted for new kingdoms, and Mrs. Fisher, viewing the Riviera as an easy introduction to London society, had guided their course thither. She had affiliations of her own in every capital, and a facility for picking them up again after long absences; and the carefully disseminated rumour of the Brys' wealth had at once gathered about them a group of cosmopolitan pleasure-seekers.

"But things are not going as well as I expected," Mrs. Fisher frankly admitted. "It 's all very well to say that everybody with money can get into society; but it would be truer to say that *nearly* everybody can. And the London market is so glutted with new Americans that, to succeed there now, they must be either very clever or awfully queer. The Brys are neither. *He* would get on well enough if she 'd let him alone; they like his slang and his brag and his blunders. But Louisa spoils it all by trying to repress him and put herself forward. If she 'd be natural herself—fat and vulgar and bouncing—it would be all right; but as soon as she meets anybody smart she tries to be slender and queenly. She tried it with the Duchess of Beltshire and Lady Skiddaw, and they fled. I 've done my best to make her see her mistake—I 've said to her again and again: 'Just let yourself go, Louisa'; but she keeps up the humbug even with me—I believe she keeps on being queenly in her own room, with the door shut.

"The worst of it is," Mrs. Fisher went on, "that she thinks it 's all *my* fault. When the Dorsets turned up here six weeks ago, and everybody began to make a fuss about Lily Bart, I could see Louisa thought that if she 'd had Lily in tow instead of me she would have been hob-nobbing with all the royalties by this time. She does n't realize that it 's Lily's beauty that does it: Lord Hubert tells me Lily is thought even handsomer than when he knew her at Aix ten years ago. It seems she was tremendously admired there. An Italian Prince, rich and the real thing, wanted to marry her; but just at the critical moment a good-looking step-son turned up, and Lily was silly enough to flirt with him while her marriage-settlements with the step-father were being drawn up. Some people said the young man did it on purpose. You can fancy the scandal: there was an awful row between the men, and people began to look at Lily so queerly that Mrs. Peniston had to pack up and finish her cure elsewhere. Not that *she* ever understood: to this day she thinks that Aix did n't suit her, and mentions her having been sent there as proof of the incompetence of French doctors. That 's Lily all over, you know: she works like a slave preparing the ground and sowing her seed; but the day she ought to be reaping the harvest she over-sleeps herself or goes off on a picnic."

Mrs. Fisher paused and looked reflectively at the deep shimmer of sea between the cactus-flowers. "Sometimes," she added, "I think it 's just flightiness—and sometimes I think it 's because, at heart, she despises the things she 's trying for. And it 's the difficulty of deciding that makes her such an interesting study." She glanced tentatively at Selden's motionless profile, and resumed with a slight sigh: "Well, all I can say is, I wish she 'd give *me* some of her discarded opportunities. I wish we could change places now, for instance. She could make a very good thing out of the Brys if she managed them properly, and I should know just how to look after George Dorset while Bertha is reading Verlaine with Neddy Silverton."

She met Selden's sound of protest with a sharp derisive glance. "Well, what 's the use of mincing matters? We all know that 's what Bertha brought her abroad for. When Bertha wants to have a good time she has to provide occupation for George. At first I thought Lily was going to play her cards well *this* time, but there are rumours that Bertha is jealous of her success here and at Cannes, and I should n't be surprised if there were a break any day. Lily's only safeguard is that Bertha needs her badly—oh, very badly. The Silverton affair is in the acute stage: it 's necessary that George's attention should be pretty continuously distracted. And I 'm bound to say Lily *does* distract it: I believe he 'd marry her tomorrow if he found out there was anything wrong with Bertha. But you know him—he 's as blind as he 's jealous; and of course Lily's present business is to keep him blind. A clever woman might know just the right moment to tear off the bandage: but Lily is n't clever in that way, and when George does open his eyes she 'll probably contrive not to be in his line of vision."

Selden tossed away his cigarette. "By Jove—it 's time for my train," he exclaimed, with a glance at his watch; adding, in reply to Mrs. Fisher's surprised comment—"Why, I thought of course you were at Monte!"—a murmured word to the effect that he was making Nice his head-quarters.

"The worst of it is, she snubs the Brys now," he heard irrelevantly flung after him.

Ten minutes later, in the high-perched bedroom of an hotel overlooking the Casino, he was tossing his effects into a couple of gaping portmanteaux, while the porter waited outside to transport them to the cab at the door. It took but a brief plunge down the steep white road to the station to land him safely in the afternoon express for Nice; and not till he was installed in the corner of an empty carriage, did he exclaim to himself, with a reaction of self-contempt: "What the deuce am I running away from?"

The pertinence of the question checked Selden's fugitive impulse before the train had started. It was ridiculous to be flying like an emotional coward from an infatuation his reason had conquered. He had instructed his bankers to forward some important business letters to Nice, and at Nice he would quietly await them. He was already annoyed with himself for having left Monte Carlo, where he had intended to pass the week which remained to him before sailing; but it would now be difficult to return on his steps without an appearance of inconsistency from which his pride recoiled. In his inmost heart he was not sorry to put himself beyond the probability of meeting Miss Bart. Completely as he had detached himself from her, he could not yet regard her merely as a social instance; and viewed in a more personal way she was not likely to be a reassuring object of study. Chance encounters, or even the repeated mention of her name, would send his thoughts back into grooves from which he had resolutely detached them; whereas, if she could be entirely excluded from his life, the pressure of new and varied impressions, with which no thought of her was connected, would soon complete the work of separation. Mrs. Fisher's conversation had, indeed, operated to that end; but the treatment was too painful to be voluntarily chosen while milder remedies were untried; and Selden thought he could trust himself to return gradually to a reasonable view of Miss Bart, if only he did not see her.

Having reached the station early, he had arrived at this point in his reflections before the increasing throng on the platform warned him that he could not hope to preserve his privacy; the next moment there was a hand on the door, and he turned to confront the very face he was fleeing.

Miss Bart, glowing with the haste of a precipitate descent upon the train, headed a group composed of the Dorsets, young Silverton, and Lord Hubert Dacey, who had barely time to spring into the carriage, and envelop Selden in ejaculations of surprise and welcome, before the whistle of departure sounded. The party, it appeared, were hastening to Nice in response to a sudden summons to dine with the Duchess of Beltshire and to see the water-fête in the bay; a plan evidently improvised—in spite of Lord Hubert's protesting "Oh, I say, you know,"—for the express purpose of defeating Mrs. Bry's endeavour to capture the Duchess.

During the laughing relation of this manœuvre, Selden had time for a rapid impression of Miss Bart, who had seated herself opposite to him in the golden afternoon light. Scarcely three months had elapsed since he had parted from her on the threshold of the Brys' conservatory; but a subtle change had passed over the quality of her beauty. Then it had had a transparency through which the fluctuations of the spirit were sometimes tragically visible; now its impenetrable surface suggested a process of crystallization which had fused her whole being into one hard brilliant substance. The change had struck Mrs. Fisher as a rejuvenation: to Selden it seemed like that moment of pause and arrest when the warm fluidity of youth is chilled into its final shape.

He felt it in the way she smiled on him, and in the readiness and competence with which, flung unexpectedly into his presence, she took up the thread of their intercourse as though that thread had not been snapped with a violence from which he still reeled. Such facility sickened him—but he told himself that it was with the pang which precedes recovery. Now he would really get well—would eject the last drop of poison from his blood. Already he felt himself calmer in her presence than he had learned to be in the thought of her. Her assumptions and elisions, her short-cuts and long *détours,* the skill with which she contrived to meet him at a point from which no inconvenient glimpses of the past were visible, suggested what opportunities she had had for practising such arts since their last meeting. He felt that she had at last arrived at an understanding with herself: had made a pact with her rebellious impulses, and achieved a uniform system of self-government, under which all vagrant tendencies were either captive or forced into the service of the state.

And he saw other things too in her manner: saw how it had adjusted itself to the hidden intricacies of a situation in which, even after Mrs. Fisher's elucidating flashes, he still felt himself agrope. Surely Mrs. Fisher could no longer charge Miss Bart with neglecting her opportunities! To Selden's exasperated observation she was only too completely alive to them. She was "perfect" to every one: subservient to Bertha's anxious predominance, good-naturedly watchful of Dorset's moods, brightly companionable to Silverton and Dacey, the latter of whom met her on an evident footing of old admiration, while young Silverton, portentously self-absorbed, seemed conscious of her only as of something vaguely obstructive. And suddenly, as Selden noted the fine shades of manner by which she harmonized herself with her surroundings, it flashed on him that, to need such adroit handling, the situation must indeed be desperate. She was on the edge of something—that was the impression left with him. He seemed to see her poised on the brink of a chasm, with one graceful foot advanced to assert her unconsciousness that the ground was failing her.

On the Promenade des Anglais, where Ned Silverton hung on him for the half hour before dinner, he received a deeper impression of the general insecurity. Silverton was in a mood of Titanic pessimism. How any one could come to such a damned hole as the Riviera—any one with a grain of imagination—with the whole Mediterranean to choose from: but then, if one's estimate of a place depended on the way they broiled a spring chicken! Gad! what a study might be made of the tyranny of the stomach—the way a sluggish liver or insufficient gastric juices might affect the whole course of the universe, overshadow everything in reach—chronic dyspepsia ought to be among the "statutory causes"; a woman's life might be ruined by a man's inability to digest fresh bread. Grotesque? Yes—and tragic—like most absurdities. There 's nothing grimmer than the tragedy that wears a comic mask. . . . Where was he? Oh—the reason they chucked Sicily and rushed back? Well—partly, no doubt, Miss Bart's desire to get back to bridge and smartness. Dead as a stone to art and poetry—the light never *was* on sea or land for her! And of course she persuaded Dorset that the Italian food was bad for him. Oh, she could make him believe anything—*anything!* Mrs. Dorset was aware of it—oh, perfectly: nothing *she* did n't see! But she could hold her tongue—she 'd had to, often enough. Miss Bart was an intimate friend—she would n't hear a word against her. Only it hurts a woman's pride—there are some things one does n't get used to . . . All this in confidence, of course? Ah—and there were the ladies signalling from the balcony of the hotel. . . . He plunged across the Promenade, leaving Selden to a meditative cigar.

The conclusions it led him to were fortified, later in the evening, by some of those faint corroborative hints that generate a light of their own in the dusk of a doubting mind. Selden, stumbling on a chance acquaintance, had dined with him, and adjourned, still in his company, to the brightly lit Promenade, where a line of crowded stands commanded the glittering darkness of the waters. The night was soft and persuasive. Overhead hung a summer sky furrowed with the rush of rockets; and from the east a late moon, pushing up beyond the lofty bend of the coast, sent across the bay a shaft of brightness which paled to ashes in the red glitter of the illuminated boats. Down the lantern-hung Promenade, snatches of band-music floated above the hum of the crowd and the soft tossing of boughs in dusky gardens; and between these gardens and the backs of the stands there flowed a stream of people in whom the vociferous carnival mood seemed tempered by the growing languor of the season.

Selden and his companion, unable to get seats on one of the stands
facing the bay, had wandered for a while with the throng, and then
found a point of vantage on a high garden-parapet above the Promenade. Thence they caught but a triangular glimpse of the water, and of
the flashing play of boats across its surface; but the crowd in the street
was under their immediate view, and seemed to Selden, on the whole,
of more interest than the show itself. After a while, however, he wearied
of his perch and, dropping alone to the pavement, pushed his way to the
first corner and turned into the moonlit silence of a side street. Long
garden-walls overhung by trees made a dark boundary to the pavement;
an empty cab trailed along the deserted thoroughfare, and presently Selden saw two persons emerge from the opposite shadows, signal to the
cab, and drive off in it toward the centre of the town. The moonlight
touched them as they paused to enter the carriage, and he recognized
Mrs. Dorset and young Silverton.

Beneath the nearest lamp-post he glanced at his watch and saw that
the time was close on eleven. He took another cross street, and without
breasting the throng on the Promenade, made his way to the fashionable club which overlooks that thoroughfare. Here, amid the blaze of
crowded baccarat tables, he caught sight of Lord Hubert Dacey, seated
with his habitual worn smile behind a rapidly dwindling heap of gold.
The heap being in due course wiped out, Lord Hubert rose with a
shrug, and joining Selden, adjourned with him to the deserted terrace
of the club. It was now past midnight, and the throng on the stands was
dispersing, while the long trails of red-lit boats scattered and faded beneath a sky repossessed by the tranquil splendour of the moon.

Lord Hubert looked at his watch. "By Jove, I promised to join the
Duchess for supper at the *London House;* but it's past twelve, and I
suppose they've all scattered. The fact is, I lost them in the crowd soon
after dinner, and took refuge here, for my sins. They had seats on one of
the stands, but of course they could n't stop quiet: the Duchess never
can. She and Miss Bart went off in quest of what they call adventures—
gad, it ain't their fault if they don't have some queer ones!" He added
tentatively, after pausing to grope for a cigarette: "Miss Bart's an old
friend of yours, I believe? So she told me.—Ah, thanks—I don't seem
to have one left." He lit Selden's proffered cigarette, and continued, in
his high-pitched drawling tone: "None of my business, of course, but I
did n't introduce her to the Duchess. Charming woman, the Duchess,
you understand; and a very good friend of mine; but *rather* a liberal
education."

Selden received this in silence, and after a few puffs Lord Hubert

broke out again: "Sort of thing one can't communicate to the young
lady—though young ladies nowadays are so competent to judge
for themselves; but in this case—I 'm an old friend too, you know . . .
and there seemed no one else to speak to. The whole situation 's a
little mixed, as I see it—but there used to be an aunt somewhere, a
diffuse and innocent person, who was great at bridging over chasms she
did n't see . . . Ah, in New York, is she? Pity New York 's such a long
way off!"

II

Miss Bart, emerging late the next morning from her cabin, found
herself alone on the deck of the Sabrina.

The cushioned chairs, disposed expectantly under the wide awning,
showed no signs of recent occupancy, and she presently learned from
a steward that Mrs. Dorset had not yet appeared, and that the gentlemen—separately—had gone ashore as soon as they had breakfasted.
Supplied with these facts, Lily leaned awhile over the side, giving herself
up to a leisurely enjoyment of the spectacle before her. Unclouded sunlight enveloped sea and shore in a bath of purest radiancy. The purpling
waters drew a sharp white line of foam at the base of the shore; against
its irregular eminences, hotels and villas flashed from the greyish verdure of olive and eucalyptus; and the background of bare and finely-
pencilled mountains quivered in a pale intensity of light.

How beautiful it was—and how she loved beauty! She had always
felt that her sensibility in this direction made up for certain obtusenesses
of feeling of which she was less proud; and during the last three months
she had indulged it passionately. The Dorsets' invitation to go abroad
with them had come as an almost miraculous release from crushing difficulties; and her faculty for renewing herself in new scenes, and casting
off problems of conduct as easily as the surroundings in which they had
arisen, made the mere change from one place to another seem, not
merely a postponement, but a solution of her troubles. Moral complications existed for her only in the environment that had produced them;
she did not mean to slight or ignore them, but they lost their reality
when they changed their background. She could not have remained in
New York without repaying the money she owed to Trenor; to acquit
herself of that odious debt she might even have faced a marriage with
Rosedale; but the accident of placing the Atlantic between herself and
her obligations made them dwindle out of sight as if they had been
milestones and she had travelled past them.

Her two months on the Sabrina had been especially calculated to aid this illusion of distance. She had been plunged into new scenes, and had found in them a renewal of old hopes and ambitions. The cruise itself charmed her as a romantic adventure. She was vaguely touched by the names and scenes amid which she moved, and had listened to Ned Silverton reading Theocritus by moonlight, as the yacht rounded the Sicilian promontories, with a thrill of the nerves that confirmed her belief in her intellectual superiority. But the weeks at Cannes and Nice had really given her more pleasure. The gratification of being welcomed in high company, and of making her own ascendency felt there, so that she found herself figuring once more as the "beautiful Miss Bart" in the interesting journal devoted to recording the least movements of her cosmopolitan companions—all these experiences tended to throw into the extreme background of memory the prosaic and sordid difficulties from which she had escaped.

If she was faintly aware of fresh difficulties ahead, she was sure of her ability to meet them: it was characteristic of her to feel that the only problems she could not solve were those with which she was familiar. Meanwhile she could honestly be proud of the skill with which she had adapted herself to somewhat delicate conditions. She had reason to think that she had made herself equally necessary to her host and hostess; and if only she had seen any perfectly irreproachable means of drawing a financial profit from the situation, there would have been no cloud on her horizon. The truth was that her funds, as usual, were inconveniently low; and to neither Dorset nor his wife could this vulgar embarrassment be safely hinted. Still, the need was not a pressing one; she could worry along, as she had so often done before, with the hope of some happy change of fortune to sustain her; and meanwhile life was gay and beautiful and easy, and she was conscious of figuring not unworthily in such a setting.

She was engaged to breakfast that morning with the Duchess of Beltshire, and at twelve o'clock she asked to be set ashore in the gig. Before this she had sent her maid to enquire if she might see Mrs. Dorset; but the reply came back that the latter was tired, and trying to sleep. Lily thought she understood the reason of the rebuff. Her hostess had not been included in the Duchess's invitation, though she herself had made the most loyal efforts in that direction. But her grace was impervious to hints, and invited or omitted as she chose. It was not Lily's fault if Mrs. Dorset's complicated attitudes did not fall in with the Duchess's easy gait. The Duchess, who seldom explained herself, had not formulated her objection beyond saying: "She 's rather a bore, you know. The only one of your friends I like is that little Mr. Bry—*he* 's funny—" but Lily knew enough not to press the point, and was not altogether sorry to be thus distinguished at her friend's expense. Bertha certainly *had* grown tiresome since she had taken to poetry and Ned Silverton.

On the whole, it was a relief to break away now and then from the Sabrina; and the Duchess's little breakfast, organized by Lord Hubert with all his usual virtuosity, was the pleasanter to Lily for not including her travelling-companions. Dorset, of late, had grown more than usually morose and incalculable, and Ned Silverton went about with an air that seemed to challenge the universe. The freedom and lightness of the ducal intercourse made an agreeable change from these complications, and Lily was tempted, after luncheon, to adjourn in the wake of her companions to the hectic atmosphere of the Casino. She did not mean to play; her diminished pocket-money offered small scope for the adventure; but it amused her to sit on a divan, under the doubtful protection of the Duchess's back, while the latter hung above her stakes at a neighbouring table.

The rooms were packed with the gazing throng which, in the afternoon hours, trickles heavily between the tables, like the Sunday crowd in a lion-house. In the stagnant flow of the mass, identities were hardly distinguishable; but Lily presently saw Mrs. Bry cleaving her determined way through the doors, and, in the broad wake she left, the light figure of Mrs. Fisher bobbing after her like a row-boat at the stern of a tug. Mrs. Bry pressed on, evidently animated by the resolve to reach a certain point in the rooms; but Mrs. Fisher, as she passed Lily, broke from her towing-line, and let herself float to the girl's side.

"Lose her?" she echoed the latter's query, with an indifferent glance at Mrs. Bry's retreating back. "I daresay—it does n't matter: I *have* lost her already." And, as Lily exclaimed, she added: "We had an awful row this morning. You know, of course, that the Duchess chucked her at dinner last night, and she thinks it was my fault—my want of management. The worst of it is, the message—just a mere word by telephone—came so late that the dinner had to be paid for; and Bécassin *had* run it up—it had been so drummed into him that the Duchess was coming!" Mrs. Fisher indulged in a faint laugh at the remembrance. "Paying for what she does n't get rankles so dreadfully with Louisa: I can't make her see that it 's one of the preliminary steps to getting what you have n't paid for—and as I was the nearest thing to smash, she smashed me to atoms, poor dear!"

Lily murmured her commiseration. Impulses of sympathy came naturally to her, and it was instinctive to proffer her help to Mrs. Fisher.

"If there 's anything I can do—if it 's only a question of meeting the Duchess! I heard her say she thought Mr. Bry amusing——"

But Mrs. Fisher interposed with a decisive gesture. "My dear, I have my pride: the pride of my trade. *I* could n't manage the Duchess, and I can't palm off your arts on Louisa Bry as mine. I 've taken the final step: I go to Paris tonight with the Sam Gormers. *They 're* still in the elementary stage; an Italian Prince is a great deal more than a Prince to them, and they 're always on the brink of taking a courier for one. To save them from that is my present mission." She laughed again at the picture. "But before I go I want to make my last will and testament—I want to leave you the Brys."

"Me?" Miss Bart joined in her amusement. "It 's charming of you to remember me, dear; but really——"

"You 're already so well provided for?" Mrs. Fisher flashed a sharp glance at her. "*Are* you, though, Lily—to the point of rejecting my offer?"

Miss Bart coloured slowly. "What I really meant was, that the Brys would n't in the least care to be so disposed of."

Mrs. Fisher continued to probe her embarrassment with an unflinching eye. "What you really meant was that you 've snubbed the Brys horribly; and you know that they know it——"

"Carry!"

"Oh, on certain sides Louisa bristles with perceptions. If you 'd even managed to have them asked once on the Sabrina—especially when royalties were coming! But it 's not too late," she ended earnestly, "it 's not too late for either of you."

Lily smiled. "Stay over, and I 'll get the Duchess to dine with them."

"I shan't stay over—the Gormers have paid for my *salon-lit*," said Mrs. Fisher with simplicity. "But get the Duchess to dine with them all the same."

Lily's smile again flowed into a slight laugh: her friend's importunity was beginning to strike her as irrelevant. "I 'm sorry I have been negligent about the Brys——" she began.

"Oh, as to the Brys—it 's you I 'm thinking of," said Mrs. Fisher abruptly. She paused, and then, bending forward, with a lowered voice: "You know we all went on to Nice last night when the Duchess chucked us. It was Louisa's idea—I told her what I thought of it."

Miss Bart assented. "Yes—I caught sight of you on the way back, at the station."

"Well, the man who was in the carriage with you and George

Dorset—that horrid little Dabham who does 'Society Notes from the Riviera'—had been dining with us at Nice. And he 's telling everybody that you and Dorset came back alone after midnight."

"Alone—? When he was with us?" Lily laughed, but her laugh faded into gravity under the prolonged implication of Mrs. Fisher's look. "We *did* come back alone—if that 's so very dreadful! But whose fault was it? The Duchess was spending the night at Cimiez with the Crown Princess; Bertha got bored with the show, and went off early, promising to meet us at the station. We turned up on time, but she did n't—she did n't turn up at all!"

Miss Bart made this announcement in the tone of one who presents, with careless assurance, a complete vindication; but Mrs. Fisher received it in a manner almost inconsequent. She seemed to have lost sight of her friend's part in the incident: her inward vision had taken another slant.

"Bertha never turned up at all? Then how on earth did she get back?"

"Oh, by the next train, I suppose; there were two extra ones for the *fête*. At any rate, I know she 's safe on the yacht, though I have n't yet seen her; but you see it was not my fault," Lily summed up.

"Not your fault that Bertha did n't turn up? My poor child, if only you don't have to pay for it!" Mrs. Fisher rose—she had seen Mrs. Bry surging back in her direction. "There 's Louisa, and I must be off—oh, we 're on the best of terms externally; we 're lunching together; but at heart it 's *me* she 's lunching on," she explained; and with a last hand-clasp and a last look, she added; "Remember, I leave her to you; she 's hovering now, ready to take you in."

Lily carried the impression of Mrs. Fisher's leave-taking away with her from the Casino doors. She had accomplished, before leaving, the first step toward her reinstatement in Mrs. Bry's good graces. An affable advance—a vague murmur that they must see more of each other—an allusive glance to a near future that was felt to include the Duchess as well as the Sabrina—how easily it was all done, if one possessed the knack of doing it! She wondered at herself, as she had so often wondered, that, possessing the knack, she did not more consistently exercise it. But sometimes she was forgetful—and sometimes, could it be that she was proud? Today, at any rate, she had been vaguely conscious of a reason for sinking her pride, had in fact even sunk it to the point of suggesting to Lord Hubert Dacey, whom she ran across on the Casino steps, that he might really get the Duchess to dine with the Brys, if *she* undertook to have them asked on the Sabrina. Lord Hubert had promised his help, with the readiness on which she could always count: it was his only way of ever reminding her that he had once been ready to do so much more for her. Her path, in short, seemed to smooth itself before her as she advanced; yet the faint stir of uneasiness persisted. Had it been produced, she wondered, by her chance meeting with Selden? She thought not—time and change seemed so completely to have relegated him to his proper distance. The sudden and exquisite reaction from her anxieties had had the effect of throwing the recent past so far back that even Selden, as part of it, retained a certain air of unreality. And he had made it so clear that they were not to meet again; that he had merely dropped down to Nice for a day or two, and had almost his foot on the next steamer. No—that part of the past had merely surged up for a moment on the fleeing surface of events; and now that it was submerged again, the uncertainty, the apprehension persisted.

They grew to sudden acuteness as she caught sight of George Dorset descending the steps of the Hôtel de Paris and making for her across the square. She had meant to drive down to the quay and regain the yacht; but she now had the immediate impression that something more was to happen first.

"Which way are you going? Shall we walk a bit?" he began, putting the second question before the first was answered, and not waiting for a reply to either before he directed her silently toward the comparative seclusion of the lower gardens.

She detected in him at once all the signs of extreme nervous tension. The skin was puffed out under his sunken eyes, and its sallowness had paled to a leaden white against which his irregular eyebrows and long reddish moustache were relieved with a saturnine effect. His appearance, in short, presented an odd mixture of the bedraggled and the ferocious.

He walked beside her in silence, with quick precipitate steps, till they reached the embowered slopes to the east of the Casino; then, pulling up abruptly, he said: "Have you seen Bertha?"

"No—when I left the yacht she was not yet up."

He received this with a laugh like the whirring sound in a disabled clock. "Not yet up? Had she gone to bed? Do you know at what time she came on board? This morning at seven!" he exclaimed.

"At seven?" Lily started. "What happened—an accident to the train?"

He laughed again. "They missed the train—all the trains—they had to drive back."

"Well——?" She hesitated, feeling at once how little even this necessity accounted for the fatal lapse of hours.

"Well, they could n't get a carriage at once—at that time of night, you know—" the explanatory note made it almost seem as though as he were putting the case for his wife—"and when they finally did, it was only a one-horse cab, and the horse was lame!"

"How tiresome! I see," she affirmed, with the more earnestness because she was so nervously conscious that she did not; and after a pause she added: "I 'm so sorry—but ought we to have waited?"

"Waited for the one-horse cab? It would scarcely have carried the four of us, do you think?"

She took this in what seemed the only possible way, with a laugh intended to sink the question itself in his humorous treatment of it. "Well, it would have been difficult; we should have had to walk by turns. But it would have been jolly to see the sunrise."

"Yes: the sunrise *was* jolly," he agreed.

"Was it? You saw it, then?"

"I saw it, yes; from the deck. I waited up for them."

"Naturally—I suppose you were worried. Why did n't you call on me to share your vigil?"

He stood still, dragging at his moustache with a lean weak hand. "I don't think you would have cared for its *dénouement*," he said with sudden grimness.

Again she was disconcerted by the abrupt change in his tone, and as in one flash she saw the peril of the moment, and the need of keeping her sense of it out of her eyes.

"*Dénouement*—is n't that too big a word for such a small incident? The worst of it, after all, is the fatigue which Bertha has probably slept off by this time."

She clung to the note bravely, though its futility was now plain to her in the glare of his miserable eyes.

"Don't—don't——!" he broke out, with the hurt cry of a child; and while she tried to merge her sympathy, and her resolve to ignore any cause for it, in one ambiguous murmur of deprecation, he dropped down on the bench near which they had paused, and poured out the wretchedness of his soul.

It was a dreadful hour—an hour from which she emerged shrinking and seared, as though her lids had been scorched by its actual glare. It was not that she had never had premonitory glimpses of such an outbreak; but rather because, here and there throughout the three months,

the surface of life had shown such ominous cracks and vapours that her
fears had always been on the alert for an upheaval. There had been
moments when the situation had presented itself under a homelier yet
more vivid image—that of a shaky vehicle, dashed by unbroken steeds
over a bumping road, while she cowered within, aware that the harness
wanted mending, and wondering what would give way first. Well—
everything had given way now; and the wonder was that the crazy outfit
had held together so long. Her sense of being involved in the crash,
instead of merely witnessing it from the road, was intensified by the way
in which Dorset, through his furies of denunciation and wild reactions
of self-contempt, made her feel the need he had of her, the place she
had taken in his life. But for her, what ear would have been open to his
cries? And what hand but hers could drag him up again to a footing of
sanity and self-respect? All through the stress of the struggle with him,
she had been conscious of something faintly maternal in her efforts to
guide and uplift him. But for the present, if he clung to her, it was not
in order to be dragged up, but to feel some one floundering in the
depths with him: he wanted her to suffer with him, not to help him to
suffer less.

Happily for both, there was little physical strength to sustain his
frenzy. It left him, collapsed and breathing heavily, to an apathy so deep
and prolonged that Lily almost feared the passers-by would think it the
result of a seizure, and stop to offer their aid. But Monte Carlo is, of all
places, the one where the human bond is least close, and odd sights are
the least arresting. If a glance or two lingered on the couple, no intrusive sympathy disturbed them; and it was Lily herself who broke the
silence by rising from her seat. With the clearing of her vision the sweep
of peril had extended, and she saw that the post of danger was no longer
at Dorset's side.

"If you won't go back, I must—don't make me leave you!" she
urged.

But he remained mutely resistant, and she added: "What are you
going to do? You really can't sit here all night."

"I can go to an hotel. I can telegraph my lawyers." He sat up,
roused by a new thought. "By Jove, Selden 's at Nice—I 'll send for
Selden!"

Lily, at this, reseated herself with a cry of alarm. "No, no, *no!*" she
protested.

He swung round on her distrustfully. "Why not Selden? He 's a lawyer, is n't he? One will do as well as another in a case like this."

"As badly as another, you mean. I thought you relied on *me* to help you."

"You do — by being so sweet and patient with me. If it had n't been for you I 'd have ended the thing long ago. But now it 's got to end." He rose suddenly, straightening himself with an effort. "You can't want to see me ridiculous."

She looked at him kindly. "That 's just it." Then, after a moment's pondering, almost to her own surprise she broke out with a flash of inspiration: "Well, go over and see Mr. Selden. You 'll have time to do it before dinner."

"Oh, *dinner*——" he mocked her; but she left him with the smiling rejoinder: "Dinner on board, remember; we 'll put it off till nine if you like."

It was past four already; and when a cab had dropped her at the quay, and she stood waiting for the gig to put off for her, she began to wonder what had been happening on the yacht. Of Silverton's whereabouts there had been no mention. Had he returned to the Sabrina? Or could Bertha — the dread alternative sprang on her suddenly — could Bertha, left to herself, have gone ashore to rejoin him? Lily's heart stood still at the thought. All her concern had hitherto been for young Silverton, not only because, in such affairs, the woman's instinct is to side with the man, but because his case made a peculiar appeal to her sympathies. He was so desperately in earnest, poor youth, and his earnestness was of so different a quality from Bertha's, though hers too was desperate enough. The difference was that Bertha was in earnest only about herself, while he was in earnest about her. But now, at the actual crisis, this difference seemed to throw the weight of destitution on Bertha's side, since at least he had her to suffer for, and she had only herself. At any rate, viewed less ideally, all the disadvantages of such a situation were for the woman; and it was to Bertha that Lily's sympathies now went out. She was not fond of Bertha Dorset, but neither was she without a sense of obligation, the heavier for having so little personal liking to sustain it. Bertha had been kind to her, they had lived together, during the last months, on terms of easy friendship, and the sense of friction of which Lily had recently become aware seemed to make it the more urgent that she should work undividedly in her friend's interest.

It was in Bertha's interest, certainly, that she had despatched Dorset to consult with Lawrence Selden. Once the grotesqueness of the situation accepted, she had seen at a glance that it was the safest in which

Dorset could find himself. Who but Selden could thus miraculously combine the skill to save Bertha with the obligation of doing so? The consciousness that much skill would be required made Lily rest thankfully in the greatness of the obligation. Since he would *have* to pull Bertha through she could trust him to find a way; and she put the fulness of her trust in the telegram she managed to send him on her way to the quay.

Thus far, then, Lily felt that she had done well; and the conviction strengthened her for the task that remained. She and Bertha had never been on confidential terms, but at such a crisis the barriers of reserve must surely fall: Dorset's wild allusions to the scene of the morning made Lily feel that they were down already, and that any attempt to rebuild them would be beyond Bertha's strength. She pictured the poor creature shivering behind her fallen defences and awaiting with suspense the moment when she could take refuge in the first shelter that offered. If only that shelter had not already offered itself elsewhere! As the gig traversed the short distance between the quay and the yacht, Lily grew more than ever alarmed at the possible consequences of her long absence. What if the wretched Bertha, finding in all the long hours no soul to turn to—but by this time Lily's eager foot was on the side-ladder, and her first step on the Sabrina showed the worst of her apprehensions to be unfounded; for there, in the luxurious shade of the after-deck, the wretched Bertha, in full command of her usual attenuated elegance, sat dispensing tea to the Duchess of Beltshire and Lord Hubert.

The sight filled Lily with such surprise that she felt that Bertha, at least, must read its meaning in her look, and she was proportionately disconcerted by the blankness of the look returned. But in an instant she saw that Mrs. Dorset had, of necessity, to look blank before the others, and that, to mitigate the effect of her own surprise, she must at once produce some simple reason for it. The long habit of rapid transitions made it easy for her to exclaim to the Duchess: "Why, I thought you 'd gone back to the Princess!" and this sufficed for the lady she addressed, if it was hardly enough for Lord Hubert.

At least it opened the way to a lively explanation of how the Duchess was, in fact, going back the next moment, but had first rushed out to the yacht for a word with Mrs. Dorset on the subject of tomorrow's dinner—the dinner with the Brys, to which Lord Hubert had finally insisted on dragging them.

"To save my neck, you know!" he explained, with a glance that appealed to Lily for some recognition of his promptness; and the Duchess added, with her noble candour: "Mr. Bry has promised him a tip, and he says if we go he 'll pass it on to us."

This led to some final pleasantries, in which, as it seemed to Lily, Mrs. Dorset bore her part with astounding bravery, and at the close of which Lord Hubert, from half way down the side-ladder, called back, with an air of numbering heads: "And of course we may count on Dorset too?"

"Oh, count on him," his wife assented gaily. She was keeping up well to the last—but as she turned back from waving her adieux over the side, Lily said to herself that the mask must drop and the soul of fear look out.

Mrs. Dorset turned back slowly; perhaps she wanted time to steady her muscles; at any rate, they were still under perfect control when, dropping once more into her seat behind the tea-table, she remarked to Miss Bart with a faint touch of irony: "I suppose I ought to say good morning."

If it was a cue, Lily was ready to take it, though with only the vaguest sense of what was expected of her in return. There was something unnerving in the contemplation of Mrs. Dorset's composure, and she had to force the light tone in which she answered: "I tried to see you this morning, but you were not yet up."

"No—I got to bed late. After we missed you at the station I thought we ought to wait for you till the last train." She spoke very gently, but with just the least tinge of reproach.

"You missed us? You waited for us at the station?" Now indeed Lily was too far adrift in bewilderment to measure the other's words or keep watch on her own. "But I thought you did n't get to the station till after the last train had left!"

Mrs. Dorset, examining her between lowered lids, met this with the immediate query: "Who told you that?"

"George—I saw him just now in the gardens."

"Ah, is that George's version? Poor George—he was in no state to remember what I told him. He had one of his worst attacks this morning, and I packed him off to see the doctor. Do you know if he found him?"

Lily, still lost in conjecture, made no reply, and Mrs. Dorset settled herself indolently in her seat. "He 'll wait to see him; he was horribly frightened about himself. It 's very bad for him to be worried, and whenever anything upsetting happens, it always brings on an attack."

This time Lily felt sure that a cue was being pressed on her; but it was put forth with such startling suddenness, and with so incredible an air of ignoring what it led up to, that she could only falter out doubtfully: "Anything upsetting?"

"Yes—such as having you so conspicuously on his hands in the small hours. You know, my dear, you 're rather a big responsibility in such a scandalous place after midnight."

At that—at the complete unexpectedness and the inconceivable audacity of it—Lily could not restrain the tribute of an astonished laugh.

"Well, really—considering it was you who burdened him with the responsibility!"

Mrs. Dorset took this with an exquisite mildness. "By not having the superhuman cleverness to discover you in that frightful rush for the train? Or the imagination to believe that you 'd take it without us—you and he all alone—instead of waiting quietly in the station till we *did* manage to meet you?"

Lily's colour rose: it was growing clear to her that Bertha was pursuing an object, following a line she had marked out for herself. Only, with such a doom impending, why waste time in these childish efforts to avert it? The puerility of the attempt disarmed Lily's indignation: did it not prove how horribly the poor creature was frightened?

"No; by our simply all keeping together at Nice," she returned.

"Keeping together? When it was you who seized the first opportunity to rush off with the Duchess and her friends? My dear Lily, you are not a child to be led by the hand!"

"No—nor to be lectured, Bertha, really; if that 's what you are doing to me now."

Mrs. Dorset smiled on her reproachfully. "Lecture you—I? Heaven forbid! I was merely trying to give you a friendly hint. But it 's usually the other way round, is n't it? I 'm expected to take hints, not to give them: I 've positively lived on them all these last months."

"Hints—from me to you?" Lily repeated.

"Oh, negative ones merely—what not to be and to do and to see. And I think I 've taken them to admiration. Only, my dear, if you 'll let me say so, I did n't understand that one of my negative duties was *not* to warn you when you carried your imprudence too far."

A chill of fear passed over Miss Bart: a sense of remembered treachery that was like the gleam of a knife in the dusk. But compassion, in a moment, got the better of her instinctive recoil. What was this outpouring of senseless bitterness but the tracked creature's attempt to cloud the medium through which it was fleeing? It was on Lily's lips to exclaim: "You poor soul, don't double and turn—come straight back to me, and we 'll find a way out!" But the words died under the impenetrable insolence of Bertha's smile. Lily sat silent, taking the brunt of it quietly, letting it spend itself on her to the last drop of its accumulated falseness; then, without a word, she rose and went down to her cabin.

III

Miss Bart's telegram caught Lawrence Selden at the door of his hotel; and having read it, he turned back to wait for Dorset. The message necessarily left large gaps for conjecture; but all that he had recently heard and seen made these but too easy to fill in. On the whole he was surprised; for though he had perceived that the situation contained all the elements of an explosion, he had often enough, in the range of his personal experience, seen just such combinations subside into harmlessness. Still, Dorset's spasmodic temper, and his wife's reckless disregard of appearances, gave the situation a peculiar insecurity; and it was less from the sense of any special relation to the case than from a purely professional zeal, that Selden resolved to guide the pair to safety. Whether, in the present instance, safety for either lay in repairing so damaged a tie, it was no business of his to consider: he had only, on general principles, to think of averting a scandal, and his desire to avert it was increased by his fear of its involving Miss Bart. There was nothing specific in this apprehension; he merely wished to spare her the embarrassment of being ever so remotely connected with the public washing of the Dorset linen.

How exhaustive and unpleasant such a process would be, he saw even more vividly after his two hours' talk with poor Dorset. If anything came out at all, it would be such a vast unpacking of accumulated moral rags as left him, after his visitor had gone, with the feeling that he must fling open the windows and have his room swept out. But nothing should come out; and happily for his side of the case, the dirty rags, however pieced together, could not, without considerable difficulty, be turned into a homogeneous grievance. The torn edges did not always fit—there were missing bits, there were disparities of size and colour, all of which it was naturally Selden's business to make the most of in putting them under his client's eye. But to a man in Dorset's mood the completest demonstration could not carry conviction, and Selden saw that for the moment all he could do was to soothe and temporize, to offer sympathy and to counsel prudence. He let Dorset depart charged to the brim with the sense that, till their next meeting, he must maintain a strictly noncommittal attitude; that, in short, his share in the game consisted for the present in looking on. Selden knew, however, that he could not long keep such violences in equilibrium; and he promised to meet Dorset, the next morning, at an hotel in Monte Carlo. Meanwhile he counted not a little on the reaction of weakness and self-distrust that, in such natures, follows on every unwonted expenditure of moral force; and his telegraphic reply to Miss Bart consisted simply in the injunction: "Assume that everything is as usual."

On this assumption, in fact, the early part of the following day was lived through. Dorset, as if in obedience to Lily's imperative bidding, had actually returned in time for a late dinner on the yacht. The repast had been the most difficult moment of the day. Dorset was sunk in one of the abysmal silences which so commonly followed on what his wife called his "attacks" that it was easy, before the servants, to refer it to this cause; but Bertha herself seemed, perversely enough, little disposed to make use of this obvious means of protection. She simply left the brunt of the situation on her husband's hands, as if too absorbed in a grievance of her own to suspect that she might be the object of one herself. To Lily this attitude was the most ominous, because the most perplexing, element in the situation. As she tried to fan the weak flicker of talk, to build up, again and again, the crumbling structure of "appearances," her own attention was perpetually distracted by the question: "What on earth can she be driving at?" There was something positively exasperating in Bertha's attitude of isolated defiance. If only she would have given her friend a hint they might still have worked together successfully; but how could Lily be of use, while she was thus obstinately shut out from participation? To be of use was what she honestly wanted; and not for her own sake but for the Dorsets'. She had not thought of her own situation at all: she was simply engrossed in trying to put a little order in theirs. But the close of the short dreary evening left her with a sense of effort hopelessly wasted. She had not tried to see Dorset alone: she had positively shrunk from a renewal of his confidences. It was Bertha whose confidence she sought, and who should as eagerly have invited her own; and Bertha, as if in the infatuation of self-destruction, was actually pushing away her rescuing hand.

Lily, going to bed early, had left the couple to themselves; and it seemed part of the general mystery in which she moved that more than an hour should elapse before she heard Bertha walk down the silent passage and regain her room. The morrow, rising on an apparent continuance of the same conditions, revealed nothing of what had occurred between the confronted pair. One fact alone outwardly proclaimed the change they were all conspiring to ignore; and that was the non-appearance of Ned Silverton. No one referred to it, and this tacit avoidance of the subject kept it in the immediate foreground of consciousness. But there was another change, perceptible only to Lily; and that was that Dorset now avoided her almost as pointedly as his wife. Perhaps he was repenting his rash outpourings of the previous day; perhaps only trying, in his clumsy way, to conform to Selden's counsel to behave "as usual." Such instructions no more make for easiness of attitude than the photographer's behest to "look natural"; and in a creature as unconscious as poor Dorset of the appearance he habitually presented, the struggle to maintain a pose was sure to result in queer contortions.

It resulted, at any rate, in throwing Lily strangely on her own resources. She had learned, on leaving her room, that Mrs. Dorset was still invisible, and that Dorset had left the yacht early; and feeling too restless to remain alone, she too had herself ferried ashore. Straying toward the Casino, she attached herself to a group of acquaintances from Nice, with whom she lunched, and in whose company she was returning to the rooms when she encountered Selden crossing the square. She could not, at the moment, separate herself definitely from her party, who had hospitably assumed that she would remain with them till they took their departure; but she found time for a momentary pause of enquiry, to which he promptly returned: "I 've seen him again — he 's just left me."

She waited before him anxiously. "Well? What has happened? What *will* happen?"

"Nothing as yet — and nothing in the future, I think."

"It 's over, then? It 's settled? You 're sure?"

He smiled. "Give me time. I 'm not sure — but I 'm a good deal surer." And with that she had to content herself, and hasten on to the expectant group on the steps.

Selden had in fact given her the utmost measure of his sureness, had even stretched it a shade to meet the anxiety in her eyes. And now, as he turned away, strolling down the hill toward the station, that anxiety remained with him as the visible justification of his own. It was not, indeed, anything specific that he feared: there had been a literal truth in his declaration that he did not think anything would happen. What troubled him was that, though Dorset's attitude had perceptibly changed, the change was not clearly to be accounted for. It had certainly not been produced by Selden's arguments, or by the action of his own soberer reason. Five minutes' talk sufficed to show that some alien influence had been at work, and that it had not so much subdued his resentment as weakened his will, so that he moved under it in a state of apathy, like a dangerous lunatic who has been drugged. Temporarily, no doubt, however exerted, it worked for the general safety: the question was how long it would last, and by what kind of reaction it was likely to be followed. On these points Selden could gain no light; for he saw that one effect of the transformation had been to shut him off from free communion with Dorset. The latter, indeed, was still moved by the irresistible desire to discuss his wrong; but, though he revolved about it with the same forlorn tenacity, Selden was aware that something always restrained him from full expression. His state was one to produce first weariness and then impatience in his hearer; and when their talk was over, Selden began to feel that he had done his utmost, and might justifiably wash his hands of the sequel.

It was in this mind that he had been making his way back to the station when Miss Bart crossed his path; but though, after his brief word with her, he kept mechanically on his course, he was conscious of a gradual change in his purpose. The change had been produced by the look in her eyes; and in his eagerness to define the nature of that look, he dropped into a seat in the gardens, and sat brooding upon the question. It was natural enough, in all conscience, that she should appear anxious: a young woman placed, in the close intimacy of a yachting-cruise, between a couple on the verge of disaster, could hardly, aside from her concern for her friends, be insensible to the awkwardness of her own position. The worst of it was that, in interpreting Miss Bart's state of mind, so many alternative readings were possible; and one of these, in Selden's troubled mind, took the ugly form suggested by Mrs. Fisher. If the girl was afraid, was she afraid for herself or for her friends? And to what degree was her dread of a catastrophe intensified by the sense of being fatally involved in it? The burden of offence lying manifestly with Mrs. Dorset, this conjecture seemed on the face of it gratuitously unkind; but Selden knew that in the most one-sided matrimonial quarrel there are generally counter-charges to be brought, and that they are brought with the greater audacity where the original grievance is so emphatic. Mrs. Fisher had not hesitated to suggest the likelihood of Dorset's marrying Miss Bart if "anything happened"; and though Mrs. Fisher's conclusions were notoriously rash, she was shrewd enough in reading the signs from which they were drawn. Dorset had apparently shown marked interest in the girl, and this interest might be used to cruel advantage in his wife's struggle for rehabilitation. Selden knew that Bertha would fight to the last round of powder: the rashness of her conduct was illogically combined with a cold determination to escape its consequences. She could be as unscrupulous in fighting for herself as she was reckless in courting danger, and whatever came to her hand at such moments was likely to be used as a defensive missile. He did not, as yet, see clearly just what course she was likely to take, but his perplexity increased his apprehension, and with it the sense that, before leaving, he must speak again with Miss Bart. Whatever her share in the situation — and he had always honestly tried to resist judging her by her surroundings — however free she might be from any personal connection with it, she would be better out of the way of a possible crash; and since she had appealed to him for help, it was clearly his business to tell her so.

This decision at last brought him to his feet, and carried him back to the gambling rooms, within whose doors he had seen her disappearing; but a prolonged exploration of the crowd failed to put him on her traces. He saw instead, to his surprise, Ned Silverton loitering somewhat ostentatiously about the tables; and the discovery that this actor in the drama was not only hovering in the wings, but actually inviting the exposure of the footlights, though it might have seemed to imply that all peril was over, served rather to deepen Selden's sense of foreboding. Charged with this impression he returned to the square, hoping to see Miss Bart move across it, as every one in Monte Carlo seemed inevitably to do at least a dozen times a day; but here again he waited vainly for a glimpse of her, and the conclusion was slowly forced on him that she had gone back to the Sabrina. It would be difficult to follow her there, and still more difficult, should he do so, to contrive the opportunity for a private word; and he had almost decided on the unsatisfactory alternative of writing, when the ceaseless diorama of the square suddenly unrolled before him the figures of Lord Hubert and Mrs. Bry.

Hailing them at once with his question, he learned from Lord Hubert that Miss Bart had just returned to the Sabrina in Dorset's company; an announcement so evidently disconcerting to him that Mrs. Bry, after a glance from her companion, which seemed to act like the pressure on a spring, brought forth the prompt proposal that he should come and meet his friends at dinner that evening — "At Bécassin's — a little dinner to the Duchess," she flashed out before Lord Hubert had time to remove the pressure.

Selden's sense of the privilege of being included in such company brought him early in the evening to the door of the restaurant, where he paused to scan the ranks of diners approaching down the brightly lit terrace. There, while the Brys hovered within over the last agitating alternatives of the *menu,* he kept watch for the guests from the Sabrina, who at length rose on the horizon in company with the Duchess, Lord and Lady Skiddaw and the Stepneys. From this group it was easy for him to detach Miss Bart on the pretext of a moment's glance into one of the brilliant shops along the terrace, and to say to her, while they lingered together in the white dazzle of a jeweller's window: "I stopped over to see you—to beg of you to leave the yacht."

The eyes she turned on him showed a quick gleam of her former fear. "To leave—? What do you mean? What has happened?"

"Nothing. But if anything should, why be in the way of it?"

The glare from the jeweller's window, deepening the pallour of her face, gave to its delicate lines the sharpness of a tragic mask. "Nothing will, I am sure; but while there 's even a doubt left, how can you think I would leave Bertha?"

The words rang out on a note of contempt—was it possibly of contempt for himself? Well, he was willing to risk its renewal to the extent of insisting, with an undeniable throb of added interest: "You have yourself to think of, you know—" to which, with a strange fall of sadness in her voice, she answered, meeting his eyes: "If you knew how little difference that makes!"

"Oh, well, nothing *will* happen," he said, more for his own reassurance than for hers; and "Nothing, nothing, of course!" she valiantly assented, as they turned to overtake their companions.

In the thronged restaurant, taking their places about Mrs. Bry's illuminated board, their confidence seemed to gain support from the familiarity of their surroundings. Here were Dorset and his wife once more presenting their customary faces to the world, she engrossed in establishing her relation with an intensely new gown, he shrinking with dyspeptic dread from the multiplied solicitations of the *menu*. The mere fact that they thus showed themselves together, with the utmost openness the place afforded, seemed to declare beyond a doubt that their differences were composed. How this end had been attained was still matter for wonder, but it was clear that for the moment Miss Bart rested confidently in the result; and Selden tried to achieve the same view by telling himself that her opportunities for observation had been ampler than this own.

Meanwhile, as the dinner advanced through a labyrinth of courses, in which it became clear that Mrs. Bry had occasionally broken away from Lord Hubert's restraining hand, Selden's general watchfulness began to lose itself in a particular study of Miss Bart. It was one of the days when she was so handsome that to be handsome was enough, and all the rest—her grace, her quickness, her social felicities—seemed the overflow of a bounteous nature. But what especially struck him was the way in which she detached herself, by a hundred undefinable shades, from the persons who most abounded in her own style. It was in just such company, the fine flower and complete expression of the state she aspired to, that the differences came out with special poignancy, her grace cheapening the other women's smartness as her finely-discriminated silences made their chatter dull. The strain of the last hours had restored to her face the deeper eloquence which Selden had lately missed in it, and the bravery of her words to him still fluttered in her voice and eyes. Yes, she was matchless—it was the one word for her; and he could give his admiration the freer play because so little personal feeling remained in it. His real detachment from her had taken place, not at the lurid moment of disenchantment, but now, in the sober after-light of discrimination, where he saw her definitely divided from him by the crudeness of a choice which seemed to deny the very differences he felt in her. It was before him again in its completeness—the choice in which she was content to rest: in the stupid costliness of the food and the showy dulness of the talk, in the freedom of speech which never arrived at wit and the freedom of act which never made for romance. The strident setting of the restaurant, in which their table seemed set apart in a special glare of publicity, and the presence at it of little Dabham of the "Riviera Notes," emphasized the ideals of a world where conspicuousness passed for distinction, and the society column had become the roll of fame.

It was as the immortalizer of such occasions that little Dabham, wedged in modest watchfulness between two brilliant neighbours, suddenly became the centre of Selden's scrutiny. How much did he know of what was going on, and how much, for his purpose, was still worth finding out? His little eyes were like tentacles thrown out to catch the floating intimations with which, to Selden, the air at moments seemed thick; then again it cleared to its normal emptiness, and he could see nothing in it for the journalist but leisure to note the elegance of the ladies' gowns. Mrs. Dorset's, in particular, challenged all the wealth of Mr. Dabham's vocabulary: it had surprises and subtleties worthy of what he would have called "the literary style." At first, as Selden had noticed, it had been almost too preoccupying to its wearer; but now she was in full command of it, and was even producing her effects with unwonted freedom. Was she not, indeed, too free, too fluent, for perfect naturalness? And was not Dorset, to whom his glance had passed by a natural transition, too jerkily wavering between the same extremes? Dorset indeed was always jerky; but it seemed to Selden that tonight each vibration swung him farther from his centre.

The dinner, meanwhile, was moving to its triumphant close, to the evident satisfaction of Mrs. Bry, who, throned in apoplectic majesty between Lord Skiddaw and Lord Hubert, seemed in spirit to be calling on Mrs. Fisher to witness her achievement. Short of Mrs. Fisher her audience might have been called complete; for the restaurant was crowded with persons mainly gathered there for the purpose of spectatorship, and accurately posted as to the names and faces of the celebrities they had come to see. Mrs. Bry, conscious that all her feminine guests came under that heading, and that each one looked her part to admiration, shone on Lily with all the pent-up gratitude that Mrs. Fisher had failed to deserve. Selden, catching the glance, wondered what part Miss Bart had played in organizing the entertainment. She did, at least, a great deal to adorn it; and as he watched the bright security with which she bore itself, he smiled to think that he should have fancied her in need of help. Never had she appeared more serenely mistress of the situation than when, at the moment of dispersal, detaching herself a little from the group about the table, she turned with a smile and a graceful slant of the shoulders to receive her cloak from Dorset.

The dinner had been protracted over Mr. Bry's exceptional cigars and a bewildering array of liqueurs, and many of the other tables were empty; but a sufficient number of diners still lingered to give relief to the leave-taking of Mrs. Bry's distinguished guests. This ceremony was drawn out and complicated by the fact that it involved, on the part of the Duchess and Lady Skiddaw, definite farewells, and pledges of speedy reunion in Paris, where they were to pause and replenish their wardrobes on the way to England. The quality of Mrs. Bry's hospitality, and of the tips her husband had presumably imparted, lent to the manner of the English ladies a general effusiveness which shed the rosiest light over their hostess's future. In its glow Mrs. Dorset and the Stepneys were also visibly included, and the whole scene had touches of intimacy worth their weight in gold to the watchful pen of Mr. Dabham.

A glance at her watch caused the Duchess to exclaim to her sister that they had just time to dash for their train, and the flurry of this departure over, the Stepneys, who had their motor at the door, offered to convey the Dorsets and Miss Bart to the quay. The offer was accepted, and Mrs. Dorset moved away with her husband in attendance. Miss Bart had lingered for a last word with Lord Hubert, and Stepney, on whom Mr. Bry was pressing a final, and still more expensive, cigar, called out: "Come on, Lily, if you 're going back to the yacht."

Lily turned to obey; but as she did so, Mrs. Dorset, who had paused on her way out, moved a few steps back toward the table.

"Miss Bart is not going back to the yacht," she said in a voice of singular distinctness.

A startled look ran from eye to eye; Mrs. Bry crimsoned to the verge of congestion, Mrs. Stepney slipped nervously behind her husband, and Selden, in the general turmoil of his sensations, was mainly conscious of a longing to grip Dabham by the collar and fling him out into the street.

Dorset, meanwhile, had stepped back to his wife's side. His face was white, and he looked about him with cowed angry eyes. "Bertha! — Miss Bart . . . this is some misunderstanding . . . some mistake . . . "

"Miss Bart remains here," his wife rejoined incisively. "And, I think, George, we had better not detain Mrs. Stepney any longer."

Miss Bart, during this brief exchange of words, remained in admirable erectness, slightly isolated from the embarrassed group about her. She had paled a little under the shock of the insult, but the discomposure of the surrounding faces was not reflected in her own. The faint disdain of her smile seemed to lift her high above her antagonist's reach, and it was not till she had given Mrs. Dorset the full measure of the distance between them that she turned and extended her hand to her hostess.

"I am joining the Duchess tomorrow," she explained, "and it seemed easier for me to remain on shore for the night."

She held firmly to Mrs. Bry's wavering eye while she gave this explanation, but when it was over Selden saw her send a tentative glance from one to another of the women's faces. She read their incredulity in their averted looks, and in the mute wretchedness of the men behind them, and for a miserable half-second he thought she quivered on the brink of failure. Then, turning to him with an easy gesture, and the pale bravery of her recovered smile — "Dear Mr. Selden," she said, "you promised to see me to my cab."

Outside, the sky was gusty and overcast, and as Lily and Selden moved toward the deserted gardens below the restaurant, spurts of warm rain blew fitfully against their faces. The fiction of the cab had been tacitly abandoned; they walked on in silence, her hand on his arm, till the deeper shade of the gardens received them, and pausing beside a bench, he said: "Sit down a moment."

She dropped to the seat without answering, but the electric lamp at the bend of the path shed a gleam on the struggling misery of her face. Selden sat down beside her, waiting for her to speak, fearful lest any word he chose should touch too roughly on her wound, and kept also from free utterance by the wretched doubt which had slowly renewed itself within him. What had brought her to this pass? What weakness had placed her so abominably at her enemy's mercy? And why should

Bertha Dorset have turned into an enemy at the very moment when she so obviously needed the support of her sex? Even while his nerves raged at the subjection of husbands to their wives, and at the cruelty of women to their kind, reason obstinately harped on the proverbial relation between smoke and fire. The memory of Mrs. Fisher's hints, and the corroboration of his own impressions, while they deepened his pity also increased his constraint, since, whichever way he sought a free outlet for sympathy, it was blocked by the fear of committing a blunder.

Suddenly it struck him that his silence must seem almost as accusatory as that of the men he had despised for turning from her; but before he could find the fitting word she had cut him short with a question.

"Do you know of a quiet hotel? I can send for my maid in the morning."

"An hotel — *here* — that you can go to alone? It 's not possible."

She met this with a pale gleam of her old playfulness. "What *is,* then? It 's too wet to sleep in the gardens."

"But there must be some one —— "

"Some one to whom I can go? Of course — any number — but at *this* hour? You see my change of plan was rather sudden —— "

"Good God — if you 'd listened to me!" he cried, venting his helplessness in a burst of anger.

She still held him off with the gentle mockery of her smile. "But have n't I?" she rejoined. "You advised me to leave the yacht, and I 'm leaving it."

He saw then, with a pang of self-reproach, that she meant neither to explain nor to defend herself; that by his miserable silence he had forfeited all chance of helping her, and that the decisive hour was past.

She had risen, and stood before him in a kind of clouded majesty, like some deposed princess moving tranquilly to exile.

"Lily!" he exclaimed, with a note of despairing appeal; but — "Oh, not now," she gently admonished him; and then, in all the sweetness of her recovered composure: "Since I must find shelter somewhere, and since you 're so kindly here to help me —— "

He gathered himself up at the challenge. "You will do as I tell you? There 's but one thing, then; you must go straight to your cousins, the Stepneys."

"Oh — " broke from her with a movement of instinctive resistance; but he insisted: "Come — it 's late, and you must appear to have gone there directly."

He had drawn her hand into his arm, but she held him back with a last gesture of protest. "I can't—I can't—not that—you don't know Gwen: you must n't ask me!"

"I *must* ask you—you must obey me," he persisted, though infected at heart by her own fear.

Her voice sank to a whisper: "And if she refuses"—but, "Oh, trust me—trust me!" he could only insist in return; and yielding to his touch, she let him lead her back in silence to the edge of the square.

In the cab they continued to remain silent through the brief drive which carried them to the illuminated portals of the Stepneys' hotel. Here he left her outside, in the darkness of the raised hood, while his name was sent up to Stepney, and he paced the showy hall, awaiting the latter's descent. Ten minutes later the two men passed out together between the gold-laced custodians of the threshold; but in the vestibule Stepney drew up with a last flare of reluctance.

"It 's understood, then?" he stipulated nervously, with his hand on Selden's arm. "She leaves tomorrow by the early train—and my wife 's asleep, and can't be disturbed."

IV

The blinds of Mrs. Peniston's drawing-room were drawn down against the oppressive June sun, and in the sultry twilight the faces of her assembled relatives took on a fitting shadow of bereavement.

They were all there: Van Alstynes, Stepneys and Melsons—even a stray Peniston or two, indicating, by a greater latitude in dress and manner, the fact of remoter relationship and more settled hopes. The Peniston side was, in fact, secure in the knowledge that the bulk of Mr. Peniston's property "went back"; while the direct connection hung suspended on the disposal of his widow's private fortune and on the uncertainty of its extent. Jack Stepney, in his new character as the richest nephew, tacitly took the lead, emphasizing his importance by the deeper gloss of his mourning and the subdued authority of his manner; while his wife's bored attitude and frivolous gown proclaimed the heiress's disregard of the insignificant interests at stake. Old Ned Van Alstyne, seated next to her in a coat that made affliction dapper, twirled his white moustache to conceal the eager twitch of his lips; and Grace Stepney, red-nosed and smelling of crape, whispered emotionally to Mrs. Herbert Melson: "I could n't *bear* to see the Niagara anywhere else!"

A rustle of weeds and quick turning of heads hailed the opening of the door, and Lily Bart appeared, tall and noble in her black dress, with Gerty Farish at her side. The women's faces, as she paused interrogatively on the threshold, were a study in hesitation. One or two made faint motions of recognition, which might have been subdued either by the solemnity of the scene, or by the doubt as to how far the others meant to go; Mrs. Jack Stepney gave a careless nod, and Grace Stepney, with a sepulchral gesture, indicated a seat at her side. But Lily, ignoring the invitation, as well as Jack Stepney's official attempt to direct her, moved across the room with her smooth free gait, and seated herself in a chair which seemed to have been purposely placed apart from the others.

It was the first time that she had faced her family since her return from Europe, two weeks earlier; but if she perceived any uncertainty in their welcome, it served only to add a tinge of irony to the usual composure of her bearing. The shock of dismay with which, on the dock, she had heard from Gerty Farish of Mrs. Peniston's sudden death, had been mitigated, almost at once, by the irrepressible thought that now, at last, she would be able to pay her debts. She had looked forward with considerable uneasiness to her first encounter with her aunt. Mrs. Peniston had vehemently opposed her niece's departure with the Dorsets, and had marked her continued disapproval by not writing during Lily's absence. The certainty that she had heard of the rupture with the Dorsets made the prospect of the meeting more formidable; and how should Lily have repressed a quick sense of relief at the thought that, instead of undergoing the anticipated ordeal, she had only to enter gracefully on a long-assured inheritance? It had been, in the consecrated phrase, "always understood" that Mrs. Peniston was to provide handsomely for her niece; and in the latter's mind the understanding had long since crystallized into fact.

"She gets everything, of course—I don't see what we 're here for," Mrs. Jack Stepney remarked with careless loudness to Ned Van Alstyne; and the latter's deprecating murmur— "Julia was always a just woman"— might have been interpreted as signifying either acquiescence or doubt.

"Well, it 's only about four hundred thousand," Mrs. Stepney rejoined with a yawn; and Grace Stepney, in the silence produced by the lawyer's preliminary cough, was heard to sob out: "They won't find a towel missing—I went over them with her the very day——"

Lily, oppressed by the close atmosphere, and the stifling odour of fresh mourning, felt her attention straying as Mrs. Peniston's lawyer, solemnly erect behind the Buhl table at the end of the room, began to rattle through the preamble of the will.

"It 's like being in church," she reflected, wondering vaguely where Gwen Stepney had got such an awful hat. Then she noticed how stout Jack had grown—he would soon be almost as plethoric as Herbert Melson, who sat a few feet off, breathing puffily as he leaned his black-gloved hands on his stick.

"I wonder why rich people always grow fat—I suppose it 's because there 's nothing to worry them. If I inherit, I shall have to be careful of my figure," she mused, while the lawyer droned on through a labyrinth of legacies. The servants came first, then a few charitable institutions, then several remoter Melsons and Stepneys, who stirred consciously as their names rang out, and then subsided into a state of impassiveness befitting the solemnity of the occasion. Ned Van Alstyne, Jack Stepney, and a cousin or two followed, each coupled with the mention of a few thousands: Lily wondered that Grace Stepney was not among them. Then she heard her own name—"to my niece Lily Bart ten thousand dollars—" and after that the lawyer again lost himself in a coil of unintelligible periods, from which the concluding phrase flashed out with startling distinctness: "and the residue of my estate to my dear cousin and name-sake, Grace Julia Stepney."

There was a subdued gasp of surprise, a rapid turning of heads, and a surging of sable figures toward the corner in which Miss Stepney wailed out her sense of unworthiness through the crumpled ball of a black-edged handkerchief.

Lily stood apart from the general movement, feeling herself for the first time utterly alone. No one looked at her, no one seemed aware of her presence; she was probing the very depths of insignificance. And under her sense of the collective indifference came the acuter pang of hopes deceived. Disinherited—she had been disinherited—and for Grace Stepney! She met Gerty's lamentable eyes, fixed on her in a despairing effort at consolation, and the look brought her to herself. There was something to be done before she left the house: to be done with all the nobility she knew how to put into such gestures. She advanced to the group about Miss Stepney, and holding out her hand said simply: "Dear Grace, I am so glad."

The other ladies had fallen back at her approach, and a space created itself about her. It widened as she turned to go, and no one advanced to fill it up. She paused a moment, glancing about her, calmly taking the measure of her situation. She heard some one ask a question about the date of the will; she caught a fragment of the lawyer's answer—something about a sudden summons, and an "earlier instrument." Then the tide of dispersal began to drift past her; Mrs. Jack Stepney and Mrs.

Herbert Melson stood on the doorstep awaiting their motor; a sympa-
thizing group escorted Grace Stepney to the cab it was felt to be fitting
she should take, though she lived but a street or two away; and Miss
Bart and Gerty found themselves almost alone in the purple drawing-
room, which more than ever, in its stuffy dimness, resembled a well-
kept family vault, in which the last corpse had just been decently deposited.

In Gerty Farish's sitting-room, whither a hansom had carried the two
friends, Lily dropped into a chair with a faint sound of laughter: it struck
her as a humorous coincidence that her aunt's legacy should so nearly
represent the amount of her debt to Trenor. The need of discharging
that debt had reasserted itself with increased urgency since her return to
America, and she spoke her first thought in saying to the anxiously hovering Gerty: "I wonder when the legacies will be paid."

But Miss Farish could not pause over the legacies; she broke into a
larger indignation. "Oh, Lily, it 's unjust; it 's cruel — Grace Stepney
must *feel* she has no right to all that money!"

"Any one who knew how to please Aunt Julia has a right to her
money," Miss Bart rejoined philosophically.

"But she was devoted to you — she led every one to think —— "
Gerty checked herself in evident embarrassment, and Miss Bart turned
to her with a direct look. "Gerty, be honest: this will was made only six
weeks ago. Had she heard of my break with the Dorsets?"

"Every one heard, of course, that there had been some disagreement — some misunderstanding —— "

"Did she hear that Bertha turned me off the yacht?"

"Lily!"

"That was what happened, you know. She said I was trying to marry
George Dorset. She did it to make him think she was jealous. Is n't that
what she told Gwen Stepney?"

"I don't know — I don't listen to such horrors."

"I *must* listen to them — I must know where I stand." She paused,
and again sounded a faint note of derision. "Did you notice the women?
They were afraid to snub me while they thought I was going to get the
money — afterward they scuttled off as if I had the plague." Gerty remained silent, and she continued: "I stayed on to see what would happen. They took their cue from Gwen Stepney and Lulu Melson — I saw
them watching to see what Gwen would do. — Gerty, I must know just
what is being said of me."

"I tell you I don't listen——"

"One hears such things without listening." She rose and laid her resolute hands on Miss Farish's shoulders. "Gerty, are people going to cut me?"

"Your *friends*, Lily—how can you think it?"

"Who are one's friends at such a time? Who, but you, you poor trustful darling? And heaven knows what *you* suspect me of!" She kissed Gerty with a whimsical murmur. "You 'd never let it make any difference—but then you 're fond of criminals, Gerty! How about the irreclaimable ones, though? For I 'm absolutely impenitent, you know."

She drew herself up to the full height of her slender majesty, towering like some dark angel of defiance above the troubled Gerty, who could only falter out: "Lily, Lily—how can you laugh about such things?"

"So as not to weep, perhaps. But no—I 'm not of the tearful order. I discovered early that crying makes my nose red, and the knowledge has helped me through several painful episodes." She took a restless turn about the room, and then, reseating herself, lifted the bright mockery of her eyes to Gerty's anxious countenance.

"I should n't have minded, you know, if I 'd got the money—" and at Miss Farish's protesting "Oh!" she repeated calmly: "Not a straw, my dear; for, in the first place, they would n't have quite dared to ignore me; and if they had, it would n't have mattered, because I should have been independent of them. But now—!" The irony faded from her eyes, and she bent a clouded faced upon her friend.

"How can you talk so, Lily? Of course the money ought to have been yours, but after all that makes no difference. The important thing——" Gerty paused, and then continued firmly: "The important thing is that you should clear yourself—should tell your friends the whole truth."

"The whole truth?" Miss Bart laughed. "What is truth? Where a woman is concerned, it 's the story that 's easiest to believe. In this case it 's a great deal easier to believe Bertha Dorset's story than mine, because she has a big house and an opera box, and it 's convenient to be on good terms with her."

Miss Farish still fixed her with an anxious gaze. "But what *is* your story, Lily? I don't believe any one knows it yet."

"My story?—I don't believe I know it myself. You see I never thought of preparing a version in advance as Bertha did—and if I had, I don't think I should take the trouble to use it now."

But Gerty continued with her quiet reasonableness: "I don't want a version prepared in advance—but I want you to tell me exactly what happened from the beginning."

"From the beginning?" Miss Bart gently mimicked her. "Dear Gerty, how little imagination you good people have! Why, the beginning was in my cradle, I suppose—in the way I was brought up, and the things I was taught to care for. Or no—I won't blame anybody for my faults: I 'll say it was in my blood, that I got it from some wicked pleasure-loving ancestress, who reacted against the homely virtues of New Amsterdam, and wanted to be back at the court of the Charleses!" And as Miss Farish continued to press her with troubled eyes, she went on impatiently: "You asked me just now for the truth—well, the truth about any girl is that once she 's talked about she 's done for; and the more she explains her case the worse it looks.—My good Gerty, you don't happen to have a cigarette about you?"

In her stuffy room at the hotel to which she had gone on landing, Lily Bart that evening reviewed her situation. It was the last week in June, and none of her friends were in town. The few relatives who had stayed on, or returned, for the reading of Mrs. Peniston's will, had taken flight again that afternoon to Newport or Long Island; and not one of them had made any proffer of hospitality to Lily. For the first time in her life she found herself utterly alone except for Gerty Farish. Even at the actual moment of her break with the Dorsets she had not had so keen a sense of its consequences, for the Duchess of Beltshire, hearing of the catastrophe from Lord Hubert, had instantly offered her protection, and under her sheltering wing Lily had made an almost triumphant progress to London. There she had been sorely tempted to linger on in a society which asked of her only to amuse and charm it, without enquiring too curiously how she had acquired her gift for doing so; but Selden, before they parted, had pressed on her the urgent need of returning at once to her aunt, and Lord Hubert, when he presently reappeared in London, abounded in the same counsel. Lily did not need to be told that the Duchess's championship was not the best road to social rehabilitation, and as she was besides aware that her noble defender might at any moment drop her in favour of a new *protégée,* she reluctantly decided to return to America. But she had not been ten minutes on her native shore before she realized that she had delayed too long to regain it. The Dorsets, the Stepneys, the Brys—all the actors and witnesses in the miserable drama—had preceded her with their version of the case; and, even had she seen the least chance of gaining a hearing for her own, some obscure disdain and reluctance would have restrained her. She knew it was not by explanations and counter-charges that she could ever hope to recover her lost standing; but even had she felt the least trust in their efficacy, she would still have been held back by the feeling which had kept her from defending herself to Gerty Farish—a feeling that was half pride and half humiliation. For though she knew she had been ruthlessly sacrificed to Bertha Dorset's determination to win back her husband, and though her own relation to Dorset had been that of the merest good-fellowship, yet she had been perfectly aware from the outset that her part in the affair was, as Carry Fisher brutally put it, to distract Dorset's attention from his wife. That was what she was "there for": it was the price she had chosen to pay for three months of luxury and freedom from care. Her habit of resolutely facing the facts, in her rare moments of introspection, did not now allow her to put any false gloss on the situation. She had suffered for the very faithfulness with which she had carried out her part of the tacit compact, but the part was not a handsome one at best, and she saw it now in all the ugliness of failure.

She saw, too, in the same uncompromising light, the train of consequences resulting from that failure; and these became clearer to her with every day of her weary lingering in town. She stayed on partly for the comfort of Gerty Farish's nearness, and partly for lack of knowing where to go. She understood well enough the nature of the task before her. She must set out to regain, little by little, the position she had lost; and the first step in the tedious task was to find out, as soon as possible, on how many of her friends she could count. Her hopes were mainly centred on Mrs. Trenor, who had treasures of easy-going tolerance for those who were amusing or useful to her, and in the noisy rush of whose existence the still small voice of detraction was slow to make itself heard. But Judy, though she must have been apprised of Miss Bart's return, had not even recognized it by the formal note of condolence which her friend's bereavement demanded. Any advance on Lily's side might have been perilous: there was nothing to do but to trust to the happy chance of an accidental meeting, and Lily knew that, even so late in the season, there was always a hope of running across her friends in their frequent passages through town.

To this end she assiduously showed herself at the restaurants they frequented, where, attended by the troubled Gerty, she lunched luxuriously, as she said, on her expectations.

"My dear Gerty, you would n't have me let the head-waiter see that I 've nothing to live on but Aunt Julia's legacy? Think of Grace

Stepney's satisfaction if she came in and found us lunching on cold mutton and tea! What sweet shall we have today, dear — *Coupe Jacques* or
Pêches à la Melba?"

She dropped the *menu* abruptly, with a quick heightening of colour,
and Gerty, following her glance, was aware of the advance, from an
inner room, of a party headed by Mrs. Trenor and Carry Fisher. It was
impossible for these ladies and their companions — among whom Lily
had at once distinguished both Trenor and Rosedale — not to pass, in
going out, the table at which the two girls were seated; and Gerty's
sense of the fact betrayed itself in the helpless trepidation of her manner.
Miss Bart, on the contrary, borne forward on the wave of her buoyant
grace, and neither shrinking from her friends nor appearing to lie in wait
for them, gave to the encounter the touch of naturalness which she
could impart to the most strained situations. Such embarrassment as
was shown was on Mrs. Trenor's side, and manifested itself in the
mingling of exaggerated warmth with imperceptible reservations. Her
loudly affirmed pleasure at seeing Miss Bart took the form of a nebulous
generalization, which included neither enquiries as to her future nor the
expression of a definite wish to see her again. Lily, well-versed in the
language of these omissions, knew that they were equally intelligible to
the other members of the party: even Rosedale, flushed as he was with
the importance of keeping such company, at once took the temperature
of Mrs. Trenor's cordiality, and reflected it in his off-hand greeting of
Miss Bart. Trenor, red and uncomfortable, had cut short his salutations
on the pretext of a word to say to the head-waiter; and the rest of the
group soon melted away in Mrs. Trenor's wake.

It was over in a moment — the waiter, *menu* in hand, still hung on
the result of the choice between *Coupe Jacques* and *Pêches à la Melba* —
but Miss Bart, in the interval, had taken the measure of her fate. Where
Judy Trenor led, all the world would follow; and Lily had the doomed
sense of the castaway who has signalled in vain to fleeing sails.

In a flash she remembered Mrs. Trenor's complaints of Carry
Fisher's rapacity, and saw that they denoted an unexpected acquaintance with her husband's private affairs. In the large tumultuous disorder
of the life at Bellomont, where no one seemed to have time to observe
any one else, and private aims and personal interests were swept along
unheeded in the rush of collective activities, Lily had fancied herself
sheltered from inconvenient scrutiny; but if Judy knew when Mrs.
Fisher borrowed money of her husband, was she likely to ignore the
same transaction on Lily's part? If she was careless of his affections she

was plainly jealous of his pocket; and in that fact Lily read the explanation of her rebuff. The immediate result of these conclusions was the passionate resolve to pay back her debt to Trenor. That obligation discharged, she would have but a thousand dollars of Mrs. Peniston's legacy left, and nothing to live on but her own small income, which was considerably less than Gerty Farish's wretched pittance; but this consideration gave way to the imperative claim of her wounded pride. She must be quits with the Trenors first; after that she would take thought for the future.

In her ignorance of legal procrastinations she had supposed that her legacy would be paid over within a few days of the reading of her aunt's will; and after an interval of anxious suspense, she wrote to enquire the cause of the delay. There was another interval before Mrs. Peniston's lawyer, who was also one of the executors, replied to the effect that, some questions having arisen relative to the interpretation of the will, he and his associates might not be in a position to pay the legacies till the close of the twelvemonth legally allotted for their settlement. Bewildered and indignant, Lily resolved to try the effect of a personal appeal; but she returned from her expedition with a sense of the powerlessness of beauty and charm against the unfeeling processes of the law. It seemed intolerable to live on for another year under the weight of the debt; and in her extremity she decided to turn to Miss Stepney, who still lingered in town, immersed in the delectable duty of "going over" her benefactress's effects. It was bitter enough for Lily to ask a favour of Grace Stepney, but the alternative was bitterer still; and one morning she presented herself at Mrs. Peniston's, where Grace, for the facilitation of her pious task, had taken up a provisional abode.

The strangeness of entering as a suppliant the house where she had so long commanded, increased Lily's desire to shorten the ordeal; and when Miss Stepney entered the darkened drawing-room, rustling with the best quality of crape, her visitor went straight to the point: would she be willing to advance the amount of the expected legacy?

Grace, in reply, wept and wondered at the request, bemoaned the inexorableness of the law, and was astonished that Lily had not realized the exact similarity of their positions. Did she think that only the payment of the legacies had been delayed? Why, Miss Stepney herself had not received a penny of her inheritance, and was paying rent—yes, actually!—for the privilege of living in a house that belonged to her. She was sure it was not what poor dear cousin Julia would have wished— she had told the executors so to their faces; but they were inaccessible to reason, and there was nothing to do but to wait. Let Lily take example by her, and be patient—let them both remember how beautifully patient cousin Julia had always been.

Lily made a movement which showed her imperfect assimilation of this example. "But you will have everything, Grace—it would be easy for you to borrow ten times the amount I am asking for."

"Borrow—easy for me to borrow?" Grace Stepney rose up before her in sable wrath. "Do you imagine for a moment that I would raise money on my expectations from cousin Julia, when I know so well her unspeakable horror of every transaction of the sort? Why, Lily, if you must know the truth, it was the idea of your being in debt that brought on her illness—you remember she had a slight attack before you sailed. Oh, I don't know the particulars, of course—I don't *want* to know them—but there were rumours about your affairs that made her most unhappy—no one could be with her without seeing that. I can't help it if you are offended by my telling you this now—if I can do anything to make you realize the folly of your course, and how deeply *she* disapproved of it, I shall feel it is the truest way of making up to you for her loss."

V

It seemed to Lily, as Mrs. Peniston's door closed on her, that she was taking a final leave of her old life. The future stretched before her dull and bare as the deserted length of Fifth Avenue, and opportunities showed as meagrely as the few cabs trailing in quest of fares that did not come. The completeness of the analogy was, however, disturbed as she reached the sidewalk by the rapid approach of a hansom which pulled up at sight of her.

From beneath its luggage-laden top, she caught the wave of a signalling hand; and the next moment Mrs. Fisher, springing to the street, had folded her in a demonstrative embrace.

"My dear, you don't mean to say you 're still in town? When I saw you the other day at Sherry's I did n't have time to ask——" She broke off, and added with a burst of frankness: "The truth is I was *horrid*, Lily, and I 've wanted to tell you so ever since."

"Oh——" Miss Bart protested, drawing back from her penitent clasp; but Mrs. Fisher went on with her usual directness: "Look here, Lily, don't let 's beat about the bush: half the trouble in life is caused by pretending there is n't any. That 's not my way, and I can only say I 'm thoroughly ashamed of myself for following the other women's lead.

But we 'll talk of that by and bye — tell me now where you 're staying and what your plans are. I don't suppose you 're keeping house in there with Grace Stepney, eh? — and it struck me you might be rather at loose ends."

In Lily's present mood there was no resisting the honest friendliness of this appeal, and she said with a smile: "I *am* at loose ends for the moment, but Gerty Farish is still in town, and she 's good enough to let me be with her whenever she can spare the time."

Mrs. Fisher made a slight grimace. "H'm — that 's a temperate joy. Oh, I know — Gerty 's a trump, and worth all the rest of us put together; but *à la longue* you 're used to a little higher seasoning, are n't you, dear? And besides, I suppose she 'll be off herself before long — the first of August, you say? Well, look here, you can't spend your summer in town; we 'll talk of that later too. But meanwhile, what do you say to putting a few things in a trunk and coming down with me to the Sam Gormers' tonight?"

And as Lily stared at the breathless suddenness of the suggestion, she continued with her easy laugh: "You don't know them and they don't know you; but that don't make a rap of difference. They 've taken the Van Alstyne place at Roslyn, and I 've got *carte blanche* to bring my friends down there — the more the merrier. They do things awfully well, and there 's to be rather a jolly party there this week —— " she broke off, checked by an undefinable change in Miss Bart's expression. "Oh, I don't mean *your* particular set, you know: rather a different crowd, but very good fun. The fact is, the Gormers have struck out on a line of their own: what they want is to have a good time, and to have it in their own way. They gave the other thing a few months' trial, under my distinguished auspices, and they were really doing extremely well — getting on a good deal faster than the Brys, just because they did n't care as much — but suddenly they decided that the whole business bored them, and that what they wanted was a crowd they could really feel at home with. Rather original of them, don't you think so? Mattie Gormer *has* got aspirations still; women always have; but she 's awfully easy-going, and Sam won't be bothered, and they both like to be the most important people in sight, so they 've started a sort of continuous performance of their own, a kind of social Coney Island, where everybody is welcome who can make noise enough and does n't put on airs. *I* think it 's awfully good fun myself — some of the artistic set, you know, any pretty actress that 's going, and so on. This week, for instance, they have Audrey Anstell, who made such a hit last spring in 'The Winning of Winny'; and Paul Morpeth — he 's painting Mattie Gormer — and the

Dick Bellingers, and Kate Corby—well, every one you can think of who 's jolly and makes a row. Now don't stand there with your nose in the air, my dear—it will be a good deal better than a broiling Sunday in town, and you 'll find clever people as well as noisy ones—Morpeth, who admires Mattie enormously, always brings one or two of his set."

Mrs. Fisher drew Lily toward the hansom with friendly authority. "Jump in now, there 's a dear, and we 'll drive round to your hotel and have your things packed, and then we 'll have tea, and the two maids can meet us at the train."

It was a good deal better than a broiling Sunday in town—of that no doubt remained to Lily as, reclining in the shade of a leafy verandah, she looked seaward across a stretch of greensward picturesquely dotted with groups of ladies in lace raiment and men in tennis flannels. The huge Van Alstyne house and its rambling dependencies were packed to their fullest capacity with the Gormers' week-end guests, who now, in the radiance of the Sunday forenoon, were dispersing themselves over the grounds in quest of the various distractions the place afforded: distractions ranging from tennis-courts to shooting-galleries, from bridge and whiskey within doors to motors and steam-launches without. Lily had the odd sense of having been caught up into the crowd as carelessly as a passenger is gathered in by an express train. The blonde and genial Mrs. Gormer might, indeed, have figured the conductor, calmly assigning seats to the rush of travellers, while Carry Fisher represented the porter pushing their bags into place, giving them their numbers for the dining-car, and warning them when their station was at hand. The train, meanwhile, had scarcely slackened speed—life whizzed on with a deafening rattle and roar, in which one traveller at least found a welcome refuge from the sound of her own thoughts.

The Gormer *milieu* represented a social out-skirt which Lily had always fastidiously avoided; but it struck her, now that she was in it, as only a flamboyant copy of her own world, a caricature approximating the real thing as the "society play" approaches the manners of the drawing-room. The people about her were doing the same things as the Trenors, the Van Osburghs, and the Dorsets: the difference lay in a hundred shades of aspect and manner, from the pattern of the men's waistcoats to the inflexion of the women's voices. Everything was pitched in a higher key, and there was more of each thing: more noise, more colour, more champagne, more familiarity—but also greater good-nature, less rivalry, and a fresher capacity for enjoyment.

Miss Bart's arrival had been welcomed with an uncritical friendliness that first irritated her pride and then brought her to a sharp sense of her own situation—of the place in life which, for the moment, she must accept and make the best of. These people knew her story—of that her first long talk with Carry Fisher had left no doubt: she was publicly branded as the heroine of a "queer" episode—but instead of shrinking from her as her own friends had done, they received her without question into the easy promiscuity of their lives. They swallowed her past as easily as they did Miss Anstell's, and with no apparent sense of any difference in the size of the mouthful: all they asked was that she should—in her own way, for they recognized a diversity of gifts—contribute as much to the general amusement as that graceful actress, whose talents, when off the stage, were of the most varied order. Lily felt at once that any tendency to be "stuck-up," to mark a sense of differences and distinctions, would be fatal to her continuance in the Gormer set. To be taken in on such terms—and into such a world!—was hard enough to the lingering pride in her; but she realized, with a pang of self-contempt, that to be excluded from it would, after all, be harder still. For, almost at once, she had felt the insidious charm of slipping back into a life where every material difficulty was smoothed away. The sudden escape from a stifling hotel in a dusty deserted city to the space and luxury of a great country-house fanned by sea breezes, had produced a state of moral lassitude agreeable enough after the nervous tension and physical discomfort of the past weeks. For the moment she must yield to the refreshment her senses craved—after that she would reconsider her situation, and take counsel with her dignity. Her enjoyment of her surroundings was, indeed, tinged by the unpleasant consideration that she was accepting the hospitality and courting the approval of people she had disdained under other conditions. But she was growing less sensitive on such points: a hard glaze of indifference was fast forming over her delicacies and susceptibilities, and each concession to expediency hardened the surface a little more.

On the Monday, when the party disbanded with uproarious adieux, the return to town threw into stronger relief the charms of the life she was leaving. The other guests were dispersing to take up the same existence in a different setting: some at Newport, some at Bar Harbour, some in the elaborate rusticity of an Adirondack camp. Even Gerty Farish, who welcomed Lily's return with tender solicitude, would soon be preparing to join the aunt with whom she spent her summers on Lake George: only Lily herself remained without plan or purpose, stranded in a backwater of the great current of pleasure. But Carry Fisher, who had insisted on transporting her to her own house, where she herself was to perch for a day or two on the way to the Brys' camp, came to the rescue with a new suggestion.

"Look here, Lily—I 'll tell you what it is: I want you to take my place with Mattie Gormer this summer. They 're taking a party out to Alaska next month in their private car, and Mattie, who is the laziest woman alive, wants me to go with them, and relieve her of the bother of arranging things; but the Brys want me too—oh, yes, we 've made it up: did n't I tell you?—and, to put it frankly, though I like the Gormers best, there 's more profit for me in the Brys. The fact is, they want to try Newport this summer, and if I can make it a success for them they— well, they 'll make it a success for *me*." Mrs. Fisher clasped her hands enthusiastically. "Do you know, Lily, the more I think of my idea the better I like it—quite as much for you as for myself. The Gormers have both taken a tremendous fancy to you, and the trip to Alaska is—well— the very thing I should want for you just at present."

Miss Bart lifted her eyes with a keen glance. "To take me out of my friends' way, you mean?" she said quietly; and Mrs. Fisher responded with a deprecating kiss: "To keep you out of their sight till they realize how much they miss you."

Miss Bart went with the Gormers to Alaska; and the expedition, if it did not produce the effect anticipated by her friend, had at least the negative advantage of removing her from the fiery centre of criticism and discussion. Gerty Farish had opposed the plan with all the energy of her some- what inarticulate nature. She had even offered to give up her visit to Lake George, and remain in town with Miss Bart, if the latter would renounce her journey; but Lily could disguise her real distaste for this plan under a sufficiently valid reason.

"You dear innocent, don't you see," she protested, "that Carry is quite right, and that I must take up my usual life, and go about among people as much as possible? If my old friends choose to believe lies about me I shall have to make new ones, that 's all; and you know beg- gars must n't be choosers. Not that I don't like Mattie Gormer—I *do* like her: she 's kind and honest and unaffected; and don't you suppose I feel grateful to her for making me welcome at a time when, as you 've yourself seen, my own family have unanimously washed their hands of me?"

Gerty shook her head, mutely unconvinced. She felt not only that Lily was cheapening herself by making use of an intimacy she would never have cultivated from choice, but that, in drifting back now to her former manner of life, she was forfeiting her last chance of ever escaping from it. Gerty had but an obscure conception of what Lily's actual experience had been: but its consequences had established a lasting hold on her pity since the memorable night when she had offered up her own secret hope to her friend's extremity. To characters like Gerty's such a sacrifice constitutes a moral claim on the part of the person in whose behalf it has been made. Having once helped Lily, she must continue to help her; and helping her, must believe in her, because faith is the mainspring of such natures. But even if Miss Bart, after her renewed taste of the amenities of life, could have returned to the barrenness of a New York August, mitigated only by poor Gerty's presence, her worldly wisdom would have counselled her against such an act of abnegation. She knew that Carry Fisher was right: that an opportune absence might be the first step toward rehabilitation, and that, at any rate, to linger on in town out of season was a fatal admission of defeat.

From the Gormers' tumultuous progress across their native continent, she returned with an altered view of her situation. The renewed habit of luxury—the daily waking to an assured absence of care and presence of material ease—gradually blunted her appreciation of these values, and left her more conscious of the void they could not fill. Mattie Gormer's undiscriminating good-nature, and the slap-dash sociability of her friends, who treated Lily precisely as they treated each other—all these characteristic notes of difference began to wear upon her endurance; and the more she saw to criticize in her companions, the less justification she found for making use of them. The longing to get back to her former surroundings hardened to a fixed idea; but with the strengthening of her purpose came the inevitable perception that, to attain it, she must exact fresh concessions from her pride. These, for the moment, took the unpleasant form of continuing to cling to her hosts after their return from Alaska. Little as she was in the key of their *milieu,* her immense social facility, her long habit of adapting herself to others without suffering her own outline to be blurred, the skilled manipulation of all the polished implements of her craft, had won for her an important place in the Gormer group. If their resonant hilarity could never be hers, she contributed a note of easy elegance more valuable to Mattie Gormer than the louder passages of the band. Sam Gormer and his special cronies stood indeed a little in awe of her; but Mattie's following, headed by Paul Morpeth, made her feel that they prized her for the very qualities they most conspicuously lacked. If Morpeth, whose social indolence was as great as his artistic activity, had abandoned himself to the easy current of the Gormer existence, where the minor exactions of politeness where unknown or ignored, and a man could either break his engagements, or keep them in a painting-jacket and slippers, he still preserved his sense of differences, and his appreciation of graces he had no time to cultivate. During the preparations for the Brys' *tableaux* he had been immensely struck by Lily's plastic possibilities — "not the face: too self-controlled for expression; but the rest of her — gad, what a model she 'd make!" — and though his abhorrence of the world in which he had seen her was too great for him to think of seeking her there, he was fully alive to the privilege of having her to look at and listen to while he lounged in Mattie Gormer's dishevelled drawing-room.

Lily had thus formed, in the tumult of her surroundings, a little nucleus of friendly relations which mitigated the crudeness of her course in lingering with the Gormers after their return. Nor was she without pale glimpses of her own world, especially since the breaking-up of the Newport season had set the social current once more toward Long Island. Kate Corby, whose tastes made her as promiscuous as Carry Fisher was rendered by her necessities, occasionally descended on the Gormers, where, after a first stare of surprise, she took Lily's presence almost too much as a matter of course. Mrs. Fisher, too, appearing frequently in the neighbourhood, drove over to impart her experiences and give Lily what she called the latest report from the weather-bureau; and the latter, who had never directly invited her confidence, could yet talk with her more freely than with Gerty Farish, in whose presence it was impossible even to admit the existence of much that Mrs. Fisher conveniently took for granted.

Mrs. Fisher, moreover, had no embarrassing curiosity. She did not wish to probe the inwardness of Lily's situation, but simply to view it from the outside, and draw her conclusions accordingly; and these conclusions, at the end of a confidential talk, she summed up to her friend in the succinct remark: "You must marry as soon as you can."

Lily uttered a faint laugh — for once Mrs. Fisher lacked originality. "Do you mean, like Gerty Farish, to recommend the unfailing panacea of 'a good man's love'?"

"No — I don't think either of my candidates would answer to that description," said Mrs. Fisher after a pause of reflection.

"Either? Are there actually two?"

"Well, perhaps I ought to say one and a half — for the moment."

Miss Bart received this with increasing amusement. "Other things being equal, I think I should prefer a half-husband: who is he?"

"Don't fly out at me till you hear my reasons — George Dorset."

"Oh——" Lily murmured reproachfully; but Mrs. Fisher pressed

on unrebuffed. "Well, why not? They had a few weeks' honeymoon when they first got back from Europe, but now things are going badly with them again. Bertha has been behaving more than ever like a mad-woman, and George's powers of credulity are very nearly exhausted. They 're at their place here, you know, and I spent last Sunday with them. It was a ghastly party—no one else but poor Neddy Silverton, who looks like a galley-slave (they used to talk of my making that poor boy unhappy!)—and after luncheon George carried me off on a long walk, and told me the end would have to come soon."

Miss Bart made an incredulous gesture. "As far as that goes, the end will never come—Bertha will always know how to get him back when she wants him."

Mrs. Fisher continued to observe her tentatively. "Not if he has any one else to turn to! Yes—that 's just what it comes to: the poor creature can't stand alone. And I remember him such a good fellow, full of life and enthusiasm." She paused, and went on, dropping her glance from Lily's: "He would n't stay with her ten minutes if he *knew*——"

"Knew——?" Miss Bart repeated.

"What *you* must, for instance—with the opportunities you 've had! If he had positive proof, I mean——"

Lily interrupted her with a deep blush of displeasure. "Please let us drop the subject, Carry: it 's too odious to me." And to divert her companion's attention she added, with an attempt at lightness: "And your second candidate? We must not forget him."

Mrs. Fisher echoed her laugh. "I wonder if you 'll cry out just as loud if I say—Sim Rosedale?"

Miss Bart did not cry out: she sat silent, gazing thoughtfully at her friend. The suggestion, in truth, gave expression to a possibility which, in the last weeks, had more than once recurred to her; but after a moment she said carelessly: "Mr. Rosedale wants a wife who can establish him in the bosom of the Van Osburghs and Trenors."

Mrs. Fisher caught her up eagerly. "And so *you* could—with his money! Don't you see how beautifully it would work out for you both?"

"I don't see any way of making him see it," Lily returned, with a laugh intended to dismiss the subject.

But in reality it lingered with her long after Mrs. Fisher had taken leave. She had seen very little of Rosedale since her annexation by the Gormers, for he was still steadily bent on penetrating to the inner Paradise from which she was now excluded; but once or twice, when nothing better offered, he had turned up for a Sunday, and on these

occasions he had left her in no doubt as to his view of her situation.
That he still admired her was, more than ever, offensively evident; for in
the Gormer circle, where he expanded as in his native element, there
were no puzzling conventions to check the full expression of his approval. But it was in the quality of his admiration that she read his
shrewd estimate of her case. He enjoyed letting the Gormers see that he
had known "Miss Lily"—she was "Miss Lily" to him now—before
they had had the faintest social existence: enjoyed more especially im-
pressing Paul Morpeth with the distance to which their intimacy dated
back. But he let it be felt that that intimacy was a mere ripple on the
surface of a rushing social current, the kind of relaxation which a man of
large interests and manifold preoccupations permits himself in his hours
of ease.

The necessity of accepting this view of their past relation, and of
meeting it in the key of pleasantry prevalent among her new friends, was
deeply humiliating to Lily. But she dared less than ever to quarrel with
Rosedale. She suspected that her rejection rankled among the most unforgettable of his rebuffs, and the fact that he knew something of her
wretched transaction with Trenor, and was sure to put the basest construction on it, seemed to place her hopelessly in his power. Yet at Carry
Fisher's suggestion a new hope had stirred in her. Much as she disliked
Rosedale, she no longer absolutely despised him. For he was gradually
attaining his object in life, and that, to Lily, was always less despicable
than to miss it. With the slow unalterable persistency which she had
always felt in him, he was making his way through the dense mass of
social antagonisms. Already his wealth, and the masterly use he had
made of it, were giving him an enviable prominence in the world of
affairs, and placing Wall Street under obligations which only Fifth Avenue could repay. In response to these claims, his name began to figure
on municipal committees and charitable boards; he appeared at ban-
quets to distinguished strangers, and his candidacy at one of the fashionable clubs was discussed with diminishing opposition. He had figured once or twice at the Trenor dinners, and had learned to speak with
just the right note of disdain of the big Van Osburgh crushes; and all he
now needed was a wife whose affiliations would shorten the last tedious
steps of his ascent. It was with that object that, a year earlier, he had
fixed his affections on Miss Bart; but in the interval he had mounted
nearer to the goal, while she had lost the power to abbreviate the remaining steps of the way. All this she saw with the clearness of vision
that came to her in moments of despondency. It was success that dazzled her—she could distinguish facts plainly enough in the twilight of

failure. And the twilight, as she now sought to pierce it, was gradually lighted by a faint spark of reassurance. Under the utilitarian motive of Rosedale's wooing she had felt, clearly enough, the heat of personal inclination. She would not have detested him so heartily had she not known that he dared to admire her. What, then, if the passion persisted, though the other motive had ceased to sustain it? She had never even tried to please him—he had been drawn to her in spite of her manifest disdain. What if she now chose to exert the power which, even in its passive state, he had felt so strongly? What if she made him marry her for love, now that he had no other reason for marrying her?

VI

As became persons of their rising consequence, the Gormers were engaged in building a country-house on Long Island; and it was a part of Miss Bart's duty to attend her hostess on frequent visits of inspection to the new estate. There, while Mrs. Gormer plunged into problems of lighting and sanitation, Lily had leisure to wander, in the bright autumn air, along the tree-fringed bay to which the land declined. Little as she was addicted to solitude, there had come to be moments when it seemed a welcome escape from the empty noises of her life. She was weary of being swept passively along a current of pleasure and business in which she had no share; weary of seeing other people pursue amusement and squander money, while she felt herself of no more account among them than an expensive toy in the hands of a spoiled child.

It was in this frame of mind that, striking back from the shore one morning into the windings of an unfamiliar lane, she came suddenly upon the figure of George Dorset. The Dorset place was in the immediate neighbourhood of the Gormers' newly-acquired estate, and in her motor-flights thither with Mrs. Gormer, Lily had caught one or two passing glimpses of the couple; but they moved in so different an orbit that she had not considered the possibility of a direct encounter.

Dorset, swinging along with bent head, in moody abstraction, did not see Miss Bart till he was close upon her; but the sight, instead of bringing him to a halt, as she had half-expected, sent him toward her with an eagerness which found expression in his opening words.

"Miss Bart!—You 'll shake hands, won't you? I 've been hoping to meet you—I should have written to you if I 'd dared." His face, with its tossed red hair and straggling moustache, had a driven uneasy look, as though life had become an unceasing race between himself and the thoughts at his heels.

The look drew a word of compassionate greeting from Lily, and he pressed on, as if encouraged by her tone: "I wanted to apologize—to ask you to forgive me for the miserable part I played——"

She checked him with a quick gesture. "Don't let us speak of it: I was very sorry for you," she said, with a tinge of disdain which, as she instantly perceived, was not lost on him.

He flushed to his haggard eyes, flushed so cruelly that she repented the thrust. "You might well be; you don't know—you must let me explain. I was deceived: abominably deceived——"

"I am still more sorry for you, then," she interposed, without irony; "but you must see that I am not exactly the person with whom the subject can be discussed."

He met this with a look of genuine wonder. "Why not? Is n't it to you, of all people, that I owe an explanation——"

"No explanation is necessary: the situation was perfectly clear to me."

"Ah——" he murmured, his head drooping again, and his irresolute hand switching at the underbrush along the lane. But as Lily made a movement to pass on, he broke out with fresh vehemence: "Miss Bart, for God's sake don't turn from me! We used to be good friends—you were always kind to me—and you don't know how I need a friend now."

The lamentable weakness of the words roused a motion of pity in Lily's breast. She too needed friends—she had tasted the pang of loneliness; and her resentment of Bertha Dorset's cruelty softened her heart to the poor wretch who was after all the chief of Bertha's victims.

"I still wish to be kind; I feel no ill-will toward you," she said. "But you must understand that after what has happened we can't be friends again—we can't see each other."

"Ah, you *are* kind—you 're merciful—you always were!" He fixed his miserable gaze on her. "But why can't we be friends—why not, when I 've repented in dust and ashes? Is n't it hard that you should condemn me to suffer for the falseness, the treachery of others? I was punished enough at the time—is there to be no respite for me?"

"I should have thought you had found complete respite in the reconciliation which was effected at my expense," Lily began, with renewed impatience; but he broke in imploringly: "Don't put it in that way—when that 's been the worst of my punishment. My God! what could I do—was n't I powerless? You were singled out as a sacrifice: any word I might have said would have been turned against you——"

"I have told you I don't blame you; all I ask you to understand is that, after the use Bertha chose to make of me—after all that her behaviour has since implied—it 's impossible that you and I should meet."

He continued to stand before her, in his dogged weakness. "Is it—need it be? Might n't there be circumstances——?" he checked himself, slashing at the wayside weeds in a wider radius. Then he began again: "Miss Bart, listen—give me a minute. If we 're not to meet again, at least let me have a hearing now. You say we can't be friends after—after what has happened. But can't I at least appeal to your pity? Can't I move you if I ask you to think of me as a prisoner—a prisoner you alone can set free?"

Lily's inward start betrayed itself in a quick blush: was it possible that this was really the sense of Carry Fisher's adumbrations?

"I can't see how I can possibly be of any help to you," she murmured, drawing back a little from the mounting excitement of his look.

Her tone seemed to sober him, as it had so often done in his stormiest moments. The stubborn lines of his face relaxed, and he said, with an abrupt drop to docility: "You *would* see, if you 'd be as merciful as you used to be: and heaven knows I 've never needed it more!"

She paused a moment, moved in spite of herself by this reminder of her influence over him. Her fibres had been softened by suffering, and the sudden glimpse into his mocked and broken life disarmed her contempt for his weakness.

"I am very sorry for you—I would help you willingly; but you must have other friends, other advisers."

"I never had a friend like you," he answered simply. "And besides—can't you see?—you 're the only person"—his voice dropped to a whisper—"the only person who knows."

Again she felt her colour change; again her heart rose in precipitate throbs to meet what she felt was coming.

He lifted his eyes to her entreatingly. "You do see, don't you? You understand? I 'm desperate—I 'm at the end of my tether. I want to be free, and you can free me. I know you can. You don't want to keep me bound fast in hell, do you? You can't want to take such a vengeance as that. You were always kind—your eyes are kind now. You say you 're sorry for me. Well, it rests with you to show it; and heaven knows there 's nothing to keep you back. You understand, of course—there would n't be a hint of publicity—not a sound or a syllable to connect you with the thing. It would never come to that, you know: all I need is

to be able to say definitely: 'I know this—and this—and this'—and
the fight would drop, and the way be cleared, and the whole abomina-
ble business swept out of sight in a second."

He spoke pantingly, like a tired runner, with breaks of exhaustion
between his words; and through the breaks she caught, as through the
shifting rents of a fog, great golden vistas of peace and safety. For there
was no mistaking the definite intention behind his vague appeal; she
could have filled up the blanks without the help of Mrs. Fisher's insinuations. Here was a man who turned to her in the extremity of his loneliness and his humiliation: if she came to him at such a moment he
would be hers with all the force of his deluded faith. And the power to
make him so lay in her hand—lay there in a completeness he could not
even remotely conjecture. Revenge and rehabilitation might be hers at
a stroke—there was something dazzling in the completeness of the opportunity.

She stood silent, gazing away from him down the autumnal stretch
of the deserted lane. And suddenly fear possessed her—fear of herself,
and of the terrible force of the temptation. All her past weaknesses were
like so many eager accomplices drawing her toward the path their feet
had already smoothed. She turned quickly, and held out her hand to
Dorset.

"Goodbye—I 'm sorry; there 's nothing in the world that I can
do."

"Nothing? Ah, don't say that," he cried; "say what 's true: that you
abandon me like the others. You, the only creature who could have
saved me!"

"Goodbye—goodbye," she repeated hurriedly; and as she moved
away she heard him cry out on a last note of entreaty: "At least you 'll
let me see you once more?"

Lily, on regaining the Gormer grounds, struck rapidly across the lawn
toward the unfinished house, where she fancied that her hostess might
be speculating, not too resignedly, on the cause of her delay; for, like
many unpunctual persons, Mrs. Gormer disliked to be kept waiting.

As Miss Bart reached the avenue, however, she saw a smart phaeton
with a high-stepping pair disappear behind the shrubbery in the direction of the gate; and on the doorstep stood Mrs. Gormer, with a glow
of retrospective pleasure on her open countenance. At sight of Lily the
glow deepened to an embarrassed red, and she said with a slight laugh:
"Did you see my visitor? Oh, I thought you came back by the avenue.

It was Mrs. George Dorset—she said she 'd dropped in to make a neighbourly call."

Lily met the announcement with her usual composure, though her experience of Bertha's idiosyncrasies would not have led her to include the neighbourly instinct among them; and Mrs. Gormer, relieved to see that she gave no sign of surprise, went on with a deprecating laugh: "Of course what really brought her was curiosity—she made me take her all over the house. But no one could have been nicer—no airs, you know, and so good-natured: I can quite see why people think her so fascinating."

This surprising event, coinciding too completely with her meeting with Dorset to be regarded as contingent upon it, had yet immediately struck Lily with a vague sense of foreboding. It was not in Bertha's habits to be neighbourly, much less to make advances to any one outside the immediate circle of her affinities. She had always consistently ignored the world of outer aspirants, or had recognized its individual members only when prompted by motives of self-interest; and the very capriciousness of her condescensions had, as Lily was aware, given them special value in the eyes of the persons she distinguished. Lily saw this now in Mrs. Gormer's unconcealable complacency, and in the happy irrelevance with which, for the next day or two, she quoted Bertha's opinions and speculated on the origin of her gown. All the secret ambitions which Mrs. Gormer's native indolence, and the attitude of her companions, kept in habitual abeyance, were now germinating afresh in the glow of Bertha's advances; and whatever the cause of the latter, Lily saw that, if they were followed up, they were likely to have a disturbing effect upon her own future.

She had arranged to break the length of her stay with her new friends by one or two visits to other acquaintances as recent; and on her return from this somewhat depressing excursion she was immediately conscious that Mrs. Dorset's influence was still in the air. There had been another exchange of visits, a tea at a country-club, an encounter at a hunt ball; there was even a rumour of an approaching dinner, which Mattie Gormer, with an unnatural effort at discretion, tried to smuggle out of the conversation whenever Miss Bart took part in it.

The latter had already planned to return to town after a farewell Sunday with her friends; and, with Gerty Farish's aid, had discovered a small private hotel where she might establish herself for the winter. The hotel being on the edge of a fashionable neighbourhood, the price of the few square feet she was to occupy was considerably in excess of her

means; but she found a justification for her dislike of poorer quarters in
the argument that, at this particular juncture, it was of the utmost importance to keep up a show of prosperity. In reality, it was impossible
for her, while she had the means to pay her way for a week ahead, to
lapse into a form of existence like Gerty Farish's. She had never been so
near the brink of insolvency; but she could at least manage to meet her
weekly hotel bill, and having settled the heaviest of her previous debts
out of the money she had received from Trenor, she had a still fair margin of credit to go upon. The situation, however, was not agreeable
enough to lull her to complete unconsciousness of its insecurity. Her
rooms, with their cramped outlook down a sallow vista of brick walls
and fire-escapes, her lonely meals in the dark restaurant with its sur-
charged ceiling and haunting smell of coffee — all these material discomforts, which were yet to be accounted as so many privileges soon to
be withdrawn, kept constantly before her the disadvantages of her state;
and her mind reverted the more insistently to Mrs. Fisher's counsels.
Beat about the question as she would, she knew the outcome of it was
that she must try to marry Rosedale; and in this conviction she was fortified by an unexpected visit from George Dorset.

She found him, on the first Sunday after her return to town, pacing
her narrow sitting-room to the imminent peril of the few knick-knacks
with which she had tried to disguise its plush exuberances; but the sight
of her seemed to quiet him, and he said meekly that he had n't come to
bother her — that he asked only to be allowed to sit for half an hour and
talk of anything she liked. In reality, as she knew, he had but one subject: himself and his wretchedness; and it was the need of her sympathy
that had drawn him back. But he began with a pretence of questioning
her about herself, and as she replied, she saw that, for the first time, a
faint realization of her plight penetrated the dense surface of his self-
absorption. Was it possible that her old beast of an aunt had actually cut
her off? That she was living alone like this because there was no one else
for her to go to, and that she really had n't more than enough to keep
alive on till the wretched little legacy was paid? The fibres of sympathy
were nearly atrophied in him, but he was suffering so intensely that he
had a faint glimpse of what other sufferings might mean — and, as she
perceived, an almost simultaneous perception of the way in which her
particular misfortunes might serve him.

When at length she dismissed him, on the pretext that she must
dress for dinner, he lingered entreatingly on the threshold to blurt out:
"It 's been such a comfort — do say you 'll let me see you again — " But

to this direct appeal it was impossible to give an assent; and she said with friendly decisiveness: "I 'm sorry—but you know why I can't."

He coloured to the eyes, pushed the door shut, and stood before her embarrassed but insistent. "I know how you might, if you would— if things were different—and it lies with you to make them so. It 's just a word to say, and you put me out of my misery!"

Their eyes met, and for a second she trembled again with the nearness of the temptation. "You 're mistaken; I know nothing; I saw nothing," she exclaimed, striving, by sheer force of reiteration, to build a barrier between herself and her peril; and as he turned away, groaning out "You sacrifice us both," she continued to repeat, as if it were a charm: "I know nothing—absolutely nothing."

Lily had seen little of Rosedale since her illuminating talk with Mrs. Fisher, but on the two or three occasions when they had met she was conscious of having distinctly advanced in his favour. There could be no doubt that he admired her as much as ever, and she believed it rested with herself to raise his admiration to the point where it should bear down the lingering counsels of expediency. The task was not an easy one; but neither was it easy, in her long sleepless nights, to face the thought of what George Dorset was so clearly ready to offer. Baseness for baseness, she hated the other least: there were even moments when a marriage with Rosedale seemed the only honourable solution of her difficulties. She did not indeed let her imagination range beyond the day of plighting: after that everything faded into a haze of material well-being, in which the personality of her benefactor remained mercifully vague. She had learned, in her long vigils, that there were certain things not good to think of, certain midnight images that must at any cost be exorcised—and one of these was the image of herself as Rosedale's wife.

Carry Fisher, on the strength, as she frankly owned, of the Brys' Newport success, had taken for the autumn months a small house at Tuxedo; and thither Lily was bound on the Sunday after Dorset's visit. Though it was nearly dinner-time when she arrived, her hostess was still out, and the firelit quiet of the small silent house descended on her spirit with a sense of peace and familiarity. It may be doubted if such an emotion had ever before been evoked by Carry Fisher's surroundings; but, contrasted to the world in which Lily had lately lived, there was an air of repose and stability in the very placing of the furniture, and in the quiet competence of the parlour-maid who led her up to her room. Mrs.

Fisher's unconventionality was, after all, a merely superficial divergence from an inherited social creed, while the manners of the Gormer circle represented their first attempt to formulate such a creed for themselves.

It was the first time since her return from Europe that Lily had found herself in a congenial atmosphere, and the stirring of familiar associations had almost prepared her, as she descended the stairs before dinner, to enter upon a group of her old acquaintances. But this expectation was instantly checked by the reflection that the friends who remained loyal were precisely those who would be least willing to expose her to such encounters; and it was hardly with surprise that she found, instead, Mr. Rosedale kneeling domestically on the drawing-room hearth before his hostess's little girl.

Rosedale in the paternal rôle was hardly a figure to soften Lily; yet she could not but notice a quality of homely goodness in his advances to the child. They were not, at any rate, the premeditated and perfunctory endearments of the guest under his hostess's eye, for he and the little girl had the room to themselves; and something in his attitude made him seem a simple and kindly being compared to the small critical creature who endured his homage. Yes, he would be kind—Lily, from the threshold, had time to feel—kind in his gross, unscrupulous, rapacious way, the way of the predatory creature with his mate. She had but a moment in which to consider whether this glimpse of the fireside man mitigated her repugnance, or gave it, rather, a more concrete and intimate form; for at sight of her he was immediately on his feet again, the florid and dominant Rosedale of Mattie Gormer's drawing-room.

It was no surprise to Lily to find that he had been selected as her only fellow-guest. Though she and her hostess had not met since the latter's tentative discussion of her future, Lily knew that the acuteness which enabled Mrs. Fisher to lay a safe and pleasant course through a world of antagonistic forces was not infrequently exercised for the benefit of her friends. It was, in fact, characteristic of Carry that, while she actively gleaned her own stores from the fields of affluence, her real sympathies were on the other side—with the unlucky, the unpopular, the unsuccessful, with all her hungry fellow-toilers in the shorn stubble of success.

Mrs. Fisher's experience guarded her against the mistake of exposing Lily, for the first evening, to the unmitigated impression of Rosedale's personality. Kate Corby and two or three men dropped in to dinner, and Lily, alive to every detail of her friend's method, saw that such opportunities as had been contrived for her were to be deferred till she had, as it were, gained courage to make effectual use of them. She had a sense of acquiescing in this plan with the passiveness of a sufferer resigned to the surgeon's touch; and this feeling of almost lethargic helplessness continued when, after the departure of the guests, Mrs. Fisher followed her upstairs.

"May I come in and smoke a cigarette over your fire? If we talk in my room we shall disturb the child." Mrs. Fisher looked about her with the eye of the solicitous hostess. "I hope you 've managed to make yourself comfortable, dear? Is n't it a jolly little house? It 's such a blessing to have a few quiet weeks with the baby."

Carry, in her rare moments of prosperity, became so expansively maternal that Miss Bart sometimes wondered whether, if she could ever get time and money enough, she would not end by devoting them both to her daughter.

"It 's a well-earned rest: I 'll say that for myself," she continued, sinking down with a sigh of content on the pillowed lounge near the fire. "Louisa Bry is a stern task-master: I often used to wish myself back with the Gormers. Talk of love making people jealous and suspicious— it 's nothing to social ambition! Louisa used to lie awake at night wondering whether the women who called on us called on *me* because I was with her, or on *her* because she was with me; and she was always laying traps to find out what I thought. Of course I had to disown my oldest friends, rather than let her suspect she owed me the chance of making a single acquaintance—when, all the while, that was what she had me there for, and what she wrote me a handsome cheque for when the season was over!"

Mrs. Fisher was not a woman who talked of herself without cause, and the practice of direct speech, far from precluding in her an occasional resort to circuitous methods, served rather, at crucial moments, the purpose of the juggler's chatter while he shifts the contents of his sleeves. Through the haze of her cigarette smoke she continued to gaze meditatively at Miss Bart, who, having dismissed her maid, sat before the toilet-table shaking out over her shoulders the loosened undulations of her hair.

"Your hair 's wonderful, Lily. Thinner—? What does that matter, when it 's so light and alive? So many women's worries seem to go straight to their hair—but yours looks as if there had never been an anxious thought under it. I never saw you look better than you did this evening. Mattie Gormer told me that Morpeth wanted to paint you— why don't you let him?"

Miss Bart's immediate answer was to address a critical glance to the reflection of the countenance under discussion. Then she said, with a slight touch of irritation: "I don't care to accept a portrait from Paul Morpeth."

Mrs. Fisher mused. "N—no. And just now, especially—well, he can do you after you 're married." She waited a moment, and then went on: "By the way, I had a visit from Mattie the other day. She turned up here last Sunday—and with Bertha Dorset, of all people in the world!"

She paused again to measure the effect of this announcement on her hearer, but the brush in Miss Bart's lifted hand maintained its unwavering stroke from brow to nape.

"I never was more astonished," Mrs. Fisher pursued. "I don't know two women less predestined to intimacy—from Bertha's standpoint, that is; for of course poor Mattie thinks it natural enough that she should be singled out—I 've no doubt the rabbit always thinks it is fascinating the anaconda. Well, you know I 've always told you that Mattie secretly longed to bore herself with the really fashionable; and now that the chance has come, I see that she 's capable of sacrificing all her old friends to it."

Lily laid aside her brush and turned a penetrating glance upon her friend. "Including *me?*" she suggested.

"Ah, my dear," murmured Mrs. Fisher, rising to push back a log from the hearth.

"That 's what Bertha means, is n't it?" Miss Bart went on steadily. "For of course she always means something; and before I left Long Island I saw that she was beginning to lay her toils for Mattie."

Mrs. Fisher sighed evasively. "She has her fast now, at any rate. To think of that loud independence of Mattie's being only a subtler form of snobbishness! Bertha can already make her believe anything she pleases—and I 'm afraid she 's begun, my poor child, by insinuating horrors about you."

Lily flushed under the shadow of her drooping hair. "The world is too vile," she murmured, averting herself from Mrs. Fisher's anxious scrutiny.

"It 's not a pretty place; and the only way to keep a footing in it is to fight it on its own terms—and above all, my dear, not alone!" Mrs. Fisher gathered up her floating implications in a resolute grasp. "You 've told me so little that I can only guess what has been happening; but in the rush we all live in there 's no time to keep on hating any one without a cause, and if Bertha is still nasty enough to want to injure you with other people it must be because she 's still afraid of you. From her standpoint there 's only one reason for being afraid of you; and my own idea is that, if you want to punish her, you hold the means in your hand. I believe you can marry George Dorset tomorrow; but if you don't care for that particular form of retaliation, the only thing to save you from Bertha is to marry somebody else."

VII

The light projected on the situation by Mrs. Fisher had the cheerless distinctness of a winter dawn. It outlined the facts with a cold precision unmodified by shade or colour, and refracted, as it were, from the blank walls of the surrounding limitations: she had opened windows from which no sky was ever visible. But the idealist subdued to vulgar necessities must employ vulgar minds to draw the inferences to which he cannot stoop; and it was easier for Lily to let Mrs. Fisher formulate her case than to put it plainly to herself. Once confronted with it, however, she went the full length of its consequences; and these had never been more clearly present to her than when, the next afternoon, she set out for a walk with Rosedale.

It was one of those still November days when the air is haunted with the light of summer, and something in the lines of the landscape, and in the golden haze which bathed them, recalled to Miss Bart the September afternoon when she had climbed the slopes of Bellomont with Selden. The importunate memory was kept before her by its ironic contrast to her present situation, since her walk with Selden had represented an irresistible flight from just such a climax as the present excursion was designed to bring about. But other memories importuned her also; the recollection of similar situations, as skilfully led up to, but through some malice of fortune, or her own unsteadiness of purpose, always failing of the intended result. Well, her purpose was steady enough now. She saw that the whole weary work of rehabilitation must begin again, and against far greater odds, if Bertha Dorset should succeed in breaking up her friendship with the Gormers; and her longing for shelter and security was intensified by the passionate desire to triumph over Bertha, as only wealth and predominance could triumph over her. As the wife of Rosedale—the Rosedale she felt it in her power to create—she would at least present an invulnerable front to her enemy.

She had to draw upon this thought, as upon some fiery stimulant, to keep up her part in the scene toward which Rosedale was too frankly tending. As she walked beside him, shrinking in every nerve from the

way in which his look and tone made free of her, yet telling herself that
this momentary endurance of his mood was the price she must pay for
her ultimate power over him, she tried to calculate the exact point at
which concession must turn to resistance, and the price *he* would have
to pay be made equally clear to him. But his dapper self-confidence
seemed impenetrable to such hints, and she had a sense of something
hard and self-contained behind the superficial warmth of his manner.

They had been seated for some time in the seclusion of a rocky glen
above the lake, when she suddenly cut short the culmination of an impassioned period by turning upon him the grave loveliness of her gaze.

"I *do* believe what you say, Mr. Rosedale," she said quietly; "and I
am ready to marry you whenever you wish."

Rosedale, reddening to the roots of his glossy hair, received this announcement with a recoil which carried him to his feet, where he halted
before her in an attitude of almost comic discomfiture.

"For I suppose that is what you do wish," she continued, in the
same quiet tone. "And, though I was unable to consent when you spoke
to me in this way before, I am ready, now that I know you so much
better, to trust my happiness to your hands."

She spoke with the noble directness which she could command on
such occasions, and which was like a large steady light thrown across the
tortuous darkness of the situation. In its inconvenient brightness
Rosedale seemed to waver a moment, as though conscious that every
avenue of escape was unpleasantly illuminated.

Then he gave a short laugh, and drew out a gold cigarette-case, in
which, with plump jewelled fingers, he groped for a gold-tipped cigarette. Selecting one, he paused to contemplate it a moment before saying: "My dear Miss Lily, I 'm sorry if there 's been any little misappre-
hension between us—but you made me feel my suit was so hopeless
that I had really no intention of renewing it."

Lily's blood tingled with the grossness of the rebuff; but she
checked the first leap of her anger, and said in a tone of gentle dignity:
"I have no one but myself to blame if I gave you the impression that my
decision was final."

Her word-play was always too quick for him, and this reply held him
in puzzled silence while she extended her hand and added, with the
faintest inflection of sadness in her voice: "Before we bid each other
goodbye, I want at least to thank you for having once thought of me as
you did."

The touch of her hand, the moving softness of her look, thrilled a
vulnerable fibre in Rosedale. It was her exquisite inaccessibleness, the

sense of distance she could convey without a hint of disdain, that made it most difficult for him to give her up.

"Why do you talk of saying goodbye? Ain't we going to be good friends all the same?" he urged, without releasing her hand.

She drew it away quietly. "What is your idea of being good friends?" she returned with a slight smile. "Making love to me without asking me to marry you?"

Rosedale laughed with a recovered sense of ease. "Well, that 's about the size of it, I suppose. I can't help making love to you — I don't see how any man could; but I don't mean to ask you to marry me as long as I can keep out of it."

She continued to smile. "I like your frankness; but I am afraid our friendship can hardly continue on those terms."

She turned away, as though to mark that its final term had in fact been reached, and he followed her for a few steps with a baffled sense of her having after all kept the game in her own hands.

"Miss Lily——" he began impulsively; but she walked on without seeming to hear him.

He overtook her in a few quick strides, and laid an entreating hand on her arm. "Miss Lily — don't hurry away like that. You 're beastly hard on a fellow; but if you don't mind speaking the truth I don't see why you should n't allow me to do the same."

She had paused a moment with raised brows, drawing away instinctively from his touch, though she made no effort to evade his words.

"I was under the impression," she rejoined, "that you had done so without waiting for my permission."

"Well — why should n't you hear my reasons for doing it, then? We 're neither of us such new hands that a little plain speaking is going to hurt us. I 'm all broken up on you: there 's nothing new in that. I 'm more in love with you than I was this time last year; but I 've got to face the fact that the situation is changed."

She continued to confront him with the same air of ironic composure. "You mean to say that I 'm not as desirable a match as you thought me?"

"Yes; that 's what I do mean," he answered resolutely. "I won't go into what 's happened. I don't believe the stories about you — I don't *want* to believe them. But they 're there, and my not believing them ain't going to alter the situation."

She flushed to her temples, but the extremity of her need checked the retort on her lip and she continued to face him composedly. "If they are not true," she said, "does n't *that* alter the situation?"

He met this with a steady gaze of his small stock-taking eyes, which made her feel herself no more than some superfine human merchandise. "I believe it does in novels; but I 'm certain it don't in real life. You know that as well as I do: if we 're speaking the truth, let 's speak the whole truth. Last year I was wild to marry you, and you would n't look at me: this year—well, you appear to be willing. Now, what has changed in the interval? Your situation, that 's all. Then you thought you could do better; now——"

"You think you can?" broke from her ironically.

"Why, yes, I do: in one way, that is." He stood before her, his hands in his pockets, his chest sturdily expanded under its vivid waistcoat. "It 's this way, you see: I 've had a pretty steady grind of it these last years, working up my social position. Think it 's funny I should say that? Why should I mind saying I want to get into society? A man ain't ashamed to say he wants to own a racing stable or a picture gallery. Well, a taste for society 's just another kind of hobby. Perhaps I want to get even with some of the people who cold-shouldered me last year— put it that way if it sounds better. Anyhow, I want to have the run of the best houses; and I 'm getting it too, little by little. But I know the quickest way to queer yourself with the right people is to be seen with the wrong ones; and that 's the reason I want to avoid mistakes."

Miss Bart continued to stand before him in a silence that might have expressed either mockery or a half-reluctant respect for his candour, and after a moment's pause he went on: "There it is, you see. I 'm more in love with you than ever, but if I married you now I 'd queer myself for good and all, and everything I 've worked for all these years would be wasted."

She received this with a look from which all tinge of resentment had faded. After the tissue of social falsehoods in which she had so long moved it was refreshing to step into the open daylight of an avowed expediency.

"I understand you," she said. "A year ago I should have been of use to you, and now I should be an encumbrance; and I like you for telling me so quite honestly." She extended her hand with a smile.

Again the gesture had a disturbing effect upon Mr. Rosedale's self-command. "By George, you 're a dead game sport, you are!" he exclaimed; and as she began once more to move away, he broke out suddenly—"Miss Lily—stop. You know I don't believe those stories— I believe they were all got up by a woman who did n't hesitate to sacrifice you to her own convenience——"

Lily drew away with a movement of quick disdain: it was easier to endure his insolence than his commiseration.

"You are very kind; but I don't think we need discuss the matter farther."

But Rosedale's natural imperviousness to hints made it easy for him to brush such resistance aside. "I don't want to discuss anything; I just want to put a plain case before you," he persisted.

She paused in spite of herself, held by the note of a new purpose in his look and tone; and he went on, keeping his eyes firmly upon her: "The wonder to me is that you 've waited so long to get square with that woman, when you 've had the power in your hands." She continued silent under the rush of astonishment that his words produced, and he moved a step closer to ask with low-toned directness: "Why don't you use those letters of hers you bought last year?"

Lily stood speechless under the shock of the interrogation. In the words preceding it she had conjectured, at most, an allusion to her supposed influence over George Dorset; nor did the astonishing indelicacy of the reference diminish the likelihood of Rosedale's resorting to it. But now she saw how far short of the mark she had fallen; and the surprise of learning that he had discovered the secret of the letters left her, for the moment, unconscious of the special use to which he was in the act of putting his knowledge.

Her temporary loss of self-possession gave him time to press his point; and he went on quickly, as though to secure completer control of the situation: "You see I know where you stand—I know how completely she 's in your power. That sounds like stage-talk, don't it?—but there 's a lot of truth in some of those old gags; and I don't suppose you bought those letters simply because you 're collecting autographs."

She continued to look at him with a deepening bewilderment: her only clear impression resolved itself into a scared sense of his power.

"You 're wondering how I found out about 'em?" he went on, answering her look with a note of conscious pride. "Perhaps you 've forgotten that I 'm the owner of the Benedick—but never mind about that now. Getting on to things is a mighty useful accomplishment in business, and I 've simply extended it to my private affairs. For this *is* partly my affair, you see—at least, it depends on you to make it so. Let 's look the situation straight in the eye. Mrs. Dorset, for reasons we need n't go into, did you a beastly bad turn last spring. Everybody knows what Mrs. Dorset is, and her best friends would n't believe her on oath where their own interests were concerned; but as long as they 're out of the row it 's much easier to follow her lead than to set themselves against it, and you 've simply been sacrificed to their laziness and selfishness. Is n't that a pretty fair statement of the case? — Well, some people say you 've got the neatest kind of an answer in your hands: that George Dorset would marry you tomorrow, if you 'd tell him all you know, and give him the chance to show the lady the door. I daresay he would; but you don't seem to care for that particular form of getting even, and, taking a purely business view of the question, I think you 're right. In a deal like that, nobody comes out with perfectly clean hands, and the only way for you to start fresh is to get Bertha Dorset to back you up, instead of trying to fight her."

He paused long enough to draw breath, but not to give her time for the expression of her gathering resistance; and as he pressed on, expounding and elucidating his idea with the directness of the man who has no doubts of his cause, she found the indignation gradually freezing on her lip, found herself held fast in the grasp of his argument by the mere cold strength of its presentation. There was no time now to wonder how he had heard of her obtaining the letters: all her world was dark outside the monstrous glare of his scheme for using them. And it was not, after the first moment, the horror of the idea that held her spellbound, subdued to his will; it was rather its subtle affinity to her own inmost cravings. He would marry her tomorrow if she could regain Bertha Dorset's friendship; and to induce the open resumption of that friendship, and the tacit retractation of all that had caused its withdrawal, she had only to put to the lady the latent menace contained in the packet so miraculously delivered into her hands. Lily saw in a flash the advantage of this course over that which poor Dorset had pressed upon her. The other plan depended for its success on the infliction of an open injury, while this reduced the transaction to a private understanding, of which no third person need have the remotest hint. Put by Rosedale in terms of business-like give-and-take, this understanding took on the harmless air of a mutual accommodation, like a transfer of property or a revision of boundary lines. It certainly simplified life to view it as a perpetual adjustment, a play of party politics, in which every concession had its recognized equivalent: Lily's tired mind was fascinated by this escape from fluctuating ethical estimates into a region of concrete weights and measures.

Rosedale, as she listened, seemed to read in her silence not only a gradual acquiescence in his plan, but a dangerously far-reaching perception of the chances it offered; for as she continued to stand before him without speaking, he broke out, with a quick return upon himself: "You see how simple it is, don't you? Well, don't be carried away by the idea that it 's *too* simple. It is n't exactly as if you 'd started in with a clean bill of health. Now we 're talking let 's call things by their right names, and clear the whole business up. You know well enough that Bertha Dorset could n't have touched you if there had n't been — well — questions asked before — little points of interrogation, eh? Bound to happen to a good-looking girl with stingy relatives, I suppose; anyhow, they *did* happen, and she found the ground prepared for her. Do you see where I 'm coming out? You don't want these little questions cropping up again. It 's one thing to get Bertha Dorset into line — but what you want is to keep her there. You can frighten her fast enough — but how are you going to keep her frightened? By showing her that you 're as powerful as she is. All the letters in the world won't do that for you as you are now; but with a big backing behind you, you 'll keep her just where you want her to be. That 's *my* share in the business — that 's what I 'm offering you. You can't put the thing through without me — don't run away with any idea that you can. In six months you 'd be back again among your old worries, or worse ones; and here I am, ready to lift you out of 'em tomorrow if you say so. *Do* you say so, Miss Lily?" he added, moving suddenly nearer.

The words, and the movement which accompanied them, combined to startle Lily out of the state of tranced subservience into which she had insensibly slipped. Light comes in devious ways to the groping consciousness, and it came to her now through the disgusted perception that her would-be accomplice assumed, as a matter of course, the likelihood of her distrusting him and perhaps trying to cheat him of his share of the spoils. This glimpse of his inner mind seemed to present the whole transaction in a new aspect, and she saw that the essential baseness of the act lay in its freedom from risk.

She drew back with a quick gesture of rejection, saying, in a voice that was a surprise to her own ears: "You are mistaken — quite mistaken — both in the facts and in what you infer from them."

Rosedale stared a moment, puzzled by her sudden dash in a direction so different from that toward which she had appeared to be letting him guide her.

"Now what on earth does that mean? I though we understood each other!" he exclaimed; and to her murmur of "Ah, we do *now*," he retorted with a sudden burst of violence: "I suppose it 's because the letters are to *him*, then? Well, I 'll be damned if I see what thanks you 've got from him!"

VIII

The autumn days declined to winter. Once more the leisure world was in transition between country and town, and Fifth Avenue, still deserted at the week-end, showed from Monday to Friday a broadening stream of carriages between house-fronts gradually restored to consciousness.

The Horse Show, some two weeks earlier, had produced a passing semblance of reanimation, filling the theatres and restaurants with a human display of the same costly and high-stepping kind as circled daily about its ring. In Miss Bart's world the Horse Show, and the public it attracted, had ostensibly come to be classed among the spectacles disdained of the elect; but, as the feudal lord might sally forth to join in the dance on his village green, so society, unofficially and incidentally, still condescended to look in upon the scene. Mrs. Gormer, among the rest, was not above seizing such an occasion for the display of herself and her horses; and Lily was given one or two opportunities of appearing at her friend's side in the most conspicuous box the house afforded. But this lingering semblance of intimacy made her only the more conscious of a change in the relation between Mattie and herself, of a dawning discrimination, a gradually formed social standard, emerging from Mrs. Gormer's chaotic view of life. It was inevitable that Lily herself should constitute the first sacrifice to this new ideal, and she knew that, once the Gormers were established in town, the whole drift of fashionable life would facilitate Mattie's detachment from her. She had, in short, failed to make herself indispensable; or rather, her attempt to do so had been thwarted by an influence stronger than any she could exert. That influence, in its last analysis, was simply the power of money: Bertha Dorset's social credit was based on an impregnable bank-account.

Lily knew that Rosedale had overstated neither the difficulty of her own position nor the completeness of the vindication he offered: once Bertha's match in material resources, her superior gifts would make it easy for her to dominate her adversary. An understanding of what such domination would mean, and of the disadvantages accruing from her rejection of it, was brought home to Lily with increasing clearness during the early weeks of the winter. Hitherto, she had kept up a semblance of movement outside the main flow of the social current; but with the return to town, and the concentrating of scattered activities, the mere fact of not slipping back naturally into her old habits of life marked her as being unmistakably excluded from them. If one were not a part of the season's fixed routine, one swung unsphered in a void of social non-

existence. Lily, for all her dissatisfied dreaming, had never really conceived the possibility of revolving about a different centre: it was easy
enough to despise the world, but decidedly difficult to find any other
habitable region. Her sense of irony never quite deserted her, and she
could still note, with self-directed derision, the abnormal value suddenly
acquired by the most tiresome and insignificant details of her former
life. Its very drudgeries had a charm now that she was involuntarily released from them: card-leaving, note-writing, enforced civilities to the
dull and elderly, and the smiling endurance of tedious dinners—how
pleasantly such obligations would have filled the emptiness of her days!
She did indeed leave cards in plenty; she kept herself, with a smiling and
valiant persistence, well in the eye of her world; nor did she suffer any of
those gross rebuffs which sometimes produce a wholesome reaction of
contempt in their victim. Society did not turn away from her, it simply
drifted by, preoccupied and inattentive, letting her feel, to the full measure of her humbled pride, how completely she had been the creature of
its favour.

She had rejected Rosedale's suggestion with a promptness of scorn
almost surprising to herself: she had not lost her capacity for high flashes
of indignation. But she could not breathe long on the heights; there
had been nothing in her training to develop any continuity of moral
strength: what she craved, and really felt herself entitled to, was a situation in which the noblest attitude should also be the easiest. Hitherto
her intermittent impulses of resistance had sufficed to maintain her self-
respect. If she slipped she recovered her footing, and it was only afterward that she was aware of having recovered it each time on a slightly
lower level. She had rejected Rosedale's offer without conscious effort;
her whole being had risen against it; and she did not yet perceive that,
by the mere act of listening to him, she had learned to live with ideas
which would once have been intolerable to her.

To Gerty Farish, keeping watch over her with a tenderer if less discerning eye than Mrs. Fisher's, the results of the struggle were already distinctly visible. She did not, indeed, know what hostages Lily had already
given to expediency; but she saw her passionately and irretrievably
pledged to the ruinous policy of "keeping up." Gerty could smile now
at her own early dream of her friend's renovation through adversity: she
understood clearly enough that Lily was not of those to whom privation
teaches the unimportance of what they have lost. But this very fact, to
Gerty, made her friend the more piteously in want of aid, the more exposed to the claims of a tenderness she was so little conscious of needing.

Lily, since her return to town, had not often climbed Miss Farish's
stairs. There was something irritating to her in the mute interrogation
of Gerty's sympathy: she felt the real difficulties of her situation to be
incommunicable to any one whose theory of values was so different
from her own, and the restrictions of Gerty's life, which had once had
the charm of contrast, now reminded her too painfully of the limits to
which her own existence was shrinking. When at length, one afternoon,
she put into execution the belated resolve to visit her friend, this sense
of shrunken opportunities possessed her with unusual intensity. The
walk up Fifth Avenue, unfolding before her, in the brilliance of the hard
winter sunlight, an interminable procession of fastidiously-equipped
carriages—giving her, through the little squares of brougham-windows,
peeps of familiar profiles bent above visiting-lists, of hurried hands dispensing notes and cards to attendant footmen—this glimpse of the
ever-revolving wheels of the great social machine made Lily more than
ever conscious of the steepness and narrowness of Gerty's stairs, and of
the cramped blind-alley of life to which they led. Dull stairs destined
to be mounted by dull people: how many thousands of insignificant
figures were going up and down such stairs all over the world at that
very moment—figures as shabby and uninteresting as that of the
middle-aged lady in limp black who descended Gerty's flight as Lily
climbed to it!

"That was poor Miss Jane Silverton—she came to talk things over
with me: she and her sister want to do something to support themselves," Gerty explained, as Lily followed her into the sitting-room.

"To support themselves? Are they so hard up?" Miss Bart asked with
a touch of irritation: she had not come to listen to the woes of other
people.

"I 'm afraid they have nothing left: Ned's debts have swallowed up
everything. They had such hopes, you know, when he broke away from
Carry Fisher; they thought Bertha Dorset would be such a good influence, because she does n't care for cards, and—well, she talked quite
beautifully to poor Miss Jane about feeling as if Ned were her younger
brother, and wanting to carry him off on the yacht, so that he might
have a chance to drop cards and racing, and take up his literary work
again."

Miss Farish paused with a sigh which reflected the perplexity of her
departing visitor. "But that is n't all; it is n't even the worst. It seems
that Ned has quarrelled with the Dorsets; or at least Bertha won't allow
him to see her, and he is so unhappy about it that he has taken to gam-

bling again, and going about with all sorts of queer people. And cousin Grace Van Osburgh accuses him of having had a very bad influence on Freddy, who left Harvard last spring, and has been a great deal with Ned ever since. She sent for Miss Jane, and made a dreadful scene; and Jack Stepney and Herbert Melson, who were there too, told Miss Jane that Freddy was threatening to marry some dreadful woman to whom Ned had introduced him, and that they could do nothing with him because now he 's of age he has his own money. You can fancy how poor Miss Jane felt—she came to me at once, and seemed to think that if I could get her something to do she could earn enough to pay Ned's debts and send him away—I 'm afraid she has no idea how long it would take her to pay for one of his evenings at bridge. And he was horribly in debt when he came back from the cruise—I can't see why he should have spent so much more money under Bertha's influence than Carry's: can you?"

Lily met this query with an impatient gesture. "My dear Gerty, I always understand how people can spend much more money—never how they can spend any less!"

She loosened her furs and settled herself in Gerty's easy-chair, while her friend busied herself with the tea-cups.

"But what can they do—the Miss Silvertons? How do they mean to support themselves?" she asked, conscious that the note of irritation still persisted in her voice. It was the very last topic she had meant to discuss—it really did not interest her in the least—but she was seized by a sudden perverse curiosity to know how the two colourless shrinking victims of young Silverton's sentimental experiments meant to cope with the grim necessity which lurked so close to her own threshold.

"I don't know—I am trying to find something for them. Miss Jane reads aloud very nicely—but it 's so hard to find any one who is willing to be read to. And Miss Annie paints a little—— "

"Oh, I know—apple-blossoms on blotting-paper; just the kind of thing I shall be doing myself before long!" exclaimed Lily, starting up with a vehemence of movement that threatened destruction to Miss Farish's fragile tea-table.

Lily bent over to steady the cups; then she sank back into her seat. "I 'd forgotten there was no room to dash about in—how beautifully one does have to behave in a small flat! Oh, Gerty, I was n't meant to be good," she sighed out incoherently.

Gerty lifted an apprehensive look to her pale face, in which the eyes shone with a peculiar sleepless lustre.

"You look horribly tired, Lily; take your tea, and let me give you this cushion to lean against."

Miss Bart accepted the cup of tea, but put back the cushion with an impatient hand.

"Don't give me that! I don't want to lean back—I shall go to sleep if I do."

"Well, why not, dear? I 'll be as quiet as a mouse," Gerty urged affectionately.

"No—no; don't be quiet; talk to me—keep me awake! I don't sleep at night, and in the afternoon a dreadful drowsiness creeps over me."

"You don't sleep at night? Since when?"

"I don't know—I can't remember." She rose and put the empty cup on the tea-tray. "Another, and stronger, please; if I don't keep awake now I shall see horrors tonight—perfect horrors!"

"But they 'll be worse if you drink too much tea."

"No, no—give it to me; and don't preach, please," Lily returned imperiously. Her voice had a dangerous edge, and Gertie noticed that her hand shook as she held it out to receive the second cup.

"But you look so tired: I 'm sure you must be ill——"

Miss Bart set down her cup with a start. "Do I look ill? Does my face show it?" She rose and walked quickly toward the little mirror above the writing-table. "What a horrid looking-glass—it 's all blotched and discoloured. Any one would look ghastly in it!" She turned back, fixing her plaintive eyes on Gerty. "You stupid dear, why do you say such odious things to me? It 's enough to make one ill to be told one looks so! And looking ill means looking ugly." She caught Gerty's wrists, and drew her close to the window. "After all, I 'd rather know the truth. Look me straight in the face, Gerty, and tell me: am I perfectly frightful?"

"You 're perfectly beautiful now, Lily: your eyes are shining, and your cheeks have grown so pink all of a sudden——"

"Ah, they *were* pale, then—ghastly pale, when I came in? Why don't you tell me frankly that I 'm a wreck? My eyes are bright now because I 'm so nervous—but in the mornings they look like lead. And I can see the lines coming in my face—the lines of worry and disappointment and failure! Every sleepless night leaves a new one—and how can I sleep, when I have such dreadful things to think about?"

"Dreadful things—what things?" asked Gerty, gently detaching her wrists from her friend's feverish fingers.

"What things? Well, poverty, for one—and I don't know any that 's more dreadful." Lily turned away and sank with sudden weariness into the easy-chair near the tea-table. "You asked me just now if I could understand why Ned Silverton spent so much money. Of course I understand—he spends it on living with the rich. You think we live *on* the rich, rather than with them: and so we do, in a sense—but it 's a privilege we have to pay for! We eat their dinners, and drink their wine, and smoke their cigarettes, and use their carriages and their opera-boxes and their private cars—yes, but there 's a tax to pay on every one of those luxuries. The man pays it by big tips to the servants, by playing cards beyond his means, by flowers and presents—and—and—lots of other things that cost; the girl pays it by tips and cards too—oh, yes, I 've had to take up bridge again—and by going to the best dress-makers, and having just the right dress for every occasion, and always keeping herself fresh and exquisite and amusing!"

She leaned back for a moment, closing her eyes, and as she sat there, her pale lips slightly parted, and the lids dropped above her fagged brilliant gaze, Gerty had a startled perception of the change in her face—of the way in which an ashen daylight seemed suddenly to extinguish its artificial brightness. She looked up, and the vision vanished.

"It does n't sound very amusing, does it? And it is n't—I 'm sick to death of it! And yet the thought of giving it all up nearly kills me—it 's what keeps me awake at night, and makes me so crazy for your strong tea. For I can't go on in this way much longer, you know—I 'm nearly at the end of my tether. And then what can I do—how on earth am I to keep myself alive? I see myself reduced to the fate of that poor Silverton woman—slinking about to employment agencies, and trying to sell painted blotting-pads to Women's Exchanges! And there are thousands and thousands of women trying to do the same thing already, and not one of the number who has less idea how to earn a dollar than I have!"

She rose again with a hurried glance at the clock. "It 's late, and I must be off—I have an appointment with Carry Fisher. Don't look so worried, you dear thing—don't think too much about the nonsense I 've been talking." She was before the mirror again, adjusting her hair with a light hand, drawing down her veil, and giving a dexterous touch to her furs. "Of course, you know, it has n't come to the employment agencies and the painted blotting-pads yet; but I 'm rather hard-up just for the moment, and if I could find something to do—notes to write and visiting-lists to make up, or that kind of thing—it would tide me over till the legacy is paid. And Carry has promised to find somebody

who wants a kind of social secretary—you know she makes a specialty
of the helpless rich."

Miss Bart had not revealed to Gerty the full extent of her anxiety. She
was in fact in urgent and immediate need of money: money to meet the
vulgar weekly claims which could neither be deferred nor evaded. To
give up her apartment, and shrink to the obscurity of a boarding-house,
or the provisional hospitality of a bed in Gerty Farish's sitting-room,
was an expedient which could only postpone the problem confronting
her; and it seemed wiser as well as more agreeable to remain where she
was and find some means of earning her living. The possibility of having
to do this was one which she had never before seriously considered, and
the discovery that, as a bread-winner, she was likely to prove as helpless
and ineffectual as poor Miss Silverton, was a severe shock to her self-
confidence.

Having been accustomed to take herself at the popular valuation, as
a person of energy and resource, naturally fitted to dominate any situation in which she found herself, she vaguely imagined that such gifts
would be of value to seekers after social guidance; but there was unfortunately no specific head under which the art of saying and doing the
right thing could be offered in the market, and even Mrs. Fisher's re-
sourcefulness failed before the difficulty of discovering a workable vein
in the vague wealth of Lily's graces. Mrs Fisher was full of indirect expedients for enabling her friends to earn a living, and could conscien-
tiously assert that she had put several opportunities of this kind before
Lily; but more legitimate methods of bread-winning were as much out
of her line as they were beyond the capacity of the sufferers she was
generally called upon to assist. Lily's failure to profit by the chances
already afforded her might, moreover, have justified the abandonment
of farther effort on her behalf; but Mrs. Fisher's inexhaustible good-
nature made her an adept at creating artificial demands in response to
an actual supply. In the pursuance of this end she at once started on a
voyage of discovery in Miss Bart's behalf; and as the result of her explorations she now summoned the latter with the announcement that she
had "found something."

Left to herself, Gerty mused distressfully upon her friend's plight, and
her own inability to relieve it. It was clear to her that Lily, for the present, had no wish for the kind of help she could give. Miss Farish could
see no hope for her friend but in a life completely reorganized and de-

tached from its old associations; whereas all Lily's energies were centred in the determined effort to hold fast to those associations, to keep herself visibly identified with them, as long as the illusion could be maintained. Pitiable as such an attitude seemed to Gerty, she could not judge it as harshly as Selden, for instance, might have done. She had not forgotten the night of emotion when she and Lily had lain in each other's arms, and she had seemed to feel her very heart's blood passing into her friend. The sacrifice she had made had seemed unavailing enough; no trace remained in Lily of the subduing influences of that hour; but Gerty's tenderness, disciplined by long years of contact with obscure and inarticulate suffering, could wait on its object with a silent forbearance which took no account of time. She could not, however, deny herself the solace of taking anxious counsel with Lawrence Selden, with whom, since his return from Europe, she had renewed her old relation of cousinly confidence.

Selden himself had never been aware of any change in their relation. He found Gerty as he had left her, simple, undemanding and devoted, but with a quickened intelligence of the heart which he recognized without seeking to explain it. To Gerty herself it would once have seemed impossible that she should ever again talk freely with him of Lily Bart; but what had passed in the secrecy of her own breast seemed to resolve itself, when the mist of the struggle cleared, into a breaking down of the bounds of self, a deflecting of the wasted personal emotion into the general current of human understanding.

It was not till some two weeks after her visit from Lily that Gerty had the opportunity of communicating her fears to Selden. The latter, having presented himself on a Sunday afternoon, had lingered on through the dowdy animation of his cousin's tea-hour, conscious of something in her voice and eye which solicited a word apart; and as soon as the last visitor was gone Gerty opened her case by asking how lately he had seen Miss Bart.

Selden's perceptible pause gave her time for a slight stir of surprise.

"I have n't seen her at all—I 've perpetually missed seeing her since she came back."

This unexpected admission made Gerty pause too; and she was still hesitating on the brink of her subject when he relieved her by adding: "I 've wanted to see her—but she seems to have been absorbed by the Gormer set since her return from Europe."

"That 's all the more reason: she 's been very unhappy."

"Unhappy at being with the Gormers?"

"Oh, I don't defend her intimacy with the Gormers; but that too is at an end now, I think. You know people have been very unkind since Bertha Dorset quarrelled with her."

"Ah——" Selden exclaimed, rising abruptly to walk to the window, where he remained with his eyes on the darkening street while his cousin continued to explain: "Judy Trenor and her own family have deserted her too—and all because Bertha Dorset has said such horrible things. And she is very poor—you know Mrs. Peniston cut her off with a small legacy, after giving her to understand that she was to have everything."

"Yes—I know," Selden assented curtly, turning back into the room, but only to stir about with restless steps in the circumscribed space between door and window. "Yes—she 's been abominably treated; but it 's unfortunately the precise thing that a man who wants to show his sympathy can't say to her."

His words caused Gerty a slight chill of disappointment. "There would be other ways of showing your sympathy," she suggested.

Selden, with a slight laugh, sat down beside her on the little sofa which projected from the hearth. "What are you thinking of, you incorrigible missionary?" he asked.

Gerty's colour rose, and her blush was for a moment her only answer. Then she made it more explicit by saying: "I am thinking of the fact that you and she used to be great friends—that she used to care immensely for what you thought of her—and that, if she takes your staying away as a sign of what you think now, I can imagine its adding a great deal to her unhappiness."

"My dear child, don't add to it still more—at least to your conception of it—by attributing to her all sorts of susceptibilities of your own." Selden, for his life, could not keep a note of dryness out of his voice; but he met Gerty's look of perplexity by saying more mildly: "But, though you immensely exaggerate the importance of anything I could do for Miss Bart, you can't exaggerate my readiness to do it—if you ask me to." He laid his hand for a moment on hers, and there passed between them, on the current of the rare contact, one of those exchanges of meaning which fill the hidden reservoirs of affection. Gerty had the feeling that he measured the cost of her request as plainly as she read the significance of his reply; and the sense of all that was suddenly clear between them made her next words easier to find.

"I do ask you, then; I ask you because she once told me that you had been a help to her, and because she needs help now as she has never needed it before. You know how dependent she has always been on ease and luxury—how she has hated what was shabby and ugly and uncomfortable. She can't help it—she was brought up with those ideas, and has never been able to find her way out of them. But now all the things she cared for have been taken from her, and the people who taught her to care for them have abandoned her too; and it seems to me that if some one could reach out a hand and show her the other side—show her how much is left in life and in herself——" Gerty broke off, abashed at the sound of her own eloquence, and impeded by the difficulty of giving precise expression to her vague yearning for her friend's retrieval. "I can't help her myself: she 's passed out of my reach," she continued. "I think she 's afraid of being burden to me. When she was last here, two weeks ago, she seemed dreadfully worried about her future: she said Carry Fisher was trying to find something for her to do. A few days later she wrote me that she had taken a position as private secretary, and that I was not to be anxious, for everything was all right, and she would come in and tell me about it when she had time; but she has never come, and I don't like to go to her, because I am afraid of forcing myself on her when I 'm not wanted. Once, when we were children, and I had rushed up after a long separation, and thrown my arms about her, she said: 'Please don't kiss me unless I ask you to, Gerty'— and she *did* ask me, a minute later; but since then I 've always waited to be asked."

Selden had listened in silence, with the concentrated look which his thin dark face could assume when he wished to guard it against any involuntary change of expression. When his cousin ended, he said with a slight smile: "Since you 've learned the wisdom of waiting, I don't see why you urge me to rush in——" but the troubled appeal of her eyes made him add, as he rose to take leave: "Still, I 'll do what you wish, and not hold you responsible for my failure."

Selden's avoidance of Miss Bart had not been as unintentional as he had allowed his cousin to think. At first, indeed, while the memory of their last hour at Monte Carlo still held the full heat of his indignation, he had anxiously watched for her return; but she had disappointed him by lingering in England, and when she finally reappeared it happened that business had called him to the West, whence he came back only to learn that she was starting for Alaska with the Gormers. The revelation of this suddenly-established intimacy effectually chilled his desire to see her. If, at a moment when her whole life seemed to be breaking up, she could cheerfully commit its reconstruction to the Gormers, there was no reason why such accidents should ever strike her as irreparable. Every step she took seemed in fact to carry her farther from the region where,

once or twice, he and she had met for an illumined moment; and the
recognition of this fact, when its first pang had been surmounted, produced in him a sense of negative relief. It was much simpler for him to
judge Miss Bart by her habitual conduct than by the rare deviations
from it which had thrown her so disturbingly in his way; and every act
of hers which made the recurrence of such deviations more unlikely,
confirmed the sense of relief with which he returned to the conventional
view of her.

But Gerty Farish's words had sufficed to make him see how little
this view was really his, and how impossible it was for him to live quietly
with the thought of Lily Bart. To hear that she was in need of help—
even such vague help as he could offer—was to be at once repossessed
by that thought; and by the time he reached the street he had sufficiently convinced himself of the urgency of his cousin's appeal to turn
his steps directly toward Lily's hotel.

There his zeal met a check in the unforeseen news that Miss Bart
had moved away; but, on his pressing his enquiries, the clerk remembered that she had left an address, for which he presently began to
search through his books.

It was certainly strange that she should have taken this step without
letting Gerty Farish know of her decision; and Selden waited with a
vague sense of uneasiness while the address was sought for. The process
lasted long enough for uneasiness to turn to apprehension; but when at
length a slip of paper was handed him, and he read on it: "Care of Mrs.
Norma Hatch, Emporium Hotel," his apprehension passed into an incredulous stare, and this into the gesture of disgust with which he tore
the paper in two, and turned to walk quickly homeward.

IX

When Lily woke on the morning after her translation to the Emporium Hotel, her first feeling was one of purely physical satisfaction. The
force of contrast gave an added keenness to the luxury of lying once
more in a soft-pillowed bed, and looking across a spacious sunlit room
at a breakfast-table set invitingly near the fire. Analysis and introspection
might come later; but for the moment she was not even troubled by the
excesses of the upholstery or the restless convolutions of the furniture.
The sense of being once more lapped and folded in ease, as in some
dense mild medium impenetrable to discomfort, effectually stilled the
faintest note of criticism.

When, the afternoon before, she had presented herself to the lady to whom Carry Fisher had directed her, she had been conscious of entering a new world. Carry's vague presentment of Mrs. Norma Hatch (whose reversion to her Christian name was explained as the result of her latest divorce), left her under the implication of coming "from the West," with the not unusual extenuation of having brought a great deal of money with her. She was, in short, rich, helpless, unplaced: the very subject for Lily's hand. Mrs. Fisher had not specified the line her friend was to take; she owned herself unacquainted with Mrs. Hatch, whom she "knew about" through Melville Stancy, a lawyer in his leisure moments, and the Falstaff of a certain section of festive club life. Socially, Mr. Stancy might have been said to form a connecting link between the Gormer world and the more dimly-lit region on which Miss Bart now found herself entering. It was, however, only figuratively that the illumination of Mrs. Hatch's world could be described as dim: in actual fact, Lily found her seated in a blaze of electric light, impartially projected from various ornamental excrescences on a vast concavity of pink damask and gilding, from which she rose like Venus from her shell. The analogy was justified by the appearance of the lady, whose large-eyed prettiness had the fixity of something impaled and shown under glass. This did not preclude the immediate discovery that she was some years younger than her visitor, and that under her showiness, her ease, the aggression of her dress and voice, there persisted that ineradicable innocence which, in ladies of her nationality, so curiously coexists with startling extremes of experience.

The environment in which Lily found herself was as strange to her as its inhabitants. She was unacquainted with the world of the fashionable New York hotel—a world over-heated, over-upholstered, and over-fitted with mechanical appliances for the gratification of fantastic requirements, while the comforts of a civilized life were as unattainable as in a desert. Through this atmosphere of torrid splendour moved wan beings as richly upholstered as the furniture, beings without definite pursuits or permanent relations, who drifted on a languid tide of curiosity from restaurant to concert-hall, from palm-garden to music-room, from "art exhibit" to dress-maker's opening. High-stepping horses or elaborately equipped motors waited to carry these ladies into vague metropolitan distances, whence they returned, still more wan from the weight of their sables, to be sucked back into the stifling inertia of the hotel routine. Somewhere behind them, in the background of their lives, there was doubtless a real past, peopled by real human activities:

they themselves were probably the product of strong ambitions, persistent energies, diversified contacts with the wholesome roughness of life; yet they had no more real existence than the poet's shades in limbo.

Lily had not been long in this pallid world without discovering that Mrs. Hatch was its most substantial figure. That lady, though still floating in the void, showed faint symptoms of developing an outline; and in this endeavour she was actively seconded by Mr. Melville Stancy. It was Mr. Stancy, a man of large resounding presence, suggestive of convivial occasions and of a chivalry finding expression in "first-night" boxes and thousand dollar bonbonnières, who had transplanted Mrs. Hatch from the scene of her first development to the higher stage of hotel life in the metropolis. It was he who had selected the horses with which she had taken the blue ribbon at the Show, had introduced her to the photographer whose portraits of her formed the recurring ornament of "Sunday Supplements," and had got together the group which constituted her social world. It was a small group still, with heterogeneous figures suspended in large unpeopled spaces; but Lily did not take long to learn that its regulation was no longer in Mr. Stancy's hands. As often happens, the pupil had outstripped the teacher, and Mrs. Hatch was already aware of heights of elegance as well as depths of luxury beyond the world of the Emporium. This discovery at once produced in her a craving for higher guidance, for the adroit feminine hand which should give the right turn to her correspondence, the right "look" to her hats, the right succession to the items of her *menus*. It was, in short, as the regulator of a germinating social life that Miss Bart's guidance was required; her ostensible duties as secretary being restricted by the fact that Mrs. Hatch, as yet, knew hardly any one to write to.

The daily details of Mrs. Hatch's existence were as strange to Lily as its general tenor. The lady's habits were marked by an Oriental indolence and disorder peculiarly trying to her companion. Mrs. Hatch and her friends seemed to float together outside the bounds of time and space. No definite hours were kept; no fixed obligations existed: night and day flowed into one another in a blur of confused and retarded engagements, so that one had the impression of lunching at the tea-hour, while dinner was often merged in the noisy after-theatre supper which prolonged Mrs. Hatch's vigil till day-light.

Through this jumble of futile activities came and went a strange throng of hangers-on—manicures, beauty-doctors, hair-dressers, teachers of bridge, of French, of "physical development": figures sometimes indistinguishable, by their appearance, or by Mrs. Hatch's relation to them, from the visitors constituting her recognized society. But strangest of all to Lily was the encounter, in this latter group, of several of her acquaintances. She had supposed, and not without relief, that she was passing, for the moment, completely out of her own circle; but she found that Mr. Stancy, one side of whose sprawling existence over-lapped the edge of Mrs. Fisher's world, had drawn several of its bright-est ornaments into the circle of the Emporium. To find Ned Silverton among the habitual frequenters of Mrs. Hatch's drawing-room was one of Lily's first astonishments; but she soon discovered that he was not Mr. Stancy's most important recruit. It was on little Freddy Van Os-burgh, the small slim heir of the Van Osburgh millions, that the atten-tion of Mrs. Hatch's group was centred. Freddy, barely out of college, had risen above the horizon since Lily's eclipse, and she now saw with surprise what an effulgence he shed on the outer twilight of Mrs. Hatch's existence. This, then, was one of the things that young men "went in" for when released from the official social routine; this was the kind of "previous engagement" that so frequently caused them to dis-appoint the hopes of anxious hostesses. Lily had an odd sense of being behind the social tapestry, on the side where the threads were knotted and the loose ends hung. For a moment she found a certain amusement in the show, and in her own share of it: the situation had an ease and unconventionality distinctly refreshing after her experience of the irony of conventions. But these flashes of amusement were but brief reactions from the long disgust of her days. Compared with the vast gilded void of Mrs. Hatch's existence, the life of Lily's former friends seemed packed with ordered activities. Even the most irresponsible pretty woman of her acquaintance had her inherited obligations, her conven-tional benevolences, her share in the working of the great civic machine; and all hung together in the solidarity of these traditional functions. The performance of specific duties would have simplified Miss Bart's position; but the vague attendance on Mrs. Hatch was not without its perplexities.

It was not her employer who created these perplexities. Mrs. Hatch showed from the first an almost touching desire for Lily's approval. Far from asserting the superiority of wealth, her beautiful eyes seemed to urge the plea of inexperience: she wanted to do what was "nice," to be taught how to be "lovely." The difficulty was to find any point of con-tact between her ideals and Lily's.

Mrs. Hatch swam in a haze of indeterminate enthusiasms, of aspira-tions culled from the stage, the newspapers, the fashion-journals, and a gaudy world of sport still more completely beyond her companion's ken. To separate from these confused conceptions those most likely to

advance the lady on her way, was Lily's obvious duty; but its performance was hampered by rapidly-growing doubts. Lily was in fact becoming more and more aware of a certain ambiguity in her situation. It
was not that she had, in the conventional sense, any doubt of Mrs.
Hatch's irreproachableness. The lady's offences were always against
taste rather than conduct; her divorce record seemed due to geograph-
ical rather than ethical conditions; and her worst laxities were likely to
proceed from a wandering and extravagant good-nature. But if Lily did
not mind her detaining her manicure for luncheon, or offering the
"Beauty-Doctor" a seat in Freddy Van Osburgh's box at the play, she
was not equally at ease in regard to some less apparent lapses from convention. Ned Silverton's relation to Stancy seemed, for instance, closer
and less clear than any natural affinities would warrant; and both appeared united in the effort to cultivate Freddy Van Osburgh's growing
taste for Mrs. Hatch. There was as yet nothing definable in the situation, which might well resolve itself into a huge joke on the part of the
other two; but Lily had a vague sense that the subject of their experiment was too young, too rich, and too credulous. Her embarrassment
was increased by the fact that Freddy seemed to regard her as
coöperating with himself in the social development of Mrs. Hatch: a
view that suggested, on his part, a permanent interest in the lady's future. There were moments when Lily found an ironic amusement in this
aspect of the case. The thought of launching such a missile as Mrs.
Hatch at the perfidious bosom of society was not without its charm:
Miss Bart had even beguiled her leisure with visions of the fair Norma
introduced for the first time to a family banquet at the Van Osburghs'.
But the thought of being personally connected with the transaction was
less agreeable; and her momentary flashes of amusement were followed
by increasing periods of doubt.

The sense of these doubts was uppermost when, late one afternoon,
she was surprised by a visit from Lawrence Selden. He found her alone
in the wilderness of pink damask, for in Mrs. Hatch's world the tea-hour
was not dedicated to social rites, and the lady was in the hands of her
masseuse.

Selden's entrance had caused Lily an inward start of embarrassment;
but his air of constraint had the effect of restoring her self-possession,
and she took at once the tone of surprise and pleasure, wondering
frankly that he should have traced her to so unlikely a place, and asking
what had inspired him to make the search.

Selden met this with an unusual seriousness: she had never seen him
so little master of the situation, so plainly at the mercy of any obstruc-

tions she might put in his way. "I wanted to see you," he said; and she could not resist observing in reply that he had kept his wishes under remarkable control. She had in truth felt his long absence as one of the chief bitternesses of the last months: his desertion had wounded sensibilities far below the surface of her pride.

Selden met the challenge with directness. "Why should I have come, unless I thought I could be of use to you? It is my only excuse for imagining you could want me."

This struck her as a clumsy evasion, and the thought gave a flash of keenness to her answer. "Then you have come now because you think you can be of use to me?"

He hesitated again. "Yes: in the modest capacity of a person to talk things over with."

For a clever man it was certainly a stupid beginning; and the idea that his awkwardness was due to the fear of her attaching a personal significance to his visit, chilled her pleasure in seeing him. Even under the most adverse conditions, that pleasure always made itself felt: she might hate him, but she had never been able to wish him out of the room. She was very near hating him now; yet the sound of his voice, the way the light fell on his thin dark hair, the way he sat and moved and wore his clothes—she was conscious that even these trivial things were inwoven with her deepest life. In his presence a sudden stillness came upon her, and the turmoil of her spirit ceased; but an impulse of resistance to this stealing influence now prompted her to say: "It 's very good of you to present yourself in that capacity; but what makes you think I have anything particular to talk about?"

Though she kept the even tone of light intercourse, the question was framed in a way to remind him that his good offices were unsought; and for a moment Selden was checked by it. The situation between them was one which could have been cleared up only by a sudden explosion of feeling; and their whole training and habit of mind were against the chances of such an explosion. Selden's calmness seemed rather to harden into resistance, and Miss Bart's into a surface of glittering irony, as they faced each other from the opposite corners of one of Mrs. Hatch's elephantine sofas. The sofa in question, and the apartment peopled by its monstrous mates, served at length to suggest the turn of Selden's reply.

"Gerty told me that you were acting as Mrs. Hatch's secretary; and I knew she was anxious to hear how you were getting on."

Miss Bart received this explanation without perceptible softening. "Why did n't she look me up herself, then?" she asked.

"Because, as you did n't send her your address, she was afraid of being importunate." Selden continued with a smile: "You see no such scruples restrained me; but then I have n't as much to risk if I incur your displeasure."

Lily answered his smile. "You have n't incurred it as yet; but I have an idea that you are going to."

"That rests with you, does n't it? You see my initiative does n't go beyond putting myself at your disposal."

"But in what capacity? What am I to do with you?" she asked in the same light tone.

Selden again glanced about Mrs. Hatch's drawing-room; then he said, with a decision which he seemed to have gathered from this final inspection: "You are to let me take you away from here."

Lily flushed at the suddenness of the attack; then she stiffened under it and said coldly: "And may I ask where you mean me to go?"

"Back to Gerty in the first place, if you will; the essential thing is that it should be away from here."

The unusual harshness of his tone might have shown her how much the words cost him; but she was in no state to measure his feelings while her own were in a flame of revolt. To neglect her, perhaps even to avoid her, at a time when she had most need of her friends, and then suddenly and unwarrantably to break into her life with this strange assumption of authority, was to rouse in her every instinct of pride and self-defence.

"I am very much obliged to you," she said, "for taking such an interest in my plans; but I am quite contented where I am, and have no intention of leaving."

Selden had risen, and was standing before her in an attitude of uncontrollable expectancy.

"That simply means that you don't know where you are!" he exclaimed.

Lily rose also, with a quick flash of anger. "If you have come here to say disagreeable things about Mrs. Hatch——"

"It is only with your relation to Mrs. Hatch that I am concerned."

"My relation to Mrs. Hatch is one I have no reason to be ashamed of. She has helped me to earn a living when my old friends were quite resigned to seeing me starve."

"Nonsense! Starvation is not the only alternative. You know you can always find a home with Gerty till you are independent again."

"You show such an intimate acquaintance with my affairs that I suppose you mean — till my aunt's legacy is paid?"

"I do mean that; Gerty told me of it," Selden acknowledged without embarrassment. He was too much in earnest now to feel any false constraint in speaking his mind.

"But Gerty does not happen to know," Miss Bart rejoined, "that I owe every penny of that legacy."

"Good God!" Selden exclaimed, startled out of his composure by the abruptness of the statement.

"Every penny of it, and more too," Lily repeated; "and you now perhaps see why I prefer to remain with Mrs. Hatch rather than take advantage of Gerty's kindness. I have no money left, except my small income, and I must earn something more to keep myself alive."

Selden hesitated a moment; then he rejoined in a quieter tone: "But with your income and Gerty's—since you allow me to go so far into the details of the situation—you and she could surely contrive a life together which would put you beyond the need of having to support yourself. Gerty, I know, is eager to make such an arrangement, and would be quite happy in it——"

"But I should not," Miss Bart interposed. "There are many reasons why it would be neither kind to Gerty nor wise for myself." She paused a moment, and as he seemed to await a farther explanation, added with a quick lift of her head: "You will perhaps excuse me from giving you these reasons."

"I have no claim to know them," Selden answered, ignoring her tone; "no claim to offer any comment or suggestion beyond the one I have already made. And my right to make that is simply the universal right of a man to enlighten a woman when he sees her unconsciously placed in a false position."

Lily smiled, "I suppose," she rejoined, "that by a false position you mean one outside of what we call society; but you must remember that I had been excluded from those sacred precincts long before I met Mrs. Hatch. As far as I can see, there is very little real difference in being inside or out, and I remember your once telling me that it was only those inside who took the difference seriously."

She had not been without intention in making this allusion to their memorable talk at Bellomont, and she waited with an odd tremor of the nerves to see what response it would bring; but the result of the experiment was disappointing. Selden did not allow the allusion to deflect him from his point; he merely said with completer fulness of emphasis: "The question of being inside or out is, as you say, a small one, and it happens to have nothing to do with the case, except in so far as Mrs. Hatch's desire to be inside may put you in the position I call false."

In spite of the moderation of his tone, each word he spoke had the effect of confirming Lily's resistance. The very apprehensions he aroused hardened her against him: she had been on the alert for the note of personal sympathy, for any sign of recovered power over him; and his attitude of sober impartiality, the absence of all response to her appeal, turned her hurt pride to blind resentment of his interference. The conviction that he had been sent by Gerty, and that, whatever straits he conceived her to be in, he would never voluntarily have come to her aid, strengthened her resolve not to admit him a hair's breadth farther into her confidence. However doubtful she might feel her situation to be, she would rather persist in darkness than owe her enlightenment to Selden.

"I don't know," she said, when he had ceased to speak, "why you imagine me to be situated as you describe; but as you have always told me that the sole object of a bringing-up like mine was to teach a girl to get what she wants, why not assume that that is precisely what I am doing?"

The smile with which she summed up her case was like a clear barrier raised against farther confidences: its brightness held him at such a distance that he had a sense of being almost out of hearing as he rejoined: "I am not sure that I have ever called you a successful example of that kind of bringing-up."

Her colour rose a little at the implication, but she steeled herself with a light laugh.

"Ah, wait a little longer—give me a little more time before you decide!" And as he wavered before her, still watching for a break in the impenetrable front she presented: "Don't give me up; I may still do credit to my training!" she affirmed.

X

Look at those spangles, Miss Bart—every one of 'em sewed on crooked."

The tall forewoman, a pinched perpendicular figure, dropped the condemned structure of wire and net on the table at Lily's side, and passed on to the next figure in the line.

There were twenty of them in the work-room, their fagged profiles, under exaggerated hair, bowed in the harsh north light above the utensils of their art; for it was something more than an industry, surely, this creation of ever-varied settings for the face of fortunate womanhood. Their own faces were sallow with the unwholesomeness of hot air and sedentary toil, rather than with any actual signs of want: they were employed in a fashionable millinery establishment, and were fairly well clothed and well paid; but the youngest among them was as dull and colourless as the middle-aged. In the whole work-room there was only one skin beneath which the blood still visibly played; and that now burned with vexation as Miss Bart, under the lash of the forewoman's comment, began to strip the hat-frame of its over-lapping spangles.

To Gerty Farish's hopeful spirit a solution appeared to have been reached when she remembered how beautifully Lily could trim hats. Instances of young lady-milliners establishing themselves under fashionable patronage, and imparting to their "creations" that indefinable touch which the professional hand can never give, had flattered Gerty's visions of the future, and convinced even Lily that her separation from Mrs. Norma Hatch need not reduce her to dependence on her friends.

The parting had occurred a few weeks after Selden's visit, and would have taken place sooner had it not been for the resistance set up in Lily by his ill-starred offer of advice. The sense of being involved in a transaction she would not have cared to examine too closely had soon afterward defined itself in the light of a hint from Mr. Stancy that, if she "saw them through," she would have no reason to be sorry. The implication that such loyalty would meet with a direct reward had hastened her flight, and flung her back, ashamed and penitent, on the broad bosom of Gerty's sympathy. She did not, however, propose to lie there prone, and Gerty's inspiration about the hats at once revived her hopes of profitable activity. Here was, after all, something that her charming listless hands could really do; she had no doubt of their capacity for knotting a ribbon or placing a flower to advantage. And of course only these finishing touches would be expected of her: subordinate fingers, blunt, grey, needle-pricked fingers, would prepare the shapes and stitch the linings, while she presided over the charming little front shop — a shop all white panels, mirrors, and moss-green hangings — where her finished creations, hats, wreaths, aigrettes and the rest, perched on their stands like birds just poising for flight.

But at the very outset of Gerty's campaign this vision of the green-and-white shop had been dispelled. Other young ladies of fashion had been thus "set-up," selling their hats by the mere attraction of a name and the reputed knack of tying a bow; but these privileged beings could command a faith in their powers materially expressed by the readiness to pay their shop-rent and advance a handsome sum for current expenses. Where was Lily to find such support? And even could it have been found, how were the ladies on whose approval she depended to be induced to give her their patronage? Gerty learned that whatever sympathy her friend's case might have excited a few months since had been imperilled, if not lost, by her associations with Mrs. Hatch. Once again, Lily had withdrawn from an ambiguous situation in time to save her self-respect, but too late for public vindication. Freddy Van Osburgh was not to marry Mrs. Hatch; he had been rescued at the eleventh hour—some said by the efforts of Gus Trenor and Rosedale—and despatched to Europe with old Ned Van Alstyne; but the risk he had run would always be ascribed to Miss Bart's connivance, and would somehow serve as a summing-up and corroboration of the vague general distrust of her. It was a relief to those who had hung back from her to find themselves thus justified, and they were inclined to insist a little on her connection with the Hatch case in order to show that they had been right.

Gerty's guest, at any rate, brought up against a solid wall of resistance; and even when Carry Fisher, momentarily penitent for her share in the Hatch affair, joined her efforts to Miss Farish's, they met with no better success. Gerty had tried to veil her failure in tender ambiguities; but Carry, always the soul of candour, put the case squarely to her friend.

"I went straight to Judy Trenor; she has fewer prejudices than the others, and besides she's always hated Bertha Dorset. But what *have* you done to her, Lily? At the very first word about giving you a start she flamed out about some money you'd got from Gus; I never knew her so hot before. You know she'll let him do anything but spend money on his friends: the only reason she's decent to me now is that she knows I'm not hard up.—He speculated for you, you say? Well, what's the harm? He had no business to lose. He *did n't* lose? Then what on earth—but I never *could* understand you, Lily!"

The end of it was that, after anxious enquiry and much deliberation, Mrs. Fisher and Gerty, for once oddly united in their effort to help their friend, decided on placing her in the work-room of Mme. Regina's renowned millinery establishment. Even this arrangement was not effected without considerable negotiation, for Mme. Regina had a strong prejudice against untrained assistance, and was induced to yield only by the fact that she owed the patronage of Mrs. Bry and Mrs. Gormer to Carry Fisher's influence. She had been willing from the first to employ Lily in the show-room: as a displayer of hats, a fashionable beauty might be a valuable asset. But to this suggestion Miss Bart opposed a negative which Gerty emphatically supported, while Mrs. Fisher, inwardly unconvinced, but resigned to this latest proof of Lily's unreason, agreed that perhaps in the end it would be more useful that she should learn the trade. To Regina's work-room Lily was therefore committed by her friends, and there Mrs. Fisher left her with a sigh of relief, while Gerty's watchfulness continued to hover over her at a distance.

Lily had taken up her work early in January: it was now two months later, and she was still being rebuked for her inability to sew spangles on a hat-frame. As she returned to her work she heard a titter pass down the tables. She knew she was an object of criticism and amusement to the other work-women. They were, of course, aware of her history—the exact situation of every girl in the room was known and freely discussed by all the others—but the knowledge did not produce in them any awkward sense of class distinction: it merely explained why her untutored fingers were still blundering over the rudiments of the trade. Lily had no desire that they should recognize any social difference in her; but she had hoped to be received as their equal, and perhaps before long to show herself their superior by a special deftness of touch, and it was humiliating to find that, after two months of drudgery, she still betrayed her lack of early training. Remote was the day when she might aspire to exercise the talents she felt confident of possessing; only experienced workers were entrusted with the delicate art of shaping and trimming the hat, and the forewoman still held her inexorably to the routine of preparatory work.

She began to rip the spangles from the frame, listening absently to the buzz of talk which rose and fell with the coming and going of Miss Haines's active figure. The air was closer than usual, because Miss Haines, who had a cold, had not allowed a window to be opened even during the noon recess; and Lily's head was so heavy with the weight of a sleepless night that the chatter of her companions had the incoherence of a dream.

"I *told* her he 'd never look at her again; and he did n't. I would n't have, either—I think she acted real mean to him. He took her to the Arion Ball, and had a hack for her both ways. . . . She 's taken ten bottles, and her headaches don't seem no better—but she 's written a testimonial to say the first bottle cured her, and she got five dollars and her picture in the paper. . . . Mrs. Trenor's hat? The one with the green Paradise? Here, Miss Haines—it 'll be ready right off. . . . That was one of the Trenor girls here yesterday with Mrs. George Dorset. How 'd I know? Why, Madam sent for me to alter the flower in that Virot hat— the blue tulle: she 's tall and slight, with her hair fuzzed out—a good deal like Mamie Leach, on'y thinner. . . . "

On and on it flowed, a current of meaningless sound, on which, startlingly enough, a familiar name now and then floated to the surface.

It was the strangest part of Lily's strange experience, the hearing of these names, the seeing the fragmentary and distorted image of the world she had lived in reflected in the mirror of the working-girls' minds. She had never before suspected the mixture of insatiable curiosity and contemptuous freedom with which she and her kind were discussed in this underworld of toilers who lived on their vanity and self-indulgence. Every girl in Mme. Regina's work-room knew to whom the headgear in her hands was destined, and had her opinion of its future wearer, and a definite knowledge of the latter's place in the social system. That Lily was a star fallen from that sky did not, after the first stir of curiosity had subsided, materially add to their interest in her. She had fallen, she had "gone under," and true to the ideal of their race, they were awed only by success—by the gross tangible image of material achievement. The consciousness of her different point of view merely kept them at a little distance from her, as though she were a foreigner with whom it was an effort to talk.

"Miss Bart, if you can't sew those spangles on more regular I guess you 'd better give the hat to Miss Kilroy."

Lily looked down ruefully at her handiwork. The forewoman was right: the sewing on of the spangles was inexcusably bad. What made her so much more clumsy than usual? Was it a growing distaste for her task, or actual physical disability? She felt tired and confused: it was an effort to put her thoughts together. She rose and handed the hat to Miss Kilroy, who took it with a suppressed smile.

"I 'm sorry; I 'm afraid I am not well," she said to the forewoman.

Miss Haines offered no comment. From the first she augured ill of Mme. Regina's consenting to include a fashionable apprentice among her workers. In that temple of art no raw beginners were wanted, and Miss Haines would have been more than human had she not taken a certain pleasure in seeing her forebodings confirmed.

"You 'd better go back to binding edges," she said drily.

Lily slipped out last among the band of liberated work-women. She did not care to be mingled in their noisy dispersal: once in the street, she always felt an irresistible return to her old standpoint, an instinctive shrinking from all that was unpolished and promiscuous. In the days— how distant they now seemed!—when she had visited the Girls' Club with Gerty Farish, she had felt an enlightened interest in the working-classes; but that was because she looked down on them from above, from the happy altitude of her grace and her beneficence. Now that she was on a level with them, the point of view was less interesting.

She felt a touch on her arm, and met the penitent eye of Miss Kilroy.

"Miss Bart, I guess you can sew those spangles on as well as I can when you 're feeling right. Miss Haines did n't act fair to you."

Lily's colour rose at the unexpected advance: it was a long time since real kindness had looked at her from any eyes but Gerty's.

"Oh, thank you: I 'm not particularly well, but Miss Haines was right. I *am* clumsy."

"Well, it 's mean work for anybody with a headache." Miss Kilroy paused irresolutely. "You ought to go right home and lay down. Ever try orangeine?"

"Thank you." Lily held out her hand. "It 's very kind of you — I mean to go home."

She looked gratefully at Miss Kilroy, but neither knew what more to say. Lily was aware that the other was on the point of offering to go home with her, but she wanted to be alone and silent — even kindness, the sort of kindness that Miss Kilroy could give, would have jarred on her just then.

"Thank you," she repeated as she turned away.

She struck westward through the dreary March twilight, toward the street where her boarding-house stood. She had resolutely refused Gerty's offer of hospitality. Something of her mother's fierce shrinking from observation and sympathy was beginning to develop in her, and the promiscuity of small quarters and close intimacy seemed, on the whole, less endurable than the solitude of a hall bedroom in a house where she could come and go unremarked among other workers. For a while she had been sustained by this desire for privacy and independence; but now, perhaps from increasing physical weariness, the lassitude brought about by hours of unwonted confinement, she was beginning to feel acutely the ugliness and discomfort of her surroundings. The day's task done, she dreaded to return to her narrow room, with its blotched wall-paper and shabby paint; and she hated every step of the walk thither, through the degradation of a New York street in the last stages of decline from fashion to commerce.

But what she dreaded most of all was having to pass the chemist's at the corner of Sixth Avenue. She had meant to take another street: she had usually done so of late. But today her steps were irresistibly drawn toward the flaring plate-glass corner; she tried to take the lower crossing, but a laden dray crowded her back, and she struck across the street obliquely, reaching the sidewalk just opposite the chemist's door.

Over the counter she caught the eye of the clerk who had waited on her before, and slipped the prescription into his hand. There could be no question about the prescription: it was a copy of one of Mrs.

Hatch's, obligingly furnished by that lady's chemist. Lily was confident that the clerk would fill it without hesitation; yet the nervous dread of a refusal, or even of an expression of doubt, communicated itself to her restless hands as she affected to examine the bottles of perfume stacked on the glass case before her.

The clerk had read the prescription without comment; but in the act of handing out the bottle he paused.

"You don't want to increase the dose, you know," he remarked.

Lily's heart contracted. What did he mean by looking at her in that way?

"Of course not," she murmured, holding out her hand.

"That 's all right: it 's a queer-acting drug. A drop or two more, and off you go — the doctors don't know why."

The dread lest he should question her, or keep the bottle back, choked the murmur of acquiescence in her throat; and when at length she emerged safely from the shop she was almost dizzy with the intensity of her relief. The mere touch of the packet thrilled her tired nerves with the delicious promise of a night of sleep, and in the reaction from her momentary fear she felt as if the first fumes of drowsiness were already stealing over her.

In her confusion she stumbled against a man who was hurrying down the last steps of the elevated station. He drew back, and she heard her name uttered with surprise. It was Rosedale, fur-coated, glossy and prosperous — but why did she seem to see him so far off, and as if through a mist of splintered crystals? Before she could account for the phenomenon she found herself shaking hands with him. They had parted with scorn on her side and anger upon his; but all trace of these emotions seemed to vanish as their hands met, and she was only aware of a confused wish that she might continue to hold fast to him.

"Why, what 's the matter, Miss Lily? You 're not well!" he exclaimed; and she forced her lips into a pallid smile of reassurance.

"I 'm a little tired — it 's nothing. Stay with me a moment, please," she faltered. That she should be asking this service of Rosedale!

He glanced at the dirty and unpropitious corner on which they stood, with the shriek of the "elevated" and the tumult of trams and waggons contending hideously in their ears.

"We can't stay here; but let me take you somewhere for a cup of tea. The *Longworth* is only a few yards off, and there 'll be no one there at this hour."

A cup of tea in quiet, somewhere out of the noise and ugliness, seemed for the moment the one solace she could bear. A few steps brought them to the ladies' door of the hotel he had named, and a moment later he was seated opposite to her, and the waiter had placed the tea-tray between them.

"Not a drop of brandy or whiskey first? You look regularly done up, Miss Lily. Well, take your tea strong, then; and, waiter, get a cushion for the lady's back."

Lily smiled faintly at the injunction to take her tea strong. It was the temptation she was always struggling to resist. Her craving for the keen stimulant was forever conflicting with that other craving for sleep—the midnight craving which only the little phial in her hand could still. But today, at any rate, the tea could hardly be too strong: she counted on it to pour warmth and resolution into her empty veins.

As she leaned back before him, her lids drooping in utter lassitude, though the first warm draught already tinged her face with returning life, Rosedale was seized afresh by the poignant surprise of her beauty. The dark pencilling of fatigue under her eyes, the morbid blue-veined pallour of the temples, brought out the brightness of her hair and lips, as though all her ebbing vitality were centred there. Against the dull chocolate-coloured background of the restaurant, the purity of her head stood out as it had never done in the most brightly-lit ball-room. He looked at her with a startled uncomfortable feeling, as though her beauty were a forgotten enemy that had lain in ambush and now sprang out on him unawares.

To clear the air he tried to take an easy tone with her. "Why, Miss Lily, I have n't seen you for an age. I did n't know what had become of you."

As he spoke he was checked by an embarrassing sense of the complications to which this might lead. Though he had not seen her he had heard of her; he knew of her connection with Mrs. Hatch, and of the talk resulting from it. Mrs. Hatch's *milieu* was one which he had once assiduously frequented, and now as devoutly shunned.

Lily, to whom the tea had restored her usual clearness of mind, saw what was in his thoughts and said with a slight smile: "You would not be likely to know about me. I have joined the working classes."

He stared in genuine wonder. "You don't mean——? Why, what on earth are you doing?"

"Learning to be a milliner—at least *trying* to learn," she hastily qualified the statement.

Rosedale suppressed a low whistle of surprise. "Come off—you ain't serious, are you?"

"Perfectly serious. I 'm obliged to work for my living."

"But I understood—I thought you were with Norma Hatch."

"You heard I had gone to her as her secretary?"

"Something of the kind, I believe." He leaned forward to refill her cup.

Lily guessed the possibilities of embarrassment which the topic held for him, and raising her eyes to his, she said suddenly: "I left her two months ago."

Rosedale continued to fumble awkwardly with the tea-pot, and she felt sure that he had heard what had been said of her. But what was there that Rosedale did not hear?

"Was n't it a soft berth?" he enquired, with an attempt at lightness.

"Too soft—one might have sunk in too deep." Lily rested one arm on the edge of the table, and sat looking at him more intently than she had ever looked before. An uncontrollable impulse was urging her to put her case to this man, from whose curiosity she had always so fiercely defended herself.

"You know Mrs. Hatch, I think? Well, perhaps you can understand that she might make things too easy for one."

Rosedale looked faintly puzzled, and she remembered that allusiveness was lost on him.

"It was no place for you, anyhow," he agreed, so suffused and immersed in the light of her full gaze that he found himself being drawn into strange depths of intimacy. He who had had to subsist on mere fugitive glances, looks winged in flight and swiftly lost under covert, now found her eyes settling on him with a brooding intensity that fairly dazzled him.

"I left," Lily continued, "lest people should say I was helping Mrs. Hatch to marry Freddy Van Osburgh—who is not in the least too good for her—and as they will continue to say it, I see that I might as well have stayed where I was."

"Oh, Freddy——" Rosedale brushed aside the topic with an air of its unimportance which gave a sense of the immense perspective he had acquired. "Freddy don't count—but I knew *you* were n't mixed up in that. It ain't your style."

Lily coloured slightly: she could not conceal from herself that the words gave her pleasure. She would have liked to sit there, drinking more tea, and continuing to talk of herself to Rosedale. But the old habit of observing the conventions reminded her that it was time to bring their colloquy to an end, and she made a faint motion to push back her chair.

Rosedale stopped her with a protesting gesture. "Wait a minute— don't go yet; sit quiet and rest a little longer. You look thoroughly played out. And you have n't told me——" He broke off, conscious of going farther than he had meant. She saw the struggle and understood it; understood also the nature of the spell to which he yielded as, with his eyes on her face, he began again abruptly: "What on earth did you mean by saying just now that you were learning to be a milliner?"

"Just what I said. I am an apprentice at Regina's."

"Good Lord—*you?* But what for? I knew your aunt had turned you down: Mrs. Fisher told me about it. But I understood you got a legacy from her——"

"I got ten thousand dollars; but the legacy is not to be paid till next summer."

"Well, but—look here: you could *borrow* on it any time you wanted."

She took her head gravely. "No; for I owe it already."

"Owe it? The whole ten thousand?"

"Every penny." She paused, and then continued abruptly, with her eyes on his face: "I think Gus Trenor spoke to you once about having made some money for me in stocks."

She waited, and Rosedale, congested with embarrassment, muttered that he remembered something of the kind.

"He made about nine thousand dollars," Lily pursued, in the same tone of eager communicativeness. "At the time, I understood that he was speculating with my own money: it was incredibly stupid of me, but I knew nothing of business. Afterward I found out that he had *not* used my money—that what he said he had made for me he had really given me. It was meant in kindness, of course; but it was not the sort of obligation one could remain under. Unfortunately I had spent the money before I discovered my mistake; and so my legacy will have to go to pay it back. That is the reason why I am trying to learn a trade."

She made the statement clearly, deliberately, with pauses between the sentences, so that each should have time to sink deeply into her hearer's mind. She had a passionate desire that some one should know the truth about this transaction, and also that the rumour of her intention to repay the money should reach Judy Trenor's ears. And it had suddenly occurred to her that Rosedale, who had surprised Trenor's confidence, was the fitting person to receive and transmit her version of the facts. She had even felt a momentary exhilaration at the thought of thus relieving herself of her detested secret; but the sensation gradually faded in the telling, and as she ended her pallour was suffused with a deep blush of misery.

Rosedale continued to state at her in wonder; but the wonder took the turn she had least expected.

"But see here—if that 's the case, it cleans you out altogether?"

He put it to her as if she had not grasped the consequences of her act; as if her incorrigible ignorance of business were about to precipitate her into a fresh act of folly.

"Altogether—yes," she calmly agreed.

He sat silent, his thick hands clasped on the table, his little puzzled eyes exploring the recesses of the deserted restaurant.

"See here—that 's fine," he exclaimed abruptly.

Lily rose from her seat with a deprecating laugh. "Oh, no—it 's merely a bore," she asserted, gathering together the ends of her feather scarf.

Rosedale remained seated, too intent on his thoughts to notice her movement. "Miss Lily, if you want any backing—I like pluck——" broke from him disconnectedly.

"Thank you." She held out her hand. "Your tea has given me a tremendous backing. I feel equal to anything now."

Her gesture seemed to show a definite intention of dismissal, but her companion had tossed a bill to the waiter, and was slipping his short arms into his expensive overcoat.

"Wait a minute—you 've got to let me walk home with you," he said.

Lily uttered no protest, and when he had paused to make sure of his change they emerged from the hotel and crossed Sixth Avenue again. As she led the way westward past a long line of areas which, through the distortion of their paintless rails, revealed with increasing candour the *disjecta membra* of bygone dinners, Lily felt that Rosedale was taking contemptuous note of the neighbourhood; and before the doorstep at which she finally paused he looked up with an air of incredulous disgust.

"This is n't the place? Some one told me you were living with Miss Farish."

"No: I am boarding here. I have lived too long on my friends."

He continued to scan the blistered brown stone front, the windows draped with discoloured lace, and the Pompeian decoration of the muddy vestibule; then he looked back at her face and said with a visible effort: "You 'll let me come and see you some day?"

She smiled, recognizing the heroism of the offer to the point of being frankly touched by it. "Thank you—I shall be very glad," she made answer, in the first sincere words she had ever spoken to him.

That evening in her own room Miss Bart—who had fled early from the heavy fumes of the basement dinner-table—sat musing upon the impulse which had led her to unbosom herself to Rosedale. Beneath it she discovered an increasing sense of loneliness—a dread of returning to the solitude of her room, while she could be anywhere else, or in any company but her own. Circumstances, of late, had combined to cut her off more and more from her few remaining friends. On Carry Fisher's part the withdrawal was perhaps not quite involuntary. Having made her final effort on Lily's behalf, and landed her safely in Mme. Regina's work-room, Mrs. Fisher seemed disposed to rest from her labours; and Lily, understanding the reason, could not condemn her. Carry had in fact come dangerously near to being involved in the episode of Mrs. Norma Hatch, and it had taken some verbal ingenuity to extricate herself. She frankly owned to having brought Lily and Mrs. Hatch together, but then she did not know Mrs. Hatch—she had expressly warned Lily that she did not know Mrs. Hatch—and besides, she was not Lily's keeper, and really the girl was old enough to take care of herself. Carry did not put her own case so brutally, but she allowed it to be thus put for her by her latest bosom friend, Mrs. Jack Stepney: Mrs. Stepney, trembling over the narrowness of her only brother's escape, but eager to vindicate Mrs. Fisher, at whose house she could count on the "jolly parties" which had become a necessity to her since marriage had emancipated her from the Van Osburgh point of view.

Lily understood the situation and could make allowances for it. Carry had been a good friend to her in difficult days, and perhaps only a friendship like Gerty's could be proof against such an increasing strain. Gerty's friendship did indeed hold fast; yet Lily was beginning to avoid her also. For she could not go to Gerty's without risk of meeting Selden; and to meet him now would be pure pain. It was pain enough even to think of him, whether she considered him in the distinctness of her waking thoughts, or felt the obsession of his presence through the blur of her tormented nights. That was one of the reasons why she had turned again to Mrs. Hatch's prescription. In the uneasy snatches of her natural dreams he came to her sometimes in the old guise of fellowship and tenderness; and she would rise from the sweet delusion mocked and emptied of her courage. But in the sleep which the phial procured she sank far below such half-waking visitations, sank into depths of dreamless annihilation from which she woke each morning with an obliterated past.

Gradually, to be sure, the stress of the old thoughts would return; but at least they did not importune her waking hour. The drug gave her a momentary illusion of complete renewal, from which she drew strength to take up her daily work. The strength was more and more needed as the perplexities of her future increased. She knew that to Gerty and Mrs. Fisher she was only passing through a temporary period of probation, since they believed that the apprenticeship she was serving at Mme. Regina's would enable her, when Mrs. Peniston's legacy was paid, to realize the vision of the green-and-white shop with the fuller competence acquired by her preliminary training. But to Lily herself, aware that the legacy could not be put to such a use, the preliminary training seemed a wasted effort. She understood clearly enough that, even if she could ever learn to compete with hands formed from childhood for their special work, the small pay she received would not be a sufficient addition to her income to compensate her for such drudgery. And the realization of this fact brought her recurringly face to face with the temptation to use the legacy in establishing her business. Once installed, and in command of her own work-women, she believed she had sufficient tact and ability to attract a fashionable *clientèle;* and if the business succeeded she could gradually lay aside money enough to discharge her debt to Trenor. But the task might take years to accomplish, even if she continued to stint herself to the utmost; and meanwhile her pride would be crushed under the weight of an intolerable obligation.

These were her superficial considerations; but under them lurked the secret dread that the obligation might not always remain intolerable. She knew she could not count on her continuity of purpose, and what really frightened her was the thought that she might gradually accommodate herself to remaining indefinitely in Trenor's debt, as she had accommodated herself to the part allotted her on the Sabrina, and as she had so nearly drifted into acquiescing with Stancy's scheme for the advancement of Mrs. Hatch. Her danger lay, as she knew, in her old incurable dread of discomfort and poverty; in the fear of that mounting tide of dinginess against which her mother had so passionately warned her. And now a new vista of peril opened before her. She understood that Rosedale was ready to lend her money; and the longing to take advantage of his offer began to haunt her insidiously. It was of course impossible to accept a loan from Rosedale; but proximate possibilities hovered temptingly before her. She was quite sure that he would come and see her again, and almost sure that, if he did, she could bring him to the point of offering to marry her on the terms she had previously rejected. Would she still reject them if they were offered? More and more, with every fresh mischance befalling her, did the pursuing furies seem to take the shape of Bertha Dorset; and close at hand, safely locked among her papers, lay the means of ending their pursuit. The temptation, which her scorn of Rosedale had once enabled her to reject, now insistently returned upon her; and how much strength was left her to oppose it?

What little there was must at any rate be husbanded to the utmost; she could not trust herself again to the perils of a sleepless night. Through the long hours of silence the dark spirit of fatigue and loneliness crouched upon her breast, leaving her so drained of bodily strength that her morning thoughts swam in a haze of weakness. The only hope of renewal lay in the little bottle at her bed-side; and how much longer that hope would last she dared not conjecture.

XI

Lily, lingering for a moment on the corner, looked out on the afternoon spectacle of Fifth Avenue.

It was a day in late April, and the sweetness of spring was in the air. It mitigated the ugliness of the long crowded thoroughfare, blurred the gaunt roof-lines, threw a mauve veil over the discouraging perspective of the side streets, and gave a touch of poetry to the delicate haze of green that marked the entrance to the Park.

As Lily stood there, she recognized several familiar faces in the passing carriages. The season was over, and its ruling forces had disbanded; but a few still lingered, delaying their departure for Europe, or passing through town on their return from the South. Among them was Mrs. Van Osburgh, swaying majestically in her C-spring barouche, with Mrs. Percy Gryce at her side, and the new heir to the Gryce millions enthroned before them on his nurse's knees. They were succeeded by Mrs. Hatch's electric victoria, in which that lady reclined in the lonely splendour of a spring toilet obviously designed for company; and a moment or two later came Judy Trenor, accompanied by Lady Skiddaw, who had come over for her annual tarpon fishing and a dip into "the street."

This fleeting glimpse of her past served to emphasize the sense of aimlessness with which Lily at length turned toward home. She had nothing to do for the rest of the day, nor for the days to come; for the season was over in millinery as well as in society, and a week earlier Mme. Regina had notified her that her services were no longer required. Mme. Regina always reduced her staff on the first of May, and Miss

Bart's attendance had of late been so irregular—she had so often been unwell, and had done so little work when she came—that it was only as a favour that her dismissal had hitherto been deferred.

Lily did not question the justice of the decision. She was conscious of having been forgetful, awkward and slow to learn. It was bitter to acknowledge her inferiority even to herself, but the fact had been brought home to her that as a bread-winner she could never compete with professional ability. Since she had been brought up to be ornamental, she could hardly blame herself for failing to serve any practical purpose; but the discovery put an end to her consoling sense of universal efficiency.

As she turned homeward her thoughts shrank in anticipation from the fact that there would be nothing to get up for the next morning. The luxury of lying late in bed was a pleasure belonging to the life of ease; it had no part in the utilitarian existence of the boarding-house. She liked to leave her room early, and to return to it as late as possible; and she was walking slowly now in order to postpone the detested approach to her doorstep.

But the doorstep, as she drew near it, acquired a sudden interest from the fact that it was occupied—and indeed filled—by the conspicuous figure of Mr. Rosedale, whose presence seemed to take on an added amplitude from the meanness of his surroundings.

The sight stirred Lily with an irresistible sense of triumph. Rosedale, a day or two after their chance meeting, had called to enquire if she had recovered from her indisposition; but since then she had not seen or heard from him, and his absence seemed to betoken a struggle to keep away, to let her pass once more out of his life. If this were the case, his return showed that the struggle had been unsuccessful, for Lily knew he was not the man to waste his time in an ineffectual sentimental dalliance. He was too busy, too practical, and above all too much preoccupied with his own advancement, to indulge in such unprofitable asides.

In the peacock-blue parlour, with its bunches of dried pampas grass, and discoloured steel engravings of sentimental episodes, he looked about him with unconcealed disgust, laying his hat distrustfully on the dusty console adorned with a Rogers statuette.

Lily sat down on one of the plush and rosewood sofas, and he deposited himself in a rocking-chair draped with a starched antimacassar which scraped unpleasantly against the pink fold of skin above his collar.

"My goodness—you can't go on living here!" he exclaimed.

Lily smiled at his tone. "I am not sure that I can; but I have gone over my expenses very carefully, and I rather think I shall be able to manage it."

"Be able to manage it? That 's not what I mean — it's no place for you!"

"It 's what *I* mean; for I have been out of work for the last week."

"Out of work — out of work! What a way for you to talk! The idea of your having to work — it 's preposterous." He brought out his sentences in short violent jerks, as though they were forced up from a deep inner crater of indignation. "It 's a farce — a crazy farce," he repeated, his eyes fixed on the long vista of the room reflected in the blotched glass between the windows.

Lily continued to meet his expostulations with a smile. "I don't know why I should regard myself as an exception —— " she began.

"Because you *are;* that 's why; and your being in a place like this is a damnable outrage. I can't talk of it calmly."

She had in truth never seen him so shaken out of his usual glibness; and there was something almost moving to her in his inarticulate struggle with his emotions.

He rose with a start which left the rocking-chair quivering on its beam ends, and placed himself squarely before her.

"Look here, Miss Lily, I 'm going to Europe next week: going over to Paris and London for a couple of months — and I can't leave you like this. I can't do it. I know it 's none of my business — you 've let me understand that often enough; but things are worse with you now than they have been before, and you must see that you 've got to accept help from somebody. You spoke to me the other day about some debt to Trenor. I know what you mean — and I respect you for feeling as you do about it."

A blush of surprise rose to Lily's pale face, but before she could interrupt him he had continued eagerly: "Well, I 'll lend you the money to pay Trenor; and I won't — I — see here, don't take me up till I 've finished. What I mean is, it 'll be a plain business arrangement, such as one man would make with another. Now, what have you got to say against that?"

Lily's blush deepened to a glow in which humiliation and gratitude were mingled; and both sentiments revealed themselves in the unexpected gentleness of her reply.

"Only this: that it is exactly what Gus Trenor proposed; and that I can never again be sure of understanding the plainest business arrangement." Then, realizing that this answer contained a germ of injustice, she added, even more kindly: "Not that I don't appreciate your kindness—that I 'm not grateful for it. But a business arrangement between us would in any case be impossible, because I shall have no security to give when my debt to Gus Trenor has been paid."

Rosedale received this statement in silence: he seemed to feel the note of finality in her voice, yet to be unable to accept it as closing the question between them.

In the silence Lily had a clear perception of what was passing through his mind. Whatever perplexity he felt as to the inexorableness of her course—however little he penetrated its motive—she saw that it unmistakably tended to strengthen her hold over him. It was as though the sense in her of unexplained scruples and resistances had the same attraction as the delicacy of feature, the fastidiousness of manner, which gave her an external rarity, an air of being impossible to match. As he advanced in social experience this uniqueness had acquired a greater value for him, as though he were a collector who had learned to distinguish minor differences of design and quality in some long-coveted object.

Lily, perceiving all this, understood that he would marry her at once, on the sole condition of a reconciliation with Mrs. Dorset; and the temptation was the less easy to put aside because, little by little, circumstances were breaking down her dislike for Rosedale. The dislike, indeed, still subsisted; but it was penetrated here and there by the perception of mitigating qualities in him: of a certain gross kindliness, a rather helpless fidelity of sentiment, which seemed to be struggling through the hard surface of his material ambitions.

Reading his dismissal in her eyes, he held out his hand with a gesture which conveyed something of this inarticulate conflict.

"If you 'd only let me, I 'd set you up over them all—I 'd put you where you could wipe your feet on 'em!" he declared; and it touched her oddly to see that his new passion had not altered his old standard of values.

Lily took no sleeping-drops that night. She lay awake viewing her situation in the crude light which Rosedale's visit had shed on it. In fending off the offer he was so plainly ready to renew, had she not sacrificed to one of those abstract notions of honour that might be called the conventionalities of the moral life? What debt did she owe to a social order which had condemned and banished her without trial? She had never been heard in her own defence; she was innocent of the charge on which she had been found guilty; and the irregularity of her conviction might seem to justify the use of methods as irregular in recovering her lost rights. Bertha Dorset, to save herself, had not scrupled to ruin her by an open falsehood; why should she hesitate to make private use of the facts that chance had put in her way? After all, half the opprobrium of such an act lies in the name attached to it. Call it blackmail and it becomes unthinkable; but explain that it injures no one, and that the rights regained by it were unjustly forfeited, and he must be a formalist indeed who can find no plea in its defence.

The arguments pleading for it with Lily were the old unanswerable ones of the personal situation: the sense of injury, the sense of failure, the passionate craving for a fair chance against the selfish despotism of society. She had learned by experience that she had neither the aptitude nor the moral constancy to remake her life on new lines; to become a worker among workers, and let the world of luxury and pleasure sweep by her unregarded. She could not hold herself much to blame for this ineffectiveness, and she was perhaps less to blame than she believed. Inherited tendencies had combined with early training to make her the highly specialized product she was: an organism as helpless out of its narrow range as the sea-anemone torn from the rock. She had been fashioned to adorn and delight; to what other end does nature round the rose-leaf and paint the humming-bird's breast? And was it her fault that the purely decorative mission is less easily and harmoniously fulfilled among social beings than in the world of nature? That it is apt to be hampered by material necessities or complicated by moral scruples?

These last were the two antagonistic forces which fought out their battle in her breast during the long watches of the night; and when she rose the next morning she hardly knew where the victory lay. She was exhausted by the reaction of a night without sleep, coming after many nights of rest artificially obtained; and in the distorting light of fatigue the future stretched out before her grey, interminable and desolate.

She lay late in bed, refusing the coffee and fried eggs which the friendly Irish servant thrust through her door, and hating the intimate domestic noises of the house and the cries and rumblings of the street. Her week of idleness had brought home to her with exaggerated force these small aggravations of the boarding-house world, and she yearned for that other luxurious world, whose machinery is so carefully concealed that one scene flows into another without perceptible agency.

At length she rose and dressed. Since she had left Mme. Regina's she had spent her days in the streets, partly to escape from the uncongenial promiscuities of the boarding-house, and partly in the hope that physical fatigue would help her to sleep. But once out of the house, she could not decide where to go; for she had avoided Gerty since her dismissal from the milliner's, and she was not sure of a welcome anywhere else.

The morning was in harsh contrast to the previous day. A cold grey sky threatened rain, and a high wind drove the dust in wild spirals up and down the streets. Lily walked up Fifth Avenue toward the Park, hoping to find a sheltered nook where she might sit; but the wind chilled her, and after an hour's wandering under the tossing boughs she yielded to her increasing weariness, and took refuge in a little restaurant in Fifty-ninth Street. She was not hungry, and had meant to go without luncheon; but she was too tired to return home, and the long perspective of white tables showed alluringly through the windows.

The room was full of women and girls, all too much engaged in the rapid absorption of tea and pie to remark her entrance. A hum of shrill voices reverberated against the low ceiling, leaving Lily shut out in a little circle of silence. She felt a sudden pang of profound loneliness. She had lost the sense of time, and it seemed to her as though she had not spoken to any one for days. Her eyes sought the faces about her, craving a responsive glance, some sign of an intuition of her trouble. But the sallow preoccupied women, with their bags and note-books and rolls of music, were all engrossed in their own affairs, and even those who sat by themselves were busy running over proof-sheets or devouring magazines between their hurried gulps of tea. Lily alone was stranded in a great waste of disoccupation.

She drank several cups of the tea which was served with her portion of stewed oysters, and her brain felt clearer and livelier when she emerged once more into the street. She realized now that, as she sat in the restaurant, she had unconsciously arrived at a final decision. The discovery gave her an immediate illusion of activity: it was exhilarating to think that she had actually a reason for hurrying home. To prolong her enjoyment of the sensation she decided to walk; but the distance was so great that she found herself glancing nervously at the clocks on the way. One of the surprises of her unoccupied state was the discovery that time, when it is left to itself and no definite demands are made on it, cannot be trusted to move at any recognized pace. Usually it loiters; but just when one has come to count upon its slowness, it may suddenly break into a wild irrational gallop.

She found, however, on reaching home, that the hour was still early enough for her to sit down and rest a few minutes before putting her plan into execution. The delay did not perceptibly weaken her resolve. She was frightened and yet stimulated by the reserved force of resolution which she felt within herself: she saw it was going to be easier, a great deal easier, than she had imagined.

At five o'clock she rose, unlocked her trunk, and took out a sealed packet which she slipped into the bosom of her dress. Even the contact with the packet did not shake her nerves as she had half-expected it would. She seemed encased in a strong armour of indifference, as though the vigorous exertion of her will had finally benumbed her finer sensibilities.

She dressed herself once more for the street, locked her door and went out. When she emerged on the pavement, the day was still high, but a threat of rain darkened the sky and cold gusts shook the signs projecting from the basement shops along the street. She reached Fifth Avenue and began to walk slowly northward. She was sufficiently familiar with Mrs. Dorset's habits to know that she could always be found at home after five. She might not, indeed, be accessible to visitors, especially to a visitor so unwelcome, and against whom it was quite possible that she had guarded herself by special orders; but Lily had written a note which she meant to send up with her name, and which she thought would secure her admission.

She had allowed herself time to walk to Mrs. Dorset's, thinking that the quick movement through the cold evening air would help to steady her nerves; but she really felt no need of being tranquillized. Her survey of the situation remained calm and unwavering.

As she reached Fiftieth Street the clouds broke abruptly, and a rush of cold rain slanted into her face. She had no umbrella and the moisture quickly penetrated her thin spring dress. She was still half a mile from her destination, and she decided to walk across to Madison Avenue and take the electric car. As she turned into the side street, a vague memory stirred in her. The row of budding trees, the new brick and limestone house-fronts, the Georgian flat-house with flower-boxes on its balconies, were merged together into the setting of a familiar scene. It was down this street that she had walked with Selden, that September day two years ago; a few yards ahead was the doorway they had entered together. The recollection loosened a throng of benumbed sensations — longings, regrets, imaginings, the throbbing brood of the only spring her heart had ever known. It was strange to find herself passing his house on such an errand. She seemed suddenly to see her action as he would see it — and the fact of his own connection with it, the fact that, to attain her end, she must trade on his name, and profit by a secret of his past, chilled her blood with shame. What a long way she had travelled since the day of their first talk together! Even then her feet had

been set in the path she was now following—even then she had resisted
the hand he had held out.

All her resentment of his fancied coldness was swept away in this
overwhelming rush of recollection. Twice he had been ready to help her—
to help her by loving her, as he had said—and if, the third time, he had
seemed to fail her, whom but herself could she accuse? . . . Well, that
part of her life was over; she did not know why her thoughts still clung
to it. But the sudden longing to see him remained; it grew to hunger as
she paused on the pavement opposite his door. The street was dark and
empty, swept by the rain. She had a vision of his quiet room, of the
bookshelves, and the fire on the hearth. She looked up and saw a light
in his window; then she crossed the street and entered the house.

XII

The library looked as she had pictured it. The green-shaded lamps
made tranquil circles of light in the gathering dusk, a little fire flickered
on the hearth, and Selden's easy-chair, which stood near it, had been
pushed aside when he rose to admit her.

He had checked his first movement of surprise, and stood silent,
waiting for her to speak, while she paused a moment on the threshold,
assailed by a rush of memories.

The scene was unchanged. She recognized the row of shelves from
which he had taken down his La Bruyère, and the worn arm of the chair
he had leaned against while she examined the precious volume. But
then the wide September light had filled the room, making it seem a
part of the outer world: now the shaded lamps and the warm hearth,
detaching it from the gathering darkness of the street, gave it a sweeter
touch of intimacy.

Becoming gradually aware of the surprise under Selden's silence,
Lily turned to him and said simply: "I came to tell you that I was sorry
for the way we parted—for what I said to you that day at Mrs.
Hatch's."

The words rose to her lips spontaneously. Even on her way up the
stairs, she had not thought of preparing a pretext for her visit, but she
now felt an intense longing to dispel the cloud of misunderstanding that
hung between them.

Selden returned her look with a smile. "I was sorry too that we
should have parted in that way; but I am not sure I did n't bring it on
myself. Luckily I had foreseen the risk I was taking——"

"So that you really did n't care——?" broke from her with a flash of her old irony.

"So that I was prepared for the consequences," he corrected good-humouredly. "But we 'll talk of all this later. Do come and sit by the fire. I can recommend that arm-chair, if you 'll let me put a cushion behind you."

While he spoke she had moved slowly to the middle of the room, and paused near his writing-table, where the lamp, striking upward, cast exaggerated shadows on the pallour of her delicately-hollowed face.

"You look tired—do sit down," he repeated gently.

She did not seem to hear the request. "I wanted you to know that I left Mrs. Hatch immediately after I saw you," she said, as though continuing her confession.

"Yes—yes; I know," he assented, with a rising tinge of embarrassment.

"And that I did so because you told me to. Before you came I had already begun to see that it would be impossible to remain with her—for the reasons you gave me; but I would n't admit it—I would n't let you see that I understood what you meant."

"Ah, I might have trusted you to find your own way out—don't overwhelm me with the sense of my officiousness!"

His light tone, in which, had her nerves been steadier, she would have recognized the mere effort to bridge over an awkward moment, jarred on her passionate desire to be understood. In her strange state of extra-lucidity, which gave her the sense of being already at the heart of the situation, it seemed incredible that any one should think it necessary to linger in the conventional outskirts of word-play and evasion.

"It was not that—I was not ungrateful," she insisted. But the power of expression failed her suddenly; she felt a tremor in her throat, and two tears gathered and fell slowly from her eyes.

Selden moved forward and took her hand. "You are very tired. Why won't you sit down and let me make you comfortable?"

He drew her to the arm-chair near the fire, and placed a cushion behind her shoulders.

"And now you must let me make you some tea: you know I always have that amount of hospitality at my command."

She shook her head, and two more tears ran over. But she did not weep easily, and the long habit of self-control reasserted itself, though she was still too tremulous to speak.

"You know I can coax the water to boil in five minutes," Selden continued, speaking as though she were a troubled child.

His words recalled the vision of that other afternoon when they had sat together over his tea-table and talked jestingly of her future. There were moments when that day seemed more remote than any other event in her life; and yet she could always relive it in its minutest detail.

She made a gesture of refusal. "No: I drink too much tea. I would rather sit quietly—I must go in a moment," she added confusedly.

Selden continued to stand near her, leaning against the mantelpiece. The tinge of constraint was beginning to be more distinctly perceptible under the friendly ease of his manner. Her self-absorption had not allowed her to perceive it at first; but now that her consciousness was once more putting forth its eager feelers, she saw that her presence was becoming an embarrassment to him. Such a situation can be saved only by an immediate outrush of feeling; and on Selden's side the determining impulse was still lacking.

The discovery did not disturb Lily as it might once have done. She had passed beyond the phase of well-bred reciprocity, in which every demonstration must be scrupulously proportioned to the emotion it elicits, and generosity of feeling is the only ostentation condemned. But the sense of loneliness returned with redoubled force as she saw herself forever shut out from Selden's inmost self. She had come to him with no definite purpose; the mere longing to see him had directed her; but the secret hope she had carried with her suddenly revealed itself in its death-pang.

"I must go," she repeated, making a motion to rise from her chair. "But I may not see you again for a long time, and I wanted to tell you that I have never forgotten the things you said to me at Bellomont, and that sometimes—sometimes when I seemed farthest from remembering them—they have helped me, and kept me from mistakes; kept me from really becoming what many people have thought me."

Strive as she would to put some order in her thoughts, the words would not come more clearly; yet she felt that she could not leave him without trying to make him understand that she had saved herself whole from the seeming ruin of her life.

A change had come over Selden's face as she spoke. Its guarded look had yielded to an expression still untinged by personal emotion, but full of a gentle understanding.

"I am glad to have you tell me that; but nothing I have said has really made the difference. The difference is in yourself—it will always be there. And since it *is* there, it can't really matter to you what people think: you are so sure that your friends will always understand you."

"Ah, don't say that—don't say that what you have told me has made no difference. It seems to shut me out—to leave me all alone with the other people." She had risen and stood before him, once more completely mastered by the inner urgency of the moment. The consciousness of his half-divined reluctance had vanished. Whether he wished it or not, he must see her wholly for once before they parted.

Her voice had gathered strength, and she looked him gravely in the eyes as she continued. "Once—twice—you gave me the chance to escape from my life, and I refused it: refused it because I was a coward. Afterward I saw my mistake—I saw I could never be happy with what had contented me before. But it was too late: you had judged me—I understood. It was too late for happiness—but not too late to be helped by the thought of what I had missed. That is all I have lived on—don't take it from me now! Even in my worst moments it has been like a little light in the darkness. Some women are strong enough to be good by themselves, but I needed the help of your belief in me. Perhaps I might have resisted a great temptation, but the little ones would have pulled me down. And then I remembered—I remembered your saying that such a life could never satisfy me; and I was ashamed to admit to myself that it could. That is what you did for me—that is what I wanted to thank you for. I wanted to tell you that I have always remembered; and that I have tried—tried hard. . ."

She broke off suddenly. Her tears had risen again, and in drawing out her handkerchief her fingers touched the packet in the folds of her dress. A wave of colour suffused her, and the words died on her lips. Then she lifted her eyes to his and went on in an altered voice.

"I have tried hard—but life is difficult, and I am a very useless person. I can hardly be said to have an independent existence. I was just a screw or a cog in the great machine I called life, and when I dropped out of it I found I was of no use anywhere else. What can one do when one finds that one only fits into one hole? One must get back to it or be thrown out into the rubbish heap—and you don't know what it 's like in the rubbish heap!"

Her lips wavered into a smile—she had been distracted by the whimsical remembrance of the confidences she had made to him, two years earlier, in that very room. Then she had been planning to marry Percy Gryce—what was it she was planning now?

The blood had risen strongly under Selden's dark skin, but his emotion showed itself only in an added seriousness of manner.

"You have something to tell me—do you mean to marry?" he said abruptly.

Lily's eyes did not falter, but a look of wonder, of puzzled self-

interrogation, formed itself slowly in their depths. In the light of his
question, she had paused to ask herself if her decision had really been
taken when she entered the room.

"You always told me I should have to come to it sooner or later!"
she said with a faint smile.

"And you have come to it now?"

"I shall have to come to it—presently. But there is something else I
must come to first." She paused again, trying to transmit to her voice
the steadiness of her recovered smile. "There is some one I must say
goodbye to. Oh, not *you*—we are sure to see each other again—but
the Lily Bart you knew. I have kept her with me all this time, but now
we are going to part, and I have brought her back to you—I am going
to leave her here. When I go out presently she will not go with me. I
shall like to think that she has stayed with you—and she'll be no trouble, she'll take up no room."

She went toward him, and put out her hand, still smiling. "Will you
let her stay with you?" she asked.

He caught her hand, and she felt in his the vibration of feeling that
had not yet risen to his lips. "Lily—can't I help you?" he exclaimed.

She looked at him gently. "Do you remember what you said to me
once? That you could help me only by loving me? Well—you did love
me for a moment; and it helped me. It has always helped me. But the
moment is gone—it was I who let it go. And one must go on living.
Goodbye."

She laid her other hand on his, and they looked at each other with a
kind of solemnity, as though they stood in the presence of death. Something in truth lay dead between them—the love she had killed in him
and could no longer call to life. But something lived between them also,
and leaped up in her like an imperishable flame: it was the love his love
had kindled, the passion of her soul for his.

In its light everything else dwindled and fell away from her. She
understood now that she could not go forth and leave her old self with
him: that self must indeed live on in his presence, but it must still continue to be hers.

Selden had retained her hand, and continued to scrutinize her with
a strange sense of foreboding. The external aspect of the situation had
vanished for him as completely as for her: he felt it only as one of those
rare moments which lift the veil from their faces as they pass.

"Lily," he said in a low voice, "you must n't speak in this way. I
can't let you go without knowing what you mean to do. Things may
change—but they don't pass. You can never go out of my life."

She met his eyes with an illumined look. "No," she said, "I see that now. Let us always be friends. Then I shall feel safe, whatever happens."

"Whatever happens? What do you mean? What is going to happen?"

She turned away quietly and walked toward the hearth.

"Nothing at present—except that I am very cold, and that before I go you must make up the fire for me."

She knelt on the hearthrug, stretching her hands to the embers. Puzzled by the sudden change in her tone, he mechanically gathered a handful of wood from the basket and tossed it on the fire. As he did so, he noticed how thin her hands looked against the rising light of the flames. He saw too, under the loose lines of her dress, how the curves of her figure had shrunk to angularity; he remembered long afterward how the red play of the flame sharpened the depression of her nostrils, and intensified the blackness of the shadows which struck up from her cheekbones to her eyes. She knelt there for a few moments in silence; a silence which he dared not break. When she rose he fancied that he saw her draw something from her dress and drop it into the fire; but he hardly noticed the gesture at the time. His faculties seemed tranced, and he was still groping for the word to break the spell.

She went up to him and laid her hands on his shoulders. "Good-bye," she said, and as he bent over her she touched his forehead with her lips.

XIII

The street-lamps were lit, but the rain had ceased, and there was a momentary revival of light in the upper sky. Lily walked on unconscious of her surroundings. She was still treading the buoyant ether which emanates from the high moments of life. But gradually it shrank away from her and she felt the dull pavement beneath her feet. The sense of weariness returned with accumulated force, and for a moment she felt that she could walk no farther. She had reached the corner of Forty-first Street and Fifth Avenue, and she remembered that in Bryant Park there were seats where she might rest.

That melancholy pleasure-ground was almost deserted when she entered it, and she sank down on an empty bench in the glare of an electric street-lamp. The warmth of the fire had passed out of her veins, and she told herself that she must not sit long in the penetrating dampness which struck up from the wet asphalt. But her will-power seemed to have spent itself in a last great effort, and she was lost in the blank reaction which follows on an unwonted expenditure of energy. And besides, what was there to go home to? Nothing but the silence of her cheerless room—that silence of the night which may be more racking to tired nerves than the most discordant noises: that, and the bottle of chloral by her bed. The thought of the chloral was the only spot of light in the dark prospect: she could feel its lulling influence stealing over her already. But she was troubled by the thought that it was losing its power—she dared not go back to it too soon. Of late the sleep it had brought her had been more broken and less profound; there had been nights when she was perpetually floating up through it to consciousness. What if the effect of the drug should gradually fail, as all narcotics were said to fail? She remembered the chemist's warning against increasing the dose; and she had heard before of the capricious and incalculable action of the drug. Her dread of returning to a sleepless night was so great that she lingered on, hoping that excessive weariness would reinforce the waning power of the chloral.

Night had now closed in, and the roar of traffic in Forty-second Street was dying out. As complete darkness fell on the square the lingering occupants of the benches rose and dispersed; but now and then a stray figure, hurrying homeward, struck across the path where Lily sat, looming black for a moment in the white circle of electric light. One or two of these passers-by slackened their pace to glance curiously at her lonely figure; but she was hardly conscious of their scrutiny.

Suddenly, however, she became aware that one of the passing shadows remained stationary between her line of vision and the gleaming asphalt; and raising her eyes she saw a young woman bending over her.

"Excuse me—are you sick?—Why, it 's Miss Bart!" a half-familiar voice exclaimed.

Lily looked up. The speaker was a poorly-dressed young woman with a bundle under her arm. Her face had the air of unwholesome refinement which ill-health and over-work may produce, but its common prettiness was redeemed by the strong and generous curve of the lips.

"You don't remember me," she continued, brightening with the pleasure of recognition, "but I 'd know you anywhere, I 've thought of you such a lot. I guess my folks all know your name by heart. I was one of the girls at Miss Farish's club—you helped me to go to the country that time I had lung-trouble. My name 's Nettie Struther. It was Nettie Crane then—but I daresay you don't remember that either."

Yes: Lily was beginning to remember. The episode of Nettie Crane's timely rescue from disease had been one of the most satisfying incidents of her connection with Gerty's charitable work. She had furnished the girl with the means to go to a sanatorium in the mountains: it struck her now with a peculiar irony that the money she had used had been Gus Trenor's.

She tried to reply, to assure the speaker that she had not forgotten; but her voice failed in the effort, and she felt herself sinking under a great wave of physical weakness. Nettie Struther, with a startled exclamation, sat down and slipped a shabbily-clad arm behind her back.

"Why, Miss Bart, you *are* sick. Just lean on me a little till you feel better."

A faint glow of returning strength seemed to pass into Lily from the pressure of the supporting arm.

"I 'm only tired—it is nothing," she found voice to say in a moment; and then, as she met the timid appeal of her companion's eyes, she added involuntarily: "I have been unhappy—in great trouble."

"*You* in trouble? I 've always thought of you as being so high up, where everything was just grand. Sometimes, when I felt real mean, and got to wondering why things were so queerly fixed in the world, I used to remember that *you* were having a lovely time, anyhow, and that seemed to show there was a kind of justice somewhere. But you must n't sit here too long—it's fearfully damp. Don't you feel strong enough to walk on a little ways now?" she broke off.

"Yes—yes; I must go home," Lily murmured, rising.

Her eyes rested wonderingly on the thin shabby figure at her side. She had known Nettie Crane as one of the discouraged victims of over-work and anæmic parentage: one of the superfluous fragments of life destined to be swept prematurely into that social refuse-heap of which Lily had so lately expressed her dread. But Nettie Struther's frail envelope was now alive with hope and energy: whatever fate the future reserved for her, she would not be cast into the refuse-heap without a struggle.

"I am very glad to have seen you," Lily continued, summoning a smile to her unsteady lips. "It will be my turn to think of you as happy—and the world will seem a less unjust place to me too."

"Oh, but I can't leave you like this—you're not fit to go home alone. And I can't go with you either!" Nettie Struther wailed with a start of recollection. "You see, it 's my husband's night-shift—he 's a motor-man—and the friend I leave the baby with has to step upstairs to get *her* husband's supper at seven. I did n't tell you I had a baby, did I? She 'll be four months old day after tomorrow, and to look at her you would n't think I 'd ever had a sick day. I 'd give anything to show you the baby, Miss Bart, and we live right down the street here—it 's only three blocks off." She lifted her eyes tentatively to Lily's face, and then added with a burst of courage: "Why won't you get right into the cars and come home with me while I get baby's supper? It 's real warm in our kitchen, and you can rest there, and I 'll take *you* home as soon as ever she drops off to sleep."

It *was* warm in the kitchen, which, when Nettie Struther's match had made a flame leap from the gas-jet above the table, revealed itself to Lily as extraordinarily small and almost miraculously clean. A fire shone through the polished flanks of the iron stove, and near it stood a crib in which a baby was sitting upright, with incipient anxiety struggling for expression on a countenance still placid with sleep.

Having passionately celebrated her reunion with her offspring, and excused herself in cryptic language for the lateness of her return, Nettie restored the baby to the crib and shyly invited Miss Bart to the rocking-chair near the stove.

"We' ve got a parlour too," she explained with pardonable pride; "but I guess it 's warmer in here, and I don't want to leave you alone while I 'm getting baby's supper."

On receiving Lily's assurance that she much preferred the friendly proximity of the kitchen fire, Mrs. Struther proceeded to prepare a bottle of infantile food, which she tenderly applied to the baby's impatient lips; and while the ensuing degustation went on, she seated herself with a beaming countenance beside her visitor.

"You 're sure you won't let me warm up a drop of coffee for you, Miss Bart? There 's some of baby's fresh milk left over—well, maybe you 'd rather just sit quiet and rest a little while. It 's too lovely having you here. I 've thought of it so often that I can't believe it 's really come true. I 've said to George again and again: 'I just wish Miss Bart could see me *now*—' and I used to watch for your name in the papers, and we 'd talk over what you were doing, and read the descriptions of the dresses you wore. I have n't seen your name for a long time, though, and I began to be afraid you were sick, and it worried me so that George said I 'd get sick myself, fretting about it." Her lips broke into a reminiscent smile. "Well, I can't afford to be sick again, that 's a fact: the last spell nearly finished me. When you sent me off that time I never thought I 'd come back alive, and I did n't much care if I did. You see I did n't know about George and the baby then."

She paused to readjust the bottle to the child's bubbling mouth.

"You precious—don't you be in too much of a hurry! Was it mad with mommer for getting its supper so late? Marry Anto'nette—that 's what we call her: after the French queen in that play at the Garden—I told George the actress reminded me of you, and that made me fancy the name . . . I never thought I 'd get married, you know, and I 'd never have had the heart to go on working just for myself."

She broke off again, and meeting the encouragement in Lily's eyes, went on, with a flush rising under her anæmic skin: "You see I was n't only just *sick* that time you sent me off—I was dreadfully unhappy too. I 'd known a gentleman where I was employed—I don't know as you remember I did typewriting in a big importing firm—and—well—I thought we were to be married: he 'd gone steady with me six months and given me his mother's wedding ring. But I presume he was too stylish for me—he travelled for the firm, and had seen a great deal of society. Work girls are n't looked after the way you are, and they don't always know how to look after themselves. I did n't . . . and it pretty near killed me when he went away and left off writing . . . It was then I came down sick—I thought it was the end of everything. I guess it would have been if you had n't sent me off. But when I found I was getting well I began to take heart in spite of myself. And then, when I got back home, George came round and asked me to marry him. At first I thought I could n't, because we 'd been brought up together, and I knew he knew about me. But after a while I began to see that that made it easier. I never could have told another man, and I 'd never have married without telling; but if George cared for me enough to have me as I was, I did n't see why I should n't begin over again—and I did."

The strength of the victory shone forth from her as she lifted her irradiated face from the child on her knees.

"But, mercy, I did n't mean to go on like this about myself, with you sitting there looking so fagged out. Only it 's so lovely having you here, and letting you see just how you 've helped me." The baby had sunk back blissfully replete, and Mrs. Struther softly rose to lay the bottle aside. Then she paused before Miss Bart.

"I only wish I could help *you*—but I suppose there 's nothing on earth I could do," she murmured wistfully.

Lily, instead of answering, rose with a smile and held out her arms; and the mother, understanding the gesture, laid her child in them.

The baby, feeling herself detached from her habitual anchorage, made an instinctive motion of resistance; but the soothing influences of digestion prevailed, and Lily felt the soft weight sink trustfully against her breast. The child's confidence in its safety thrilled her with a sense of warmth and returning life, and she bent over, wondering at the rosy blur of the little face, the empty clearness of the eyes, the vague tendrilly motions of the folding and unfolding fingers. At first the burden in her arms seemed as light as a pink cloud or a heap of down, but as she continued to hold it the weight increased, sinking deeper, and penetrating her with a strange sense of weakness, as though the child entered into her and became a part of herself.

She looked up, and saw Nettie's eyes resting on her with tenderness and exultation.

"Would n't it be too lovely for anything if she could grow up to be just like you? Of course I know she never *could*—but mothers are always dreaming the craziest things for their children."

Lily clasped the child close for a moment and laid her back in her mother's arms.

"Oh, she must not do that—I should be afraid to come and see her too often!" she said with a smile; and then, resisting Mrs. Struther's anxious offer of companionship, and reiterating the promise that of course she would come back soon, and make George's acquaintance, and see the baby in her bath, she passed out of the kitchen and went alone down the tenement stairs.

As she reached the street she realized that she felt stronger and happier: the little episode had done her good. It was the first time she had ever come across the results of her spasmodic benevolence, and the surprised sense of human fellowship took the mortal chill from her heart.

It was not till she entered her own door that she felt the reaction of a deeper loneliness. It was long after seven o'clock, and the light and odours proceeding from the basement made it manifest that the boarding-house dinner had begun. She hastened up to her room, lit the gas, and began to dress. She did not mean to pamper herself any longer, to go without food because her surroundings made it unpalatable. Since it was her fate to live in a boarding-house, she must learn to fall in with the conditions of the life. Nevertheless she was glad that, when she descended to the heat and glare of the dining-room, the repast was nearly over.

In her own room again, she was seized with a sudden fever of activity. For weeks past she had been too listless and indifferent to set her possessions in order, but now she began to examine systematically the contents of her drawers and cupboard. She had a few handsome dresses left—survivals of her last phase of splendour, on the Sabrina and in London—but when she had been obliged to part with her maid she had given the woman a generous share of her cast-off apparel. The remaining dresses, though they had lost their freshness, still kept the long unerring lines, the sweep and amplitude of the great artist's stroke, and as she spread them out on the bed the scenes in which they had been worn rose vividly before her. An association lurked in every fold: each fall of lace and gleam of embroidery was like a letter in the record of her past. She was startled to find how the atmosphere of her old life enveloped her. But, after all, it was the life she had been made for: every dawning tendency in her had been carefully directed toward it, all her interests and activities had been taught to centre around it. She was like some rare flower grown for exhibition, a flower from which every bud had been nipped except the crowning blossom of her beauty.

Last of all, she drew forth from the bottom of her trunk a heap of white drapery which fell shapelessly across her arm. It was the Reynolds dress she had worn in the Bry *tableaux*. It had been impossible for her to give it away, but she had never seen it since that night, and the long flexible folds, as she shook them out, gave forth an odour of violets which came to her like a breath from the flower-edged fountain where she had stood with Lawrence Selden and disowned her fate. She put back the dresses one by one, laying away with each some gleam of light, some note of laughter, some stray waft from the rosy shores of pleasure. She was still in a state of highly-wrought impressionability, and every hint of the past sent a lingering tremor along her nerves.

She had just closed her trunk on the white folds of the Reynolds dress when she heard a tap at her door, and the red fist of the Irish maid-servant thrust in a belated letter. Carrying it to the light, Lily read with surprise the address stamped on the upper corner of the envelope. It was a business communication from the office of her aunt's executors, and she wondered what unexpected development had caused them to break silence before the appointed time.

She opened the envelope and a cheque fluttered to the floor. As she stooped to pick it up the blood rushed to her face. The cheque represented the full amount of Mrs. Peniston's legacy, and the letter accompanying it explained that the executors, having adjusted the business of the estate with less delay than they had expected, had decided to anticipate the date fixed for the payment of the bequests.

Lily sat down beside the desk at the foot of her bed, and spreading out the cheque, read over and over the *ten thousand dollars* written across it in a steely business hand. Ten months earlier the amount it stood for had represented the depths of penury; but her standard of values had changed in the interval, and now visions of wealth lurked in every flourish of the pen. As she continued to gaze at it, she felt the glitter of the visions mounting to her brain, and after a while she lifted the lid of the desk and slipped the magic formula out of sight. It was easier to think without those five figures dancing before her eyes; and she had a great deal of thinking to do before she slept.

She opened her cheque-book, and plunged into such anxious calculations as had prolonged her vigil at Bellomont on the night when she had decided to marry Percy Gryce. Poverty simplifies book-keeping, and her financial situation was easier to ascertain than it had been then; but she had not yet learned the control of money, and during her transient phase of luxury at the Emporium she had slipped back into habits of extravagance which still impaired her slender balance. A careful examination of her cheque-book, and of the unpaid bills in her desk, showed that, when the latter had been settled, she would have barely enough to live on for the next three or four months; and even after that, if she were to continue her present way of living, without earning any additional money, all incidental expenses must be reduced to the vanishing point. She hid her eyes with a shudder, beholding herself at the entrance of that ever-narrowing perspective down which she had seen Miss Silverton's dowdy figure take its despondent way.

It was no longer, however, from the vision of material poverty that she turned with the greatest shrinking. She had a sense of deeper empoverishment—of an inner destitution compared to which outward conditions dwindled into insignificance. It was indeed miserable to be poor—to look forward to a shabby, anxious middle-age, leading by dreary degrees of economy and self-denial to gradual absorption in the dingy communal existence of the boarding-house. But there was something more miserable still—it was the clutch of solitude at her heart, the sense of being swept like a stray uprooted growth down the heedless current of the years. That was the feeling which possessed her now— the feeling of being something rootless and ephemeral, mere spin-drift of the whirling surface of existence, without anything to which the poor little tentacles of self could cling before the awful flood submerged them. And as she looked back she saw that there had never been a time when she had had any real relation to life. Her parents too had been rootless, blown hither and thither on every wind of fashion, without any personal existence to shelter them from its shifting gusts. She herself had grown up without any one spot of earth being dearer to her than another: there was no centre of early pieties, of grave endearing traditions, to which her heart could revert and from which it could draw strength for itself and tenderness for others. In whatever form a slowly-accumulated past lives in the blood—whether in the concrete image of the old house stored with visual memories, or in the conception of the house not built with hands, but made up of inherited passions and loyalties—it has the same power of broadening and deepening the individual existence, of attaching it by mysterious links of kinship to all the mighty sum of human striving.

Such a vision of the solidarity of life had never before come to Lily. She had had a premonition of it in the blind motions of her mating-instinct; but they had been checked by the disintegrating influences of the life about her. All the men and women she knew were like atoms whirling away from each other in some wild centrifugal dance: her first glimpse of the continuity of life had come to her that evening in Nettie Struther's kitchen.

The poor little working-girl who had found strength to gather up the fragments of her life, and build herself a shelter with them, seemed to Lily to have reached the central truth of existence. It was a meagre enough life, on the grim edge of poverty, with scant margin for possibilities of sickness or mischance, but it had the frail audacious permanence of a bird's nest built on the edge of a cliff—a mere wisp of leaves and straw, yet so put together that the lives entrusted to it may hang safely over the abyss.

Yes—but it had taken two to build the nest; the man's faith as well as the woman's courage. Lily remembered Nettie's words: *I knew he knew about me.* Her husband's faith in her had made her renewal possible—it is so easy for a woman to become what the man she loves believes her to be! Well—Selden had twice been ready to stake his faith on Lily Bart; but the third trial had been too severe for his endurance. The very quality of his love had made it the more impossible to recall to life. If it had been a simple instinct of the blood, the power of her beauty might have revived it. But the fact that it struck deeper, that it was inextricably wound up with inherited habits of thought and feeling, made it as impossible to restore to growth as a deep-rooted plant torn from its bed. Selden had given her of his best; but he was as incapable as herself of an uncritical return to former states of feeling.

There remained to her, as she had told him, the uplifting memory of his faith in her; but she had not reached the age when a woman can live on her memories. As she held Nettie Struther's child in her arms the frozen currents of youth had loosed themselves and run warm in her veins: the old life-hunger possessed her, and all her being clamoured for its share of personal happiness. Yes—it was happiness she still wanted, and the glimpse she had caught of it made everything else of no

account. One by one she had detached herself from the baser possibilities, and she saw that nothing now remained to her but the emptiness
of renunciation.

It was growing late, and an immense weariness once more possessed
her. It was not the stealing sense of sleep, but a vivid wakeful fatigue, a
wan lucidity of mind against which all the possibilities of the future were
shadowed forth gigantically. She was appalled by the intense clearness of
the vision; she seemed to have broken through the merciful veil which
intervenes between intention and action, and to see exactly what she
would do in all the long days to come. There was the cheque in her
desk, for instance—she meant to use it in paying her debt to Trenor;
but she foresaw that when the morning came she would put off doing
so, would slip into gradual tolerance of the debt. The thought terrified
her—she dreaded to fall from the height of her last moment with Lawrence Selden. But how could she trust herself to keep her footing? She
knew the strength of the opposing impulses—she could feel the countless hands of habit dragging her back into some fresh compromise with
fate. She felt an intense longing to prolong, to perpetuate, the momentary exaltation of her spirit. If only life could end now—end on this
tragic yet sweet vision of lost possibilities, which gave her a sense of
kinship with all the loving and foregoing in the world!

She reached out suddenly and, drawing the cheque from her
writing-desk, enclosed it in an envelope which she addressed to her
bank. She then wrote out a cheque for Trenor, and placing it, without
an accompanying word, in an envelope inscribed with his name, laid the
two letters side by side on her desk. After that she continued to sit at the
table, sorting her papers and writing, till the intense silence of the house
reminded her of the lateness of the hour. In the street the noise of
wheels had ceased, and the rumble of the "elevated" came only at long
intervals through the deep unnatural hush. In the mysterious nocturnal
separation from all outward signs of life, she felt herself more strangely
confronted with her fate. The sensation made her brain reel, and she
tried to shut out consciousness by pressing her hands against her eyes.
But the terrible silence and emptiness seemed to symbolize her future—
she felt as though the house, the street, the world were all empty, and
she alone left sentient in a lifeless universe.

But this was the verge of delirium . . . she had never hung so near
the dizzy brink of the unreal. Sleep was what she wanted—she remembered that she had not closed her eyes for two nights. The little bottle
was at her bed-side, waiting to lay its spell upon her. She rose and undressed hastily, hungering now for the touch of her pillow. She felt so

profoundly tired that she thought she must fall asleep at once; but as soon as she had lain down every nerve started once more into separate wakefulness. It was as though a great blaze of electric light had been turned on in her head, and her poor little anguished self shrank and cowered in it, without knowing where to take refuge.

She had not imagined that such a multiplication of wakefulness was possible: her whole past was reënacting itself at a hundred different points of consciousness. Where was the drug that could still this legion of insurgent nerves? The sense of exhaustion would have been sweet compared to this shrill beat of activities; but weariness had dropped from her as though some cruel stimulant had been forced into her veins.

She could bear it—yes, she could bear it; but what strength would be left her the next day? Perspective had disappeared—the next day pressed close upon her, and on its heels came the days that were to follow—they swarmed about her like a shrieking mob. She must shut them out for a few hours; she must take a brief bath of oblivion. She put out her hand, and measured the soothing drops into a glass; but as she did so, she knew they would be powerless against the supernatural lucidity of her brain. She had long since raised the dose to its highest limit, but tonight she felt she must increase it. She knew she took a slight risk in doing so—she remembered the chemist's warning. If sleep came at all, it might be a sleep without waking. But after all that was but one chance in a hundred: the action of the drug was incalculable, and the addition of a few drops to the regular dose would probably do no more than procure for her the rest she so desperately needed. . . .

She did not, in truth, consider the question very closely—the physical craving for sleep was her only sustained sensation. Her mind shrank from the glare of thought as instinctively as eyes contract in a blaze of light—darkness, darkness was what she must have at any cost. She raised herself in bed and swallowed the contents of the glass; then she blew out her candle and lay down.

She lay very still, waiting with a sensuous pleasure for the first effects of the soporific. She knew in advance what form they would take—the gradual cessation of the inner throb, the soft approach of passiveness, as though an invisible hand made magic passes over her in the darkness. The very slowness and hesitancy of the effect increased its fascination: it was delicious to lean over and look down into the dim abysses of unconsciousness. Tonight the drug seemed to work more slowly than usual: each passionate pulse had to be stilled in turn, and it was long before she felt them dropping into abeyance, like sentinels falling asleep at their posts. But gradually the sense of complete subjugation came over her,

and she wondered languidly what had made her feel so uneasy and excited. She saw now that there was nothing to be excited about—she
had returned to her normal view of life. Tomorrow would not be so
difficult after all: she felt sure that she would have the strength to meet
it. She did not quite remember what it was that she had been afraid to
meet, but the uncertainty no longer troubled her. She had been unhappy, and now she was happy—she had felt herself alone, and now the
sense of loneliness had vanished.

She stirred once, and turned on her side, and as she did so, she suddenly understood why she did not feel herself alone. It was odd—but
Nettie Struther's child was lying on her arm: she felt the pressure of its
little head against her shoulder. She did not know how it had come
there, but she felt no great surprise at the fact, only a gentle penetrating
thrill of warmth and pleasure. She settled herself into an easier position,
hollowing her arm to pillow the round downy head, and holding her
breath lest a sound should disturb the sleeping child.

As she lay there she said to herself that there was something she
must tell Selden, some word she had found that should make life clear
between them. She tried to repeat the word, which lingered vague and
luminous on the far edge of thought—she was afraid of not remembering it when she woke; and if she could only remember it and say it to
him, she felt that everything would be well.

Slowly the thought of the word faded, and sleep began to enfold
her. She struggled faintly against it, feeling that she ought to keep
awake on account of the baby; but even this feeling was gradually lost in
an indistinct sense of drowsy peace, through which, of a sudden, a dark
flash of loneliness and terror tore its way.

She started up again, cold and trembling with the shock: for a moment she seemed to have lost her hold of the child. But no—she was
mistaken—the tender pressure of its body was still close to hers: the
recovered warmth flowed through her once more, she yielded to it, sank
into it, and slept.

XIV

The next morning rose mild and bright, with a promise of summer
in the air. The sunlight slanted joyously down Lily's street, mellowed
the blistered house-front, gilded the paintless railings of the door-step,
and struck prismatic glories from the panes of her darkened window.

When such a day coincides with the inner mood there is intoxication
in its breath; and Selden, hastening along the street through the squalor

of its morning confidences, felt himself thrilling with a youthful sense of adventure. He had cut loose from the familiar shores of habit, and launched himself on uncharted seas of emotion; all the old tests and measures were left behind, and his course was to be shaped by new stars.

That course, for the moment, led merely to Miss Bart's boarding-house; but its shabby door-step had suddenly become the threshold of the untried. As he approached he looked up at the triple row of windows, wondering boyishly which one of them was hers. It was nine o'clock, and the house, being tenanted by workers, already showed an awakened front to the street. He remembered afterward having noticed that only one blind was down. He noticed too that there was a pot of pansies on one of the window sills, and at once concluded that the window must be hers: it was inevitable that he should connect her with the one touch of beauty in the dingy scene.

Nine o'clock was an early hour for a visit, but Selden had passed beyond all such conventional observances. He only knew that he must see Lily Bart at once — he had found the word he meant to say to her, and it could not wait another moment to be said. It was strange that it had not come to his lips sooner — that he had let her pass from him the evening before without being able to speak it. But what did that matter, now that a new day had come? It was not a word for twilight, but for the morning.

Selden ran eagerly up the steps and pulled the bell; and even in his state of self-absorption it came as a sharp surprise to him that the door should open so promptly. It was still more of a surprise to see, as he entered, that it had been opened by Gerty Farish — and that behind her, in an agitated blur, several other figures ominously loomed.

"Lawrence!" Gerty cried in a strange voice, "how could you get here so quickly?" — and the trembling hand she laid on him seemed instantly to close about his heart.

He noticed the other faces, vague with fear and conjecture — he saw the landlady's imposing bulk sway professionally toward him; but he shrank back, putting up his hand, while his eyes mechanically mounted the steep black walnut stairs, up which he was immediately aware that his cousin was about to lead him.

A voice in the background said that the doctor might be back at any minute — and that nothing, upstairs, was to be disturbed. Some one else exclaimed: "It was the greatest mercy — " then Selden felt that Gerty had taken him gently by the hand, and that they were to be suffered to go up alone.

In silence they mounted the three flights, and walked along the passage to a closed door. Gerty opened the door, and Selden went in after her. Though the blind was down, the irresistible sunlight poured a tempered golden flood into the room, and in its light Selden saw a narrow bed along the wall, and on the bed, with motionless hands and calm unrecognizing face, the semblance of Lily Bart.

That it was her real self, every pulse in him ardently denied. Her real self had lain warm on his heart but a few hours earlier—what had he to do with this estranged and tranquil face which, for the first time, neither paled nor brightened at his coming?

Gerty, strangely tranquil too, with the conscious self-control of one who has ministered to much pain, stood by the bed, speaking gently, as if transmitting a final message.

"The doctor found a bottle of chloral—she had been sleeping badly for a long time, and she must have taken an overdose by mistake. . . . There is no doubt of that—no doubt—there will be no question—he has been very kind. I told him that you and I would like to be left alone with her—to go over her things before any one else comes. I know it is what she would have wished."

Selden was hardly conscious of what she said. He stood looking down on the sleeping face which seemed to lie like a delicate impalpable mask over the living lineaments he had known. He felt that the real Lily was still there, close to him, yet invisible and inaccessible; and the tenuity of the barrier between them mocked him with a sense of helplessness. There had never been more than a little impalpable barrier between them—and yet he had suffered it to keep them apart! And now, though it seemed slighter and frailer than ever, it had suddenly hardened to adamant, and he might beat his life out against it in vain.

He had dropped on his knees beside the bed, but a touch from Gerty aroused him. He stood up, and as their eyes met he was struck by the extraordinary light in his cousin's face.

"You understand what the doctor has gone for? He has promised that there shall be no trouble—but of course the formalities must be gone through. And I asked him to give us time to look through her things first——"

He nodded, and she glanced about the small bare room. "It won't take long," she concluded.

"No—it won't take long," he agreed.

She held his hand in hers a moment longer, and then, with a last look at the bed, moved silently toward the door. On the threshold she paused to add: "You will find me downstairs if you want me."

Selden roused himself to detain her. "But why are you going? She would have wished——"

Gerty shook her head with a smile. "No: this is what she would have wished——" and as she spoke a light broke through Selden's stony misery, and he saw deep into the hidden things of love.

The door closed on Gerty, and he stood alone with the motionless sleeper on the bed. His impulse was to return to her side, to fall on his knees, and rest his throbbing head against the peaceful cheek on the pillow. They had never been at peace together, they two; and now he felt himself drawn downward into the strange mysterious depths of her tranquillity.

But he remembered Gerty's warning words—he knew that, though time had ceased in this room, its feet were hastening relentlessly toward the door. Gerty had given him this supreme half-hour, and he must use it as she willed.

He turned and looked about him, sternly compelling himself to regain his consciousness of outward things. There was very little furniture in the room. The shabby chest of drawers was spread with a lace cover, and set out with a few gold-topped boxes and bottles, a rose-coloured pin-cushion, a glass tray strewn with tortoise-shell hair-pins—he shrank from the poignant intimacy of these trifles, and from the blank surface of the toilet-mirror above them.

These were the only traces of luxury, of that clinging to the minute observance of personal seemliness, which showed what her other renunciations must have cost. There was no other token of her personality about the room, unless it showed itself in the scrupulous neatness of the scant articles of furniture: a washing-stand, two chairs, a small writing-desk, and the little table near the bed. On this table stood the empty bottle and glass, and from these also he averted his eyes.

The desk was closed, but on its slanting lid lay two letters which he took up. One bore the address of a bank, and as it was stamped and sealed, Selden, after a moment's hesitation, laid it aside. On the other letter he read Gus Trenor's name; and the flap of the envelope was still ungummed.

Temptation leapt on him like the stab of a knife. He staggered under it, steadying himself against the desk. Why had she been writing to Trenor—writing, presumably, just after their parting of the previous evening? The thought unhallowed the memory of that last hour, made a mock of the word he had come to speak, and defiled even the reconciling silence upon which it fell. He felt himself flung back on all the ugly uncertainties from which he thought he had cast loose forever.

After all, what did he know of her life? Only as much as she had chosen to show him, and measured by the world's estimate, how little that was! By what right—the letter in his hand seemed to ask—by what right was it he who now passed into her confidence through the gate which death had left unbarred? His heart cried out that it was by right of their last hour together, the hour when she herself had placed the key in his hand. Yes—but what if the letter to Trenor had been written afterward?

He put it from him with sudden loathing, and setting his lips, addressed himself resolutely to what remained of his task. After all, that task would be easier to perform, now that his personal stake in it was annulled.

He raised the lid of the desk, and saw within it a cheque-book and a few packets of bills and letters, arranged with the orderly precision which characterized all her personal habits. He looked through the letters first, because it was the most difficult part of the work. They proved to be few and unimportant, but among them he found, with a strange commotion of the heart, the note he had written her the day after the Brys' entertainment.

"When may I come to you?"—his words overwhelmed him with a realization of the cowardice which had driven him from her at the very moment of attainment. Yes—he had always feared his fate, and he was too honest to disown his cowardice now; for had not all his old doubts started to life again at the mere sight of Trenor's name?

He laid the note in his card-case, folding it away carefully, as something made precious by the fact that she had held it so; then, growing once more aware of the lapse of time, he continued his examination of the papers.

To his surprise, he found that all the bills were receipted; there was not an unpaid account among them. He opened the cheque-book, and saw that, the very night before, a cheque of ten thousand dollars from Mrs. Peniston's executors had been entered in it. The legacy, then, had been paid sooner than Gerty had led him to expect. But, turning another page or two, he discovered with astonishment that, in spite of this recent accession of funds, the balance had already declined to a few dollars. A rapid glance at the stubs of the last cheques, all of which bore the date of the previous day, showed that between four or five hundred dollars of the legacy had been spent in the settlement of bills, while the remaining thousands were comprehended in one cheque, made out, at the same time, to Charles Augustus Trenor.

Selden laid the book aside, and sank into the chair beside the desk. He leaned his elbows on it, and hid his face in his hands. The bitter waters of life surged high about him, their sterile taste was on his lips. Did the cheque to Trenor explain the mystery or deepen it? At first his mind refused to act—he felt only the taint of such a transaction between a man like Trenor and a girl like Lily Bart. Then, gradually, his troubled vision cleared, old hints and rumours came back to him, and out of the very insinuations he had feared to probe, he constructed an explanation of the mystery. It was true, then, that she had taken money from Trenor; but true also, as the contents of the little desk declared, that the obligation had been intolerable to her, and that at the first opportunity she had freed herself from it, though the act left her face to face with bare unmitigated poverty.

That was all he knew—all he could hope to unravel of the story. The mute lips on the pillow refused him more than this—unless indeed they had told him the rest in the kiss they had left upon his forehead. Yes, he could now read into that farewell all that his heart craved to find there; he could even draw from it courage not to accuse himself for having failed to reach the height of his opportunity.

He saw that all the conditions of life had conspired to keep them apart; since his very detachment from the external influences which swayed her had increased his spiritual fastidiousness, and made it more difficult for him to live and love uncritically. But at least he *had* loved her—had been willing to stake his future on his faith in her—and if the moment had been fated to pass from them before they could seize it, he saw now that, for both, it had been saved whole out of the ruin of their lives.

It was this moment of love, this fleeting victory over themselves, which had kept them from atrophy and extinction; which, in her, had reached out to him in every struggle against the influence of her surroundings, and in him, had kept alive the faith that now drew him penitent and reconciled to her side.

He knelt by the bed and bent over her, draining their last moment to its lees; and in the silence there passed between them the word which made all clear.

PART TWO

The House of Mirth:
A Case Study in
Contemporary Criticism

A Critical History of
The House of Mirth

The House of Mirth, Edith Wharton's second novel, was published in book form on October 14, 1905, a few days in advance of the November supplement of *Scribner's Magazine,* which had begun serial publication of the novel in January 1905. In its monthly installments, this story of New York high society at the turn of the century attracted a wide readership. Lily Bart, the novel's beautiful, decorative, and vulnerable heroine, won the hearts of housewives and businessmen. Across America, a middle-class reading public was as interested then as it is today in the activities of the leisured classes, and *The House of Mirth* offered an insider's view of New York society transformed by the new industrial wealth of the late nineteenth century.

Lily Bart was a child of this new world. Her father was descended from prudent Anglo-Dutch settlers, as were Edith Wharton's parents; he married beneath him, socially speaking, and he bankrupted himself trying to further his wife's social climbing pursuits. Orphaned in adolescence and now approaching her twenty-ninth birthday (she has been on the marriage market for a decade), Lily lives with her wealthy, conservative aunt, Mrs. Peniston, and makes her way virtually alone in a pleasure-seeking and self-interested environment. *The House of Mirth* charts her slow and seemingly inevitable descent from the ranks of the privileged, where she had hoped to make a good marriage, to a solitary life on the economic and social margins. Lily is the instrument of Edith Wharton's attack on an irresponsible, grasping, and morally corrupt upper class. In the final chapters of the novel, Lily uses a small bequest from her aunt to pay off various debts. Desperate for sleep, she then imbibes a large draft of chloral and falls into a slumber from which she does not awake. Lily's story, which had begun as an apparent arch comedy of manners, has, by its closing scene, turned to tragedy.

I

News of Lily Bart's death spread quickly, and readers who arrived late at their local newsstand found no available copy of *Scribner's Magazine*. Two editions of the book, 70,000 copies, sold out during the advance publication period. By early December, 140,000 copies had been sold, and Charles Scribner reported in a letter to Edith that the novel was having "the most rapid sale of any book ever published by Scribner" (20 November 1905). By year's end, she had accrued royalties of $30,000, valued at over half a million tax-free dollars today. *The House of Mirth* climbed to the top of the bestseller list, where it held place for four months, surpassing Upton Sinclair's *The Jungle*. It received serious and generally praiseworthy reviews both in America and England, where it was published by Macmillan. That the book was compelling and controversial is apparent in the spirited debate it engendered in reviews and literary columns of newspapers and magazines.

Few readers missed the moral thrust of *The House of Mirth*, whose title is taken from *Ecclesiastes* 7.4: "The heart of the wise is in the house of mourning; but the heart of fools is in the house of mirth." Edith Wharton firmly believed that good fiction must treat the "eternal laws" of life. Dr. Morgan Dix, rector of Trinity Church in Manhattan, a longtime friend and the man who had officiated at her marriage to Edward R. Wharton in April 1885, wrote her on December 1, 1905, to say that her novel was "a terrible but just arraignment of the social misconduct which begins in folly and ends in moral and spiritual death." She responded: "*No* novel worth anything can be anything but a novel 'with a purpose,' & if anyone who cared for the moral issue did not see in my work that *I* care for it, I should have no one to blame but myself—or at least my inadequate means of rendering my effects" (5 December 1905).

Literary reviewers and critics recognized the moral thrust of *The House of Mirth*, placing it in the dual tradition of social satire and the novel of manners. Early debate focused on three issues: (1) Was New York society as corrupt, and corrupting, as the novel portrayed? (2) Was a corrupt society a suitable subject for art? (3) Was it necessary for Lily Bart to die in order for the novel to make its moral point? These questions structured the literary reception of *The House of Mirth,* the terms by which it was read and understood for some sixty years following its publication.

From today's perspective, the excesses of 1905 high society may seem tame, but its primary indulgences—gambling, drinking, stock market speculation, and extra-marital affairs—are still in vogue. Was it true, however, that the "smart set" was as vain and vapid as Edith Wharton portrayed them, or the rich as devoid of passion and unprincipled as they appear in *The House of Mirth?* The banner headline in the *New York Times* literary review section for Sunday, October 15, 1905, proclaimed: "New York Society Held Up to Scorn in Three New Books." (The two other books in the review were an anonymously written novel, *Our Best Society,* and a collection of nonfiction essays, now considered a period piece, entitled *The Reign of Gilt,* by David Graham Phillips.) By late November a dispute focusing on the accuracy of Wharton's portrait of high society opened in the *New York Times Saturday Review of Books* between two readers who identified themselves as "Lenox" and "Newport." "Newport" thought the book unjustly characterized the New York social scene. "Lenox" argued that "Newport" refused to recognize the truthful, if unflattering, portrait of society and failed to see the book's "entire scheme and purpose" (24 November 1905). (The two anonymous letter writers were perhaps personally acquainted with Edith Wharton, who had a summer home in Lenox, Massachusetts. During her childhood, her family summered in Newport, Rhode Island, a fashionable society resort, and she lived there for eight years after her marriage.)

The Independent, which acknowledged that "society was, indeed, the coming field in fiction," called the book a "missionary effort" to reform "the most corrupt class of people in the world," but commented that Wharton's writing was "a fashion of the times for interpreting decadent symptoms in human nature." The review, published before *The House of Mirth* had completed its run in *Scribner's Magazine*—before Lily Bart's death stirred transatlantic debate about the power of society to corrupt individuals—concluded that "what [Wharton] says will not last, because it is simply the fashionable drawing of ephemeral types and still more ephemeral sentiments." Mary Moss, writing for *The Atlantic Monthly,* agreed with this assessment: Lily Bart could at best "only inspire interest and curiosity. You see, you understand, and you ratify, but unfortunately, you do not greatly care." But *The House of Mirth* was far more than a sermon or an exercise in didacticism. Most commentators remarked on Wharton's profound knowledge of the social scene she examined and praised the high quality of her writing and the careful workmanship of the book's structure, although several found the novel unpleasant. According to the British *Publishers' Circular,* its satire offered "a grim picture of the moneyed class in America."

British reviewers, whom Wharton believed treated her work in greater depth and seriousness than did American critics, did not doubt her portrait of New York society (one suspects a certain gleefulness in their readiness to condemn American crassness). The *English Review* praised her courage in not shrinking from "the appalling facts of life"; the *Times* of London applauded her for registering "to the last degree of delicacy the jumble of crudity and over-civilization which she finds in New York to-day." The *Manchester Guardian* noted that she had not created "lifeless puppets to illustrate a theory" but rather had "watche[d] her characters as they live[d]," and lauded her for "searching deep into the causes of things." The *Guardian, Daily Chronicle, Globe,* and *Dundee Advertiser* called her both a realist and a satirist, and the *English Review* concluded that she was "cynical but not heartless." *Woman* characterized *The House of Mirth* as "unpleasant" but "clever"; the *Westminster Gazette* called it a "dreadfully clever book"; James MacArthur in *Harper's Weekly* noted that the "low moral level" of Lily's "self-indulgent world," with its "lack of ideals," had led many to "condemn *The House of Mirth* as depressing and degrading." Comparing Wharton to Henry James, the *Outlook* remarked on the "detachment" of its authorial perspective. Writer Alice Meynell praised Wharton in the *Bookman* as a moralist but noted that her "extremity of reserve," her unwillingness to reveal herself in the book, was a major flaw.

The urgent issue for readers on both sides of the Atlantic was whether the characters Wharton had created were suitable subjects for art. With the possible exceptions of Lily Bart and Lawrence Selden, *The House of Mirth* seemed to offer no admirable characters. *The Times* of London thought Selden had the potential for moral growth (an opinion that would be disputed today), and described him as an "extremely subtle discovery of the writer's, sympathetic and cultivated, slipping in and out of the society round him, a detached spectator." *The Westminster Gazette* noted that only in the last pages of the novel, when Lily began to "develop some of the good qualities which had been overgrown with these horrid weeds, [does one] find a single character in the book who is not altogether odious." The reviewer claimed that Lily's late development was "a mistake from the artistic point of view" and gave "an air of exaggeration to a satire which is otherwise just though sardonic." *The Nation* (London) used even stronger language: "The denizens of 'The House of Mirth' are revolting." If "this is American society . . . it is utterly unsuitable for conversion into literature." The reviewer for the *Birmingham Post* suggested, deferentially, that Wharton "would have done herself greater justice had she gone to a higher plane for her people, where she might have found possibly one heroic character." (Edward L. Burlingame, editor of *Scribner's Magazine*, had early on expressed "disappointment" in "a certain monotony of motives in the [character] types" [letter to EW, 21 September 1904]). *The Saturday Review*, however, claimed that Lily Bart was Edith Wharton's stroke of genius — a "character that will haunt the imagination of the reader and live in his memory," a "masterly study of the modern American woman with her coldly corrupt nature and unhealthy charm."

One reviewer took issue with the prevalent complaint that a corrupt, pleasure-seeking society was an unfit subject for art. Hamilton Mabie, writing for the American journal *The Outlook*, set *The House of Mirth* in the literary traditions of Thackeray and George Eliot, Hawthorne, Flaubert, and Tolstoy, finding it "deeply moralized because it is deeply humanized." Calling it an "invigorating piece of work," Mabie claimed that its judgment of society was "as searching, penetrating, relentless as life itself." He emphasized both its psychological and sociological realism, and argued that the kind of society it portrayed was to be found in every city, in every generation. Mabie cautioned readers who might assume that it described "society as a whole." It did not, he said. Rather, *The House of Mirth* portrayed a section of society that is "the inevitable result of leisure and wealth without cultivated tastes and generous aims" — an observation that echoed Wharton's own beliefs. He predicted that it would take its place among the great works of fiction, but that it was too soon to recognize "its veracity, its power, its art," precisely because the novel challenged "the optimistic mood which is supposed to dominate American readers." This last statement looked forward to contemporary approaches to literature that emphasize the historical and cultural contexts out of which the novel was composed.

The third issue that troubled readers was the necessity of Lily's death. Some readers had hoped that her story would not end in tragedy. One woman wrote to the *New York Times* to say that had *she* written the story, she "could not have resisted the temptation of making Selden, during that last meeting with Lily, send surreptitiously for a clergyman to marry them forthwith. Only thus could she have escaped that fatal dose of chloral" (M.L.B., Oxford, N.J., letter to editor, 27 November

1905). Most reviewers, however, saw that Lily's fate could not be avoided. The *Spectator,* the famous and long-lived English journal founded by Joseph Addison and Sir Richard Steele in the eighteenth century, concluded thus: "The story is so closely knit, so logically carried out, that one cannot but acquiesce in its inevitableness, and admire the skill with which Mrs. Wharton has contrived to reconcile her readers to a conclusion which at first seemed mercilessly inconclusive." If there was a fault to be found with the author's method, it was in her "too elaborate . . . ingenuity in contriving that every indiscretion, however venial, should ultimately recoil on her heroine with accumulated force." Edith Wharton answered this complaint some thirty years later in *A Backward Glance* when she claimed that "a frivolous society can acquire dramatic significance *only through what its frivolity destroys* (207, emphasis added).

In general, reviewers who saw Lily as society's victim objected that the ending was too brutal and tragic (the author was "merciless"). Another group found Lily complicit with the society that had corrupted her and thus deserved to die. A third group, represented in the opinion of the *Westminster Gazette,* saw Lily as both fated and unable to live outside the "House of Mirth," even though she refused to accept its mores fully. Lily's death forced critics in 1905 to question the novel's meaning in terms of social morality, and the history of criticism on *The House of Mirth* reflects shifts in American values and politics and changing attitudes about the place of literature in modern society. Across the years, Lily Bart has been seen in sets of oppositions—rebellious and independent, on the one hand, and as victim of a corrupt society on the other; a woman who simultaneously procrastinated and acted too quickly; a symbol of an attenuated, dying culture, a tragic heroine, a figure for art in a materialistic society, a character who represents the limited choices for women in patriarchal society, and an emblem of femininity (see Tyson). Whether the novel is read as social realism or mannerist satire, psychological drama or tragicomedy, its meaning turns on the circumstances of Lily's life and death.

II

   The House of Mirth marked Edith Wharton's coming of age as a novelist and established her reputation as a major writer of the twentieth century. Her loyal readership and her editors at Scribner's wanted her to explore further "the house of mirth" theme in her future writings. But

Wharton was eager to try new subjects and settings. She returned to the contemporary New York social scene in only one other novel, *The Custom of the Country* (1913), published after she had moved to France. From 1907 on, she gradually distanced herself from modern American life—first by expatriating, then by her preoccupation with the vast network of charities she established during the first World War, and finally by fleeing Paris for seclusion in the French countryside when postwar expatriates arrived in 1919. In the 1920s, her most productive period of writing, she wrote several novels that purported to document postwar life, but her greatest successes in these years lay in works that treated mid-nineteenth-century life, the New York of her parents' generation (*The Age of Innocence,* 1921, which won the Pulitzer Prize for literature, and *Old New York,* 1924, a set of four novellas, one of which—"The Old Maid"—was adapted for the stage and won the Pulitzer Prize for drama in 1935). At her death in 1937, she was best known to younger readers as the author of *Ethan Frome,* a story of rural Massachusetts (1911), which had been issued in a cheap library edition for schools and colleges. By the 1930s, her social chronicles, *The House of Mirth* first among them, were judged as mere "curiosities"—nostalgic reminiscences, as Wilson Follett put it, of a bygone age rather than condemnations of modern mores. With the rise of fascism and the fear of war in Europe, the world had darkened, and Wharton's comedies had little to say to a generation that anticipated the collapse of civilization.

In a famous essay written less than a year after Edith Wharton's death, Edmund Wilson tried to refocus public attention on her work between 1905 and 1917, considered the "high" period of her drawing-room satires. His essay, "Justice to Edith Wharton," is often credited with renewing interest in her work and laying the ground for a serious reevaluation of her literary reputation. Although the dean of American critics, Wilson's singularly powerful voice could not alone restore wide public interest or academic regard for her writing, regard that reached a low ebb in the decade following her death. Ten years later, Diana Trilling's essay, "*The House of Mirth* Revisited," turned the tide of critical interest. Trilling, a critic on the political left, argued that Wharton's writings had meaning for postwar contemporary society. She was particularly interested in the class and economic structures that supported *The House of Mirth,* a novel she described as "one of the most telling indictments of a social system based on the chance distribution of wealth, and therefore of social privilege, that has ever been put on paper." This essay forecast the modes of Marxist, cultural, and feminist criticism that have now taken precedence in literary studies.

But Trilling, like Edmund Wilson, was going against the tide of formalism that held sway in America in the 1940s and 1950s. The New Criticism focused on literary artistry rather than subject and themes. Formalism examined works of literature as timeless art objects to be judged on aesthetic grounds (beliefs that Wharton herself held about art); its approach was ruinous to a novel like *The House of Mirth*, with its strong thematic and moral emphasis. Coupled with an entrenched reaction against women's writing in favor of male psychological fiction (a trend that began in the 1920s and lasted well into the 1960s), the prevailing tide of formalism, with its interest in literary technique, had serious consequences for Wharton's reputation. Major American critics and literary historians like F.O. Matthiessen and Van Wyck Brooks either had little to say about Wharton or tended to devalue her writing because she, like Jane Austen before her, worked on an apparently small canvas and wrote in a "minor" genre, the novel of manners.

The first major reassessment of Wharton's work after her death was Blake Nevius's *Edith Wharton: A Study of Her Fiction* (1953), still considered a valuable critical work. He argued that her writing was important because it chronicled a significant phase of social history and dramatized the conflict of ideals between the old mercantile world and the new industrial societies—a conflict that provides the background to *The House of Mirth*. Oddly enough, Nevius did not pay close attention in his study to Wharton's first "society" novel, perhaps because *The House of Mirth* had long been out of print.

In 1962, Scribner's issued a paperback edition of *The House of Mirth*, making it possible for general readers and university students to rediscover the novel that is still taught more often and read more frequently than any other of Edith Wharton's writings. In "Life Among the Ungentle Genteel," Marie Bristol assessed the implications of the reissue of *The House of Mirth* and offered cogent explanations for the long neglect of Wharton's writing: she was neglected because she was seen to be an outdated writer of the "Genteel School" and a disciple of Henry James. Praising her clear and lucid writing style, her gift for characterization and plot structure, Bristol classified Wharton in the tradition of Theodore Dreiser and naturalism and described *The House of Mirth* as a "novel of dialectics," a term drawn from Marxist thought that is now inflected by structuralist and poststructuralist uses of the term (see glossary).

It has taken many years, however, to erase the popular image of Edith Wharton as a "genteel" woman and writer, to overcome the belief that her writing was limited to the study of a narrow and dying class of

New York City society, and for her work to be treated with the seriousness and respect of her male colleagues in American literature. Indeed, the effort to see Wharton in her own terms and to chart a place for her in literary history is still ongoing. In the post-World War II years, she appeared on university reading lists represented primarily by her short fiction; in both undergraduate and graduate courses, she was inevitably paired with Henry James and seen—falsely—to be his imitator as a chronicler of Old New York. This entrenched view began to change when Richard Poirer in his influential 1965 reexamination of American literary history argued eloquently for Wharton's artistic originality and showed in how many ways her work differed from that of James. He pointed to the ways their subject matter and styles diverged, and he emphasized the relation of character and environment in Wharton's novels. Characters in *The House of Mirth*, he contended, are "propelled mostly by environmental circumstances external to them."

Poirer was not alone in trying to bring Wharton out of James's shadow; nor was he the only critic to reconsider the social contexts of Wharton's fiction. Criticism of *The House of Mirth* was slowly coming around again to issues that had drawn the attention of its earliest readers: the tension between character and situation, and the influence of gender, social class, race, and the marketplace in shaping the moral climate of society—and, by extension, the literature it produced. The social and political upheaval in the United States and Europe in the 1960s contributed to a rethinking of the canons of culture and demanded new curricula, a call for change (still echoed today) that was fueled by a profound skepticism and mistrust of the founding ideas and organizations of western society. Wharton was thought to be too upper class, too Victorian, too fixed in her late-nineteenth-century context, too representative of a wealthy, conservative elitism to excite much interest in an increasingly alienated and politically radicalized student body. She embodied for many the sexual and social repression of the WASP elitism then under attack, and the moral force of her writing—if recognized at all—was out of favor in the newly "liberated" sixties.

III

Wharton seemed to represent all that was antithetical to the social and sexual revolution of the 1960s, just as she and James in the early years of the century symbolized all that avant-garde writers wanted to overthrow. Her writings did not appear to lend themselves to structuralist and poststructuralist ways of reading, approaches that emerged in Europe in the late 1960s and the 1970s and made their way to America, where they mounted an attack on the principles and proponents of formalism. The new ideas came primarily from France, entered American universities by way of foreign language departments, and were promulgated by a small group of men in elite institutions in Paris: philosopher and literary theorist Roland Barthes (whose writing charted the shift for literary studies from structuralism to poststructuralism); philosopher and historian Michel Foucault, author of a six-volume history of sexuality, sexual repression, and penal servitude in western culture; philosopher and literary theorist Jacques Derrida, best known in America as the exponent of a textual strategy called "deconstruction" but whose larger project is "grammatology," the study of the function and status of writing; and psychoanalyst Jacques Lacan, who theorized human psychosexuality in relation to language, using Ferdinand de Saussure's work in linguistics and the writings of Surrealist poets and avant-garde novelists, many of whom were his personal friends. Taking into account a founding assumption of modern science — the observer is always part of what she or he observes — these theories undermine the belief that language and literature can provide a window onto a stable reality or that reality is wholly external to the literary text that interprets it.

Edith Wharton, schooled in eighteenth-century rationalism, would undoubtedly have resisted such theories. She had a skeptical, if frank, regard for Freud's work on human sexuality, although she used his vocabulary to explain the psychic and spiritual traumas of her friends. She was disconcerted, even shocked, by avant-garde writing, which she believed to be self-indulgent and lacking in the necessary control and conscious domination of the artistic subject that she had worked so hard to achieve in her own writing. She saw art and genius in a gendered perspective, as did many other women artists of her generation. For her, the true artist was always male and genius always masculine, and she defined her own considerable artistic talents as something other than genius. Had she still been alive to see her writing fall out of favor with formalist critics in the 1940s and 1950s, she might have agreed that they lacked the organizing aesthetic principle of genius that makes art.

Only now, thirty years after structuralism made its first forays into American university classrooms, are Wharton's works the focus of "new" theories of reading and writing. (For example, Margot Norris's essay in this volume is the first deconstructive reading of *The House of Mirth*). The road that led from formalist dismissal of her writing in the 1950s to the current renaissance in Wharton studies was paved by feminist critics, whose initial effort was to bring her writing back to public attention by focusing on the "images of women" in her works. As feminist inquiry developed and diversified over the last thirty years, influenced by European thought and forging alliances with a variety of other interpretive methods, it provided ways to see Wharton's writing as modern, even modernist. Poststructuralist feminist theories, informed by research in the biological and social sciences, emphasize the *constructed* nature of human subjectivity and demonstrate how ideological discourses interact to figure (and disfigure) human subjects. As the essays in this volume demonstrate (and all five of them could be categorized as feminist), these ways of reading have much to say about the society that both created and destroyed Lily Bart.

Lily's beauty and behavior, her attitudes and morals, are so enmeshed with her society that it is impossible to detach her from the sociohistorical framework constructed by the novel. In *The Writing of Fiction* (1925), Wharton explained that the goal of a novel of society was to "interweave individual and social analysis" so successfully that one was indistinguishable from the other" (81). In her memoir, *A Backward Glance* (1934), she spoke directly to the problem of interweaving individual and social analysis in *The House of Mirth:* "The problem was how to extract from such a subject the typical human significance which is the story-teller's reason for telling one story rather than another" (207). What was the "human significance" of "a society of irresponsible pleasure-seekers" such as those we meet in *The House of Mirth?* She found her answer in Lily Bart, a woman who is debased and destroyed by society (*Glance* 207). But Lily is not merely a victim of society's will, nor are its mores entirely external to her sensibilities. She herself represents the contested terrain of human subjectivity in which powerful social forces vie for dominance and distinction. The meaning of Lily's life and death is neither self-evident nor a given.

IV

The same might be said of Edith Wharton's life and death. But when structuralism was first staking its claims in Paris in the 1960s and Michel Foucault and Roland Barthes were declaring the "death of the Author" (whose "life," they said, is a web of fiction, a "text"), Edith Wharton had not yet been the subject of a biography. By 1971 four biographical studies were in print, none of them either a literary or a full-life study: Percy Lubbock, *Portrait of Edith Wharton*, drawn from memoirs prepared by selected friends and acquaintances; Grace Kellogg Griffith, *The Two Lives of Edith Wharton,* a biography marred by inaccurate assumptions about Wharton's intimate life, her mental health, and her writing methods; Louis Auchincloss, *Edith Wharton,* a study drawn primarily from letters and memorabilia that he owned; and Millicent Bell, *Edith Wharton and Henry James,* an influential scholarly work that situates the two writers as friends and colleagues rather than as master and disciple. These works were necessarily limited in their approaches because Wharton's personal papers, housed with her literary archive at Yale, were still under a thirty-year interdiction to protect the privacy of family members and friends, and the literary estate had not yet appointed an official biographer.

In 1967, the year the seal on the Yale archive was lifted, the Edith Wharton estate appointed R. W. B. Lewis, a Yale professor, to write a biography. Published in 1975, his *Edith Wharton* shaped a woman that both conformed to her public image as a haughty Victorian debilitated by neurasthenia and surprised the world by revealing Wharton as a woman of passion (she had a midlife love affair with William Morton Fullerton, a bisexual) and capable of writing sizzling scenes of father-daughter seduction (see the "Beatrice Palmato" fragment). Indeed, revelation of the love affair and the reprinted piece of pornography virtually eclipsed other aspects of her story—notably, the passion she had for writing. Two years later, Cynthia Griffin Wolff's *A Feast of Words,* a powerful psycholiterary biography, tried to solve the "puzzle of creativity" at the heart of Wharton's writing. Like Lewis's Pulitzer Prize-winning book, Wolff's study drew on the theories of psychologist Erik Erikson and examined the effects of Wharton's childhood sufferings and psychological illnesses on the development of her lifework.

Recent studies of Wharton's life and art have have continued this emphasis on the psychological, using a variety of approaches. Lev Raphael uses the work of Silvan Tomkins and Gershen Kaufman on shaming *(Prisoners of Shame);* Barbara White examines Wharton's short fiction in terms of incest and child-abuse studies, as does David Holbrook; Gloria Ehrlich combines Freudian theory with recent theories of mothering in *The Sexual Education of Edith Wharton.* While psychoanalytic studies have provided an important thread in Wharton criticism, they interweave with contextual and cultural analysis within the framework of American studies that was opened in 1980 with Elizabeth Ammons's feminist study, *Edith Wharton's Argument with America,* which traces Wharton's argument with patriarchal society through her life and fiction; my own literary history of expatriate Paris modernism, *Women of the Left Bank* (1986); and Susan Goodman's *Edith Wharton's Women* (1990), a study of female friendships in Wharton's life and fiction. This focus on Wharton's life and writing in their cultural-historical contexts has opened new possibilities for biographies and critical studies and renewed interest in her "neglected" writings, especially those that have been long out of print and are now being republished.

The 1980s saw an outpouring of scholarship on Wharton and increasing public interest in her. The Edith Wharton Society was founded; an international group, it arranges conferences, publishes a scholarly journal, the *Edith Wharton Review,* and encourages teaching and research on Wharton. Important scholarly and bibliographical tools appeared in the late 1980s and early 1990s, including the 1988 publication of a one-volume edition of Wharton's literary correspondence (some four hundred letters, most of them written between 1902 and 1937 and constituting about one-sixth of the total available), edited by R. W. B. Lewis and Nancy Lewis. In 1990, two important bibliographies were published: Kristin O. Lauer and Margaret P. Murray compiled an annotated secondary bibliography that brought Marlene Springer's 1899–1973 bibliography up to date; Stephen Garrison compiled a massive, authoritative, and invaluable descriptive bibliography of Wharton's writing. Other important publications of 1990 included Margaret McDowell's revised edition of her thoughtful 1976 Twayne series biography and Linda Wagner-Martin's *The House of Mirth: A Novel of Admonition* in the Twayne Masterwork Studies.

Wharton scholars now have easier access to the immense archives of unpublished materials by and about her. The fifty-thousand item Edith Wharton Collection at the Beinecke Library (Yale University) was recatalogued in 1989 and is now more accessible to scholars and students. Materials inherited by Ambassador William R. Tyler, residuary legatee of the Edith Wharton Estate, are now housed at the Lilly Library (Indiana University). Wharton's more than three hundred notes and letters to Morton Fullerton are at the Humanities Research Center (University of Texas).

An "Edith Wharton Revolution," as it has been called by Annette Zilvermitt, editor of the *Edith Wharton Review,* is underway, and it extends well beyond the borders of the academy. Wharton has again found the popular reading public that made *The House of Mirth* an overnight bestseller—a loyal readership that sustained her creatively, financially, and emotionally throughout her life. She and her work are now very much "in fashion" and in *Vogue* (literally), articles about her having appeared in art, design, and architecture publications and in all the major women's magazines in America and Great Britain during the last several years. Her novels and short stories have been made into major films *(The Children, Ethan Frome, The Age of Innocence),* and illustrated biographies and books on her travels and gardens are soon to be published by trade presses. Edith Wharton Restoration in Lenox, Massachusetts, established in the early 1980s to restore her Berkshire mansion, The Mount, attracts huge crowds of visitors every summer and has fostered renewed interest in Wharton's expertise in architectural and landscape design. A wealth of new information about her life has come to light in the last two years (the bulk of it drawn from public archives in the United States and in Europe), and recently discovered letters, diaries, and manuscripts add depth and dimension—and in some instances change entirely—our visions of Edith Wharton. More than 130 years after her birth, she continues to draw us to her while resisting our efforts to categorize her as woman and writer.

V

The following five essays provide historical backgrounds for *The House of Mirth* and discuss its characters, situation, and form (or genre). Their methods of inquiry are situated in our contemporary culture rather than the world of Wharton's novel, but these approaches are neither arbitrary nor extraneous to the novel's own concerns; each essay mirrors something already at work within the text. A feminist critic sees late-nineteenth-century attitudes toward women as constitutive—but also restrictive—forces in Lily Bart's (and Edith Wharton's) efforts to gain self-determination. A Marxist critic examines how class structures and the system of economic exchange construct and position Lily within a capitalist marketplace where she herself is not an agent of change but a commodity, an item of exchange. A cultural critic examines the place and function of gender within a "culture of capitalism" in which a double sexual standard is always at work and where a woman's capital is her "female sexual probity"—her virginity before marriage and her fidelity afterwards. A deconstructive critic shows how *The House of Mirth* misreads and misapplies its own conventions of literary realism and the novel of manners. A psychoanalytic critic explains how Edith Wharton elevates (sublimates) her suffering into art and how Edith and Lily share the "sorrow of women who do not quite fit into societal norms."

Fixed as we are in our contemporary moment, we cannot easily catapult ourselves into the historical past and read *The House of Mirth* as a mirror of everyday social reality circa 1905. By virtue of our own historical positioning, we see the world presented in the novel as an invention. We seek to understand its conventions and mechanisms, to see how it creates its subject and characters, and to know the ways in which it tells its stories. A set of sexual, social, financial, racial, moral, and psychological economies governs this world: How do they intersect, overlap, support, and undercut each other? How do they position us as readers so that we participate in creating Lily Bart and her world? The essays that follow provide insights into these questions.

Shari Benstock

WORKS CITED

Ammons, Elizabeth, ed. *The House of Mirth*. New York: Norton, 1990.

Auchincloss, Lewis. *Edith Wharton: A Woman in Her Time*. New York: Viking, 1971.

Bell, Millicent. *Edith Wharton and Henry James: The Story of Their Friendship*. New York: Braziller, 1965.

Benstock, Shari. *Women of the Left Bank: Paris 1900–1940*. Austin: U of Texas P, 1986.

Birmingham Post. Unsigned rev. 3 Nov. 1905.

Bristol, Marie. "Life Among the Ungentle Genteel: Edith Wharton's *The House of Mirth* Revisited." *Western Humanities Review* 16 (Autumn 1962): 371–74.

Brooks, Van Wyck. *The Confident Years: 1885–1915*. New York: Dutton, 1952.

Daily Chronicle (England). Unsigned rev. 6 Nov. 1905.

Dundee Advertiser (Scotland). Unsigned rev. 26 Oct. 1905.

Ehrlich, Gloria C. *The Sexual Education of Edith Wharton*. Berkeley: U of California P, 1992.

English Review. Unsigned rev. 4 Nov. 1905.

Follett, Wilson. "What Edith Wharton Did—And Might Have Done." *New York Times Book Review*. 5 Sept. 1937: 2.

Garrison, Stephen. *Edith Wharton: A Descriptive Bibliography*. Pittsburgh: U of Pittsburgh P, 1990.

Globe (England). Unsigned rev. 28 Oct. 1905.

Goodman, Susan. *Edith Wharton's Women: Friends and Rivals.* Hanover and London: UP of New England, 1990.

Griffith, Grace Kellogg. *The Two Lives of Edith Wharton: The Woman and Her Work.* New York: Appleton, 1965.

Holbrook, David. *Edith Wharton and the Unsatisfactory Man.* London: Vision, 1991.

The Independent. Unsigned rev. 10 July 1905: 113.

Lauer, Kristin O., and Margaret P. Murray. *Edith Wharton: An Annotated Secondary Bibliography.* New York: Garland, 1990.

Lewis, R. W. B. *Edith Wharton: A Biography.* New York: Harper, 1975.

Lewis, R. W. B., and Nancy Lewis, ed. *The Letters of Edith Wharton.* New York: Scribner's, 1988.

Lubbock, Percy. *Portrait of Edith Wharton.* New York: Appleton, 1947.

Mabie, Hamilton W. "A Notable Novel." *The Outlook* (21 Oct. 1905): 404–06.

MacArthur, James. "Books and Bookmen." *Harper's Weekly* 49 (2 Dec. 1905): 1750.

The Manchester Guardian. Unsigned rev. 1 Nov. 1905.

McDowell, Margaret B. *Edith Wharton.* Rev. ed. Boston: G. K. Hall, 1990.

Meynell, Alice. "The House of Mirth." *Bookman* (London) 29 (1905): 130–31.

Moss, Mary. "Notes on New Novels." *The Atlantic Monthly* 97 (1906): 52–53.

The Nation. Unsigned rev. 81 (1905): 447–48.

Nevius, Blake. *Edith Wharton: A Study of Her Fiction.* Berkeley: U California P, 1953.

Outlook (England). Unsigned rev. 4 Nov. 1905.

Poirier, Richard. "Edith Wharton's *The House of Mirth.*" *The American Novel: From James Fenimore Cooper to William Faulkner.* New York: Basic Books, 1965. Expanded and rpt. as *A World Elsewhere: The Place of Style in American Literature.* New York: Oxford UP, 1966.

Publishers' Circular (London). Unsigned rev. 25 Nov. 1905.

Raphael, Lev. *Edith Wharton's Prisoners of Shame: A New Perspective on Her Neglected Fiction.* New York: St. Martin's, 1991.

The Saturday Review (London). Unsigned rev. 101 (1906): 209–10.

The Spectator. Unsigned rev. 28 Oct. 1905.

Springer, Marlene. *Edith Wharton and Kate Chopin: A Reference Guide.* Boston: G. K. Hall, 1976).

The Times (London). Unsigned rev. 1 Dec. 1905.

Trilling, Diana. *"The House of Mirth* Revisited." *Harper's Bazaar* 81 (1947): 126–27.

Tyson, Lois. "Beyond Morality: Lily Bart, Lawrence Selden and the Aesthetic Commodity in *The House of Mirth." Edith Wharton Review* 9. 2 (Fall 1992): 3–10.

Wagner-Martin, Linda. *The House of Mirth: A Novel of Admonition.* Boston: G. K. Hall, 1990.

Westminster Gazette. (London). Unsigned rev. 25 Nov. 1905.

Wharton, Edith. *A Backward Glance.* New York: Scribner's, 1934.

———. *The Writing of Fiction.* New York: Scribner's, 1925.

White, Barbara. *Edith Wharton: A Study of the Short Fiction.* Boston: Twayne, 1991.

Wilson, Edmund. "Justice to Edith Wharton." *The New Republic* 95 (29 June 1938): 209–13.

Wolff, Cynthia Griffin. *A Feast of Words: The Triumph of Edith Wharton.* New York: Oxford UP, 1977.

Woman (England). Unsigned rev. 20 Dec. 1905.

Cultural Criticism
and
The House of Mirth

WHAT IS CULTURAL CRITICISM?

What do you think of when you think of culture? The opera or ballet? A performance of a Mozart symphony at Lincoln Center, or a Rembrandt show at the Metropolitan Museum of Art? Does the phrase "cultural event" conjure up images of young people in jeans and T-shirts or of people in their sixties dressed formally? Most people hear "culture" and think "High Culture." Consequently, most people, when they first hear of cultural criticism, assume it would be more formal than, well, say, formalism. They suspect it would be "highbrow," in both subject and style.

Nothing could be further from the truth. In fact, one of the goals of cultural criticism is to oppose Culture with a capital C, in other words, that *view* of culture which always and only equates it with what we sometimes call "high culture." Cultural critics want to make the term *culture* refer to *popular* culture as well as to that culture we associate with the so-called classics. Cultural critics are as likely to write about "Star Trek" as they are to analyze James Joyce's *Ulysses*. They want to break down the boundary between high and low, and to dismantle the hierarchy that the distinction implies. They also want to discover the (often political) reasons *why* a certain kind of aesthetic product is more valued than others.

A cultural critic writing on a revered classic might concentrate on a movie or even comic strip version. Or she might see it in light of some more common form of reading material (a novel by Jane Austen might be viewed in light of Gothic romances or ladies' conduct manuals), as the reflection of some common cultural myths or concerns (*Huckleberry Finn* might be shown to reflect and shape American myths about race, concerns about juvenile delinquency), or as an example of how texts move back and forth across the alleged boundary between "low" and "high" culture. A history play by Shakespeare, as one group of cultural critics has pointed out, may have started off as a popular work enjoyed by working people, later become a "highbrow" play enjoyed only by the privileged and educated, and, still later, due to a film version produced during World War II, become popular again — this time because it has been produced and viewed as a patriotic statement about England's greatness during wartime (Humm 6–7). Even as this introduction was being written, cultural critics were analyzing the "cultural work" being done cooperatively by Mel Gibson and Shakespeare in Franco Zeffirelli's movie, *Hamlet*.

In combating old definitions of what constitutes culture, of course, cultural critics sometimes end up combating old definitions of what constitutes the literary canon, that is, the once-agreed-upon honor roll of Great Books. They tend to do so, however, neither by adding books (and movies and television sitcoms) *to* the old list of texts that every "culturally literate" person should supposedly know, nor by substituting for it some kind of Counterculture Canon. Rather, they tend to combat the canon by critiquing the very *idea* of canon. Cultural critics want to get us away from thinking about certain works as the "best" ones produced by a given culture (and therefore as the novels that best represent American culture). They seek to be more descriptive and less evaluative, more interested in relating than rating cultural products and events.

It is not surprising, then, that in an article on "The Need for Cultural Studies," four groundbreaking cultural critics have written that "Cultural Studies should . . . abandon the goal of giving students access to that which represents a culture." Instead, these critics go on to argue, it should show works in reference to other works, economic contexts, or broad social discourses (about childbirth, women's education, rural decay, etc.) within whose contexts the work makes sense. Perhaps most important, critics doing cultural studies should counter the prevalent notion that culture is some wholeness that has already been formed. Culture, rather, is really a set of interactive *cultures*, alive and growing and changing, and cultural critics should be present- and even future-oriented. Cultural critics should be "resisting intellectuals," and cultural studies should be "an emancipatory project" (Giroux 478–80).

The paragraphs above are peppered with words like *oppose, counter, deny, resist, combat, abandon,* and *emancipatory.* What such words suggest—and quite accurately—is that a number of cultural critics view themselves in political, even oppositional, terms. Not only are cultural critics likely to take on the literary canon while offering political readings of popular films, but they are also likely to take on the institution of the university, for that is where the old definitions of culture as High Culture (and as something formed and finished and canonized) have been most vigorously preserved, defended, and reinforced.

Cultural critics have been especially critical of the departmental structure of universities, for that structure, perhaps more than anything else, has kept the study of the "arts" more or less distinct from the study of history, not to mention from the study of such things as television, film, advertising, journalism, popular photography, folklore, current affairs, shoptalk, and gossip. By doing so, the departmental structure of universities has reasserted the high/low culture distinction, implying that all the latter subjects are best left to historians, sociologists, anthropologists, linguists, and communication theorists. But such a suggestion, cultural critics would argue, keeps us from seeing the aesthetics of an advertisement as well as the propagandistic elements of a work of literature. For these reasons, cultural critics have mixed and matched the most revealing analytical procedures developed in a variety of disciplines, unabashedly jettisoning the rest. For these reasons, too, they have formed—and encouraged other scholars to form—networks other than and outside of those enforced departmentally.

Some initially loose interdisciplinary networks have, over time, solidified to become Cultural Studies programs and majors, complete with courses on comics and surveys of soaps. As this has happened, a significant if subtle danger has arisen. Cultural critics, Richard Johnson has warned, must strive diligently to keep cultural studies from becoming a discipline unto itself—one in which students encounter cartoons as a canon and belief in the importance of such popular forms as an "orthodoxy" (39). The only principles that critics doing cultural studies can doctrinally espouse, Johnson suggests, are the two that have thus far been introduced: namely, the principle that "culture" has been an "inegalitarian" concept, a "tool" of "condescension," and the belief that a new, "interdisciplinary (and sometimes antidisciplinary)" approach to *true* culture (that is, to the forms in which culture actually lives now) is required now that history and art and media are so complex and inter-related (42).

Johnson, ironically, played a major part in the institutionalization of cultural studies. Together with Stuart Hall and Richard Hoggart, he developed the Centre for Contemporary Cultural Studies, founded by Hoggart and Hall at Birmingham University, in England, in 1964. The fact that the Centre was founded in the mid-1960s is hardly surprising; cultural criticism, based as it is on a critique of elitist definitions of culture, spoke powerfully to and gained great energy and support from a decade of student unrest and revolt. The fact that the first center for cultural studies was founded in England, in Europe, is equally unsurprising. Although the United States has probably contributed more than any other nation to the *media* through which culture currently lives, critics in Europe, drawing upon the ideas of both Marxist and non-Marxist theorists, first articulated the need for something like what we now call cultural criticism or cultural studies. Indeed, to this day, European critics are more involved than Americans, not only in the analysis of popular cultural forms and products but also in the analysis of human subjectivity or consciousness *as* a form or product of culture. ("Subjectivities," Johnson argues, are "produced, not given, and are . . . objects of inquiry" inevitably related to "social practices," whether those involve factory rules, supermarket behavior patterns, reading habits, advertisements watched, myths perpetrated, or languages and other signs to which people are exposed [44–45].)

Among the early continental critics now seen as forerunners of present-day cultural critics were those belonging to the *Annales* school, so-called because of the name of the journal that Marc Bloch and Lucien Febvre launched, in France, in 1929: *Annales: Economies, Sociétés, Civilisations.* The *Annales* school critics greatly influenced later thinkers like Michel Foucault, who, in turn, influenced other *Annales* thinkers such as Roger Chartier, Jacques Ravel, François Furet, and Robert Darnton. Both first- and second-generation *Annales* school critics warn against the development of "topics" of study by cultural critics—unless those same critics are bent on "developing . . . [a] sense of cohesion or interaction between topics" (Hunt 9). At the same time, interested as they are in cohesion, *Annales* school critics have warned against seeing the "rituals and other forms of symbolic action" as "express[ing]" a central, coherent, communal meaning." They have reminded us that texts affect different readers "in varying and individual ways" (Hunt 13–14).

Michel Foucault is another strong, continental influence on present-day cultural criticism—and perhaps *the* strongest influence on American cultural criticism and the so-called new historicism, an interdisciplinary form of historical criticism whose evolution has often paralleled that of cultural criticism. Influenced by early *Annales* critics and contemporary Marxists (but neither an *Annales* critic nor a Marxist himself), Foucault sought to study cultures in terms of power relationships. Unlike Marxists and some *Annales* school critics, he refused to see power as something exercised by a dominant over a subservient class. Indeed, he emphasized that power is not just *repressive* power: a tool of conspiracy by one individual or institution against another. Power, rather, is a whole complex of forces; it is that which produces what happens.

Thus even a tyrannical aristocrat does not simply wield power, for he is empowered by "discourses"—accepted ways of thinking, writing, and speaking—and practices that amount to power. Foucault tried to view all things, from punishment to sexuality, in terms of the widest possible variety of discourses. As a result, he traced the "genealogy" of topics he studied through texts that more traditional historians and literary critics would have overlooked, looking at (in Lynn Hunt's words) "memoirs of deviants, diaries, political treatises, architectural blueprints, court records, doctors' reports—appl[ying] consistent principles of analysis in search of moments of reversal in discourse, in search of events as loci of the conflict where social practices were transformed" (Hunt 39). Foucault tended not only to build interdisciplinary bridges but also, in the process, to bring into the study of culture the "histories of women, homosexuals, and minorities"—groups seldom studied by those interested in culture with a capital C (Hunt 45).

Of the British influences on cultural studies and criticism as it is today, several have already been mentioned. Of those who have not, two early forerunners stand out. One of these, the Marxist critic E. P. Thompson, revolutionized study of the industrial revolution by writing about its impact on human attitudes, even consciousness. He showed how a shared cultural view, specifically that of what constitutes a fair or just price, influenced crowd behavior and caused such things as the food riots and rick burnings of the nineteenth century. The other, even greater, early British influence on contemporary cultural criticism and cultural studies was the late Raymond Williams. In works like *The Long Revolution* and *Culture and Society: 1780–1950,* Williams demonstrated that culture is not a fixed and finished but, rather, a living and changing thing. One of the changes he called for was the development of a common socialist culture.

Like Marxists, with whom he often both argued and sympathized, Williams viewed culture in relation to ideologies, what he termed the "residual," "dominant," or "emerging" ways of viewing the world held by classes or individuals holding power in a given social group. But unlike Thompson and Richard Hoggart, he avoided emphasizing *social* classes and class *conflict* in discussing those forces most powerfully shaping and changing culture. And, unlike certain continental Marxists, he could never see the cultural "superstructure" as being a more or less simple "reflection" of the economic "base." Williams's tendency was to focus on people as people, on how they experience conditions they find themselves in and creatively respond to those conditions in their social practices. A believer in the resiliency of the individual, he produced a body of criticism notable for what Hall has called its "humanism" (63).

As is clear from the paragraphs above, the emergence and evolution of cultural studies or criticism are difficult to separate entirely from the development of Marxist thought. Marxism is, in a sense, the background to the background of most cultural criticism, and some contemporary cultural critics consider themselves Marxist critics as well. Thus, although Marxist criticism and its most significant practitioners are introduced elsewhere in this volume, some mention of Marxist ideas — and of the critics who developed them — is also necessary here. Of particular importance to the evolution of cultural criticism are the works of Walter Benjamin, Antonio Gramsci, Louis Althusser, and Mikhail Bakhtin.

Bakhtin was a Russian, later a Soviet, critic so original in his thinking and wide-ranging in his influence that some would say he was never a Marxist at all. He viewed language — especially literary texts — in terms of discourses and dialogues *between* discourses. Within a novel written in a society in flux, for instance, the narrative may include an official, legitimate discourse, plus another infiltrated by challenging comments and even retorts. In a 1929 book on Dostoyevsky and a 1940 study *Rabelais and His World,* Bakhtin examined what he calls "polyphonic" novels, each characterized by a multiplicity of voices or discourses. In Dostoyevsky the independent status of a given character is marked by the difference of his or her language from that of the narrator. (The narrator's voice, too, can in fact be a dialogue.) In works by Rabelais, Bakhtin finds that the (profane) language of the carnival and of other popular festivities play against and parody the more official discourses, that is, of the magistrates or the Church. Bakhtin influenced modern cultural criticism by showing, in a sense, that the conflict between "high" and "low" culture takes place not only between classic and popular texts but also between the "dialogic" voices that exist within all great books.

Walter Benjamin was a German Marxist who, during roughly the same period, attacked certain conventional and traditional literary forms that he felt conveyed a stultifying "aura" of culture. He took this position in part because so many previous Marxist critics and, in his own day, Georg Lukács, had seemed to be stuck on appreciating nineteenth-century realistic novels—and opposed to the modernist works of their own time. Benjamin not only praised modernist movements, such as Dadaism, but also saw as hopeful the development of new art forms utilizing mechanical production and reproduction. These forms, including radio and films, offered the promise of a new definition of culture via a broader, less exclusive domain of the arts.

Antonio Gramsci, an Italian Marxist best known for his *Prison Notebooks* (first published as *Lettere dal carcere* in 1947), critiqued the very concept of literature and, beyond that, of culture in the old sense, stressing not only the importance of culture more broadly defined but the need for nurturing and developing proletarian, or working-class, culture. He suggested the need to view intellectuals politically—and the need for what he called "radical organic" intellectuals. Today's cultural critics calling for colleagues to "legitimate the notion of writing reviews and books for the general public," to "become involved in the political reading of popular culture," and, in general, to "repoliticize . . . scholarship" have often cited Gramsci as an early advocate of their views (Giroux 482).

Finally, and most importantly, Gramsci related literature to the ideologies of the culture that produced it and developed the concept of "hegemony," a term he used to describe the pervasive, weblike system of meanings and values—ideologies—that shapes the way things look, what they mean and, therefore, what reality *is* for the majority of people within a culture. Gramsci did not see people, even poor people, as the helpless victims of hegemony, as ideology's idiotic robots. Rather, he believed that people have the freedom and power to struggle against ideology, to alter hegemony. As Patrick Brantlinger has suggested in *Crusoe's Footprints: Cultural Studies in Britain and America* (1990), Gramsci's thought is unspoiled by the "intellectual arrogance that views the vast majority of people as deluded zombies, the victims or creatures of ideology" (100).

Of those Marxists who, after Gramsci, explored the complex relationship between literature and ideology, the French Marxist Louis

Althusser also had a significant impact on cultural criticism. Unlike Gramsci, Althusser tended to see ideology in control of people, and not vice versa. He argued that the main function of ideology is to reproduce the society's existing relations of production, and that that function is even carried out in most literary texts, although literature is relatively autonomous from other "social formations." Dave Laing has explained Althusser's position by saying that the "ensemble of habits, moralities, and opinions" that can be found in any work of literature tend to "ensure that the work-force (and those responsible for re-producing them in the family, school, etc.) are maintained in their position of subordination to the dominant class" (91).

In many ways, though, Althusser is as good an example of where Marxism and cultural criticism part ways as he is of where cultural criticism is indebted to Marxists and their ideas. For although Althusser did argue that literature is relatively autonomous—more independent of ideology than, say, Church, press, or State—*he* meant by literature not just literature in the narrow sense but something even narrower. He meant Good Literature, certainly not the popular forms that present-day cultural critics would want to set beside Tolstoy and Joyce, Eliot and Brecht. Those popular fictions, Althusser assumed, were mere packhorses designed (however unconsciously) to carry the baggage of a culture's ideology, mere brood mares destined to reproduce it.

Thus, while cultural critics have embraced *both* Althusser's notion that works of literature reflect certain ideological formations *and* his notion that, at the same time, literary works may be relatively distant from or even resistant to ideology, they have rejected the narrow limits within which Althusser and other Marxists have defined literature. In "Marxism and Popular Fiction" (1986), Tony Bennett uses "Monty Python's Flying Circus" and another British television show, "Not the 9 o'clock News," to argue that the Althusserian notion that all forms of popular culture are to be included "among [all those] many material forms which ideology takes . . . under capitalism" is "simply not true." The "entire field" of "popular fiction"—which Bennett takes to include films and television shows as well as books—is said to be "replete with instances" of works that do what Bennett calls the "work" of "distancing." That is, they have the effect of separating the audience from, not rebinding the audience to, prevailing ideologies (249).

Although there are Marxist cultural critics (Bennett himself is one, carrying on through his writings what may be described as a lover's quarrel with Marxism), most cultural critics are not Marxists in any strict sense. Anne Beezer, in writing about such things as advertisements and women's magazines, contests the "Althusserian view of ideology as the construction of the subject" (qtd. in Punter 103). That is to say, she gives both the media she is concerned with and their audiences more credit than Althusserian Marxists presumably would. Whereas they might argue that such media make people what they are, she points out that the same magazines that may, admittedly, tell women how to please their men may, at the same time, offer liberating advice to women about how to preserve their independence by not getting too serious romantically. And, she suggests, many advertisements advertise their status as ads, just as many people who view or read them see advertising as advertising and interpret it accordingly.

The complex and subtle sort of analysis that Beezer has brought to bear on women's magazines and advertisements has been focused on paperback romance novels by Tania Modleski and Janice Radway, in *Loving with a Vengeance* (1982) and *Reading the Romance* (1984), respectively. Radway, a feminist cultural critic who uses but finally exceeds Marxist critical discourse, points out that many women who read romances do so in order to carve out a time and space that is wholly their own, not to be intruded upon by their husband or children. Also, Radway argues, such novels may end in marriage, but the marriage is usually between a feisty and independent heroine and a powerful man she has "tamed," that is, made sensitive and caring. And why do so many such stories involve such heroines and end as they do? Because, Radway demonstrates through painstaking research into publishing houses, bookstores, and reading communities, their consumers *want* them to be that way. They don't buy—or, if they buy they don't recommend—romances in which, for example, a heroine is raped: thus, in time, fewer and fewer such plots find their way onto the racks by the supermarket checkout.

Radway's reading is typical of feminist cultural criticism in that it is *political*—but not exclusively about oppression. The subjectivities of women may be "produced" by romances—that is, their thinking is governed by what they read—but the same women also govern, to some extent, what gets written or produced, thus doing "cultural work" of their own. Rather than seeing all forms of popular culture as manifestations of ideology, soon to be remanifested in the minds of victimized audiences, non-Marxist cultural critics tend to see a sometimes disheartening but always dynamic synergy between cultural forms and the culture's consumers.

Mary Poovey does this in *The Proper Lady and the Woman Writer* (1984), a book in which she traces the evolution of female "propriety."

Poovey closely connects the proprieties taught by eighteenth-century women who wrote conduct manuals, ladies' magazines, and even novels with patriarchal notions of women and men's *property*. (Since property was inherited, an unfaithful woman could threaten the disposition of a man's inheritance by giving birth to children who were not his. Therefore, writings by women that reinforced proprieties also shored up the proprietary status quo.) Finally, though, Poovey also shows that some of the women writers who reinforced proprieties and were seen as "textbook Proper Ladies" in fact "crossed the borders of that limited domain" (40). They may have written stories showing the audacity, for women, of trying to lead an imaginative, let alone audacious, life beyond the bounds of domestic propriety. But they did so imaginatively and audaciously.

In the essay that follows, Lillian S. Robinson examines *The House of Mirth* in relation to the economic structure of Wharton's society and the resulting "sexual economies" that determine gender relations. Although she calls *The House of Mirth* the most "vertical" of Wharton's novels—meaning that it represents a broader range of classes than do most of her narratives—Robinson nonetheless judges the novel's social vision to be "grotesquely top-heavy." For Wharton, "society" means *high* society—much as culture still means *high* culture for many people today.

Indeed, the social distinction Wharton makes best is between the worlds of new and old money. Whereas speculation and consumption, and their attendant volatility, are the socially acceptable habits of (comparatively) recent successful social climbers, maintenance and preservation (read stability) are the watchwords of families that have inherited wealth. While their values tend to vary, one constant unites them—the "culture of capitalism" as a "rigidly gendered phenomenon" that leads to a clear, if unspoken, sexual double standard. In a "social milieu constructed as a marketplace," "female sexual probity" (virginity before marriage and fidelity afterward) is a woman's ultimate and altogether necessary capital. "It is no accident," Robinson illustratively asserts, "that the term 'damaged goods' to describe a girl who had lost her virginity, as well as one tainted with venereal disease, became current in the popular idiom and in mass culture at this period."

"Top-heavy" though *The House of Mirth* may be, the novel does recognize and represent the existence of impoverished classes. We catch glimpses, after all, of young women "slaving in millinery shops," garment factories, and typing pools. Wharton's novel represents the broader social spectrum mainly through scattered details, however, and on a level of discourse that may not be readily obvious to most readers, especially readers of our own day. Surfacing facts pertaining to weekly wages, annual incomes, estate values, losses at cards, and monthly rents—facts few readers in our day would notice or know what to make of—she discovers "instances of massive income inequality," thereby demonstrating that as Lily "descends the economic scale," the "amount she once spent on (fill in the luxury) would now supply many months of (some necessity), or would if she had it at all."

It may seem that Robinson features aspects of *The House of Mirth* that Wharton's text would just as soon we gloss over. And, in a sense, Robinson *is* seeking to reveal what *The House of Mirth* would leave politely obscure: like most cultural critics, Robinson views her role as a political, even oppositional one. Part of her project is to make us realize that the ideology in which Wharton grew up—through which she viewed the world—was one that did not reveal but, rather, downplayed the fact that the weekly pay of skilled women workers was less than the cost, per day, of fresh flowers for an upper-class family's dining room table.

With the benefit of a cultural critique like Robinson's, we can gain what Robinson at one point calls a "double vision" of *The House of Mirth* and the culture it represents. On the level at which it enforces capitalist ideology, the novel depicts the fall of a once-prized young woman, Lily Bart, "not only against the *background* of social inequality but because of and through" it. At a level difficult if not impossible to see until a critic like Robinson has unearthed and evaluated economic evidence not always so prominent in the text and placed it in the broader contexts of the economic history of the period and place, *The House of Mirth* affords us a vision, through Lily Bart's fall, of the grotesquely broad gulf between the lives of the rich and the poor.

Focusing on "the culture of capitalism," a term she uses to refer to the social relations that capitalism engenders, Robinson makes convenient use of Marxist models and terms—as do many if not most cultural critics. (She calls *The House of Mirth* a novel that "occupies" the "space" between "base" and "superstructure," thereby using two terms that Marx and Marxists have used to distinguish economic modes of production from resulting social institutions.) But, as her analysis of popular idioms ["damaged goods," "gentlemanliness"] suggests, she is ultimately more interested in the complex currents within "mass culture" than in oppression, alienation, or class conflict. For although she recognizes the difference between working-class women and Lily Bart—even after Lily has fallen into poverty — Robinson's interest is more in gender than in class. Like many feminist cultural critics who have preceded her, her emphasis is ultimately on the affinities between the material experiences of individual women in a culture that "traffics" in them.

Ross C Murfin

CULTURAL CRITICISM: A SELECTED BIBLIOGRAPHY

General Introductions to Cultural Criticism, Cultural Studies

Brantlinger, Patrick. *Crusoe's Footprints: Cultural Studies in Britain and America*. New York: Routledge, 1990.

Desan, Philippe, Priscilla Parkhurst Ferguson, and Wendy Griswold. "Editors' Introduction: Mirrors, Frames, and Demons: Reflections on the Sociology of Literature." *Literature and Social Practice*. Ed. Desan, Ferguson, and Griswold. Chicago: U of Chicago P, 1989. 1–10.

Eagleton, Terry. "Two Approaches in the Sociology of Literature." *Critical Inquiry* 14 (1988): 469–76.

Giroux, Henry, David Shumway, Paul Smith, and James Sosnoski. "The Need for Cultural Studies: Resisting Intellectuals and Oppositional Public Spheres." *Dalhousie Review* 64.2 (1984): 472–86.

Graff, Gerald, and Bruce Robbins. "Cultural Criticism." *Redrawing the Boundaries*. Ed. Stephen Greenblatt and Giles Gunn. New York: MLA, 1992.

Gunn, Giles. *The Culture of Criticism and the Criticism of Culture*. New York: Oxford, 1987.

Hall, Stuart. "Cultural Studies: Two Paradigms." *Media, Culture and Society* 2 (1980): 57–72.

Humm, Peter, Paul Stigant, and Peter Widdowson, eds. *Popular Fictions: Essays in Literature and History*. New York: Methuen, 1986.

Hunt, Lynn, ed. *The New Cultural History: Essays*. Berkeley: U of California P, 1989.

Johnson, Richard. "What Is Cultural Studies Anyway?" *Social Text: Theory/Culture/Ideology* 16 (1986–87): 38–80.

Pfister, Joel. "The Americanization of Cultural Studies." *Yale Journal of Criticism* 4 (1991): 199–229.

Punter, David, ed. *Introduction to Contemporary Critical Studies.*
New York: Longman, 1986. See especially Punter's "Introduc-
tion: Culture and Change" 1–18, Tony Dunn's "The Evolution
of Cultural Studies" 71–91, and the essay "Methods for Cultural
Studies Students" by Anne Beezer, Jean Grimshaw, and Martin
Barker 95–118.

Cultural Studies:
Some Early British Examples

Hoggart, Richard. *Speaking to Each Other.* 2 vols. London: Chatto,
1970.
———. *The Uses of Literacy: Changing Patterns in English Mass Cul-
ture.* Boston: Beacon, 1961.
Thompson, E. P. *The Making of the English Working Class.* New York:
Pantheon, 1977.
———. *William Morris: Romantic to Revolutionary.* New York: Pan-
theon, 1977.
Williams, Raymond. *Culture and Society, 1780–1950.* New York:
Harper, 1958.
———. *The Long Revolution.* New York: Columbia UP, 1961.

Cultural Studies:
Continental and Marxist Influences

Althusser, Louis, *For Marx.* Trans. Ben Brewster. New York: Pan-
theon, 1969.
Althusser, Louis, and Etienne Balibar. *Reading Capital.* Trans. Ben
Brewster. New York: Pantheon, 1971.
Bakhtin, Mikhail. *The Dialogic Imagination: Four Essays.* Ed. Michael
Holquist. Trans. Caryl Emerson. Austin: U of Texas P, 1981.
———. *Rabelais and His World.* Cambridge: MIT P, 1968.
Benjamin, Walter. *Illuminations.* Ed. with intro. by Hannah Arendt.
Trans. H. Zohn. New York: Harcourt, 1968.
Bennett, Tony. "Marxism and Popular Fiction." *Popular Fiction: Es-
says in Literature and History.* Ed. Humm, Stigant, and Widdow-
son. New York: Methuen, 1986.
Foucault, Michel. *Discipline and Punish: The Birth of the Prison.*
Trans. Alan Sheridan. New York: Pantheon, 1978.
———. *The History of Sexuality,* vol. 1. Trans. Robert Hurley. New
York: Pantheon, 1978.

Gramsci, Antonio. *Selections from the Prison Notebooks.* Ed. Quintin Hoare and Geoffrey Nowell Smith. New York: International UP, 1971.

Modern Cultural Studies: Selected British and American Examples

Colls, Robert, and Philip Dodd, eds. *Englishness: Politics and Culture, 1880–1920.* London: Croom Helm, 1986.

Modleski, Tania. *Loving with a Vengeance: Mass-Produced Fantasies for Women.* Hamden: Archon, 1982.

Poovey, Mary. *Uneven Developments: The Ideological Work of Gender in Mid-Victorian England.* Chicago: U of Chicago P, 1988.

Radway, Janice. *Reading the Romance: Women, Patriarchy, and Popular Literature.* Chapel Hill: U of North Carolina P, 1984.

Cultural Studies of *The House of Mirth*

Ammons, Elizabeth. *Edith Wharton's Argument with America.* Athens: U of Georgia P, 1980.

DuBow, Wendy M. "The Businesswoman in Edith Wharton." *Edith Wharton Review* 8.2 (Fall 1991): 11–18.

Kaplan, Amy. "Crowded Spaces in *The House of Mirth.*" *The Social Construction of American Realism.* Chicago: U of Chicago P, 1988.

Price, Alan. "Lily Bart and Carrie Meeber: Cultural Sisters." *American Literary Realism: 1870–1910,* 13 (1980): 238–45.

Tyson, Lois. "Beyond Morality: Lily Bart, Lawrence Selden, and the Aesthetic Commodity in *The House of Mirth.*" *Edith Wharton Review* 9.2 (Fall 1992): 3–10.

Westbrook, Wayne W. "Lily-Bartering on the New York Social Exchange in *The House of Mirth.*" *Ball State University Forum* 20 (1979): 59–64.

A CULTURAL PERSPECTIVE

LILLIAN S. ROBINSON

The Traffic in Women:
A Cultural Critique of
The House of Mirth

My working title for this essay was "A Hazard of New Fortunes." As I contemplated the project, the name I had given it neatly suggested the cut-throat phase of capitalist development, while implicitly comparing it to earlier stages in the getting and husbanding of great fortunes. The title functioned as a portmanteau in which the notions of gambling and danger, both central to *The House of Mirth* and both entailed in the word "hazard," could be contained. By recalling William Dean Howells's novel, the title "A Hazard of New Fortunes" would also recall his warning against the rising culture of speculative enterprise, a menace he discerned as already present in the very period that Edith Wharton was later to label The Age of Innocence.

I hope to claim all the benefits of the original title while replacing it with one that carries even more cultural baggage. As the first title evoked Howells's, my new one echoes Wharton's contemporary Emma Goldman and her radical treatise on the sexual economies of marriage, family, and prostitution. At the same time, it refers to Gayle Rubin's appropriation of Goldman's title for a ground-breaking mid-1970s contribution to feminist social theory in which Rubin posits the existence of a "sex-gender system" underlying and administering the oppression of women in our society.[1]

Most important, the title change signals a shift in focus from base to superstructure, from productive relations to the social relations they create. It is precisely this space that *The House of Mirth* occupies, translating the new fortunes of the marketplace into the particular traffic in women that is their cultural expression. This space is also the natural habitat of cultural studies, the ground for which the approach was designed. Economic histories undoubtedly offer better descriptions of the

---

[1]William Dean Howells, *A Hazard of New Fortunes,* 1890 (rpt. New York: Boni and Liveright, 1976); Emma Goldman, "The Traffic in Women," 1911 (rpt. in *The Traffic in Women and Other Essays,* ed. Alix Kates Shulman (New York: Times Change Press, 1970); Gayle Rubin, "The Traffic in Women: Notes on the 'Political Economy' of Sex," in Rayna Reiter, ed. *Toward an Anthropology of Women* (New York: Monthly Review Press, 1975).

triumph of finance capital in the early years of this century. But Wharton's novel is without peer when it comes to defining the *culture* of capitalism, especially insofar as that culture was a rigidly gendered phenomenon.

The House of Mirth comes closer than any of Wharton's other novels to providing a vertical section of her society. Most of her narratives concentrate on the upper reaches of wealth and social influence, although her two novels set in rural New England (*Summer* and *Ethan Frome*) are concerned with characters from a considerably lower order. Lily Bart's New York is itself internally stratified by class—as her own literal poor-relation status makes abundantly clear—as well as by "old" and "new" money groupings, with their attendant implications. The highest level of society, moreover, is also contiguous with and dependent upon the many other levels that constituted New York at the turn of the century and that also become part of Lily's experience.

Nonetheless, the mere mention of Emma Goldman, who was not only Edith Wharton's contemporary but also Lily Bart's, should serve as a cautionary reminder of how grotesquely top-heavy Wharton's social vision remained. *The House of Mirth* may show us more segments of society than Wharton is accustomed to representing, but the focus is still on the secondary meaning of the word "society," the one frequently designated by the modifier "high." In fact, Wharton inverts the pyramid alluded to by two other contemporaries of hers, Ward McAllister and William Sydney Porter. McAllister denominated New York's social elite "The Four Hundred," with reference to the capacity of Mrs. William Backhouse Astor's ballroom. Porter, focusing elsewhere in the social universe, in fact, on the population of Greater New York, called one volume of the stories he signed "O. Henry" *The Four Million*. From the amount of attention Wharton devotes to individuals from different social ranks, an unwary reader might almost receive the impression that most New Yorkers in Lily Bart's time were very wealthy and that the poverty to which Lily sinks was an uncommon condition, rather than one shared by most of the population. Wharton knows and reveals several strata of poverty below Lily's—all of them, moreover, specifically female versions of poverty. But she is best able to imagine tragedy as taking place right where Aristotle tells us it does, in the rarefied upper realms where people and their actions acquire "a certain magnitude" and where the fall is therefore a precipitous descent in expectations, as well as a decline in status and income.

Wharton does not recognize the masses of young women—whether slaving in millinery shops like the one where Lily failed or typing in offices like the beneficiaries of Gerty Farish's Girls' Club or even sweating out their youth in the downtown garment factories—as potential or actual tragic figures. Only Lily Bart, when she descends to their level, possesses tragic dimensions. Yet Lily's tragedy is informed by the existence of those masses, whose being Wharton acknowledges even as she constructs her narrative on the level of capital—monetary, social, and sexual—rather than on that of labor.

The House of Mirth can be read almost as a dissertation on the cultures of rich Americans at a certain moment in economic and social history. Wharton is an astute interpreter of social climbing and its variations, as reflected in the (different) nouveaux riches strata represented by Simon Rosedale, the Wellington Brys, the Sam Gormers, and Mrs. Norma Hatch. But her focus is on two segments of the highest social level: the "old" Old New York represented by Mrs. Peniston and her Van Alstyne connections, to which people like the Gryces, after their move from Albany, are readily assimilated, and the "new" Old New York, represented by the Trenors and their circle at Bellomont. One need only consider the Van Osburghs, society rivals of the Trenors (at least on the female side of the family) but marrying Gryces and Stepneys, to recognize the interconnections between these two segments of the upper crust.

But, while showing us these interconnections, Wharton insists on the differences, particularly in the characteristic organization of social and sexual life. The Penistons and their ilk are the descendants of Dutch and English merchants, whose fortunes have long been invested in New York real estate and the kinds of stocks and bonds that gave these holdings the generic name "securities." The work of a male in this class is to oversee the protection of an inheritance, as Percy Gryce learns to "shepherd" his upon coming into the family fortune. Although it may take place right on Wall Street, this work is as far removed from the rough and tumble of stock market speculation as it is from the ancestral enterprises. These representatives of the bourgeoisie derive their income from both mercantile capital and industrial-finance capital, but they are distinctly not "in trade."

The Trenor-Dorset axis of the very rich also includes "old money," although it need not be quite as old to qualify for membership in that group. It is this circle that the social climbers seek to penetrate (or, depending on their distance, at least dream of penetrating) and, however exclusive this circle prides itself on being, it is here that some of the newly rich may possibly obtain a foothold. The economic basis of this class is inherited wealth, but the males work at increasing their patrimonies through investment in that speculative market from which the fortune of a man like Simon Rosedale derives. Indeed, Rosedale's first successful social interactions come about through his willingness to introduce men like Gus Trenor to advantageous deals. Trenor feels pressured to make more money because his wife's way of life, her level of consumption, makes new demands on his purse. In return for Rosedale's assistance in making that money, he enables Rosedale to enter the more elevated stratum and join the cycle of consumption.

Whereas for the Van Alstynes and the Penistons consumption means luxurious food and clothing and occasional travel to a stodgy country house or a European spa, to the Trenors and Dorsets it means maintaining a palatial estate and an elegant town house, extravagant dress, jewels, yachts, and the social seasons of Paris, London, and the Cote d'Azur. Possessors of the "old" old money are concerned primarily with preservation — of their capital itself and the goods it has bought them — whereas speculation and consumption are the key words describing the economic habits of the "new" old money.

Because Wharton explicitly contrasts the social glitter of the fashionable world in which Lily moves with the more solid sumptuary comforts of the older wealth, it is tempting to see the prevailing sexual morality as a vestige, a peculiar survival from the earlier culture. It is certainly true that the double standard governing male and female behavior and an exaggerated emphasis on appearances typify the values of the earlier period. In the world of the Trenors and the Dorsets, however, although the same standards prevail, they take on new meanings, meanings entirely consistent with the new phase of social evolution, so that the code is finally no more incongruous in the new century than it was in the old.

A related mistake would be to identify the sexual code as crass or hypocritical only in the Trenor-Dorset frame of reference, not in that of Mrs. Peniston and the well-fed generations before her. In fact, the two sets of meanings are almost identically crude in their discrete materialisms. Female chastity before marriage, thereafter unvarying monogamy until death, do have a theological patina for Mrs. Peniston. But conventional Christian morality comes as a form of ideological hindsight to justify the sexual and family order that preceded the theology. The only religion that this lady is actually represented as practicing is the care and worship of her possessions. The seasonal scrubbing, with its attendant inventories of linens and blankets, takes the place in her life of any more spiritually significant ritual. In this context, a bride's virginity and a wife's fidelity are part of the household inventory, property that enables the orderly inheritance of other forms of property along the lines of legitimate patriarchal descent. The baby boy whom the former Evie Van Osburgh displays in her carriage is described not as her son or even the fruit of her union with Percy Gryce, but rather as the next heir to the Gryce fortune. Particularly when millions are at stake, it is vital that the means of transfer across generational lines be secured by a transcendant security as to the purity of blood descent. (A mother's identity, after all, is rarely problematical, so the sexual morality espoused by Mrs. Peniston and her ancestors serves to provide firm assurances for the act of faith entailed in accepting paternity and, with it, the transfer of the father's property.)

If female sexual probity was also property in the older value system, it shared the essential stability of other forms of property in that system. Never the object of speculation or wild shifts in the economy surrounding it, it was like the unassailable capital of funds so securely invested that living comfortably on the interest became an object of faith in itself. One scandal that is not presented to Mrs. Peniston's sensitive ears is that of touching one's capital, treating it, along with the interest, as money to be spent. Mrs. Peniston's attitude toward both household goods and cash makes it clear how shocking she would find such behavior. Indeed, among her segment of the rich, invading capital would be tantamount to rape.

Similarly, Lily's "gambling debts" and the rumors about her financial and personal involvement with a married man are not only equally shocking to her aunt but are offenses equivalent to the principle of untouched principal. Mrs. Peniston died, Grace Stepney tells Lily, deeply troubled (and, inferentially, *because* she was deeply troubled) by "rumours about your affairs" (220). The very idea of Lily's owing money had brought on Mrs. Peniston's illness, but surely there is a double-entendre at work in those "affairs," and not a very far-fetched one, because the two kinds of imprudence are identified in a mentality to which it "was horrible of a young girl to let herself be talked about; however unfounded the charges against her, she must be to blame for their having been made" (132–33).

Lily's cousin Jack Stepney, whose former impecunious state forced him to sponsor Simon Rosedale in an attempt to serve as a bridge between the new climber and the established society of Bellomont, becomes instead a bridge backward to Mrs. Peniston's world after his marriage to a Van Osburgh underwrites his moralizing. His comment on Lily's appearance in the tableaux vivants says much more than he is aware of: "Really, you know, I 'm no prude, but when it comes to a girl standing there as if she was up at auction . . . " (158). The problem, of course, is that in both the old and the new versions of ruling class society, Lily is indeed "up at auction"; it is an auction, however, where her beauty is only an adjunct to her sexual trustworthiness, since the purpose of the proposed sale would be defeated if the wares are displayed in what the customer perceives as an overly suggestive fashion. For it is not sexual pleasure but the continuity of family and fortune that is at stake in the proposed transaction.

Although Mrs. Peniston has a seemingly infinite capacity for being shocked, her vision of good conduct has nothing to do with genuine goodness. And Stepney's hypocrisy does not reside in the fact that, as a bachelor, he lived a more modern and raucous life himself. Rather, both of them — but she especially — expect the system to be better policed, the repression to be more effective than it has become. From the Peniston point of view, the immorality of the new order is expressed as carelessness — about religious forms, expenditure, and sexual behavior. Today, it is possible to imagine all sorts of breaches of the moral code that were once unimaginable — and the imaginability is sinful enough. Next to this, purity of heart, intentions, and even actions are entirely irrelevant.

The final evidence that the older version of the code is based on — indeed, is part and parcel of — material calculation is the fact that its strictures apply only to women. Although the narrative contains no exact male parallel to Lily's situation, it abounds in cases that illustrate various aspects of the double standard. Sons of the conservative families are shepherded into suitable marriages and protected from unsuitable ones. The danger feared from a boy's sowing his wild oats is not a sexual relationship with a rich married woman but, as with Ned Silverton, it is the extravagance into which such an affair leads him; not an affair with a provincial divorcée but the threat, as with Freddy Van Osburgh, that he might marry the creature. Young men in this world are considered highly suggestible, and whether or not they can also be suggested off the primose path (Freddy, indeed, was believed to have been "saved" by the joint efforts of those moral paragons Trenor and Rosedale), the blame for their straying invariably rests with the woman. And the only consequences that are commented on are monetary, rather than moral.

The Trenor-Dorset milieu both overlaps with and continues the Peniston-Van Alstyne milieu while paying lip service to its values. Judy Trenor ostentatiously provides transportation to church for her weekend guests, and this gesture constitutes, for her, the moral equivalent of actual church attendance. The Trenors condone divorce in certain cases, but they also entertain the Bishop annually, taking care that no divorced woman (or anyone else whose liveliness Judy cherishes throughout the rest of the year) is present. Moreover, the women at Bellomont understand that, in order to win the right to be bored for life by Percy Gryce, Lily must pretend to eschew their modern ways: no playing bridge for money, no cigarettes, and church services as if they were a regular part of her life. These women all aid and abet the subterfuge, because Percy Gryce is fabulously rich and his eligibility as a husband is thereby beyond question.

These examples suggest that Bellomont pays only lip service to the *sexual* morality of the earlier generation. In fact, however, the demand for virginity among unmarried women and fidelity for married ones, with severe penalties for the mere appearance of deviation and entirely different, much looser standards for men, are an integral part of the new society. The old motives of patrimony supporting patriarchy still survive, but they are supplemented by a new approach to female sexuality that corresponds to the new manifestations of capitalism. The keynote of the Peniston-Van Alstyne way of life was security, stability—both in its culture and in the marketplace that informs the culture. By contrast, the dominant tonality of the Trenor-Dorset circle is volatility: speculation in the marketplace, what Wharton was already calling "glitter" in its cultural style. ("Under the glitter of their opportunities," Wharton states damningly, Lily "saw the poverty of their achievement" [70]).

It is not economic continuity that matters in this world but the daring transaction, at least the *successful* daring transaction. The market in female beauty and social grace, in "charm," reflects this other market, while adding consumption—the conspicuous sort anatomized by American economist Thorstein Veblen at precisely Lily Bart's moment in history—to income production as a vital component of the cultural economy. Selden sees this parallel when he remarks lightly, as Lily is preparing to leave his flat: "Ah, well, there must be plenty of capital on the look-out for such an investment [as you]. Perhaps you'll meet your fate tonight at the Trenors'" (33). And Simon Rosedale, fantasizing about marriage to Lily as a means of establishing himself socially, imagines decking her with richer clothing and jewels than the other women have. Moreover, when he begins to suspect that Lily has not, in fact, "come across" sexually in return for monetary favors from other men, she looks like an even better bargain than he had originally imagined.

It is no accident that the term "damaged goods," used to describe a girl who had lost her virginity as well as one tainted with venereal disease, became current in the popular idiom and in mass culture at this period. Lily's sexual attractiveness is undeniably a material asset in her struggle to improve her social and financial position through marriage. But ironically it is also a liability as long as it is not yet backed up by money and status. Her beauty and her need to use it make her vulnerable to false assumptions about her behavior and lessen her credibility once a nasty story is in circulation. "That the maintenance of a moral attribute should be dependent on dollars and cents made the world appear a more sordid place than she had conceived it" (169). But Lily's goal is to maintain her moral attitude and buy back her self-esteem by repaying her debt to Gus Trenor. What does her in with the Bellomont set is Bertha Dorset's ability to use Lily's combination of attractiveness and vulnerability to lay an entirely undeserved moral burden on her. And, because the ethical marketplace in which they are operating is the same "sordid place," it is one where, as Lily herself explains, "it's a great deal easier to believe Bertha Dorset's story than mine, because she has a big house and an opera box, and it's convenient to be on good terms with her" (215). In short, the omniscient narrator concludes a bit later, "Bertha Dorset's social credit was based on an impregnable bank-account" (246).

Wharton wavers between extremes of precision and vagueness in her references to money. On the one hand, we learn that Percy Gryce's income is some $800,000 a year and that Mrs. Peniston's fortune is dismissed by Gwen Van Osburgh Stepney as amounting to "only" $400,000 altogether. Lily is considered to be disinherited when she receives $10,000 in her aunt's will, yet the amount, if she were not already so indebted to Trenor, would be enough capital to start a smart hat shop. Lily loses $300 at bridge her first night at Bellomont, and it would not surprise Mrs. Peniston if her niece owed $1,000 or more to her dressmaker. The actual $9,000 owed to Gus Trenor enabled Lily to live very well. On the other hand, the amounts of small incomes like that of Lily herself or Gerty Farish are never specified, nor are the wages of those who work for a living, whether they be professionals like Selden or typists and milliners like other young women who are mentioned in the pages of *The House of Mirth*.

Those who read the novel when it was first published could be expected to know that $800,000 a year represented fabulous wealth and that only a Van Osburgh—that is, someone both very rich and very stupid—would call that merely "comfortable" or disparage a $400,000 estate. At the high end of the monetary spectrum, readers nearly a century later are still able to appreciate Gryce's income and perceive Mrs.

Peniston's legacy to Grace Stepney as substantial. (If a single woman in 1992 inherited $400,000, her unearned income would be approximately equal to the salaries of many professional women, while still leaving her, of course, with the principal intact.)

It is at the low end of the monetary scale that inflation has put us at a disadvantage in interpreting the meaning of a dollar, and where Wharton gives us far less help. When Mr. Bart comes home to announce his "ruin," his wife and daughter are discussing the cost of fresh flowers for the daily luncheon table. It would be "only" twelve dollars a day, Lily observes. Her mother thinks this is too much to spend for an amenity that does not enhance the outward impression of their wealth, while her father explodes in impotent irony, suggesting that she go ahead and spend ten times as much, because the twelve dollars is as far beyond his capacity to pay as the higher amount would be. Wharton's contemporaries may have stopped at this point to consider that skilled women workers like those in the millinery shop were unlikely to earn as much as twelve dollars a *week* at the turn of the century. As an overage apprentice, Lily must have brought home considerably less than that. The amount Lily loses at cards in a single night—admittedly a great sum to her, if not to those who won it from her—might pay the rent on Nettie Struther's railroad flat for two years. The examples could be multiplied almost indefinitely, but the only one Wharton actually uses is the matter of Lily's first contribution to the Girls' Club, which is at once somewhat less than the cost of the dressing case whose purchase she has deferred, and enough to enable the club to keep going with its charitable work for a time.

It is not clear what Wharton expected the reader to make of all these instances of massive income inequality. In Lily's own history, they create a reiterated ironic motif as she descends the economic scale: the amount she once spent on (fill in the luxury) would now supply many months of (some necessity), or would if she had it at all. But Lily's fall takes place not only against a *background* of social inequality but because of and through a system of inequality. Seen from this perspective, her plight acquires meanings that Wharton seems to be at some pains *not* to endow it with. It is—and grotesquely—as if the vast gulf between a handful of rich people and the masses of poor ones serves chiefly to dramatize Lily Bart's condition, rather than the other way around.

The House of Mirth establishes a double vision of economic inequality and its characteristic language—whether the subject is social relations, friendship, the sexual order, or a melding of these—is the language of business transactions. In recent years, since Lily can no longer depend on her beauty alone to maintain her desirability as a house guest, she has been forced to abandon her refusal to play bridge for money. "It was," Wharton explains, "one of the *taxes* she had to pay for . . . prolonged hospitality" (45; emphasis added). The longer she remains on the matrimonial market and the more precarious her combined economic and moral situation, the higher the tax becomes. Thus, on the yachting trip, Lily's "job" is "to distract Dorset's attention from his wife. That was what she was 'there for': it was the *price* she had chosen to pay for three months of luxury and freedom from care" (217; emphasis added). This kind of calculation about social exchanges revives the dead metaphor at the core of Wharton's remark about Lily's fatal ignoring of Grace Stepney: "how could she foresee that such a friend was *worth* cultivating?" (128; emphasis added).

The material transactions of social life acquire a sexual dimension when Trenor tells Lily that Rosedale is "a chap it pays to be decent to" (103), especially in a context where, since her own financial dealings with Trenor, she has begun to consider her relation to his circle in terms increasingly reminiscent of the counting house:

> It was true that during the last three or four weeks she had absented herself from Bellomont on the pretext of having other visits to pay; but she now began to feel that the reckoning she had thus contrived to evade had rolled up *interest* in the interval. (103; emphasis added)

Lily realizes too late that she erred in not allowing Rosedale to drive her to the station after their unlucky encounter outside the Benedick. The drive would not only have allowed him a few possibly titillating minutes alone in a cab with her but, far more important at this stage of his social climbing, would allow him, once on the platform, to be taken for a guest en route to Bellomont. (This mistake would have had real value to him, even though it would necessarily have been confined to those who were also not part of the house party.) Lily's impetuous hailing of her own hansom frustrates a desire that is only secondarily sexual, a desire with whose satisfaction, Wharton tells us, she "might have *purchased* his silence" (36; emphasis added) about an indiscretion he believes to be sexual in nature.

It is a mistake she does not repeat during the drive where she agrees to let Trenor make investments for her. The immediate concession, we learn, allowing him to "rest his hand reassuringly on hers, *cost* her only a momentary shiver of reluctance" (96; emphasis added). But the deal with Trenor, at least as he understands it, requires payment in a weightier coin, and he is crudely straightforward in his demands. "Hang it, the man who pays for the dinner is generally allowed to have a seat at table" (148) and "you 've got to pay up" (148), he tells her.

Wharton also enjoys a conventional discourse of paying for one's faults with repentance and reform. Such discourse is almost always backed up, however, with the language about paying with one's reputation and, in Lily's case, paying for social favors with material and personal sacrifices while paying for monetary favors with sexual ones. This way of thinking is not confined to Lily's relationships and transactions within the Bellomont circle but is made possible by a social milieu constructed as a marketplace. Indeed, Wellington Bry, that epitome of the nouveau riche, calls an entire culture a "market" when he dismisses the French for judging a restaurant by its ability to cook a commonplace (and inexpensive) dish: " '*Peas?*' said Mr. Bry contemptuously. 'Can they cook terrapin? It just shows . . . what these European markets are, when a fellow can make a reputation cooking peas!' " (180). It is neither the produce market nor the stock market he is referring to, here, but Europe itself and its values. The remark paves the way for Carry Fisher's observation a bit further on about the difficulties she has encountered in obtaining the proper entree into London Society for him and his wife: "the London market is so glutted with new Americans that, to succeed there now, they must be either very clever or awfully queer" (183). Mrs. Fisher has refined her view of the special economy of social climbing to something approaching a theory. "Paying for what she does n't get rankles so with Louisa," she observes of Mrs. Bry. "I can't make her see that it 's one of the preliminary steps to getting what you have n't paid for" (191).

Much of the monetary discourse about society centers in Lily's own consciousness or in Wharton's descriptions of Lily's situation. It parallels and points up Lily's sense of her social value and the nature of her "labor" in the orbits of the possessors' great wealth. Very early in the novel, she explains to Selden that "a woman is asked out as much for her clothes as for herself" (33). When she tries to explain to Gerty why Ned Silverton has spent so much money, she elaborates an entire theory (for Lily will have a theory of dependency, as Gerty has one of climbing) of the cost of being a hanger-on like herself and Ned:

> You think we live *on* the rich, rather than with them: and so we
> do, in a sense — but it's a privilege we have to pay for! . . . The
> man pays it by big tips to the servants, by playing cards beyond his

means, by flowers and presents—and—and—lots of other things
that cost; the girl pays it by tips and cards too . . . and having just
the right dress for every occasion, and always keeping herself fresh
and exquisite and amusing! (251)

In this sense, Lily's attractiveness is not a means to an end but an end in
itself, a form of social currency that she is required to keep on spending
as the price of admission to a matrimonial market where she is no longer
a real contender. In the Trenors' circle, it seems, where all markets are
volatile, the ante keeps being raised, while following the tendency—in
the personal, cultural realm as in the economic one—of the rate of
profit to decline.

As Lily's situation and that of young Silverton suggest, much can be
learned about Wharton's vision of great wealth by observing those who
live on its margins. Through her mother's precept and example, Lily
learned young that "living like pigs" (the only recognized alternative to
Mrs. Bart's showy lifestyle) was a matter of choice, almost a matter of
morality, because it demonstrated "the lack of any proper standard of
conduct" (49). By contrast, to Mrs. Bart "and her acquaintances there
was something heroic in living as though one were much richer than
one's bank-book denoted" (48). Consequently, poverty "seemed to her
such a confession of failure that it amounted to disgrace" (52). The
gendered relation to income in that class's culture is almost caricatured
by the Barts' marriage: he earns the money, presumably by managing
investments; she consumes it in such a way as to exhaust his economic
potency while making it look as if she has more to spend than she has.
When he is "ruined" financially, there is nothing for him to do but take
to his bed and die. (Unlike a real speculator, who might go through any
number of wipeouts and recoveries in the course of an adventurous career on Wall Street.)

Given Mr. Bart's sole masculine role, his "ruin" has a parallel with
that of a young girl whose lost virginity was the only commodity she
had to offer in the sexual marketplace. The appearance-and-reality
games Mrs. Bart plays with her husband's resources, as well as her inability to proceed with them once the "ruin" has reduced the capital to
the point where great efforts could still not produce highly visible effects, might be compared to what happens to her daughter, who is effectively "ruined" by the manipulation of appearances, even though she
has in fact held onto her original "capital," her virginity.

Lawrence Selden is set up as a counterweight to the rest of Lily's
acquaintances. He is a man with the sensitivity to see through and

beyond the world of Bellomont and also through and beyond the facade that Lily herself maintains. Still, he not only benefits from the double standard that destroys Lily but he feels free, despite his own actual affair with a married woman, to judge Lily for the appearance of a relationship with a married man. Once his hypocrisy is recognized as precisely that, as a variation on the Bellomont theme rather than an exception to or deviation from it, it is possible to read Selden's relationship to income and expenditure as an ironic parallel to Lily's, rather than a contrast to it.

Like Lily, Selden received his early training in consumption patterns from his parents, who, like hers, were relatively poor for their class. Unlike the Barts, neither of the senior Seldens "cared for money," but as Wharton is quick to add, their disdain took the familiar form "of always spending a little more than was prudent" so that "restricted means were felt only as a check on aimless profusion" (154). Wharton actually places the word "values" in quotation marks as she points out that Selden's derived from his mother, as Lily's did from hers. But there seems to be no irony in Wharton's characterization of this attitude as "detachment from the sumptuary side of life: the stoic's carelessness of material things, combined with the Epicurean's pleasure in them" (154). Moreover, the paragraphs that describe Mrs. Selden's habits of consumption are sandwiched between descriptions of her husband's and her son's profound emotional ties to her. Her charm, we are told, continues to breathe out of her portrait, and her husband was the kind of man whose delight in such charm kept her "perennially charming." The son's preference for the old home ways of "going without money" intertwines with his loving remembrance of his mother; his association of true felicity, with her style of consumption, combined with an erotic relationship to a pretty woman. It is the Oedipus complex if it had been Veblen instead of his contemporary Freud who first defined it!

Selden's purportedly more ascetic and aesthetic world view ultimately boils down to the fact that he "enjoyed spectacular effects, and was not insensible to the part money plays in their production," so that "all he asked was that the very rich should live up to their calling as stage-managers, and not spend their money in a dull way" (136). At its highest level of refinement, these values lead to his irritation, on the Riviera, with the "stupid costliness of the food" (207), there apparently being a clever—perhaps even a brilliant—costliness (or, to be fair, an elegant frugality) that would be more pleasing to his sensibilities.

On one level, Lily's affinities are clearly with all those who live, as she does, on the margins of the world of the very rich. But when her situation is likened to that of a man on those same margins, whether the man be Jack Stepney, Ned Silverton, or Lawrence Selden, all the contrasts based on gender must immediately be invoked. Consider instead Lily's affinities with the other women, regardless of their class, whose income is inadequate to their needs. Here the similarities among women are material ones, while the differences reside in the cultural meanings attributed to the conjunction of female identity, social class, and poverty.

Thus, Carry Fisher serves Judy Trenor socially in much the same way that Lily does. But she is also openly employed by people like the Brys and the Gormers, who are trying to work their way into high society. As a double divorcée with a young child, she is tainted by the combination of having had sexual experience in the past and not having a man with a solid income in the present. Her dubious history has not "ruined" her for society, but it has removed her from the sexual arena where Lily's looks, charm, and virginity are still, at the beginning of the narrative, the counters in the game of matrimony and property. Indeed, it is only after Lily's reputation has become too soiled for those counters to retain any value that Carry proposes two solutions: marriage to Dorset or Rosedale — neither of them the sort of marriage that would have been at stake in Lily's original game — or taking a share in her own business of sponsoring social climbers. The results would hardly be the same, of course, but both options become available only after Lily's status as a virgin has been challenged.

Another, quite different, manifestation of poverty within Lily's own social rank is Gerty Farish. Her (again comparative) poverty and her lack of beauty have removed her from the matrimonial stakes. In consequence, she faces neither Lily's opportunities to rise in social status through an advantageous marriage nor her risk of losing everything by failing (in a circle where auction bridge is the occupation of and the metaphor for daily life) to play her cards right. Gerty's first appearance in a narrative where she has hitherto served only as an example employed by both Lily and Selden is described in a voice suggesting that Lily has temporarily taken over from her creator the tasks of exposition and the establishment of a point of view: "Miss Gertrude Farish . . . typified the mediocre and the ineffectual. . . . Of course, being fatally poor and dingy, it was wise of Gerty to have taken up philanthropy and symphony concerts" (99). Gerty accepts her fate and even enjoys it, but special attention from Selden awakens romantic longings in her also, at least until she voluntarily abandons her cousin to Lily. Because she has neither money nor obvious sexual attractions, Gerty cannot even afford the ticket of admission to the scene where money and sex are at play. And she's not supposed to want to get in.

It is worth noting, I think, that Carry Fisher and Gerty Farish, so different in every other respect that it is supposed to be amazing and incongruous when they briefly join forces in Lily's behalf, do have one important trait in common. They are the only characters in this populous novel who show any interest in changing society. Carry has gone through socialism and Christian Science and is now, at the beginning of the narrative, concerned with civic reform. Wharton certainly treats the volatility of her fads very lightly, but Carry is nonetheless the sole member of the Bellomont circle who notices that there is something missing, something that needs to be made right. Gerty, of course, has "gone in" for philanthropy and is sincerely committed to her efforts to help working women. These social concerns on the part of the novel's two other "poor" women of the ruling class is a reminder that all the characters are living at the dawn of what was to become the Progressive Era, a period marked by the continued excesses of finance capital and a series of essentially upper-class movements to correct the system's most flagrant abuses.

Gerty's charities represent Lily's first contact with girls who are genuinely, not just comparatively, poor. Her impulsive contribution to the Girls' Club is based on her recognition, one of a series running through the novel, that she and they have something very fundamental in common. These office workers, she realizes,

> were young girls, like herself; some perhaps pretty, some not without a trace of her finer sensibilities. She pictured herself leading such a life as theirs — a life in which achievement seemed as squalid as failure — and the vision made her shudder sympathetically. (119)

On her last day of life, Lily encounters one of the young working women who had been assisted by the Girls' Club. Nettie Crane Struther had been restored to health by a stay in a sanatorium that Lily paid for with what, as soon as she recalls Nettie's story, she also ironically realizes must have been Gus Trenor's money. Her sense of the irony of the situation is only enhanced as Nettie tells the rest of her story. It turns out that she was not only anaemic (and perhaps tubercular) when she fell ill, but "dreadfully unhappy too," as the result of desertion by the man she had expected to marry, who appears to have sacrificed her to his social ambitions. Nettie's "ruin" encompassed her physical and emotional well-being but not her "reputation," so that a cure meant the return of both physical health and the right to a sexual life. She is even able to marry a good man from her own background, one who already "knows about" her. "I never could have told another man," she explains, while leaving it unclear just what there was to tell, "and I' d never have married without telling; but if George cared for me enough to have me as I was, I did n't see why I should n't begin over again" (293). It might be argued that George the motorman evinces more genuine decency than Lawrence Selden or any of the men in the Bellomont circle. And that he is enabled to act on his gentlemanly instincts because, unlike the real gentlemen, he has no consideration of inheritance and status to cloud his understanding of Nettie as another man's victim, rather than as his rival's damaged property. Nettie thus has been provided with the means to "begin again," thanks to the generosity of George as well as that of Lily, whereas there is no one generous enough to offer a true "fresh start" to Lily herself.

Meeting Nettie at this point in her own downward slide awakens Lily's sense of solidarity, even before she learns the whole story:

> She had known Nettie Crane as one of the discouraged victims of over-work and anæmic parentage: one of the superfluous fragments of life destined to be swept prematurely onto that social refuse-heap of which Lily had so lately expressed her dread. (291)

One irony resides in Nettie's persistent refusal to recognize Lily as sharing any part of her own condition. Another is summed up in her pithy observation about the sexual pitfalls from which she believes girls of Lily's class to be protected. "Work girls," she explains, "are n't looked after the way you are" (293).

Although it has no effect on Nettie's worshipful consideration of Lily as a creature from another, more rarefied universe, the encounter does at least serve to restore Lily's sense of community. This feeling had been eroded during her months at the millinery shop, when, no longer able to look down on working girls from a more elevated social position, she had lost her "enlightened interest" in them. "Now that she was on a level with them, the point of view was less interesting," (268). Lily herself announces, "I have joined the working classes" (271), but this is true only in part. Materially she is one of them, but there remains a distance across which she and her sister workers look at each other through distorting lenses. The description of the millinery workers' faces — sallow, dull, and colorless — underlines the point that the first toll such labor takes is on the youth, energy, and health of the worker. The description ends with the comment that "In the whole work-room there was only one skin beneath which the blood still visibly played; and that now burned with vexation" (265), that of Lily Bart. Even the most sympathetic description of the working classes exists principally as a foil for the exposition of Lily's differentness, which comes down to a matter of different class expectations.

Wharton does not tell us—indeed, she probably does not know— anything about the sexual lives and dreams of the millinery workers. Much of their chatter may be about their own relationships, but, just as Lily tunes them out, hearing only their gossip and speculation about the shop's customers, her own former friends who are to wear the hats, Wharton implies by the absence of talk that is personal to the workers that all the romance in their lives is at second hand. Lily is fascinated and repulsed by the work-girls' approach to the circle she used to frequent, seeing it as a "fragmentary and distorted image" (268). She herself does not figure in their gossip or even excite their interest, because she is "a star fallen from that sky" (268). After this first astronomical image, Wharton repeats only that Lily had fallen, with no more reference to stars. So surely, like other fallen sisters, she is to be understood as having experienced a fall from the norms of sexual behavior. Ultimately, the difference between Lily and her work mates is that she once had a price placed on her sexual being and has subsequently been discarded from a marketplace where these women have never figured.

Lily's sense of the material bond that connects her to other women without economic resources is always represented in very striking language. On her first night at Bellomont, having lost heavily at bridge and made her first bleak calculations, she reflects on the high cost of moving in this milieu: "in her bitter moods it sometimes struck her that she and her maid were in the same position, except that the latter received her wages more regularly" (46). When she learns the truth about her financial arrangement with Trenor, the bitterness becomes despair as she compares her transactions to the more honest dealings of a prostitute: "I 've sunk lower than the lowest," she tells the uncomprehending Gerty, "for I 've taken what they take, and not paid as they pay" (166). Perhaps the most striking image, however, one that is vividly physical without being explicitly sexual, comes after Lily glimpses Miss Jane Silverton on Gerty's staircase:

> The walk up Fifth Avenue . . . this glimpse of the ever-revolving wheels of the great social machine made Lily more than ever conscious of the steepness and narrowness of Gerty's stairs, and of the cramped blind-alley of life to which they led. Dull stairs destined

to be mounted by dull people: how many thousands of insignificant figures were going up and down such stairs all over the world
at that very moment—figures as shabby and uninteresting as that
of the middle-aged lady in limp black who descended Gerty's
flight as Lily climbed to it! (248)

It is these moments of connection, however much contempt for others
and for herself they also reveal, that lead to self-knowledge. The question then becomes, for Wharton, whether such self-knowledge can lead
anywhere but to self-destruction.

The first scene of the novel is envisaged from Selden's point of view,
so Wharton introduces Lily as she appears through his eyes. He sees her
as an object, even a product, of great value, although the production
process he imagines is a peculiarly cosmic one:

He had a confused sense that she must have cost a great deal to
make, that a great many dull and ugly people must, in some
mysterious way, have been sacrificed to produce her. (27)

The notion is fanciful, but it is not really very pretty. It is the ideal extension of his bemused realization, a few moments earlier, that Lily and
the frumpy suburban women making their way through Grand Central
Station even belonged to the same race or species. "The dinginess, the
crudity of this average section of womankind made him feel how highly
specialized she was" (27). The trouble is that "specialized" products are
manufactured for a very particular and also very limited function and
that, if they are unable, for whatever reason, to fulfill that function, they
have no use at all. An expensive machine might be retooled, but Lily has
to find other, far less glamorous and remunerative work than that for
which she was "designed."

From this perspective, it is significant that only men from her former
life express consternation and horror at Lily's needing to work for a
living. "Out of work—out of work!" Rosedale fulminates. "The idea of
your having to work— it 's preposterous" (279). And even Selden suggests that, instead, she pool her (unearned) income with Gerty's. In this
way, "you and she could surely contrive a life together which would put
you beyond the need of having to support yourself" (263). For this, to
him, is the inconceivable, that Lily Bart should in fact be like other
women—in any event, like other poor women—that the "finer clay" of
which he imagines her to be made is actually the material of sexuality as
experienced in the higher social spheres. And that, once disabled from
using those materials, Lily's body becomes, like other bodies, the subject, rather than the object of the labor process.

I do not mean to suggest that Wharton was incapable of imagining an alternative for Lily in the world of unskilled woman workers: Lily Bart, Sweatshop Operative; Lily Bart, Shirtwaist Striker; or even Miss Bart of the Women's Trade Union League. Rather, I believe that the novel's references to the masses of women who worked because they had no other possibility in life gives resonance to Lily's fate. Hers is a tragedy that could occur only to a woman from the class into which she was born, a woman whose poverty, as judged by the standards of that class, turned her only asset into a fatal liability. In their last interview, a shaken Simon Rosedale offers Lily a loan, saying that theirs would be "a plain business arrangement, such as one man would make with another" (279). *The House of Mirth,* the novel that contains this offer, and Lily Bart's life, which the novel documents, are testimony that no such arrangement can exist, that in "good" society, the workings of capital invariably have a gender—and a sex.

Marxist Criticism
and
The House of Mirth

WHAT IS MARXIST CRITICISM?

To the question "What is Marxist Criticism?" it may be tempting to respond with another question: "What does it matter?" In light of the rapid and largely unanticipated demise of Soviet-style communism in the former U.S.S.R. and throughout Eastern Europe, it might easily be supposed that Marxist literary analysis would disappear too, quickly becoming an anachronism in a world enamored with full market capitalism.

In fact, however, there is no reason why Marxist criticism should weaken, let alone disappear. It is, after all, a distinct phenomenon from Soviet and Eastern European communism, having had its beginnings nearly eighty years before the Bolshevik revolution and having thrived, since the 1940s, mainly in the West: not as a form of communist propaganda but rather as a form of critique, a discourse for interrogating *all* societies and their texts in terms of certain specific issues. Those issues — including race, class, and the attitudes shared within a given culture — are as much with us as ever, not only in contemporary Russia but also in these United States.

The argument could even be made that Marxist criticism has been strengthened by the collapse of Soviet-style communism. There was a time, after all, when few self-respecting Anglo-American journals would use Marxist terms or models, however illuminating, to analyze Western issues or problems. It smacked of sleeping with the enemy. With the collapse of the Kremlin, however, old taboos began to give way. Even the staid *Wall Street Journal* now seems comfortable using phrases like "worker alienation" to discuss the problems plaguing the American business world.

The assumption that Marxist criticism will die on the vine of a moribund political system rests in part on another mistaken assumption, namely, that Marxist literary analysis is practiced only by people who would like to see society transformed into a Marxist-communist state, one created through land reform, the redistribution of wealth, a tightly and centrally managed economy, the abolition of institutionalized religion, etc. In fact, it has never been necessary to be a communist political revolutionary to be classified as a Marxist literary critic. (Many of the critics discussed in this introduction actually fled communist societies to live in the West.) Nor is it necessary to like only those literary works with a radical social vision or to dislike books that represent or even reinforce a middle-class, capitalist world-view. It is necessary, however, to adopt what most students of literature would consider a radical definition of the purpose and function of literary criticism.

More traditional forms of criticism, according to the Marxist critic Pierre Macherey, "set . . . out to deliver the text from its own silences by coaxing it into giving up its true, latent, or hidden meaning." Inevitably, however, non-Marxist criticism "intrude[s] its own discourse between the reader and the text" (qtd. in Bennett 107). Marxist critics, by contrast, do not attempt to discover hidden meanings in texts. Or, if they do, they do so only after seeing the text, first and foremost, as a material product to be understood in broadly historical terms. That is to say, a literary work is first viewed as a product *of* work (and hence of the realm of production and consumption we call economics). Second, it may be looked upon as a work that *does* identifiable work of its own. At one level, that work is usually to enforce and reinforce the prevailing ideology, that is, the network of conventions, values, and opinions to which the majority of people uncritically subscribe.

This does not mean that Marxist critics merely describe the obvious. Quite the contrary: the relationship that the Marxist critic Terry Eagleton outlines in *Criticism and Ideology* (1978) between the soaring cost of books in the nineteenth century, the growth of lending libraries, the practice of publishing "three-decker" novels (so that three borrowers could be reading the same book at the same time), and the changing *content* of those novels is highly complex in its own way. But the complexity Eagleton finds is not that of the deeply buried meaning of the text. Rather, it is that of the complex web of social and economic relationships that were prerequisite to the work's production. Marxist criticism does not seek to be, in Eagleton's words, "a passage from text to reader." Instead, "its task is to show the text as it cannot know itself, to manifest those conditions of its making (inscribed in its very letter) about which it is necessarily silent" (43).

As everyone knows, Marxism began with Karl Marx, the nineteenth-century German philosopher best known for writing *Das Kapital,* the seminal work of the communist movement. What everyone doesn't know is that Marx was also the first Marxist literary critic (much as Sigmund Freud, who psychoanalyzed E. T. A. Hoffmann's supernatural tale "The Sandman," was the first Freudian literary critic). During the 1830s Marx wrote critical essays on writers such as Goethe and Shakespeare (whose tragic vision of Elizabethan disintegration he praised).

The fact that Marxist literary criticism began with Marx himself is hardly surprising, given Marx's education and early interests. Trained in the classics at the University of Bonn, Marx wrote literary imitations, his own poetry, a failed novel, and a fragment of a tragic drama (*Oulanem*) before turning to contemplative and political philosophy. Even after he met Friedrich Engels in 1843 and began collaborating on works such as *The German Ideology* and *The Communist Manifesto,* Marx maintained a keen interest in literary writers and their works. He and Engels argued about the poetry of Heinrich Heine, admired Hermann Freiligrath (a poet critical of the German aristocracy), and faulted the playwright Ferdinand Lassalle for writing about a reactionary knight in the Peasants' War rather than about more progressive aspects of German history.

As these examples suggest, Marx and Engels would not—indeed, could not—think of aesthetic matters as being distinct and independent from such things as politics, economics, and history. Not surprisingly, they viewed the alienation of the worker in industrialized, capitalist societies as having grave consequences for the arts. How can people mechanically stamping out things that bear no mark of their producer's individuality (people thereby "reified," turned into things themselves) be expected to recognize, produce, or even consume things of beauty? And if there is no one to consume something, there will soon be no one to produce it, especially in an age in which production (even of something like literature) has come to mean *mass* (and therefore profitable) production.

In *The German Ideology* (1846), Marx and Engels expressed their sense of the relationship between the arts, politics, and basic economic reality in terms of a general social theory. Economics, they argued, provides the "base" or "infrastructure" of society, but from that base emerges a "superstructure" consisting of law, politics, philosophy, religion, and art.

Marx later admitted that the relationship between base and superstructure may be indirect and fluid: every change in economics may not be reflected by an immediate change in ethics or literature. In *The Eighteenth Brumaire of Louis Bonaparte* (1852), he came up with the word *homology* to describe the sometimes unbalanced, often delayed, and almost always loose correspondence between base and superstructure. And later in that same decade, while working on an introduction to his *Political Economy*, Marx further relaxed the base-superstructure relationship. Writing on the excellence of ancient Greek art (versus the primitive nature of ancient Greek economics), he conceded that a gap sometimes opens up between base and superstructure—between economic forms and those produced by the creative mind.

Nonetheless, *at* base the old formula was maintained. Economics remained basic and the connection between economics and superstructural elements of society was reaffirmed. Central to Marxism and Marxist literary criticism was and is the following "materialist" insight: consciousness, without which such things as art cannot be produced, is not the source of social forms and economic conditions. It is, rather, their most important product.

Marx and Engels, drawing upon the philosopher Friedrich Hegel's theories about the dialectical synthesis of ideas out of theses and antitheses, believed that a revolutionary class war (pitting middle-class capitalists against a proletarian, antithetical class) would lead eventually to the synthesis of a new social and economic order. Placing their faith not in the idealist Hegelian dialectic but, rather, in what they called "dialectical materialism," they looked for a secular and material salvation of humanity—one in, not beyond, history—via revolution and not via divine intervention. And they believed that the communist society eventually established would be one capable of producing new forms of consciousness and belief and therefore, ultimately, great art.

The revolution anticipated by Marx and Engels did not occur in their century, let alone lifetime. When it finally did take place, it didn't happen in places where Marx and Engels had thought it might be successful: the United States, Great Britain, and Germany. It happened, rather, in 1917 Russia, a country long ruled by despotic czars, but also enlightened by the works of powerful novelists and playwrights, including Chekhov, Pushkin, Tolstoy, and Dostoyevsky.

Perhaps because of its significant literary tradition, Russia produced revolutionaries like Nikolai Lenin, who shared not only Marx's interest in literature but also his belief in literature's ultimate importance. But it was not without some hesitation that Lenin endorsed the significance of texts written during the reign of the czars. Well before 1917 he had questioned what the relationship should be between a society undergoing a revolution and the great old literature of its bourgeois past.

Lenin attempted to answer that question in a series of essays on Tolstoy that he wrote between 1908 and 1911. Tolstoy—the author of *War and Peace* and *Anna Karenina*—was an important nineteenth-century Russian writer whose views hardly accorded with those of young Marxist revolutionaries. Continuing interest in a writer like Tolstoy may be justified, Lenin reasoned, given the primitive and unenlightened economic order of the society that produced him. Since superstructure usually lags behind base (and is therefore usually *more* primitive), the attitudes of a Tolstoy look relatively progressive when viewed in light of the unenlightened, capitalist society out of which they arose.

Moreover, Lenin also reasoned, the writings of the great Russian realists would *have* to suffice, at least in the short run. Lenin looked forward, in essays like "Party Organization and Party Literature," to the day in which new artistic forms would be produced by progressive writers with revolutionary political views and agendas. But he also knew that a great proletarian literature was unlikely to evolve until a thoroughly literate proletariat had been produced by the educational system.

Lenin was hardly the only revolutionary leader involved in setting up the new Soviet state who took a strong interest in literary matters. In 1924 Leon Trotsky published a book called *Literature and Revolution,* which is still acknowledged as a classic of Marxist literary criticism.

Trotsky worried about the direction in which Marxist aesthetic theory seemed to be going. He responded skeptically to groups like Proletkult, which opposed tolerance toward pre- and nonrevolutionary writers, and which called for the establishment of a new, proletarian culture. Trotsky warned of the danger of cultural sterility and risked unpopularity by pointing out that there is no necessary connection between the quality of a literary work and the quality of its author's politics.

In 1927 Trotsky lost a power struggle with Josef Stalin, a man who believed, among other things, that writers should be "engineers" of "human souls." After Trotsky's expulsion from the Soviet Union, views held by groups like Proletkult and the Left Front of Art (LEF), and by theorists such as Nikolai Bukharin and A. A. Zhdanov, became more prevalent. Speaking at the First Congress of the Union of Soviet Writers in 1934, the Soviet author Maxim Gorky called for writing that would "make labor the principal hero of our books." It was at the same writer's congress that "socialist realism," an art form glorifying workers and the revolutionary State, was made Communist party policy and the official literary form of the USSR.

Of those critics active in the USSR after the expulsion of Trotsky and the unfortunate triumph of Stalin, two critics stand out. One, Mikhail Bakhtin, was a Russian, later a Soviet, critic who spent much of his life in a kind of internal exile. Many of his essays were written in the 1930s and not published in the West or translated until the late 1960s. His work comes out of an engagement with the Marxist intellectual tradition as well as out of an indirect, even hidden, resistance to the Soviet government. It has been important to Marxist critics writing in the West because his theories provide a means to decode submerged social critique, especially in early modern texts. He viewed language — especially literary texts — in terms of discourses and dialogues *between* discourses. Within a novel written in a society in flux, for instance, the narrative may include an official, legitimate discourse, plus another infiltrated by challenging comments and even retorts. In a 1929 book on Dostoyevsky and a 1940 study *Rabelais and His World,* Bakhtin examined what he calls "polyphonic" novels, each characterized by a multiplicity of voices or discourses. In Dostoyevsky the independent status of a given character is marked by the difference of his or her language from that of the narrator. (The narrator's voice, too, can in fact be a dialogue.) In works by Rabelais, Bakhtin finds that the (profane) language of the carnival and of other popular festivals play against and parody the more official discourses, that is, of the magistrates of the Church. Bakhtin influenced modern cultural criticism by showing, in a sense, that the conflict between "high" and "low" culture takes place not only between classic and popular texts but also between the "dialogic" voices that exist within all great books.

The other sane and subtle Marxist critic who managed to survive Stalin's dictatorship and his repressive policies was Georg Lukács. A Hungarian who had begun his career as an "idealist" critic, Lukács had converted to Marxism in 1919; renounced his earlier, Hegelian work shortly thereafter; visited Moscow in 1930–1931; and finally emigrated to the USSR in 1933, just one year before the First Congress of the Union of Soviet Writers met. Lukács was far less narrow in his views than the most strident Stalinist Soviet critics of the 1930s and 1940s. He disliked much socialist realism and appreciated prerevolutionary, realistic novels that broadly reflected cultural "totalities"—and were populated with characters representing human "types" of the author's place and time. (Lukács was particularly fond of the historical canvases painted by the early-nineteenth-century novelist Sir Walter Scott.) But like his more rigid and censorious contemporaries, he drew the line at accepting nonrevolutionary, modernist works like James Joyce's *Ulysses*. He condemned movements like Expressionism and Symbolism, preferring works with "content" over more decadent, experimental works characterized mainly by "form."

With Lukács its most liberal and tolerant critic from the early 1930s until well into the 1960s, the Soviet literary scene degenerated to the point that the works of great writers like Franz Kafka were no longer read, either because they were viewed as decadent, formal experiments or because they "engineered souls" in "nonprogressive" directions. Officially sanctioned works were generally ones in which artistry lagged far behind the politics (no matter how bad the politics were).

Fortunately for the Marxist critical movement, politically radical critics *outside* the Soviet Union were free of its narrow, constricting policies and, consequently, able fruitfully to develop the thinking of Marx, Engels, and Trotsky. It was these non-Soviet Marxists who kept Marxist critical theory alive and useful in discussing all *kinds* of literature, written across the entire historical spectrum.

Perhaps because Lukács was the best of the Soviet communists writing Marxist criticism in the 1930s and 1940s, non-Soviet Marxists tended to develop their ideas by publicly opposing those of Lukács. German dramatist and critic Bertolt Brecht countered Lukács by arguing that art ought to be viewed as a field of production, not as a container of "content." Brecht also criticized Lukács for his attempt to enshrine realism at the expense not only of other "isms" but also of poetry and drama, both of which had been largely ignored by Lukács.

Even more outspoken was Brecht's critical champion Walter Benjamin, a German Marxist who, in the 1930s, attacked those conventional and traditional literary forms conveying a stultifying "aura" of culture. Benjamin praised Dadaism and, more important, new forms of art ushered in by the age of mechanical reproduction. Those forms—

including radio and film—offered hope, he felt, for liberation from capitalist culture, for they were too new to be part of its stultifyingly ritual-
istic traditions.

But of all the anti-Lukácsians outside the USSR who made a contribution to the development of Marxist literary criticism, the most important was probably Théodor Adorno. Leader since the early 1950s of the
Frankfurt school of Marxist criticism, Adorno attacked Lukács for his
dogmatic rejection of nonrealist modern literature and for his belief in
the primacy of content over form. Art does not equal science, Adorno
insisted. He went on to argue for art's autonomy from empirical forms
of knowledge, and to suggest that the interior monologues of modernist works (by Beckett and Proust) reflect the fact of modern alienation
in a way that Marxist criticism ought to find compelling.

In addition to turning against Lukács and his overly constrictive
canon, Marxists outside the Soviet Union were able to take advantage
of insights generated by non-Marxist critical theories being developed
in post-World War II Europe. One of the movements that came to be
of interest to non-Soviet Marxists was structuralism, a scientific approach to the study of humankind whose proponents believed that all
elements of culture, including literature, could be understood as parts
of a system of signs. Using modern linguistics as a model, structuralists
like Claude Lévi-Strauss broke the myths of various cultures down into
"mythemes" in an attempt to show that there are structural correspondences or homologies between the mythical elements produced by various human communities across time.

Of the European structuralist Marxists, one of the most influential
was Lucien Goldmann, a Rumanian critic living in Paris. Goldmann
combined structuralist principles with Marx's base-superstructure
model in order to show how economics determines the mental structures of social groups, which are reflected in literary texts. Goldmann
rejected the idea of individual human genius, choosing to see works,
instead, as the "collective" products of "trans-individual" mental structures. In early studies, such as *The Hidden God* (1955), he related seven-
teenth-century French texts (such as Racine's *Phèdre*) to the ideology of
Jansenism. In later works, he applied Marx's base-superstructure model
even more strictly, describing a relationship between economic conditions and texts unmediated by an intervening, collective consciousness.

In spite of his rigidity and perhaps because of his affinities with
structuralism, Goldmann came to be seen in the 1960s as the proponent
of a kind of watered-down, "humanist" Marxism. He was certainly
viewed that way by the French Marxist Louis Althusser, a disciple not of

Lévi-Strauss and structuralism but rather of the psychoanalytic theorist Jacques Lacan and of the Italian communist Antonio Gramsci, famous for his writings about ideology and "hegemony." (Gramsci used the latter word to refer to the pervasive, weblike system of assumptions and values that shapes the way things look, what they mean, and therefore what reality *is* for the majority of people within a culture.)

Like Gramsci, Althusser viewed literary works primarily in terms of their relationship to ideology, the function of which, he argued, is to (re)produce the existing relations of production in a given society. Dave Laing, in his book on *The Marxist Theory of Art* (1978), has attempted to explain this particular insight of Althusser's by saying that ideologies, through the "ensemble of habits, moralities, and opinions" that can be found in any literary text, "ensure that the work-force (and those responsible for re-producing them in the family, school, etc.) are maintained in their position of subordination to the dominant class" (91). This is not to say that Althusser thought of the masses as a brainless multitude following only the dictates of the prevailing ideology: Althusser followed Gramsci in suggesting that even working-class people have some freedom to struggle against ideology and change history. Nor is it to say that Althusser saw ideology as being a coherent, consistent force. In fact, he saw it as being riven with contradictions that works of literature sometimes expose and even widen. Thus Althusser followed Marx and Gramsci in believing that although literature must be seen in *relation* to ideology, it—like all social forms—has some degree of autonomy.

Althusser's followers included Pierre Macherey, who in *A Theory of Literary Production* (1966) developed Althusser's concept of the relationship between literature and ideology. A realistic novelist, he argued, attempts to produce a unified, coherent text, but instead ends up producing a work containing lapses, omissions, gaps. This happens because within ideology there are subjects that cannot be covered, things that cannot be said, contradictory views that aren't recognized as contradictory. (The critic's challenge, in this case, is to supply what the text cannot say, thereby making sense of gaps and contradictions.)

But there is another reason why gaps open up and contradictions become evident in texts. Works don't just reflect ideology (which Goldmann had referred to as "myth" and which Macherey refers to as a system of "illusory social beliefs"); they are also "fictions," works of art, *products* of ideology that have what Goldmann would call a "worldview" to offer. What kind of product, Macherey implicitly asks, is identical to the thing that produced it? It is hardly surprising, then, that

Balzac's fiction shows French peasants in two different lights, only one of which is critical and judgmental, only one of which is baldly ideological. Writing approvingly on Macherey and Macherey's mentor Althusser in *Marxism and Literary Criticism* (1976), Terry Eagleton says: "It is by giving ideology a determinate form, fixing it within certain fictional limits, that art is able to distance itself from [ideology], thus revealing . . . [its] limits" (19).

A follower of Althusser, Macherey is sometimes referred to as a "post-Althusserian Marxist." Eagleton, too, is often described that way, as is his American contemporary, Fredric Jameson. Jameson and Eagleton, as well as being post-Althusserians, are also among the few Anglo-American critics who have closely followed and significantly developed Marxist thought.

Before them, Marxist interpretation in English was limited to the work of a handful of critics: Christopher Caudwell, Christopher Hill, Arnold Kettle, E. P. Thompson, and Raymond Williams. Of these, Williams was perhaps least Marxist in orientation: he felt that Marxist critics, ironically, tended too much to isolate economics from culture; that they overlooked the individualism of people, opting instead to see them as "masses"; and that even more ironically, they had become an elitist group. But if the least Marxist of the British Marxists, Williams was also by far the most influential. Preferring to talk about "culture" instead of ideology, Williams argued in works such as *Culture and Society 1780–1950* (1958) that culture is "lived experience" and, as such, an interconnected set of social properties, each and all grounded in and influencing history.

Terry Eagleton's *Criticism and Ideology* (1978) is in many ways a response to the work of Williams. Responding to Williams's statement, in *Culture and Society,* that "there are in fact no masses; there are only ways of seeing people as masses" (289), Eagleton writes: "That men and women really are now unique individuals was Williams's (unexceptionable) insistence; but it was a proposition bought at the expense of perceiving the fact that they must mass and fight to achieve their full individual humanity. One has only to adapt Williams's statement to 'There are in fact no classes; there are only ways of seeing people as classes' to expose its theoretical paucity" (*Criticism* 29).

Eagleton goes on, in *Criticism and Ideology,* to propose an elaborate theory about how history—in the form of "general," "authorial," and "aesthetic" ideology—enters texts, which in turn may revivify, open up, or critique those same ideologies, thereby setting in motion a process that may alter history. He shows how texts by Jane Austen, Matthew Arnold, Charles Dickens, George Eliot, Joseph Conrad, and T. S. Eliot deal with and transmute conflicts at the heart of the general and authorial ideologies behind them: conflicts between morality and individualism, individualism and social organicism and utilitarianism.

As all this emphasis on ideology and conflict suggests, a modern British Marxist like Eagleton, even while acknowledging the work of a British Marxist predecessor like Williams, is more nearly developing the ideas of continental Marxists like Althusser and Macherey. That holds, as well, for modern American Marxists like Fredric Jameson. For although he makes occasional, sympathetic references to the works of Williams, Thompson, and Hill, Jameson makes far more *use* of Lukács, Adorno, and Althusser as well as non-Marxist structuralist, psychoanalytic, and poststructuralist critics.

In the first of several influential works, *Marxism and Form* (1971), Jameson takes up the question of form and content, arguing that the former is "but the working out" of the latter "in the realm of superstructure" (329). (In making such a statement Jameson opposes not only the tenets of Russian Formalists, for whom content had merely been the fleshing out of form, but also those of so-called vulgar Marxists, who tended to define form as mere ornamentation or windowdressing.) In his later work *The Political Unconscious* (1981), Jameson uses what in *Marxism and Form* he had called "dialectical criticism" to synthesize out of structuralism and poststructuralism, Freud and Lacan, Althusser and Adorno, a set of complex arguments that can only be summarized reductively.

The fractured state of societies and the isolated condition of individuals, he argued, may be seen as indications that there originally existed an unfallen state of something that may be called "primitive communism." History—which records the subsequent divisions and alienations—limits awareness of its own contradictions and of that lost, Better State, via ideologies and their manifestation in texts, whose strategies essentially contain and repress desire, especially revolutionary desire, into the collective unconscious. (In Conrad's *Lord Jim*, Jameson shows, the knowledge that governing classes don't *deserve* their power is contained and repressed by an ending that metaphysically blames Nature for the tragedy and that melodramatically blames wicked Gentleman Brown.)

As demonstrated by Jameson in analyses like the one mentioned

above, textual strategies of containment and concealment may be discovered by the critic, but only by the critic practicing dialectical
criticism, that is to say, a criticism aware, among other things, of its *own*
status as ideology. All thought, Jameson concludes, is ideological; only
through ideological thought that knows itself as such can ideologies be
seen through and eventually transcended.

In the essay that follows, Wai-chee Dimock begins by showing that
Edith Wharton's *The House of Mirth* is thoroughly permeated by the
language of exchange. The power of the marketplace, however, "resides
not in its presence, which is only marginal" in the novel, "but in its
ability to reproduce itself, in its ability to assimilate everything else into
its domain." Social intercourse becomes commodified and "even the
most private affairs take on the essence of business transactions, for the
realm of human relations is fully contained within an all-encompassing
business ethic." Thus, sexual favors can represent "payment in kind,"
and invitations to a society dinner party can be like "surrogate cash payments." Everything has a price, everything eventually has to be paid for
by someone, and everything can "count as money."

In the world as represented by Wharton, prices are arbitrary and
everything is subject to barter and negotiation at a level dependent
upon the parties' relative status. "Not everyone pays half a million dollars for a dinner invitation," Dimock points out. "Some pay nothing at
all." Power rests with those who can define the rates of exchange, set
the terms of the transaction, and determine what will satisfy the obligation to make "payments in kind." Since that privilege belongs to only
one partner in a given transaction, *all* exchanges are, at base, unfair. The
"fair play" of the marketplace is thus, Dimock argues, "in fact a fiction
masking a deeper reality of unfairness."

Only Lily Bart rebels in any significant way against this all-permeat-
ing economic system. In a world where use equals abuse and nonpayment is (almost everyone's) secret motto, private morality stands defenseless. That Lily actually plays by the rules makes her, in Dimock's
phrase, a "deviant." Her "rebellion by submission" — her compliance in
faithfully following the rules everyone else tries to subvert (rules everyone is actually *expected* to subvert) — challenges the basis of exchange.
In the final analysis, however, her status (even self-acknowledged) as
"human merchandise" and the ubiquity of the marketplace make her
feeble rebellion futile. In addition, as Dimock notes, "in refusing to do
business Lily is perhaps also refusing to live." That her protests end up
"contained, absorbed, and exploited" by the very system that they at-

tempt to condemn ultimately "attests to the frightening power of the marketplace."

Throughout her essay, Dimock describes the way in which *The House of Mirth* points out anomalies and contradictions in the capitalist ethic: the "doublethink" that allows people like Bertha to be rewarded for "nonpayment of debts"; the "spectatorship" of men like Selden who, having little or no economic capital to invest, would rather admire costly women from a distance than hazard spiritual capital; the fact that "payment in kind," the basis of barter economy, is a sham in the highly developed capitalist marketplace, particularly in its social realm. Wharton does, to be sure, occasionally allude wistfully to the ideal of the ancestral home (a "transcendent order" based on "blood" and "roots"). Ultimately, though, she does not see it as a viable option, leaving undeveloped a fleeting suggestion that it might somehow be transformed and realized by the working class, victims of the unjust economic system in place. Thus, although Wharton detests the system of exchange, she also seems to feel the weight of its inevitability.

To further summarize Dimock's argument would spoil its unfolding pleasures. Suffice it to say, here, that that argument is a fundamentally Marxist one because of the way in which it: (1) sees a work of fiction (superstructure) in terms of the economic system (base) in which it was produced; (2) sees *within* the world of the work a network of private affairs and social institutions that are themselves, at base, manifestations of the economic system; and (3) sees gaps and contradictions in (and thereby sees through) various myths endemic to capitalist ideology (such as the notion of "fair play").

Dimock, to be sure, shares some of the concerns and attitudes of those feminist and (feminist) cultural critics who focus on the (de)valuation of women in capitalist society. "Many critics have suggested" that "power" in *The House of Mirth* is "patriarchal," Dimock writes, but then she begins to distance herself from her feminist and feminist culturalist colleagues. "They are right, no doubt, about the basis for power, insofar as power is economic and insofar as money making is a male prerogative, but the actual wielders of power in the book are often not men but women." Wharton, Dimock even suggests, "is most interested . . . in the mediated and socialized forms of power . . . that women do enjoy and that they use skillfully and sometimes brutally."

Dimock's argument is thus more Marxist than feminist in that her focus is less on the historical oppression of women by men than it is on the oppression of the weak by the powerful. It seems that in her view, power is determined less by gender than by class. It also seems that, in her view, everything *including* class is determined in Wharton's early-twentieth-century American world by the business of capitalistic business.

Ross C Murfin

MARXIST CRITICISM:
A SELECTED BIBLIOGRAPHY

Marx, Engels, Lenin, and Trotsky

Engels, Friedrich. *The Condition of the Working Class in England*. Ed. and trans. W. O. Henderson and W. H. Chaloner. Stanford: Stanford UP, 1968.

Lenin, V. I. *On Literature and Art*. Moscow: Progress, 1967.

Marx, Karl. *Selected Writings*. Ed. David McLellan. Oxford: Oxford UP, 1977.

Trotsky, Leon. *Literature and Revolution*. New York: Russell, 1967.

General Introductions to and Reflections on Marxist Criticism

Bennett, Tony. *Formalism and Marxism*. London: Methuen, 1979.

Demetz, Peter. *Marx, Engels and the Poets*. Chicago: U of Chicago P, 1967.

———. *Literary Theory: An Introduction*. Minneapolis: U of Minnesota P, 1983. This entire survey is informed by Eagleton's Marxist perspective.

Eagleton, Terry. *Marxism and Literary Criticism*. Berkeley: U of California P, 1976.

Elster, Jon. *An Introduction to Karl Marx*. Cambridge, Eng. and New York: Cambridge UP, 1985.

———. *Nuts and Bolts for the Social Sciences*. Cambridge, New York: Cambridge UP, 1989.

Fokkema, D. W., and Elrud Kunne-Ibsch. *Theories of Literature in the Twentieth Century: Structuralism, Marxism, Aesthetics of Reception, Semiotics*. New York: St. Martin's, 1977. See ch. 4, "Marxist Theories of Literature."

Frow, John. *Marxism and Literary History*. Cambridge: Harvard UP, 1986.

Jefferson, Ann, and David Robey. *Modern Literary Theory: A Critical*

Introduction. Totowa: Barnes, 1982. See the essay "Marxist Literary Theories" by David Forgacs.

Laing, Dave. *The Marxist Theory of Art.* Brighton, Eng.: Harvester, 1978.

Selden, Raman. *A Reader's Guide to Contemporary Literary Theory.* Lexington: U of Kentucky P, 1985. See ch. 2, "Marxist Theories."

Slaughter, Cliff. *Marxism, Ideology and Literature.* Atlantic Highlands: Humanities, 1980.

Some Classic Marxist Studies and Statements

Adorno, Théodor. *Prisms.* Trans. Samuel and Shierry Weber. Cambridge: MIT P, 1982.

Althusser, Louis. *For Marx.* Trans. Ben Brewster. New York: Pantheon, 1969.

Althusser, Louis, and Etienne Balibar. *Reading Capital.* Trans. Ben Brewster. New York: Pantheon, 1971.

Auerbach, Erich. *Mimesis: The Representation of Reality in Western Literature.* Trans. Willard R. Trask. Princeton: Princeton UP, 1953.

Bakhtin, Mikhail. *Rabelais and His World.* Cambridge: MIT P, 1968.

Benjamin, Walter, *Illuminations.* Ed. with intro. by Hannah Arendt. Trans. H. Zohn. New York: Harcourt, 1968.

Caudwell, Christopher. *Illusion and Reality.* New York: Russell, 1955.

———. *Studies in a Dying Culture.* London: Lawrence, 1938.

Goldmann, Lucien. *The Hidden God.* New York: Humanities, 1964.

———. *Towards a Sociology of the Novel.* London: Tavistock, 1975.

Gramsci, Antonio. *Selections from the Prison Notebooks.* Ed. Quintin Hoare and Geoffrey Nowell Smith. New York: International UP, 1971.

Kettle, Arnold. *An Introduction to the English Novel.* New York: Harper, 1960.

Lukács, Georg. *The Historical Novel.* Trans. H. and S. Mitchell. Boston: Beacon, 1963.

———. *Studies in European Realism.* New York: Grosset, 1964.

———. *The Theory of the Novel.* Cambridge: MIT, 1971.

Marcuse, Herbert. *One-Dimensional Man.* Boston: Beacon, 1964.

Thompson, E. P. *The Making of the English Working Class.* New York: Pantheon, 1964.

———. *William Morris: Romantic to Revolutionary.* New York: Pantheon, 1977.

Williams, Raymond. *Culture and Society 1780–1950*. New York: Harper, 1958.

———. *The Long Revolution*. New York: Columbia UP, 1961.

———. *Marxism and Literature*. Oxford: Oxford UP, 1977.

Wilson, Edmund. *To the Finland Station*. Garden City: Doubleday, 1953.

Studies by and of Post-Althusserian Marxists

Dowling, William C. *Jameson, Althusser, Marx: An Introduction to "The Political Unconscious."* Ithaca: Cornell UP, 1984.

Eagleton, Terry. *Criticism and Ideology: A Study in Marxist Literary Theory*. London: Verso, 1978.

———. *Exiles and Émigrés*. New York: Schocken, 1970.

Jameson, Fredric. *Marxism and Form: Twentieth-Century Dialectical Theories of Literature*. Princeton: Princeton UP, 1971.

———. *The Political Unconscious: Narrative as a Socially Symbolic Act*. Ithaca: Cornell UP, 1981.

Macherey, Pierre. *A Theory of Literary Production*. Trans. G. Wall. London: Routledge, 1978.

Marxist Readings of *The House of Mirth*

Quoyesser, Catherine. "The Antimodernist Unconscious: Genre and Ideology in *The House of Mirth*." *Arizona Quarterly* 44 (Winter 1989): 55–79.

Trilling, Diana. "*The House of Mirth* Revisited." *Harper's Bazaar* 81 (1947): 167–77, 181–86. Rpt. *Edith Wharton: A Collection of Critical Essays. Twentieth Century Views*. Ed. Irving Howe. Englewood Cliffs: Prentice, 1962.

A MARXIST PERSPECTIVE

WAI-CHEE DIMOCK

Debasing Exchange:
Edith Wharton's *The House of Mirth*

" . . . you got reckless—thought you could turn me inside out, and chuck me in the gutter like an empty purse. But, by gad, that ain't playing fair: that 's dodging the rules of the game. Of course I know now what you wanted—it was n't my beautiful eyes you were after—but I tell you what, Miss Lily, you 've got to pay up for making me think so——". . . .
  "Pay up?" she faltered. "Do you mean that I owe you money?"
  He laughed again. "Oh, I 'm not asking you for payment in kind. But there 's such a thing as fair play—and interest on one's money—and hang me if I 've had as much as a look from you——"

–EDITH WHARTON *The House of Mirth*

The most brutal moment in *The House of Mirth* dramatizes not so much the centrality of sex as the centrality of exchange. Sexual favors are what Gus Trenor wants, but his demands are steeped in—and legitimated by—the language of the marketplace, the language of traded benefits and reciprocal obligations. Odious as it may seem, Trenor's speech merely asserts what everyone assumes. "Investments" and "returns," "interests" and "payments": these words animate and possess Wharton's characters, even in their world of conspicuous leisure (Trilling 122). The power of the marketplace, then, resides not in its presence, which is only marginal in *The House of Mirth,* but in its ability to reproduce itself, in its ability to assimilate everything else into its domain. As a controlling logic, a mode of human conduct and human association, the marketplace is everywhere and nowhere, ubiquitous and invisible. Under its shadow, even the most private affairs take on the essence of business transactions, for the realm of human relations is fully contained within an all-encompassing business ethic. Some characters—Trenor and Rosedale, for instance—obviously speak the voice of the marketplace, but even those who hold themselves aloof (as Lawrence Selden does) turn out to be more susceptible than they think.
  Of all the characters, Lily Bart has the most puzzling and contradictory relation to the marketplace. A self-acknowledged "human

merchandise," she is busy marketing herself throughout most of the book, worried only about the price she will fetch. She tries to induce Percy Gryce to purchase her, and if she had succeeded she would have been "to him what his Americana had hitherto been: the one possession in which he took sufficient pride to spend money on it" (65). Much later, as she forces herself to accept Rosedale's attentions, she consoles herself by calculating "the price *he* would have to pay" (240). Lily is clearly caught up in the ethos of exchange. And yet her repeated and sometimes intentional failure to find a buyer, her ultimate refusal to re-alize her "asset" (52)—as her mother designates her beauty—makes her something of a rebel. She is not much of a rebel, of course, and that is precisely the point. For Lily's "rebellion," in its very feebleness and limitation, attests to the frightening power of the marketplace. It attests as well to Wharton's own politics, to her bleakness of vision in the face of a totalizing system she finds at once detestable and inevitable.

The persistent talk of "cost" and "payment" in *The House of Mirth* raises the question of *currency*. How does one compute the "cost" of an action, what constitutes a "debt," and in what form must "payments" be made? Money, the standard medium of exchange, is not the only currency in circulation. Trenor clearly does not wish to be paid back with a check. In fact, "payment in kind" is never expected in transac-tions in the social marketplace, and this unspoken rule makes for a plethora of business opportunities. A "society" dinner, for instance, is worth its weight in gold. Since the likes of Rosedale habitually "giv[e] away a half-a-million tip for a dinner" (93), Jack Stepney regularly "pay[s] his debts in dinner invitations" (37). Others—even those who protest—eventually follow Stepney's example, for the simple reason that Rosedale is "placing Wall Street under obligations which only Fifth Avenue could repay" (228). There are other expenses, other debts, and other means of payment as well. Lily's visit to Selden's bachelor apart-ment is a "luxury" that is "going to cost her rather more than she could afford" (36). Still she might have "purchased [Rosedale's] silence" if she had only allowed him to take her to the train station, since "to be seen walking down the platform at the crowded afternoon hour in the company of Miss Lily Bart would have been money in his pocket" (36). Business, in the social world, operates by what we might call the com-modification of social intercourse.[1] Everything has a price and must be

---

[1] Most recent critics have related commodification to gender issues. See Montgomery 897; Ammons 33; and Wershoven 56. But women are hardly the only ones turned into commodities; indeed, the entire fabric of social intercourse is, in my view, commodified.

paid for, just as—on the opposite end—everything can be made to "count as" money, to be dealt out and accepted in lieu of cash. Dispensed in this manner, social gestures lose their initial character and figure only as exchange values: the dinner invitations, for Stepney and Rosedale, presumably have no meaning except as surrogate cash payments. A social world predicated on business ethics is an essentially reductive world, and the power of money lies not so much in its pristine form as in its claim as a model, in its ability to define other things in its own image. The fluidity of currencies in *The House of Mirth*, the apparently endless business possibilities, attests to the reduction of human experiences to abstract equivalents for exchange (Marx 35–93).

The principle of exchange, the idea that one has to "pay" for what one gets, lays claim to a kind of quid pro quo justice, and it is this justice, this "fair play," that Trenor demands from Lily. What he does not (or chooses not to) recognize is that what he calls "fair" is by no means self-evident and certainly not computable on an absolute scale. The problem stems, of course, from the rate of exchange, from the way prices are fixed. After all, why should a single dinner cost Rosedale a tip worth half a million (why not a quarter of a million, or a million)? And, for that matter, why should a ride in the park *not* be sufficient "payment" for the money Lily owes Trenor? In both instances, the "price" for the received benefit could easily have been otherwise, since the rate of exchange is altogether variable, altogether an artificial stipulation. In other words, two items might be yoked in one equation, pronounced of equal worth, but their "equality" will always remain imputed rather than inherent. Prices will remain arbitrary as long as the exchange rests on a negotiated parity between the exchange items—negotiated according to the bargaining powers of the contracting parties. Not everyone pays half a million dollars for a dinner invitation. Some pay nothing at all. The manipulatable rate of exchange makes it a treacherous model for "fair play." Lily "owes" Trenor the payment that he now demands only according to his rate of exchange—not hers—and his ability to set the rate and impose it on Lily says nothing about fairness, only something about power.

Power in *The House of Mirth*, many critics have suggested, is partriarchical (Fetterly; Wolff 109–33). They are right, no doubt, about the basis for power, insofar as power is economic and insofar as money making is a male prerogative, but the actual wielders of power in the book are often not men but women. On the whole, Wharton is interested less in the etiology of power than in the way power comports itself, in the mode and manner of its workings. She is most interested, that is to say, in the mediated and socialized forms of power, power that women do enjoy and that they use skillfully and sometimes brutally. Within the orbits of exchange, power resides in the ability to define the terms of exchange, to make one thing "equal" to another. That privilege belongs, obviously, to only one of the partners, and this intrinsic inequity gives the lie to Trenor's notion of fairness. A presumed model of justice and mutuality, exchange really grows out of an imbalance of power, which it in turn reconstitutes. Its "fair play" is in fact a fiction masking a deeper reality of unfairness, for the rate of exchange is no more than a tautological reflection of the inequity that is the condition as well as the result of its operations.

Nowhere is the injustice of exchange more clearly demonstrated than on board the *Sabrina*. Lily's presence on the yacht is, as everyone recognizes, simply a business arrangement. "We all know that's what Bertha brought her abroad for," Carry Fisher observes. "When Bertha wants to have a good time she has to provide occupation for George. . . . and of course Lily's present business is to keep him blind" (184). Afterward Lily seems to realize this fact equally well: "That was what she was 'there for': it was the price she had chosen to pay for three months of luxury and freedom from care" (217). But the "price" turns out to be steeper than Lily thinks, for she pays eventually with her good name and, indirectly, with her aunt's inheritance. The luxurious yacht cruise is a rotten deal for Lily, but it remains a "deal." And without deviating from the model of exchange, Bertha has managed to get her money's worth from Lily; she has simply managed to get away with a good bargain. Like Trenor, Bertha has come up with a rate of exchange to suit herself; unlike Trenor, she is eminently successful in exacting payments from Lily. Thanks to her adroit management, the reconciliation with her husband is "effected at [Lily's] expense" (230). Bertha has got everything she wants without any significant expenditure. This feat is all the more remarkable because—if the logic of exchange were to be faithfully followed—she ought to have paid a heavy price for her affair with Ned Silverton. But Bertha, in her "cold determination to escape [the] consequences" of her actions, has raised nonpayment to an art.

Bertha's success summarizes the contradiction that energizes and sustains the system of exchange. The art of nonpayment requires, after all, the most brazen sort of doublethink. The principle that enables Bertha to collect payments from Lily is the same principle that enables her to shrug off her own debts, and Bertha's ability to master that contradiction entitles her to her considerable rewards. For doublethink is the very essence of the exchange system, a system in which use and abuse are the same thing, in which legislations violate and violations legislate, in which, to play by the rules, one must break the rules. Doublethink explains why a system based on exchange should have nonpayment as its secret motto.

"The hatred of expenditure," Georges Bataille has written, "is the raison d'être of and the justification for the bourgeoisie" (73). Bertha Dorset's bold miserliness—her absolute refusal to "pay"—is therefore only the extreme and ruthless version of a prevailing stinginess, observable in duller and stodgier persons. A case in point is Mrs. Peniston, Lily's aunt. She is quite willing to give her niece room and board and occasional checks for clothes in return for "the reward to which disinterestedness is entitled" (54). But she is loath to give anything else. "When I offered you a home, I did n't undertake to pay your gambling debts," she informs Lily (172). Apparently she is not ready for other kinds of expenditure either. When Lily intimates that she has "had worries," Mrs. Peniston" shut[s] her lips with the snap of a purse closing against a beggar" (169). Obviously no spendthrift, emotional or otherwise, Mrs. Peniston manages her affections economically and keeps her obligations minimal. Both her generosity and her forbearance have limits, which Lily in time exceeds. Mrs. Peniston has not bargained for the troubles Lily gets into, and she "recognize[s] no obligation" to help (172). But she is quick to detect any breach of contract on Lily's side and to retaliate accordingly. Nothing can be more logical than her eventual decision to disinherit her niece. Since Lily has failed to meet her obligations, Mrs. Peniston sees no reason to meet *hers*. If there is something hard and mechanical in the aunt's moral accounting, it is no more than what is considered "just" (212) among those who stick to business principles. Mrs. Peniston is not alone in turning away from Lily. Her conditional affection parodies that of another character. In the same chapter in which Lily looks in vain to her aunt for help, she also waits in vain for Lawrence Selden to come to her (ch. 15).

Selden has other things in common with Lily's aunt aside from their shared abandonment of Lily. Like Mrs. Peniston, who chooses to be a "looker-on" in life (126), Selden relishes his "spectatorship" and "indolent amusement" (30). In the opening scene we find him amused in just this way: he is "divert[ed]" by Lily, "enjoy[ing]" her "as a spectator" (26) "with a purely impersonal enjoyment" (31). Unlike Mrs. Peniston, however, Selden does not always remain a spectator. He has had his share of action (an affair with Bertha Dorset, for instance), and even in his indolent enjoyment of Lily he is not without other intentions. For Selden also happens to be a connoisseur, an investor in aesthetic objects, a man equipped with the "lingering, appraising, inventorial mind of the experienced collector" (Wolff 12). Selden collects, Wharton explains, "as much as a man may who has no money to spend"; now and then he "pick[s] up something in the rubbish heap; and [he goes] and look[s] on at the big sales" (32). Selden remains a spectator when he cannot afford to buy, but he is not averse to pocketing little tidbits when they can be had for a small price. The investor picks up where the spectator leaves off, and in making the most of his resources, in getting the most from exchange, Selden shows more speculative instinct than he would like to admit.

"Speculation" is precisely what draws Selden to Lily. "[H]e could never see her without a faint movement of interest," we learn as soon as the novel opens; "it was characteristic of her that she always roused speculation" (25). Selden is "interest[ed]" in Lily—curious about what she will do—but he is "interested" also in another sense, as every investor would be in an eminently collectible item. To be sure, Selden is not half as crude as the others: while they notice Lily's "outline" (139), he admires the "modelling of her little ear, the crisp upward wave of her hair," "the thick planting of her straight black lashes" (27), and "her hand, polished as a bit of old ivory, with its slender pink nails" (29; Wolff 120–33; Wershoven 46). Lily would have been a valuable acquisition, and Selden knows it. "Ah, well, there must be plenty of capital on the look-out for such an investment" (33), he muses as they discuss her marriage prospects. Selden himself, apparently, has no such "capital" to "invest" and chooses simply to look on. His "admiring spectatorship" (82) costs him nothing, involves "no risks" (87), and allows him to enjoy the goods without the responsibility of paying for them.

Why does Selden not invest in Lily? On the face of it, he cannot afford to: he has "nothing to give" her (85). That is true as far as money goes, but money is not the only asset in Selden's portfolio, nor does he always count himself indigent. What holds him back, indeed, is not so much the thought of having "nothing to give" as the thought of what he might have to lose. And Selden stands to lose a great deal. His currency is not money, of course, but spiritual stocks, and in this currency he has been saving and hoarding for so long that he is afraid there might be "a chance of his having to pay up" (153). If he has so far kept his riches to himself, he has done so "not from any poverty of feeling" (153) but from a conscious sense of his accumulated wealth and from a determination to safeguard that wealth. Lily now presents him with an opportunity to "invest," and the question for Selden is whether she can be trusted with his emotional capital, whether he can "stake his faith" on her (305). The quandary he faces is not unlike that of his friends on the stock exchange, and the way he settles the question puts him in good company, which is to say, the company of the nonpayers, the company of Mrs. Peniston and Bertha Dorset.

Selden is loath to part with his assets in the hazardous business of exchange. This self-serving conservatism comes through most vividly in a seemingly jesting moment between him and Lily:

> "Do you want to marry me?" she asked.
> He broke into a laugh. "No, I don't want to—but perhaps I should if you did!" (85)

Never is romance so unpassionate, so bluntly contractual. "Perhaps I should if you did"—the niggardly proposition epitomizes Selden's love for Lily. He will not propose to her until he knows that she will accept him; indeed, he will not love her until he knows that she will love him in return, until he can be "as sure of her surrender as of his own" (155). Short of this assurance—and all through the book Selden is never completely sure—he will not part with his spiritual capital; he will not take "risks" with it. For Selden love is a form of exchange, and he will hear of nothing but profits.

The discipline of business determines which of the two roles, spectator or investor, Selden chooses to play (Agnew 65–100). The spectator turns into the investor at the point where returns are guaranteed. These, then, are the two faces of the speculator—for Selden is no less business-minded when he "looks on" than when he "picks up" a find— and their equal congeniality enables him to perform some heady emotional flip-flops. As a spectator Selden remains cynically amused by Lily; as an investor he seeks to acquire her hand. Disparate as these sentiments may seem, for Selden they are both "options," to be taken up or put aside at will, and he trades options with daunting facility. Meeting him for the first time after Bellomont, Lily is struck by his having "gone back without an effort to the footing on which they had stood before their last talk together" (104). But such adaptability is to be expected from someone who computes his love as if it were on a balance sheet, "proportion[ing]" his expenditure to anticipated returns. Selden's "speculation" is the sort that will brook no risks (and certainly no losses), and Lily is simply not a sound enough investment for him. The sight of her emerging late at night from the Trenor house shatters his slim confidence, and Selden is quick to pull out. When they meet again he has once more become a spectator. In Monte Carlo he can "give his admiration the freer play because so little personal feeling remained in it" (207), and he sticks to this convenient role all through Lily's subsequent troubles.

Still, the investor in Selden is not quite willing to give up. As the book closes he is ready to make another move, to trust once again to his "sense of adventure" (301). Of course, he arrives just a few hours too late for the adventure to take off, but even that unfortunate fact has no meaning for him except as a "loss" to himself. Faced with Lily's death, he will only "accuse himself for having failed to reach the height of his opportunity" (305). Selden does not seem aware of his responsibility— of his complicity—in her death. Like Mrs. Peniston, he "recognize[s] no obligation" toward Lily's welfare and accords himself no blame for her demise. Indeed, the worst thing that Selden can say about himself is that he has not been enterprising enough, that he has missed his "opportunity." And so he remains, to the end, a closet speculator. Selden's lament is one that Rosedale would have understood and might even have made himself. The "republic of the spirit" turns out to be less a republic than a refined replica of the social marketplace, of which Selden is a full participating member.

Selden is a "negative hero," then, as Wharton herself admits, not a high-minded dissident but very much "one of them" (82; Wolff 111). Like the others, he too exudes a cold stinginess, a desire for acquisition without risk and without expenditure. It is not Selden but Lily, the woman he tutors and scolds, who comes closest to breaking away from the rules and premises of the marketplace. Lily is also, of course, the only one who pays routinely and scrupulously, and often with currency she can little afford. "You think we live *on* the rich, rather than with them," Lily observes to Gerty: "and so we do, in a sense—but it's a privilege we have to pay for!" (251). She is right. It is no accident that the one who pays most regularly is also the one with the scantest means, for nonpayment, as we have seen, is a privilege of the powerful, those who fix the rate of exchange. Lily is therefore the obverse of, and the needed complement to, three characters: Bertha Dorset, who avoids paying by making others foot the bill; Mrs. Peniston, who scrimps on her obligations; and Lawrence Selden, who pulls out when the deal seems overly risky. "Paying" is Lily's habitual way of being, and she is at it almost as soon as the book opens. It is she, not Selden, who has to "pay so dearly for" her visit to his apartment (36). Lily goes on to pay for her stay at Bellomont by performing "social drudgery" for Mrs. Trenor (56) as well as by incurring gambling debts. She pays for her momentary truancy from Percy Gryce. She pays Trenor, though not to his satisfaction. She pays Bertha for the cruise on the *Sabrina,* just as she pays Norma Hatch for her brief stay at the Emporium Hotel. And she pays, finally, for those extravagant sentiments she permits herself to feel toward Selden.

Lily's dutiful payments are altogether in keeping with the principle of exchange. She is merely doing what the system requires of her, what she is supposed to. And yet—such is the irony of exchange—it is precisely this strict compliance that marks her as a deviant. Lily is working, after all, within a system in which nonpayment is the norm, in which violation is the only mode of conformity. She is penalized, then, not for breaking the rules but for observing them. This sort of absurdity is the logic of nightmare, but it is just this absurd logic that makes the exchange system work. In its disfiguring light, Lily's "rebellion" takes on the correspondingly absurd form of playing by the rules, of rebellion by submission.

Lily's paradoxical conformity and deviance come across most clearly in her dealings with Trenor. Having taken almost nine thousand dollars from him and finding her obligation "not the sort . . . one could remain under" (273), she proceeds to settle her debt as soon as she receives her aunt's legacy—a decision that "cleans [her] out altogether," as Rosedale rather indelicately puts it (274). In repaying Trenor, Lily is indeed complying with the rules of exchange, but she is also challenging the very basis of exchange. Trenor never expects to be paid back in quite this way. "Payment in kind," the most primitive form of barter economy, has no place in a highly developed social marketplace, which trades on the putative equivalence between disparate entities. By paying back the exact monetary amount, by equating nine thousand dollars with nine thousand dollars, Lily at once obeys the principle of exchange and reduces it to tautology. Her nine-thousand-dollar debt is now just that: a nine-thousand-dollar debt, not some ill-defined and possibly limitless obligation. In other words, by making money its own equivalent, Lily reduces it to its own terms and defies its purchasing power. She has understood what it means to live under the "intolerable obligation" of an all-consuming system of exchange, and she now tries to exorcise its influence by facing up to what she owes—in all the crudeness and brutality of its cash amount—just to rescue from its dominion the other strands of her life. What appears as a gesture of submission turns out to be a gesture of defiance, for by adhering literally to the terms of exchange Lily turns the system on its head. And yet, as every reader must recognize, defiance of this sort is ultimately unavailing. The exchange system can easily accommodate rebellion like Lily's: Trenor, no doubt, will take the money and even circulate it anew. Lily's action hurts no one but herself. It remains a challenge to the exchange system in spirit but not in fact.

When Lily returns the money, her rebellion by submission assumes its final and characteristically self-defeating form, the only form it is permitted to take within the exchange system. We see the beginning of that pattern in her earlier and grateful refusal of the "plain business arrangement" Rosedale offers her. What Rosedale proposes is this:

> "Well, I 'll lend you the money to pay Trenor; and I won't—I—see here, don't take me up till I 've finished. What I mean is, it 'll be a plain business arrangement, such as one man would make with another. Now, what have you got to say against that?"
>
> Lily's blush deepened to a glow in which humiliation and gratitude were mingled; and both sentiments revealed themselves in the unexpected gentleness of her reply.
>
> "Only this: that it is exactly what Gus Trenor proposed; and that I can never again be sure of understanding the plainest business arrangement." Then, realizing that this answer contained a germ of injustice, she added, even more kindly: "Not that I don't appreciate your kindness—that I 'm not grateful for it. But a business arrangement between us would in any case be impossible, because I shall have no security to give when my debt to Gus Trenor has been paid." (279–80)

This reply is surely an impressive statement from someone who, not so long ago, believed that "her modest investments were to be mysteriously multiplied" with Trenor's help (96). Lily has since found out what even "the simplest business arrangement" entails, and on this occasion she is careful to keep "business" to its strictest possible definition. She is in fact blunter, more matter-of-fact than Rosedale himself, but by being so implacably businesslike, Lily paradoxically obstructs, rather than facilitates, business opportunities. By insisting on money as the only legitimate currency, she limits the field of action as well as the available material for exchange. There is something heroic in her refusal to accept money when she knows she has no money to give in return, and yet such principles are surely suicidal, when the point of exchange is to get and not to give. What is honorable from a moral point of view is plain foolishness within the context of the marketplace (Davidson 10). Like her decision to return Trenor's money, Lily's rejection of Rosedale's loan leaves the exchange system intact and hurts only herself. Where the marketplace is everywhere, in refusing to do business Lily is perhaps also refusing to live—an implication Wharton takes up at the end.

Meanwhile Lily is left to commit two more business errors. The more serious one (from a practical point of view) concerns the disposition of Bertha's letters. These are valuable assets, and Rosedale, the consummate businessman, has no doubt about how Lily should use them. "The wonder to me is that you 've waited so long to get square with that woman, when you've had the power in your hands," he declares (243). After all, Bertha had saved her own skin "at Lily's expense," she "owes" Lily, and nothing would be more natural than an attempt to right the balance. Of course, there are different ways of "getting even" (244). Going to Bertha's husband with proof of her infidelity could be one way, but from a "purely business view of the question" Rosedale does not recommend this method, since "in a deal like that, nobody comes out with perfectly clean hands" (244). He has a much better "deal" in mind. Lily is to use the letters not to destroy Bertha but to cow her, to "get [her] into line" (245). Unlike the other deal, a risky business, this one is guaranteed to work:

> [Rosedale's plan] reduced the transaction to a private understand-
> ing, of which no third person need have the remotest hint. Put by
> Rosedale in terms of business-like give-and-take, this understand-
> ing took on the harmless air of a mutual accommodation, like a
> transfer of property or a revision of boundary lines. It certainly
> simplified life to view it as a perpetual adjustment, a play of party
> politics, in which every concession had its recognized equivalent;
> Lily's tired mind was fascinated by this escape from fluctuating
> ethical estimates into a region of concrete weights and measures.
> (244)

Properly managed, even revenge can become a form of exchange. And in the hands of Rosedale, exchange will be very good business indeed—completely without risk, with profits guaranteed. Lily's grievances are to be paid back with "recognized equivalent[s]"; they are to count as credits with which to exact payment (and indeed interest) from the offending party. The past wrongs are to be set right by a little "adjustment" between the two women in the form of a "private transaction," a "transfer of property," from which Lily is to be—for once—the receiving rather than the paying party.

Lily has not always been averse to righting her balance. Much earlier, when she was contemplating marriage to Percy Gryce, she had looked forward to the "old scores she could pay off as well as old benefits she could return" (65). Still, she cannot bring herself to use Bertha's letters. Even though Rosedale will not marry her unless she is "reconciled" with Bertha and "rehabilitated" in society, and even though marriage is her only remaining hope, Lily cannot carry out the "private transaction" he has so plainly laid out. To strike a deal with Bertha, Lily is required not only to "trade on [Selden's] name, and profit by a secret of his past" (283) but to "trade on" and "profit by" her past wrongs. Rosedale's method represents the ultimate commodification of experience, the reduction and quantification of moral outrage into "concrete weights and measures" for exchange. Lily cannot do it. This, too, is a business opportunity she must reject. If she refuses to pay her debts with surrogate money, she also refuses to "cash in" on her injuries. Since she will not make Bertha "pay back" what Bertha "owes" her, she must leave the imbalance between herself and Bertha unredressed. What Lily is rejecting is not so much the idea of revenge as the degradation of revenge in the arena of exchange.

As Lily leaves Selden's apartment, she quietly slides the packet of letters into the fire. Rosedale would have been horrified. Her last "asset" is now destroyed and with it any hope of rehabilitation. But Lily has not planned to burn the letters—she does so on the spur of the moment—and her sudden decision probably has something to do with another mistake she makes during the same visit, the mistake of indulging in "the passion of her soul" (288). Hardly anyone else in the book has been guilty of this mistake, and it becomes all the more startling against the background of Selden's tepid civilities. He offers her tea— "that amount of hospitality at my command," he tells her. Lily sees that "her presence [is] becoming an embarrassment to him," she notices his "light tone" and his all-too-evident "linger[ing] in the conventional outskirts of word-play and evasion" (285). But his demeanor no longer holds her back; for once she can accept the disparity between her sentiments and his. In Wharton's wonderful phrase, Lily has "passed beyond the phase of well-bred reciprocity, in which every demonstration must be scrupulously proportioned to the emotion it elicits" (286). In destroying Bertha's letters, she is offering Selden a great deal more than he has offered her or will ever offer her. But Lily no longer weighs and "proportion[s]" her feelings; she is no longer deterred by thoughts of "profits" and "returns." As she throws away her love in an act of wanton expenditure, she is making what is perhaps her most eloquent protest against the ethics of exchange.

And yet this protest, like her other ones, is ultimately futile, ultimately contained, absorbed, and exploited by the very system against which it is directed. The exchange system has room for money foolishly returned and loans foolishly refused, just as it has room for sentiments foolishly indulged in. Far from being a threat to the system, Lily's gesture of defiance merely recapitulates its assignation—merely reaffirms its sovereignty—for in giving Selden more than she gets from him, Lily is simply reverting to her customary role within the exchange system: her role as the one who "pays."

Even more ironically, Lily's extraordinary expenditure, like her previous ones, is not valued by those who benefit from it; it literally goes unnoticed. For a man who prides himself on his spectatorship, Selden is surprisingly blind to the moral drama unfolding before his very eyes. "When she rose he fancied that he saw her draw something from her dress and drop it into the fire; but he hardly noticed the gesture at the time" (289). The gesture will never be noticed; it is not meant to be. Lily's delicacy of feeling, her rectitude and generosity—all these are lost on Selden. They will always be unrecognized, unrewarded even by his gratitude. But that, too, is only to be expected. For the nobility of her action surely lies in its fruitlessness, in its utter lack of material consequence, in its erasure from history.

With her death Lily's moral triumph evaporates as if it had never taken place. In the last chapter of *The House of Mirth,* Wharton presents us with the spectacle of Selden rummaging through Lily's papers, fretting over the check made out to Trenor, feeling sorry for himself—and remaining, all the while, abysmally ignorant of what she has done for his sake. Wharton could not have written a stronger or more bitter commentary on the loneliness and futility of Lily's "rebellion." But even if her secret had somehow been revealed, it would have made no sense to her friends. They would have dismissed it as a species of folly. Private morality is finally defenseless against an exchange system that dissolves the language of morality into its own harsh, brassy parlance. Within this totalizing system moral rectitude simply counts as another exchange value, another commodity—and an insanely expensive one, as it turns out (Howe 18). For this ultimate luxury Lily pays with her life. Her few moments of moral triumph, translated into the idiom of the marketplace, merely figure as moments of ill-advised improvidence, altogether in keeping with her lifelong habit of spending "more than she could afford" (36). Morality, in *The House of Mirth,* provides no transcendent language, no alternative way of being, but feeds directly into the mechanisms of the marketplace. Lily's rebellion, which appeals to and presupposes a transcendent moral order, is doomed for that very reason.

"A frivolous society can acquire dramatic significance only through what its frivolity destroys. Its tragic implication lies in its power of debasing people and ideas," Wharton once said about *The House of Mirth* (*Glance* 207). Such debasement and destructiveness she conveys with devastating clarity. Her difficulty arises only when she is confronted with the need to imagine an alternative to the exchange system, a positive ideal to complement her ringing critique. To do so Wharton can only invoke an absent ideal—something that it has never been Lily's privilege to experience:

> And as [Lily] looked back she saw that there had never been a time when she had had any real relation to life. Her parents too had been rootless, blown hither and thither on every wind of fashion, without any personal existence to shelter them from its shifting gusts. She herself had grown up without any one spot of earth being dearer to her than another: there was no centre of early pieties, of grave endearing traditions, to which her heart could revert and from which it could draw strength for itself and tenderness for others. In whatever form a slowly-accumulated past lives in the blood—whether in the concrete image of the old house stored with visual memories, or in the conception of the house not built with hands, but made up of inherited passions and loyalties—it has the same power of broadening and deepening the individual existence, of attaching it by mysterious links of kinship to all the mighty sum of human striving. (296–97)

Wharton's image of the sanctified ancestral home, like the house of custom and ceremony Yeats prays for, is a quintessentially aristocratic ideal. As metaphor and as fact, the ancestral house stands aloof, in all its feudal strength, from the contemporary world of commodities, the world of "the wares / Peddled in the thoroughfares."[2] It is Wharton's fantasy of a transcendent order, for an organic life based on "blood" and "root[s]" is indeed antithetical to the mechanical exchange of capitalism. Wharton's critique of the marketplace is essentially an aristocratic critique, a critique from the standpoint of "early pieties," "grave endearing traditions," and "inherited passions and loyalties." And yet, even as she articulates her ideal, she sees that it does not exist, will not exist, and indeed has never existed, either in her own experience or in

---

[2]In "A Prayer for My Daughter" Yeats, like Wharton, images a house sanctified against the corruption of the marketplace:

> And may her bridegroom bring her to a house
> Where all's accustomed, ceremonious;
> For arrogance and hatred are the wares
> Peddled in the thoroughfares.
> How but in custom and in ceremony
> Are innocence and beauty born?
> Ceremony's a name for the rich horn,
> And custom for the spreading laurel tree.

Lily's. The ideal is declared impossible even as it is invoked. The ancestral home is no alternative to the commodified "house of mirth," irrevocably present and here to stay.

Still, Wharton is not quite willing to give up the idea of transcendence. She finally compromises, ingeniously if not altogether convincingly, by grafting her ideal on a lower social order, the working class. The fantasized ancestral house does appear in the book after all, if only in the modernized and modified form of a working-class tenement. And to the occupant of this humble habitation, Nettie Struther, Wharton entrusts her vision of a life antithetical to the one she condemns. It is in Nettie's kitchen that Lily catches her "first glimpse of the continuity of life." She sees in Nettie someone who seems "to have reached the central truth of existence" (297). It is not clear how Nettie accomplishes that feat (aside from her good fortune in having found a trusting husband); nor is it clear how her haphazard life as a wage laborer can withstand the ravages of the marketplace. As an ideal, Nettie remains curiously unsubstantiated, curiously unexamined: Wharton seems to have suspended her ironic incisiveness, her withering sense of all that entraps and compromises the human spirit. She does not look more closely at Nettie, one suspects, because she cannot afford to. Wharton is not completely persuaded by the virtues of the working class, nor is she altogether sympathetic to their causes. Even though she looks instinctively to the "poor little working-girl" (297) in her search for a redemptive figure, she sees Nettie less as the representative of the working class than as the embodiment of a private ideal—Wharton's ideal. Nettie, then, is to be *from* the working class but not too militantly, not too clamorously, *of* it. To be all that Wharton wants her to be, Nettie must be abstracted from the all-contaminating exchange system. She must be romanticized and, to some extent, insulated—transported, in short, from the social realm into another realm, what we might call the realm of nature, a realm Wharton metaphorically invokes. Nettie's makeshift tenement, Wharton would have us believe, has "the frail audacious permanence of a bird's nest built on the edge of a cliff" (297). As an organic force, a principle of tenacity and continuity, Nettie takes her place with the "permanence" of natural history, at once more primitive and (Wharton hopes) more enduring than the exchange system.

A "naturalized" working class represents Wharton's best hope for an organic life beyond the marketplace. It is the only romanticism she permits herself in the book, but even this ideal is not always easy to sustain. On a number of occasions—most particularly when Nettie expresses her innocent hope that her daughter ("Marry Anto'nette") will grow up to be just like Lily—we see the corrosive vision of the ironist subverting the "alternative" she has so painstakingly set up. The book is fueled, then, by an almost exclusively critical energy directed at the marketplace Wharton disdains. She can only confusedly gesture toward a redeeming alternative: for her, the house of mirth has no exit.

WORKS CITED

Agnew, Jean-Christophe. "The Consuming Vision of Henry James." *The Culture of Consumption: Critical Essays in American History, 1880–1980.* Ed. Richard Wightman Fox and T. J. Jackson Lears. New York: Pantheon, 1983. 65–100.

Ammons, Elizabeth. *Edith Wharton's Argument with America.* Athens: U of Georgia P, 1980.

Bataille, Georges. "The Notion of Expenditure." Trans. Allan Stoekl. *Raritan* 3 (1984): 62–79.

Davidson, Cathy N. "Kept Women in *The House of Mirth.*" *Markham Review* 9 (1979): 10–13.

Fetterley, Judith. " 'Temptation to be a beautiful object': Double Standard and Double Bind in *The House of Mirth.*" *Studies in American Fiction* 5 (1977): 199–211.

Howe, Irving, ed. "Introduction: The Achievement of Edith Wharton." *Edith Wharton: A Collection of Critical Essays.* Englewood Cliffs: Prentice, 1962. 1–18.

Lewis, R. W. B. *Edith Wharton: A Biography.* New York: Harper, 1975.

Marx, Karl. *Capital.* Trans. Samuel Moore and Edward Aveling. New York: International, 1967.

McDowell, Margaret. *Edith Wharton.* Boston: Twayne, 1976.

Michaels, Walter Benn. "Dreiser's *Financier.* The Man of Business as a Man of Letters." *American Realism: New Essays.* Ed. Eric J. Sundquist. Baltimore: Johns Hopkins UP, 1982. 278–95.

Montgomery, Judith H. "American Galatea." *College English* 32 (1971): 890–99.

Trilling, Diana. "*The House of Mirth* Revisited." *American Scholar* 32 (1962–63): 113–26.

Wershoven, Carol. *The Female Intruder in the Novels of Edith Wharton.* London: Associated UP, 1982.

Wharton, Edith. *A Backward Glance.* 1933. New York: Scribner's, 1964.

Wolff, Cynthia Griffin. *A Feast of Words.* New York: Oxford UP, 1977.

Feminist Criticism
and
The House of Mirth

WHAT IS FEMINIST CRITICISM?

Feminist criticism comes in many forms, and feminist critics have a variety of goals. Some are interested in rediscovering the works of women writers overlooked by a masculine-dominated culture. Others have revisited books by male authors and reviewed them from a woman's point of view to understand how they both reflect and shape the attitudes that have held women back.

Since the early 1970s three strains of feminist criticism have emerged, strains that can be categorized as French, American, and British. These categories should not be allowed to obscure either the global implications of the women's movement or the fact that interests and ideas have been shared by feminists from France, Great Britain, and the United States. British and American feminists have examined similar problems while writing about many of the same writers and works, and American feminists have recently become more receptive to French theories about femininity and writing. Historically speaking, however, French, American, and British feminists have examined similar problems from somewhat different perspectives.

French feminists have tended to focus their attention on language, analyzing the ways in which meaning is produced. They have concluded that language as we commonly think of it is a decidedly male realm. Drawing on the ideas of the psychoanalytic philosopher Jacques Lacan, French feminists remind us that language is a realm of public discourse. A child enters the linguistic realm just as it comes to grasp its separateness from its mother, just about the time that boys identify with their father, the family representative of culture. The language learned reflects a binary logic that opposes such terms as active/passive, masculine/feminine, sun/moon, father/mother, head/heart, son/daughter, intelligent/sensitive, brother/sister, form/matter, phallus/vagina, reason/emotion. Because this logic tends to group with masculinity such qualities as light, thought, and activity, French feminists have said that the structure of language is phallocentric: it privileges the phallus and, more generally, masculinity by associating them with things and values more appreciated by the (masculine-dominated) culture. Moreover, French feminists believe, "masculine desire dominates speech and posits woman as an idealized fantasy-fulfillment for the incurable emotional lack caused by separation from the mother" (Jones 83).

In the view of French feminists, language is associated with separation from the mother. Its distinctions represent the world from the male point of view, and it systematically forces women to choose: either they can imagine and represent themselves as men imagine and represent them (in which case they may speak, but will speak as men) or they can choose "silence," becoming in the process "the invisible and unheard sex" (Jones 83).

But some influential French feminists have argued that language only *seems* to give women such a narrow range of choices. There is another possibility, namely that women can develop a *feminine* language. In various ways, early French feminists such as Annie Leclerc, Xavière Gauthier, and Marguerite Duras have suggested that there is something that may be called *l'écriture féminine:* women's writing. Recently, Julia Kristeva has said that feminine language is "semiotic," not "symbolic." Rather than rigidly opposing and ranking elements of reality, rather than symbolizing one thing but not another in terms of a third, feminine language is rhythmic and unifying. If from the male perspective it seems fluid to the point of being chaotic, that is a fault of the male perspective.

According to Kristeva, feminine language is derived from the pre-oedipal period of fusion between mother and child. Associated with the maternal, feminine language is not only threatening to culture, which is patriarchal, but is also a medium through which women may be creative in new ways. But Kristeva has paired her central, liberating claim—that truly feminist innovation in all fields requires an understanding of the relation between maternity and feminine creation—with a warning. A feminist language that refuses to participate in "masculine" discourse, that places its future entirely in a feminine, semiotic discourse, risks being politically marginalized by men. That is to say, it risks being relegated to the outskirts (pun intended) of what is considered socially and politically significant.

Kristeva, who associates feminine writing with the female body, is joined in her views by other leading French feminists. Hélène Cixous, for instance, also posits an essential connection between the woman's body, whose sexual pleasure has been repressed and denied expression, and women's writing. "Write your self. Your body must be heard," Cixous urges; once they learn to write their bodies, women will not only realize their sexuality but enter history and move toward a future based on a "feminine" economy of giving rather than the "masculine" economy of hoarding (Cixous 250). For Luce Irigaray, women's sexual pleasure (*jouissance*) cannot be expressed by the dominant, ordered, "logical," masculine language. She explores the connection between women's sexuality and women's language through the following analogy: as women's *jouissance* is more multiple than men's unitary, phallic pleasure ("woman has sex organs just about everywhere"), so "feminine" language is more diffusive than its "masculine" counterpart. ("That is undoubtedly the reason . . . her language . . . goes off in all directions and . . . he is unable to discern the coherence," Irigaray writes [101–03].)

Cixous's and Irigaray's emphasis on feminine writing as an expression of the female body has drawn criticism from other French feminists. Many argue that an emphasis on the body either reduces "the feminine" to a biological essence or elevates it in a way that shifts the valuation of masculine and feminine but retains the binary categories. For Christine Fauré, Irigaray's celebration of women's difference fails to address the issue of masculine dominance, and a Marxist-feminist, Catherine Clément, has warned that "poetic" descriptions of what constitutes the feminine will not challenge that dominance in the realm of production. The boys will still make the toys, and decide who gets to use them. In her effort to redefine women as political rather than as sexual beings, Monique Wittig has called for the abolition of sexual categories that Cixous and Irigaray retain and revalue as they celebrate women's writing.

American feminist critics have shared with French critics both an interest in and a cautious distrust of the concept of feminine writing. Annette Kolodny, for instance, has worried that the "richness and variety of women's writing" will be missed if we see in it only its "feminine mode" or "style" ("Some Notes" 78). And yet Kolodny herself proceeds, in the same essay, to point out that women *have* had their own style, which includes reflexive constructions ("she found herself crying") and particular, recurring themes (clothing and self-fashioning are two that Kolodny mentions; other American feminists have focused on madness, disease, and the demonic).

Interested as they have become in the "French" subject of feminine style, American feminist critics began by analyzing literary texts rather than philosophizing abstractly about language. Many reviewed the great works by male writers, embarking on a revisionist rereading of literary tradition. These critics examined the portrayals of women characters, exposing the patriarchal ideology implicit in such works and showing how clearly this tradition of systematic masculine dominance is inscribed in our literary tradition. Kate Millett, Carolyn Heilbrun, and Judith Fetterley, among many others, created this model for American feminist criticism, a model that Elaine Showalter came to call "the feminist critique" of "male-constructed literary history" ("Poetics" 25).

Meanwhile another group of critics including Sandra Gilbert, Susan Gubar, Patricia Meyer Spacks, and Showalter herself created a somewhat different model. Whereas feminists writing "feminist critique" have analyzed works by men, practitioners of what Showalter used to refer to as "gynocriticism" have studied the writings of those women who, against all odds, produced what she calls "a literature of their own." In *The Female Imagination* (1975), Spacks examines the female literary tradition to find out how great women writers across the ages have felt, perceived themselves, and imagined reality. Gilbert and Gubar, in *The Madwoman in the Attic* (1979), concern themselves with well-known women writers of the nineteenth century, but they too find that general concerns, images, and themes recur, because the authors that they treat wrote "in a culture whose fundamental definitions of literary authority are both overtly and covertly patriarchal" (45).

If one of the purposes of gynocriticism is to (re)study well-known women authors, another is to rediscover women's history and culture, particularly women's communities that have nurtured female creativity. Still another related purpose is to discover neglected or forgotten women writers and thus to forge an alternative literary tradition, a

canon that better represents the female perspective by better representing the literary works that have been written by women. Showalter, in *A
Literature of Their Own* (1977), admirably began to fulfill this purpose,
providing a remarkably comprehensive overview of women's writing
through three of its phases. She defines these as the "Feminine, Feminist, and Female" phases, phases during which women first imitated a
masculine tradition (1840–80), then protested against its standards and
values (1880–1920), and finally advocated their own autonomous, female perspective (1920 to the present).

With the recovery of a body of women's texts, attention has returned to a question raised a decade ago by Lillian Robinson: Doesn't
American feminist criticism need to formulate a theory of its own practice? Won't reliance on theoretical assumptions, categories, and strategies developed by men and associated with nonfeminist schools of
thought prevent feminism from being accepted as equivalent to these
other critical discourses? Not all American feminists believe that a special or unifying theory of feminist practice is urgently needed;
Showalter's historical approach to women's culture allows a feminist
critic to use theories based on nonfeminist disciplines. Kolodny has advocated a "playful pluralism" that encompasses a variety of critical
schools and methods. But Jane Marcus and others have responded that
if feminists adopt too wide a range of approaches, they may relax the
tensions between feminists and the educational establishment necessary
for political activism.

The question of whether feminism weakens or fortifies itself by emphasizing its separateness—and by developing unity through separateness—is one of several areas of debate within American feminism. Another area of disagreement touched on earlier, between feminists who
stress universal feminine attributes (the feminine imagination, feminine
writing) and those who focus on the political conditions experienced by
certain groups of women at certain times in history, parallels a larger
distinction between American feminist critics and their British counter-
parts.

While it has been customary to refer to an Anglo-American tradition
of feminist criticism, British feminists tend to distinguish themselves
from what they see as an American overemphasis on texts linking
women across boundaries and decades and an underemphasis on popular art and culture. They regard their own critical practice as more political than that of American feminists, whom they have often faulted for

being uninterested in historical detail. They would join such American critics as Myra Jehlen to suggest that a continuing preoccupation with women writers might create the danger of placing women's texts outside the history that conditions them.

In the view of British feminists, the American opposition to male stereotypes that denigrate women has often led to counterstereotypes of feminine virtue that ignore real differences of race, class, and culture among women. In addition, they argue that American celebrations of individual heroines falsely suggest that powerful individuals may be immune to repressive conditions and may even imply that *any* individual can go through life unconditioned by the culture and ideology in which she or he lives.

Similarly, the American endeavor to recover women's history—for example, by emphasizing that women developed their own strategies to gain power within their sphere—is seen by British feminists like Judith Newton and Deborah Rosenfelt as an endeavor that "mystifies" male oppression, disguising it as something that has created for women a special world of opportunities. More important from the British standpoint, the universalizing and "essentializing" tendencies in both American practice and French theory disguise women's oppression by highlighting sexual difference, suggesting that a dominant system is impervious to political change. By contrast, British feminist theory emphasizes an engagement with historical process in order to promote social change.

In the essay that follows, Frances L. Restuccia begins by reminding us that feminism takes several forms. She then proceeds to categorize *The House of Mirth* as a feminist novel containing at least two forms of feminism. There is a "practical" critique of chauvinistic men and the frilly femininity that men have imposed on women, and there is another, "theoretical" feminism that refuses to categorize existing femininity as weakness or disadvantage—and refuses to credit men for its creation. Just as various feminist discourses can clash over how to read a given novel, so the two feminisms within *The House of Mirth* create a tension that provides fertile grounds for analysis.

Restuccia associates the feminism that has generally been characterized as "French" earlier in this introduction with the character of Lily Bart (although she also claims that Lily, like *The House of Mirth* and feminism in general, is double if not "multiplicitous" in nature). Lily's feminism anticipates that of Cixous, who links writing and that form of femininity characterized by an "open, extravagant subjectivity." Whar-

ton, according to Restuccia, "identifies Lily's multifariousness as feminine and inscribes such femininity in her writing."

Lily is misunderstood by characters like the legalistic Selden, for
whom "she was so evidently the victim of the civilization which had
produced her, that the links of her bracelet seemed like manacles chaining her to her fate" (29). And she is equally misunderstood by critics
(including "practical" feminists) who would see her in much the same
way, as one "transmogrified into a static art object" designed and built
in accordance with patriarchal definitions of femininity. Such observers,
uncomfortable with Lily's oscillation and ambiguity, try to clarify "what
persists in remaining opaque" by reducing Lily to a one-dimensional
character. But Lily, Restuccia argues, cannot be so easily reduced. For
one thing, she has an unusually sharp—and uncharacteristic—"awareness of the sexism of her society." Thus, "*if* Lily is victimized,"
Restuccia insists, "she is intelligent about it."

Restuccia's argument also associates Lily and her mode of femininity with literariness, textuality, and writing. As Restuccia explains,
"Beginning and ending with scenes of Lily in the library, the novel
encourages us to imagine her as possessing a literary consciousness or
sensibility. . . . Like a piece of fiction, she makes the boundary of the
natural and artificial unsurveyable." Writing, unlike speech, is indefinite,
freed from authority, open to interpretation. Restuccia thus compares
Lily to a literary text in that her "suppleness" and "indefiniteness" of
character make her difficult to summarize or interpret easily; in this way,
Lily "rebel[s] against reification." Gerty at one point challenges her to
sum herself up: "But what *is* your story, Lily? I don't believe any one
knows it yet. . . . I want you to tell me exactly what happened from the
beginning." Lily avoids answering the question by lightly mocking her
questioner. "'From the beginning?' Miss Bart gently mimicked her.
'Dear Gerty, how little imagination you good people have!'" Restuccia,
who comments on the scene by saying that "Lily resists Gerty's compulsion to totalize" what she instinctively recognizes as "irreducible," goes
on to draw a connection between that act of resistance and Wharton's
act of writing the novel. Wharton, she suggests, wrote fiction "in large
part . . . to counterpose gossip and the law, the female and male versions
of reductive storytelling . . . Unlike gossips and lawyers, Wharton refuses to produce penetrable story of a woman's experience" (216).

Lily's story cannot be made fully penetrable because it deals with
one who oscillates endlessly between a culturally constructed "flightiness" on the one hand and a nature that "frees" her from all the dead-
ening "fixities" that that same patriarchal culture would impose on the

other. Feminist criticism, Restuccia suggests, and feminism in general will have to somehow come to terms with and even value Lily's liberating femininity if it is not to make merely cosmetic alterations in the order of things, thereby extending the old, stultifying code to the point that it simply includes and coopts women.

Restuccia's essay takes up a number of fascinating matters, including law and gossip, fate and luck, "clarity" and "polyvalence," and the relationship of all these pairings to speech and writing, masculinity and femininity, and the two opposed feminist readings of Lily (as a kittenish product of oppression on the one hand and as one who playfully avoids oppression on the other). It would be reductive if not impossible to try to summarize the richness and complexity of those discussions in an introduction such as this. Suffice it to say that Restuccia's argument takes sides in that conflict between feminisms that she sees going on within and beyond the walls of *The House of Mirth,* although it acknowledges that poststructuralist and practical feminisms need each other, calling any attempt to make them "mutually exclusive" a "fatal error."

In the final analysis, Restuccia may be said to write from a poststructuralist, even deconstructive, French-style feminist perspective. Such a critique prefers to see in a character like Lily more playfulness than pathos and ultimately tends not to see the world of the text in terms of rigid oppositions (masculinity and femininity, fate and luck, law and gossip), but rather to see through and deconstruct such oppositions — as she believes *The House of Mirth* does and as she believes feminist criticism can and soon must do. For it is only in the avoidance of such strict dichotomies and definitions that feminism will emerge from and subvert, once and for all, the myriad patterns that have held women back.

Ross C Murfin

FEMINIST CRITICISM: A SELECTED BIBLIOGRAPHY

French Feminist Theories

Beauvoir, Simone de. *The Second Sex.* 1953. Trans. and ed. H. M. Parshley. New York: Bantam, 1961.

Cixous, Hélène. "The Laugh of the Medusa." Trans. Keith Cohen and Paula Cohen. *Signs* 1 (1976): 875–94.

Cixous, Hélène, and Catherine Clément. *The Newly Born Woman.* Trans. Betsy Wing. Minneapolis: U of Minnesota P, 1986.

French Feminist Theory. Special issue, *Signs* 7.1 (1981).

Irigaray, Luce. *This Sex Which Is Not One.* Trans. Catherine Porter. Ithaca: Cornell UP, 1985.

Jones, Ann Rosalind. "Writing the Body: Toward an Understanding of *L'Écriture féminine.*" Showalter, *New Feminist Criticism* 361–77.

Kristeva, Julia. *Desire in Language: A Semiotic Approach to Literature and Art.* Ed. Leon S. Roudiez. Trans. Thomas Gora, Alice Jardine, and Roudiez. New York: Columbia UP, 1980.

Marks, Elaine, and Isabelle de Courtivron, eds. *New French Feminisms: An Anthology,* Amherst: U of Massachusetts P, 1980.

Moi, Toril, ed. *French Feminist Thought: A Reader.* Oxford: Basil Blackwell, 1987.

British and American Feminist Theories

Belsey, Catherine, and Jane Moore, eds. *The Feminist Reader: Essays in Gender and the Politics of Literary Criticism.* New York: Basil Blackwell, 1989.

Benhabib, Seyla, and Drucilla Cornell, eds. *Feminism as Critique: On the Politics of Gender.* Minneapolis: U of Minnesota P, 1987.

Collins, Patricia Hill. *Black Feminist Thought: Knowledge, Consciousness, and the Politics of Empowerment.* Boston: Unwin Hyman, 1990.

de Lauretis, Teresa, ed. *Feminist Studies/Critical Studies.* Bloomington: Indiana UP, 1986.

Feminist Readings: French Texts/American Contexts. Special issue, *Yale French Studies* 62 (1982). Essays by Jardine and Spivak.

Fuss, Diana. *Essentially Speaking: Feminism, Nature, and Difference.* New York: Routledge, 1989.

Herndl, Diana Price, and Robyn Warhol, eds. *Feminisms: An Anthology of Literary Theory and Criticism.* New Brunswick, NJ: Rutgers UP, 1991.

hooks, bell, *Ain't I a Woman?: Black Women and Feminism.* Boston: South End, 1981.

Keohane, Nannerl O., Michelle Z. Rosaldo, and Barbara C. Gelpi, eds. *Feminist Theory: A Critique of Ideology.* Chicago: U of Chicago P, 1982.

Kolodny, Annette. "Dancing Through the Minefield: Some Observations on the Theory, Practice, and Politics of a Feminist Literary Criticism." Showalter, *New Feminist Criticism* 144–67.

The Lesbian Issue. Special issue, *Signs* 9 (Summer 1984).

Malson, Micheline, et al., eds. *Feminist Theory in Practice and Process.* Chicago: U of Chicago P, 1986.

Rich, Adrienne. *On Lies, Secrets, and Silence: Selected Prose, 1966–1979.* New York: Norton, 1979.

Showalter, Elaine. "Toward a Feminist Poetics." Showalter, *New Feminist Criticism* 125–43.

———, ed. *The New Feminist Criticism: Essays on Women, Literature, and Theory.* New York: Pantheon, 1985.

The Feminist Critique

Fetterley, Judith. *The Resisting Reader: A Feminist Approach to American Fiction.* Bloomington: Indiana UP, 1978.

Greer, Germaine. *The Female Eunuch.* New York: McGraw, 1971.

Millett, Kate. *Sexual Politics.* Garden City: Doubleday, 1970.

Robinson, Lillian S. *Sex, Class, and Culture.* 1978. New York: Methuen, 1986.

Wittig, Monique. *Les Guérillères.* 1969. Trans. David Le Vay. New York: Avon, 1973.

Woolf, Virginia. *A Room of One's Own.* New York: Harcourt, 1929.

Women's Writing and Creativity

Abel, Elizabeth, ed. *Writing and Sexual Difference.* Chicago: U of Chicago P, 1982.

Abel, Elizabeth, Marianne Hirsch, and Elizabeth Langland, eds. *The Voyage In: Fictions of Female Development.* Hanover: UP of New England, 1983.

Auerbach, Nina. *Communities of Women: An Idea in Fiction.* Cambridge: Harvard UP, 1978.

Christian, Barbara. *Black Feminist Criticism: Perspectives on Black Women Writers.* New York: Pergamon, 1985.

Gilbert, Sandra M., and Susan Gubar. *The Madwoman in the Attic: The Woman Writer and the Nineteenth-Century Literary Imagination.* New Haven: Yale UP, 1979.

Jacobus, Mary, ed. *Women Writing and Writing about Women.* New York: Barnes, 1979.

Miller, Nancy K., ed. *The Poetics of Gender,* New York: Columbia UP, 1986.

Newton, Judith Lowder. *Women, Power and Subversion: Social Strategies in British Fiction, 1778–1860.* Athens: U of Georgia P, 1981.

Poovey, Mary. *The Proper Lady and the Woman Writer: Ideology as Style in the Works of Mary Wollstonecraft, Mary Shelley, and Jane Austen.* Chicago: U of Chicago P, 1984.

Showalter, Elaine. *A Literature of Their Own: British Women Novelists from Brontë to Lessing.* Princeton: Princeton UP, 1977.

Marxist and Class Analysis

Barrett, Michèle. *Women's Oppression Today: Problems in Marxist Feminist Analysis.* London: Verso, 1980.

Delphy, Christine. *Close to Home: A Materialist Analysis of Women's Oppression.* Trans. and ed. Diana Leonard. Amherst: U of Massachusetts P, 1984.

Hartsock, Nancy C. M. *Money, Sex, and Power: Toward a Feminist Historical Materialism.* Boston: Northeastern UP, 1985.

Kaplan, Cora. *Sea Changes: Culture and Feminism.* London: Verso, 1986.

Mitchell, Juliet. *Woman's Estate.* New York: Pantheon, 1971.

Newton, Judith, and Deborah Rosenfelt, eds. *Feminist Criticism and Social Change: Sex, Class and Race in Literature and Culture.* New York: Methuen, 1985.

Sargent, Lydia, ed. *Women and Revolution: A Discussion of the Unhappy Marriage of Marxism and Feminism.* Montreal: Black Rose, 1981.

Women's History/Women's Studies

Bridenthal, Renate, and Claudia Koonz, eds. *Becoming Visible: Women in European History.* Boston: Houghton, 1977.

Farnham, Christie, ed. *The Impact of Feminist Research in the Academy.* Bloomington: Indiana UP, 1987.

Kelly, Joan. *Women, History and Theory.* Chicago: U of Chicago P, 1984.

McConnell-Ginet, Sally, et al., eds. *Women and Language in Literature and Society.* New York: Praeger, 1980.

Mitchell, Juliet, and Ann Oakley, eds. *The Rights and Wrongs of Women.* London: Penguin, 1976.

Newton, Judith L., et al., eds. *Sex and Class in Women's History.* London: Routledge, 1983.

Riley, Denise. *"Am I That Name?": Feminism and the Category of "Women" in History.* Minneapolis: U of Minnesota P, 1988.

Rowbotham, Sheila. *Women's Consciousness, Man's World.* Harmondsworth: Penguin, 1973.

Schipper, Mineke, ed. *Unheard Words: Women and Literature in Africa, the Arab World, Asia, the Caribbean, and Latin America.* London: Allison, 1985.

Scott, Joan Wallach. *Gender and the Politics of History.* New York: Columbia UP, 1988.

Smith-Rosenberg, Carroll. *Disorderly Conduct: Visions of Gender in Victorian America.* New York: Knopf, 1985.

Feminism and Other Critical Approaches

Armstrong, Nancy, ed. *Literature as Women's History I.* A special issue of *Genre* 19–20 (1986–87).

Benstock, Shari. *Textualizing the Feminine: On the Limits of Genre.* Norman: U of Oklahoma P, 1991.

Diamond, Irene, and Lee Quinby, eds. *Feminism and Foucault: Reflections on Resistance.* Boston: Northeastern UP, 1988.

Elliot, Patricia. *From Mastery to Analysis: Theories of Gender in Psychoanalytic Criticism.* Ithaca: Cornell UP, 1990.

Feminist Studies 14 (1988). Special issue on feminism and deconstruction.

Gallop, Jane. *The Daughter's Seduction: Feminism and Psychoanalysis.* Ithaca: Cornell UP, 1982.

Keller, Evelyn Fox. *Reflections on Gender and Science.* New Haven: Yale UP, 1985.

Meese, Elizabeth, and Alice Parker, eds. *The Difference Within: Feminism and Critical Theory.* Amsterdam/Philadelphia: John Benjamins, 1989.

Penley, Constance, ed. *Feminism and Film Theory.* New York: Routledge, 1988.

Feminist Approaches to *The House of Mirth*

Benstock, Shari. "'The Word Which Made All Clear': The Silent Close of *The House of Mirth.*" *Famous Last Words: Women Against Novelistic Endings.* Ed. Alison Booth. Charlottesville: UP of Virginia, 1993.

Brazin, Nancy Topping. "The Destruction of Lily Bart: Capitalism, Christianity, and Male Chauvinism." *Denver Quarterly* 17.4 (Winter 1983): 97–108.

Fetterly, Judith. "The Temptation to Be a Beautiful Object: Double Standard and Double Bind in *The House of Mirth.*" *Studies in American Fiction* 5 (1977): 199–211. Rpt. in *Fiction by American Women: Recent Views.* Ed. Winifred Farrant Bevilacqua. Port Washington: Associate Faculty P, 1983.

Gilbert, Sandra M., and Susan Gubar. *No Man's Land: The Place of the Woman Writer in the Twentieth Century.* Vol. 2, *Sexchanges.* New Haven: Yale UP, 1989.

Joslin, Katherine. *Women Writers: Edith Wharton.* London: Macmillan, 1991.

Lidoff, Joan. "Another Sleeping Beauty: Narcissism in *The House of Mirth.*" *American Quarterly* 32 (1980): 519–32. Rpt. *American Realism: New Essays.* Ed. Eric J. Sundquist. Baltimore: Johns Hopkins UP, 1982.

Olin-Ammenthorp, Julie. "Edith Wharton's Challenge to Feminist Criticism." *Studies in American Fiction* 16. 2 (Autumn 1988): 237–44.

Showalter, Elaine. "The Death of the Lady (Novelist): Wharton's *House of Mirth.*" *Representations* 9 (Winter 1985): 133–139. Rpt. in *Edith Wharton.* Ed. Harold Bloom. New York: Chelsea, 1986; *Edith Wharton: New Critical Essays.* Ed. Alfred Bendixon and Annette Zilversmit. New York: Garland, 1992; *The House of Mirth.* Ed. Elizabeth Ammons. New York: Norton, 1990: 357–72.

Wershoven, Carol. *The Female Intruder in the Novels of Edith Wharton.* London: Associated UP, 1982.

A FEMINIST PERSPECTIVE

FRANCES L. RESTUCCIA

The Name of the Lily:
Edith Wharton's Feminism(s)

"Lily . . . returned from her expedition with a sense of the powerlessness of beauty and charm against the unfeeling processes of
the law."

> –EDITH WHARTON *The House of Mirth*

"Writing, space of dispersion of desire, where Law is dismissed."

> –ROLAND BARTHES *Image Music Text*

"This is to call for, then, a decentered vision (*theoria*) but a centered action that will not result in a renewed invisibility."

> –NANCY K. MILLER "The Text's Heroine:
> A Feminist Critic and Her Fictions"

Edith Wharton's *The House of Mirth* is a feminist novel comprising—
perhaps by definition, since feminism often envisions itself as multiple—
at least two feminisms. The story may be read as a social fable that indicts fashionable, fin-de-siècle New York society for producing human
feminine ornaments that it has no qualms about crushing. "In the first
Donnée Book," Cynthia Griffin Wolff informs us, "*The House of Mirth*
went by the title 'A Moment's Ornament' "; and Wolff herself pinpoints
a "pernicious form of femininity" — "femininity as the art of 'being' " —
"as the subject of . . . *the House of Mirth*" (109). Wharton's novel conveys the practical feminist message that women bred to be frilly decora-
tions run risks of various sorts of death. But even as Wharton proffers
this warning, she floats the view that a firm position is unattractively
masterful, not female (or feminine), and that the suppleness of indecision is preferable to the phallogocentrism demonstrated in *The House of
Mirth* by one male suitor after another who attempts to capture, clarify,
and crystallize Lily Bart. While femininity in the first reading (Irigaray's
femininity that *"occurs only within models and laws devised by male subjects"* [86, emphasis added]) is a liability, in the second (Irigaray's femininity "external to the laws of exchange" [85]) it metamorphoses into
an asset: "Misfortune had made Lily supple instead of hardening her,
and a pliable substance is less easy to break than a stiff one" (54).

The tension between Wharton's feminisms, then, has a contemporary avatar: the apparent incommensurability of a humanist feminism — holding out for female subjectivity and agency — that advances a position (in this case, women who yield to "'the temptation to be a beautiful object' . . . [are] destroyed by the consequences of that temptation," as Judith Fetterley writes [200]), and a poststructuralist feminism that refuses definitive positions for their masterliness, preferring to luxuriate in a perpetual openness and inaccessibility. Translating this ambivalence toward definitive positions into academic terms, Peggy Kamuf explains in "Replacing Feminist Criticism" that "feminist thought has yet to decide where to situate itself on the map of the known world's divisions — either in a canonical mainstream with its centers of learning and culture, or in an outlying and unexplored region" (46). And so one must beware of the inadequacy of even "feminist" readings of Lily Bart that stress single-mindedly her ontology as an art object, as they resemble tellingly (disturbingly) the Lily Bart perceived by Lawrence Selden — practitioner of the law. Like *The House of Mirth* itself, Lily Bart is duplicitous, if not multiplicitous (hence [she] cannot be reduced to an art *object*). Anticipating Cixous, who writes in *Sorties* that "there is a link between the economy of femininity — the open, extravagant subjectivity, that relationship to the other in which the gift doesn't calculate its influence — and the possibility of love; and a link today between this 'libido of the other' and writing" (91–92), Wharton identifies Lily's multifariousness as feminine and inscribes such femininity in her writing.

In an early book on Wharton, *Edith Wharton: A Study of Her Fiction,* Blake Nevius sets up a pertinent opposition: he reads Lily (commonly enough) as the product of her environment and has trouble with her indeterminacy. He cannot take it seriously: "Her vacillation between the claims of the spirit represented by Selden and the prospect of a wealthy marriage is never quite convincing" (56–57). To retain his image of Lily as a helpless, victimized product of her society, Nevius must discount her movement, her oscillation, which, even in dismissing it, he deprecates as "vacillation." Like Selden, Nevius shrinks Lily to "an essentially lightweight and static protagonist . . . [whose] fate, if not tragic according to any satisfactory definition of the term, at least impresses us with the sense of infinite and avoidable waste" (55). (Avoidable by society, not by Lily.) Her equivocation, which Nevius certainly recognizes, threatens this reduction; hence he must dismiss it.

Yet the first page of the novel reveals that Lily Bart is not constituted by, but stands *"behind"* (as Barthes says of the "text"), "the limit of the *doxa*": "Taking the word literally, it may be said that [Lily] is always *paradoxical"* (157–58). In the opening scene of *The House of Mirth*, Selden (like Nevius) is disoriented by Lily. He cannot fix what transfixes him: "What was Miss Bart doing in town at that season? If she had appeared to be catching a train, he might have inferred that he had come on her in the act of transition between one and another of the country-houses which disputed her presence after the close of the Newport season; but her desultory air perplexed him" (25). Selden is disquieted by Lily's duplicity: "She stood apart from the crowd, . . . wearing an air of irresolution which might, as he surmised, be the mask of a very definite purpose" (25); "There was nothing new about Lily Bart, yet he could never see her without a faint movement of interest: it was characteristic of her that she always roused speculation, that her simplest acts seemed the result of far-reaching intentions" (25); "He knew that if she did not wish to be seen she would contrive to elude him" (26).

But as soon as he finds himself by Lily's lithe side, strolling elegantly along Madison Avenue, Selden (like Nevius) lapses into reifying her as an artistic product of her social milieu: he takes

> a luxurious pleasure . . . in the modelling of her little ear, the crisp upward wave of her hair—was it ever so slightly brightened by art?—and the thick planting of her straight black lashes. . . . He had a confused sense that she must have cost a great deal to make, that a great many dull and ugly people must . . . have been sacrificed to produce her. He was aware that the qualities distinguishing her from the herd of her sex were chiefly external: as though a fine glaze of beauty and fastidiousness had been applied to vulgar clay. (27)

(He then changes his mind, though not his basic conception, deciding that the "material" must have been "fine" in the first place.) Once Lily and Selden enter and settle into his dark, cheerful library, Selden articulates the theme that Blake Nevius considers to be uppermost: "She was so evidently the victim of the civilization which had produced her, that the links of her bracelet seemed like manacles chaining her to her fate" (29). Muddled as to whether Lily or "dull and ugly people"are the more abused victims of civilization, Selden is certain that Lily is an aesthetic commodity of an industrial process. Are the remaining three hundred pages of the novel merely a dramatic unfolding of this early assessment?[1]

In chapter I Lily has a feminist moment of lucidity and verbal felicity

[1]For an analysis of *The House of Mirth* as testimony to "the frightening power of the marketplace," whose "ethos of exchange" Lily is "clearly caught up in" (376), see Waichee Dimock's "Debasing Exchange: Edith Wharton's *The House of Mirth.*"

that demonstrates how deftly she can capture the essence of Selden's reflex taxonomy. She makes plain her awareness of the sexism of her society by spelling out the difference between an insufficiently rich man and an insufficiently rich woman: "Ah, there 's the difference—a girl must [marry], a man may if he chooses." A man's shabby coat won't lose him a dinner invitation, but "a woman [Lily understands perfectly] is asked out as much for her clothes as for herself" (33). These are Lily's, not just Wharton's, words; *if* Lily is victimized, she is intelligent about it.

And how victimized is she? Wharton offers a plethora of clues that Lily eludes triumphantly the attempted encapsulizations of her male observers. Beginning and ending with scenes of Lily in the library, the novel encourages us to imagine her as possessing a literary consciousness or sensibility ("Lily, who prided herself on her broad-minded recognition of literature, . . . always carried an Omar Khayyam in her travelling-bag" [79])—as being literary and therefore resistant to legalistic hermeneutics. (If there is irony in the Omar Khayyám reference, at least Lily's tastes tend toward the literature of pleasure.) Like a piece of fiction, she makes the boundary of the natural and artificial unsurveyable: she "had the art of blushing at the right time" (28); there is a "streak of sylvan freedom in her nature that lent such savour to her artificiality" (34); "Miss Bart . . . gave to the encounter the touch of naturalness which she could impart to the most strained situations" (218). Alive to subtexts, "Miss Bart had the gift of following an undercurrent of thought while she appeared to be sailing on the surface of conversation" (41). In a late tête-à-tête with Rosedale, during which she attempts to revive his marriage proposal and fails (Rosedale clears this up with his unequivocal "I had really no intention of renewing it"), Lily comments, "I have no one but myself to blame if I gave you the impression that my decision was final" (Lily's decisions are never final); and the narrator explains Rosedale's "puzzled silence" by remarking that "Her word-play was always too quick for him" (240). Likewise: "Her sense of irony never quite deserted her" (247). If Wharton invites us to apprehend Lily as an analogue of art, we must take care in constructing the parallel, avoiding the traditional legalistic tendency to ascribe univocal meanings to things, to wash away their ambiguity—in this case to regard Lily as an art object, or in other terms, as a "work" rather than a "text" (the latter being, as Barthes elaborates in "From Work to Text," "an object that can[not] be computed" [156]).

Perhaps Wharton best identifies her—or a female—version of Barthes's "work" in a climactic conversation between Gerty and Lily just after Lily's Aunt Peniston disinherits her, at a time when Lily's reputation is sullied by rumors of her flirting too ambitiously with George Dorset. Altruistic, naive Gerty wishes to squeeze the truth out of Miss Bart: "'The important thing is that you should clear yourself—should tell your friends the whole truth'" (215). Lily's initial impulse in responding to Gerty is to point out that with women, "truth" takes a special form: the form of gossip, a reductive story, "an object that can be computed." Lily's shrewdness extends to knowing that the credibility of gossip hinges on money and power: "'The whole truth?' Miss Bart laughed. 'What is truth? Where a woman is concerned, it's the story that's easiest to believe. In this case it's a great deal easier to believe Bertha Dorset's story than mine, because she has a big house and an opera box, and it's convenient to be on good terms with her'" (215).

Determined to get beyond this impasse, Gerty inquires tenaciously: "But what *is* your story, Lily? I don't believe any one knows it yet" (215). This is a conundrum for Lily herself. Gerty persists: "I want you to tell me exactly what happened from the beginning" (216). Unable to articulate her origin, and equally unable to explain the impossibility of articulating such an aporia, Lily evades Gerty by reproaching her: "'From the beginning?' Miss Bart gently mimicked her. 'Dear Gerty, how little imagination you good people have!'" (216). Lily's story, as they refer to it and as Lily seems instinctively to comprehend, is an irreducible one. "Good people," however, to do good, to make the necessary social corrections, must acknowledge specific truths, certain moral axioms, which, to Lily's way of thinking, results in the constriction of a more "imaginative" (to borrow her term) apprehension of what constitutes an origin, a cause, an account of a person's life. Good people are merely gossips with more elevating reductions.

Kamuf converts Lily's French feminism *avant la lettre* into the terminology of feminist theory: "If . . . the empirical rectification of an empirical error can only result in yet another form of that error which is the possibility of a totalizing reference to an object—whether masculine, feminine or somehow both—then what is put in question . . . is perhaps the idea that feminist criticism can seek to define its object and still practice an effective critique of power structures" (44). Lily resists Gerty's compulsion to totalize; and Wharton, it seems to me, shares Lily's complex vision of female subjectivity, having in large part written *The House of Mirth* to counterpose gossip and the law, the female and male versions of reductive storytelling, with a (Barthesian) textual rendering of Lily Bart's life. Unlike gossips and lawyers, Wharton refuses to produce another penetrable story of a woman's experience.

And unlike Selden and even Gerty, at least one character *in* the book shows an appreciation of Lily's duplicity, multiplicity, elusiveness. Carry Fisher recounts, to Selden, Lily's experience with an Italian Prince— "rich and the real thing, [he] wanted to marry her; but just at the critical moment a good-looking step-son turned up, and Lily was silly enough to flirt with him while her marriage-settlements with the step-father were being drawn up" (183)—to illustrate the general principle about Lily that "she works like a slave preparing the ground and sowing her seed; but the day she ought to be reaping the harvest she over-sleeps herself or goes off on a picnic" (183). Lily, of course, slips away from the fixity, the clamp, the containment of marriage not only with this Italian Prince but also with Selden, Dorset, Gryce, and Rosedale. She seems dedicated to a certain freedom from (especially connubial) defini- tion: Paul Morpeth "had been immensely struck by Lily's plastic possi- bilities" (226); "It was her exquisite inaccessibleness, the sense of dis- tance she could convey . . . that made it most difficult for [Rosedale] to give her up" (240–41). Perhaps, as Judith Fetterley comments, "she cannot project herself as a wife, she cannot imagine life after the plunge because she cannot finally face the price she would have to pay for it: acceptance of a system which makes of her an object and treats her as a possession" (205). Lily's elusive behavior adumbrates questions such as Kamuf's about the value of working within already existing patriarchal institutions: "If feminist theory can be content to propose cosmetic modifications on the face of humanism and its institutions [in this case marriage], will it have done anything more than reproduce the structure of woman's exclusion in the same code which has been extended to include her?" (45). Carry Fisher seems to position herself within this feminist dilemma. Unlike Blake Nevius, she reaps pleasure from Lily's oscillation, which keeps her free. Carry attempts to offer Selden a less determinate conception of Lily: "Sometimes, . . . I think it 's just flight- iness—and sometimes I think it 's because, at heart, she despises the things she 's trying for. And it 's the difficulty of deciding that makes her such an interesting study" (183–84).

But Selden takes no cues from Carry Fisher, even though his expe- rience with Lily corroborates Carry's sense of Lily's irreducibility. En- gaged in his own "particular study of Miss Bart" at dinner on the Rivi- era, he characterizes her as "matchless," undoubtedly oblivious to the aptness of his pun. At this point in their jaded relationship, "he could give his admiration the freer play because so little personal feeling re- mained in it" (207). The more emotionally invested Selden is in Lily, the more he tries to mold her into his romantic ideal; the less invested, the more he allows Lily a freer play as cause and corollary of the free play of his admiration. He is throughout the novel striving to be "on her traces" (205)—she wonders that "he should have traced her to so unlikely a place" as the world of Mrs. Hatch, where he locates Lily "in the wilderness of pink damask" (260)—without ever realizing that the traces are all he has. At the final moment of his encounter with Lily at Mrs. Hatch's Hotel, where Lily grows "more aware of a certain ambiguity in her situation" (260), Selden seeks (in language of incipient rape) "a break in the impenetrable front she presented" (264).

He never finds the fantasy figure he desires and so resorts to forging it. Lily resents the "strange . . . authority" he attempts to wield over her at Mrs. Hatch's residence (he insists that she leave immediately) (262), an authority with which Selden tries to smother Lily once she is dead and unable, in a sense, to resist. Just before discovering her corpse, he recalls "the word he meant to say to her" (301), as if he might solve everything with a single word—Selden's transcendental signifier. (It is true that, just before dying, Lily "said to herself that there was something she must tell Selden, some word she had found that should make life clear between them." But she struggles "to repeat the word, which lingered vague and luminous on the far edge of thought" and dies "afraid of not remembering it when she woke." Unlike Selden's word, Lily's remains unobtainable: "Slowly the thought of the word faded, and sleep began to enfold her" ([300]). This is the stifling, maudlin note on which the novel ends: "He knelt by the bed and bent over her, draining their last moment to its lees; and in the silence there passed between them the word which made all clear" (305).

Wharton makes it unmistakable that Selden's alleged final communication with Lily is his limited lachrymose conception. He has already done a mawkish reading of himself with Lily: "Yes, he could now *read into* that farewell [the day before, when she kissed his forehead] all that his heart craved to find there" (305, emphasis added). From the start, Selden has been straining to commodify Lily as an objet d'art (the only way, obtuse playboy that he is, he can enjoy her); and now that she is dead, his reconstruction of Lily—as a "work"—can ossify. In Cynthia Griffin Wolff's words, "The 'real' Lily—the *only* Lily he can tolerate—is the beautiful idealized memory he carries of her, the most superb piece in his collection" (131–32).

Incorrigible sentimentalist, Selden interprets Lily's story as a romantic tragedy: he deludes himself into believing that "all the conditions of life had conspired to keep them apart," that "the moment had been fated to pass from them before they could seize it" (305). His preoccupation with the theme of fate serves his strenuous but futile effort to supply an explanation, a cause, a beginning for Lily's downfall. Advocate of the law, he wishes to make transparent what persists in remaining opaque.

Wharton goes to elaborate lengths to undermine Selden's theme of fate. Fate — or metaphysical law, a concept to mollify a lawyer's desire for lawfulness — must do battle in the novel with a much more arbitrary, playful agency, that of luck. It may be wrong in fact to conceive of luck as an "agency" at all: for the concept gravitates in the direction of "chance" and is invoked for events that cannot be exactly predicted or controlled. On the other hand, fate *is* an agency, and the term gravitates in the direction of "doom." Fate and luck begin by posing as synonyms, upon consideration seem as incongruous as inexorable law and free will, and end by appearing as hopelessly antithetical as death and life. Selden's "fate" is merely one provisional focal point within a fluctuating perspective manifest in *The House of Mirth* from beginning to end. Wharton's attempt to keep Lily alive in spirit and free from society's determination to predict omnisciently and control omnipotently — to construct the world, including Lily, as work and not as text — takes the form of a conceptual oscillation between fate and luck. Selden appears not to have internalized Lily's first words to him in the novel — "Mr. Selden — what good luck!" (26) — despite the fact that he repeats her sentiment upon meeting her at the Van Osburgh wedding: " 'This is luck,' he said smiling" (104). Lily reiterates the motif immediately: " 'What luck!' she repeated" (26). Although vis-à-vis Lily's luck motif Selden introduces the motif of fate — "Perhaps you 'll meet your fate to-night at the Trenors' " (33) — Rosedale prefers to see serendipity. His first words to Lily are, "Miss Bart? Well — of all people! This *is* luck" (35).

Fate and luck are flung around as explanations for events in *The House of Mirth* to the point of sabotaging Selden's legalistic position. Such deconstruction may also serve to dissolve the political opposition between Gerty and Lily, who prefigure the division in feminism roughly seven decades later between what we might term, for brevity's sake, praxis and theory. Fate, according to this translation of the fate-luck duality, would signify the idea that women groomed to be ladies are doomed to stunted growth or stagnation, if not to death. Oddly enough, this practical, socially oriented feminism converges with the positions of Nevius and Selden: law is fate, and society is its minion; the law that needs modifying is acknowledged. Luck, on the other hand, like theoretically oriented feminism, like the French *féminité* (kinetic, overflowing), subverts all pattern, shakes any firm ground.

It turns out that Lily, oscillating in imitation of the text that incarnates her, is the chief dismantler of the fate-luck antinomy. Early on, not only does she take bumping into Selden to be "good luck," but she thinks of "having [Gryce] to herself in the train" as "luck" (38); to Lily's analogical mind, a stroke of luck even links her fortuitous encounters with the two men: "The 'points' [on Americana] she had had the presence of mind to glean from Selden, in anticipation of this very contingency [of meeting Gryce], were serving her to such good purpose that she began to think her visit to him had been the luckiest incident of the day" (40). But the cheeriness that upholds Lily's faith in luck dwindles as Gryce fills her with ennui. Her metaphysics of happy contingencies begins to mix with a gloomier outlook: she swings from the thought that she "must submit to more boredom . . . on the bare chance that [Gryce] might ultimately decide to do her the honour of boring her for life" to the conclusion that that ",was a hateful fate" (44). Even before her luck at cards and the stock market goes sour (luck obviously enters the novel's philosophical field by way of auction bridge and Wall Street), Lily, like her mother, develops an "anger against fate" (51) that surfaces periodically: "She was beginning to have fits of angry rebellion against fate, when she longed to drop out of the race and make an independent life for herself" (56). Here her "fate" presumably requires her prostitution to the immediate world of aristocratic New York and its beauty and marriage contests: Lily feels fated to lose.

To blame fate, however, is to be inconsistent, though that hardly constitutes an objection in Lily's mind to doing so: "She was not above the inconsistency of charging fate, rather than herself, with her own misfortunes" (52). All it takes is an upward swoop of her life for Fortuna to replace the Fates in her mythic imagination. Lily receives a dividend check from Trenor with a renewed faith in luck: "The world was not so stupid· and blundering after all: now and then a stroke of luck came to the unluckiest. At the thought her spirits began to rise: it was characteristic of her that one trifling piece of good fortune should give wings to all her hopes" (102). Only three pages later, Lily again shifts philosophical ground: "It seemed to be her fate to appear at her worst to Selden" (104). And when Mrs. Haffen offers Bertha Dorset's letters to Lily, both chance and fate loom large: "Bertha Dorset's letters were nothing to her—they might go where the current of chance carried them! But Selden was inextricably involved in their fate" (113).

Lily's vertiginous movement from fate to luck and back again never flags. Toward the close of the novel, on the evening of her ambiguous death, "In the mysterious nocturnal separation from all outward signs of life, [Lily] felt herself more strangely confronted with her fate" (298); in the last accounting of her death, we are nevertheless directed to its statistical improbability: "If sleep came at all, it might be a sleep without waking. But after all that was but one chance in a hundred" (299). I say "last" and not "final" since I see no justification for privileging chance over fate as the reason for Lily's death. That both alternatives ought to be held in suspense is one lesson of Lily's book-long oscillation.

While Lily refuses positions of stability, Selden (creature of his profession) locates them where they are nonexistent. Selden must transform opacity to transparency, as he does in his refashioning of Lily's story. We might consequently expect that, given the instability—the constitutive ambiguity—of the written word, Selden would shy away from writing. (Barthes pronounces that "The spoken word is 'clear'; the banishment of polysemy [such banishment being the definition of 'clarity'] serves the Law—*all speech is on the side of the Law*" [191; emphasis added].) Compelled to locate Lily to suppress the eruption of something terrible and irrevocable surrounding the Dorset-Lily affair, Selden accordingly "almost decided on the *unsatisfactory alternative of writing*, when the ceaseless diorama of the square suddenly unrolled before him the figures of Lord Hubert and Mrs. Bry" (214; emphasis added). He typically prefers to speak rather than to write; polysemy is lost on Selden, as it is on Rosedale. When Lily says to Rosedale, during their tea together at the *Longworth*, "You know Mrs. Hatch, I think? Well, perhaps you can understand that she might make things too easy for one," "Rosedale [again] looked faintly puzzled, and she remembered that allusiveness was lost on him" (272).[2]

In contrast, Wharton not only implicates Lily and Carry Fisher in polyvalence, in literariness, but even Bertha Dorset seems a member of the novel's literary guild. (Wharton may wish to rescue female gossips from self-incarceration in restrictive stories.) Bertha's membership is established in a way that aligns femininity and writing. To Bécassin's, for the dinner honoring the Duchess, Bertha wears the most lavish piece of clothing in the novel—a dress in "the literary style." Although it is Selden who recognizes the gown's literariness, he predictably ends up being troubled by the excessive freedom it lends to Bertha: Mrs. Dorset's gown, "in particular, challenged all the wealth of Mr.

---

[2] In "The Death of the Lady (Novelist)," Elaine Showalter notices what she calls Lily's "inability to rise above the 'word-play and evasion' . . . that restrict her conversations with Selden and to tell her own story"; to Showalter, Lily "can only speak in parables [Selden] is totally unable to comprehend" (136). But we must strive to comprehend the parables that surpass Selden's understanding.

Dabham's [the *Riviera Notes*'s journalist's] vocabulary: it had surprises and subtleties worthy of what he would have called 'the literary style.' At first, as Selden had noticed, it had been almost too preoccupying to its wearer; but now she was in full command of it, and was even producing her effects with unwonted freedom. Was she not, indeed, too free, too fluent, for perfect naturalness?" (207). It is as if Selden perceives in Bertha's extravagant dress the threat of a suspension of univocal truths and meanings, an attempt, to quote Irigaray in *This Sex Which Is Not One*, "to wrest [femininity] away from the economy of the logos," thus releasing it to generate *"disruptive excess"* (78).

This identification of an elegant gown—metonymy for femininity—with writing is not anomalous. In her last dwelling place, Lily takes out her dresses and reads them as if they were musty autobiographical novels: "The remaining dresses, though they had lost their freshness, still kept the long unerring lines, the sweep and amplitude of the great artist's stroke, and as she spread them out on the bed the scenes in which they had been worn rose vividly before her. An association lurked in every fold: each fall of lace and gleam of embroidery was like a letter in the record of her past" (294–95). Lily draws forth the white Reynolds dress from her trunk last of all: its "long flexible folds" record her romantic evening next to "the flower-edged fountain ["falling among lilies"] where she had stood with Lawrence Selden" (295). The conflation of femininity and Wharton's writing is here italicized, as other former "ghosts" (besides Selden) of Lily's past haunt the scene, their presences evoked through linguistic play, specifically puns. Lily "put back the dresses one by one, laying away with each some gleam of light, some note of laughter, some stray waft from the *rosy* shores of pleasure. She was still in a state of highly-wrought impressionability, and every hint of the past sent a lingering *tremor* along her nerves" (295; emphases added).

As Rosedale and Trenor are conjured up, Wharton's writing paronomastically joins with Lily's dresses in the task of enfolding her past. The doubleness of Lily, epitome of femininity, is mirrored in the doubleness of Wharton's prose. The two—Lily/femininity and Wharton's writing/writing—again coalesce in what is perhaps the most uncanny scene of the book: on the evening of her death, after Lily wraps up her bank business, "she continued to sit at [her writing-desk], sorting her papers and writing, till the intense silence of the house reminded her of the lateness of the hour" (298). What is she writing? It is as if Wharton momentarily slides into Lily's body here (as if Lily's body were a dress) and takes up her pen, to stress the kinship of femininity and writing—both of which, to invoke Hélène Cixous, "freed from law, unencumbered by moderation, [exceed] phallic authority" (86).

I have suggested that Wharton's writing is textual, rather than naturalistic, that it may be aligned with femininity, or play, or luck, rather than with law or fate. In arguing that Wharton represents in *The House of Mirth* the tension underlying her novel between practical and theoretical feminist loyalties—since her representation takes the form of an oscillating motion throughout the book—it would seem I am claiming that Wharton prefers a posthumanist feminism that insists on the instability of all ground, which, in Nancy Miller's conception, "rethink[s] the very locations of the center and the periphery, and within that fragile topology, the stability of the subject" (53). But this is just half of Miller's proposal, as it is half (or one) of Wharton's feminism(s). Wharton, like Miller, values simultaneously the idea that "we must live out (the hortatory always returns) a practical politics within the institution" (53). Wharton does not present the oscillation between fate—agent of the doom predicted for ornamental women by practical feminists—and luck—the notion more congenial to poststructuralist feminists for whom plurivocality is liberation—as *itself* an example of plurivocality. If she had, the oscillation would then indicate a triumph of the literary dimension of the book at the expense of the social and would paradoxically calm itself. Wharton refuses a merely "textual" synthesis of "text" and "work," as if the social ground of the novel finally could be swallowed up by a vaster textuality. For we have a woman's death on our hands—a sort of ultimate stability of the subject and victory of the institution.

It is not exactly that Lily's elusiveness, her refusal to become fixed, is suicidal. Her demise is instead the result of her being born into a patriarchal world in which a woman is pinned down, transmogrified into a static art object if she is beautiful, and has to be married, as Lily complains, in any case. Lily cannot survive, far less flourish, in this world of frozen female identities. The society of *The House of Mirth* either forces women into its slots or rejects them. Lily's suppleness, her indefiniteness, protects her from being forced in, so she is tossed out. But while we may take pleasure and pride in the purity of Lily's rebellion against reification, death is an exorbitant price to pay.

As a way of balancing Lily's literariness, which enhances her vulnerability to annihilation, Wharton has drawn a couple of female characters in *The House of Mirth* who, to use Cixous's trope, "wear sensible shoes."[3] Gerty Farish, with her philanthropic work for young women, for one. And there is a second, perhaps similarly unglamorous, heroine who no doubt is sensibly clad: Nettie Struther. I have been treating Lily as an ex-centric character who emblematizes ex-centricity: "She [in fact] had grown up without any one spot of earth being dearer to her than another: there was no centre of early pieties, of grave endearing traditions, to which her heart could revert and from which it could draw strength for itself and tenderness for others" (296). Put this way, more from a domestic than a philosophical vantage point, however, the loss entailed in Lily's polymorphousness becomes apparent. In Nettie Struther's kitchen toward the end of the novel, a drained, jaundiced Lily samples her first taste of a humanly centered existence: "All the men and women she knew were like atoms whirling away from each other in some wild centrifugal dance: her first glimpse of the continuity of life had come to her that evening in Nettie Struther's kitchen" (297). Lily even considers Nettie's blissfully centripetal domestic space to be the appropriate setting of an oracle: "The poor little working-girl . . . seemed to Lily to have reached the central truth of existence" (297). What happened, we may wonder, to the sophisticated theorist tutoring Gerty in the impossibility of truth telling, especially for women?

Yet the idea that Nettie Struther's household expresses a "central truth of existence" is almost as facile as Selden's romantic tragedy. Wharton arouses hope in Nettie's domestic arrangement even as she revokes it through the saccharinity of the scene. Wharton allows *The House of Mirth* to come into focus provisionally as a "work" rather than a "text" when Gerty's and Nettie's heroinisms emerge, so that we must acknowledge the beneficence of "good people." These young women, unlike Lily, after all, will continue the progressive efforts of women (the Barthesian "work" implies here "social work"). But socially crucial as Gerty and Nettie may be, they are at the same time not only intellectually unappealing but ultimately unthreatening to male laws and power structures.

At the end of "The Text's Heroine: A Feminist Critic and Her Fictions," Miller proposes that "What we might wish for . . . is a female

---

[3]In "The Text's Heroine," Miller sees the opposition, also named by Elaine Marks, between "the American, empirical and social science model of Women's Studies [and] the French ludic endeavor" as a "problematic that can be understood in relation to *shoes:* as in the sturdy, sensible sort worn by American feminists, and the more elegant sort worn by [Hélène] Cixous." Miller is referring to an informal presentation at Barnard in 1979, in which Cixous used this shoe paradigm "to make a point about difference and recuperation" (48–49).

materialism attentive to the needs of the body as well as the luxuries of the mind. Can we imagine, or should we, a position that speaks in tropes and walks in sensible shoes?" (53). Or, I would add, one that speaks sensibly and walks stylishly? Wharton shares this double wish for women, realizing in advance that a poststructuralist feminism needs the action of a real-world feminism, while a practically oriented feminism needs the intellectual vitality of poststructuralist feminism immune to extant patriarchal structures and values. (Both sides are, of course, political.)

The fatal error is to treat these feminisms as mutually exclusive. A sociopolitical feminism alone, working for improvement within the law, would kill off the dazzling multiplicity of a Lily, turning her into a drab Gerty. (To quote Judith Fetterley, "One might wish Lily to follow Gerty's example, . . . but she could do so only at the cost of being a lily" [203]—floating free.) A sociopolitical feminism alone might destroy Lily as effectively as the sociopolitical structure it tries to reform, the sole difference being that the death she would be condemned to would be a death-in-life. Of course, activist feminists are apt not to be as impressed as Francophile feminists with the importance of keeping a dazzling Lily in full bloom; the point Wharton makes to them by locating the law within Lawrence Selden and art within Lily Bart is that it is lawfulness itself, not any particular set of laws, that is antipathetic to Lily, and the "literary" alone that can vivify her. Indeed, Lily continues to bloom for us only because Wharton's literary presentation of her is more labyrinthine than Selden's legalistic interpretations, whether they happen to condemn or justify her. Even improved laws, even laws that would find Lily innocent, would kill her.[4]

But Lily is murdered one way or the other. In point of fact, it *is* one particular set of laws that condemns and destroys Lily, which is the inevitable result of her trying to step outside it. Textuality may be revolutionary when planted within the law; outside it, merely juxtaposed with it, creating a binary pair literature/law, it is entirely weak. "The need," Barthes writes (speaking of pedagogy) at the end of *Image Music Text*,

---

[4]In *Gender Trouble*, Judith Butler disputes the idea that feminist subversions of conventional gender roles cannot occur within the terms of power. She advocates "a repetition of the law which is not its consolidation, but its displacement" (30), believing that prediscursive subversions are futile gestures and that change must occur within the terms of culture. Yet in a double move (akin to what I am proposing) that weds the humanist insistence upon agency and the postmodernist suspicion of stability, Butler argues that the phantasmatic construction of identity "opens up other configurations, not only of genders and bodies, but of politics itself" (142). "I" may be asserted through "the structure of signification . . . " (143).

"is to work at patiently tracing out a pure form, that of a *floating* (the very form of the signifier); a floating which would not destroy anything but would be content simply to disorientate the Law" (215). Lily floats with the very form of the signifier—but the law does not thereby suffer a perceivable disorientation, for the law is nothing if not hostile to textuality. Until the utopia of textualized law, feminism has no choice but doubleness (at least—a double life in the world of law and the world of letters—a doubleness that will be enervating to feminism, a source merely of endless interfeminist disputation, until its necessity is taken for granted.

WORKS CITED

Barthes, Roland. "From Work to Text." *Image Music Text*. Trans. Stephen Heath. New York: Hill and Wang, 1977. 155–64.

———. "Writers, Intellectuals, Teachers." *Image Music Text*. 190–215.

Butler, Judith. *Gender Trouble*. London: Routledge, 1990.

Cixous, Hélène, and Catherine Clément. *The Newly Born Woman*. Trans. Betsy Wing. Minneapolis: U of Minnesota P, 1986.

Dimock, Wai-chee. "Debasing Exchange: Edith Wharton's *The House of Mirth*." *PMLA* 100 (October 1985): 783–92. [Dimock's essay is also reprinted in this volume on pp. 375–90]

Fetterley, Judith. " 'The Temptation To Be a Beautiful Object': Double Standard and Double Bind in *The House of Mirth*." *Studies in American Fiction* 5 (Autumn 1977): 199–211.

Irigaray, Luce. *This Sex Which Is Not One*. Trans. Catherine Porter with Carolyn Burke. Ithaca: Cornell UP, 1985.

Kamuf, Peggy. "Replicating Feminist Criticism." *Diacritics* 12 (Summer 1982): 42–47.

Miller, Nancy K. "The Text's Heroine: A Feminist Critic and Her Fictions." *Diacritics* 12 (Summer 1982): 48–53.

Nevius, Blake. *Edith Wharton: A Study of Her Fiction*. Berkeley: U of California P, 1953.

Showalter, Elaine. "The Death of the Lady (Novelist): Wharton's *The House of Mirth*." *Representations* 9 (Winter 1985): 133–49.

Wharton, Edith. *The House of Mirth*. New York: Scribner's, 1905.

Wolff, Cynthia Griffin. *A Feast of Words: The Triumph of Edith Wharton*. New York: Oxford UP, 1977.

Deconstruction
and
The House of Mirth

WHAT IS DECONSTRUCTION?

Deconstruction has a reputation for being the most complex and forbidding of contemporary critical approaches to literature, but in fact almost all of us have, at one time, either deconstructed a text or badly wanted to deconstruct one. Sometimes when we hear a lecturer effectively marshal evidence to show that a book means primarily one thing, we long to interrupt and ask what he or she would make of other, conveniently overlooked passages, passages that seem to contradict the lecturer's thesis. Sometimes, after reading a provocative critical article that *almost* convinces us that a familiar work means the opposite of what we assumed it meant, we may wish to make an equally convincing case for our former reading of the text. We may not think that the poem or novel in question better supports our interpretation, but we may recognize that the text can be used to support *both* readings. And sometimes we simply want to make that point: texts can be used to support seemingly irreconcilable positions.

To reach this conclusion is to feel the deconstructive itch. J. Hillis Miller, the preeminent American deconstructor, puts it this way: "Deconstruction is not a dismantling of the structure of a text, but a demonstration that it has already dismantled itself. Its apparently solid ground is no rock but thin air" ("Stevens' Rock" 341). To deconstruct a text isn't to show that all the high old themes aren't there to be found in it. Rather, it is to show that a text—not unlike DNA with its double helix—can have intertwined, opposite "discourses"—strands of narrative, threads of meaning.

Ultimately, of course, deconstruction refers to a larger and more complex enterprise than the practice of demonstrating that a text means contradictory things. The term refers to a way of reading texts practiced by critics who have been influenced by the writings of the French philosopher Jacques Derrida. It is important to gain some understanding of Derrida's project and of the historical backgrounds of his work before reading the deconstruction that follows, let alone attempting to deconstruct a text. But it is important, too, to approach deconstruction with anything but a scholar's sober and almost worshipful respect for knowledge and truth. Deconstruction offers a playful alternative to traditional scholarship, a confidently adversarial alternative, and deserves to be approached in the spirit that animates it.

Derrida, a philosopher of language who coined the term "deconstruction," argues that we tend to think and express our thoughts in terms of opposites. Something is black but not white, masculine and therefore not feminine, a cause rather than an effect, and so forth. These mutually exclusive pairs of dichotomies are too numerous to list but would include beginning/end, conscious/unconscious, presence/absence, speech/writing, and construction/destruction (the last being the opposition that Derrida's word deconstruction tries to contain and subvert). It we think hard about these dichotomies, Derrida suggests, we will realize that they are not simply oppositions; they are also hierarchies in miniature. In other words, they contain one term that our culture views as being superior and one term viewed as negative or inferior. Sometimes the superior term seems only subtly superior (*speech, masculine, cause*), whereas sometimes we know immediately which term is culturally preferable (*presence* and *beginning* and *consciousness* are easy choices). But the hierarchy always exists.

Of particular interest to Derrida, perhaps because it involves the language in which all the other dichotomies are expressed, is the hierarchical opposition speech/writing. Derrida argues that the "privileging" of speech, that is, the tendency to regard speech in positive terms and writing in negative terms, cannot be disentangled from the privileging of presence. (Postcards are written by absent friends; we read Plato because he cannot speak from beyond the grave.) Furthermore, according to Derrida, the tendency to privilege both speech and presence is part of the Western tradition of *logocentrism*, the belief that in some ideal beginning were creative *spoken* words, words such as "Let there be light," spoken by an ideal, *present* God. According to logocentric tradition, these words can now only be represented in unoriginal speech or writing (such as the written phrase in quotation marks above). Derrida doesn't seek to reverse the hierarchized opposition between speech and writing, or presence and absence, or early and late, for to do so would be to fall into a trap of perpetuating the same forms of thought and expression that he proposes to deconstruct. Rather, his goal is to erase the boundary between oppositions such as speech and writing, and to do so in such a way as to throw the order and values implied by the opposition into question.

Returning to the theories of Ferdinand de Saussure, who invented the modern science of linguistics, Derrida reminds us that the association of speech with present, obvious, and ideal meaning and writing with absent, merely pictured, and therefore less reliable meaning is suspect, to say the least. As Saussure demonstrated, words are *not* the things they name and, indeed, they are only arbitrarily associated with those things. Neither spoken nor written words have present, positive, identifiable attributes themselves; they have meaning only by virtue of their difference from other words (*red, read, reed*). In a sense, meanings emerge from the gaps or spaces between them. Take *read* as an example. To know whether it is the present or past tense of the verb — whether it rhymes with *red* or *reed*—we need to see it in relation to some other word (for example, *yesterday*).

Because the meanings of words lie in the differences between them and in the differences between them and the things they name, Derrida suggests that all language is constituted by *différance*, a word he has coined that puns on two French words meaning "to differ" and "to defer": words are the deferred presences of the things they "mean," and their meaning is grounded in difference. Derrida, by the way, changes the *e* in the French word *différence* to an *a* in his neologism *différance;* the change, which can be seen in writing but cannot be heard in spoken French, is itself a playful, witty challenge to the notion that writing is inferior or "fallen" speech.

In *De la grammatologie* [*Of Grammatology*] (1967) and *Dissemination* (1972), Derrida begins to redefine writing by deconstructing some old definitions. In *Dissemination,* he traces logocentrism back to Plato, who in the *Phaedrus* has Socrates condemn writing and who, in all the great dialogues, powerfully postulates that metaphysical longing for origins and ideals that permeates Western thought. "What Derrida does in his reading of Plato," Barbara Johnson points out, "is to unfold dimensions of Plato's *text* that work against the grain of (Plato's own) Platonism" (xxiv). Remember: that is what deconstruction does according to Miller; it shows a text dismantling itself.

In *Of Grammatology,* Derrida turns to the *Confessions* of Jean-Jacques Rousseau and exposes a grain running against the grain. Rousseau, another great Western idealist and believer in innocent, noble origins, on one hand condemned writing as mere representation, a corruption of the more natural, childlike, direct, and therefore undevious speech. On the other hand, Rousseau admitted his own tendency to lose self-presence and blurt out exactly the wrong thing in public. He confesses that, by writing at a distance from his audience, he often expressed himself better: "If I were present, one would never know what I was worth," Rousseau admitted (Derrida, *Of Grammatology* 142). Thus, writing is a *supplement* to speech that is at the same time *necessary.* Barbara Johnson, sounding like Derrida, puts it this way: "Recourse to writing . . . is necessary to recapture a presence whose lack has not been preceded by any fullness" (Derrida, *Dissemination* xii). Thus, Derrida shows that one strand of Rousseau's discourse made writing seem a secondary, even treacherous supplement, while another made it seem necessary to communication.

Have Derrida's deconstructions of *Confessions* and the *Phaedrus* explained these texts, interpreted them, opened them up and shown us what they mean? Not in any traditional sense. Derrida would say that anyone attempting to find a single, correct meaning in a text is simply imprisoned by that structure of thought that would oppose two readings and declare one to be right and not wrong, correct rather than incorrect. In fact, any work of literature that we interpret defies the laws of Western logic, the laws of opposition and noncontradiction. In the views of poststructuralist critics, texts don't say "A and not B." They say "A and not-A," as do texts written by literary critics, who are also involved in producing creative writing.

Miller has written that the purpose of deconstruction is to show "the existence in literature of structures of language which contradict the law of non-contradiction." Why find the grain that runs against the grain? To restore what Miller has called "the strangeness of literature," to reveal the "capacity of each work to surprise the reader," to demonstrate that "literature continually exceeds any formula or theory with which the critic is prepared to encompass it" (Miller, *Fiction* 5).

Although its ultimate aim may be to critique Western idealism and logic, deconstruction began as a response to structuralism and to formalism, another structure-oriented theory of reading. (Deconstruction, which is really only one kind of a poststructuralist criticism, is sometimes referred to as poststructuralist criticism, or even as poststructuralism.)

Structuralism, Robert Scholes tells us, may now be seen as a reaction to modernist alienation and despair (3). Using Saussure's theory as Derrida was to do later, European structuralists attempted to create a *semiology,* or science of signs, that would give humankind at once a scientific and a holistic way of studying the world and its human inhabitants. Roland Barthes, a structuralist who later shifted toward poststructuralism, hoped to recover literary language from the isolation in which it had been studied and to show that the laws that govern it govern all signs, from road signs to articles of clothing. Claude Lévi-Strauss, a structural anthropologist who studied everything from village structure to the structure of myths, found in myths what he called *mythemes,* or building blocks, such as basic plot elements. Recognizing that the same mythemes occur in similar myths from different cultures, he suggested that all myths may be elements of one great myth being written by the collective human mind.

Derrida could not accept the notion that structuralist thought might someday explain the laws governing human signification and thus provide the key to understanding the form and meaning of everything from an African village to a Greek myth to Rousseau's *Confessions.* In his view, the scientific search by structural anthropologists for what unifies humankind amounts to a new version of the old search for the lost ideal, whether that ideal be Plato's bright realm of the Idea or the Paradise of Genesis or Rousseau's unspoiled Nature. As for the structuralist belief that texts have "centers" of meaning, in Derrida's view that derives from the logocentric belief that there is a reading of the text that accords with "the book as seen by God." Jonathan Culler, who thus translates a difficult phrase from Derrida's *L'Écriture et la différence* [*Writing and Difference*] (1967) in his book *Structuralist Poetics* (1975), goes on to explain what Derrida objects to in structuralist literary criticism:

> [When] one speaks of the structure of a literary work, one does so from a certain vantage point: one starts with notions of the meaning or effects of a poem and tries to identify the structures responsible for those effects. Possible configurations or patterns that make no contribution are rejected as irrelevant. That is to say, an intuitive understanding of the poem functions as the "centre" . . . : it is both a starting point and a limiting principle. (244)

For these reasons, Derrida and his poststructuralist followers reject the very notion of "linguistic competence" introduced by Noam Chomsky, a structural linguist. The idea that there is a competent reading "gives a privileged status to a particular set of rules of reading, . . . granting pre-eminence to certain conventions and excluding from the realm of language all the truly creative and productive violations of those rules" (Culler, *Structuralist Poetics* 241).

Poststructuralism calls into question assumptions made about literature by formalist, as well as by structuralist, critics. Formalism, or the New Criticism as it was once commonly called, assumes a work of literature to be a freestanding, self-contained object, its meanings found in the complex network of relations that constitute its parts (images, sounds, rhythms, allusions, and so on). To be sure, deconstruction is somewhat like formalism in several ways. Both the formalist and the deconstructor focus on the literary text; neither is likely to interpret a poem or a novel by relating it to events in the author's life, letters, historical period, or even culture. And formalists, long before deconstructors, discovered counterpatterns of meaning in the same text. Formalists find ambiguity and irony, deconstructors find contradiction and undecidability.

Here, though, the two groups part ways. Formalists believe a complete understanding of a literary work is possible, an understanding in which even the ambiguities will fulfill a definite, meaningful function. Poststructuralists confront the apparently limitless possibilities for the production of meaning that develop when the language of the critic enters the language of the text. They cannot accept the formalist view that a work of literary art has organic unity (therefore, structuralists would say, a "center"), if only we could find it.

Undecidability, as Paul de Man came to define it, is a complex notion easily misunderstood. There is a tendency to assume it refers to readers who, when forced to decide between two or more equally plausible and conflicting readings motivated by the same text, throw up their hands and decide that the choice can't be made. But undecidability in fact debunks this whole notion of reading as a decision-making process carried out on texts by readers. To say we are forced to choose or decide—or that we are unable to do so—is to locate the problem of undecidability falsely outside ourselves, and to make it reside within a text to which we come as another. The poststructuralist concept of undecidability, we might say, deconstructs the either/or distinction or opposition that structuralists and formalists have made between reader and text. It entails what de Man calls the "mutual obliteration" not only of propositions apparently opposed but also of the subject/object relation.

Poststructuralists break with formalists, too, over an issue they have debated with structuralists. The issue involves metaphor and metonymy, two terms for different kinds of rhetorical *tropes*, or figures of speech. *Metonymy* refers to a figure that is chosen to stand for something that it is commonly associated with, or with which it happens to be contiguous or juxtaposed. When said to a waitress, "I'll have the cold plate today" is a metonymic figure of speech for "I'll eat the cold food you're serving today." We refer to the food we want as a plate simply because plates are what food happens to be served on and because everyone understands that by *plate* we mean food. A *metaphor,* on the other hand, is a figure of speech that involves a special, intrinsic, nonarbitrary relationship with what it represents. When you say you are blue, if you believe that there is an intrinsic, timeless likeness between that color and melancholy feeling—a likeness that just doesn't exist between sadness and yellow—then you are using the word *blue* metaphorically.

Although both formalists and structuralists make much of the difference between metaphor and metonymy, Derrida, Miller and de Man have contended with the distinction deconstructively. They have questioned not only the distinction but also, and perhaps especially, the privilege we grant to metaphor, which we tend to view as the positive and superior figure of speech. De Man, in *Allegories of Reading* (1979), analyzes a passage from Proust's *Swann's Way,* arguing that it is about the nondistinction between metaphor and metonymy—and that it makes its claim metonymically. In *Fiction and Repetition: Seven English Novels* (1982), Miller connects the belief in metaphorical correspondences with other metaphysical beliefs, such as those in origins, endings, transcendence, and underlying truths. Isn't it likely, deconstructors keep implicitly asking, that every metaphor was once a metonym, but that we have simply forgotten what arbitrary juxtaposition or contiguity gave rise to the association that now seems mysteriously special?

The hypothesis that what we call metaphors are really old metonyms may perhaps be made clearer by the following example. We used the word *Watergate* as a metonym to refer to a political scandal that began in the Watergate building complex. Recently, we have used part of the building's name (*gate*) to refer to more recent scandals (*Irangate*). However, already there are people who use and "understand" these terms who are unaware that Watergate is the name of a building. In the future, isn't it possible that *gate,* which began as part of a simple metonym, will seem like the perfect metaphor for scandal — a word that suggests corruption and wrongdoing with a strange and inexplicable rightness?

This is how deconstruction works: by showing that what was prior and privileged in the old hierarchy (for instance, metaphor and speech) can just as easily seem secondary, the deconstructor causes the formerly privileged term to exchange properties with the formerly devalued one. Causes become effects and (d)evolutions become origins, but the result is neither the destruction of the old order or hierarchy nor the construction of a new one. It is, rather, *deconstruction*. In Robert Scholes's words, "If either cause or effect can occupy the position of an origin, then origin is no longer originary; it loses its metaphorical privilege" (88).

Once deconstructed, literal and figurative can exchange properties, so that the prioritizing between them is erased: all words, even dog and cat, are understood to be figures. It's just that we have used some of them so long that we have forgotten how arbitrary and metonymic they are. And, just as literal and figurative can exchange properties, criticism can exchange properties with literature, in the process coming to be seen not merely as a supplement — the second, negative, and inferior term in the binary opposition creative writing/literary criticism — but rather as an equally creative form of work. Would we write if there were not critics — intelligent readers motivated and able to make sense of what is written? Who, then, depends on whom?

"It is not difficult to see the attractions" of deconstructive reading, Jonathan Culler has commented. "Given that there is no ultimate or absolute justification for any system or for the interpretations from it," the critic is free to value "the activity of interpretation itself, . . . rather than any results which might be obtained" (*Structuralist Poetics* 248). Not everyone, however, has so readily seen the attractions of deconstruction. Two eminent critics, M. H. Abrams and Wayne Booth, have observed that a deconstructive reading "is plainly and simply parasitical" on what Abrams calls "the obvious or univocal meaning" (Abrams 457–58). In other words, there would be no deconstructors if critics did not already exist who can see and show central and definite meanings in texts. Miller responded in an essay entitled "The Critic as Host," in which he deconstructed not only the oppositional hierarchy (host/parasite) but also the two terms themselves, showing that each derives from two definitions meaning nearly opposite things. *Host* means "hospitable welcomer" and "military horde." *Parasite* originally had a positive connotation; in Greek, *parasitos* meant "beside the grain" and referred to a friendly guest. Finally, Miller suggests, the words *parasite* and *host* are inseparable, depending on one another for their meaning in a given work, much as do hosts and parasites, authors and critics, structuralists and poststructuralists.

In the essay that follows, Margot Norris discusses what, in her first paragraph, she calls the "deconstructive gesture" of *The House of Mirth*. For one thing, the text "unmask[s] the moral, social, and aesthetic order," showing it to be a set of contradictions. It reads the world, in other words, much as deconstructor would read a text, and in the process manages to call into question oppositions like text/world, fiction/fact.

At the same time, Norris argues, the novel deconstructs itself, undermining the very generic conventions that would seem to provide it with novelistic form and a means with which to expose the world as fiction or text. Wharton's realistic novel of manners is ultimately foiled by its own plot and "fails," finally, "as a reliable guide to social stability." It indicts itself through its sexual double standard wherein an innocent Lily (who in fact "recognizes, respects, and internalizes" the authority that causes her ruin) stands punished while a guilty Selden goes free, but is nonetheless allowed to judge her. The novel thus simultaneously "unmasks" reality, showing its solemnly held truths to be fictions, and recognizes "itself as an instrument for misunderstanding its own social foundation and function."

Recounting the myriad ways in which *The House of Mirth* is a novel of and about "speculation," Norris plays creatively with the root of the word, showing two of its derivatives (spectacles and speculum, or mirror) to be at once opposite and apt descriptions of the novel. Ultimately, her reading does what she says "a deconstructive reading of the novel" should do: it "replaces the notion that novels are mirrors of reality . . . with the notion that novels are mirrors of discourses or ways of speaking about reality that have acquired authority by concealing their inability to speak a 'truth' or represent an inherent 'meaning.' "

Of those discourses that, by Wharton's day, had acquired authority by effectively concealing their own representational weaknesses or failures, Norris discusses the scientific discourse first. Science, by the late nineteenth century, was not only a discourse *mirrored* by the novel, it was also—as Norris's deconstruction shows us—the novel's mirror. At the same time, however, the novel was looking at—and through—a wholly different discourse, the aesthetic discourse of the day, which said that art (and, by extension, the novel) should exist for its own sake and have no relationship to reality.

Each of these discourses is shown, by Wharton's reading of *The House of Mirth,* to be fraught with internal contradictions. At the same time, Norris's deconstruction *of* the novel shows how it is itself "implicated in the collapse of the discourses of science and art that are intended to invest the narration with their authority." As a result, we see that the novel "is without 'any real relation to life.'" We can see the artificiality of the text through the spectacles of Norris's analysis, because it shows us how the novel deconstructively mirrors, or critically speculates on, itself. From the "vantage point" of its scientific discourse, it is too much "an objet d'art, . . . a hermetically sealed room"; from that of its aesthetic discourse, it is sentimental naturalism, at once "vulgar and cheap." And from the vantage point of a novel at once reflecting and seeing through both discourses (in both senses of the phrase), it is a medium able only to see the truth of its own *inability* to see the truth in a world in which the discourse of business triumphs as science and art destroy one another. Science and art have, after all, served only to "mask the crass financial and social commerce at society's heart."

Typically deconstructive (though deconstructors would say nothing is typical) is Norris's tendency to view the world in terms of its discourses and to view texts not in terms of their unity or coherence but, rather, in terms of their internal oppositions. But it is also deconstructive in the way it plays with etymologies and shows "slippages" in the meanings of words. Introducing her discussion of two pivotal episodes in Lily Bart's life, one involving "her triumphant enactment of a painting . . . at the Wellington Brys' ball," the other "her subsequent misinterpretation by Lawrence Selden," Norris promises at once to "make use of" and "demonstrate" the metaphysical insight provided by deconstruction that allows it to offer a radically different conception of language and poetics. That is, that language is anchored to no intrinsic meaning and has no source, and that all language must be thought of as founded on an absence, rather than a presence, of meaning. For in one of these scenes, speculation means risky investment; in the other, it means risky conjecture. Meanwhile, in both—and *through* both— *The House of Mirth* shows us a world in which morality has been "bankrupted by duplicity and hypocrisy," a world in which signs and seemings are only appearances without "value or truth" as their "foundation[s]."

Ross C Murfin

DECONSTRUCTION: A SELECTED BIBLIOGRAPHY

Deconstruction, Postructuralism, and Structuralism: Introduction, Guides, and Surveys

Arac, Jonathan, Wlad Godzich, and Wallace Martin, eds. *The Yale Critics: Deconstruction in America*. Minneapolis: U of Minnesota P, 1983. See especially the essays of Bové, Godzich, Pease, and Corngold.

Berman, Art. *From the New Criticism to Deconstruction: The Reception of Structuralism and Post-Structuralism*. Urbana: U of Illinois P, 1988.

Cain, William E. "Deconstruction in America: The Recent Literary Criticism of J. Hillis Miller." *College English* 41 (1979): 367–82.

Culler, Jonathan. *On Deconstruction: Theory and Criticism After Structuralism*. Ithaca: Cornell UP, 1982.

———. *Structuralist Poetics: Structuralism, Linguistics and the Study of Literature*. Ithaca: Cornell UP, 1975. See especially ch. 10.

Gasché, Rodolphe. "Deconstruction as Criticism." *Glyph* 6 (1979): 177–215.

Jefferson, Ann. "Structuralism and Post Structuralism." *Modern Literary Theory: A Comparative Introduction*. Totowa, NJ: Barnes, 1982. 84–112.

Leitch, Vincent B. *Deconstructive Criticism: An Advanced Introduction and Survey*. New York: Columbia UP, 1983.

Lentricchia, Frank. *After the New Criticism*. Chicago: U of Chicago P, 1981.

Melville, Stephen W. *Philosophy Beside Itself: On Deconstruction and Modernism*. Theory and History of Literature 27. Minneapolis: U of Minnesota P, 1986.

Norris, Christopher. *Deconstruction and the Interests of Theory*. Oklahoma Project for Discourse and Theory 4. Norman: U of Oklahoma P, 1989.

———. *Deconstruction: Theory and Practice*. London: Methuen, 1982.

Raval, Suresh. *Metacriticism*. Athens: U of Georgia P, 1981.

Scholes, Robert. *Structuralism in Literature: An Introduction*. New Haven: Yale UP, 1974.

Sturrock, John. *Structuralism and Since*. Oxford; New York: Oxford UP, 1975.

Selected Works by Jacques Derrida and Paul de Man

de Man, Paul. *Allegories of Reading*. New Haven: Yale UP, 1979. See especially ch. 1 ("Semiology and Rhetoric").

———. *Blindness and Insight*. New York: Oxford UP, 1971. Minneapolis: U of Minnesota P, 1983. The 1983 edition contains important essays not included in the original edition.

———. *The Resistance to Theory*. Minneapolis: U of Minnesota P, 1986.

Derrida, Jacques. *Dissemination*. 1972. Trans. Barbara Johnson. Chicago: U of Chicago P, 1981. See especially the concise, incisive "Translator's Introduction," which provides a useful point of entry into this work and others by Derrida.

———. *Of Grammatology*. Trans. Gayatri C. Spivak. Baltimore: Johns Hopkins UP, 1976. Trans. of *De la Grammatologie*. 1967.

———. *The Postcard: From Socrates to Freud and Beyond*. Trans. with intro. Alan Bass. Chicago: U of Chicago P, 1987.

———. *Speech and Phenomena, and Other Essays on Husserl's Theory of Signs*. 1973. Trans. David B. Allison. Evanston: Northwestern UP, 1978.

———. *Writing and Difference*. 1967. Trans. Alan Bass. Chicago: U of Chicago P, 1978.

Essays in Deconstruction and Poststructuralism

Barthes, Roland. *S/Z*. Trans. Richard Miller. New York: Hill, 1974. In this influential work, Barthes turns from a structuralist to a poststructuralist approach.

Bloom, Harold, et al., eds. *Deconstruction and Criticism*. New York: Seabury, 1979. Includes essays by Bloom, de Man, Derrida, Miller, and Hartman.

Chase, Cynthia. *Decomposing Figures*. Baltimore: Johns Hopkins UP, 1986.

Harari, Josué, ed. *Textual Strategies: Perspectives in Post-Structuralist Criticism*. Ithaca: Cornell UP, 1979.

Johnson, Barbara. *The Critical Difference: Essays in the Contemporary Rhetoric of Reading*. Baltimore: Johns Hopkins UP, 1980.

———. *A World of Difference*. Baltimore: Johns Hopkins UP, 1987.

Krupnick, Mark, ed. *Displacement: Derrida and After*. Bloomington: Indiana UP, 1987.

Miller, J. Hillis. "Ariadne's Thread: Repetition and the Narrative Line." *Critical Inquiry* 3 (1976): 57–77.

————. Introduction. *Bleak House*. By Charles Dickens. Ed. Norman Page. Harmondsworth: Penguin, 1971. 11–34.

————. *The Ethics of Reading: Kant, de Man, Eliot, Trollope, James, and Benjamin*. New York: Columbia UP, 1987.

————. *Fiction and Repetition: Seven English Novels*. Cambridge: Harvard UP, 1982.

————. "*Heart of Darkness* Revisited." In *"Heart of Darkness": Case Studies in Contemporary Criticism*. Ed. Ross C Murfin. Boston: Bedford-St. Martin's, 1989. 209–24.

————. "Stevens' Rock and Criticism as Cure." *The Georgia Review* 30 (1976): 5–31, 330–48.

Ulmer, Gregory L. *Applied Grammatology*. Baltimore: Johns Hopkins UP, 1985.

**Other Work Referred to in
"What Is Deconstruction?"**

Abrams, M. H. "Rationality and the Imagination in Cultural History." *Critical Inquiry* 2 (1976): 447–64.

A DECONSTRUCTIONIST PERSPECTIVE

MARGOT NORRIS

Death by Speculation: Deconstructing
The House of Mirth

I

"She always roused speculation," (25) the first page of *The House of Mirth* tells us of Lily Bart, and by the last page we have come to understand that *speculation,* in its complex, shifting, and manifold meanings in the novel (Steiner 284) has killed her. Thematically all the various operations of plot and character that contribute to Lily's death — society's erroneous conjectures about her morality, her debts to gambling and to Gus Trenor's financial investments on her behalf, her unsuccessful speculation with her own beauty to secure a profitable match, her misjudgments of her own nature and the characters of other people, as well as her fatal miscalculation of the potency of chloral — function as forms of speculation that founder on a universe of arbitrary value, power, and meaning. This unmasking of a moral, social, and aesthetic order that might be thought of as an economy without a figurative gold standard to give it a stable, intrinsic ground or centered meaning, constitutes what we may call the deconstructive gesture of the novel. To explore this gesture, I will use the function of speculation in the text to demonstrate how *The House of Mirth* deconstructs itself generically as a novel of manners and as realism, by turning itself into a speculum, an instrument for dilating its own textual strategies and lethal speculations on women. In this way, the radical instabilities of the text's own interpretive positions may seem to double as Wharton's feminist project.

A deconstructive reading of this or any novel would consider in the first place *how* the text attempts to produce meaning, and would, secondly, uncover the inability of the novelistic genre's premises and presuppositions to contain or guarantee its meaning. In the case of *The House of Mirth,* such an aim is greatly abetted by the novel itself, as it turns a lens (spectacles) or mirror (speculum) on itself by questioning whether it can sustain the generic project its narrative texture (detailed attention to customs and social behavior) and plot (the social and moral consequences of sexual behavior) promise. Wharton's text pretends to exert the social control of a novel of manners and a novel of adultery — both genres appropriate to the late nineteenth century in which the novel is set — by enforcing social conformity and normative behavior through the expulsion of deviants. The plot alone, however, foils this object. Like the traditional heroine of an adultery novel, Lily Bart is punished and dies for transgressing society's mores, even though she has, in fact, preserved both virtue and virginity. The novel thus rotates about a generic perversity. It has misread and misapplied its own plot conventions, and failed as a reliable guide to social stability. Indeed, it is forced to recognize itself as an instrument for misunderstanding its own social foundation and function, and as the destroyer of its own ideological premises. In violating the rules and conventions that traditionally allow novels to create fictions about the conditions of social stability, *The House of Mirth* focuses attention specifically on how novels *use* the figure of woman as a carrier or code of value — that is, as a *sign.* Thus the novel, as a traditional genre, both *speculates about* woman, by conjecturing the nature of her social role and value, and *speculates with* woman, by using its construction and manipulation of her roles and values to produce certain social outcomes that will validate its authority. A deconstructive reading of the novel replaces the notion that novels are mirrors of reality (that, for example, *The House of Mirth* is best read as a history or chronicle of late-nineteenth-century New York society) with the notion that novels are mirrors of discourses or ways of speaking about reality that have acquired authority by concealing their inability to speak a "truth" or represent an inherent "meaning."

II

In *The House of Mirth,* the narrative voice and its surrogates quite openly betray their own historical discourses, which, not surprisingly for fin de siècle America, are the languages of business, science, and art. But the novel does not intend them, I believe, to be equal, and it is worthwhile to examine these discourses and their relative power separately, in order to track the internal intellectual dynamism of the novel. Science and art are seemingly put forward in their most modern, up-to-date, and ostensibly progressive guises in order to lend the novel's dominant point of view—which can readily be gendered male, at least at the outset—the twin authority of reason and sensibility, of rigorous objectivity and cultivated subjectivity. This double expertise and the confidence it inspires shapes Lawrence Selden's authority in judging Lily Bart—an authority that to her ruin she recognizes, respects, and internalizes. "She was moved by this sudden glimpse into the laboratory where his faiths were formed," the narration describes Lily's response to hearing Selden speak of "the republic of the spirit" (83). Selden views Lily Bart from the vantage points of science and art, as a naturalist and as a connoisseur, and these perspectives transform her into a specimen ("Was it possible that she belonged to the same race?") and an objet d'art ("as though a fine glaze of beauty and fastidiousness had been applied to vulgar clay" (27). But while she too sees him at times as a specimen— "like flies in a bottle, and having once flown in, could never again regain their freedom"—she endows him with an autonomy and agency that privileges his perspective, and makes her see herself through his eyes:

> It was Selden's distinction that he had never forgotten the way out. That was the secret of his way of readjusting her vision. Lily, turning her eyes from him, found herself scanning her little world through his retina. (70)

Selden, who is described as a man "who had renounced sentimental experiments" (82), does not refrain from conducting moral experiments on Lily Bart. His moral pressures upon her are shaped by his judgment, as naturalist and connoisseur, that she is a rare organism and a rare artifact. His insistence that she maintain the superiority of an absolutely *fine* spirit ultimately costs her her life, and costs the novel—given the moral disqualification produced by Selden's own adultery—its authority.

As the sources of Selden's authority, modern science and art shape the authority of the modern novel as well, and I believe it is the continental male tradition—as much or more than the nineteenth-century female traditions of novelistic writing (Showalter)—that *The House of Mirth* enacts and subverts in the discourses it deploys. After its utter transformation in the latter nineteenth century at the hands of Emile Zola and Gustave Flaubert, the modern novel assimilated the objectivity of science, its empirically descriptive and unsentimental gaze—troped, in the case of naturalism, as the examination of human life with a microscopic lens—to give its realism and naturalism the progressive cachet of a more modern way of recording reality. The novel was thus assimilated to the progressive ethos—a faith that science and technology would effect continuous linear improvement in social and cultural life—that accompanied the capitalistic expansions of the late nineteenth century. This same period saw the flowering of aestheticism in the arts, as art was no longer required to serve religion or morality, and was becoming autonomous—existing for its own sake, *l'art pour l'art*. Aestheticism, promoted in England by Oscar Wilde in literature and by the American James McNeill Whistler in painting (he titled the painting of his mother *Arrangement in Gray and Black*), severed art's relationship to nature and reality by concentrating on its pure formalism. "Art begins with abstract decoration, with purely imaginative and pleasurable work dealing with what is unreal and non-existent," Oscar Wilde wrote in the voice of one of his aesthetes. Art in the late nineteenth century was permitted to become exquisitely useless, and thus free to aspire to its own perfection as pure beauty—much like Lily Bart herself. Against attempts to place the novel within the F. R. Leavis "great tradition" of the novel, and its mandate of high moral seriousness (Dixon 217), *The House of Mirth* could be read as endowed with no moral message or meaning other than its celebration of its own beautifully crafted formal perfection.

But Wharton insures that these historical discourses of science and art directing the novel's philosophy collapse from their own internal contradictions, and reveal themselves to be governed by a hidden regime of economy (Dimock) that allows the discourse of business, in the end, to achieve a Pyrrhic philosophical victory. Before their collapse at the end of the novel, the discourses of science and aesthetics have become so thoroughly entwined—by using the naturalist's language to account for Lily's beauty—that they destroy each other. "In judging

Miss Bart," we are told of Selden in the opening pages of the novel, "he had always made use of 'the argument from design'" (27). The anachronistic folly of this pre-Darwinian theory, which held that the manifold adjustments of an organism to its environment were evidence of the guiding hand of the Creator, is of course amply elaborated and proven by the plot. The narration concedes its failure at the end of the novel, when it describes the limit of Lily's powers of adaptation ("an organism as helpless out of its narrow range as the sea-anemone torn from the rock" [281]) to refute her ability to sustain "the purely decorative mission"—that is, her explicitly aestheticist role—in life. "She had been fashioned to adorn and delight; to what other end does nature round the rose-leaf and paint the humming-bird's breast?" (281). But the novelistic plot stages a far more brutally Darwinian theory (Lewis 56–57) of natural selection and survival of the fittest, that makes it clear that Lily is not a natural organism at all but a horticultural artifact, "some rare flower grown for exhibition, a flower from which every bud had been nipped except the crowning blossom of her beauty" (295), unable to survive outside the hothouse element created by wealth—"Her whole being dilated in an atmosphere of luxury; it was the background she required, the only climate she could breathe in" (45). At novel's end, Lily's last philosophical vision of herself confirms that there has been neither Providence nor the wherewithal for survival in a world whose final natural tropes become those of the wasteland ("the feeling of being something rootless and ephemeral"), the deluge ("mere spin-drift of the whirling surface of existence, without anything to which the poor little tentacles of self could cling before the awful flood submerged them" [296]) and the entropy of chaos ("All the men and women she knew were like atoms whirling away from each other in some wild centrifugal dance" [297]). The only trope of fragile hope is her image of Nettie Struther's tattered family suspended above the abyss—"a bird's nest built on the edge of a cliff" (297).

The House of Mirth, as a novel, becomes implicated in the collapse of the discourses of science and art that are intended to invest the narration with their authority. If the novel of manners is thought to symbolize a society that feels itself to be secure, *The House of Mirth* demonstrates itself to possess the treacherous security of a hermetically sealed room—the stifling intellectual self-enclosure troped in the Gryce fortune made from "a patent device for excluding fresh air from hotels" (42) and doubled in its mirror of "the Gryce library in a fire-proof annex that looked like a mausoleum" (41). Indeed, the metaphor of the hermetically sealed room contains other figures of self-enclosure that reveal the novel's social life, culture, and art to share in Lily Bart's own final self-revelation, that "there had never been a time when she had had any real relation to life" (296). The novel of manners too is without "any real relation to life," since it mirrors the unnatural environment of the hot-house whose orchids depend upon the artificial separation of inside and outside, of culture and nature — of "society" as it has aesthetically constructed itself as an "inside," with the mass of workers necessary to maintain its aesthetics on its outside:

> She had always accepted with philosophic calm the fact that existences such as hers were pedestalled on foundations of obscure humanity. The dreary limbo of dinginess lay all around and beneath that little illuminated circle in which life reached its finest efflorescence, as the mud and sleet of a winter night enclose a hot-house filled with tropical flowers. (152)

The novel, of course, thematically ruptures this social self-enclosure, not only with invasions of the nouveaux riches, but when it thrusts Lily Bart to the mud and sleet outside to join the milliners, dressmakers, and charwomen who had once invisibly produced the *matériel* for her beauty. The novel formally ruptures its own aestheticist self-enclosure as well, when it breaks its formalistic restraint at novel's end to dabble in the sentimentality and naturalism of generic forms that, from the vantage of the novel of manners, appear vulgar and cheap. The sentimental heroism of Nellie Struthers is pure Dickens, and the shift in register is less a symptom of Wharton's aesthetic lapse than a deliberate contamination of her text with preaestheticist generic forms.

Like a speculum, *The House of Mirth* turns a mirror to its inside, and reveals itself too — as an objet d'art, a perfectly crafted and exquisite thing — to resemble a hermetically sealed room. Its mirror image becomes the library of country houses whose books are not intended to be read — "The library at Bellomont was in fact never used for reading" (73) — and, conversely, the library as "collection" of books valued as rare material commodities rather than for their intellectual contents: " 'I don't suppose the buyers of Americana sit up reading them all night — old Jefferson Gryce certainly did n't' " (32). Lily assimilates herself quite explicitly to this book "collection" in order to market herself to the connoisseur: "she determined to be to him what his Americana had hitherto been, the one possession in which he took sufficient pride to spend money on it" (65). She would be to Percy Gryce one of the exquisite volumes she finds in Selden's library, with "ripe tints of good tooling and old morocco" (31), valued for the rarity of its beauty without being read or understood—by anyone but Selden, the only reader of book and woman in the novel. Lily thus comes to stand for the novel of manners, including *The House of Mirth* itself, as an exquisite object whose interior is merely an exquisite exterior, and whose function is to produce the cachet of possession, to serve as object of pure intellectual acquisitiveness unburdened by understanding. When books in country houses *are* read, on occasion, they risk ripping apertures to horror inside the minds of their readers. "She had once picked up, in a house where she was staying, a translation of the *Eumenides*, and her imagination had been seized by the high terror of the scene where Orestes, in the cave of the oracle, finds his implacable huntresses asleep, and snatches an hour's repose" (150). Thus unread libraries may be figured as caves lined with sleeping tormentors that let one rest only if one does not rouse them from their shelves. One does not read books, *The House of Mirth* seems to be saying: books read us, and they may read us violently. Or rather books may read themselves. *The House of Mirth* reads its outside, its status as an aesthetic and intellectual commodity—its "femininity," we might call it, given how commodification is gendered in the novel—as its inside. The collapse of the authority of its historical discourses of science and art, and the triumph of economy and business, allow the novel to glimpse the *truth* of its inability to produce *truth* (Dixon), that becomes its specular insight into its own condition.

III

In order to trace in *The House of Mirth* the underlying slippages of meaning along the hidden etymological track of seeing and observation—the way speculation and the spectacular rotate around an axis of interpretation based on exteriority and its observation—it may be helpful to look closely at the central pivotal episodes (chapters XII and XIII) that mark the plot's peripeteia and Lily's reversal of fortune. This exercise will simultaneously make use of, and demonstrate, the metaphysical insight provided by deconstruction that allows it to offer a radically different conception of language and poetics: namely, that language is anchored to no intrinsic meaning and has no source, and that all language must be thought of as founded on an absence, rather than a presence, of meaning. In consequence, language itself is necessarily figurative and poetic. In examining the pivotal episodes of Lily's tableau vivant and its effects, her triumphant enactment of a painting by Sir Joshua Reynolds at the Wellington Brys's ball and her subsequent misinterpretation by Lawrence Selden, the absence of an origin or ground in language may be figured as an insight into the doubleness or repetition or secondary condition (a secondary condition without a primary) of art's ability to *re*-present, but not *present*. The text's presentation of these pivotal episodes of Lily's life marks its own *re*-presentational necessity with a conspicuous repetition: it narrates the same incidents twice, giving us two accounts, two perspectives, two interpretations—Lily's and Selden's, woman's and man's, the private and the public, one inside the house and one outside—of Lily's triumph and fall. The novel thus stages its tragedy as a staged tragedy, transforming its implied "author" into a puppeteer, perhaps one of the "battered wire-pullers like Mrs. Fisher" (94). In pointing to itself as tragedy, Wharton's text signals its own complicity with the use and abuse of the "classic" by the very society the novel critiques.

The doubly narrated events at the turning point of the novel overlap two forms of speculation—speculation as risky investment and speculation as risky conjecture—that have in common an intense preoccupation and confusion about the relationship between inner and outer, the essential and the representational that, in both cases, is figured as art. The Wellington Brys's ball is itself a speculative venture, a great risk or gamble mounted in the interest of catapulting them (to preserve the military jargon stimulated by their eponym) into social acceptance— "To attack society collectively, when one's means of approach are limited to a few acquaintances, is like advancing into a strange country with an insufficient number of scouts; but such rash tactics have sometimes led to brilliant victories" (135). Their stratagem is art, the tableaux vivants in which Lily triumphs, and the episode is concluded when Van Alstyne and Selden see Lily Bart leaving Gus Trenor's empty house and risk the dangerous conjecture that she is guilty of the colossal impropriety imputed to her: that she accepts money from a married man in return for her favors. Both spectacles, the Wellington Brys's ball and the scene witnessed by Van Alstyne and Selden, are troped in the figures of art, architecture, theater, and other forms of representation, to focus the issue on the problematical nature of what is true, genuine, original, valuable, real, and its impossible interpretation.

Selden attends the Wellington Brys's ball precisely for the artificiality of the art it offers—"he enjoyed spectacular effects, and was not insensible to the part money plays in their production: all he asked was that the very rich should live up to their calling as stage-managers, and not spend their money in a dull way" (136). But this notion of the rich as stage-managers of spectacles, and their homes as theatrical spaces, challenges the implicitly held belief that social ascendance has an intrinsic origin or source: "blood" and ancestry, a hermetically sealed "inside" that grounds social value in the innermost genetic life of the body. A volatile social mobility ("the Vanderbilts had married all over the lot, and even the Goulds were almost respectable," Louis Auchincloss wrote in the Afterword to the 1964 edition of the book) was produced by capitalistic speculation in late-nineteenth-century America — for example, Jay Gould's dangerous speculations with gold that caused the panic of "Black Friday" in 1869. Wharton's novel argues that in the absence of the innate taste guaranteed by family and breeding, the taste of the nouveaux riches was exteriorized by explicit allusions to classical art — or, rather, varieties of neoclassical art, the art of the Renaissance or the eighteenth century — in houses and their furnishings. The Wellington Brys's house is described as "as well-designed for the display of a festal assemblage as one of those airy pleasure-halls which the Italian architects improvised to set off the hospitality of princes" (136) and its ceiling, Gerty Farish is told, is "by Veronese" (137). Ned Van Alstyne makes the motive behind the Brys's house design explicit: "the desire to imply that one has been to Europe, and has a standard. I 'm sure Mrs. Bry thinks her house a copy of the *Trianon*" (161). Art as representation of taste takes the place of the missing origin in blood and breeding.

The Wellington Brys's ball becomes a *mise en abyme,* or infinite regress of representation without a fixed origin or point of value. The offer of joyous entertainment transforms their house into a self-contradictory "house of mirth" — self-contradictory because its mirth is without spontaneity, its merry entertainment an imitation of earlier houses of mirth: the aristocratic great houses of the eighteenth century with their tableaux vivants, celebrated in such neoclassical novels as Goethe's *Elective Affinities.* The Brys's own neoclassicism is a re-version of neoclassicisms: a modern imitation of eighteenth century imitations of Renaissance classicisms. Lily Bart ultimately represents a tableau vivant of a tableau vivant, for Sir Joshua Reynolds's *Mrs. Lloyd* is not a portrait of a lady but a portrait of a lady impersonating a classical dryad. [See the portrait on p. 440.] In the phase of his career that Ellis Waterhouse calls his "unfortunate portrait style," Sir Joshua Reynolds painted aristocratic women as classical figures:

> the Duchess of Manchester as "Diana" removing a bow from her infant son as "Cupid" (taken from Albano); Lady Blake as Juno receiving the cestus from Venus (from a Roman statue); two ladies moralizing at a tomb inscribed "Et ego in Arcadia" (a fancy from Guernico); and an exercise in the manner of Correggio with the title of "Hope nursing Love." (227)

Sir Joshua Reynolds, *Mrs. Lloyd*. 1775.

This style was inspired by his study of the classical subjects of the Italian Renaissance. Reynolds's portraits are not of real women but of real women as figures of other paintings: that is, portraits of representations of representations. The narrative voice is therefore utterly ironic in describing Lily's tableau of Reynolds's *Mrs. Lloyd* as "when the curtain suddenly parted on a picture which was simply and undisguisedly the portrait of Miss Bart" (138). These words imply that the scene possesses great realism, and that, as Gerty Farish observes, "It makes her look like the real Lily" (139). But the deeper implication is that the tableau's "realism" derives from the fact that Lily never looks like a "real" woman at all, that she always looks like a portrait of a woman, an idealized and aesthetically interpreted version of what a "real" beautiful woman looks like, a representation of herself rather than herself. Indeed, Lily Bart has impersonated Mrs. Lloyd once before, when, leaning against the mantle in Selden's drawing room at the novel's beginning, she assumes the attitude of Mrs. Lloyd's dryad: "The attitude revealed the long slope of her slender sides, which gave a kind of wild-wood grace to her outline — as though she were a captured dryad subdued to the conventions of the drawing-room" (34). Selden's response to Lily's tableau — "for the first time he seemed to see before him the real Lily Bart" (139) — is therefore doubly ironic, because he sees before him the same artificial picture he saw earlier in his drawing room, of Lily as drawing-room dryad, whose model is *Mrs. Lloyd*, with "the long dryad-like curves that swept upward from her poised foot to her lifted arm" (139). The irony is further deepened when we realize that the classical scene Mrs. Lloyd impersonates — Angelica, from Ariosto's *Orlando*, carving the name of her lover into a tree (Steiner 293) — mirrors Bertha Dorset, Selden's previous lover, writing the love letters that have, already, fallen into Lily's hands. When we learn of Selden that "before the curtain fell, he had time to feel the whole tragedy of her life" (139), one is prodded to wonder if Selden is not merely imposing one Reynolds on another in his perception of Lily's tableau — perhaps Reynolds's *Sarah Siddons as the Tragic Muse.*

The narrative itself remarks that the theatricality of the Wellington Brys's house of mirth makes it difficult to retrieve any reality from marble that appears *faux* and chairs that look like trompe l'oeil — "so rapidly-evoked was the whole *mise-en-scène* that one had to touch the marble columns to learn they were not of cardboard, to seat one's self in one of the damask-and-gold arm-chairs to be sure it was not painted against the wall" (136). When reality is retrieved from the tableaux vivants, therefore, it produces a shock that derives from recognizing that the "real" and the "living" are retrievable only as a negation or an absence. Lily's ability to draw attention to her "flesh and blood loveliness," her living beauty rather than the beauty of her artifice, is described precisely in terms of its opposite, as her ability to impersonate the representation of Mrs. Lloyd: "It was as though she had stepped, not out of, but into, Reynolds's canvas, banishing the phantom of his dead beauty by the beams of her living grace" (138–39). Mrs. Lloyd is dead, a phantom who exists in the painting only as the present absence of a re-presentation. But the narrative statement is self-reflexive, as we are sharply reminded that at the moment of telling, Lily Bart, too, is a dead beauty (though we learn of her death only at novel's end) and the vivid portrait of her tableau vivant only a specular and refracted re-presentation. Indeed, *The House of Mirth* as novel might be construed as a mausoleum of dead beauties that can be made to live only in the representations of their representations. Males, for that matter, are not exempt: Percy Gryce is described as looking like "a clever pupil's drawing from a plaster-cast" (64).

The dead beauties in *The House of Mirth* owe their continued existence to art, and specifically to the permanence of literature and its inscribed representation of painting as opposed to the ephemeral and perishable nature of the tableau vivant. This memorializing of beauty in the art of portraiture is doubly inflected by wealth and class. The tableau vivant is such an expensive and wasteful form of art — consuming tremendous resources for a totally transitory and perishable effect — that it marks the surplus and excess wealth of its producers. But the society portrait produced by the English classical painters of the eighteenth century is likewise a mark of conspicuous consumption, as Rosedale makes quite explicit: "My God, Mrs. Fisher, if I could get Paul Morpeth to paint her like that, the picture 'd appreciate a hundred per cent in ten years" (159). New York society's anti-Semitism toward Rosedale (Mac-Dowell 24–26) contains a hidden self-reflexive specularity: Rosedale exteriorizes both the money-making and the semiology of value ("He had his race's accuracy in the appraisal of values" [36]) that makes the social prerogatives of taste and breeding possible — but whose operations must be hidden and disavowed to preserve their aesthetic effects. Rosedale's innocence in articulating the repressed truth of New York society's desires and values turns him into the mirror of its own unaestheticized heart. What must be added to the money, in order to transform it into symbolic social value, is precisely the surplus or excess of art in its own most profitable and transactionable form — as classic. Lily would have added the necessary art to Rosedale's money ("to be seen walking . . . in the company of Miss Lily Bart would have been money in his pocket, as he might himself have phrased it" [36]), would have masked, and taught him to mask, its operation. This is the function of the novel's classical intertextuality, then: to reveal classical art as a detachable and reattachable semiological marker of cultural superiority to mask the crass financial and social commerce of society's heart.

"Deuced bold thing to show herself in that get-up; but gad, there is n't a break in the lines anywhere," (139) Ned Van Alstyne comments on Lily's appearance—thereby himself breaking the classical lines of Lawrence Selden's aesthetic meditation on Lily's tableau. Just as Lily's body breaks out of the classical draperies that shroud her and thrusts the reality of her living contours—that she is a woman and not a painting—into the consciousness of the men, so does the narrative break its aesthetic line with the utterance of the libidinal perception of the male connoisseurs who see her. The paradigm remains classical—Pygmalion and Galatea, the sculptor who falls in love with his beautiful statue—but the response is philistine: men seeing veiled nakedness in classicism's veiled nudity. "I never knew till tonight what an outline Lily has," Ned Van Alstyne confesses, and from art the scandal of a repressed interiority whose eruption would scandalize art lovers ("Damned bad taste, I call it" [142] Trenor curses) breaks the lines of the text. Selden separates himself from the philistines precisely by clinging to the classical intertexts he put in place at the ball, when he transformed the Brys's conservatory into the set of Shakespeare's *A Midsummer Night's Dream,* and rebuffed the men's insinuations with a sense of cultural superiority troped in *The Tempest*—"Does one go to Caliban for a judgment on Miranda?" (139). But his allusion to *The Tempest*—Shakespeare's colonial allegory, as it is often read—conceals truths that Selden represses and that the text itself insists on placing in the foreground. At Carry Fisher's dinner the night after the ball, there is plantation music, and Jack Stepney evokes Lily's tableau in the very different image of the slave on the auction block, "Really, you know, I 'm no prude, but when it comes to a girl standing there as if she was up at auction" (158). Only Selden ignores these persistent colonial metaphors of Lily's political reality, the veiled homology of Lily's auctioning her beauty on the marriage market, to pornography, prostitution, and slavery—"the links of her bracelet seemed like manacles chaining her to her fate" (29). When Selden revisits them with thoughts of rescuing Lily and taking her to the *Beyond!* of her seal that might unseal her fate, he returns to the classical trope, "He knew that Perseus's task is not done when he has loosed Andromeda's chains" (159). The trope turns up, like many of Selden's values, in an internalized form in Lily's self-estimation — "She seemed a stranger to herself, or rather there were two selves in her, the one she had always known, and a new abhorrent being to which it found itself chained" (150).

The perceptual structures that shape the plot of the novel's climax — the refractive optics of outer and inner seeing, spectacle and speculum — govern the reader's speculative interpretations throughout the dénouement and novel's end. The novel gives two consecutive versions of what happens at the Trenor house the day after the Wellington Brys's ball — an interior and an exterior, executed as witness inside and outside the house — that succeed in destroying Selden's moral authority, and with it, the solidity or locatability of the reader's own moral locus. The novel first makes us privy to the shock of Lily's *anagnorisis* — her recognition that her financial dependence on Trenor has compromised her sufficiently to make her vulnerable to his threatened rape — by sliding us along the transition from the imitation high art of the Brys's tableaux to the imitation low art of Carry Fisher's plantation music, to the raw melodrama ("You must pay the rent!" — "but I tell you what, Miss Lily, you 've got to pay up for making me think so" [149]) of the Trenors's domestic sanctum. While this scene transpires, Ned Van Alstyne is explicating the Trenor house to Selden as though he were an art historian offering a slide show — " 'Now for the Trenors, you remember, he chose the Corinthian: exuberant, but based on the best precedent.' . . . The walking-stick which Van Alstyne swung in demonstration dropped to a startled 'Hallo!' as the door opened and two figures were seen silhouetted against the hall-light" (161). The narration itself introduces the trope of the stereopticon, the double magic lantern that combines two images of the same scene upon a screen in order to create a single image with the solidity of a three-dimensional figure, to describe what Van Alstyne and Selden think they see. Selden, who had been harboring a contradictory image of Lily ("He was no less conscious than before of what was said of Lily Bart, but he could separate the woman he knew from the vulgar estimate of her" [155]) now merges his double vision with Van Alstyne's to create the consensus of a single solid figure of a fallen Lily. The compact of their consolidated perception is sealed rhetorically with an antinomous compact, their agreement — when they have never had such absolute faith in their eyes — to keep silent about what they saw because "appearances are deceptive" (161).

This scene at the Trenor house — whose cost remains private and confined to Selden's lost respect — is reenacted publicly, in a highly dramatic scene, some months later when Bertha Dorset impugns Lily's virtue by forbidding her return to the yacht in the harbor of Monte Carlo. The scene's moral structure—the false imputation of adultery to Lily—is identical to the Trenor house scene, but the damage of an implicit accusation delivered before Selden, an assortment of *haute monde* guests, and the gossip reporter for *Society Notes from the Riviera,* is fatal. The scene is the outcome of a thoroughgoing theatricalization of social transgression, as the Dorsets's yacht becomes the mise en scène of a transparent charade by which Bertha panders Lily to her husband in order to mask her own affair with Ned Silverton. But the narrative fails to give the dramatic moment of accusation its full moral due when it refuses to foreground and underline the grossly apparent double standard of its own gender mores that the novel's redoubling of earlier scenarios makes explicit. Bertha Dorset has contrived to use an "innocent" affair to front a guilty one, and it was Lawrence Selden, Lily's judge throughout the novel ("you had judged me—I understood" [287]), who stood precisely in Ned Silverton's adulterous place only a year or so earlier. Indeed, the text underlines the consistency of Bertha Dorset's taste in men, as Neddy Silverton, spouting Verlaine and Theocritus, is shown to be a would-be poet-scholar not unlike the bookish and allusive Lawrence Selden himself. The novel's plot has all along retrieved the "fact" of Selden's adultery from conjecture and speculation by investing it not in the deceptive and manipulable scenario of a spectacle—like Lily's alleged scandals—but by sealing it instead in the interiority of speech and folding it into the envelopes of Bertha Dorset's love letters to Selden, which fall into Lily's hands; "the words, scrawled in heavy ink on pale-tinted note-paper, smote on Lily's ear as though she had heard them spoken" (112). It takes both sexes to commit adultery, and by pairing man and woman as true and false adulterous doubles—a guilty Selden allowed to deliver moral judgments upon Lily's dead body, an innocent Lily murdered by the plot for an adultery she did not commit, Wharton's *House of Mirth* indicts itself, and its own adherence to the forms of the adultery novel, for having murdered a woman twice, thematically and rhetorically.

Lily dies without justice, for justice would have demanded not only that Selden see the beam in his own eye but that the novel, standing in for her hypocritical society, of which Lily thinks "it is for having betrayed its connivance that the body social punishes the offender who is found out" (113), see it too. The novel's gesture in repeating Lily's own refusal to use the letters to expose Selden as her true adulterous double is therefore problematized in the same way: not as a heroic self-sacrificing act that entitled the novel to assume a tragic posture, to become a "tragic novel," but as a doubling of the woman's own internalizing and naturalizing of a vicious and murderous double standard. The novel's final grotesque self-righteousness—letting us "forgive" a tragic Lily for an imaginary crime because she has protected a sexual double standard with her life—repeats Selden's own hypocrisy. Selden's utter innocence of the irony of his own judgmentalisms is borrowed from what was surely one of his own classics: Hamlet leaping histrionically into Ophelia's grave to declare his love while conveniently forgetting that he killed her with tormenting and unjust imputations and accusations. The novel, too, leaps into the graves of the dead beauties of the nineteenth-century adultery novel tradition to celebrate their tragedy—but at least it theatricalizes its own gesture and catches it in the feminist speculum. Its authoritative narrative discourses neutralized, its plot theatricalized as a *mise en abyme* of representation, its social "world" collapsed onto an empty stage, and its "morality" bankrupted by duplicity and hypocrisy, *The House of Mirth* has exposed the absence of value or truth as its foundation. The final posthumous communication it promises—through an exchange of a mysterious, transcendent "word" (Dixon) that will give the "tragedy" meaning—offers not the gold standard of "love" but merely the counterfeit of a wooden nickel.

Works Cited

Auchincloss, Louis. Afterword. *The House of Mirth*. New York: New American Library, 1964. 344–49.

Dimock, Wai-chee. "Debasing Exchange: Edith Wharton's *The House of Mirth*. In *Modern Critical Views: Edith Wharton*. Ed. Harold Bloom. New York: Chelsea House, 1986. 123–37. [Dimock's essay is also reprinted in this volume on pp. 375–90.]

Dixon, Roslyn. "Reflecting Vision in *The House of Mirth*." *Twentieth Century Literature* 33 (Summer 1987): 211–22.

Lewis, R. W. B. *Edith Wharton: A Biography*. New York: Harper, 1975.

McDowell, Margaret B. *Edith Wharton*. Boston: Twayne Publishers, 1991.

Showalter, Elaine. "The Death of a Lady (Novelist): Wharton's *House of Mirth*." In *Modern Critical Views: Edith Wharton*. Ed. Harold Bloom. New York: Chelsea House, 1986.

Steiner, Wendy. "The Causes of Effect: Edith Wharton and the Economics of Ekphrasis." *Poetics Today* 10 (Summer 1989): 279–97.

Waterhouse, Ellis. *Painting in Britain 1530–1790*. New York: Viking Penguin, 1988.

Psychoanalytic Criticism
and
The House of Mirth

WHAT IS PSYCHOANALYTIC CRITICISM?

It seems natural to think about novels in terms of dreams. Like dreams, novels are fictions, inventions of the mind that, although based on reality, are by definition not literally true. Like a novel, a dream may have some truth to tell, but, like a novel, it may need to be interpreted before that truth can be grasped. Many novels contain dreams and reveal important aspects of character through dreams.

There are other reasons why it seems natural to make an analogy between dreams and novels. We can live vicariously through romantic fictions, much as we can through daydreams. Terrifying novels and nightmares affect us in much the same way, plunging us into an atmosphere that continues to cling, even after the last chapter has been read — or the alarm clock has sounded. Thus it is not surprising to hear someone say in class that Mary Shelley's *Frankenstein* is a nightmarish tale. Nor are we likely to be surprised by the claim of Frederick Karl, Joseph Conrad's biographer, that *Heart of Darkness* is characterized by the same kind of distortion, condensation, and displacement that Sigmund Freud described in his *Interpretation of Dreams* (1900).

Karl, who invokes Conrad's text and psychoanalytic theory in the same breath, is a Freudian literary critic. But what about the reader who simply compares *Frankenstein* to a nightmare, or Emily Brontë's *Wuthering Heights* to a dream? Is such a reader a Freudian as well? Is he or she, too, a psychoanalytic critic?

To some extent the answer to both questions has to be yes. We are all Freudians, really, whether or not we have read a single work by the famous Austrian psychoanalyst. At one time or another, most of us have referred to ego, libido, complexes, unconscious desires, and sexual repression. The premises of Freud's thought have changed the way the Western world thinks about itself. Psychoanalytic criticism has influenced the teachers our teachers studied with, the works of scholarship and criticism they read, and the critical and creative writers *we* read as well.

What Freud did was develop a language that described, a model that explained, a theory that encompassed human psychology. Many of the elements of psychology he sought to describe and explain are present in the literary works of various ages and cultures, from Sophocles' *Oedipus Rex* to Shakespeare's *Hamlet* to works being written in our own day. When the great novel of the twenty-first century is written, many of these same elements of psychology will probably inform its discourse as well. If, by understanding human psychology according to Freud, we can appreciate literature on a new level, then we should acquaint ourselves with his insights.

Freud's theories are either directly or indirectly concerned with the nature of the unconscious mind. Freud didn't invent the notion of the unconscious; others before him had suggested that even the supposedly "sane" human mind was conscious and rational only at times, and even then at possibly only one level. But Freud went further, suggesting that the powers motivating men and women are *mainly* and *normally* unconscious.

Freud, then, powerfully developed an old idea: that the human mind is essentially dual in nature. He called the predominantly passional, irrational, unknown, and unconscious part of the psyche the *id*, or "it." The *ego*, or "I," was his term for the predominantly rational, logical, orderly, conscious part. Another aspect of the psyche, which he called the *superego*, is really a projection of the ego. The superego almost seems to be outside of the self, making moral judgments, telling us to make sacrifices for good causes even though self-sacrifice may not be quite logical or rational. And, in a sense, the superego *is* "outside," since much of what it tells us to do or think we have learned from our parents, our schools, or our religious institutions.

What the ego and superego tell us *not* to do or think is repressed, forced into the unconscious mind. One of Freud's most important contributions to the study of the psyche, the theory of repression, goes something like this: much of what lies in the unconscious mind has been put there by consciousness, which acts as a censor, driving underground unconscious or conscious thoughts or instincts that it deems unacceptable. Censored materials often involve infantile sexual desires, Freud postulated. Repressed to an unconscious state, they emerge only in disguised forms: in dreams, in language (so-called Freudian slips), in creative activity that may produce art (including literature), and in neurotic behavior.

According to Freud, all of us have repressed wishes and fears; we all have dreams in which repressed feelings and memories emerge disguised, and thus we are all potential candidates for dream analysis. One of the unconscious desires most commonly repressed is the childhood wish to displace the parent of our own sex and take his or her place in the affections of the parent of the opposite sex. This desire really involves a number of different but related wishes and fears. (A boy — and it should be remarked in passing that Freud here concerns himself mainly with the male — may fear that his father will castrate him, and he may wish that his mother would return to nursing him.) Freud referred to the whole complex of feelings by the word "oedipal," naming the complex after the Greek tragic hero Oedipus, who unwittingly killed his father and married his mother.

Why are oedipal wishes and fears repressed by the conscious side of the mind? And what happens to them after they have been censored? As Roy P. Basler puts it in *Sex, Symbolism, and Psychology in Literature* (1975), "from the beginning of recorded history such wishes have been restrained by the most powerful religious and social taboos, and as a result have come to be regarded as 'unnatural,'" even though "Freud found that such wishes are more or less characteristic of normal human development":

> In dreams, particularly, Freud found ample evidence that such wishes persisted. . . . Hence he conceived that natural urges, when identified as "wrong," may be repressed but not obliterated. . . . In the unconscious, these urges take on symbolic garb, regarded as nonsense by the waking mind that does not recognize their significance. (14)

Freud's belief in the significance of dreams, of course, was no more original than his belief that there is an unconscious side to the psyche.

Again, it was the extent to which he developed a theory of how dreams work—and the extent to which that theory helped him, by analogy, to understand far more than just dreams—that made him unusual, important, and influential beyond the perimeters of medical schools and psychiatrists' offices.

The psychoanalytic approach to literature not only rests on the theories of Freud; it may even be said to have *begun* with Freud, who was interested in writers, especially those who relied heavily on symbols. Such writers regularly cloak or mystify ideas in figures that make sense only when interpreted, much as the unconscious mind of a neurotic disguises secret thoughts in dream stories or bizarre actions that need to be interpreted by an analyst. Freud's interest in literary artists led him to make some unfortunate generalizations about creativity; for example, in the twenty-third lecture in *Introductory Lectures on Psycho-Analysis* (1922), he defined the artist as "one urged on by instinctive needs that are too clamorous" (314). But is also led him to write creative literary criticism of his own, including an influential essay on "The Relation of a Poet to Daydreaming" (1908) and "The Uncanny" (1919), a provocative psychoanalytic reading of E. T. A. Hoffmann's supernatural tale "The Sandman."

Freud's application of psychoanalytic theory to literature quickly caught on. In 1909, only a year after Freud had published "The Relation of a Poet to Daydreaming," the psychoanalyst Otto Rank published *The Myth of the Birth of the Hero*. In that work, Rank subscribes to the notion that the artist turns a powerful, secret wish into a literary fantasy, and he uses Freud's notion about the "oedipal" complex to explain why the popular stories of so many heroes in literature are so similar. A year after Rank had published his psychoanalytic account of heroic texts, Ernest Jones, Freud's student and eventual biographer, turned his attention to a tragic text: Shakespeare's *Hamlet.* In an essay first published in the *American Journal of Psychology,* Jones, like Rank, makes use of the oedipal concept: he suggests that Hamlet is a victim of strong feelings toward his mother, the queen.

Between 1909 and 1949 numerous other critics decided that psychological and psychoanalytic theory could assist in the understanding of literature. I. A. Richards, Kenneth Burke, and Edmund Wilson were among the most influential to become interested in the new approach. Not all of the early critics were committed to the approach; neither were all of them Freudians. Some followed Alfred Adler, who believed that writers wrote out of inferiority complexes, and others applied the ideas of Carl Gustav Jung, who had broken with Freud over Freud's emphasis on sex and who had developed a theory of the *collective* unconscious. According to Jungian theory, a great work of literature is not a disguised expression of its author's personal, repressed wishes; rather, it is a manifestation of desires once held by the whole human race but now repressed because of the advent of civilization.

It is important to point out that among those who relied on Freud's models were a number of critics who were poets and novelists as well. Conrad Aiken wrote a Freudian study of American literature, and poets such as Robert Graves and W. H. Auden applied Freudian insights when writing critical prose. William Faulkner, Henry James, James Joyce, D. H. Lawrence, Marcel Proust, and Toni Morrison are only a few of the novelists who have either written criticism influenced by Freud or who have written novels that conceive of character, conflict, and creative writing itself in Freudian terms. The poet H. D. (Hilda Doolittle) was actually a patient of Freud's and provided an account of her analysis in her book *Tribute to Freud*. By giving Freudian theory credibility among students of literature that only they could bestow, such writers helped to endow psychoanalytic criticism with the largely Freudian orientation that, one could argue, it still exhibits today.

The willingness, even eagerness, of writers to use Freudian models in producing literature and criticism of their own consummated a relationship that, to Freud and other pioneering psychoanalytic theorists, had seemed fated from the beginning; after all, therapy involves the close analysis of language. René Wellek and Austin Warren included "psychological" criticism as one of the five "extrinsic" approaches to literature described in their influential book, *Theory of Literature* (1942). Psychological criticism, they suggest, typically attempts to do at least one of the following: provide a psychological study of an individual writer; explore the nature of the creative process; generalize about "types and laws present within works of literature"; or theorize about the psychological "effects of literature upon its readers" (81). Entire books on psychoanalytic criticism even began to appear, such as Frederick J. Hoffman's *Freudianism and the Literary Mind* (1945).

Probably because of Freud's characterization of the creative mind as "clamorous" if not ill, psychoanalytic criticism written before 1950 tended to psychoanalyze the individual author. Poems were read as fantasies that allowed authors to indulge repressed wishes, to protect themselves from deep-seated anxieties, or both. A perfect example of author analysis would be Marie Bonaparte's 1933 study of Edgar Allan Poe. Bonaparte found Poe to be so fixated on his mother that his repressed longing emerges in his stories in images such as the white spot on a black cat's breast, said to represent mother's milk.

A later generation of psychoanalytic critics often paused to analyze the characters in novels and plays before proceeding to their authors. But not for long, since characters, both evil and good, tended to be seen by these critics as the author's potential selves, or projections of various repressed aspects of his or her psyche. For instance, in *A Psychoanalytic Study of the Double in Literature* (1970), Robert Rogers begins with the view that human beings are double or multiple in nature. Using this assumption, along with the psychoanalytic concept of "dissociation" (best known by its result, the dual or multiple personality), Rogers concludes that writers reveal instinctual or repressed selves in their books, often without realizing that they have done so.

In the view of critics attempting to arrive at more psychological insights into an author than biographical materials can provide, a work of literature is a fantasy or a dream — or at least so analogous to daydream or dream that Freudian analysis can help explain the nature of the mind that produced it. The author's purpose in writing is to gratify secretly some forbidden wish, in particular an infantile wish or desire that has been repressed into the unconscious mind. To discover what the wish is, the psychoanalytic critic employs many of the terms and procedures developed by Freud to analyze dreams.

The literal surface of a work is sometimes spoken of as its "manifest content" and treated as a "manifest dream" or "dream story" would be treated by a Freudian analyst. Just as the analyst tries to figure out the "dream thought" behind the dream story — that is, the latent or hidden content of the manifest dream — so the psychoanalytic literary critic tries to expose the latent, underlying content of a work. Freud used the words *condensation* and *displacement* to explain two of the mental processes whereby the mind disguises its wishes and fears in dream stories. In condensation several thoughts or persons may be condensed into a single manifestation or image in a dream story; in displacement, an anxiety, a wish, or a person may be displaced onto the image of another, with which or whom it is loosely connected through a string of associations that only an analyst can untangle. Psychoanalytic critics treat metaphors as if they were dream condensations; they treat metonyms — figures of speech based on extremely loose, arbitrary associations — as if they were dream displacements. Thus figurative literary language in general is treated as something that evolves as the writer's conscious mind resists what the unconscious tells it to picture or describe.

A symbol is, in Daniel Weiss's words, "a meaningful concealment of truth as the truth promises to emerge as some frightening or forbidden idea" (20).

In a 1970 article entitled "The 'Unconscious' of Literature," Norman Holland, a literary critic trained in psychoanalysis, succinctly sums up the attitudes held by critics who would psychoanalyze authors, but without quite saying that it is the *author* that is being analyzed by the psychoanalytic critic. "When one looks at a poem psychoanalytically," he writes, "one considers it as though it were a dream or as though some ideal patient [were speaking] from the couch in iambic pentameter." One "looks for the general level or levels of fantasy associated with the language. By level I mean the familiar stages of childhood development—oral [when desires for nourishment and infantile sexual desires overlap], anal [when infants receive their primary pleasure from defecation], urethral [when urinary functions are the locus of sexual pleasure], phallic [when the penis or, in girls, some penis substitute is of primary interest], oedipal." Holland continues by analyzing not Robert Frost but Frost's poem "Mending Wall" as a specifically oral fantasy that is not unique to its author. "Mending Wall" is "about breaking down the wall which marks the separated or individuated self so as to return to a state of closeness to some Other"—including and perhaps essentially the nursing mother ("Unconscious" 136, 139).

While not denying the idea that the unconscious plays a role in creativity, psychoanalytic critics such as Holland began to focus more on the ways in which authors create works that appeal to *our* repressed wishes and fancies. Consequently, they shifted their focus away from the psyche of the author and toward the psychology of the reader and the text. Holland's theories, which have concerned themselves more with the reader than with the text, have helped to establish another school of critical theory: reader-response criticism. Elizabeth Wright explains Holland's brand of modern psychoanalytic criticism in this way: "What draws us as readers to a text is the secret expression of what we desire to hear, much as we protest we do not. The disguise must be good enough to fool the censor into thinking that the text is respectable, but bad enough to allow the unconscious to glimpse the unrespectable" (117).

Holland is one of dozens of critics who have revised Freud significantly in the process of revitalizing psychoanalytic criticism. Another such critic is D. W. Winnicott, an "object relations" theorist who has had a significant impact on literary criticism. Critics influenced by

Winnicott and his school have questioned the tendency to see reader/text as an either/or construct; instead, they have seen reader and text (or audience and play) in terms of a *relationship* taking place in what Winnicott calls a "transitional" or "potential space"—space in which binary terms like *real* and *illusory, objective* and *subjective,* have little or no meaning.

Psychoanalytic theorists influenced by Winnicott see the transitional or potential reader/text (or audience/play) space as being *like* the space entered into by psychoanalyst and patient. More important, they also see it as being similar to the space between mother and infant: a space characterized by trust in which categorizing terms such as "knowing" and "feeling" mix and merge and have little meaning apart from one another.

Whereas Freud saw the mother-son relationship in terms of the son and his repressed oedipal complex (and saw the analyst-patient relationship in terms of the patient and the repressed "truth" that the analyst could scientifically extract), object-relations analysts see both relationships as *"dyadic,"* as being dynamic in both directions. Consequently, they don't depersonalize analysis or their analyses. It is hardly surprising, therefore, that contemporary literary critics who apply object-relations theory to the texts they discuss don't depersonalize critics or categorize their interpretations as "truthful"—at least, not in any objective or scientific sense. In the view of such critics, interpretations are made of language—itself a transitional object—and are themselves the mediating terms or transitional objects of a relationship.

Like critics of the Winnicottian School, the French structuralist theorist Jacques Lacan focuses on language and language-related issues. He treats the unconscious *as* a language and, consequently, views the dream not as Freud did (as a form and symptom of repression) but, rather, as a form of discourse. Thus we may study dreams psychoanalytically in order to learn about literature, even as we may study literature in order to learn more about the unconscious. In Lacan's seminar on Poe's "The Purloined Letter," a pattern of repetition like that used by psychoanalysts in their analyses is used to arrive at a reading of the story. According to Wright, "the new psychoanalytic structural approach to literature" employs "analogies from psychoanalysis . . . to explain the workings of the text as distinct from the workings of a particular author's, character's, or even reader's mind" (125).

Lacan, however, did far more than extend Freud's theory of dreams, literature, and the interpretation of both. More significantly, he took Freud's whole theory of psyche and gender and added to it a crucial third term—that of language. In the process, he both used and significantly developed Freud's ideas about the oedipal stage and complex.

Lacan points out that the pre-oedipal stage, in which the child at first does not even recognize its independence from its mother, is also a pre*verbal* stage, one in which the child communicates without the medium of language, or—if we insist on calling the child's communications a language—in a language that can only be called *literal*. (Coos, certainly, cannot be said to be figurative or symbolic.) Then, while still in the pre-oedipal stage, the child enters the *mirror* stage.

During the mirror period, the child comes to view itself and its mother, later other people as well, *as* independent selves. This is the stage in which the child is first able to fear the aggressions of another, to desire what is recognizably beyond the self (initially the mother), and, finally, to want to compete with another for the same desired object. This is also the stage at which the child first becomes able to feel sympathy with another being who is being hurt by a third, to cry when another cries. All of these developments, of course, involve projecting beyond the self and, by extension, constructing one's own self (or "ego" or "I) as others view one—that is, as *another*. Such constructions, according to Lacan, are just that: constructs, products, artifacts—fictions of coherence that in fact hide what Lacan calls the "absence" or "lack" of being.

The mirror stage, which Lacan also refers to as the *Imaginary* stage, is fairly quickly succeeded by the oedipal stage. As in Freud, this stage begins when the child, having come to view itself as self and the father and mother as separate selves, perceives gender and gender differences between its parents and between itself and one of its parents. For boys, gender awareness involves another, more powerful recognition, for the recognition of the father's phallus as the mark of his difference from the mother involves, at the same time, the recognition that his older and more powerful father is also his rival. That, in turn, leads to the understanding that what once seemed wholly his and even indistinguishable from himself is in fact someone else's: something properly desired only at a distance and in the form of socially acceptable *substitutes*.

The fact that the oedipal stage roughly coincides with the entry of the child into language is extremely important for Lacan. For the linguistic order is essentially a figurative or "Symbolic order"; words are not the things they stand for but are, rather, stand-ins or substitutes for those things. Hence boys, who in the most crucial period of their development have had to submit to what Lacan calls the "Law of the Father"—a law that prohibits direct desire for and communicative intimacy with what has been the boy's whole world — enter more easily into the realm of language and the Symbolic order than do girls, who have never really had to renounce that which once seemed continuous with the self: the mother. The gap that has been opened up for boys, which includes the gap between signs and what they substitute for — the gap marked by the phallus and encoded with the boy's sense of his maleness — has not opened up for girls, or has not opened up in the same way, to the same degree.

For Lacan, the father need not be present to trigger the oedipal stage; nor does his phallus have to be seen to catalyze the boy's (easier) transition into the Symbolic order. Rather, Lacan argues, a child's recognition of its gender is intricately tied up with a growing recognition of the system of names and naming, part of the larger system of substitutions we call language. A child has little doubt about who its mother is, but who is its father, and how would one know? The father's claim rests on the mother's *word* that he is in fact the father; the father's relationship to the child is thus established through language and a system of marriage and kinship — names — that in turn is basic to rules of everything from property to law. The name of the father (*nom du père,* which in French sounds like *non du père*) involves, in a sense, nothing of the father: nothing, that is, except his word or name.

Lacan's development of Freud has had several important results. First, his sexist-seeming association of maleness with the Symbolic order, together with his claim that women cannot therefore enter easily into the order, has prompted feminists not to reject his theory out of hand but, rather, to look more closely at the relation between language and gender, language and women's inequality. Some feminists have gone so far as to suggest that the social and political relationships between male and female will not be fundamentally altered until language itself has been radically changed. (That change might begin dialectically, with the development of some kind of "feminine language" grounded in the presymbolic — the literal-to-imaginary — communication between mother and child.)

Second, Lacan's theory has proved of interest to deconstructors and other poststructuralists, in part because it holds that the ego (which in Freud's view is as necessary as it is natural) is a product or construct. The ego-artifact, produced during the mirror stage, *seems* at once unified, consistent, and organized around a determinate center. But the unified self, or ego, is a fiction, according to Lacan. The yoking together of fragments and destructively dissimilar elements takes its psychic toll, and it is the job of the Lacanian psychoanalyst to "deconstruct," as it were, the ego, to show its continuities to be contradictions as well.

In the essay that follows, Ellie Ragland Sullivan begins by discussing the relationship between sublimation (the modification of the natural expression of an instinctual impulse in a socially acceptable manner) and the production of art. For Freud, sublimation generally involved the transformation of sexual impulse, but Ragland Sullivan prefers Lacan's broader theory that sublimation "concerns an impasse between the desire for being . . . and the drive for satisfaction." Sublime experiences, in other words, result from the painful clash between what we want in the short run and what we feel we are in the long run. When those clashes occur, we sense a gap or lack in the self; ordinary language, which normally obscures painful discontinuities, suddenly breaks. This failure makes art possible.

Suffering, that "irreducible problem" all humans face but that only artists—through the sublime—can transcend, thus functions as the catalyst that transforms language into art. "Art" is "not neurosis but," rather, "the effort to exit from an *unconscious* dilemma." That dilemma, not surprisingly, is rooted in childhood. In a Lacanian move, Ragland Sullivan suggests that "art might be defined as the invention of scenarios that offer potentially new identifications, new signifiers for being."

But if, according to Lacan, suffering is what "drives one to elevate language to the level of art," and if sexual identification is not what is sublimated in the process (or, rather, if it is desexualized in the process), then what *is* sublimated? For Lacan, it is the drive for fusion with the mother, the feeling of consistency or oneness that Lacan calls *jouissance*. And what *jouissance* gets sublimated in—what it becomes when it is desexualized—is culture, language, that which Lacan has called the Name of the Father. In culture and language, desires and drives are transferred from one thing to another in a system of deferrals and substitutions. Thus, even when we *think* we get what we want, we don't quite, and the sense that "something is lacking," namely *being* (Lacan would speak of the lack of [or in] being) can lead to neurosis.

In *The House of Mirth*, Ragland Sullivan argues, Edith Wharton seeks to define the artist in a novel that grows out of *jouissance* and its sublimation. Ragland Sullivan sees the novel's struggle to define being as grounded in Wharton's own life—a life that included rejection by her mother and close and long-lasting identification with her father. In writing *The House of Mirth*, Wharton transforms language to fill in what was lacking in her own childhood family novel: a worthy place for her father. At the same time, she depicts a "frivolous society" as a "stand-in" for "a mother who does not love her child."

In the process, *The House of Mirth* (which Ragland Sullivan considers a "clearly autobiographical" novel) reveals that its author grappled with "the identification problem . . . Lacan found at the basis of the neurosis Freud called hysteria." Drawing on both Freud and Lacan, Ragland Sullivan suggests that the particular neurosis known as hysteria has its "dialectical basis" in the situation where a daughter has been emotionally abandoned by her mother to the point that the daughter identifies primarily with her father. As an hysteric herself, Wharton wrote *The House of Mirth* to "sublimate the pain of being an outsider in the society in which she grew up . . . [and] to find a way to bear the pain of not having an adequate signifier by which to link gender to being."

Although *The House of Mirth* "speaks the discourse of the hysteric," it also represents hysterics and hysteria from a wider perspective. Wharton depicts the female hysteric specifically in Lily Bart and, more generally, in "the sorrow of women who do not quite fit into societal norms." Hysteria is shown to result from a "split in gender identification": although the hysteric "knows she is a woman, she unconsciously identifies with men." The "desire to know how to be as a woman" drives Wharton; Lily Bart, the heroine she creates to "incarnate the enigmatic suffering peculiar to the hysteric," reveals the all-important — and also ambiguous — nature of gender difference. Lily, "infused with Edith's own soul," is thus her character in more than one sense, burdened with "only two signifiers by which to represent herself in the world: beauty and money."

Wharton herself avoided the tragedy entailed by this terrible lack of self-signifiers (woman's being is not beauty, and it certainly cannot be represented by money) by transforming neurosis into art. "Writing becomes a way of inventing a signifier where there is none." For Wharton, writing functions as a mode of catharsis to free her from suffering, but it cannot be a true signifier — for none exists. Indeed, "writing reproduces the very lack from which the drive comes in the first place: the drive to be satisfied at the level of *being*." Writing instead "satisfies the drive for *jouissance*" because it helps Wharton "work with her desire to know what niggles at the borders of her consciousness." It is not a cure, however, since the artist "never knows for sure precisely what troubles her."

Ragland Sullivan ends by focusing on Lily and on her constant failure to do the socially appropriate thing within a society that considers her an enigma at best. The hysteric, driven by the "logic or rationality" of her neurosis and identifying with "socially unacceptable males," *cannot* do the socially appropriate thing. As soon as she tries to follow the expected course, she "sees through the hypocrisies in the social game" and "her desire to please" is thwarted by her recognition of the game as "a sham." So she inevitably sets herself on "an oppositional course that seems irrational to others." As a nonconformist, Lily, like Wharton, thus stands as one of "a race apart."

Ross C Murfin

PSYCHOANALYTIC CRITICISM: A SELECTED BIBLIOGRAPHY

Some Short Introductions to Psychological and Psychoanalytic Criticism

Holland, Norman. "The 'Unconscious' of Literature." *Contemporary Criticism.* Ed. Norman Bradbury and David Palmer. Stratford-upon-Avon Series 12. New York: St. Martin's, 1970. 131–54.

Natoli, Joseph, and Frederik L. Rusch, comps. *Psychocriticism: An Annotated Bibliography.* Westport: Greenwood, 1984.

Scott, Wilbur. *Five Approaches to Literary Criticism.* London: Collier-Macmillan, 1962. See the essays by Burke and Gorer as well as Scott's introduction to the section "The Psychological Approach: Literature in the Light of Psychological Theory."

Wellek, René, and Austin Warren. *Theory of Literature.* New York: Harcourt, 1942. See the chapter "Literature and Psychology" in pt. 3, "The Extrinsic Approach to the Study of Literature."

Wright, Elizabeth. "Modern Psychoanalytic Criticism." *Modern Literary Theory: A Comparative Introduction.* Ed. Ann Jefferson and David Robey. Totowa: Barnes, 1982. 113–33.

Freud, Lacan, and Their Influence

Basler, Roy P. *Sex, Symbolism, and Psychology in Literature.* New York: Octagon, 1975. See especially 13–19.

Clément, Catherine. *The Lives and Legends of Jacques Lacan.* Trans. Arthur Goldhammer. New York: Columbia UP, 1983.

Freud, Sigmund. *Introductory Lectures on Psycho-Analysis.* Trans. Joan Riviere. London: Allen, 1922.

Gallop, Jane. *Reading Lacan.* Ithaca: Cornell UP, 1985.

Hoffman, Frederick J. *Freudianism and the Literary Mind.* Baton
Rouge: Louisiana State UP, 1945.

Hogan, Patrick Colm, and Lalita Pandit, eds. *Lacan and Criticism: Essays and Dialogue on Language, Structure, and the Unconscious.*
Athens: U of Georgia P, 1990.

Kazin, Alfred. "Freud and His Consequences." *Contemporaries.* Boston: Little, 1962. 351–93.

Lacan, Jacques. *Écrits: A Selection.* Trans. Alan Sheridan. New York:
Norton, 1977.

———. *Feminine Sexuality: Lacan and the école freudienne.* Ed. Juliet
Mitchell and Jacqueline Rose. Trans. Rose. New York: Norton,
1982.

———. *The Four Fundamental Concepts of Psychoanalysis.* Trans. Alan
Sheridan. London: Penguin, 1980.

Macey, David. *Lacan in Contexts.* New York: Verso, 1988.

Meisel, Perry, ed. *Freud: A Collection of Critical Essays.* Englewood
Cliffs: Prentice, 1981.

Muller, John P., and William J. Richardson. *Lacan and Language: A
Reader's Guide to "Écrits."* New York: International UP, 1982.

Porter, Laurence M. *"The Interpretation of Dreams": Freud's Theories
Revisited.* Twayne's Masterwork Studies Series. Boston: G. K.
Hall, 1986.

Ragland Sullivan, Ellie. *Jacques Lacan and the Philosophy of Psychoanalysis.* U of Illinois P, 1986.

Ragland Sullivan, Ellie, and Mark Bracher, eds. *Lacan and the Subject
of Language.* New York: Routledge, 1991.

Reppen, Joseph, and Maurice Charney. *The Psychoanalytic Study of Literature.* Hillsdale: Analytic, 1985.

Schneiderman, Stuart. *Jacques Lacan: The Death of an Intellectual
Hero.* Cambridge: Harvard UP, 1983.

———. *Returning to Freud: Clinical Psychoanalysis in the School of
Lacan.* New Haven: Yale UP, 1980.

Selden, Raman. *A Reader's Guide to Contemporary Literary Theory.*
2nd ed. Lexington: U of Kentucky P, 1989. See "Jacques Lacan:
Language and the Unconscious."

Trilling, Lionel. "Art and Neurosis." *The Liberal Imagination.* New
York: Scribner's, 1950. 160–80.

Wilden, Anthony. "Lacan and the Discourse of the Other." In Lacan,
Speech and Language in Psychoanalysis. Trans. Wilden. Baltimore:
Johns Hopkins UP, 1981. (Published as *The Language of the Self*
in 1968.) 159–311.

Psychoanalysis, Feminism, and Literature

Chodorow, Nancy. *The Reproduction of Mothering: Psychoanalysis and the Sociology of Gender*. Berkeley: U of California P, 1978.

Gallop, Jane. *The Daughter's Seduction: Feminism and Psychoanalysis*. Ithaca: Cornell UP, 1982.

Garner, Shirley Nelson, Claire Kahane, and Madelon Sprengnether. *The (M)other Tongue: Essays in Feminist Psychoanalytic Interpretation*. Ithaca: Cornell UP, 1985.

Irigaray, Luce. *This Sex Which Is Not One*. Trans. Catherine Porter. Ithaca: Cornell UP, 1985.

———. *The Speculum of the Other Woman*. Trans. Gillian C. Gill. Ithaca: Cornell UP, 1985.

Jacobus, Mary. "Is There a Woman in This Text?" *New Literary History* 14 (1982): 117–41.

Kristeva, Julia. *The Kristeva Reader*. Ed. Toril Moi. New York: Columbia UP, 1986. See especially the selection from *Revolution in Poetic Language*, 89–136.

Mitchell, Juliet. *Psychoanalysis and Feminism*. New York: Random, 1974.

Mitchell, Juliet, and Jacqueline Rose, "Introduction I" and "Introduction II." Lacan, *Feminine Sexuality: Jacques Lacan and the école freudienne*. 1–26, 27–57.

Sprengnether, Madelon. *The Spectral Mother: Freud, Feminism, and Psychoanalysis*. Ithaca: Cornell UP, 1990.

Psychological and Psychoanalytic Studies of Literature

Bettelheim, Bruno. *The Uses of Enchantment: The Meaning and Importance of Fairy Tales*. New York: Knopf, 1976. Although this book is about fairy tales instead of literary works written for publication, it offers model Freudian readings of well-known stories.

Crews, Frederick C. *Out of My System: Psychoanalysis, Ideology, and Critical Method*. New York: Oxford UP, 1975.

———. *Relations of Literary Study*. New York: MLA, 1967. See the chapter "Literature and Psychology."

Diehl, Joanne Feit. "Re-Reading *The Letter*: Hawthorne, the Fetish, and the (Family) Romance." *Nathaniel Hawthorne, The Scarlet Letter*. Ed. Ross C Murfin. Case Studies in Contemporary Criticism Series. Ed. Ross C Murfin. Boston: Bedford–St. Martin's, 1991. 235–51.

Hallman, Ralph. *Psychology of Literature: A Study of Alienation and Tragedy.* New York: Philosophical Library, 1961.

Hartman, Geoffrey, ed. *Psychoanalysis and the Question of the Text.* Baltimore: Johns Hopkins UP, 1978. See especially the essays by Hartman, Johnson, Nelson, and Schwartz.

Hertz, Neil. *The End of the Line: Essays on Psychoanalysis and the Sublime.* New York: Columbia UP, 1985.

Holland, Norman N. *Dynamics of Literary Response.* New York: Oxford UP, 1968.

———. *Poems in Persons: An Introduction to the Psychoanalysis of Literature.* New York: Norton, 1973.

Kris, Ernest. *Psychoanalytic Explorations in Art.* New York: International, 1952.

Lucas, F. L. *Literature and Psychology.* London: Cassell, 1951.

Natoli, Joseph, ed. *Psychological Perspectives on Literature: Freudian Dissidents and Non-Freudians: A Casebook.* Hamden: Archon Books–Shoe String, 1984.

Phillips, William, ed. *Art and Psychoanalysis.* New York: Columbia UP, 1977.

Rogers, Robert. *A Psychoanalytic Study of the Double in Literature.* Detroit: Wayne State UP, 1970.

Skura, Meredith. *The Literary Use of the Psychoanalytic Process.* New Haven: Yale UP, 1981.

Strelka, Joseph P. *Literary Criticism and Psychology.* University Park: Pennsylvania State UP, 1976. See especially the essays by Lerner and Peckham.

Weiss, Daniel. *The Critic Agonistes: Psychology, Myth, and the Art of Fiction.* Ed. Eric Solomon and Stephen Arkin. Seattle: U of Washington P, 1985.

Lacanian Psychoanalytic Studies of Literature

Collings, David. "The Monster and the Imaginary Mother: A Lacanian Reading of *Frankenstein*." *Mary Shelley, Frankenstein.* Ed. Johanna M. Smith. Case Studies in Contemporary Criticism Series. Ed. Ross C Murfin. Boston: Bedford–St. Martin's, 1992. 245–58.

Davis, Robert Con, ed. *The Fictional Father: Lacanian Readings of the Text.* Amherst: U of Massachusetts P, 1981.

———, ed. "Lacan and Narration." *Modern Language Notes* 5 (1983): 843–1063.

Feldman, Shoshana, ed. *Jacques Lacan and the Adventure of Insight:*

Psychoanalysis in Contemporary Culture. Cambridge: Harvard UP, 1987.

———. *Literature and Psychoanalysis: The Question of Reading: Otherwise.* Baltimore: Johns Hopkins UP, 1982.

Froula, Christine. "When Eve Reads Milton: Undoing the Canonical Economy." *Canons.* Ed. Robert von Hallberg. Chicago: U of Chicago P, 1984. 149–75.

Homans, Margaret. *Bearing the Word: Language and Female Experience in Nineteenth-Century Women's Writing.* Chicago: U of Chicago P, 1986.

Muller, John P., and William J. Richardson, eds. *The Purloined Poe: Lacan, Derrida, and Psychoanalytic Reading.* Baltimore: Johns Hopkins UP, 1988. Includes Lacan's seminar on Poe's "The Purloined Letter."

Psychoanalytic Readings of *The House of Mirth*

Blum, Virginia L. "Edith Wharton's Erotic Other World." *Literature and Psychology* 33 (1987): 12–29.

Leonard, Garry M. "The Paradox of Desire: Jacques Lacan and Edith Wharton." *Edith Wharton Review* 7.2 (Winter 1990): 13–16.

Ehrlich, Gloria C. *The Sexual Education of Edith Wharton.* Berkeley: U of California P, 1992.

Wershoven, Carol J. "*The Awakening* and *The House of Mirth:* Studies of Arrested Development." *American Literary Realism 1870–1910.* 19.3 (Spring 1987): 27–41.

Wolff, Cynthia Griffin. "Lily Bart and the Beautiful Death." *American Literature* 46 (1974): 40. Rpt. *A Feast of Words: The Triumph of Edith Wharton.* New York: Oxford UP, 1977.

A PSYCHOANALYTIC PERSPECTIVE

ELLIE RAGLAND SULLIVAN

The Daughter's Dilemma:
Psychoanalytic Interpretation and Edith Wharton's
The House of Mirth

My subject is how literary art—represented here by Edith Wharton's *The House of Mirth*—and psychoanalysis, in particular theories
of hysteria and sublimation, mutually inform each other. I will examine
Wharton's novel in light of the French psychoanalyst Jacques Lacan's
redefinition of Freud's notion of hysteria as a neurosis that primarily
afflicts women. Lacan stresses the role of language in the constitution of
human subjectivity; he defines hysteria as the lack of a signifier or representation for *being* as a woman. Hysteria, then, has a certain structure
that is revealed through language and can be interpreted. I believe that
Edith Wharton, both as woman and artist, was driven by the unconscious dilemma that structures hysteria: the desire to know *how to be* as
a woman. Revealing in her literary creation Lily Bart the enigmatic suffering peculiar to hysteria, Wharton has transformed—or sublimated—
her own hysteria into art. One can see hysteria at work in *The House of
Mirth* in the logic of an identificatory structure of subjectivity in the
mother-daughter relation and in the marks or material traits of desire in
language that form around Lily's (and Edith Wharton's) quest to know
what is missing in the Other. By "Other" I mean, what is missing in her
own unconscious about which she has, by definition, no conscious
knowledge.

From this perspective, memorable literary characters tell the story of
a dilemma, a thorny problem that drives the author to write in order to
try to understand her own enigma. There is no one-to-one correspondence between the biographical material of the author's life and the
power of a literary work; yet sometimes a writer's work is so clearly autobiographical that the critic can make use of psychoanalysis to shed
light on the artistic process, to help explain how art arises as a testimony
to the same suffering that the psychoanalytic clinic treats. This is the
situation with Edith Wharton's writing, as biographers and critics have
long recognized (see Lewis, Wolff, Showalter).

Lacan reconceptualized the neurosis of hysteria away from Sigmund

Freud's idea of it as sexual repression and masochism, defining it instead as a split in gender identification, evident at the level of discourse (in language and speech), in which a daughter identifies with her father in order to compensate for lack of attention from her mother and also to *deny* her father's denigration by the mother. This pattern fits Edith Wharton's description of her own familial identifications (see *Backward Glance* and "Life and I"). Although Lacan says little about the role of the mother in hysteria, I suggest that the dialectical basis of hysteria in which the daughter identifies primarily with her opposite-sex parent arises out of the mother's emotional abandonment of her child. One can interpret *The House of Mirth,* then, as an artistic sublimation (or elevation) of neurotic suffering into art. The novel poses an ongoing series of questions about the sorrows of women who do not quite fit societal norms, and it illustrates how artists — who are also not comfortable within social norms and conventions — enshrine the knowledge of this suffering into art.

Art, Hysteria, and Sublimation

The words *sublimation, sublimate,* and the *sublime* have long been used to try to pin down what links art to life. Although the concept of the sublime remains enigmatic even today, it was first articulated by Longinus in the first century A.D., coined as a German verb by Goethe in the eighteenth century, and borrowed by Freud to try to link the mysteries of art to psychoanalysis. Lacan was also interested in the connections between art and psychoanalysis, but unlike Freud he did not try to "prove" through art the existence of the unconscious (that which is repressed in our conscious waking life because it is too painful for us to bear). Rather, he believed that art actively demonstrates what psychoanalysis has uncovered: art is the effort of the artist to exit from an *unconscious* dilemma in subjectivity and identity by reweaving childhood identifications ("Kanzer Seminar," 21–22). Seen in this way, art might be defined as the invention of scenarios that offer potentially new identifications, new signifiers for being. According to Lacan, human suffering is what drives the artist to elevate language to the level of art.

Responding to Freud on the problem of how art is linked to life, Lacan also answered a question that Aristotle worried about but could never answer: How do spectators or readers identify with a literary work *as if it were true?* He answers that the work *is* literally true at the level of psychic sublimation. He defined sublimation as a non-concept (an

Unbegriff) that concerns not what *is* but *what is missing* (in the unconscious). Sublimation concerns an impasse between one's ideal self-image (the desire for a particular recognition, achieved through identifications with others) and the drive for satisfaction (located in language by the mode in which one demands recognition). Sublimation points to a lack, or absence, of the necessary identifications by which to constitute a satisfactory image of "self." Seen this way, literature can be "literally true" — first because it provides representations or characters and situations from which the artist projects a universe (thereby reweaving old identifications); second because it provides an image of what will gratify the demand — in language — for satisfaction or recognition at the level of the desire for identification with ideals. This explanation is very different from Freud's idea that in art, as well as in hysteria, sexuality was sublimated (in his terms, repressed). Lacan showed that the process of sublimation, which works through language and representations, *desexualizes* the aim of the drive for satisfaction. The drive aims for libidinal fusion or *jouissance* (oneness) with the mother, who is represented by partial objects of desire. An infant craves her breast, her gaze, her voice, etc. Sublimation of primary, primordial objects (Lacan calls them "object *a*") results in an identificatory modification, or rerouting, of the subject of desire (Trobas 17).

In its psychological sense, the verb "sublimate" means "to modify the natural expression of (an instinctual impulse) in a socially acceptable manner," from Latin *sublimare,* meaning to raise or elevate (*The American Heritage Dictionary*). Art elevates the specific suffering in an author's life, says Lacan, as the author gives verbal form to something intangible, *transforming* an irreducible problem, some piece of (unconscious) knowledge that resists symbolization, into a kind of writing we call art. But the question that has plagued psychoanalysts and aesthetic theorists since Freud is why some people can transform their suffering into art, when most of us cannot.

At the same moment that Sigmund Freud was trying to define sublimation (1905), Wharton published *The House of Mirth,* the novel that first made her famous. It poses a series of questions about the place of women in society and the role of art in culture. What is an artist? Who is this human being who differs from others, from seemingly normative, conventional people, but does not know why? How is the artist's vision superior? (Early reviews of the book focused on these issues in relation to Wharton's critique of society.) Before finally settling on the title of the book, she abandoned two earlier working titles, "A Moment's Ornament" and "The Year of the Rose," both of which suggest that she was concerned to draw society's picture of what a woman *should* be—decorative and beautiful, even if only for a moment.

The House of Mirth title is taken from Ecclesiastes 7:3–4: "Sorrow is better than laughter: for by sadness of the countenance the heart is made better. / The heart of the wise is in the house of mourning; but the heart of fools is in the house of mirth." As the title and epigraph to the novel suggest, Wharton draws attention to the mourning that lies on the underside of mirth, in particular the mourning that accompanies what we might call the "gender problematic" of the hysteric, who identifies with the parent of the opposite sex, often because she has been emotionally abandoned by the parent of her own sex. What exactly *is* being mourned here? Why does a house of mourning produce wisdom—what kind of wisdom, and for whom? Wharton uses words to work on the Real, trying to untie the particular knots in language that indicate an underlying trauma where sexuality and gender intersect. This is precisely where sublimation occurs in her work of art, the place of impasse where language breaks, where her words (and Lily's) stumble over a repetitious trauma that is registered as a knot or enigma in language and which remains opaque even at the level of *unconscious* knowledge (see Laurent).

At the moment of sublimation, the artist's words constitute an image that stuns, an image that stops even the artist in her tracks and confronts her (and her readers) with the disconcerting fact that certain things in one's life are roadblocks. Such impasses open onto a psychic hole or void that people try to fill up with words—to cover over the gap in being that surfaces as a gap in language. Lacan calls such a stopgap "object *a*," referring to something that momentarily attenuates one's awareness of loss in its myriad manifestations. People seek to annul loss in order to main a bodily feeling of *jouissance,* of consistency or oneness. In *The House of Mirth* this occurs twice, first in the tableaux vivants scene in which Lily appears as Reynolds's "Mrs. Lloyd," (see p. 440) where Lily's beauty stuns those who see her, and the second time in the death scene, where Selden is at a loss for words. Words cannot always mitigate the pain of existence that appears in such moments, when the gap between internal ideals (to be the perfect daughter, defined in this case as being beautiful) and external realities (a mother who doesn't recognize or approve of you) shows its face in stark despair—a despair that in Lily's case leads to her death. Such moments appear in artistic language as riddles or enigma; they are the soul of the author's own symptom, which she has intimately experienced but does not understand. One could characterize sublimation as the artist's effort to make such gaps or impasses speak, enunciate their cause, show the "why" of the problem. Why, for example, does Lily Bart fail when she seems to have every possibility of winning?

The answer lies in Lily's childhood drama, which is only briefly glimpsed in the novel. She can find no exit from it in adult life, and this impasse leads to her death—a death that is not an atypical fate for a hysteric. In order to "hear" the complex truths spoken in Lily's discourse, we need to know precisely what is at stake in it. For Lacan, the hysteric is the only one who always speaks the truth of suffering in *being,* because she is situated as a speaking agent precisely at the impasse where language is split between conscious and unconscious knowledge systems, split at the point where a signifier (or representation) for sexual difference *qua* gender identity is not symbolized. The hysteric bears a message in sufferance (from old French *souffrance,* meaning suffering and also a "nowhere" place in which a letter, for example, is unclaimed, awaiting delivery); she lives the unbearable problem of identifying with the split in sexual difference. Although she does not understand her own sorrow, her experience shows that the issue of sexual difference is the burning question for her. Across time and space, hysterics have posed questions to supposed masters (doctors, priests) about what it means to be a woman, and history has responded by calling them witches, madwomen, fakes, actresses, and inventors of make-believe. The hysteric who cannot sublimate her suffering as an artist, as Wharton could, can only painfully and mortally embody it.

The difference between Edith Wharton and Lily Bart is that Wharton found a way out of her own deadly childhood drama by dramatizing her history in art. Wharton was born to a mother who was on the eve of her thirty-seventh birthday, who already had two adolescent sons and was not happy to have a third child, especially one she described as an awkward and ungraceful daughter. Thus, Wharton had the challenge of learning to live with a mother displeased by her daughter's very presence (Wolff xii–xiii). She displeased her mother in two additional ways—as a female and as a budding artist, a creator of make-believe stories. We can surmise that Edith was driven to write about what was lacking in (her) being, to grapple with a poverty of signifiers by which to represent herself at the level of being as a woman.

I would argue that Lily Bart comes alive in art because she is infused with her creator's own soul or passion—that is, the irreducible kernel of sorrow in Edith's being that has turned to a lifelong suffering. Lily has only two signifiers by which to represent herself in the world—beauty and money. Her mother had taught her that her beauty would take care of her at the level of existence, that she could use her beauty to buy security and social success. But Lily is "mentally paralyzed" in not knowing how to put her beauty to use in her search for love, a husband, money, a protector, a sponsor, even a career. This is the particular suffering of the hysteric, who is unable to assume (to know or act on) her own desire. Others always speak for Lily and decide for her. In Lacanian terms, she is spoken by the Other—by the unconscious desires of her childhood familiars.

Working with the problem of the lack of an innate signifier for gender identification, Wharton weaves Lily out of identificatory features she had taken on from her own mother (Lacan calls these features the first traits of sublimation, which form one's own "ideal ego"), thus weaving together the threads of Wharton's own being. Lily is not as intelligent and creative as Edith Wharton was. But she fits Wharton's mother's ideal of beauty as the key to success. Wharton herself was not "beautiful," as she thought her mother to have been. Thus, Lily incarnates in a static manner (visualized in the tableaux vivants scene) what Edith herself must have taken to be the essence of a woman—beauty. Trying to answer the hysteric's question—What is a woman?—at the level of physical beauty, Wharton describes Lily at the Wellington Brys's party, where she is dressed as a simple portrait:

> The unanimous "Oh!" of the spectators was a tribute, not to the brush-work of Reynolds's "Mrs. Lloyd" but to the flesh and blood loveliness of Lily Bart. She had shown her artistic intelligence in selecting a type so like her own that . . . it was as though she had stepped, not out of, but into, Reynolds's canvas, banishing the phantom of his dead beauty by the beams of her living grace. (138–39)

Mr. Ned Van Alstyne, "experienced connoisseur," says: "Deuced bold thing to show herself in that get-up; but, gad, there is n't a break in the lines anywhere, and I suppose she wanted us to know it!" (139).

At the place where the unconscious insists (or pushes) in conscious life in an attempt to supply an answer to an unknown, to what is missing in one's own story, Edith Wharton knew that beauty alone did not constitute a woman. But represented in her family by only one signifier (she was a "creator of make-believe"), how was she to define herself as a woman? Edith Wharton's scanty knowledge about how to link woman to gender and sexuality translates into Lily Bart's tragedy, thereby transforming hysteria into a question, or discourse, about the innocence of those—like Lily/Edith—who do not know how to play the social game and the sexual masquerade at which ordinary, conformist subjects are so adept. These women are indeed a race apart.

Sublimation as elevation into art was also the name Lacan gave to a lack of absence of knowledge when it overlaps with another lack. For Wharton, the lack of a signifier for *being* as a woman intersects with her lack of satisfaction in the field of the drives. Writing offered her a way of inventing a signifier where there was none: through writing, she sought a name for herself as a *woman*. Did the process of writing free Wharton, or provide catharsis, from emotional pain? By attenuating the anxiety caused by the incorporation of judgmental gazes and voices that constitute any person's subjective network of ideals and fantasies from within a highly personal signifying history, sublimation can be said to calm the body. But sublimation cannot elide the void at the center of language. By *representing* an enigma (what is missing in one's life), sublimation, instead, elevates the Real object of one's desire (to be the ideal one's mother wanted, for example) to the level of the drive (where the demand for resolution becomes a demand for *being*). Such demands are carried by language, which reproduces the very lack from which the drive comes in the first place; that is, language reproduces the drive as the wish to be satisfied at the level of an ideal *being* (to be what the other person wanted one to be). All people ask for or demand satisfaction by the way they are used by language. But even when we get what we want, something is still lacking, some tension still remains. The quest for satisfaction has not ended. Driven to reproduce the quest for unconsciously repressed ideals, language always falls short of its aim to satisfy because its very structures are founded on lack: we speak (or write) because something is missing in us, because some "lack" creates a demand that is momentarily filled by the word (as an object *a*), which provides a sense of consistency with the world.

Drive is a montage made up of words, images, and bodily effects whose aim, paradoxically, is satisfied at the same time that it is inhibited. Writing satisfied Wharton's drive for *jouissance,* or consistency and wholeness, insofar as it helped her work on her desire to know what niggled at the borders of her consciousness. Still, the writing process never revealed to her precisely what troubled her; thus there was no ultimate resolution to her pain. Writing fiction is not equivalent to a psychoanalytic cure, or even a substitution for it. But sublimation achieved through art is, nonetheless, unique because it brings a different satisfaction to the drive than the obvious or "natural" goal of the drive, which is to be recognized in a certain way by the "Other" (in Wharton's case, to be recognized by her mother and to identify with how her mother attracted her own husband, Edith's father). Unable to fulfill her mother's desire that she be pretty and feminine, unable to fulfill her own desire to be recognized and loved, Wharton instead gained recognition for herself in the larger world as an artist.

Shame and Suffering

I have argued that *The House of Mirth* not only sublimates Wharton's pain of being an outsider in the society in which she grew up but also helped her to find a way to bear the pain of lacking an adequate signifier by which to link gender to being. Her creation of Lily Bart—a daughter whose mother is emotionally absent—is not a regression to Wharton's own archaic, childhood past but rather a testimonial to the fact that childhood sorrows live on in our everyday language. Because we are first constituted in and by language, we can later use language to remake the painful identifications taken on in the past and which weigh us down in the present. In reworking her unconscious identifications with beautiful, shallow women like her mother, Wharton—quite literally—invented new ideals, new images, new signifiers for *her own being*.

One can see the paradox in Edith Wharton's dilemma. She is caught in the gap between the desire *to be* seen in a particular way at the level of the gaze (which refers not to ocular seeing but to the sense of "self" constituted by the judgments of others and the words they use to describe one) and the impossibility of realizing the ideals imposed on her by someone else (her mother as representative of Old New York society). Critics of her day portrayed her as a complaining, conservative woman whom life had passed by, but contemporary critics are now looking closely at the crisis of gender identification in her lifework and its associated pain. In *The Female Intruder in the Novels of Edith Wharton* (1982), Carol Wershoven, typifying a new breed of critic who has begun to read Wharton seriously, described her women characters as intruders, outsiders, the outcasts from society. In *Edith Wharton's Prisoners of Shame* (1991), Lev Raphael reveals the shame that lies at the core of Wharton's own sense of being: "A terrible pall of futility hangs over Wharton's correspondence with Fullerton [her midlife lover], so much of which Wharton felt was 'cast into the void.' Her early rejoicing over the intellectual and physical communion with Fullerton is gradually overshadowed by 'recurring expressions of subservience.' The dominant notes are her sense of unworthiness and being left to feel like 'a course served & cleared away!'" (1).

Having brilliantly charted the power of shame in Wharton's life,

Raphael—like Wershoven in describing Wharton as an intruder—fails to explain what caused it. In her introduction to Raphael's book, Cynthia Griffin Wolff asks: "Why might potential issues of shame be gender-linked? (xii–xiii). Lacan's work on hysteria gives an answer to Wolff's question: shame is the affect (or emotional value) that arises when one can find no signifier for being *worthy* as a woman. He notes that insofar as sexual being is not constituted symmetrically for women and men, the male response to being unworthy takes a different path— sexual perversion, aggressivity, alcoholism, etc.

Finding no answer in her conscious life to why she was so displeasing to her mother or why her father was in some way disempowered in the family (not "there" for her), the act of writing became for Wharton not only the terrain of a question about being but a place of catharsis, where she tried to exorcise pain and suffering. Lacan pointed out that catharsis also means purgation (*Seminar* VII); spitting out the words, casting off the images, Wharton purges herself of negative identifications that depress her, images drawn from the parts of a familiar life script that otherwise would have been lethally repeated in her life (as they were in Lily's) "beyond the pleasure principle"—the title of the book in which Freud unveiled his theory of the death drive. Lacan calls the death drive *jouissance,* or the drive for consistency and oneness, a drive based on repetitions of self-destructive thoughts that persist long after their initial causes had disappeared.

My picture of Edith Wharton/Lily Bart, who suffered because of a mother's deficient love and an absent father, would not appeal to the strain of feminist criticism that has castigated Wharton for the images of mother and child represented in the scene between Lily and Nettie or in Lily's deathbed hallucinations of holding her friend's baby. Patricia Spacks has characterized the deathbed scene as sentimental and regressive, an "escapist fantasy of motherhood," while Cynthia Wolff describes Lily's deathbed thoughts of "Nettie Struther's child . . . lying on her arm . . . [feeling] the pressure of its little head against her shoulder" (300) as a sign of Lily's retreat into the safety of infantilization (Spacks 20; Wolff 323).

In Lacanian theory, the primordial material that forms the earliest imagos (or representations) of being, the ideal ego, are sublimations of the mother. At the bedrock level of the corporal lie maternal introjects, her voice, gaze, bosom, smell; here images vacillate and language bumps into the earliest wisps of memory. This is the primordial *lalangue* (Lacan's name for the primordial mother who can never be recalled to memory as such), and one could say that the genre of poetry is itself the effort to incarnate *lalangue* (an invented French word that means "mothertongue") into language. Wharton's lesson, taught via Lily, is that yearning for the mother as the primary Good, for union with the primordial mother as the principle of constancy, never disappears. But her insight is double-edged and more biting than any supposed transcendence over the maternal might be. If, as I have argued, Wharton as artist was driven by the suffering specific to the hysteric, she unveiled a paradoxical truth: Her drive to write came from insufficient "self" definition at the level where everyone is the most vulnerable — gender and sexuality. In the arena of social advancement of women, this is also a bitter lesson, for it suggests that happiness as a woman and career success have little to do with one another. The tragic and black side of *The House of Mirth* lies in Wharton's unconscious effort to answer a question that no daughter can bear to ask outright: What is wrong with me that my mother finds me displeasing? Writing becomes a displacement of that question, a sublimation of that in oneself which is both horrible and impossible to bear — an excess of pain.

The secret of the power embodied in Wharton's women characters lies precisely, I maintain, in her own efforts to answer the unconscious question that plagues her: What is woman? Lily Bart is constituted by a strange mixture of traits, combining the fashion-plate beauty and shallowness of Edith's own mother with the stunned innocence and disbelief that mark the countenance of an unloved (or badly loved) child. Insofar as hysteria is an inability to play the social game of love and sex by the rules of conventional expectations, Lily's flaw lies in her not seeing that there is a game to play. So thoroughly encased is she in the cocoon of incapacity to constitute her own desire, that she fails to see that one "gets on" in the world by living from appearances. She does not understand that the social masquerade is precisely a network of tacitly agreed-upon lies. Or, perhaps, she decides — for reasons unknown even to herself — not to play the game.

Lily's disappointment when she discovers that her Aunt Julia Peniston has disinherited her dramatizes the hysteric's confusion about why things do not work out for her. Attentive to her aunt over the years, Lily nonetheless took no care to protect her reputation from sexual taint. Not sure how to identify with women, the hysteric by definition does not understand the only crime that normatively repressed subjects (that is, most people) will not forgive: not playing by their notions, or rules, of what constitutes discretion. Because the hysteric cannot do the socially appropriate thing within the sexual masquerade — for she does not identify with women who take their value from being wives, mothers, mistresses, social hostesses — she becomes an enigma to social adepts, and also a subject for gossip. In this, the hysteric shares much with Edith Wharton and her mother, Lucretia Jones, both of whom were subjects of sexual gossip.

One could easily romanticize Lily's truthfulness, her lack of hypocrisy. Asking Gerty Farish what gossip is circulating about her, Lily says: "I should n't have minded, you know, if I 'd got the money" (215). Gerty replies in shocked horror: " 'How can you talk so, Lily? Of course the money ought to have been yours, but after all that makes no difference. The important thing——' Gerty paused, and then continued firmly: 'The important thing is that you should clear yourself — should tell your friends the whole truth.' 'The whole truth?' Miss Bart laughed. 'What is truth? Where a woman is concerned, it 's the story that 's easiest to believe.' . . . Miss Farish still fixed her with an anxious gaze. 'But what *is* your story, Lily? I don't believe any one knows it yet.' 'My story? — I don't believe I know it myself'" (215). Gerty presses Lily to tell her story from the beginning. "The beginning was in my cradle, I suppose — in the way I was brought up," Lily says, "and the things I was taught to care for" (216).

Wanting to please her friends, to do what is expected of her, Lily tries to make herself marry Percy Gryce. But just as Mr. Gryce is about to propose, delighted with the image of Lily as a religious woman going to church, Lily follows Lawrence Selden instead. Wharton writes that Lily's "duty to go to church" was entirely too reasonable a course not to inspire her to rebellion (72). Lacan shows us what Wharton could not systematize or fully explain: the logic or rationality of hysteria. Emotionally abandoned by her mother, the hysteric compensates by an excessive concern to please the men with whom she instead identifies. But her desire to please is supported by the knowledge that the social game is itself a sham. No sooner does the hysteric try to live up to society's picture of the ideally well-behaved girl than she sees through the hypocrisies of the social game. This knowledge determines her on an oppositional course that seems irrational to others.

Since the hysteric identifies with socially unacceptable males (her father being the prototypical model of a man denigrated by his wife), she follows what she defines as a "superior" man — one who disdains social conventions — thereby placing love over respectability, and excitement over well-being. Although Lawrence Selden, whom Lily loves, is not a worthless man, he is unacceptable to the social world Lily inhabits, one where males are prized for money and power. As if foreshadowing Wharton's real-life love affair with Morton Fullerton (begun in 1907) and her disillusionment with him later, Selden's value to Lily is that he reminds her of her father, who loved poetry, and he excites her sexually *because* he is aloof and rejecting.

The Structure of Hysteria

Until Lacan returned to Freud's texts, no one had yet pinpointed the precise identificatory bind that constitutes hysteria. But prior to psychoanalysis, women writers—and some men writers—had documented the painful existence of the hysteric, someone who does not fit. Jean-Pierre Klotz writes that the hysteric's question—Am I am man or a woman?—teaches us that the human subject as such has no inherent sexual identity. That is, hysteria is not a matter of biological sex. Even if one answers the question of whether one is a man or a woman by saying "I am a man" or "I am a woman," one still suffers at the point where sex itself is not symbolizable—one suffers in the Real. In place of a given sexual identity, one has, at most, sexual *identifications* (Klotz 52–53).

As Wharton faithfully depicts, the hysteric asks that someone take seriously her story of pain, her life lived from colliding identifications that constitute what she calls *being*. Most people follow the script that society writes for them, the norms (usually male) being the laws of convention. Neurotic and psychotic subjects live outside the bounds of conventions, without knowing it or caring about it if they do suspect it. Lily Bart is one of these:

> Miss Bart had in fact been treading a devious way, and none of her critics could have been more alive to the fact than herself; but she had a fatalistic sense of being drawn from one wrong turning to another, without ever perceiving the right road till it was too late to take it. Lily, who considered herself above narrow prejudices, had not imagined that the fact of letting Gus Tenor make a little money for her would ever disturb her self-complacency. (133)

Although *The House of Mirth* faithfully depicts the vanity and futility of New York society prior to World War I, its extra note of bitterness and despair comes, I believe, from the unbearable pain a daughter suffers when she has no position of value in the eyes of either her mother or her father. Edith Wharton transforms or sublimates this neurotic problem—the lack of a signifier for being as a woman—into unforgettable women characters like Lily Bart, a woman who vacillates about placing her sexuality on the line. Clueless about sexual relations, she silently asks, What is a woman? In relation to men, she seems a child-woman, unsure of how sex and love are carried out between women and men.

Like other women hysterics, Wharton takes a position in language that fills in for what was lacking in her own childhood family novel—a worthy place for the father—and she identifies with his suffering. Elaine Showalter writes: "Wharton's critique of the marriage system is not limited to the economic dependency of women but also extends to consider the loneliness, dehumanization, and anxiety of men. Lily's father . . . is a dim and pathetic fixture of Lily's scant childhood memories" (14–15).

Like Edith Wharton's childhood home, Lily's was an emotional desert, described in *The House of Mirth* as a place where everyone was always coming and going. "Ruling the turbulent element called home was the vigorous and determined figure of a mother still young enough to dance her ball-dresses to rags, while the hazy outline of a neutral-tinted father filled an intermediate space between the butler and the man who came to wind the clocks. Even to the eyes of infancy, Mrs. Hudson Bart had appeared young; but Lily could not recall the time when her father had not been bald and slightly stooping, with streaks of grey in his hair, and a tired walk" (47). Further characterizing Lily's father, Wharton describes his "fagged step," his being "effaced and silent" (48). "But for the most part," she continues, "he was never mentioned or thought of till his patient stooping figure presented itself on the New York dock as a buffer between the magnitude of his wife's luggage and the restrictions of the American custom-house" (48).

Lily's father does not offer an identificatory base from which a daughter can build a picture of a relationship with men based on understanding or the straightforward love of a daughter for her father. Such incomprehensions and confusions regarding men are characteristic of the hysteric, whom Lacan describes as not having introjected (or psychically incorporated) the signifiers—the signifying chain of meaning—that would tell her what in the social conventions of a given moment a woman is supposed to be to a man. Lily errs in thinking of men as harmless, as only wishing her well. When Gus Trenor makes it clear that he expects some kind of sexual favor in repayment for "investing" her money, she is shocked and stunned.

Similarly, she seems unaware that presenting her physical beauty in its sheer perfection (in the tableaux vivants, for example) might inspire either male desire or female jealousy. Wharton paints "the long dryad-like curves that swept upward from her poised foot to her lifted arm.

The noble buoyancy of her attitude, its suggestion of soaring grace, re-vealed the touch of poetry in her beauty" (139). Selden responds to Lily as "the real Lily Bart, divested of the trivialities of her little world, and catching for a moment a note of that eternal harmony of which her beauty was a part" (139). One can imagine that Wharton combined her image of her mother's beauty with an Aristotelian definition of the po-etic aesthetic—formal harmony of the parts creating beauty—in an ef-fort to understand the enigma posed by her own invention, Lily Bart. If one follows Lacan's idea that artistic beauty—the sublime—comes from an image that stuns, one can propose a different source of Lily's beauty. In confronting her author with the impossible—a dilemma from which she can find no way out—Lily presents the face of tragedy in human life. It is not her beauty in itself that stuns or compels. Her beauty is, rather, a symptom of her dilemma. To survive, she needs to *use* her beauty: to marry a man who will support her or to marry a man she loves. And she can do neither.

David Holbrook writes that Edith Wharton "felt unable to discover who she was because of the ignorance imposed on her by her mother and by her attachment to her father" (15). But Holbrook makes a literal translation between the confused sexuality of Wharton's female charac-ters and Edith's warm relationship with her own father; he ends by ac-cusing George Frederic Jones of committing incest with his daughter. In Lacan's teaching, the child's proximity to the primary object (the primordial mother) creates hysteria if the child experiences too great a rejection by the mother, thus pushing her to identify with males instead of females, or creates psychosis if there is no psychic distance between the mother and child. Whatever the effects of this distancing, the first object of desire—a desire for the mother's love—*remains* a problem for everyone long after childhood. I would argue that Lacan's picture of hysteria makes more sense of the neurotic problems Wharton raises to the level of sublimation in her art than does Holbrook's explanation of her gender confusion as the result of actual incest with her father.

Years later, ruminating about the success of *The House of Mirth,* Wharton wrote:

> A frivolous society can acquire dramatic significance only through what its frivolity destroys. Its tragic implication lies in its power of debasing people and ideals. The answer, in short, was my heroine, Lily Bart. (207)

The psychoanalytic question is: How can a frivolous society destroy a character who is herself frivolous? The answer, at the level of Wharton's own life, was one of masking. What does "frivolous society" stand in for? A mother who does not love her child. Lily's mother (and also Edith's) valued only one thing—feminine physical beauty. One might say that Lily's tragedy was not the lack of a career or money *per se,* but the lack of a signifier telling her how to translate her own physical beauty—symbolizing Woman for the society that Wharton described—into the currency of love or marriage. The failure of Lily's beauty to bring her either marriage or money defines Wharton's question: What *is* a woman? Living from only one signifier, only one identificatory paradigm (her mother's belief that beauty would automatically enable her to have whatever she wanted or needed) Lily Bart's tragedy lies in a kind of innocence, the innocence of the neurotic who continues to obey parental dicta in adult life as if she were a child.

In *The Mother's Recompense* (1925), Wharton refers indirectly to her love affair with Morton Fullerton, an affair that ended in bitter disappointment for her:

> For the first time, when she met him, her soul's lungs seemed full of air. Life still dated for her from that day—in spite of the way he had hurt her, of his having inflicted on her the bitterest pain she had ever suffered, he had given her more than he could take away. *At thirty-nine her real self had been born;* without him she would never have had a self. . . . And yet, at what cost she had bought it. (557; emphasis added)

But in *The House of Mirth,* published in 1905, Edith Wharton could not yet infuse a character with the knowledge of sexual passion linked to love. The closest she could come were Lily's seemingly uninterpretable sexual responses to Lawrence Selden, described in myriad passages where Lily's pulse quickens, her blood rises, and so on. Indeed, one could say that part of what one might call the mourning of the house of sorrow—as opposed to the laughter in the house of mirth—is precisely Lily's lack of awareness of the power of sexuality.

But I would disagree with Elaine Showalter's picture of Lily as "the perfect lady." Showalter thinks Lily does the right thing at every turn. True, she does accept not to make a fuss: she does not expose the Bertha Dorsets of society, for example, or tell Gus Trenor what she thinks of him, or tell Selden the truth. But the price of her silence is that she remains in a house of mourning—the place of the primal scene of her childhood—where knowledge of how to live in the social world is absent. If living at the level of unconscious lack is a virtue—living out of the "I don't know" that marks the place of the unconscious in anyone's knowledge—then Lily is virtuous.

But Edith Wharton is more perplexed by Lily than convinced. The subject of her novel is enunciated clearly at the end in the word that neither Selden nor Lily can find, though Selden does find it at the end, too late; the word, presumably, is love. The novel asks two questions: What is a woman? What is love? It never answers either question, and this perhaps explains why Lily cannot find the solution to her dilemma through love: Wharton herself had not yet found her own solution at this date.

Does this fact bear on what Wharton sublimates? What lack does she seek to re-produce in her fiction? Although Lily wants to tell Selden the truth about herself, about her feelings, she never does so. After she has taken the sleeping medication, Lily "said to herself that there was something she must tell Selden, some word she had found that should make life clear between them. She tried to repeat the word, which lingered vague and luminous on the far edge of thought. . . . if she could only remember it and say it to him, she felt everything would be well" (300). That she does not succeed in this is one more example of how art sublimates the pain of neurosis into a profound truth about human relations. The psychoanalytic clinic repeats one story over and over: that there is no natural or pre-given sexual harmony or proportion (no *rapport,* as Lacan calls it) between lovers. There are moments of joy and despair, mistakes and miscalculations. But there is no Oneness of symmetrical harmony between men and women.

Lacan elevated the hysteric's discourse—which speaks from absence, loss, and deprivation—to the position of the unconscious itself. Wharton puts the words of the hysteric's sorrow into Lily Bart's mouth at the end of *The House of Mirth.* "She saw that nothing now remains to her but the emptiness of renunciation. . . . But the terrible silen and emptiness seemed to symbolize her future—she felt as though house, the street, the world were all empty, and she alone left se in a lifeless universe" (298). These words describe the hysteric terrain, one Edith Wharton described for her own interior li times. One might view neurosis as the condition of not bei hide the fact that the fundamental relation each person ha edge is the family identifications in which their language meshed. But Wharton is not (only) Lily Bart. Although sh suffering, Wharton was the artist who did not die an unti is not neurosis, for art raises the tediousness of the anal level of tragedy, comedy, story and poem, wringing from us laughter, tears, and shivers of joy and pain.

Works Cited

Alvarengo, Elisa. "Distinctions entre sublimation et perversion." *Quarto* 40/41 (1990); 51–53.

Holbrook, David. *Edith Wharton and the Unsatisfactory Man.* London: Vision, 1991.

Klotz, Jean-Pierre. "Sex and Identity." *Newsletter of the Freudian Field* 5 (1991): 50–58.

Lacan, Jacques. "The agency of the letter in the unconscious or reason since Freud." *Ecrits: A Selection.* Trans. Alan Sheridan. New York: Norton, 1978.

———. *The Four Fundamental Concepts of Psycho-Analysis.* Trans. Alan Sheridan. New York: Norton, 1978.

———. "Intervention on Transference." *Feminine Sexuality.* Ed. Juliet Mitchell and Jacqueline Roe. Trans. J. Rose. New York: Norton, 1985. 61–73.

———. "Kanzer Seminar, Yale University." *Scilicet* 6/7 (1976): 7–31. Section I includes several lectures and discussions given by Lacan in North American universities in 1975.

———. *Le Séminaire,* Livre XXIII. *Le sinthome,* 1975–76. Unpublished seminar. See Jacques Aubert, ed., *Joyce avec Lacan.* Paris: Navarin, 1987. Two selections from *Le sinthome* are published in collection.

ᵗᵉ Seminar of Jacques Lacan: Book VII. *The Ethics of Psycho-* ᵗ959–1960. Ed. Jacques-Alain Miller. Trans. Dennis Por-ᵏ: Norton, 1992.

ⁿ savoir nouveau en psychanalyse? Unpublished ᵗment of Psychoanalysis, Paris VIII, 1991–92.

ᵗton: A Biography. New York: Harper and

ᵗsoners of Shame: A New Perspective ᵗrtin's, 1991.

ᵈy (Novelist): Wharton's *Critical Essays.* Ed. Alfred York: Garland, 1992.

Quarto 40/41 (1990): 16–

der in the Novels of Edith Whar- ᵗ982.

Wolff, Cynthia Griffin. *A Feast of Words: The Triumph of Edith Wharton*. New York: Oxford UP, 1977.

Wharton, Edith. *A Backward Glance*. New York: Scribner's, 1934.

———. "Life and I." *Edith Wharton: Novellas and Other Writings*. Ed. Cynthia Griffin Wolff. New York: Library of America, 1990. 1071–96.

———. *A Mother's Recompense. Edith Wharton: Novellas and Other Writings*. 551–765.

Glossary of Critical and Theoretical Terms

Most terms have been glossed parenthetically where they first appear in the text. Mainly, the glossary lists terms that are too complex to define in a phrase or a sentence or two. A few of the terms listed are discussed at greater length elsewhere (feminist criticism, for instance); these terms are defined succinctly and a page reference to the longer discussion is provided.

AFFECTIVE FALLACY   First used by William K. Wimsatt and Monroe C. Beardsley to refer to what they regarded as the erroneous practice of interpreting texts according to the psychological responses of readers. "The Affective Fallacy," they wrote in a 1946 essay later republished in the *Verbal Icon* (1954), "is a confusion between the poem and its *results* (what it *is* and what it *does*). . . . It begins by trying to derive the standards of criticism from the psychological effects of a poem and ends in impressionism and relativism." The affective fallacy, like the intentional fallacy (confusing the meaning of a work with the author's expressly intended meaning), was one of the main tenets of the New Criticism, or formalism. The affective fallacy has recently been contested by reader-response critics, who have deliberately dedicated their efforts to describing the way individual readers and "interpretive communities" go about "making sense" of texts.
See also: Authorial Intention, Formalism, Reader-Response Criticism.

AUTHORIAL INTENTION   Defined narrowly, an author's intention in writing a work, as expressed in letters, diaries, interviews, and conversations. Defined more broadly, "intentionality" involves unexpressed motivations, designs, and purposes, some of which may have remained unconscious.

The debate over whether critics should try to discern an author's intentions (conscious or otherwise) is an old one. William K. Wimsatt and Monroe C. Beardsley, in an essay first published in the 1940s, coined the term "intentional fallacy" to refer to the practice of basing interpretations on the expressed or implied intentions of authors, a practice they judged to be erroneous. As proponents of the New Criticism, or formalism, they argued that a work of literature is an object in itself and should be studied as such. They believed that it is sometimes helpful to learn what an author intended, but the critic's real purpose is to show what is actually in the text, not what an author intended to put there.

See also: Affective Fallacy, Formalism.

BASE *See* Marxist Criticism.

BINARY OPPOSITIONS *See* Oppositions.

BLANKS *See* Gaps.

CANON Since the fourth century, used to refer to those books of the Bible that the Christian church accepts as being Holy Scripture. The term has come to be applied more generally to those literary works given special status, or "privileged," by a culture. Works we tend to think of as "classics" or the "Great Books" produced by Western culture — texts that are found in every anthology of American, British, and world literature — would be among those that constitute the canon.

Recently, Marxist, feminist, minority, and Third World critics have argued that, for political reasons, many excellent works never enter the canon. Canonized works, they claim, are those that reflect — and respect — the culture's dominant ideology and/or perform some socially acceptable or even necessary form of "cultural work." Attempts have been made to broaden or redefine the canon by discovering valuable texts, or versions of texts, that were repressed or ignored for political reasons. These have been published both in traditional and in nontraditional anthologies. The more outspoken critics of the canon, especially radical critics practicing cultural criticism, have called into question the whole concept of canon or "canonicity." Privileging no form of artistic expression that reflects and revises the culture, these critics treat cartoons, comics, and soap operas with the same cogency and respect they accord novels, poems, and plays.

See also: Cultural Criticism, Feminist Criticism, Ideology, Marxist Criticism.

CONFLICTS, CONTRADICTIONS *See* Gaps.

CULTURAL CRITICISM A critical approach that is sometimes referred to as "cultural studies" or "cultural critique." Practitioners of cultural criticism oppose "high" definitions of culture and take seriously popular cultural forms. Grounded in a variety of continental European influences, cultural criticism nonetheless gained institutional force in England, in 1964, with the founding of the Centre for Contemporary Cultural Studies at Birmingham University. Broadly interdisciplinary in its scope and approach, cultural criticism views the text as the locus and catalyst of a complex network of political and economic discourses. Cultural critics share with Marxist critics an interest in the ideological contexts of cultural forms. See "What Is Cultural Criticism?" pp. 326–37.

DECONSTRUCTION A poststructuralist approach to literature that is strongly influenced by the writings of the French philosopher Jacques Derrida. Deconstruction, partly in response to structuralism and formalism, posits the undecidability of meaning for all texts. In fact, as the deconstructionist critic J. Hillis Miller points out, "deconstruction is not a dismantling of the structure of a text but a demonstration that it has already dismantled itself." See "What Is Deconstruction?" pp. 419–28.

DIALECTIC Originally developed by Greek philosophers, mainly Socrates and Plato, as a form and method of logical argumentation; the term later came to denote a philosophical notion of evolution. The German philosopher G. W. F. Hegel described dialectic as a process whereby a thesis, when countered by an antithesis, leads to the synthesis of a new idea. Karl Marx and Friedrich Engels, adapting Hegel's idealist theory, used the phrase "dialectical materialism" to discuss the way in which a revolutionary class war might lead to the synthesis of a new social economic order. The American Marxist critic Fredric Jameson has coined the phrase "dialectical criticism" to refer to a Marxist critical approach that synthesizes structuralist and poststructuralist methodologies.

See also: Marxist Criticism, Structuralism, Poststructuralism.

DIALOGIC *See* Discourse.

DISCOURSE Used specifically, can refer to (1) spoken or written discussion of a subject or area of knowledge; (2) the words in, or text of, a narrative as opposed to its story line; or (3) a "strand" within a given narrative that argues a certain point or defends a given value system.

More generally, "discourse" refers to the language in which a subject or area of knowledge is discussed or a certain kind of business is transacted. Human knowledge is collected and structured in discourses. Theology and medicine are defined by their discourses, as are politics, sexuality, and literary criticism.

A society is generally made up of a number of different discourses or "discourse communities," one or more of which may be dominant or serve the dominant ideology. Each discourse has its own vocabulary, concepts, and rules, knowledge of which constitutes power. The psychoanalyst and psychoanalytic critic Jacques Lacan has treated the unconscious as a form of discourse, the patterns of which are repeated in literature. Cultural critics, following Mikhail Bakhtin, use the word "dialogic" to discuss the dialogue *between* discourses that takes place within language or, more specifically, a literary text.

See also: Cultural Criticism, Ideology, Narrative, Psychoanalytic Criticism.

FEMINIST CRITICISM An aspect of the feminist movement whose primary goals include critiquing masculine-dominated language and literature by showing how they reflect a masculine ideology; writing the history of unknown or undervalued women writers, thereby earning them their rightful place in the literary canon; and helping create a climate in which women's creativity may be fully realized and appreciated. See "What Is Feminist Criticism?" pp. 391–98.

FIGURE *See* Metaphor, Metonymy, Symbol.

FORMALISM Also referred to as the New Criticism, formalism reached its height during the 1940s and 1950s but it is still practiced today. Formalists treat a work of literary art as if it were a self-contained, self-referential object. Rather than basing their interpretations of a text on the reader's response, the author's stated intentions, or parallels between the text and historical contexts (such as the author's life), formalists concentrate on the relationships *within* the text that give it its own distinctive character or form. Special attention is paid to repetition, particularly of images or symbols, but also of sound effects and rhythms in poetry.

Because of the importance placed on close analysis and the stress on the text as a carefully crafted, orderly object containing observable formal patterns, formalism has often been seen as an attack on Romanticism and impressionism, particularly impressionistic criticism. It has sometimes even been called an "objective" approach to literature. Formalists are more likely than certain other critics to believe and say that the meaning of a text can be known objectively. For instance, reader-response critics see meaning as a function either of each reader's experience or of the norms that govern a particular "interpretive community," and deconstructors argue that texts mean opposite things at the same time.

Formalism was originally based on essays written during the 1920s and 1930s by T. S. Eliot, I. A. Richards, and William Empson. It was significantly developed later by a group of American poets and critics, including R. P. Blackmur, Cleanth Brooks, John Crowe Ransom, Allen Tate, Robert Penn Warren, and William K. Wimsatt. Although we associate formalism with certain principles and terms (such as the "Affective Fallacy" and the "Intentional Fallacy" as defined by Wimsatt and Monroe C. Beardsley), formalists were trying to make a cultural statement rather than establish a critical dogma. Generally Southern, religious, and culturally conservative, they advocated the inherent value of literary works (particularly of literary works regarded as beautiful art objects) because they were sick of the growing ugliness of modern life and contemporary events. Some recent theorists even suggest that the rising popularity of formalism after World War II was a feature of American isolationism, the formalist tendency to isolate literature from biography and history being a manifestation of the American fatigue with wider involvements.

See also: Affective Fallacy, Authorial Intention, Deconstruction, Reader-Response Criticism, Symbol.

GAPS When used by reader-response critics familiar with the theories of Wolfgang Iser, refers to "blanks" in texts that must be filled in by readers. A gap may be said to exist whenever and wherever a reader perceives something to be missing between words, sentences, paragraphs, stanzas, or chapters. Readers respond to gaps actively and creatively, explaining apparent inconsistencies in point of view, accounting for jumps in chronology, speculatively supplying information missing from plots, and resolving problems or issues left ambiguous or "indeterminate" in the text.

Reader-response critics sometimes speak as if a gap actually exists in a text; a gap is, of course, to some extent a product of readers' perceptions. Different readers may find gaps in different texts, and different gaps in the same text. Furthermore, they may fill in these gaps in different ways, which is why, a reader-response critic might argue, works are interpreted in different ways.

Although the concept of the gap has been used mainly by reader-response critics, it has also been used by critics taking other theoretical approaches. Practitioners of deconstruction might use "gap" when speaking of the radical contradictoriness of a text. Marxists have used the term to speak of everything from the gap that opens up between economic base and cultural superstructure to the two kinds of conflicts or contradictions to be found in literary texts. The first of these, they would argue, results from the fact that texts reflect ideology, within which certain subjects cannot be covered, things cannot be said, contradictory views cannot be recognized as contradictory. The second kind of conflict, contradiction, or gap within a text results from the fact that works don't just reflect ideology: they are also fictions that, consciously or unconsciously, distance themselves from the same ideology.

See also: Deconstruction, Ideology, Marxist Criticism, Reader-Response Criticism.

GENRE A French word referring to a kind or type of literature. Individual works within a genre may exhibit a distinctive form, be governed by certain conventions, and/or represent characteristic subjects. Tragedy, epic, and romance are all genres.

Perhaps inevitably, the term "genre" is used loosely. Lyric poetry is a genre, but so are characteristic *types* of the lyric, such as the sonnet, the ode, and the elegy. Fiction is a genre, as are detective fiction and science fiction. The list of genres grows constantly as critics establish new lines of connection between individual works and discern new categories of works with common characteristics. Moreover, some writers form hybrid genres by combining the characteristics of several in a single work.

Knowledge of genres helps critics to understand and explain what is conventional and unconventional, borrowed and original, in a work.

HEGEMONY Given intellectual currency by the Italian communist Antonio Gramsci, the word (a translation of *egemonia*) refers to the pervasive system of assumptions, meanings, and values — the web of ideologies, in other words — that shapes the way things look, what they mean, and therefore what reality *is* for the majority of people within a given culture.

See also: Ideology, Marxist Criticism.

IDEOLOGY A set of beliefs underlying the customs, habits, and/or practices common to a given social group. To members of that group, the beliefs seem obviously true, natural, and even universally applicable. They may seem just as obviously arbitrary, idiosyncratic, and even false to outsiders or members of another group who adhere to another ideology. Within a society, several ideologies may coexist, or one or more may be dominant.

Ideologies may be forcefully imposed or willingly subscribed to. Their component beliefs may be held consciously or unconsciously. In either case, they come to form what Johanna M. Smith has called "the unexamined ground of our experience." Ideology governs our perceptions, judgments, and prejudices — our sense of what is acceptable, normal, and deviant. Ideology may cause a revolution; it may also allow discrimination and even exploitation.

Ideologies are of special interest to sociologically oriented critics of literature because of the way in which authors reflect or resist prevailing views in their texts. Some Marxist critics have argued that literary texts reflect and reproduce the ideologies that produced them; most, however, have shown how ideologies are riven with contradictions that works of literature manage to expose and widen. Still other Marxists have focused on the way in which texts themselves are characterized by gaps, conflicts, and contradictions between their ideological and anti-ideological functions.

Feminist critics have addressed the question of ideology by seeking to expose and thereby call into question) the patriarchal ideology mirrored or inscribed in works written by men—even men who have sought to counter sexism and break down sexual stereotypes. New historicists have been interested in demonstrating the ideological underpinnings not only of literary representations but also of our interpretations of them. Fredric Jameson, an American Marxist critic, argues that all thought is ideological, but that ideological thought that knows itself as such stands the chance of seeing through and transcending ideology.

See also: Cultural Criticism, Feminist Criticism, Marxist Criticism, New Historicism.

IMAGINARY ORDER In Lacanian theory, one of the three essential orders of the psychoanalytic field (see Real and Symbolic Order). It is most closely associated with the senses (sight, sound, touch, taste, and smell). The infant, who by comparison to many other animals is born prematurely and thus is wholly dependent on others for a prolonged period, stitches together an ego or self by identifying with images, words, and the effects of loss (separation, cut) on the body, effects that produce both the drive and the *jouissance* (or pain/pleasure threshold) attached to such losses. The specific traits of *jouissance* that link "being," body, and meaning bind an infant to its surrounding world in unary traits (or master signifiers). The Imaginary Order is this multiplaned mapping of the body by images, language, drives, and libido. As images are joined to a name (language), the infant gradually experiences a unity of body parts and motor control that empowers physical development. This "mirror stage" or "mirror phase," in which the child anticipates mastery of its inchoate body by identification with the outside world, usually occurs between six and eighteen months. An emerging sense of self emerges from the feeling that one is both similar to and different from others. This feeling arises primarily from one's primordial relation to the mother (or primary caretaker) and establishes the illusion of wholeness—a mirroring and also a "mirage of maturation"—reflected in the eyes of others. Highly dependent on the visual order, the Imaginary (which maps, or imposes, meaning on the biological organism) is always organized in relation to the Real. Because human subjects are always fundamentally separate from others and also internally divided (consious/unconcious), the apparent coherence of the Imaginary, its fullness and grandiosity, is always false, a *mis*recognition that the ego (or "me") tries to deny by imagining itself as coherent and capable. The Imaginary operates in conjunction with the Real and Symbolic and is not a "stage" or development equivalent to Freud's "pre-oedipal stage," nor is it prelinguistic.

See also: Psychoanalytic Criticism, Real, Symbolic Order.

IMPLIED READER A phrase used by some reader-response critics in place of the phrase "the reader." Whereas "the reader" could refer to any idiosyncratic individual who happens to have read or to be reading the text, "the implied reader" is *the* reader intended, even created, by the text. Other reader-response critics seeking to describe this more generally conceived reader have spoken of the "informed reader" or the "narratee," who is "the necessary counterpart of a given narrator."

See Reader-Response Criticism.

INTENTIONAL FALLACY   *See* Authorial Intention.

INTENTIONALITY   *See* Authorial Intention.

INTERTEXTUALITY   The condition of interconnectedness among texts. Every author has been influenced by others, and every work contains explicit and implicit references to other works. Writers may consciously or unconsciously echo a predecessor or precursor; they may also consciously or unconsciously disguise their indebtedness, making intertextual relationships difficult for the critic to trace.

Reacting against the formalist tendency to view each work as a free-standing object, some poststructuralist critics suggested that the meaning of a work only emerges intertextually, that is, within the context provided by other works. But there has been a reaction, too, against this type of intertextual criticism. Some new historicist critics suggest that literary history is itself too narrow a context and that works should be interpreted in light of a larger set of cultural contexts.

There is, however, a broader definition of intertextuality, one that refers to the relationship between works of literature and a wide range of narratives and discourses that we don't usually consider literary. Thus defined, intertextuality could be used by a new historicist to refer to the significant interconnectedness between a literary text and nonliterary discussions of or discourses about contemporary culture. Or it could be used by a poststructuralist to suggest that a work can only be recognized and read within a vast field of signs and tropes that is *like* a text and that makes any single text self-contradictory and "undecidable."

See also: Discourse, Formalism, Narrative, New Historicism, Poststructuralism, Trope.

MARXIST CRITICISM   An approach that treats literary texts as material products, describing them in broadly historical terms. In Marxist criticism, the text is viewed in terms of its production and consumption, as a product *of* work that does identifiable cultural work of its own. Following Karl Marx, the founder of communism, Marxist critics have used the terms "base" to refer to economic reality and "superstructure" to refer to the corresponding or "homologous" infrastructure consisting of politics, law, philosophy, religion, and the arts. Also following Marx, they have used the word "ideology" to refer to that set of cultural beliefs that literary works at once reproduce, resist, and revise. See "What Is Marxist Criticism?" pp. 359–72.

METAPHOR   The representation of one thing by another related or similar thing. The image (or activity or concept) used to represent or "figure" something else is known as the "vehicle" of the metaphor; the thing represented is called the "tenor." In other words, the vehicle is what we substitute for the tenor. The relationship between vehicle and tenor can provide much additional meaning. Thus, instead of saying, "Last night I read a book," we might say, "Last night I plowed through a book." "Plowed through" (or the activity of plowing) is the vehicle of our metaphor; "read" (or the act of reading) is the tenor, the thing being figured. The increment in meaning through metaphor is fairly obvious. Our audience knows not only *that* we read but also *how* we read, because to read a book in the way that a plow rips through earth is surely to read in a relentless, unreflective way. Note that in the sentence above, a new metaphor — "rips through" — has been used to explain an old one. This serves (which is a metaphor) as an example of just how thick (another metaphor) language is with metaphors!

Metaphor is a kind of "trope" (literally, a "turning," i.e., a figure that alters or "turns" the meaning of a word or phrase). Other tropes include allegory, conceit, metonymy, personification, simile, symbol, and synecdoche. Traditionally, metaphor and symbol have been viewed as the principal tropes; minor tropes have been categorized as *types* of these two major ones. Similes, for instance, are usually defined as simple metaphors that usually employ "like" or "as" and state the tenor outright, as in "My love is like a red, red rose." Synecdoche involves a vehicle that is a *part* of the tenor, as in "I see a sail" meaning "I see a boat." Metonymy is viewed as a metaphor involving two terms commonly if arbitrarily associated with (but not fundamentally or intrinsically related to) each other. Recently, however, deconstructors such as Paul de Man and J. Hillis Miller have questioned the "privilege" granted to metaphor and the metaphor/metonymy distinction or "opposition." They have suggested that all metaphors are really metonyms and that all figuration is arbitrary.

See also: Deconstruction, Metonymy, Oppositions, Symbol.

METONYMY The representation of one thing by another that is commonly and often physically associated with it. To refer to a writer's handwriting as his or her "hand" is to use a metonymic "figure" or "trope." The image or thing used to represent something else is known as the "vehicle" of the metonym; the thing represented is called the "tenor."

Like other tropes (such as metaphor), metonymy involves the replacement of one word or phrase by another. Liquor may be referred to as "the bottle," a monarch as "the crown." Narrowly defined, the vehicle of a metonym is arbitrarily, not intrinsically, associated with the tenor. In other words, the bottle just happens to be what liquor is stored in and poured from in our culture. The hand may be involved in the production of handwriting, but so are the brain and the pen. There is no special, intrinsic likeness between a crown and a monarch; it's just that crowns traditionally sit on monarchs' heads and not on the heads of university professors. More broadly, "metonym" and "metonymy" have been used by recent critics to refer to a wide range of figures and tropes. Deconstructors have questioned the distinction between metaphor and metonymy.

See also: Deconstruction, Metaphor, Trope.

NARRATIVE A story or a telling of a story, or an account of a situation or of events. A novel and a biography of a novelist are both narratives, as are Freud's case histories.

Some critics use the word "narrative" even more generally; Brook Thomas, a new historicist, has critiqued "narratives of human history that neglect the role human labor has played."

NEW CRITICISM *See* Formalism.

NEW HISTORICISM One of the most recent developments in contemporary critical theory, its practitioners share certain convictions, the major ones being that literary critics need to develop a high degree of historical consciousness and that literature should not be viewed apart from other human creations, artistic or otherwise.

See also: Authorial Intention, Deconstruction, Formalism, Ideology, Poststructuralism, Psychoanalytic Criticism.

OPPOSITIONS A concept highly relevant to linguistics, since linguists maintain that words (such as "black" and "death") have meaning not in themselves but in relation to other words ("white" and "life"). Jacques Derrida, a poststructuralist philosopher of language, has suggested that in the West we think in terms of these "binary oppositions" or dichotomies, which on examination turn out to be evaluative hierarchies. In other words, each opposition — beginning/end, presence/absence, or consciousness/unconsciousness — contains one term that our culture views as superior and one term that we view as negative or inferior.

Derrida has "deconstructed" a number of these binary oppositions, including two — speech/writing and signifier/signified — that he believes to be central to linguistics in particular and Western culture in general. He has concurrently critiqued the "law" of noncontradiction, which is fundamental to Western logic. He and other deconstructors have argued that a text can contain opposed strands of discourse and, therefore, mean opposite things: reason *and* passion, life *and* death, hope *and* despair, black *and* white. Traditionally, criticism has involved choosing between opposed or contradictory meanings and arguing that one is present in the text and the other absent.

French feminists have adopted the ideas of Derrida and other deconstructors, showing not only that we think in terms of such binary oppositions as male/female, reason/emotion, and active/passive, but that we also associate reason and activity with masculinity and emotion and passivity with femininity. Because of this, they have concluded that language is "phallocentric," or masculine-dominated.

See also: Deconstruction, Discourse, Feminist Criticism, Poststructuralism.

PHALLUS Freud assigned the penis the Symbolic value of organizing libidinal development; he described the phallic stage as important to the constitution of human subjectivity. Lacan viewed the Phallus as the representative of the value assigned to difference itself — that is to say, as the masculine valued over the feminine. Difference stands for culture or "law" and is the principal of psychic division (consious/unconsious), which gives rise to sexual difference (masculine/feminine) and to the differential categories of desire: psychosis, neurosis, perversion. The Symbolic order (see Symbolic Order) is ruled by the Phallus, which of itself has no inherent meaning *apart from* its differential value, on which societies are based and are represented by the Name of the Father as lawgiver and namer.

POSTSTRUCTURALISM The general attempt to contest and subvert structuralism initiated by deconstructors and certain other critics associated with psychoanalytic, Marxist, and feminist theory. Structuralists, using linguistics as a model and employing semiotic (sign) theory, posit the possibility of knowing a text systematically and revealing the "grammar" behind its form and meaning. Poststructuralists argue against the possibility of such knowledge and description. They counter that texts can be shown to contradict not only structuralist accounts of them but also themselves. In making their adversarial claims, they rely on close readings of texts and on the work of theorists such as Jacques Derrida and Jacques Lacan.

Poststructuralists have suggested that structuralism rests on distinctions between "signifier" and "signified" (signs and the things they point toward), "self" and "language" (or "text"), texts and other texts, and text and world that are overly simplistic, if not patently inaccurate. Poststructuralists have shown how all signifieds are also signifiers, and they have treated texts as "intertexts." They have viewed the world as if it *were* a text (we desire a certain car because it *symbolizes* achievement) and the self as the subject, as well as the user, of language; for example, we may shape and speak through language, but it also shapes and speaks through us.

See also: Deconstruction, Feminist Criticism, Intertextuality, Psychoanalytic Criticism, Semiotics, Structuralism.

PSYCHOANALYTIC CRITICISM Grounded in the psychoanalytic theories of Sigmund Freud, it is one of the oldest critical methodologies still in use. Freud's view that works of literature, like dreams, express secret, unconscious desires led to criticism that interpreted literary works as manifestations of the authors' neuroses. More recently, psychoanalytic critics have come to see literary works as skillfully crafted artifacts that may appeal to *our* neuroses by tapping into our repressed wishes and fantasies. Other forms of psychological criticism that diverge from Freud, although they ultimately derive from his insights, include those based on the theories of Carl Jung and Jacques Lacan. See "What Is Psychoanalytic Criticism?" pp. 447–59.

READER-RESPONSE CRITICISM An approach to literature that, as its name implies, considers the way readers respond to texts, as they read. Stanley Fish describes the method by saying that it substitutes for one question, "What does this sentence mean?" a more operational question, "What does this sentence do?" Reader-response criticism shares with deconstruction a strong textual orientation and a reluctance to define a single meaning for a work. Along with psychoanalytic criticism, it shares an interest in the dynamics of mental response to textual cues.

REAL In Lacanian psychoanalysis, one of the three orders that constitute subjectivity (the other two are Imaginary Order and Symbolic Order), the Real is the intractable and substantial world of traumatic knowledge that resists and exceeds interpretation. The Real cannot be imagined, symbolized, or known directly. It constantly eludes our efforts to name it (death, gravity, sexual difference, and the physical effects of trauma are examples of the Real) and thus creates blocks both in the Imaginary and Symbolic orders. The Real is fundamentally "Other," the mark of the cut or divide within conscious and unconscious life and is signaled in language by gaps, slips, speechlessness, and the sense of the uncanny. The Real is not what we call "reality." It is the stumbling block of the Imaginary (which thinks its can "imagine" anything, including the Real) and of the Symbolic, which tries to bring the Real under its laws (the Real exposes the "phallacy" of the Law of the Phallus). The Real is frightening; we try to tame it with laws and language and call it "reality."

See also: Imaginary Order, Psychoanalytic Criticism.

SEMIOLOGY, SEMIOTIC *See* Semiotics.

SEMIOTICS The study of signs and sign systems and the way meaning is derived from them. Structuralist anthropologists, psychoanalysts, and literary critics developed semiotics during the decades following 1950, but much of the pioneering work had been done at the turn of the century by the founder of modern linguistics, Ferdinand de Saussure, and the American philosopher Charles Sanders Peirce.

Semiotics is based on several important distinctions, including the distinction between "signifier" and "signified" (the sign and what it points toward) and the distinction between "langue" and "parole." *Langue* (French for "tongue," as in "native tongue," meaning language) refers to the entire system within which individual utterances or usages of language have meaning; *parole* (French for "word") refers to the particular utterances or usages. A principal tenet of semiotics is that signs, like words, are not significant in themselves, but instead have meaning only in relation to other signs and the entire system of signs, or langue.

The affinity between semiotics and structuralist literary criticism derives from this emphasis placed on langue, or system. Structuralist critics, after all, were reacting against formalists and their procedure of focusing on individual words as if meanings didn't depend on anything external to the text.

Poststructuralists have used semiotics but questioned some of its underlying assumptions, including the opposition between signifier and signified. The feminist poststructuralist Julia Kristeva, for instance, has used the word "semiotic" to describe feminine language, a highly figurative, fluid form of discourse that she sets in opposition to rigid, symbolic masculine language.

See also: Deconstruction, Feminist Criticism, Formalism, Poststructuralism, Oppositions, Structuralism, Symbol.

SIMILE *See* Metaphor.

SOCIOHISTORICAL CRITICISM *See* New Historicism.

STRUCTURALISM A science of humankind whose proponents attempted to show that all elements of human culture, including literature, may be understood as parts of a system of signs. Structuralism, according to Robert Scholes, was a reaction to " 'modernist' alienation and despair."

Using Ferdinand de Saussure's linguistic theory, European structuralists such as Roman Jakobson, Claude Lévi-Strauss, and Roland Barthes (before his shift toward poststructuralism) attempted to develop a "semiology" or "semiotics" (science of signs). Barthes, among others, sought to recover literature and even language from the isolation in which they had been studied and to show that the laws that govern them govern all signs, from road signs to articles of clothing.

Particularly useful to structuralists were two of Saussure's concepts: the idea of "phoneme" in language and the idea that phonemes exist in two kinds of relationships: "synchronic" and "diachronic." A phoneme is the smallest consistently significant unit in language; thus, both "a" and "an" are phonemes, but "n" is not. A diachronic relationship is that which a phoneme has with those that have preceded it in time and those that will follow it. These "horizontal" relationships produce what we might call discourse or narrative and what Saussure called "parole." The synchronic relationship is the "vertical" one that a word has in a given instant with the entire system of language ("langue") in which it may generate meaning. "An" means what it means in English because those of us who speak the language are using it in the same way at a given time.

Following Saussure, Lévi-Strauss studied hundreds of myths, breaking them into their smallest meaningful units, which he called "mythemes." Removing each from its diachronic relations with other mythemes in a single myth (such as the myth of Oedipus and his mother), he vertically aligned those mythemes that he found to be homologous (structurally correspondent). He then studied the relationships within as well as between vertically aligned columns, in an attempt to understand scientifically, through ratios and proportions, those thoughts and processes that humankind has shared, both at one particular time and across time. One could say, then, that structuralists followed Saussure in preferring to think about the overriding langue or language of myth, in which each mytheme and mytheme-constituted myth fits meaningfully, rather than about isolated individual paroles or narratives. Structuralists followed Saussure's lead in believing what the poststructuralist Jacques Derrida later decided he could not subscribe to — that sign systems must be understood in terms of binary oppositions. In analyzing myths and texts to find basic structures, structuralists tended to find that opposite terms modulate until they are finally resolved or reconciled by some intermediary third term. Thus, a structuralist reading of *Paradise Lost* would show that the war between God and the bad angels becomes a rift between God and sinful, fallen man, the rift then being healed by the Son of God, the mediating third term.

See also: Deconstruction, Discourse, Narrative, Poststructuralism, Semiotics.

SUPERSTRUCTURE *See* Marxist Criticism.

SYMBOL A thing, image, or action that, although it is of interest in its own right, stands for or suggests something larger and more complex — often an idea or a range of interrelated ideas, attitudes, and practices.

Within a given culture, some things are understood to be symbols: the flag of the United States is an obvious example. More subtle cultural symbols might be the river as a symbol of time and the journey as a symbol of life and its manifold experiences.

Instead of appropriating symbols generally used and understood within their culture, writers often create symbols by setting up, in their works, a complex but identifiable web of associations. As a result, one object, image, or action suggests others, and often, ultimately, a range of ideas.

A symbol may thus be defined as a metaphor in which the "vehicle," the thing, image, or action used to represent something else, represents many related things (or "tenors") or is broadly suggestive. The urn in Keats's "Ode on a Grecian Urn" suggests many interrelated concepts, including art, truth, beauty, and timelessness.

Symbols have been of particular interest to formalists, who study how meanings emerge from the complex, patterned relationships between images in a work, and psychoanalytic critics, who are interested in how individual authors and the larger culture both disguise and reveal unconscious fears and desires through symbols. Recently, French feminists have also focused on the symbolic. They have suggested that, as wide-ranging as it seems, symbolic language is ultimately rigid and restrictive. They favor semiotic language and writing, which, they contend, is at once more rhythmic, unifying, and feminine.

See also: Feminist Criticism, Metaphor, Psychoanalytic Criticism, Trope.

SYMBOLIC ORDER In Lacanian psychoanalysis, one of the three orders of subjectivity (see Imaginary and Real): it is the realm of law, language, and society, and the repository of generally held cultural beliefs. Its symbolic system is language, whose agent is the father or lawgiver, the one who has the power of naming. The human subject is commanded into this order, a pre-established language that defines a cultural context. Long before children can speak, they must submit to the Symbolic order of communication and its rules (grammar, syntax, etc.). They internalize and embody the Symbolic order, which determines subjectivity according to a primary law of referentiality and takes the masculine sign (see Phallus) as its ordering principle. Lacan states that both sexes must submit to the Law of the Phallus (the law of order, language, and differentiation), but their individual relation to the Law and to castration determines whether they see themselves — and are seen by others — as normative, neurotic, psychotic, or perverse. The Symbolic institutes repression (of the Imaginary), thus creating the unconsious, which itself is structured by the language of the Symbolic and follows laws similar to those of language, such as metaphor and metonymy. The unconscious, a timeless realm in which desire is ineradicable and cannot be known directly, is understood by a kind of translation that takes place constantly in language. Psychoanalysis "talks" about the desire that makes itself felt in daily life and the *jouissance* that ceaselessly tries to understand the unknown (the *Unbewusste*) in one's own thought processes. The Symbolic is not a "stage" of development (as is Freud's "Oedipal stage") nor is it set in place once and for all in human life. We constantly negotiate its threshold (in sleep, in drunkenness), and we can "fall out" of it altogether in psychosis.

See also: Imaginary Order, Psychoanalytic Criticism, Real.

SYNECDOCHE *See* Metaphor, Metonymy.

TENOR *See* Metaphor, Metonymy, Symbol.

TROPE A figure, as in "figure of speech." Literally a "turning," i.e., a turning or twisting of a word or phrase to make it mean something else. Principal tropes include metaphor, metonymy, simile, personification, and synecdoche.

See also: Metaphor, Metonymy.

VEHICLE *See* Metaphor, Metonymy, Symbol.

About the Contributors

THE VOLUME EDITOR

Shari Benstock is professor of English and women's studies at the University of Miami. She is author of *Women of the Left Bank* (1986) and *Textualizing the Feminine* (1991), editor of *The Private Self* (1988) and *Feminist Issues in Literary Scholarship* (1987), and co-author and co-editor of several books on James Joyce. She is currently completing a revisionist biography of Edith Wharton (forthcoming, 1994), and *Modernism Made Manifest: The Impact of Periodical Publication 1890–1940* for the University of Texas Press. She is former editor of *Tulsa Studies in Women's Literature* and founding co-editor of "Reading Women Writing," a feminist book series at Cornell University Press.

THE CRITICS

Wai-chee Dimock is associate professor of English at Brandeis University. Her publications include *Empire for Liberty: Melville and the Poetics of Individualism* and *Cognition and History: American Literature, Law, Political Theory,* forthcoming from the University of California Press.

Margot Norris is professor of English and comparative literature at the University of California, Irvine. She is author of two books on James

Joyce, *The Decentered Universe of Finnegans Wake* (1976) and *Joyce's Web: The Social Unraveling of Modernism* (1992). She also wrote *Beasts of the Modern Imagination: Darwin, Nietzsche, Kafka, Ernst and Lawrence* (1985). Her current work focuses on representations of mass warfare in modern literature, with a special focus on World War I.

Ellie Ragland Sullivan is chair and professor in the English Department at the University of Missouri. Among her books are *Jacques Lacan and the Philosophy of Psychoanalysis* (1986), *Lacan and the Subject of Language* (1991), and *Essays on the Pleasures of Death: From Freud to Lacan* (1993). She has written over eighty articles, held various grants, and is editor of the official Anglophone Lacan journal, *Newsletter of the Freudian Field.* Her forthcoming book is *Lacan and Sexuality.*

Francis L. Restuccia is associate professor of English at Boston College. She is the author of *James Joyce and the Law of the Father* (1989) and articles on the convergence of modernism and feminism in Virginia Woolf, E. M. Forster, and Milan Kundera. She is completing a book (supported by the American Association of University Women's Founders Fellowship) on women and pain in contemporary women's literature, theory, and everyday life.

Lillian S. Robinson, 1993–1994 C. C. Garvin Professor of English at Virginia Polytechnic Institute and State University, has held visiting chairs at the Université de Paris III, Albright College, Scripps College, San Diego State University, and the University of Hawaii. Among her publications are *Sex, Class, and Culture* (1978, reissued 1986) and *Monstrous Regiment* (1985), and a co-author of *Feminist Scholarship: Kindling in the Groves of Academe* (1985). Her articles, essays, and reviews have appeared in a number of periodicals and anthologies, and she is a frequent contributor to *The Nation* and *Women's Review of Books.*

THE SERIES EDITOR

Ross C Murfin, general editor of the Case Studies in Contemporary Criticism and volume editor of Joseph Conrad's *Heart of Darkness* and Nathaniel Hawthorne's *The Scarlet Letter* in the series, is provost and vice president for academic affairs at Southern Methodist University. He has taught at the University of Miami, Yale University, and the University of Virginia and has published scholarly studies of Joseph Conrad, Thomas Hardy, and D. H. Lawrence.